# A BIBLIOGRAPHICAL GUIDE
# TO TWENTY-FOUR
# MODERN ANGLO-WELSH WRITERS

# A BIBLIOGRAPHICAL GUIDE

# TO TWENTY-FOUR

# MODERN ANGLO-WELSH WRITERS

John Harris

Assisted by E. John Davies

CARDIFF
UNIVERSITY OF WALES PRESS
1994

British Library Cataloguing-in-Publication Data.

A catalogue record for this book is available from the British Library.

ISBN 0-7083-1233-0

**Published with the financial support of the Welsh Arts Council**

Jacket design by Design Principle, Cardiff
Typeset by Action Typesetting Limited, Gloucester
Printed in Great Britain by the Cromwell Press, Melksham, Wiltshire

# CONTENTS

# INTRODUCTION

This bibliography, jointly sponsored by the Welsh Arts Council and the Welsh Academy, provides a guide to publications by and about twenty-four English-language writers of Wales. The shape of the bibliography reflects the thinking of an advisory panel (Meic Stephens, Sally Roberts Jones, Ned Thomas, John Harris) which in 1987 drew up a list of authors who might qualify for inclusion in any large-scale bibliography of modern Anglo-Welsh writing. More than fifty names were forthcoming, a number which had dramatically to be reduced if the bulk of entries was to be gathered within one year (the period for which funding had been obtained). A short-list evolved, reflecting above all a wish to see treated at the first opportunity those writers whose *oeuvre* is now more or less established. Alas, even here a further whittling down proved unavoidable, so that some significant names are absent from the final tally. We regret such omissions, more the result (we would stress) of an eye on the clock than of any grand canonic aspirations on the part of the panel.

As it happened, a bibliographical assault on twenty-four authors proved challenge enough, even though the project was fortunately able to recruit for a year the services of Edward John Davies, a researcher whose enthusiasm for literature matched his skills in database construction. With his departure in 1988, work on the bibliography became a part-time affair, the aim now to incorporate publications up to and including 1991 (in the event some 1992-1993 publications have also been included.)

From the outset it was agreed that bibliographical records should be held in electronic form and very quickly the project built up a substantial database from which entries for this printed bibliography have been generated. The successful harnessing of computers for bibliographic work has been a feature of the past decade, with ever more library catalogues and published indexes becoming available in machine-readable form. The temptation is to take on trust someone else's citations, in particular the critical writing so impressively marshalled in the current international bibliographies of language and literature. A proportion of entries in this bibliography have been received in this way, transferred from reputable sources, though wherever possible items recorded, both primary and secondary (publications *by* and *about* an author), have been inspected at first hand. (Aberystwyth is a town well supplied with literary journals, as with Welsh periodicals and newspapers.)

The twenty-four author bibliographies are prefaced by two contextual sections, one accommodating collections of imaginative writing, the other a range of general critical and background studies. The bibliographies cannot claim to be definitive, though for the majority of authors they constitute the fullest listing yet available. A word of explanation regarding the A(ii) sections (selected contributions to books and periodicals) is particularly called for. These are conceived as very much supplementary to A(i), being largely listings of *uncollected* material, or publications not yet incorporated into a writer's monographic *oeuvre*. The overall aim has been to present the bulk of an author's work in what is taken to be its most accessible form, rather than systematically to document stages in a publishing career. (Even the A(i) sections, which *are* designed to be comprehensive, should be seen as first steps towards full-dress author bibliographies: those vital accounts, drawing substantially on publishers' records, which analyse editions, signal textual changes, and document a book's reception via reference to contemporary reviews.)

One further aspect of the A(ii) sections needs explanation: the varying degree of fullness with which this uncollected material has been listed. Each author presents a distinctive bibliographical profile, most obviously in the volume and range of output and the amount of bibliographical work already undertaken upon it. Where reliable bibliographies exist, the present lists build around them; where they do not, the thoroughness of treatment under A(ii) reflects in part the assistance of author specialists and, in some notable instances, the co-operation of authors themselves. The rooted imbalance as between guides to primary and secondary material has long troubled literary bibliographers, who know how very much easier it is to build up a bank of references to critical writing about an author (*any* critical writing about *any* author) than to track down the fugitive output of that author, especially in the periodicals and newspapers. Certainly without the help of particular authors, and experts on authors, many sections listing primary publications would be conspicuously the poorer.

## Scope of the Bibliography

*Books:* The bibliography seeks to record all of an author's publications in book form, in all British editions. Details of some American editions are also appended. (However, no attempt has been made to distinguish impressions, issues and states, as understood in bibliographical usage.)

*Contributions to Books and Periodicals:* As explained, the listing is selective. Generally, the appearance in periodicals of items later reprinted in book form is not recorded (this rule is occasionally broken, mostly where the periodical volume may be judged as accessible as the book). Likewise there is usually no indication of an author's appearance in anthologies of poetry and prose (other than those of an Anglo-Welsh nature).

*Translations:* The bibliographical control of translations is shaky and no library possesses anything remotely approaching a comprehensive stock of those relating to Anglo-Welsh literature. Such translations as are held by the National Library of Wales have been inspected, but these present lists rely heavily on entries in *Index Translationum*.

*Radio, film and television items; sound recordings:* A good many references to such non-print material were collected along the way and in the case of Emyr Humphreys, John Ormond and Alun Richards it seemed useful to issue partial lists of their work for television.

*Critical writing:* The intention here has been to provide a detailed guide to critical writing on our twenty-four authors, with an emphasis on more recent publications and those in periodicals not systematically indexed for the major current literary bibliographies. With one or two exceptions reviews as a category are excluded, though review articles can appear as part of a critic's output.

*Anthologies of Welsh writing in English:* The opening section is self-explanatory though it should be emphasized that only the major regional anthologies have been included; there are, for instance, no school anthologies nor collections from writers' circles.

## Arrangement

Arrangement of individual bibliographies separates publications by the author from those about an author, the author's output being further divided (in the majority of cases) into books, and contributions to books and periodicals. It is hoped that such a straightforward method of organization, and the provision of duplicate entries, goes some way towards obviating the lack of a general index.

*Section A. Books:* Arrangement is chronological by date of publication, both of an author's total corpus and, within entries for individual works, of editions listed beneath the first. (English and American editions are grouped separately.) Generally *books edited* are listed with *books written* though in the case of authors whose contribution as editors has been significant, *books edited* comprise a separate section.

*Section A. Contributions to books and periodicals:* Again arrangement is broadly chronological. Within an individual year, contributions to books take precedence over contributions to periodicals, which are themselves arranged chronologically (in the case of newspapers and monthlies) or by title of periodical (in the case of bi-monthlies, quarterlies and periodicals of longer frequency).

*Section A. Translations:* A translation of a work is given as part of the entry for that work, except in the case of Richard Hughes, Dylan Thomas and Raymond Williams, where translations are so numerous as to warrant a separate section (this arranged by language).

*Section B. Critical writing.* Arrangement is alphabetical by surname of critic, then chronological where two or more publications by a single critic are listed.

## Form of Entry

The basic elements are present – author; title of book/periodical article; imprint/name of periodical; date of publication, pagination details. No abstracts are attempted, though certain books (e.g. collections of essays) have their contents listed, and occasionally other supplementary notes are provided. These are descriptive rather than evaluative, and mostly of a bibliographical nature. Monographs by our twenty-four authors are described a little more fully, with details of binding and any International Standard Book Number.

# ACKNOWLEDGEMENTS

I am grateful to the Literature Committee of the Welsh Arts Council and to the Welsh Academy for the financial assistance which initiated this project, and for the forbearance shown by their respective officers throughout the period of the Bibliography's compilation. The Yapp Foundation also kindly provided a grant towards early research.

It is a pleasure to record my thanks to the many specialists who individually have looked over drafts for particular authors and offered helpful comment: they include Sam Adams, Sandra Anstey, Jonathan Barker, Yoko Bednar, David Callard, Don Dale-Jones, James A. Davies, Keri Edwards, Eugene England, Greg Hill, Islwyn Jenkins, Dafydd Johnston, Bernard Jones, J. Lawrence Mitchell, Paul Bennett Morgan, the late Michael Parnell, John Pikoulis, Richard Poole, Pat Power, Ruth Pryor and Dai Smith. I owe a special debt to Meic Stephens and M. Wynn Thomas for their many useful suggestions on the Bibliography as a whole. I have in addition received invaluable guidance from Elinor Humphreys (on Emyr Humphreys), Glyn Jones, Gwyn Jones, Roland Mathias, Leslie Norris, Alun Richards, and Harri Webb (via Meic Stephens).

Mona Gilbey and Steve Owen gave assistance on an earlier bibliographical project, and I am pleased that a portion of their research has been incorporated in the entries from the *Western Mail* and other Welsh newspapers. More recently, an Aberystwyth postgraduate student Suzanne Humphries kindly volunteered assistance with a section of the Dylan Thomas bibliography. Librarians too have been unfailingly helpful, including Gari Melville, HTV Cardiff, and Gareth Morris, BBC Wales. The staff in the Department of Printed Books, National Library of Wales, should also be singled out for their ready appreciation of the demands on service that such a project entails; in all, the National Library proved an indispensable archival base.

Closer to home, the Department of Information and Library Studies, University of Wales Aberystwyth, under the direction of D. Hywel E. Roberts, has supplied essential technical and material support. Without this kind of backing, and the generous help of those listed above, the bibliography would have been still longer in the making and all the more imperfect.

John Harris, September 1993.

# ABBREVIATIONS

| | |
|---|---|
| *AWR* | *Anglo-Welsh Review* |
| *BNW* | *Book News from Wales* |
| *BWA* | *Bulletin of the Welsh Academy* |
| *DL* | *Dock Leaves* |
| *HW* | *Herald of Wales* |
| *PP* | *Picture Post* |
| *PW˙* | *Poetry Wales* |
| *NWR* | *New Welsh Review* |
| *TLS* | *Times Literary Supplement* |
| *THSC* | *Transactions of the Honourable Society of Cymmrodorion* |
| *UTQ* | *University of Toronto Quarterly* |
| *WR* | *Welsh Review* |
| *WM* | *Western Mail* |

Abbreviations relating to physical description are standard and in the main self-explanatory. 'Pamph.' indicates a pamphlet (an item comprising a single gathering), while 'ppb.' describes a work bound in printed paper boards.

# WELSH WRITING IN ENGLISH: ANTHOLOGIES

A. Poetry and prose

B. Poetry

C. Prose

D. Regional

E. Periodicals: some special issues

F. Translations

## A. Anthologies: Poetry and Prose

*A book of Wales,* ed. D.M. and E.M. Lloyd. London: Collins, 1953. 384 p.: ill.

*Wales,* ed. Jan Morris. Oxford: Oxford University Press, 1982. v, 114 p.: ill. (Small Oxford books). ISBN: 0-19-214118-X.

*A book called hiraeth: longing for Wales,* ed. Dora Polk. Port Talbot: Alun Books, 1982. 133 p.: ill. ISBN: 0-907117-09-0.

*A book of Wales: an anthology*, ed. Meic Stephens. London: Dent, 1987. xiii, 322 p. ISBN: 0-460-7002-9.

*Wales: an anthology,* ed. Alice Thomas Ellis. London: Collins, 1989. xvi, 286 p: ill. ISBN: 0-00-217730-7. With illustrations by Kyffin Williams.

*Love from Wales: an anthology,* ed. Tony Curtis and Siân James. Bridgend: Seren Books, 1991. 175 p.: hbk & pbk. ISBN: 1-85411-064-0 hbk, 1-85411-067-5 pbk. Selections from 74 authors on the theme of love. – Cover artwork by Jonah Jones.

## B. Anthologies: Poetry

*Welsh poets: a representative English selection from contemporary writers,* ed. A.G. Prys-Jones. London: Erskine Macdonald, 1917. 94 p. Incl.: H. Idris Bell – Wilma Buckley – Hylda C. Cole – E.J. Francis Davies – Oliver Davies – W.H. Davies – R. Edwards-James – R.A. Griffith [Elphin] – T. Gwynn Jones – Elinor Jenkins – P.M. Jones – Ellen Lloyd-Williams

– Hon. Evan Morgan – A.G. Prys-Jones – Cecil Roberts – R. Silyn Roberts – Brian Rhys – Ernest Rhys – Gilbert Thomas – Alfred Williams – D.G. Williams – Iolo Aneurin Williams.

*Modern Welsh poetry,* ed. Keidrych Rhys. London: Faber, 1944. 146 p. Incl.: Davies Aberpennar – Brenda Chamberlain – Charles Davies – Constance Davies – Idris Davies – Rhys Davies – Walter Dowding – H.L.R. Edwards – Ken Etheridge – David Evans – George Ewart Evans – Charles Fisher – Wyn Griffith – Peter Hellings – Robert Herring – Nigel Heseltine – Emyr Humphries [sic] – David Jones – Glyn Jones – Alan Pryce Jones [sic] – S.G. Leonard – Alban A. Levy – Alun Lewis – Roland Mathias – Huw Menai – B.J. Morse – John Prichard – Goronwy Rees – Keidrych Rees – Lynette Roberts – Dylan Thomas – Ormond Thomas [i.e. John Ormond] – R.S. Thomas – Henry Treece – Meurig Walters – Vernon Watkins – George Woodcock.

*Presenting Welsh poetry: an anthology of Welsh verse in translation and of English verse by Welsh poets,* ed. Gwyn Williams. London: Faber, 1959. 128 p. Modern poets incl.: Ernest Rhys – Edward Thomas – W.H. Davies – David Jones – Alun Lewis – Vernon Watkins – Brenda Chamberlain – Glyn Jones – Dannie Abse – Dylan Thomas.

*Dragons and daffodils: an anthology of verse,* ed. John Stuart Williams and Richard Milner. Llandybïe: Christopher Davies, 1960. 56 p. Incl.: Dannie Abse – S.L. Bethell – Lisbeth David – Andrew David – John C. Griffiths – Terry Hawkes – G. Ingli James – Glyn Jones – Iwan Myles Jones – Trevor Jones – Mimi Josephson – Barbara Leech – Alban Levy – Richard Milner – Robin Moffet – Douglas Phillips – A.G. Prys-Jones – W.A. Rathkey – E.H. Ray – Peter Schirmer – Pamela Scott – John Stuart Williams – George Thomas.

*Welsh voices: an anthology of new poetry from Wales,* ed. Bryn Griffiths. London: Dent, 1967. x, 94 p. Incl.: Dannie Abse – Anthony Conran – Raymond Garlick – Bryn Griffiths – Peter Gruffydd – David Jones – Glyn Jones – Roland Mathias – Robert Morgan – Leslie Norris – A.G. Prys-Jones – Sally Roberts – Meic Stephens – R.S. Thomas – John Tripp – Vernon Watkins – Harri Webb – Herbert Williams – John Stuart Williams.

*This world of Wales: an anthology of Anglo-Welsh poetry from the seventeenth to the twentieth century,* ed. Gerald Morgan. Cardiff: University of Wales Press, 1968. xxiii, 227 p. ISBN 0-900768-15-0. Incl.: Introduction, by Gerald Morgan, pp. xv-xxiii – Biographies of and selections from: Henry Vaughan – John Dyer – Evan Lloyd – Gerard Manley Hopkins – W.H. Davies – Edward Thomas – David Jones – Idris Davies – Glyn Jones – Vernon Watkins – R.S. Thomas – Dylan Thomas – Alun Lewis – Solos; poems by Morgan Llwyd, Lewis Morris, Edward Davies, Brenda Chamberlain, Henry Treece, Leslie Norris, T.H. Jones, Anthony Conran, Meic Stephens, A.G. Prys-Jones – Notes, pp. 209-227.

*The lilting house: an anthology of Anglo-Welsh poetry, 1917-67,* ed. John Stuart Williams and Meic Stephens. London: Dent; Llandybïe: Christopher Davies, 1969. xxi, 215 p. ISBN: 460-04903-8. Incl.: Introduction, by Raymond Garlick, pp. xix-xxi – Selections from: W.H. Davies – Edward Thomas – Huw Menai – A.G. Prys-Jones – Wyn Griffith – David Jones – Gwyn Williams – Idris Davies – Glyn Jones – Vernon Watkins – Tom Earley – Brenda Chamberlain – R.S. Thomas – Dylan Thomas – Alun Lewis – Roland Mathias – Cyril Hodges – Keidrych Rhys – Lynette Roberts – Nigel Heseltine – Harri Webb – John Stuart Williams – T.H. Jones – Leslie Norris – Henry Treece – Robert Morgan – Peter Hellings – Dannie Abse – John Ormond – Alison Bielski – Raymond Garlick – John Tripp – Douglas Phillips – Anthony Conran – Herbert Williams – John Ackerman – Bryn Griffiths – Peter Gruffydd – Sally Roberts – Peter Preece – Alun Rees – John Idris Jones – Meic Stephens.

*Poems '69,* ed. John Stuart Williams. Llandysul: Gwasg Gomer, 1969. 85 p. Incl. poems by: Dannie Abse – Alison Bielski – Roy Burnett – Anthony Conran – Elwyn Davies – Gloria Evans Davies – Tom Early – Peter Finch – Raymond Garlick – Peter Gruffydd – Cyril Hodges – Glyn Jones – John Idris Jones – Roland Mathias – Valerie Minogue – Robert Morgan – Leslie Norris – John Ormond – Alan Perry – Sally Roberts – Meic Stephens – R.S. Thomas – John Tripp – Harri Webb – Herbert Williams – John Stuart Williams.

*Poems '70,* ed. Wyn Binding. Llandysul: Gwasg Gomer, 1970. 90 p. Incl.: Euros Bowen – David Charles – Tony Curtis – Elwyn Davies – Raymond Garlick – Emyr Humphreys – Robert Hunter – Bramwell Jones – Roland Mathias – Leslie Norris – John Ormond – Douglas Phillips – John Pook – John Richardson – Sally Roberts – Meic Stephens – Ned Thomas – Peter Thomas – R.S. Thomas – John Tripp – Harri Webb – Evan Gwyn Williams – Gwyn Williams – Herbert Williams – John Stuart Williams.

*Poems '71,* ed. Jeremy Hooker. Llandysul: Gwasg Gomer, 1971. 117 p. ISBN: 0-85088-108-0. Incl.: Sam Adams – Ruth Bidgood – Alison J. Bielski – Gillian Clarke – Anthony Conran – Tony Curtis – Elwyn Davies – John Davies – Robin Fulton – Raymond Garlick – Peter Gruffydd – Glyn Hughes – Emyr Humphreys – Glyn Jones – Derec Llwyd Morgan – Roland Mathias – P.J. Neville-Havins – Leslie Norris – John Ormond – Philip Pacey – Alan Perry – A.G. Prys-Jones – Meic Stephens – R.S. Thomas – John Tripp – Harri Webb – Evan Gwyn Williams – Gwyn Williams – Herbert Williams – John Stuart Williams.

*Poems '72,* ed. John Ackerman. Llandysul: Gwasg Gomer, 1972. 92 p. ISBN: 0-85088-149-8. Incl.: Dannie Abse – John Ackerman – Sam Adams – Graham Allen – David Barrett – Ruth Bidgood – Joseph P. Clancy – Gillian Clarke – Anthony Conran – T. Glynne Davies – Maureen Duffy – Tom Earley – Richard Evans – Raymond Garlick – Peter Gruffydd –

Cyril Hodges – Emyr Humphreys – Cliff James – B.S. Johnston – Glyn Jones – Roland Mathias – Leslie Norris – John Ormond – Meic Stephens – R.S. Thomas – John Tripp – Harri Webb – Evan Gwyn Williams – Gwyn Williams – Herbert Williams – John Stuart Williams.

*Poems '73,* ed. Gwyn Ramage. Llandysul: Gwasg Gomer, 1973. 105 p. ISBN: 0-85088-214-1. Incl.: Dannie Abse – Sam Adams – Ruth Bidgood – Alison Bielski – Gillian Clarke – Tony Curtis – John Davies – Tom Earley – Raymond Garlick – Michael Haines – Cyril Hodges – Jeremy Hooker – Emyr Humphreys – Glyn Jones – Moelwyn Merchant – Roland Mathias – Robert Morgan – Leslie Norris – John Ormond – Philip Pacey – John Pook – Sally Roberts Jones – Meic Stephens – R.S. Thomas – John Tripp – Gwyn Williams – John Stuart Williams.

*Ten Anglo-Welsh poets: an anthology . . . ,* ed. Sam Adams. Manchester: Carcanet, 1974. 136 p.: hbk & pbk. ISBN: 0-85635-085-0 hbk, 0-85635-086-9 pbk. Incl. poems by: Gwyn Williams – Glyn Jones – Roland Mathias – Harri Webb – Leslie Norris – John Ormond – Raymond Garlick – John Tripp – Gillian Clarke – John Pook – Notes, pp. 132-136.

*Poems '74: an anthology of Anglo-Welsh poetry, Summer 1973-Spring 1974,* ed. Peter Elfed Lewis. Llandysul: Gomer Press, 1974. 146 p.: pbk. ISBN: 0-85088-264-8. Incl.: Peter Abbs – John Benyon – Ruth Bidgood – Alison Bielski – Duncan Bush – Gillian Clarke – Gloria Evans Davies – J.C. Evans – Raymond Garlick – Cyril Hodges – Jeremy Hooker – Bramwell Jones – David Jones – Glyn Jones – M.A.B. Jones – Sally Roberts Jones – Sheila Jones – Roland Mathias – Robert Morgan – Leslie Norris – John Ormond – Douglas Phillips – Dora Polk – John Pook – S.M. Pugh – Alun Rees – Moira Rish – A.C. Stairs – Meic Stephens – Graham Thomas – R.S. Thomas – John Tripp – Harri Webb – Richard B. White – Jean Williams – John Stuart Williams.

*Twelve modern Anglo-Welsh poets,* ed. Don Dale-Jones and Randal Jenkins. London: University of London Press, 1975. 204 p: hbk & pbk. ISBN: 0-340-19517-7 hbk, 0-340-19518-5 pbk. Incl. poems by: Idris Davies – Vernon Watkins – R.S. Thomas – Dylan Thomas – Alun Lewis – Roland Mathias – Harri Webb – Leslie Norris – T. Harri Jones – John Ormond – Dannie Abse – Raymond Garlick – Bibliography, incl. gramophone records, pp. 201-204.

*Dragon's hoard: an anthology of modern poetry for Welsh secondary schools,* ed. Sam Adams and Gwilym Rees Hughes. Llandysul: Gwasg Gomer, 1976. 133 p. ISBN: 0-85088-322-9. Incl. poems and translations by: Dannie Abse – Sam Adams – John Ackerman – Ruth Bidgood – Alison Bielski – Euros Bowen – Joseph Clancy – Gillian Clarke – Elwyn Davies – Gareth Alban Davies – T. Glynne Davies – Pennar Davies – Tom Earley – Peter Gruffydd – Gwilym Rees Hughes – Richard Hughes – Bobi Jones – R. Gerallt Jones – Sally Roberts Jones – Alun Llywelyn-Williams – Roland Mathias – Robert Morgan – James Nicholas – Leslie Norris – John

Ormond – T.H. Parry-Williams – Alan Perry – John Pook – A.G. Prys-Jones – Gilbert Ruddock – Meic Stephens – Gwyn Thomas (1936-) – R.S. Thomas – John Tripp – J.P. Ward – Harri Webb – Gwyn Williams – Herbert Williams – John Stuart Williams.

*Poems '76: an anthology of poems by Welsh writers selected from work which has appeared during the last two years,* ed. Glyn Jones. Llandysul: Gomer Press, 1976. 89 p.: pbk. ISBN: 8-5088-000-0. Incl.: Dannie Abse – John Ackerman – Sam Adams – Graham Allen – Ruth Bidgood – Alison Bielski – Joseph P. Clancy – Gillian Clarke – Anthony Conran – Tony Curtis – Elwyn Davies – Jon Dressel – Tom Earley – Raymond Garlick – Jeremy Hooker – Emyr Humphreys – Nigel Jenkins – Sally Roberts Jones – Edward Lloyd – Roland Mathias – Robert Minhinnick – Robert Morgan – Leslie Norris – John Ormond – Richard Poole – A.G. Prys-Jones – S.M. Pugh – Meic Stephens – R.S. Thomas – John Tripp – J.P. Ward – Harri Webb – Gwyn Williams – John Stuart Williams.

*Wales today: a collection of poems and pictures for children,* ed. Don Dale-Jones and Randal Jenkins. Llandysul: Gomer Press, 1976. 144 p.: pbk. ISBN: 0-850880-022-9. Incl.: Alison Bielski – Eleanor Boniface – W.J.T. Collins – E. Crawshay Williams – D.G. Davies – Idris Davies – Noelle Davies – T.E.C. Davies – W.H. Davies – Tom Earley – Dewi Emrys – Ken Etheridge – Raymond Garlick – D.E. Grandfield – Cyril Gwynn – E.H. Harris – Myfanwy Haycock – Gerard Manley Hopkins – Richard Hughes – E.M. Jones – Glyn Jones – Gwyn Jones (translator) – John Idris Jones – Alun Lewis – Gwerfyl Mechain – Huw Menai – Leslie Norris – Robert Nye – Goronwy Owen – Alan Perry – A.G. Prys-Jones – Meic Stephens – Dylan Thomas – Edward Thomas – R.S. Thomas – Vernon Watkins – Harri Webb – John S. Williams.

*The Oxford book of Welsh verse in English,* ed. Gwyn Jones. Oxford: Oxford University Press, 1977. xxxvii, 313 p. ISBN: 0-19-211858-7. Incl.: Introduction, by Gwyn Jones, pp. xvii-xxi – Selections from the following modern English-language writers: Ernest Rhys – W.H. Davies – John Cowper Powys – Edward Thomas – Huw Menai – A.G. Prys-Jones – Wilfred Owen – David Jones – Richard Hughes – Gwyn Williams – Idris Davies – Glyn Jones – Vernon Watkins – Gwyn Jones – Margiad Evans – Tom Earley – Henry Treece – Brenda Chamberlain – R.S. Thomas – Dylan Thomas – Alun Lewis – Roland Mathias – Emyr Humphreys – T.H. Jones – Leslie Norris – Dannie Abse – John Ormond – Gloria Evans Davies. – Reissued 1983, pbk. ISBN: 0-19-281397-8.

*Poems '78: an anthology of poems by Welsh writers from work which has appeared over the past two years,* ed. Graham Allen. Llandysul: Gomer Press, 1978. 94 p.: pbk. ISBN: 0-85088-660-0. Incl.: Dannie Abse – Sam Adams – John Beynon – Ruth Bidgood – Alison Bielski – Gillian Clarke – Tony Curtis – John Davies – Jon Dressel – Tom Earley – Raymond Garlick – Steve Griffiths – Jeremy Hooker – Emyr Humphreys – Glyn

Jones – Nigel Jenkins – Bramwell Jones – Peter Thabit Jones – Sally
Roberts Jones – Roland Mathias – Robert Minhinnick – Robert Morgan
– Brian Morris – Leslie Norris – Christopher O'Neill – John Ormond
– Alan Perry – Sheenagh Pugh – Alun Rees – Elizabeth Saxon – Meic
Stephens – R.S. Thomas – John Tripp – J.P. Ward – Harri Webb –
Evan Gwyn Williams – Gwyn Williams.

*Green horse: an anthology by young poets of Wales,* ed. Meic Stephens
and Peter Finch. Swansea: Christopher Davies, 1978. 221 p.: hbk & pbk.
ISBN: 0-7154-0502-0 hbk, 0-7154-0401-2 pbk. Incl. Introduction, by Roland
Mathias, pp. 15-22 – Selections from: Graham Allen – John Beynon –
Duncan Bush – Gillian Clarke – Tony Curtis – John Davies – Paul
Evans – Richard Evans – Peter Finch – John Freeman – Roger Garfitt
– Steve Griffiths – Paul Groves – Michael Haines – Jeremy Hooker –
Cliff James – John James – Nigel Jenkins – Phillip Jenkins – Bramwell
Jones – John Idris Jones – Peter Thabit Jones – Peter Elfed Lewis –
Paul Merchant – Robert Minhinnick – Christopher Morgan – Robert
Nisbet – Christopher O'Neill – Philip Owens – Alan Perry – John
Pook – Richard Poole – Sheenagh Pugh – Alun Rees – A.M. Rhys
– Michael Senior – Iain Sinclair – Meic Stephens – Graham Thomas
– Peter Thomas – Chris Torrance – Robert Walton – J.P. Ward –
Nigel Wells – Evan Gwyn Williams – Penny Windsor.

*Wales in verse,* ed. Dannie Abse. London: Secker & Warburg, 1983. xiii,
91 p. ISBN: 0-436-00030-X. Incl.: Introduction, by Dannie Abse, pp. xi-
xiii – Poems by: Dannie Abse – Sam Adams – Michael Barn – Ruth
Bidgood – Gillian Clarke – Anthony Conran – Tony Curtis – Dafydd
ap Gwilym – Edward Davies – Idris Davies – John Davies – Raymond
Garlick – Robert Graves – Mike Jenkins – Nigel Jenkins – Glyn Jones
– D. Gwenallt Jones – T. Harri Jones – Jeremy Hooker – Gerard
Manley Hopkins – Alun Lewis – Lewis Glyn Cothi – Roland Mathias
– Robert Minhinnick – Leslie Norris – John Ormond – John Pook –
Lynette Roberts – Sally Roberts – Meic Stephens – Dylan Thomas –
R.S. Thomas – Henry Treece – John Tripp – J.P. Ward – Vernon
Watkins – Harri Webb – Herbert Williams – John Stuart Williams. –
'The poems in this anthology are, in the main, about the landscape of dif-
ferent Welsh locations.'

*Anglo-Welsh poetry, 1480-1980,* ed. Raymond Garlick and Roland Mathias.
Bridgend: Poetry Wales Press, 1984. 377 p.: hbk & pbk. ISBN: 0-907476-
21-X hbk, 0-907476-22-8 pbk. Incl.: Introduction, by Raymond Garlick and
Roland Mathias, pp. 27-44 – Selections from the following modern poets:
Ernest Rhys – W.H. Davies – E. Howard Harries – Oliver Davies –
Huw Menai – A.G. Prys-Jones – Wyn Griffith – Dudley G. Davies –
David Jones – Eiluned Lewis – Theodore Nicholl – Evan J. Thomas –
Gwyn Williams – Idris Davies – Glyn Jones – Vernon Watkins – Lynette
Roberts – Jean Earle – Ken Etheridge – Tom Earley – Elwyn Davies –
Brenda Chamberlain – R.S. Thomas – Dylan Thomas – Clifford Dyment
– Alun Lewis – Cyril Hodges – Keidrych Rhys – Roland Mathias –

Emyr Humphreys – John Stuart Williams – Harri Webb – Robert Morgan – Leslie Norris – T. Harri Jones – Ruth Bidgood – Dannie Abse – John Ormond – Alison Bielski – Raymond Garlick – John Tripp – Joseph P. Clancy – Douglas Phillips – Brian Morris – Anthony Conran – Gloria Evans Davies – Herbert Williams – Jon Dressel – Sam Adams – Peter Gruffydd – Sally Roberts Jones – Peter Preece – Gillian Clarke – Alun Rees – J.P. Ward – Evan Gwyn Williams – John Idris Jones – Meic Stephens – Graham Allen – Peter Thomas – Bramwell Jones – Chris Torrance – Jeremy Hooker – John Pook – John Beynon – Cliff James – Graham Thomas – John Davies – Nigel Wells – Richard Poole – Tony Curtis – Duncan Bush – Peter Finch – Ian Hughes – Philip Owens – Robert Walton – Steve Griffiths – Nigel Jenkins – Sheenagh Pugh – Peter Thabit Jones – Robert Minhinnick – Mike Jenkins.

*Common ground: poets in a Welsh landscape,* ed. Susan Butler. Bridgend: Poetry Wales Press, 1985. 223 p.: ill. ISBN: 0-907476-47-3. Incl.: Introduction, by Anthony Conran, pp. 11-16 – Selections from Roland Mathias, Robert Minhinnick, John Tripp, Gillian Clarke, Jeremy Hooker, Nigel Jenkins, Anne Stevenson – Interviews with the seven poets, pp. 181-216 – Notes, pp. 217-221. – Photographs by Susan Butler, Rosie Waite and Ian Walker accompany the poems.

*Poetry Wales: 25 years,* ed. Cary Archard. Bridgend: Seren Books. 1990. 257 p.: pbk. ISBN: 1-85411-031-4. Selections from 25 years of *Poetry Wales.* – 'This anthology concentrates on the poetry and on the poets. Almost ninety writers are included … [with] a limit of two, or at most three, of an individual's items being included. The material has been arranged chronologically, and an effort made to fairly represent each editor's period at the magazine.'

*The bright field: an anthology of contemporary poetry from Wales,* ed. Meic Stephens. Manchester: Carcanet, 1991. 310 p.: pbk. ISBN: 0-85635-907-6. Selections from: Bryan Aspden – John Barnie – Duncan Bush – Gillian Clarke – Tony Curtis – John Davies – Christine Evans – Peter Finch – Catherine Fisher – Steve Griffiths – Paul Groves – Douglas Houston – Mike Jenkins – Nigel Jenkins – Huw Jones – Stephen Knight – Hilary Llewellyn-Williams – Christopher Meredith – Robert Minhinnick – Sheenagh Pugh – Oliver Reynolds – Graham Thomas – Chris Torrance – J.P. Ward – Nigel Wells – Penny Windsor. – 'The editor invited poets to choose the poem or poems by which they would like to be represented and to provide reasons for their choice.'

# C. Anthologies: Prose

*Welsh short stories: an anthology.* London: Faber, 1937. 491 p. Contents: The stranger, by Richard Hughes – The conquered, by Dorothy Edwards – Resurrection, by Rhys Davies – A summer day, by Kate Roberts [tr. Dafydd Jenkins] – Davis, by Siân Evans – Janet Ifans' donkey, by Geraint Goodwin – The shining pyramid, by Arthur Machen – Shacki Thomas, by Gwyn Jones – The strange apeman, by E. Tegla Davies [tr. Ll. Wyn Griffith] – The poacher, by Eiluned Lewis – The black rat, by Frank Richards – The way of the earth, by Caradoc Evans – A life's chase, by Allen Raine – Big business, by J. Ellis Williams – Wil Thomas, by Glyn Jones – An idyll without an end, by Herbert M. Vaughan – Country dance, by Margiad Evans – Something to be thankful for, by Jack Griffith – The wild horses and fair maidens of Llanganoch, by Ifan Pughe – The bull giant head, by Blanche Devereux – A good year, by D.J. Williams [tr. Ll. Wyn Griffith] – A hewer of stone, by Richard Pryce – Siôn William, by Richard Hughes Williams [tr. Ll. Wyn Griffith] – The orchards, by Dylan Thomas – The five eggs, by Hywel Davies – A thing of nought, by Hilda Vaughan. – 'Has been compiled on the advice of a small corps of Welsh advisers.'

*Welsh short stories,* ed. Gwyn Jones. Harmondsworth: Penguin, 1940. 169 p.: pbk. Contents: Samuel Jones's harvest thanksgiving, by E. Tegla Davies [tr. Dafydd Jenkins] – Caleb's ark, by Rhys Davies – A mighty man in Sion, by Caradoc Evans – Let dogs delight, by George Ewart Evans – Davis, by Siân Evans – The lost land, by Geraint Goodwin – Dripping leaves, by W.J. Gruffydd [tr. J. Walter Jones] – A night at a cottage, by Richard Hughes – Eben Isaac, by Glyn Jones – Shacki Thomas, by Gwyn Jones – The wanderers, by Alun Lewis – The cosy room, by Arthur Machen – Worthy is the lamb, by A. Edward Richards – Sisters, by Kate Roberts [tr. Walter Dowding] – A prospect of the sea, by Dylan Thomas – Pwll-yr-Onnen, by D.J. Williams [tr. Dafydd Jenkins] – Notes on authors, pp. 166-169. – Another edition, 1941. 154 p.

*Celtic story: number one,* ed. Aled Vaughan. London: Pendulum Publications, 1946. 167 p. Incl.: Canute, by Rhys Davies – The insufferables, by Hugh V. Gill – I know a bank, by William Glynne-Jones – The rocking chair, by M.L. Turner – The feud, by Aled Vaughan – Two at the table, by Henry Treece – The hedgehog, by Cledwyn Hughes – Baboons, by Howell Davies – Unquiet dwelling, by Con Morgan – Homecoming, by Nigel Heseltine.

*Welsh short stories,* ed. Gwyn Jones. London: Oxford University Press, 1956. xv, 330 p. (World's classics; 551). Contents: Introduction, by Gwyn Jones, pp. ix-xv – The nature of man, by Rhys Davies – The benefit concert, by Rhys Davies – Be this her memorial, by Caradoc Evans – A father in Sion, by Caradoc Evans – Possessions, by George Ewart Evans – All through the night, by Margiad Evans – A sitting of eggs, by Geraint Goodwin – Ifan Owen and the grey rider, by Wyn Griffith – The stranger, by Richard Hughes – Wat Pantathro, by Glyn Jones – Price-Parry, by Glyn Jones – A night at Galon-Uchaf, by Gwyn Jones – The brute creation, by Gwyn Jones – The wanderers, by Alun Lewis – They came, by Alun Lewis – The shining pyramid, by Arthur Machen – Worthy is the lamb, by A. Edward Richards – Old age, by Kate Roberts [tr. Ll. Wyn Griffith] – Two storms, by Kate Roberts [tr. Dafydd Jenkins] – The enemies, by Dylan Thomas – A visit to Grandpa's, by Dylan Thomas – And a spoonful of grief to taste, by Gwyn Thomas – Thy need, by Gwyn Thomas – The white dove, by Aled Vaughan – Pwll-yr-Onnen, by D.J. Williams [tr. Dafydd Jenkins] – Wil Thomas's cap, by Islwyn Williams [tr. the author].

*Welsh short stories,* ed. George Ewart Evans. London: Faber, 1959. 288 p. Contents: Introduction, by George Ewart Evans, pp. 9-15 – The dilemma of Catherine Fuchsias, by Rhys Davies – A summer day, by Kate Roberts [tr. Dafydd Jenkins] – It's not by a beak you judge a woodcock, by Glyn Jones – Janet Ifans' donkey, by Geraint Goodwin – Death at Christmas, by Glyn Daniel – Goronwy's house of gold, by Gwyn Jones – The way of the earth, by Caradoc Evans – Immortality, by Henry Mansel – The orchards, by Dylan Thomas – The girl in the heather, by Islwyn Ffowc Elis [tr. the author] – Where my dark lover lies, by Gwyn Thomas – The investment, by Aled Vaughan – The orange grove, by Alun Lewis – The medal, by George Ewart Evans – Hangman's assistant, by David Alexander – Flaming tortoises, by Nigel Heseltine – The first snow, by Cledwyn Hughes – Up-ladle at three, by William Glynne-Jones – The conquered, by Dorothy Edwards – The court cupboard, by D.J. Williams [tr. Dafydd Jenkins] – Gone fishing, by John Wright – Mrs. Armitage, by Emyr Humphreys – A night for the curing, by Roland Mathias – A view across the valley, by Dilys Rowe – The stranger, by Richard Hughes.

*The shining pyramid and other stories by Welsh authors,* ed. Sam Adams and Roland Mathias. Llandysul: Gwasg Gomer, 1970. xvi, 163 p. ISBN: 0-85088-079-3. Contents: Introduction, by Sam Adams and Roland Mathias, pp. xi-xvi – The shining pyramid, by Arthur Machen – The talent thou gavest, by Caradoc Evans – Poor man's inn, by Richard Hughes – Nightgown, by Rhys Davies – The lost land, by Geraint Goodwin – Ward 'O' 3(b), by Alun Lewis – A white birthday, by Gwyn Jones – A story, by Dylan Thomas – Arrayed like one of these, by Gwyn Thomas – The boy in the bucket, by Glyn Jones – The rigours of inspection, by Emyr Humphreys – Snowdrops, by Leslie Norris – Notes on the authors, pp. 158-163.

*Twenty-five Welsh short stories,* ed. Gwyn Jones and Islwyn Ffowc Elis. London: Oxford University Press, 1971. xvi, 239 p.: pbk. ISBN: 0-19-281099-5. Contents: Introduction, by Gwyn Jones, pp. ix-xvi – Canute, by Rhys Davies – The wedding, by John Gwilym Jones [tr. Islwyn Ffowc Elis] – Cats at an auction, by Kate Roberts [tr. Ll. Wyn Griffith] – Let dogs delight, by George Ewart Evans – The dress, by Dylan Thomas – O brother man, by Gwyn Thomas – The letter, by R. Gerallt Jones [tr. the author] – A moment of time, by Richard Hughes – Song of a pole, by Islwyn Ffowc Elis [tr. the author] – Hangman's assistant, by David Alexander – Adjudication, by Islwyn Williams [tr. the author] – The miracle, by Harri Pritchard Jones – A party for the nightingale, by Margiad Evans – It's not by his beak you can judge a woodcock, by Glyn Jones – Ward 'O' 3(b), by Alun Lewis – The last ditch, by Bobi Jones [tr. Elizabeth Edwards] – China boy, by Idwal Jones – The pit, by Gwyn Jones – Davis, by Siân Evans – Samuel Jones's harvest thanksgiving, by E. Tegla Davies [tr. Dafydd Jenkins] –

Joseph's house, by Caradoc Evans – Deprivation, by Eigra Lewis Roberts [tr. Enid R. Morgan] – The man who lost his Boswell, by David Monger – A good year, by D.J. Williams [tr. Ll. Wyn Griffith] – The white farm, by Geraint Goodwin. – 'This is the fifth anthology of Welsh short stories to appear in the English language, and the first with any real claim to be true to its title or representative of its subject.' – Reissued 1992, as *Classic Welsh short stories.* pbk. ISBN: 0-19-282940-8.

*Welsh tales of terror,* ed. R. Chetwynd-Hayes. London: Fontana, 1973. 188 p.: pbk. ISBN: 0-00-613224-3. Incl.: Introduction, by R. Chetwynd-Hayes, pp. 9-11 – Jordan, by Glyn Jones – A cry of children, by John Christopher – The shining pyramid, by Arthur Machen – Animal or human beings, by Angus Wilson – The Morgan Trust, by Richard Bridgeman – Water-horses and spirits of the mist, by Marc Trevelyan – Be this her memorial, by Caradoc Evans – The lost gold mine, by Hazel F. Looker – Mrs Jones, by Dorothy K. Haynes – The Reverend John Jones and the ghostly horseman, by Ronald Seth – Cadi Hughes, by Glyn Jones – Black goddess, by Jack Griffith – The stranger, by Richard Hughes – Lord Dunwilliam and the Cwn Annwn, by R. Chetwynd-Hayes.

*The Magic Valley travellers: Welsh stories of fantasy and horror,* ed. Peter Haining. London: Gollancz, 1974. 256 p. ISBN: 0-575-01686-8. Contents: Foreword, by Richard Hughes, pp. 13-15 – Lludd and Llevelys [trad.] – Merlin and the magicians, by Geoffrey of Monmouth – Arthur and Gorlagon [anon.] – The living dead man, by Walter Map – The fairy people, by Giraldus Cambrensis – The sin eater, by John Aubrey – The fatal prediction, by Ann of Swansea – The invisible girl, by Mary Shelley – The dylluan, by George Borrow – The curse of the Pantannas, by Sir John Rhys – The treasure ghost, by Elias Owen – The corpse candle, by Wirt Sykes – The chronic argonauts, by H.G. Wells – The gift of tongues, by Arthur Machen – The coffin, by Caradoc Evans – A stray from Cathay, by John Wyndham – The stranger, by Richard Hughes – The school for witches, by Dylan Thomas – The sabbath, by Charles Williams – Week-end at Cwm Tatws, by Robert Graves – Jordan, by Glyn Jones – The dark isle, by Robert Bloch – The dark world, by Rhys Davies.

*The old man of the mist and other stories: an anthology of new writing from Wales,* ed. Lynn Hughes. London: Martin, Brian & O'Keefe, 1974. 163 p. ISBN: 0-85616-270-1. Contents: The old man of the mist, by Fletcher Watkins – New boots, by Diana Gruffydd Williams – Entertaining, by Diana Gruffydd Williams – Small boat distress signal, by John Tripp – Apricot sponge with a sage, by John Tripp – Matt Prytherch, by John Tripp – Gran and the roaring boys, by Jenny Sullivan – Perhaps I might have been different, by Jenny Sullivan – All gone, by Paula Griffiths – Marlene Biddle and the dead men, by Paula Griffiths – Born under Leo, by Paula Griffiths – Change of direction, by Ray John – Gay, by Cliff James – Lizzie, by Cliff James – And let the rest of the world go by, by Cliff James – Did anyone ever ask Beatrice?, by Byron Rogers – Long grey day, by Roderic Rees – The shell, by B.A. Westall – A suitable gift for a lady, by Joan Hughes – When I was eleven, by P.M. Cockerill – Love theme number one, by Hugh Joshua – The bread board, by Paul Keidrych Bevan.

*The Penguin book of Welsh short stories,* ed. Alun Richards. Harmondsworth: Penguin, 1976. 358 p.: pbk. ISBN: 0-1400-4061-7. Contents: Introduction, by Alun Richards, pp. 7-9 – The fashion plate, by Rhys Davies – The golden pony, by Glyn Jones – Acting captain, by Alun Lewis – Saturday night, by Geraint Goodwin – The loss, by Kate Roberts [tr. Walter Dowding] – The brute creation, by Gwyn Jones – Extraordinary little cough, by Dylan Thomas – A successful year, by D.J. Williams [tr. Glyn Jones] – The teacher, by Gwyn Thomas – The strange apeman, by E. Tegla Davies [tr. Ll. Wyn Griffith] – Be this her memorial, by Caradoc Evans – The return, by Brenda Chamberlain – Twenty tons of coal, by B.L. Coombes – The squire of Havilah, by T. Hughes Jones [tr. T. Glynne Davies] – An overdose of sun, by Eigra Lewis Roberts [tr. the author] – The house in Builth Crescent, by Moira Dearnley – Blind date, by Jane Edwards [tr. D. Llwyd Morgan] – Morfydd's celebration, by Harri Pritchard Jones [tr. Harri Webb] – A writer came to our place, by John Morgan – A roman spring, by Leslie Norris – Before forever after, by Ron Berry – Hon. Sec. (RFC), by Alun Richards – Black barren, by Islwyn Ffowc Elis [tr. the author] – Mel's secret love, by Emyr Humphreys.

*Short stories from Wales,* ed. David Elias. Exeter: Wheaton, 1978. 72 p.: ill.: pbk. ISBN: 0-08-021865-2. Contents: Christmas journey, by Kate Roberts – Snowdrops, by Leslie Norris – The letter, by R. Gerallt Jones – Cross purposes, by Dafydd Wyn – Will Thomas's cap, by Islwyn Williams – Gran and the roaring boys, by Jenny Sullivan – Curly Jones, by Robert Morgan – Possessions, by George Ewart Evans – A white birthday, by Gwyn Jones – Mrs Jones, by Dorothy K. Haynes – Resurrection, by Rhys Davies – Siôn William, by Richard Hughes Williams.

*My favourite stories of Wales,* ed. Jan Morris. Guildford: Lutterworth Press, 1980. 127 p.: ill. ISBN: 0-7188-2406-7. Modern stories selected incl: The followers, by Dylan Thomas – Tea in the heather, by Kate Roberts [tr. Ll. Wyn Griffith] – A sitting of eggs, by Geraint Goodwin – Cadi Hughes, by Glyn Jones – The brute creation, by Gwyn Jones. – With line drawings by Peter McClure.

*Pieces of eight: contemporary Anglo-Welsh short stories,* ed. Robert Nisbet. Llandysul: Gomer Press, 1982. 143 p.: pbk. ISBN: 0-85088-555-8. Contents: Foreword, by Robert Nisbet, pp. 9-11 – When you were you, by Graham Allen – Rough justice, by Graham Allen – Time spent, by Ron Berry – Left behind, by Ron Berry – Natives, by Ron Berry – A visit to Lizzie's, by Tony Curtis – The way back, by Tony Curtis – The fish-in, by Christine Furnival – For Sheenagh with love, by Christine Furnival – Hell of a man, by Eifion Jenkins – The killing, by Eifion Jenkins – Golden Jubilee, by Sally Roberts Jones – The inheritance, by Sally Roberts Jones

– Reconnaissance, by Robert Nisbet – Sunshine and Saturday, by Robert Nisbet – Go home, Davy Tuck, by John Tripp – No peace for Dando, by John Tripp.

***The green bridge: stories from Wales,*** ed. John Davies. Bridgend: Seren Books, 1988. 271 p.: hbk. & pbk. ISBN: 0-907476-93-7 hbk, 0-907476-94-5 pbk. Contents: Introduction, by John Davies, pp. 7-9 – The wild horses and fair maidens of Llanganoch, by Ifan Pughe – The conquered, by Dorothy Edwards – Gothic halls, by Nigel Heseltine – The flying hours are gone, by Geraint Goodwin – Three men from Horeb, by Caradoc Evans – The old woman and the wind, by Margiad Evans – Possessions, by George Ewart Evans – The pit, by Gwyn Jones – Arrayed like one of these, by Gwyn Thomas – Jordan, by Glyn Jones – Patricia, Edith and Arnold, by Dylan Thomas – Davis, by Siân Evans – The raid, by Alun Lewis – The swans, by Richard Hughes – The chosen one, by Rhys Davies – The return, by Brenda Chamberlain – Rosebud Prosser, by Ron Berry – My father's red indian, by Dannie Abse – The arrest, by Emyr Humphreys – Scream, scream, by Glenda Beagan – Fly half, by Alun Richards – Sing it again, Wordsworth, by Leslie Norris – The other side of summer, by Jaci Stephen – Boss, by Duncan Bush – Losing, by Clare Morgan – Notes on contributors, pp. 268-270.

***Wales on the wireless: a broadcasting anthology,*** ed. Patrick Hannan. Llandysul: Gomer in assoc. with BBC Cymru/Wales, 1988. xxii, 200 p.: ill. ISBN: 0-86383-447-7. Incl.: Incident in a bookshop (1938), by Rhys Davies, pp. 1-2 – A proper nation (1938), by Goronwy Rees, pp. 6-7 – Minority culture (1955) by Dannie Abse, p. 10 – Carwyn (1983), by Alun Richards, pp. 24-27 – Alun Lewis (1944), by Gwyn Jones, pp. 27-28 – David Jones (1965), by Harman Grisewood, pp. 29-31 – Caradoc Evans (1948), by George Bullock, pp. 31-33 – Gwyn Thomas (1981), by Gwyn Jones, pp. 33-34 – Rhondda (1980), by Gwyn Thomas, pp. 48-50 – Merthyr Tydfil (1983), by Leslie Norris, pp. 51-52 – Valleys (1943), by Idris Davies, pp. 55-56 -Swansea (1961), by Vernon Watkins, pp. 57-58 – Picturegoers (1980), by John Ormond, pp. 58-60 – Return journey (1947), by Dylan Thomas, pp. 61-63 – Aberfan (1967), by Gwyn Thomas, pp. 63-64 – Quite early one morning (1945), by Dylan Thomas, pp. 69-71 – Rats, birds and bare knuckles (1964), by Jack Jones, p. 85 – Gazooka (1953), by Gwyn Thomas, pp. 93-94 – Women in adversity (1941), by Jack Jones, p. 103 – War (1940), by Idris Davies, pp. 108-109 – A negation of humanity (1964), by Jack Jones, p. 111 – Understanding nationalism (1938), by Goronwy Rees, pp. 133-135 – Self-awareness (1950), by Richard Hughes, p. 135 – The survival of Welsh (1977), by Gwyn Jones, pp. 140-143 – Disappearing Wales (1963), by Alun Richards, pp. 152-154 – A medium-sized poet (1960), by Dannie Abse, pp. 154-157 – The working-class writer, by Bert Coombes (1947), pp. 157-159 – Terrible (1951), by Richard Hughes, pp. 159-160 – Arlott on Dylan (1983), by John Arlott, pp. 161-162 – Another Dylan (1987), by Kingsley Amis, p. 164 – Poetry of meaning (1966), by Glyn Jones, pp. 165-166 – *Selected poems* (1987), by John Ormond, pp. 166-168 – Coming back (1953), by Goronwy Rees, pp. 180-181 – Come off it, Mr Chips (1960), by Gwyn Thomas, pp. 184-185 – Lawrence of Oxford (1946), by A.G. Prys-Jones, pp. 192-194. – Excerpts from the BBC's Welsh archive.

*The new Penguin book of Welsh short stories,* ed. Alun Richards. London: Viking, 1993. xi, 400 p. ISBN: 0-670-84530-2. Contents: Introduction, by Alun Richards, pp. ix-xi – The white farm by Geraint Goodwin – The condemned, by Kate Roberts [tr. Joseph P. Clancy] – Blodwen, by Rhys Davies – A white birthday, by Gwyn Jones – Oscar, by Gwyn Thomas – A story, by Dylan Thomas – The orange grove, by Alun Lewis – Wat Pantathro, by Glyn Jones – Good-for-nothing, by Dic Tryfan [tr. Dafydd Rowlands] – A father in Sion, by Caradoc Evans – Relatives, by Alun T. Lewis [tr. Hywel Teifi Edwards] – The Mecca of the nation, by D.J. Williams [tr. R. Gerallt Jones] – A fine room to be ill in, by Raymond Williams – Twenty tons of coal, by B.L. Coombes – The suspect, by Emyr Humphreys – Self-pity, by Islwyn Ffowc Elis [tr. the author] – The former Miss Merthyr Tydfil, by Alun Richards – A house divided, by Leslie Norris – Sorry, Miss Crouch, by Dannie Abse – Fool's paradise, by Harri Pritchard Jones [tr. the author] – November kill, by Ron Berry – Waiting for the rain to break, by Jane Edwards [tr. Elin Williams] – Jennifer's baby, by Penny Windsor – Do you remember Jamie?, by Eigra Lewis Roberts – Losing, by Clare Morgan – Hopkins, by Duncan Bush – The last thrush, by Glenda Beagan – Barbecue, by Catherine Merriman – Notes on the authors, pp. 396-400.

# D. Anthologies: Regional

*Monmouthshire poetry: an anthology relating to the county or composed by writers associated with Monmouthshire,* ed. Lawrence W. Hockey. Newport: R.H. Johns, [1949]. 148 p. Selections from 34 poets, including Idris Davies, W.H. Davies, A.G. Prys-Jones, Huw Menai, Edward Thomas.

*Triongl/Triangle: blodeugerdd o gerddi'r de-orllewin: an anthology of poems from the south-west,* ed. W. Rhys Nicholas. Llandysul: Gomer Press, 1977. 104 p.: pbk. Comprises Welsh and English sections, the latter containing poems by: Graham Allen – Tony Curtis – Don Dale-Jones – Dudley G. Davies – Jon Dressel – J.C. Evans – Leslie Evans – Raymond Garlick – Jeremy Hooker – Ray Howard-Jones – Nigel Jenkins – Peter Thabit Jones – Sally Roberts Jones – Moelwyn Merchant – Robert Nisbet – John Ormond – Malcolm Parr – Kusha Petts – Alan Perry – Douglas Phillips – Peter Preece – J.P. Ward – Harri Webb – Gwyn Williams.

*Dismays and rainbows: an anthology of short stories from West Wales,* ed. Robert Nisbet. West Wales Association for the Arts, 1979. 108 p.: pbk. ISBN: 0-85088-941-3. Contents: Editor's foreword, pp. 8-9 – When you were you, by Graham Allen – Film night, by Tony Curtis – Requiem, by Moira Dearnley – Mari, by Christine Furnival – The wicker cage, by Martin Haslehurst – Leaves, by Cliff James – Hell of a man, by Eifion

Jenkins – A pigeon for Old Bember, by Peter Thabit Jones – Edward, by Sally Roberts Jones – Barber shop blues, by Robert Nisbet – The bird: a story, by Alan Perry – Protector of the people, by Ted Wilkins – Biographical notes, pp. 106-108.

*Here in North Wales*, ed. John Davies and John Pook; design and illustration by Alwyn Dempster Jones. Mold: Clwyd Centre for Educational Technology, 1982. 73 p.: ill.: pbk. ISBN: 0-904444-96-1. Selections from: Arnold Bennett – Tony Connor – Anthony Conran – Alexander Cordell – Cynan – John Davies – T. Glynne Davies – Islwyn Ffowc Elis – Nerys Hughes – Robert Graves – Clyde Holmes – T. Rowland Hughes – Emyr Humphreys – John Idris Jones – R. Gerallt Jones – Alan Llwyd – R. Williams Parry – T.H. Parry-Williams – Ken Price – Kate Roberts – Gwyn Thomas – R.S. Thomas – D.J. Thorp – John Tripp – John Wain – Harri Webb. – Arranged in two sections, The coast, The hills. – 'An anthology of twentieth-century poetry and prose intended for use in secondary schools. Focusing on a region which ... extends from Abersoch in the west to Gresford in the east, and from the coast down to Bala.'

*The valleys*, ed. John Davies and Mike Jenkins. Bridgend: Poetry Wales Press, 1984. 141 p.: hbk & pbk. ISBN: 0-907476-28-7 hbk, 0-907476-31-7 pbk. Incl. works by and extracts from: Sam Adams – Graham Allen – Ron Berry – Roy Burnett – A.J. Cronin – Bryan Martin Davies – Idris Davies – John Davies – J. Kitchener Davies – Rhys Davies – Jean Earle – Tom Earley – John Fairfax – John L. Hughes – Emyr Humphreys – Mike Jenkins – D. Gwenallt Jones – Jack Jones – Glyn Jones – Gwyn Jones – Lewis Jones – Alun Lewis – Saunders Lewis – Robert Minhinnick – Robert Morgan – Leslie Norris – Alun Richards – Meic Stephens – Gwyn Thomas – John Tripp – Vernon Watkins – Harri Webb – Islwyn Williams.

*A Cardiff anthology*, ed. Meic Stephens. Bridgend: Seren Books, 1988. 197 p.: pbk. ISBN: 0-907476-84-8. Incl. works by and extracts from: Dannie Abse – Duncan Bush – Gillian Clarke – Alexander Cordell – Tony Curtis – Roald Dahl – Idris Davies – Tom Davies – Siôn Eirian – Peter Finch – W.J. Gruffydd – Geraint Jarman – R.T. Jenkins – Bobi Jones – Harri Pritchard Jones – Glyn Jones – Goronwy Jones – Gwyn Jones – Jack Jones – Douglas Houston – Emyr Humphreys – Geraint Jarman – Eric Linklater – Alun Llywelyn-Williams – R.M. Lockley – Robert Minhinnick – Jan Morris – Iorwerth C. Peate – Alun Rees – Goronwy Rees – Oliver Reynolds – Alun Richards – Bernice Rubens – Gilbert Ruddock – Howard Spring – Gwyn Thomas – W.C. Elvet Thomas – John Tripp – Harri Webb – Herbert Williams – John Stuart Williams.

*The poetry of Pembrokeshire*, ed. Tony Curtis. Bridgend: Seren Books, 1989. 100 p.: pbk. ISBN: 1-85411-007-1. Incl.: Introduction, by Tony Curtis, pp. 7-9 – Poems by: Alison Bielski – Duncan Bush – Phil Carradice – Gillian Clarke – Tony Curtis – Jean Earle – Peter Finch – Raymond

Garlick – Cliff James – A.G. Prys-Jones – Roland Mathias – Sir Lewis Morris – T.E. Nicholas – Leslie Norris – John Ormond – Douglas Phillips – Peter Preece – Dylan Thomas – John Tripp – J. Stuart Williams – Waldo Williams.

*The poetry of Snowdonia,* ed. Tony Curtis. Bridgend: Seren Books, 1989. 134 p.: pbk. ISBN: 1-85411-008-X. Selections from 51 poets, including translations from the Welsh.

*Black harvest: an anthology of contemporary poetry from the South Wales valleys,* ed. John Evans. Pontypridd: Underground Press, 1992. [54] p.: ill.: pbk. ISBN: 1-897607-00-8. Incl.: Foreword, by Dai Smith – Poems by: Duncan Bush – John Evans – Peter Finch – Basil Griffiths – Mike Jenkins – Nigel Jenkins – Robert Minhinnick – Phil Rees – Oliver Reynolds – Labi Siffre – Chris Torrance – Barbara Walters – John Watkins – Herbert Williams – Mogg Williams. – Each poem accompanied by a Paul Nurse photograph.

**Note.** This section omits school anthologies and collections from local writers' circles. Other regional anthologies, with lesser 'Anglo-Welsh' content, include:

*Letters from Swansea,* ed. J.E. Ross. Swansea: Christopher Davies, 1969. 140 p.

*A Gower anthology,* ed. David Rees. Swansea: Christopher Davies, 1977. 208 p. ISBN: 0-7154-0407-5.

*A Pembrokeshire anthology,* ed. Dillwyn Miles. Llandybïe: Hughes, 1983. 269 p.: ill. ISBN: 0-85284-018-7.

*A Carmarthenshire anthology,* ed. Lynn Hughes. Llandybïe: Christopher Davies, 1984. xxiii, 470 p.: ill. ISBN: 0-7154-0643-4.

*The mountains of Wales: an anthology in verse and prose,* ed. Ioan Bowen Rees. Newton: Gwasg Gregynog, 1987. 189 p.: ill. ISBN: 0-948714-13-1 quarter-vellum, 0-948714-14-X special binding. Watercolour illustrations by Revd John Parker. – 'This edition consists of 275 copies … 20 in a special binding … and 255 in quarter-vellum.'
—— Cardiff: University of Wales Press, 1992. xvii, 299 p.: hbk & pbk. ISBN: 0-7083-1162-8 hbk, 0-7083-1163-6 pbk. 'A number of pieces have been added to the original Gregynog edition.' – This enlarged edition is unillustrated.

# E. Periodicals: Some Special Issues

*Life and Letters Today* (from vol. 46, 1945, *Life and Letters*). Under the editorship of Robert Herring this periodical generously covered Anglo-Welsh writing, particularly in the years 1938-1950. The following are specifically Welsh numbers: 24,31 (Mar 1940); 36, 67 (Mar 1943); 48,103 (Mar 1946); 52,115 (Mar 1947); 58,133 (Sep 1948).

*The Poetry Review* 13,2 (1922): 'South Wales number', ed. M.J. James and the Barry Council. Incl.: Welsh poets and poetry: an editorial note, by M.J. James, pp. 73-75 – Wales and English poetry, by A.G. Prys-Jones, pp. 76-87 – Some South Walian poets of today, by T.J. Thomas (Sarnicol), pp. 88-93 – Glamorgan boasts of many a bard well-skilled in harp and vocal glee, by Ellen Evans, pp. 94-98 – Poetry by: Idris Bell – Elfyn Williams David – Dudley G. Davies – Lewis Davies – Alfred Edmunds – E. Howard Harris – Richard Hughes – Wil Ifan – Edwin Stanley James – M.J. James – E. MacBean – Huw Menai – Nancy Morris – A. J. Perman – Mrs B. Price-Hughes – A.G. Prys-Jones – Bessie May Stephens – D. Vaughan Thomas – Percy Thomas – Stephen Harvard Thomas – T.J. Thomas (Sarnicol).

*Rann* 19 (1953): 'Welsh number'. Incl. poetry by: David Bell – Idris Bell – Henry Birkhead – Oonah Cuming – Raymond Garlick – Peter Hellings – Edmund Hughes – Emyr Humphreys – Glyn Jones – Roland Mathias – A.G. Prys-Jones – Morwyth Rees – R.S. Thomas – Henry Treece – Vernon Watkins.

*Poetry Book Magazine* 6,5 (1954): 'Poetry from Wales, gathered together and introduced by Raymond Garlick'. Incl.: Poetry from Wales: an introduction, pp. 1-3 – Poems by: Dannie Abse – Idris Bell – Anthony Conran – Idris Davies – Pennar Davies – Peter Hellings – Emyr Humphreys – Bobi Jones – David Jones – D. Gwenallt Jones – Glyn Jones – T. Harri Jones – Saunders Lewis – D.M. Lloyd – Alun Llywelyn-Williams – Roland Mathias – Huw Menai – Idris Parry – John Cowper Powys – Peter Preece – A.G. Prys-Jones – Lynette Roberts – Peter John Stephens – R.S. Thomas – Vernon Watkins.

*The Poetry Review,* Winter 1964, 217-227: supplement on Anglo-Welsh poetry. Incl.: Welsh writing today, by Bryn Giffiths – Poetry by: Alison J. Bielski – Anthony Conran – Gloria Evans Davies – David Elias – Lawrence Griffiths – Dedwydd Jones – Robert Morgan – Peter Preece – Bryn G. Roberts – Meic Stephens – John Tripp – Harri Webb.

*Poet: An International Monthly* [Madras], Apr 1969: 'Welsh number', ed. Peter Finch. Incl. poetry by Dannie Abse, Raymond Garlick, Glyn Jones, Roland Mathias, Leslie Norris, R.S. Thomas, John Tripp, Harri Webb and others.

*Akros* 12 (1970): special issue on Anglo-Welsh poetry. Incl. Introduction: An Anglo-Welsh renaissance, by John Tripp, pp. 5-9 – Poetry by: Raymond Garlick – Roland Mathias – Leslie Norris – Meic Stephens – John Tripp – Harri Webb.

*Transatlantic Review* 42-43 (1972) 65-96: 'A retrospective of Anglo-Welsh poetry'. Incl.: Introduction, by B.S. Johnston – Poetry by: Sam Adams – Anthony Conran – Raymond Garlick – Bryn Griffiths – John Idris Jones – Roland Mathias – Leslie Norris – John Ormond – Douglas Phillips – Meic Stephens – Ned Thomas – Peter Thomas – John Tripp – Harri Webb – Gwyn Williams – Herbert Williams – John Stuart Williams.

*Spirit: A Magazine of Poetry* 41,2 (1974-75): 'Sixteen Welsh poets'. Incl: Editorial note, by Roland Mathias – Poetry by: Dannie Abse – Sam Adams – Ruth Bidgood – Gillian Clarke – Raymond Garlick – Glyn Jones – Sally Roberts Jones – Roland Mathias – Leslie Norris – John Ormond – Meic Stephens – R.S. Thomas – John Tripp – Harri Webb – Gwyn Williams – John Stuart Williams.

*New England Review and Bread Loaf Quarterly* 10,4 (1988): 'Writers of Wales'. Incl.: Confessions of an Anglo-Welsh reader, by Jill Farringdon, pp. 381-402 – Poetry as performance in South Wales, by Peter Finch, pp. 440-446 – Poetry by: Dannie Abse – Chris Bendon – Ruth Bidgood – Euros Bowen – Duncan Bush – Gillian Clarke – Tony Curtis – John Davies – Peter Finch – Mike Jenkins – Peter Thabit Jones – Gwyneth Lewis – Christopher Meredith – Catherine Merriman – Robert Nisbet – Leslie Norris – Richard Poole – Sheenagh Pugh – Oliver Reynolds – Steve Short – R.S. Thomas. – Review: *Planet* 77 (1989) 98-99 (David Lloyd).

*North Dakota Quarterly* 57,2 (1989): 'Anglo-Welsh poetry: a selection'. Incl.: A preface to Anglo-Welsh poetry, by Raymond Garlick, pp. 3-8 – Anglo-Welsh poetry: Dylan and after, by Tony Curtis, pp. 9-14 – Poetry by: Dannie Abse – Ruth Bidgood – Gillian Clarke – Tony Conran – Tony Curtis – John Davies – Jon Dressel – Raymond Garlick – Mike Jenkins – Glyn Jones – Roland Mathias – Robert Minhinnick – Leslie Norris – John Ormond – R.S. Thomas – Harri Webb – Gwyn Williams. – This 76-page supplement edited by Raymond Garlick and Tony Curtis.

# F. Anthologies: Translations

*Poetry* [Shih Feng Association, Hong Kong] 109 (1981). Incl.: Interview with Glyn Jones, pp. i-v – Chinese translations of and introductions to poems by: Dannie Abse – Euros Bowen – Tony Curtis – Pennar Davies – Peter Finch – Raymond Garlick – Bobi Jones – Glyn Jones – Alun Llewelyn-Williams – Roland Mathias – Robert Morgan – Leslie Norris – John Ormond – Gwyn Thomas – John Tripp – Harri Webb – Gwyn Williams.

*Valliysky rasskaz: Welsh story*, ed. E. Genieva. Moscow: Izvestiya, 1983. 142 p.: pbk. (Library of foreign literature). Incl.: Nightshirt, by Rhys Davies – The shining pyramid, by Arthur Machen – In the snare, by Gwyn Jones – Rhysie at Auntie Kezia's, by Glyn Jones – Jordan, by Glyn Jones – Note on Anglo-Welsh writing, by Glyn Jones. – Also stories by George

Ewart Evans, Islwyn Ffowc Elis, E. Tegla Davies and Aled Vaughan. – With introduction by E. Genieva. – Translations by A. Melnikov.

*Revue Svetovej Literatúry* 1 (1984). Incl.: Neznámy Wales, by Katarina Karovicová, pp. 9-12 – Stories by: Rhys Davies – Gwyn Jones – Jane Edwards – Glyn Jones

*Erkundungen: 28 walisische Erzähler*, ed. Hans Petersen. Berlin: Volk und Welt, 1988. 405 p.: pbk. ISBN: 3-353-00361-4. Contents: Der Herde gleich, vom Hirten fern, by Gwyn Jones – Genau wie die Hunde auch, by Dylan Thomas – Der Champion, by Alun Richards – Katzen bei einer Auktion, by Kate Roberts – Soldat Jones, by Alun Lewis – Bis zum letzten Atemzug, by Bobi Jones – Im fernen, fernen China, by Leslie Norris – Gesang von einem Telegraphenmast, by Islwyn Ffowc Elis – Ein Mann des Schicksals, by Herbert Williams – Die Heimkehr, by Roland Mathias – Tennis bei den Robinsons, by Tony Curtis – Leute machen Kleider, by Gwyn Thomas – Das Dorf, by Duncan Bush – Ihr werdet eurer Sünde innewerden, wenn sie euch finden wird, by Caradoc Evans – Der Handel des Jahres, by D.J. Williams – Verausgabt, by Ron Berry – Cynthia, by Peter Finch – Ein früher Morgen, by Penny Windsor – Ap Towyns grosser Auftritt, by Geraint Goodwin – Wasser, by Robert Morgan – Eine erfreuliche Nachricht, by Emyr Humphreys – Lasst den Hunden doch ihren Spass, by George Ewart Evans – Morfydds Feier, by Harri Pritchard Jones – Strata Florida, by Ned Thomas – Der Weg nach Haus, by Robert Nisbet – Wat Pantathro, by Glyn Jones – Kanut, by Rhys Davies – Freuen Sie sich!, by Carl Tighe – Afterword, by Hans Petersen, pp. 365-375 – Biographical notes, pp. 377-389 – Notes, pp. 391-402. – Review: *Powys Review* 24 (1989) 69-70 (Anthony Bushell).

# WELSH WRITING IN ENGLISH: GENERAL CRITICISM

A. Bibliography and reference

B. General studies

C. Poetry

D. Prose

E. Regional guides

F. Anglo-Welsh literature in education

## A. Bibliography and Reference

JONES, Brynmor. *A bibliography of Anglo-Welsh literature, 1900-1965.* Library Association (Wales and Monmouthshire Branch), 1970. viii, 139 p. Incl.: Section A. Anglo-Welsh literature; Anthologies, Individual authors – Section B. Bibliographical and critical works; Anglo-Welsh literature in general, Individual authors, Dissertations and unpublished sources – Section C. Children's stories – Indexes; Regional, General. – The bibliography admits literature with a Welsh setting written by non-Welsh authors.

*LITERATURE in twentieth-century Wales: a guide to the field, 1.* Aberystwyth: University College of Wales (Department of English), 1979. 59 p. Incl. bibliographies of: Caradoc Evans – Idris Davies – Kate Roberts – Gwenallt – D.J. Williams – Emyr Humphreys – R.S. Thomas – Brenda Chamberlain. – With introductory section on sources in English for the study of literature in twentieth-century Wales.

JONES, Glyn and John Rowlands. *Profiles: a visitor's guide to writing in twentieth-century Wales.* Llandysul: Gomer Press, 1980. xxxi, 382 p. ISBN: 0-85088-713-5. Incl. profiles of: Arthur Machen – W.H. Davies – John Cowper Powys – Caradoc Evans – Jack Jones – David Jones – Richard Hughes – Rhys Davies – Geraint Goodwin – Gwyn Williams – Idris Davies – Glyn Jones – Vernon Watkins – Gwyn Jones – Gwyn Thomas – R.S. Thomas – Dylan Thomas – Alun Lewis – Roland Mathias – Emyr Humphreys – Harri Webb – Ron Berry – T.H. Jones – Leslie Norris – Dannie Abse – John Ormond – Raymond Garlick – John Tripp – Alun Richards – Anthony Conran – Raymond Williams.

*THE OXFORD companion to the literature of Wales,* ed. Meic Stephens. Oxford: Oxford University Press, 1986. xvi, 682 p. ISBN: 0-19-211586-3. 'A comprehensive introduction to Welsh and Anglo-Welsh literature from the sixth century to the present day.' – Reviews: *Author*, Autumn 1986, 24-25 (Gillian Clarke); *Books and Bookmen*, Apr 1986, 9 (Paul Ferris); *BNW*,

Spring 1986, 3-5 (M. Wynn Thomas); *Daily Telegraph*, 28 Feb 1986, 12 (Anthony Powell); *Guardian*, 27 Feb 1986, 23 (Raymond Williams); *Modern Language Review* 83 (1988) 713-715 (James A. Davies); *Planet* 56 (1986) 88-101 (A.M. Allchin); *Sunday Telegraph*, 9 Mar 1986, 12 (Michael Wharton); *TLS*, 6 Jun 1986, 624 (Dick Davies). Welsh version: *Cydymaith i lenyddiaeth Cymru,* ed. Meic Stephens. Caerdydd: Gwasg Prifysgol Cymru, 1986. xii, 662 p. ISBN: 0-7083-0915-1. Reviews: *Poetry Wales* 21,4 (1986) 125-129 (Rheinallt Llwyd); *Studia Celtica* 20-21 (1985-86) 297-303 (J.E. Caerwyn Williams); *Y Traethodydd*, Gor/Jul 1987, 163-165 (Brynley F. Roberts).

HOLT, Constance Wall. *Welsh women: an annotated bibliography of women in Wales and women of Welsh descent in America.* Metuchen, N.J.: Scarecrow Press, 1993. xxv, 834 p. ISBN: 0-8108-2610-0. Over 2000 entries in all, fully annotated and indexed – Parts 10.1, and 14.4 cover Literature.

JENKINS, David Clay. An index to *The Welsh Review. Journal of the Welsh Bibliographical Society* 9,4 (1965) 188-210.

MADDEN, G.M. *Index to Planet, nos. 1-27* [1970-1975]. Llangeitho: *Planet,* [1976]. 32 p.

—— *Planet: index to nos. 28-50.* Aberystwyth: *Planet,* 1980. 20 p.

ROBERTS, D. Hywel E. *Poetry Wales, 1-14 (1964-1979): an index.* Welsh Library Association, 1980. 136 p. ISBN: 0-8536713-0.

# B. General Studies

[ANON]. The two literatures of Wales. *TLS*, 5 Aug 1955, xii.

ARCHARD, Cary. Publishing in Wales, 2: Cary Archard interviewed by David Lloyd. *Planet* 96 (1992) 35-41. Concerning the Welsh literary publishers, Seren Books.

BARNIE, John. Where next? The direction of Welsh writing in English. *Planet* 91 (1992) 3-10. See also comment on the future of literature in the nineties from Ned Thomas, Joseph Clancy, Richard Poole, John Osmond, David Bartlett, Nicholas Murray, Rob Watson and D.A. Callard, pp. 112-120 (in response to Dai Smith and Robert Minhinnick, *Planet* 90).

BOORE, W.H. This Welshness. *AWR* 16,38 (1968) 142-146.

CONRAN, Anthony. A Welsh strategy for literature. *NWR* 4,3 [15] (1991-1992) 52-58. On ways in which Welsh writing in English and its funding should develop in the 1990s. – A statement on behalf of the Welsh Union of Writers.

DAVIES, Elwyn. The magazine that never was. *AWR* 81 (1985) 97-106. On attempts in 1934 to found a literary magazine.

DAVIES, James A. Under a rainbow sky: literary history. In *Swansea: an illustrated history,* ed. Glanmor Williams. Swansea: Christopher Davies, 1990. pp. 177-213.

DAVIES, Pennar. Literature in Wales in the twentieth century. In *Literature in Celtic Countries,* ed. J.E. Caerwyn Williams. Cardiff: University of Wales Press, 1971. pp. 61-76.

DAVIES, Rhys. *My Wales.* London: Jarrolds, 1937. Incl. Words, pp. 204-228.

EVANS, B. Ifor. The collective genius of English literature, 1. Wales. *Author*, Jan 1949, 7-9.

EVANS, George Ewart. The emergent national literature. *Wales* 2nd ser. 2 (1943) 50-53.

FARRINGDON, Jill. Confessions of an Anglo-Welsh reader. *New England Review and Bread Loaf Quarterly* 10,4 (1988) [Writers of Wales special issue] 381-402.

—— The language of gender. *PW* 24,3 (1988) 23-25.

GARLICK, Raymond. Editorial. *DL* 2,6 (1951) 1-4.

—— Editorial. *DL* 3,7 (1952) 1-6. On *Dock Leaves* and Anglo-Welsh literature in libraries and education.

—— Editorial. *DL* 4,11 (1953) 1-7.

—— *DL* 5,15 (1954) 1-6. On 17th-century Anglo-Welsh literature.

—— Editorial. *DL* 6,17 (1955) 1-6. On literary periodicals.

—— Editorial. *AWR* 9,23 [1958] 3-8. Discusses Gwyn Jones, *The first forty years: some notes on Anglo-Welsh literature.*

—— Editorial. *AWR* 10,25 [1959] 3-8.

—— Editorial. *AWR* 10,26 [1960] 3-9.

—— An Anglo-Welsh accidence. *University of Wales Review*, Summer 1965, 18-20.

—— Letter. *PW* 2,2 (1966) 41-43. Replies: Harri Webb, *PW* 2,3 (1966) 35-38; Raymond Garlick, PW 2,3 (1966) 39-42.

—— Welsh literature, 2. English. In *New Catholic Encyclopedia*. Vol. 14. New York: McGraw Hill, 1967. p. 872.

—— Is there an Anglo-Welsh literature? In *Literature in Celtic Countries*, ed. J.E.CaerwynWilliams.Cardiff:UniversityofWalesPress,1971.pp.195-213. With Appendix: Some Anglo-Welsh poets born between 1550 and 1850.

—— Vale atque ave. *NWR* 1,1 [1] (1988) 47-49. On demise of *The Anglo-Welsh Review.*

'GWLADGARWR'. The non Welsh-speaking Welsh. *Y Ddinas*, Oct 1958, 9-10,17.

GRIFFITH, Ll. Wyn. A note on 'Anglo-Welsh'. *Wales* 2nd ser. 1 (1943) 15-16.

—— *The Welsh*. Harmondsworth: Penguin, 1950. Incl. Welsh writers in English, pp. 102-115.

GRUFFYDD, Dyfed Elis. Publishing in Wales, 1: Dyfed Elis Gruffydd interviewed by David Lloyd. *Planet* 95 (1992) 25-29. The Gwasg Gomer editor touches upon Welsh writing in English.

HARRIS, John. Letters from the cultural battlefront: Keidrych Rhys and the *Western Mail. Planet 65* (1987) 21-26. Discusses background to *Wales.*

—— Not a *Trysorfa fach*: Keidrych Rhys and the launching of *Wales. NWR* 3,3 [11] (1991) 28-33.

HILL, Greg. What is distinctive about Welsh literature in English? *PW* 24,4 (1989) 46-48.

—— Drowned voices: post-modernism and the decline of the idea of culture. *Planet* 92 (1992) 61-70. In the context of Welsh writing in English.

JENKINS, David Clay. Writing in twentieth century Wales: a defense of the Anglo-Welsh. PhD thesis. State University of Iowa, 1956. vi, 295, 50 p. Contents: Backgrounds to writing in twentieth century Wales, pp. 8-81 –

Caradoc Evans' distorting mirror, pp. 82-116 – Richard Hughes: a study in bland criticism, pp. 117-150 – *Wales* and *The Welsh Review*, pp. 151-170 – The Welshness of Dylan Thomas, pp. 171-213 – Conclusions, pp. 214-221 – Notes, pp. 222-249 – Appendix A. Dylan Thomas's contributions to *Wales*, p. 250 – Appendix B. Annals of modern Anglo-Welsh writing, pp. 252-254 – Bibliography, pp. 255-271 – A bio-bibliography of modern Welsh authors, pp. 272-295 – An index to the *Welsh Review* [50 p.].

JENKINS, Mike. Editorial. *PW* 24,1 (1988) 2. On the term 'Anglo-Welsh'.

JENKINS, Nigel. Signposting a tradition. *Arcade*, 16 Oct 1981, 18-19. Discusses the Writers of Wales series (particularly Alan Rudrum, *Henry Vaughan*).

JOHNSTON, Dafydd. Dwy lenyddiaeth Cymru yn y tridegau. In *Sglefrio ar eiriau*, ed. John Rowlands. Llandysul: Gwasg Gomer, 1992. pp. 42-62. Comparative study of Welsh and Anglo-Welsh literature during the 1930s, with emphasis on Idris Davies and Lewis Jones.

JONES, Bobi. The Anglo-Welsh. *DL* 4,10 (1953) 23-28.

—— Anglo-Welsh: more definition. *Planet* 16 (1973) 11-23.

—— Demise of the Anglo-Welsh? *PW* 28,3 (1993) 14-18. Shortened version of his essay, Tranc yr Eingl-Gymry? *Barddas*, Ebr/Apr 1992. – See also comment by Richard Poole, *PW* 28,3 (1993) 2.

JONES, Brynmor. Letter. *PW* 3,1 (1967) 45-48. On Anglo-Welsh literature and bibliography.

JONES, Glyn. Y llenorion Eingl-Gymreig. *Taliesin* 9 (1964) 50-63. [The Anglo-Welsh writers].

—— *The dragon has two tongues: essays on Anglo-Welsh writers and writings.* London: Dent, 1968. ix, 221 p. ISBN: 0-460-03650-5. Contents: Letter to Keidrych, pp. 1-4 – Autobiography, pp. 5-38 – Background, pp. 39-48 – Introduction to short stories and novels, pp. 49-63 – Three prose writers; Caradoc Evans, Jack Jones, Gwyn Thomas, pp. 64-123 – Introduction to poetry, pp. 124-139 – Three poets; Huw Menai, Idris Davies, Dylan Thomas, pp. 140-203 – Conclusion, p. 204 – Bibliographical note, pp. 209-213.

—— Notes on Anglo-Welsh writing. *Études Anglaises* 23,3 (1970) 332-334.

—— Yr Eingl-Gymry heddiw. *Y Faner*, 6 Mai/May 1977, 12-13. [The Anglo-Welsh today].

—— *Setting out: a memoir of literary life in Wales.* Cardiff: University College Cardiff (Dept. of Extra-Mural Studies), 1982. iv, 16 p. (Park Place papers; 13). ISBN: 0-946045-17-8. Discusses outlets for Anglo-Welsh writing in the twenties and thirties.

JONES, G.O. Wales, Welsh ... *NWR* 1,1 [1] (1988) 56-60.

JONES, Gwyn. Editorial. *WR* 5 (1946) 5-7. On position of the Welsh writer in English.

—— Language, style and the Anglo-Welsh. *Essays and Studies* 6 (1953) 102-114. On Dylan Thomas, Gwyn Thomas, Glyn Jones and Caradoc Evans.

—— *The first forty years: some notes on Anglo-Welsh literature.* Cardiff: University of Wales Press, 1957. 28 p. (W.D. Thomas memorial lecture). Reprinted in *Triskel one: essays on Welsh and Anglo-Welsh literature*, ed. Sam Adams and Gwilym Rees Hughes (1971), pp. 75-95.

—— Forum needed for Welsh writers. *WM*, 27 Aug 1960, 5:A-E.

—— The Anglo-Welsh: as it was and may be. In *St David's National Festival Souvenir 1965*. London: London Welsh Trust, 1965. pp. 7-8.

—— Sense of place, 2. Writing for Wales and the Welsh. *TLS*, 28 Jul 1972, 869-870.

—— *Being and belonging: some notes on language, literature and the Welsh*. BBC Publications, 1977. 25 p. (BBC Wales annual radio lecture). ISBN: 0-563-17473-0.

—— *Babel and the dragon's tongue:* thc eighth Gwilym James memorial lecture of the University of Southampton, delivered on Thursday, 19th February, 1981. Southampton: University of Southampton, 1981. 21 p. ISBN: 0-85432-217-5.

—— Anglo-Welsh literature, 1934-46: a personal view. *THSC* (1987) 177-192. Reprinted in Gwyn Jones, *Background to Dylan Thomas* (1992), pp. 1-19.

JONES, Harri Pritchard. *PW* 4,3 (1969) 45-50. Review article on Glyn Jones, *The dragon has two tongues*.

JONES, Jack. Welsh writers and critics. *WM*, 26 Feb 1937, 11:C-E.

JONES, Noel A. The Anglo-Welsh. *DL* 4,11 (1953) 20-26.

JONES, Sally Roberts. Lost writers. *BWA* 22 (1991) 14. Argues for a widening of the Anglo-Welsh canon.

LEWIS, E. Glyn. Some aspects of Anglo-Welsh literature. *WR* 5 (1946) 176-186.

LEWIS, Saunders. *Is there an Anglo-Welsh literature?* Cardiff: University of Wales Guild of Graduates, 1939. 14 p.

LLOYD, D. Tecwyn. Dail y pren pwdr. *Barn*, Rha/Dec 1962, 36, 59. [Leaves of the rotting wood].

—— Yr Eingl-Gymry. *Barn*, Maw/Mar 1963, 141. In response to Aneirin Talfan Davies, Ion/Jan 1963, 68; Chw/Feb 1963, 100-101. – Davies replies, Ebr/Apr 1963, 168.

—— *Llên cyni a rhyfel a thrafodion eraill*. Llandysul: Gwasg Gomer, 1987. Incl. Parodi ar Gymru, pp. 191-216. – Suggests that much Anglo-Welsh writing has, from its beginnings in the Act of Union, constructed a parody of Welsh life.

MATHIAS, Roland. Editorial. *AWR* 18,41 (1969) 3-10. On development of *Dock Leaves* and the *Anglo-Welsh Review*.

—— Editorial. *AWR* 19,43 (1970) 3-11. Discusses Anglo-Welsh literature, including T.L. Williams, *Caradoc Evans*.

—— Thin spring and tributary: Welshmen writing in English. In *Anatomy of Wales*, ed. R. Brinley Jones. Peterston Super Ely: Gwerin Press, 1972. pp. 187-205.

—— The Welsh language and the English language. In *The Welsh language today*, ed. Meic Stephens. Llandysul: Gomer Press, 1973. pp. 32-63.

—— Editorial. *AWR* 23,52 (1974) 3-7.

—— Literature in English. In *The arts in Wales*, 1950-75, ed. Meic Stephens. Cardiff: Welsh Arts Council, 1979. pp. 207-238. – Welsh version: Llenyddiaeth yn Saesneg. In *Y celfyddydau yng Nghymru, 1950-75*, ed. Meic Stephens. Caerdydd: Cyngor Celfyddydau Cymru, 1979. pp. 217-250.

—— Prospects for Wales. *Author* 92, Spring 1981, 16-18.

—— *The lonely editor: a glance at Anglo-Welsh magazines.* Cardiff: University College of Cardiff Press, 1984. 18 p. (Annual Gwyn Jones lecture). ISBN: 0-906449-63-4.

—— *A ride through the wood: essays on Anglo-Welsh literature.* Bridgend: Poetry Wales Press, 1985. 320 p. ISBN: 0-907476-50-3. Contents: David Jones: towards the holy diversities, pp. 13-56 – Lord Cutglass, twenty years after [on Dylan Thomas], pp. 57-78 – Any minute or dark day now: the writing of *Under Milk Wood*, pp. 79-87 – Grief and the circus horse: a study of the mythic and Christian themes in the early poetry of Vernon Watkins, pp. 88-124 – The black spot in focus: a study of the poetry of Alun Lewis, pp.125-157 – The Caseg letters: a commentary [Brenda Chamberlain, Alun Lewis], pp. 158-185 – Philosophy and religion in the poetry of R.S. Thomas, pp. 186-205 – Channels of grace: a view of the earlier novels of Emyr Humphreys, pp. 206-233 – Address for the Henry Vaughan service 1977, pp. 237-249 – Under the threatening train of steam engines and schoolmasters: the predicament of some Anglo-Welsh poets in the nineteenth century, pp. 250-288 – The lonely editor: a glance at Anglo-Welsh magazines, pp. 289-307.

—— *Anglo-Welsh literature: an illustrated history.* Bridgend: Poetry Wales Press, 1987. 142 p.: ill. (The illustrated history of the literatures of Wales; 4). ISBN: 0-907476-64-3.

MERCHANT, W. Moelwyn. The relevance of the Anglo-Welsh. *Wales* 2nd ser. 1 (1943) 17-19.

MILLS, Christopher. *Radical anti-sheepism (revised, expanded and unexpurgated).* Cardiff: Red Sharks Press, 1992. 24 p. On Welsh writing in English and Arts Council funding, particularly as it relates to publishing.

MINHINNICK, Robert. My petition to the zoo keeper. *Planet* 90 (1991) 13-17. On ways in which Welsh writing in English and its funding should develop in the 1990s. – Article commissioned by the Welsh Arts Council. – Responses from Ned Thomas, Joseph Clancy, Richard Poole, John Osmond, David Bartlett, Nicholas Murray, Rob Watson and D.A. Callard, *Planet* 91 (1992) 112-120.

MORGAN, Kenneth O. *Rebirth of a nation: Wales, 1880-1980.* Oxford: Oxford University Press; [Cardiff]: University of Wales Press, 1981. Chapt. 9, Welsh and Anglo-Welsh, pp. 240-271.

POWYS, John Cowper. Welsh culture. *WR* 1 (1939) 255-262.

REES, Ioan Bowen. Wales and the Anglo-Welsh. *Welsh Anvil* 4 (1952) 20-31. English version of lecture to Cymdeithas Dafydd ap Gwilym, Jesus College Oxford, 16 Jan 1950.

RHYS, Keidrych. Letter from Wales. *Twentieth Century Verse* 18 (1939) 58-61.

—— Contemporary Welsh literature. *British Annual of Literature* 3 (1946) 618-622.

RICHARDS, Alun. Place and the writer. *Listener*, 18 Jul 1963, 89-90.

ROBERTS, Glyn. The Welsh school of writers. *Bookman*, Aug 1933, 248-249.

ROWE, Dilys. Thoughts on the tenth anniversary of *Wales*. *Wales* 2nd ser. 7,28 (1948) 442-451.

SMITH, Dai. The wherewithal of Welshness, *TLS*, 4 Mar 1977, 247.

—— *Wales! Wales?* London: Allen & Unwin, 1984. Discusses Idris Davies, Jack Jones, Lewis Jones and Gwyn Thomas, pp. 134-151.

—— Writing Wales. In *Wales between the wars*, ed. Trevor Herbert and Gareth Elwyn Jones. Cardiff: University of Wales Press; Open University, 1988. (Welsh history and its sources). pp. 186-278. Introductory essay, with selections from Geraint Goodwin, Raymond Williams, Gwyn Jones, Idris Davies, Alun Lewis, Lewis Jones, Gwyn Thomas, Dannie Abse, Emyr Humphreys and others.

—— Silent readers: invisible writers. *Planet* 90 (1991) 7-12. On ways in which literature and its funding should develop in the 1990s. – Article commissioned by the Welsh Arts Council. – Responses from Ned Thomas, Joseph Clancy, Richard Poole, John Osmond, David Bartlett, Nicholas Murray, Rob Watson and D.A. Callard, *Planet* 91 (1992) 112-120.

SMITH, Kenneth R. Women, criticism and the Anglo-Welsh. *PW* 20,3 (1985) 60-66.

SMITH, Peter Macdonald. Prologue to an adventure: fifty years since Keidrych Rhys' *Wales. PW* 22,4 (1987) 7-11.

—— The making of the Anglo-Welsh tradition. *NWR* 1,1 [1] (1988) 61-65.

—— A tale of two literatures: the periodicals and the Anglo-Welsh tradition. *NWR* 1,2 [2] (1988) 68-70.

—— Poetry, politics and the use of English: the periodicals and the Anglo-Welsh tradition. *NWR* 1,3 [3] (1988) 63-67.

STEPHENS, Meic. Yr Academi Gymreig and Cymdeithas Cymru Newydd. *PW* 4,3 (1968) [7-11].

—— Editorial. *PW* 6,3 (1970) 3-5.

—— Crumbs from the black swans: a reply to Mr John Gwilym Jones. *Lookout* [UCNW, Bangor], 5 Dec 1961, 4.

—— The status of the Anglo-Welsh. *Y Wawr* 12 (1962) 22-28.

—— Interview with Meic Stephens. *PW* 14,2 (1978) 19-32. J.P. Ward interviews the Literature Director on Welsh Arts Council support for publishing and poetry.

THOMAS, M. Wynn. Airs on a shoe string. *Planet* 63 (1987) 3-8. Discusses literary finance and administration within the Welsh Arts Council.

—— Literature in English. In *Glamorgan County history. Vol. VI. Glamorgan society, 1780-1980*, ed. Prys Morgan. Cardiff: Glamorgan History Trust and University of Wales Press, 1988. pp. 353-365.

—— *Internal difference: twentieth-century writing in Wales.* Cardiff: University of Wales Press, 1992. xv, 196 p. ISBN: 0-7083-1152-0. Contents: All change: the new Welsh drama before the Great War, pp. 11-24 – Writing Glamorgan, pp. 25-48 – The two Aluns [on Alun Llywelyn-Williams and Alun Lewis], pp. 49-67 – Flintshire and the regional weather forecast [on Emyr Humphreys and Emlyn Williams], pp. 68-81 – A corner of Wales [on Emyr Humphreys], pp. 82-106 – R.S. Thomas: the poetry of the Sixties, pp. 107-129 – Songs of ignorance and praise: R.S. Thomas's poems about the four people in his life, pp. 130-155 – Prison, hotel and pub: three images of contemporary Wales, pp. 156-179. – The last essay considers Mary

Jones, *Resistance*, Angharad Tomos, *Yma o hyd* and Kingsley Amis, *The old devils*.

THOMAS, Ned. *The Welsh extremist: a culture in crisis*. London: Gollancz, 1971. Incl. The Welsh and the Anglo-Welsh, pp. 99-113.

—— Is 'Anglo-Welsh' Commonwealth literature? *Planet* 11 (1972) 24-26.

—— Images of ourselves. In *The national question again: Welsh political identity in the 1980s,* ed. John Osmond. Llandysul: Gomer Press, 1985. pp. 307-319.

THOMAS, R.S. Anglo-Welsh literature. *Welsh Nationalist*, Dec 1948, 3:B-C.

—— Llenyddiaeth Eingl-Cymreig. *Y Fflam* 11 (1952) 7-9. [Anglo-Welsh literature]. – English translation in R.S. Thomas, *Selected prose*, ed. Sandra Anstey (1983), pp. 51-53.

—— The creative writer's suicide. *Planet* 41 (1987) 30-33. Reprinted in R.S. Thomas, *Selected prose*, ed. Sandra Anstey (1983), pp. 169-174. – Original Welsh text: *Taliesin* 35 (1977) 109-113.

TREWIN, J.C. The two literatures of Wales. *TLS*, 5 Aug 1955, xii.

*TRISKEL one: essays on Welsh and Anglo-Welsh literature,* ed. Sam Adams and Gwilym Rees Hughes. Swansea: Christopher Davies, 1971. 197 p.: ill. Contents: The short stories of Kate Roberts, by Pennar Davies, pp. 11-26 – History as imagination: some aspects of the poetry of David Jones, by Jeremy Hooker, pp. 27-42 – Welsh poetry since 1945, by Dafydd Glyn Jones, pp. 43-64 – The poetry of R. Williams Parry, by R. Gerallt Jones, pp. 65-74 – *The first forty years: some notes on Anglo-Welsh literature*, by Gwyn Jones, pp. 75-95 – Grief and the circus horse: a study of mythic and Christian themes in the early poetry of Vernon Watkins, by Roland Mathias, pp. 96-138 – R.T. Jenkins: the historian as author, by Prys Morgan, pp. 139-163 – The poetry of Edward Thomas, by Leslie Norris, pp. 164-178 – The poetry of Euros Bowen, by Dafydd Elis Thomas, pp. 179-185 – Humanus sum: a second look at R.S. Thomas, by R. George Thomas, pp. 186-197.

*TRISKEL two: essays on Welsh and Anglo-Welsh literature*, ed. Sam Adams and Gwilym Rees Hughes. Llandybïe: Christopher Davies, 1973. 181 p.: ill. ISBN: 7154-0046-0. Contents: The role of nature in the poetry of Dylan Thomas, by John Ackerman, pp. 9-25 – Saunders Lewis: morality playwright, by Pennar Davies, pp. 26-41 – The mythology of the mining valleys, by Glyn Tegai Hughes, pp. 42-61 – The poetry of Thomas Parry-Williams, by R. Gerallt Jones, pp. 62-87 – Seeing eternity: Vernon Watkins and the poet's task, by Leslie Norris, pp. 88-110 – Pennar Davies: more than a poeta doctus, by J. Gwyn Griffiths, pp. 111-127 – The poetry of Alun Lewis, by David Shayer, pp. 128-165 – The poetry of Gwyn Thomas, by Elan Clos Stephens, pp. 166-181.

WADE-EVANS, A.W. Anglo-Welsh. *Wales* 2nd ser. 6,3 [23] (1946) 29-39.

WAY, Brian. Anglo-Welsh writing. *Adult Education* 32 (1960) 290-293.

*THE WELSH connection:* essays by past and present members of the Department of English Language and Literature, University College of North Wales, Bangor, ed. William Tydeman. Llandysul: Gomer Press, 1986. 211 p. ISBN: 0-86383-395-0. Incl.: Gerard Hopkins as an Anglo-Welsh poet, by Anthony Conran, pp. 110-129 – Impersonality and the soldier poet: Alun Lewis and Keith Douglas, by Richard Poole, pp. 130-158 – Language, poetry and silence:

some themes in the poetry of R.S. Thomas, by Tony Brown, pp. 159-185 – The modernism of Anthony Conran, by Ian Gregson, pp. 186-208.

WILLIAMS, Ioan. Writers of Wales. *Planet* 26-27 (1974) 14-22. On the Welsh Arts Council series.

WILLIAMS, Waldo. Anglo-Welsh and Welsh. *DL* 4,12 (1953) 31-35.

## C. Poetry

ADAMS, Sam. Poets in the classroom. *PW* 12,2 (1976) 4-15. On Welsh teacher-poets.

BARNIE, John. Memory and Anglo-Welsh poetry. *PW* 12,3 (1977) 12-15.

–––– The Anglo-Welsh tradition. *PW* 20,2 (1984) 85-94. Review article on *Anglo-Welsh poetry, 1480-1980*, ed. Raymond Garlick and Roland Mathias. – Reprinted in John Barnie, *The king of ashes* (1989), pp. 42-51.

BEAGAN, Glenda. A different nourishment: exploring the effects of language loss. *PW* 29,2 (1993) 46-51.

BELL, Ian. Diminished cities: contemporary poetry in Wales and Scotland. *PW* 27,2 (1991) 28-30.

BURNHAM, Richard. *The Dublin Magazine*'s Welsh poets. *AWR* 27,60 (1978) 49-63. With discussion of Glyn Jones, R.S. Thomas, Alun Lewis, Brenda Chamberlain and T.Harri Jones.

CASTAY, Marie-Thérèse. English enriched by Celtic poets. *Spoken English* 10,3 (1977) 101-108.

–––– Développement de la poésie anglo-galloise, 1930-1980. *Caliban* 18 (1981) 21-32.

–––– La poésie anglo-galloise et la tradition galloise. In *Pays de Galles, Écosse, Irlande: actes du Congrès de Brest, Mai 1986*. Brest: Centre de Recherches Bretonnes et Celtiques, 1987. (Cahiers de Bretagne Occidentale; 7). pp. 19-32.

CLARKE, Gillian. A musical nation. *Poetry Review* 72,2 (1982) 48-51.

CONRAN, Anthony. The English poet in Wales, 1. The alien corn. AWR 10,25 (1959) 28-35.

–––– The English poet in Wales, 2. Boys of summer in their ruin. *AWR* 10,26 (1960) 11-21. Considers Dylan Thomas, Vernon Watkins and R.S. Thomas.

–––– Anglo-Welsh poetry today, Part one. *PW* 4,3 (1969) 11-16.

–––– Anglo-Welsh poetry today, Part two. *PW* 5,1 (1969) 9-12.

–––– The first Anglo-Welsh anthology? *AWR* 22,49 (1973) 198-200. Letter on *Lyra Celtica*, ed. E.A. Sharp and J. Matthay (1896).

–––– *The cost of strangeness: essays on the English poets of Wales.* Llandysul: Gomer Press, 1982. 330 p. ISBN: 0-85088-865-4. Contents: The poetry of Ernest Rhys and the Celtic revival in Wales, pp. 1-19 – The tramp poems of W.H. Davies, pp. 21-51 – The Anglo-Welsh poems of Edward Thomas, pp. 52-63 – Welsh 'English poems' and English 'Welsh' poems, pp. 64-76 – Huw Menai: trapped between worlds, pp. 77-103 – The achievement of Idris Davies, pp. 104-154 – A note on Caradoc Evans, pp. 155-161 –

Anglo-Welsh poetry and the 'Welsh way of life', pp. 162-168 – The age of Dylan Thomas, pp. 169-180 – After the funeral: the praise poetry of Dylan Thomas, pp. 180-187 – Lynette Roberts: war poet, pp. 188-200 – The writings of Brenda Chamberlain, pp. 201-211 – Gwyn Williams the translator, pp. 212-219 – Aspects of R.S. Thomas, pp. 220-262 – By the waters of Babylon: exile in Anglo-Welsh poetry, 1953-1965, pp. 263-295 – The 'second flowering' and the role of the magazine editors, pp. 296-306 – Raymond Garlick: the poetry of Anglo-Welsh opinion, pp. 307-315 – *Hiraeth* and after: a review of verse-pamphlets by Meic Stephens, Sam Adams and Bryn Griffiths, pp. 316-323.

—— Ye Brytish poets: some observations on early Anglo-Welsh poetry. *AWR* 84 (1986) 8-18.

—— Modernism in Anglo-Welsh poetry. In *The works: the Welsh Union of Writers annual, 1991*, ed. Nigel Jenkins. Cardiff: Welsh Union of Writers, 1991. pp. 13-24. – Reprinted in *Bête Noire* [Hull] 12-13 (1991-92) 384-391.

—— Tony Conran interview. *Materion Dwyieithog: Bilingual Matters* [Coleg Ceredigion] 3 (1991) 11-17. Discusses Anglo-Welsh writing and its future.

CRITICISM in Wales. *PW* 15,2 (1979) 7-41. On the state of criticism of Anglo-Welsh poetry. – Contributions by Brian Morris, Glyn Jones, Peter Elfed Lewis, John Idris Jones, Désirée Hurst, Steve Griffiths, Tony Curtis, Brian Martin Davies, Roland Mathias, Belinda Humfrey, Ruth Bidgood, Robert Minhinnick, Ian Gregson, Diane Davies, John Pikoulis, John Tripp, Greg Hill, Gwen Watkins.

CURTIS, Tony. Grafting the sour to sweetness: Anglo-Welsh poetry in the last twenty-five years. In *Wales: the imagined nation: studies in cultural and national identity*, ed. Tony Curtis. Bridgend: Poetry Wales Press, 1986. pp. 99-126.

—— Anglo-Welsh poetry: Dylan and after. *North Dakota Quarterly* 57,2 (1989) [Anglo-Welsh poetry supplement] 9-14.

DAVIES, John. How to write Anglo-Welsh poetry. *PW* 11,4 (1976) 22-23. For responses to this poem see: Jon Dressel, *PW* 12,3 (1977) 8-11; Stephen Tunicliffe, John Matthias, Alun Rees, *PW* 12,3 (1977) 7.

DAVIES, Lewis. The soul of Wales: a plea for sane criticism. *Welsh Outlook*, Jul 1922, 169-172. Discusses the *Poetry Review* special issue on Anglo-Welsh poetry (Mar 1922). – Reply: H. Idris Bell, Aug 1922, 196; with response by editor.

—— The Anglo-Cymric school of poets. *Welsh Outlook*, Jan 1926, 21-22.

DRESSEL, Jon. U.S. viewpoint. *PW* 15,3 (1979) 24-29.

FINCH, Peter. Diamonds in the dust: the background of *Second Aeon*. *PW* 4,2 (1968) 56-57.

—— Performance poetry in South Wales. *PW* 22,2 (1987) 40-47.

—— Poetry as performance in south Wales. *New England Review and Bread Loaf Quarterly* 10,4 (1988) [Writers of Wales special issue] 440-446.

—— On Welsh writing in English: an interview with Peter Finch. *PW* 28,3 (1993) 48-53. Interviewed by David Lloyd.

GARLICK, Raymond. Seventy Anglo-Welsh poets. *Welsh Anvil* 6 (1954) 76-84. Isolates an earlier Anglo-Welsh tradition, 'an extensive and distinctive minor poetry'. – In reply to Ioan Bowen Rees, *Welsh Anvil* 6 (1952) 20-31.

—— *An introduction to Anglo-Welsh literature.* University of Wales Press [for] the Welsh Arts Council, 1972. 92 p. ISBN: 0-7083-0510-5. Incl. brief details of 70 poets from 15th century onwards, pp. 81-89. – Almost exclusively concerned with poetry. – Revised edition of a work first published 1970 in the Writers of Wales series.

—— A preface to Anglo-Welsh poetry. *North Dakota Quarterly* 57,2 (1989) [Anglo-Welsh poetry supplement] 3-8.

GRIFFITHS, Bryn. What stirs the lyrical kick in the Welsh. *WM*, 11 Apr 1964, 5:A-D.

HOOKER, Jeremy. Image and argument. *AWR* 18,42 (1970) 65-76. Review article on *The lilting house: an anthology of Anglo-Welsh poetry, 1917-76*, ed. John Stuart Williams and Meic Stephens.

—— *The poetry of place: essays and reviews, 1970-1981.* Manchester: Carcanet, 1982. 197 p. ISBN: 0-85635-409-0. Contents: Matthew Arnold: on the study of Celtic literature, pp. 17-20 – Edward Thomas: the sad passion, pp. 20-31 – David Jones; Ends and new beginnings, On *The anathemata*, Brut's Albion, pp. 32-65 – Philip Pacey: landscape of fire, pp. 66-70 – Seamus Heaney: *North*, pp. 71-74 – John Cowper Powys: Welsh ambassador, pp. 75-79 – T.F. Powys: the bass note, pp. 80-92 – Emyr Humphreys: a seeing belief, pp. 93-105 – Raymond Williams: a dream of a country, pp. 106-115 – Edward Thomas, pp. 116-119 – Honouring Ivor Gurney, pp. 120-129 – Frances Bellerby in place, pp. 130-136 – English Auden, pp. 137-147 – Charles Olson: to open the mind, pp. 148-152 – John Riley: *The collected works*, pp. 153-158 – Living in Wales, pp. 159-168 – An autobiographical essay, pp. 169-179 – Poem and place, pp. 180-190 – Bibliography, pp. 191-193.

—— *The presence of the past: essays on modern British and American poetry.* Bridgend: Poetry Wales Press, 1987. 228 p. ISBN: 0-907476-71-6. Incl.: The presence of the past [on David Jones, Basil Bunting, Geoffrey Hill], pp. 9-32 – John Ormond: the accessible song, pp. 107-113 – The poetry of Anthony Conran, pp. 114-122 – John Tripp: *Collected poems, 1958-1978*, pp. 123-127 – R.S. Thomas: Prytherch and after, pp. 128-140 – Roland Mathias: the strong remembered words, pp. 141-150 – A big sea running in a shell: the poetry of Gillian Clarke, pp. 151-155 – The poetry of nearness: Anglo-Welsh poetry in the 1960s, pp. 156-176 – Resistant voices: five young Anglo-Welsh poets [Robert Minhinnick, Nigel Jenkins, Mike Jenkins, Steve Griffiths, John Davies], pp. 177-198.

—— Questions of identity. *Planet* 87 (1991) 59-65. Review article on *The bright field*, ed. Meic Stephens.

Is there a women's poetry? *PW* 23,1 (1987) 30-55. Symposium with contributions from Sheenagh Pugh, Gloria Evans Davies, Christine Evans, Sally Roberts Jones and Val Warner.

JENKINS, Nigel. The tradition that might be. *Planet* 72 (1988) 9-16. On the folk-poets of English-speaking Wales.

JENKINS, Randal. The new Anglo-Welsh poets. *PW* 8,2 (1972) 5-16.

JONES, Glyn. Slim volumes for a slim public. *WM*, 23 Jul 1960, 5:B-E. On the audience for poetry.

—— 'Second flowering': poetry in Wales. In *British poetry since 1960: a critical survey*, ed. M. Schmidt and G. Lindop. Manchester: Carcanet, 1972. pp. 122-131. Discusses Anglo-Welsh poets of the 1960s and their concern for national identity.

LEWIS, Peter Elfed. Poetry in the thirties: a view of the 'first flowering'. *AWR* 71 (1982) 50-74.

LLWYD, Alan. Cynghanedd and English poetry. *PW* 14,1 (1978) 23-58.

MATHIAS, Roland. Editorial. *AWR* 21,47 (1972) 3-8. On *Welsh poets*, ed. A.G. Prys-Jones (1917).

—— A separated place: Roland Mathias surveys the current Anglo-Welsh poetry scene. *Poetry Society Newsletter*, Oct 1985, 5.

O'NEILL, Chris. After Ward's. *Arcade*, 16 Jan 1981, 18. On J.P. Ward's editorship of *Poetry Wales*.

*POETRY WALES* 7,3 (1971) 7-51. Letters to the editor on the state of Anglo-Welsh poetry from Glyn Jones, Pennar Davies, Leslie Norris, Roland Mathias, Anthony Conran, Duncan Glen, Jeremy Hooker, B.S. Johnson, Raymond Garlick, Harri Webb, Dafydd Elis Thomas and Ned Thomas.

POOLE, Richard. Poetry and nationalism in Wales: a disinterested view. *PW* 23,2-3 (1987) 63-67.

PRYS-JONES, A.G. Anglo-Welsh poetry. *DL* 2,5 (1951) 5-9.

—— *Welsh poets:* how it happened. *London Welshman*, Dec 1964, 11-12. On background to his 1917 anthology.

SMITH, Dai. Confronting the minotaur: politics and poetry in twentieth-century Wales. *PW* 15,3 (1979) 4-23.

SMITH, Kenneth R. Welsh women poets: the portrait poem: reproduction of mothering. *PW* 24,1 (1988) 48-54. Discusses Sally Roberts Jones, Ruth Bidgood, Jean Earle and Gillian Clarke.

—— Praise of the past: the myth of eternal return in women writers. *PW* 24,4 (1989) 50-58. Incl. comment on Ruth Bidgood, Gillian Clarke and Sally Roberts Jones.

STEPHENS, Meic. The second flowering. *PW* 3,3 (1967) 2-9. Recalls circumstances under which he launched *Poetry Wales*. – See also Peter Gruffydd, Further to the second flowering, *PW* 4,1 (1968) 4-5.

THOMAS, Dylan. *The broadcasts*, ed. Ralph Maud. London: Dent, 1991. Incl. Welsh poetry, pp. 31-49. – Brief comment on Henry Vaughan, Edward Thomas, W.H. Davies, Idris Davies, Glyn Jones, Alun Lewis.

THOMAS, M. Wynn. Barddonia[i]th Saesneg yn y Gymru gyfoes. *Taliesin* 83 (1993) 102-107. [English poetry in contemporary Wales].

TRIPP, John. An Anglo-Welsh renaissance. *Akros* 12 (1970) [Special issue on Anglo-Welsh poetry] 5-9.

WARD, J.P. Editorial. *PW* 13,1 (1977) 3-11.

—— *Poetry Wales*: the twenty-first year. *PW* 21,1 (1985) 7-8.

WEBB, Harri. New Anglo-Welsh poets. *WM*, 10 Jul 1965, 10:E-G.

THE WELSH language and Anglo-Welsh poets: a symposium. *PW* 20,1 (1984) 4-18. Contributions by Duncan Bush, Tony Curtis, Steve Griffiths, Mike Jenkins, Christopher Meredith, Robert Minhinnick and Graham Thomas.

# D. Prose

[Anon]. Anglo-Welsh attitudes. *TLS*, 1 Jun 1956, 328. Review article on *Welsh short stories*, ed. Gwyn Jones.

ADAM, G.F. *Three contemporary Anglo-Welsh novelists: Jack Jones, Rhys Davies and Hilda Vaughan*. Bern: A. Franke, [1948]. 109 p. Contents: A short survey of the regional novel in English literature, pp. 5-13 – Wales and Anglo-Welsh literature, pp. 13-31 – Jack Jones' documentary realism, pp. 31-48 – Rhys Davies: regionalism as an expression of universal values, pp. 48-76 – Hilda Vaughan's neo-romantic regionalism, pp. 76-100 – Conclusion, pp. 101-104 – Bibliography, pp. 107-109.

EDWARDS, J.I. A study of the periodicals *Wales* and the *Welsh Review*, 1937-1949, and their contribution to the development of the Anglo-Welsh short story. MA thesis. University of Wales (Swansea), 1987.

EVANS, Beriah Gwynfe. Wales and its novelists. *Wales*, May 1911, 35-38.

GOODWIN, Geraint. Thoughts on the Welsh novel. *Welsh Outlook*, Mar 1930, 72-74.

JONES, Glyn. The literary scene. *Wales* 3rd ser., Dec 1959, 15-17. In response to Alun Richards, *Wales* 3rd ser., Oct 1959, 27-29.

JONES, Gwyn. Notes on the Welsh short story writers. *Life and Letters Today* 34 (1942) 172-180. Continued: *LLT* 36 (1943) 156-163.

JONES, Jack. Nofelau'r Cymry Seisnig. *Tir Newydd*, Mai/May 1937, 5-9. [Anglo-Welsh novels].

KNIGHT, Stephen. How red was my story?: the working class novel in Wales. *Planet* 98 (1993) 83-94. A broad survey, including comment on Rhys Davies, Gwyn Thomas, Jack Jones and Lewis Jones.

LEWIS, Ivor. The people and the latent wish (with a note on some Welsh writers as a cross-section). *Wales* 2nd ser. 5,8-9 [21] (1945) 46-52.

—— Writers' countries. *Wales* 2nd ser. 6,24 (1946) 74-79.

LLOYD, D. Tecwyn. Traethawd ar natur a datblygiad y dehongliad o Gymru gan awduron Eingl-Gymreig mewn rhyddiaith ... MA thesis. University of Liverpool, 1961. 431 p. Contents: Hen ddeunydd, pp. 12-32 – Y cyfraniad rhamantaidd, pp. 33-106 – Y cylchgronau, pp. 107-298 – Y nofelau, pp. 299-414 – Cloi, pp. 415-419 – Atodiadau; Cyhoeddi 'Wales' (O.M. Edwards), Lluniau rhamantaidd cyfoes, pp. 420-424 – Llyfryddiaeth, pp. 425-431. [Essay on the nature and development of the interpretation of Wales by Anglo-Welsh authors in prose].

—— The romantic parody. *Planet* 31 (1976) 29-36. 'Only recently has Anglo-Welsh literature begun to outgrow the distorting images imposed by English romanticism.'

'MULCIBER'. The future of the industrial novel in Great Britain. *WR* 2 (1939) 154-158.

PRUISCHUTZ, Hildegard. *Sensualismus als Stilelement in der modernen anglo-walisischen Prosadichtung*. Munich: Mikrokopie, 1955. 167 p. 'Inaugural Dissertation der Philosophischen Fakultat der Friedrich-Alexander-Universitat'. – [Sensualism as an element of style in Anglo-Welsh prose fiction].

REES, William. The bizarre and melodramatic in the work of Anglo-Welsh novelists. MA thesis. University of Wales (Swansea), 1972. 238 p.

Discusses: Caradoc Evans – Rhys Davies – Hilda Vaughan – Richard Vaughan – Geraint Goodwin – Richard Llewellyn – Jack Jones – Gwyn Thomas – Cledwyn Hughes – Emyr Humphreys – Glyn Jones – Gwyn Jones – Menna Gallie – W.H. Boore – Ron Berry.

RICHARDS, Alun. The never-never land. *Wales* 3rd ser., Oct 1959, 27-29. On the Wales of the Anglo-Welsh short story.

ROWE, Dilys. Some variations on a main theme. *Wales* 2nd ser. 4,6 (1944-45) 9-12. On novels of Welsh life in the Allen Raine tradition.

—— The significance of the Welsh short story writers. *Wales* 2nd ser. 5,8-9 [21] (1945) 96-100.

SMITH, Dai. Myth and meaning in the literature of the South Wales coalfield: the 1930s. *AWR* 25,56 (1976) 21-42. Refers particularly to Richard Llewellyn, *How green was my valley*.

—— A novel history. In *Wales the imagined nation: studies in cultural and national identity*, ed. Tony Curtis. Bridgend: Poetry Wales Press, 1986. pp. 131-158.

VAUGHAN, Herbert M. Wales and the historical novel. *Welsh Outlook*, Sep 1931, 247-248.

WILLIAMS, David Marcel. The presentation of character in the Anglo-Welsh novel: a study of techniques and influences. MA thesis. University of Wales (Swansea), 1959.

WILLIAMS, Michael. Welsh voices in the short story. *WR* 6 (1947) 290-298.

WILLIAMS, Raymond. *The Welsh industrial novel: the inaugural Gwyn Jones lecture*. Cardiff: University College Cardiff Press, 1979. 20 p. ISBN: 0-906449-02-2.

—— Working-class, proletarian, socialist: problems in some Welsh novels. In *The socialist novel in Britain: towards the recovery of a tradition*, ed. H. Gustav Klaus. Brighton: Harvester Press, 1982. pp. 110-121.

# E. Regional Guides

COLLINS, W.J. Townsend. *Monmouthshire writers: a literary history and anthology*. Newport: R.H. Johns, 1945. 162 p.: ill.

—— *More Monmouthshire writers: a literary history and anthology: second volume*. Newport: R.H. Johns, 1948. 176 p.: ill.

*WRITERS of the west / Llenorion y gorllewin. 1. Pembroke / Penfro*, ed. Prys Morgan. Carmarthen: West Wales Association for the Arts, 1974. 72 p.: ill. Contains the following literary tours: South Pembrokeshire, by Dillwyn Miles, pp. 4-18 – North-west Pembrokeshire, by W. Rhys Nicholas, pp. 20-44 – North Pembrokeshire, by W. Rhys Nicholas, pp. 46-71. – Bilingual text. – Drawings by Aylwin Sampson.

*WRITERS of the west / Llenorion y gorllewin. 2. Carmarthen / Caerfyrddin*, ed. Prys Morgan. Carmarthen: West Wales Association for the Arts, 1974. 69 p.: ill. Contains the following literary tours: South and east Carmarthenshire, by Gomer M. Roberts, pp. 4-17 – Carmarthen to Whitland, by D.M. Price, pp. 18-29 – Towy Valley, by Prys Morgan, pp. 30-49 – North-west Carmarthenshire, by Alun Page, pp. 50-69. – Bilingual text. – Drawings by Aylwin Sampson.

*WRITERS of the west / Llenorion y gorllewin. 3. Cardigan / Ceredigion*, ed. Prys
   Morgan. Carmarthen: West Wales Association for the Arts, 1974. 67 p.:
   ill. Contains the following literary tours, all by Gwilym Thomas: Cardigan
   to Newcastle Emlyn, pp. 4-11 – Three short tours from Llandysul, pp.
   12-20 – Three short tours from Lampeter, pp. 22-45 – Three short tours
   from Aberystwyth, pp. 46-67. – Bilingual text. – Drawings by Aylwin
   Sampson.
*WRITERS of the west / Llenorion y gorllewin. 4. West Glamorgan / Gorllewin Morgannwg*,
   ed. Prys Morgan. Carmarthen: West Wales Association for the Arts, 1974.
   59 p.: ill. Contains the following literary tours: Neath and Tawe valleys,
   by Prys Morgan, pp. 4-27 – Afan district and Tir Iarll, by Sally Roberts
   Jones – Gower and the lower valley of the Llwchwr, by Sally Roberts
   Jones, pp. 46-59. – Bilingual text. – Drawings by Aylwin Sampson.

# F. Anglo-Welsh Literature in Education

DALE-JONES, Don. Anglo-Welsh literature in the schools of Wales. *Planet* 45-46
   (1978) 26-34. Report on survey commissioned by the Literature
   Committee, Welsh Arts Council.
DAVIES, Huw. *Welsh writing in English: twenty-four themes in poetry: an index of
   resources*. Treforest: WJEC National Language Unit of Wales, 1988. 144 p.
   '24 themes and the recommended poets and poems within each category
   are arranged in alphabetical order.'
DAVIES, James A. Examiner's report: the WJEC and A level English. *Planet*
   55 (1986) 6-12.
GARLICK, Raymond. The vicious circle. *PW* 4,1 (1968) [53-55]. Review of
   Gerald Morgan, *English literature in the schools of Wales*.
——— Anglo-Welsh literature and the WJEC. *PW* 9,2 (1973) 127-131.
   Reprints letter to *The Bulletin* [magazine of Undeb Cenedlaethol Athrawon
   Cymru].
JONES, P. Bernard. A sense of place: the literature of Wales in secondary
   schools. *Planet* 68 (1988) 32-35.
LEWIS, Helen. The national curriculum: a Welsh curriculum? *PW* 25,4
   (1990) 11-14.
MATHIAS, Roland. Editorial. *AWR* 25,56 (1976) 3-11. On Anglo-Welsh lit-
   erature in higher education. – Replies: Belinda Humfrey, Sheenagh Pugh,
   *AWR* 26,57 (1976) 280-286 (with response from Roland Mathias).
MORGAN, Gerald. *English literature in the schools of Wales*. Aberystwyth: Uni-
   versity College of Wales (Faculty of Education), 1967. 12 p.
PARTRIDGE, Colin. Smouldering bush. *Planet* 28 (1975) 2-7. On approaches
   to literature in higher education.
PIKOULIS, John. Welsh writing taken seriously. *BNW*, Spring 1989, 6. On
   aims of the University of Wales Association for the Study of Welsh Writing
   in English.
——— The ideology of Anglo-Welsh. *Planet* 74 (1989) 41-51. Reflections on
   Welsh Academy project, *The literature of Wales in secondary schools*.
POETRY in education: what can be achieved. *PW* 12,2 (1976) 35-59. Transcript
   of taped discussion on poetry in secondary education, with contributions

by Cary Archard, John Beynon, Tony Curtis, Marion Glastonbury, Sue Harries and Stephen Tunnicliffe.

POOLE, Richard. Letter. *PW* 23,1 (1987) 57-58. On the literature of Wales in schools. – Replies: Mike Jenkins, *PW* 23, 2-3 (1987) 2-3; Richard Poole, *PW* 23,4 (1988) 54-55.

PUGH, Sheenagh. Letter. *AWR* 26,57 (1976) 281-284. On Anglo-Welsh literature in higher education. – Reply by Roland Mathias, pp. 284-286.

*THE STREETS and the stars: an anthology of writing from Wales*, ed. John Davies and Melvyn Jones. Bridgend: Seren Books, 1993. 190 p.: ill.: pbk. ISBN: 1-85411-976-4. 'This English course book for fourteen to sixteen year-olds draws its source material from both literatures and also includes responses to Wales by some English-born writers ... the selections include short stories, poetry, reportage, and extracts from radio plays.'

WARD, Caryl. Anglo-Welsh studies: why the apathy? *NWR* 5,3 [19] (1992-93) 87. Letter on Anglo-Welsh literature courses at university level. – Reply by Belinda Humfrey, p. 87. – Further replies by Tony Brown, Linden Peach and Angela Fish, *NWR* 5,4 [20] (1993) 86-88.

WARD, J.P. All very serious stuff plus 'Under Milk Wood': Welsh poetry in English and university education in Wales. *PW* 25,4 (1990) 14-19.

WELSH Academy. *Writing in Wales: a Welsh Academy resource pack*, ed. Tony Curtis and Cliff James. Cardiff: Welsh Academy, 1985. ISBN: 0-906906-06-7. Contents: Writers reading their own work: an audio cassette, with accompanying notes – Anglo-Welsh writing: a poster map – An introduction to Anglo-Welsh literature, by Roland Mathias – Individual sheets on Dannie Abse, Ruth Bidgood, Emyr Humphreys, Mike Jenkins, Nigel Jenkins, Sally Roberts Jones, Robert Minhinnick, Alun Richards, John Tripp, Harri Webb – Poem in draft: Fires on Llŷn, by Gillian Clarke – Poem in draft: Crane-flies, by Tony Curtis – *Writers on tour* (Welsh Arts Council booklet) – The write information: selected bibliography and sources – Notes for teachers. – Cover design by Jonah Jones.

WELSH Academy. *The literature of Wales in secondary schools: project undertaken by the Welsh Academy on behalf of the Welsh Office.* Cardiff: Welsh Office; Welsh Academy, 1987. 142 p. Incl.: The place of Anglo-Welsh literature and Welsh literature in translation within the English classroom, pp. 1-6 – Beginning at home [survey of early Anglo-Welsh literature], by Roland Mathias, pp. 98-110 – The Welsh literary tradition: a survey, by R. Brinley Jones, pp. 112-126 – Bibliography, pp. 127-142. – Detailed proposed syllabus for various secondary school levels, with comment on individual writers.

WILLIAMS, Rhys. Two cheers for Anglo-Welsh literature in schools. *BNW*, Spring 1989, 5-6.

# IDRIS DAVIES (1905-1953)

A. Publications by Idris Davies
  (i)  Books
  (ii) Selected contributions to books and periodicals

B. Publications about Idris Davies


## A (i). Publications by Idris Davies: Books

*Gwalia Deserta.* London: Dent, 1938. 26 p.

*The angry summer: a poem of 1926.* London: Faber, 1943. 55 p.
—— / introduction and notes by Tony Conran. Cardiff: University of Wales Press, 1993. xxxii, 74 p.: ill.: hbk & pbk. ISBN: 0-7083-1090-7 hbk, 0-7083-1080-X pbk. Incl.: Preface, by Tony Conran, pp. vii-x – A note on illustrative material, by Liz Powell, pp. xi-xii – Introduction, pp. xiii-xxxii – Notes, Reading list, pp. 67-74. – An edition of the poem illustrated with photographs, newspaper cuttings and eyewitness accounts.

Swedish trans.: *Vredens sommar: en dikt ur 1926*, tr. Per Holmer and Per Lindgren. Lund: Cavefors, 1978. 89 p.

*Tonypandy and other poems.* London: Faber, 1945. 70 p.

*Selected poems of Idris Davies.* London: Faber, 1953. 68 p. Contents: selections from *Gwalia deserta, The angry summer, Tonypandy and other poems* – New poems. – Selection made by T.S. Eliot.

*Send out your homing pigeons, Dai.* Cheltenham: Robert Alwyn Hughes, 1969. [15] p.: ill. Poem, with six photographs by Robert Alwyn Hughes. – No. 1 of proposed series of eight booklets featuring Idris Davies poems.

*Collected poems of Idris Davies* / edited by Islwyn Jenkins. Llandysul: Gomerian Press, 1972. xxxii, 190 p.: hbk & pbk. ISBN: 0-85088-143-9 hbk, 0-85088-141-2 pbk. Incl. Introduction, by R. George Thomas, pp. xv-xxxii. – Reprints contents of four earlier volumes, adding poems published in newspapers and periodicals and a selection of unpublished poems. – Reissued 1980, pbk.

*Fe'm ganed i yn Rhymni: cyfrol deyrnged Idris Davies / I was born in Rhymney: Idris Davies memorial volume.* Llandysul: Gomer, 1990. 68 p.: ill.: hbk & pbk. ISBN: 0-86383-623-2 hbk, 0-86383-698-4 pbk. Incl.: Introduction, by R. George Thomas, pp. 15-19 – Prose extracts – 22 poems by Idris Davies (5 in Welsh). – With Welsh translations of selected poems. – Bilingual volume, illustrated by Olwen Hughes, on the occasion of the National Eisteddfod at Rhymney Valley.


## A (ii). Publications by Idris Davies: Selected Contributions to Books and Periodicals

Rhywle yng Nghymru. *Merthyr Express*, 28 May 1927, 21:C.

Impressions. *Merthyr Express*, 17 Sep 1927, 22:C.

Thanksgiving. *Merthyr Express*, 15 Oct 1927, 21:E.

The ceaseless call. *Merthyr Express*, 26 Jan 1929, 22:C.

The skylark's adieu. *Merthyr Express*, 5 Oct 1929, 22:B.

The song of songs. *Merthyr Express*, 12 Oct 1929, 20:C.

War. *Merthyr Express*, 19 Oct 1929, 22:B.

The seven churches of Asia. *Merthyr Express*, 28 Dec 1929, 20:C.

An English youth. *Merthyr Express*, 19 Apr 1930, 21:A.

Brecknock Beacons. *Merthyr Express*, 10 May 1930, 22:D.

The winged fancy. *Merthyr Express*, 24 May 1930, 3:B.

After the rains. *Merthyr Express*, 31 May 1930, 22:A.

Amy Johnson. *Merthyr Express*, 7 Jun 1930, 21:B.

Cân Cymro bach. *Merthyr Express*, 5 Jul 1930, 22:A.

Devonshire reverie. *Merthyr Express*, 22 Aug 1930, 21:A.

Rhymney bridge. *Merthyr Express*, 30 Aug 1930, 3:C.

Trafalgar Square, London. *Merthyr Express*, 15 Nov 1930, 23:B.

Pro patria. *The Limit* [Magazine of Loughborough Training College] 13,1 (1930) 9.

The firs of Blaen Rhymni. *Merthyr Express*, 18 Jul 1931, 23:C.

The bookman's psalm. *Merthyr Express*, 29 Aug 1931, 23:C.

In time of crisis. *Merthyr Express*, 5 Sep 1931, 21:A.

The bay is calm and bright the moon – One silver night. *The Gong* [Magazine of Nottingham University] 21,1 (1931) 16, 22.

Our vegetarians. *The Limit* [Magazine of Loughborough Training College] 13,2 (1931) 80.

The perfect lecturer. *The Limit* [Magazine of Loughborough Training College] 14,1 (1931) 41.

Brecknock Beacons. *Merthyr Express*, 2 Jan 1932, 23:E.

Respice finem – Reunion. *Welsh Outlook*, Apr 1932, 36, 98.

What porridge had John Keats? – Second year June. *The Gong* [Magazine of Nottingham University] 21,2 (1932) 15, 36.

Then temple and the wind – Adieu – The fruit shop. *The Gong* [Magazine of Nottingham University] 21,3 (1932) 8, 31, 32.

A city of illusions (from the Welsh of J. Morris Jones) – G.K.C. – Education and the social order. *The Gong* [Magazine of Nottingham University] 22,1 (1932) 9, 15, 23.

Holiday morning. *The Limit* [Magazine of Loughborough Training College] 14,3 (1932) 128.

At Twickenham (January 21, 1933). *Merthyr Express*, 28 Jan 1933, 21:E.

Back to Brecknock. *Brecon and Radnor Express*, 24 Aug 1933, 4:G.

A memory. *Merthyr Express*, 4 Aug 1934, 22:B.

Psalm at evening. *Merthyr Express*, 1 Sep 1934, 3:E.

Francis Drake. *Adelphi* 8 (1934) 100.

Jubilee morning. *Merthyr Express*, 11 May 1935, 3:C.

Old men of the Wye. *Merthyr Express*, 10 Aug 1935, 3:D.

Near Talgarth. *Brecon and Radnor Express*, 12 Sep 1935, 2:H.

In a rural church. *Merthyr Express*, 19 Oct 1935, 3:B.

For mother. *Merthyr Express*, 30 Nov 1935, 2:E.

On the crest. *Merthyr Express*, 11 Jan 1936, 3:B.

Rhymney to Merthyr. *Merthyr Express*, 18 Jan 1936, 2:E.

Gwalia deserta. *Comment*, 19 Sep 1936, 92. Prose.

A preface – Llangorse – Talybont-on-Usk – Village on the Usk. *Brecon and Radnor Express*, 1 Oct 1936, 10:G.

Souvenirs from Erin. *Wales* 2 (1937) 56-60. Prose.

Shadows and cakes. *Wales* 3 (1937) 115-116. Prose.

Hen fenyw fach – Er cof. *Merthyr Express*, 7 May 1938, 22:A.

Again and again. *Brecon and Radnor Express*, 9 Jun 1938, 8:F.

Land of my mothers. *Wales* 4 (1938) 141-144. Prose.

Dai's Empire. *Wales* 4 (1938) 152-153.

The gate of death. *Cornhill Magazine*, Mar 1939, 399.

Two framed pictures. *Life and Letters Today* 21 (1939) 49.

Review of B. L. Coombes, *I am a miner*. *Life and Letters Today* 21 (1939) 110-111.

Simplicity, difficulty, obscurity, experience. *New Verse* n.s. 1 (1939) 30-31. Letter in response to Geoffrey Grigson's review of *Gwalia deserta*, *New Verse* 31-32 (1938) 24-26.

Dowlais. *Poetry and the People* [Stepney Green] 8 (1939) 5.

Morning comes again to wake the valleys. *Wales* 10 (1939) 271.

Mining valley – The poet. *WR* 2 (1939) 140.

Early morning. In *Rhyme and reason: 34 poems*, ed. David Martin. London: Fore Publications, 1944.

The valley lights. *WM*, 9 Oct 1944, 2:H.

Snowflake. *WR* 3 (1944) 249.

The black tips of Rhondda. In *Bristol packet 2*. Bristol: Bristol Writers' and Artists' Association, 1945. p. 24.

The daily —— – The day is come to choose your creed – In Cheltenham – The year of victory – Summer holiday. In *New lyrical ballads anthology:*

*ballad book 1*, ed. Maurice Carpenter and others. London: Editions Poetry, 1945. pp. 125-130.

On Victory Day. *WM*, 4 May 1945, 2:H.

The true victor – 'D.L.-G.' – The victim's epitaph. *WM*, 29 Oct 1945, 2:H.

Gilwern. *WM*, 14 Nov 1945, 2:H.

The seeker. *Wales* 2nd ser. 5,7 (1945) 68.

Childhood. In *Writing today 3*, ed. Denys Val Baker. London: Staples Press, 1946. p. 38.

Epigrams: Alun Lewis – Chaucer – The tramp. *WM*, 21 Jan 1946, 2:H.

Pontwelly, Llandyssul. *WM*, 22 Mar 1946, 2:H.

Adam's lament – Eve's confession – The last epitaph. *WM*, 17 May 1946, 2:H.

Platform five, St. Pancras. *WM*, 1 Jul 1946, 2:H.

The crooner – W.B. Yeats – Dean Swift. *WM*, 3 Aug 1946, 2:H.

Dafydd ap Gwilym – Emily Bronte – The unfortunate actor. *WM*, 26 Aug 1946, 2:H.

The road to Brecon. *WM*, 30 Sep 1946, 2:H.

George Bernard Shaw – Robert Williams Parry – Sophistication. *WM*, 14 Oct 1946, 2:H.

Genius – Dai. *WM*, 25 Nov 1946, 2:H.

Ty'r agent – Ynysddu – The bore – The ambitious boxer. *WM*, 13 Dec 1946, 2:H.

Derby day. *Wales* 2nd ser. 6,24 (1946) 17.

Ffair y waun (the fair once held on the moorland). *The Wind and the Rain* 3,2 (1946) 76.

Elfed – Insomnia – The fine arts. *WM*, 18 Jan 1947, 2:H.

Iolo Morganwg – Surprise. *WM*, 1 Feb 1947, 2:H.

Hywel Harries – Llanelly – Who said cold? *WM*, 15 Feb 1947, 2:H.

Aberystwyth. *WM*, 13 Mar 1947, 2:H.

Thomas Jones, C.H. – Wales day by day – Italy. *WM*, 14 Apr 1947, 2:H.

Williams Pantycelyn – The mathematician – Brecon. *WM*, 21 Apr 1947, 2:H.

Queen Street, Cardiff. *WM*, 3 May 1947, 2:H.

Sir John Morris Jones – Cwmscwt – Miss So-and-so. *WM*, 26 May 1947, 2:H.

Thomas Gwyn Jones – Adolf Hitler – Bird life in South Wales. *WM*, 25 Jun 1947, 2:H.

Nicholas y Glais – Owain Glyndŵr – The House of Commons. *WM*, 5 Aug 1947, 2:H.

Thomas Hardy – Harlech – Who said hot? *WM*, 25 Aug 1947, 2:H.

The demagogue – Alec James – Glamorgan to Carmarthen. *WM*, 19 Sep 1947, 2:H.

Dr. Price Llantrisant – Nantgarw – Cwmsyfiog. *WM*, 22 Oct 1947, 2:H.

Supper in Soho. *WM*, 8 Nov 1947, 2:H.

The leopard – Pembroke coast. *Modern Reading* 14 (1947) 103-104.

Tenth anniversary year message. *Wales* 2nd ser 7,26 (1947) 258. Letter.

The Christmas tree – George Borrow – Edinburgh. *WM*, 7 Jan 1948, 2:H.

Gloucester – Gandhi – Charlie Chaplain. *WM*, 19 Jan 1948, 2:H.

One after another – The plagiarists – Cork. *WM*, 16 Feb 1948, 2:H.

A village called Cardiff. *WM*, 14 Apr 1948, 2:H.

The feast. *The Wind and the Rain* 5,2 (1948) 104.

Monmouthshire – Islwyn – Bedwellty Church – Rhymney Bridge. In *Monmouthshire poetry: an anthology of poetry relating to the county or composed by writers associated with Monmouthshire,* ed. Lawrence W. Hockey. Newport: R.H. Johns, 1949. pp. 29, 55, 85, 122.

A capital idea! *South Wales Echo*, 17 Jan 1949, 2:E.

The facts. *WM*, 8 Feb 1950, 2:G.

In the polling booth. *WM*, 23 Feb 1950, 4:G.

Poets then and now. *Observer*, 26 Feb 1950, 5:A. Letter on the marketability of poetry.

'And I felt my veins were at one with the earth'. *WM*, 3 Apr 1950, 2:G.

The choirs of Rhymney. *WM*, 23 Jun 1950, 4:H.

Summer 1950. *WM*, 23 Sep 1950.

In memoriam. In *New poems 1952: a P.E.N. anthology*, ed. Clifford Dyment and others. London: Joseph, 1952. p. 101.

Celia. *AWR* 26,57 (1976) 47. Written May 1937.

*Poetry Wales* 16,4 (1981). This Idris Davies issue includes: The valleys of my fathers – Six uncollected poems; Dai's empire, Morning comes again, Mining valley, The poet, In Cheltenham, Derby day 1946, pp. 9-23 – Photographs of the poet and extracts from his diary 1930, 1939-1940, 1948, pp. 28-47.

Valleys (1943) – War (1940). In *Wales on the wireless: a broadcasting anthology*, ed. Patrick Hannan. Llandysul: Gomer in assoc. with BBC Cymru/Wales, 1988. pp. 55-56; 108-109. Text of broadcast talks.

The valleys revisited. *Planet* 74 (1989) 20-23. Text of talk broadcast 4 Jan 1943.

A chapter of boyhood. *Planet* 75 (1989) 45-49. Text of talk broadcast 2 May 1940.

A holiday at home. *Planet* 76 (1989) 55-58. Text of talk broadcast 1 Oct 1941.

Memories of childhood. *Planet* 77 (1989) 81-85. Text of talk broadcast 9 Apr 1945.

## B. Publications about Idris Davies.

[ANON]. *WM*, 8 Apr 1953, 4:C. Obituary.
ABRAHAMS, Arthur. A study of Idris Davies. *Poetry and Drama Magazine* 9,2 (1957) 14-17.

BIANCHI, Tony. Idris Davies and the politics of anger. *PW* 16,4 (1981) 112-136.

CAMPBELL, Terry. Poet who captured shine and shadow of valley towns. *WM*, 12 Feb 1987. 14:B-E. Review article on Islwyn Jenkins, *Idris Davies of Rhymney: a personal memoir.*

COLLINS, W.J. Townsend. *Monmouthshire writers: a literary history and anthology.* Newport: R.H. Johns, 1945. Incl. Idris Davies of Rhymney, pp. 147-150.

CONRAN, Anthony. *The cost of strangeness: essays on the English poets of Wales.* Llandysul: Gomer Press, 1982. Incl. The achievement of Idris Davies, pp. 104-154.

—— Idris Davies: an attempt at assessment. *Mabon* [English] 1,6 (1973) 16-29.

DAVIES, Aneirin Talfan. Idris Davies: y bardd o Sir Fynwy. *Barn*, Aws/Aug 1972, 263-264. [Idris Davies: the poet of Monmouthshire].

EDWARDS, E.E. *Echoes of Rhymney.* Risca: Starling Press, 1974. 93 p.: ill. Background to Idris Davies.

HARDING, Joan N. The life and work of Idris Davies of Rhymney. *Presenting Monmouthshire* 13 (1962) 15-24.

—— Dau fardd Sir Fynwy. *Barn*, Chw/Feb 1973, 156-157. On W.H. Davies and Idris Davies.

HARRIS, Sylvia. A bibliography of Idris Davies. *PW* 16,4 (1981) 137-145. Lists publications by and about Davies and his poetry on record.

HOCKEY, Lawrence W. A gifted Rhymney boy who became the poet of the Welsh miner. *South Wales Argus*, 9 Oct 1953, 6:A-D. Discusses selection of poems for *Monmouthshire poetry*, ed. Lawrence W. Hockey (1949).

ISAAC, Nora. Successful struggle. *WM*, 24 Feb 1987, 13:A-B. Letter on Davies's support for Welsh-language education.

JENKINS, Islwyn. The life and works of Idris Davies, Rhymney. MA thesis. University of Wales, 1957. 293 p. Contents: Historical background of Rhymney, pp. 1-28 – Idris Davies: his life, pp. 29-170 – Published works, pp. 171-221 – Unpublished works, pp. 222-237 – Special features; The Anglo-Welsh aspect, The social quality, The religious conflict, pp. 238-266 – An assessment, pp. 267-281 – Bibliography of published and unpublished works, pp. 282-293.

—— 'The nectar of an unborn joy'. *Poetry and Drama Magazine* 9,2 (1957) 11-13. Touches on friendship with Dylan Thomas and Davies's idea of the poet's function.

—— Idris Davies: poet of Rhymney. *AWR* 9,23 (1958) 13-21.

—— *Idris Davies.* Cardiff: University of Wales Press [for] the Welsh Arts Council, 1972. 81 p.: front. port. (Writers of Wales). Incl. bibliography, pp. 77-79. – 'Limited to 800 copies'.

—— *PW* 13,4 (1978) 107. Letter on the possible influence of Edward Thomas.

—— Bells of Rhymney. *PW* 16,4 (1981) 96-103.

—— *Idris Davies of Rhymney: a personal memoir.* Llandysul: Gomer, 1986. xix, 273 p.: ill. Incl. Foreword, by Neil Kinnock, pp. vii-viii.

JENKINS, Nigel. Apocalyptic bravado. *Arcade*, 7 Aug 1981, 20-21. Review article on *Poetry Wales* 16,4 (1981), Idris Davies issue.

JOHNSTON, Dafydd. Dwy lenyddiaeth Cymru yn y tridegau. In *Sglefrio ar eiriau*, ed. John Rowlands. Llandysul: Gwasg Gomer, 1992. Compares Idris Davies with Gwenallt, pp. 51-62.

—— Idris Davies and the orchestras of history. *NWR* 6,1 [21] (1993) 16-18. Review article on *The angry summer: a poem of 1926*, ed. Tony Conran.

JONES, Brynmor. *Bibliographies of Anglo-Welsh literature: Idris Davies, 1905-1953: bibliographical note, original works and contributions to periodicals, critical articles.* [Cardiff]: Welsh Arts Council Literature Department, 1969. [4] p.

JONES, Glyn. 'I was born in Rhymney': Idris Davies, the man and his work. *Poetry and Drama Magazine* 9,2 (1957) 6-10.

—— Idris Davies: the man and the poet. *Y Ddinas*, Jun 1959, 10-11. Incl. Will Griffiths's memories of Idris Davies's early days in London.

—— *The dragon has two tongues: essays on Anglo-Welsh writers and writing.* London: Dent, 1968. Incl. Idris Davies, pp. 154-171.

—— Some letters of Idris Davies. *PW* 16,4 (1981) 76-84. Extracts from letters to Glyn Jones, with linking commentary.

LEWIS, Peter Elfed. *PW* 8,1 (1972) 89-98. Review article on Idris Davies, *Collected poems*, Islwyn Jenkins, *Idris Davies*.

NAKANO, Yoko [as Y.N. Bednar]. Idris Davies: a study of a South Wales valley poet. MLitt thesis. University of Oxford, 1988. 171 p. Incl. bibliography, pp. 157-171.

—— An obscure subject: on discovering Anglo-Welsh literature and Idris Davies in particular. *Planet* 77 (1989) 86-90.

PIKOULIS, John. East and east and east: Alun Lewis and the vocation of poetry. *AWR* 63 (1978) 39-65. Compares 'Gwalia deserta. VI' with Alun Lewis's 'The mountain over Aberdare'.

—— The watcher on the mountain: the poetry of Idris Davies. *PW* 16,4 (1981) 85-91.

—— Poetry and propaganda. *AWR* 87 (1988) 91-104. Review article on Islwyn Jenkins, *Idris Davies of Rhymney*.

POOLE, Richard. Idris Davies, the bitter dreamer. *PW* 16,4 (1981) 48-75.

PUGH, Sheenagh. Idris Davies: dreams and realities. *PW* 13,1 (1977) 34-39.

—— The political poet: is he a myth? *PW* 16,4 (1981) 92-95.

RAYMOND, David. Trwbadwr y cwm du. *Y Cymro*, 17 Ebr/Apr 1953, 6. [Troubador of the black valley].

SMITH, Dai. *Wales! Wales?* London: Allen & Unwin, 1984. Includes discussion of Idris Davies, Jack Jones, Lewis Jones and Gwyn Thomas, pp. 134-151.

STEPHENS, Peter John. Introduction [to three essays on Idris Davies]. *Poetry and Drama Magazine* 9,2 (1957) 3-4.

STEPHENS-JONES, Roger. *The angry summer:* an essay on the structure of Idris Davies's poem. *Planet* 37-38 (1977) 21-28.

THOMAS, Dylan. *The broadcasts*, ed. Ralph Maud. London: Dent, 1991. Brief comment on Idris Davies, pp. 43-45.

THOMAS, Ned. *The Welsh extremist.* London, 1971. Incl. discussion of Idris Davies, pp. 103-107.

—— Okot p'Bitek, Idris Davies, Waldo and Mr. Eliot: or poetry in the University of Wales. *PW* 12,2 (1976) 67-74.

TOLLEY, A.T. *The poetry of the thirties.* London: Gollancz, 1975. Incl. discussion of Idris Davies, pp. 325-327.

WADE, Stephen. Idris Davies and proletarian literature. *AWR* 24,53 (1974) 26-30.

WILLIAMS, Angela. A kind of angry poetry. *Planet* 51 (1985) 15-24. Considers Davies's poetry in the context of the 1984 miners' strike.

WILLIAMS, D.T. *WM*, 29 Jun 1953, 6:H. Obituary.

WILLIAMS, Ioan. Two Welsh poets: James Kitchener Davies (1902-52); Idris Davies (1905-53). *PW* 16,4 (1981) 104-111.

WILLIAMS, John Roberts. Idris Davies visits the Eisteddfod. *Planet* 82 (1990) 26-28. On his appearance at Bangor 1944. – Includes 'Thanksgiving', a poem by Idris Davies.

WILLIAMS, Phil. Good bad poetry. *Planet* 13 (1972) 56-60. Review article on Idris Davies, *Collected poems*, Islwyn Jenkins, *Idris Davies*.

YOUNG, Robin. Idris Davies in Swedish. *Planet* 49-50 (1980) 132-134. Reviews *Vredens sommar: en dikt ur 1926.*

# RHYS DAVIES (1901-1978)

A. Publications by Rhys Davies
  (i) Books
  (ii) Selected contributions to books and periodicals

B. Publications about Rhys Davies

## A (i). Publications by Rhys Davies: Books

*The song of songs and other stories*. London: E. Archer, [1927]. 53 p.: front. port.: pbk. Contents: A gift of death – The sisters – Mrs. Evans number six – History – The lily – The song of songs. – Frontispiece portrait by William Roberts. – '900 copies for sale'; also signed edition, '100 copies privately printed.'

*Aaron*. London: E. Archer, 1927. 11 p: pamph. 'One hundred copies privately printed'. – This story also appeared in *New Coterie* 6 (1927) 37-45.

*The withered root*. London: R. Holden, 1927. 280 p. Novel.

U.S. ed.: New York: Holt, 1928. 335 p.

*A bed of feathers* / frontispiece wood engraving by Lionel Ellis. London: Mandrake Press, [1929]. 93 p.: ill. 'A dramatic story of love in the Welsh coalfields'. – First published in *London Aphrodite* 2 (1928) 129-150.

*Tale*. London: E. Lahr, [1930]. 15 p.: pamph. (Blue moon booklets; 2). Two issues: (a) 7.5 x 5″, list of author's publications opposite title-page, ( b) 9 x 6″, with list replaced by limitation statement ('100 copies') and author's signature; cover title and diagonal stripe printed in red.

*Rings on her fingers*. London: Shaylor, 1930. 256 p. Also signed edition, 'limited to 175 copies'. – Novel.
—— Bath: Chivers, 1969. (Portway reprints).

U.S. ed.: New York: Harcourt, Brace, 1930. 278 p.

*The stars, the world and the women* / with a foreword by Liam O'Flaherty; and an illustration by Frank C. Pape. London: William Jackson, 1930. 53 p.: ill. (The Furnival books; 4). 'Of this book there have been printed at the Chiswick Press 550 copies, signed by the author, of which 500 only are for sale.' – Story.

*Arfon*. London: Foyle, [1931]. 68 p. 'Limited to four hundred copies

numbered one to four hundred, and twelve copies lettered A to L.'
– Story.

*A pig in a poke: stories*. London: Joiner & Steele, 1931. 280 p. Contents:
Revelation – Death in the family – A pig in a poke – The new garment
– Conflict in Morfa – The song of songs – The stars, the world and the
women – The lily – Mrs. Evans number six – The sisters – A gift of
death – Evelyn and Ivor – The doctor's wife – Blodwen – Hunger.
– 'First edition limited to one thousand numbered copies'. – Also signed
edition; 'seventy copies have been printed, of which numbers 1 to 50 are
for sale in Great Britain, and numbers 51 to 70 in the United States.'

*A woman*. London: Capell at the Bronze Snail Press, 1931. 39 p. 'Of this
first edition there have been printed 165 copies for sale, each numbered and
signed by the author ... Seventeen copies for presentation have also been
printed and lettered A to L.' – Story.

*The woman among women*. London: [E. Lahr], 1931. [4] p.: pamph. 'Blue
Moon poem for Christmas 1931. '100 signed copies for sale'. – Also edition
of 100 copies, with drawing by Frederick Carter, p. [2].

*Count your blessings*. London: Putnam, 1932. 319 p. Novel.

U.S. ed.: New York: Covici, Friede, 1932. 319 p.

*The red hills*. London: Putnam, 1932. 250 p. Novel.
—— Bath: Chivers, 1970. (Portway reprints).
—— Bath: Chivers, 1977. 299 p. ISBN: 0-85997-268-2. Large print
edition.

U.S. ed.: New York: Covici, Friede, 1933. 308 p.

German ed.: Leipzig: Tauchnitz, 1934. 280 p.

*Daisy Matthews and three other tales* / with wood engravings by Agnes Miller
Parker. Waltham Saint Lawrence: Golden Cockerel Press, 1932. 64p.: ill.
Contents: Daisy Matthews – The wanderer – The sleeping beauty –
Lovers. – 'The edition is limited to 325 copies.'

*Two loves I have*. London: Cape, 1933. 284 p. Novel. – Published under
the pseudonym, Owen Pitman.

*Love provoked*. London: Putnam, 1933. 301 p. Contents: Daisy Matthews
– The romantic policewoman – Lovers – Doris in Gomorrah – The
journey – The wanderer – The bard – The sleeping beauty – A bed
of feathers – Faggots – Arfon.

*One of Norah's early days*. London: Grayson & Grayson, 1935. [37] p.:
front. Frontispiece by Joy Lloyd. – '285 copies of this first edition ... have

been printed: 250 of these, numbered and signed by the author, are for sale.'
– Story.

*Honey and bread*. London: Putnam, 1935. 365 p. Novel.
—— Bath: Chivers, 1970. (Portway reprints).

*A bed of feathers* and *Tale*. New York: Black Hawk Press, 1935. 99 p.: ill.
Privately printed for subscribers, 'limited to 900 copies'. – National Library
of Wales copy collected in Black Hawk volume with Havelock Ellis, *Kanga
Creek*, James Hanley, *A passion before death*, and Norman Davey, *The ultimate
adventure.*

*The things men do: short stories*. London: Heinemann, 1936. 266 p. Contents: The two friends – The contraption – Wrath – Cherry-blossom
on the Rhine – The friendly creature – Glimpses of the moon – The
funeral – Caleb's ark – Resurrection – Half-holiday – The farm – On
the tip.

*The skull*. Chepstow: Tintern Press, 1936. 14 p.: ill. 'The wood engravings
are by Sylvia Marshall, who also designed the binding ... There are ninety-
five copies in buckram and fifteen in pigskin.' – Story.

*A time to laugh*. London: Heinemann, 1937. 432 p. Novel. – Reissued
1938, 'cheap edition'.

U.S. ed.: New York: Stackpole, 1938. 394 p.

*My Wales*. London: Jarrolds, 1937. 288 p.: ill. Contents: Prelude –
Eisteddfod – The South Wales workers – Welsh players – Three Welsh
characters; Dr. William Price, The maid of Cefn Ydfa, Twm Shon Catti
– Words – Holiday trip.

U.S. ed.: New York: Funk & Wagnalls, 1938. 305 p.: ill.

*Drama: Y ferch o Gefn Ydfa* / troswyd i'r Gymraeg gan T. J. Williams-
Hughes. Liverpool: Gwasg y Brython, 1938. 109 p.: pbk. (Dramau cyfres
y Brython; 66). Welsh translation of otherwise unpublished play based on
the story of the Maid of Cefn Ydfa.

*Jubilee blues*. London: Heinemann, 1938. 315 p. Novel.
—— Bath: Chivers, 1969. (Portway reprints).

*Sea urchin: adventures of Jörgen Jörgensen* ... London: Duckworth, 1940.
288 p.: ill. Biography.

Icelandic trans.: Jörundur hundadagakongur, aevintyri hans og aeviraunir.
Reykjavík: Bókfellsútgáfan h. f., 1943. 279 p.: Ill.

*Under the rose*. London: Heinemann, 1940. 333 p. Novel.

*Tomorrow to fresh woods*. London: Heinemann, 1941. 315 p. Novel.

*A finger in every pie*. London: Heinemann, 1942. 177 p. Contents: The wages of love – Abraham's glory – Charity – Mourning for Ianto – The nature of man – A pearl of great price – Nightgown – Alice's pint – The dark world – Ancient courtship – Over at Rainbow Bottom – The pits are on the top – Weep not, my wanton – The zinnias – Pleasures of the table – Tomos and the harp – The parrot – Queen of the Cote d'Azur.

*The story of Wales*. London: Collins, 1943. 48 p.: ill. (Britain in pictures).

U.S. ed.: New York: Hastings House, 1943. 47 p.

*The black Venus*. London: Heinemann, 1944. 200 p. Novel.
—— Readers Union, 1948. 298 p.
—— Pan, 1950. 254 p.: pbk.
—— Bath: Chivers, 1966. 204 p. (Portway reprints).

U.S. ed.: New York: Howell Soskin, [1946]. 325 p.

Danish trans.: *Den sorte Venus*, tr. Kirsten Heerup. København: P. Branner, 1947. 230 p.

Swedish trans.: *Den svarta Venus*, tr. Nils Holmberg. Stockholm: Fritzes Bokförlog; Helsingfors: Söderström, 1948.

*Selected stories*. London; Dublin: Fridberg, 1945. 126 p.: pbk. (Hourglass library). Contents: Resurrection – The contraption – Revelation – Death in the family – Conflict in Morfa – Wrath – Arfon – The bard – The journey – Cherry-blossom on the Rhine.

*The trip to London: stories*. London: Heinemann, 1946. 128 p. Contents: The benefit concert – A dangerous remedy – The last struggle – Price of a wedding ring – The trip to London – Gents only – The public house – River, flow gently – Spectre de la rose – Death of a canary – Orestes.
—— Bath: Chivers, 1966. (Portway reprints).

U.S. ed.: New York: Howell Soskin, [1946]. 214 p.

*The dark daughters*. London: Heinemann, 1947. 298 p. Novel. – Extract: Petticoat House. In *Modern Reading 15* (1947) 89-105.
—— Readers Union, 1948.

U.S. ed.: New York: Doubleday, 1948. 279 p.

Swedish trans.: *De mörka döttrarna*, tr. Eva Marstander. Stockholm: Folket i bilds förlag, 1951. 306 p.

*Boy with a trumpet*. London: Heinemann, 1949. 265 p. Contents: The dilemma of Catherine Fuchsias – Boy with a trumpet – Canute – A human condition – Fear – The fashion plate – A man in haste – Tomorrow – One of Norah's early days – The foolish one – The beard – Wigs, costumes, masks.

U.S. ed.: *Boy with a trumpet and other selected short stories* / with an introduction by Bucklin Moon. New York: Doubleday, 1951. 304 p.

German trans.: *Der Junge mit der Trompete*, tr. Siegfried Schmitz. München: Nymphenburger Verlagshandl, 1960. 149 p.

*Marianne*. London: Heinemann, 1951. 301 p. Novel.
—— Popular Library, 1952.

U.S. ed.: New York: Doubleday, 1952. 288 p.

*The painted king*. London: Heinemann, 1954. 250 p. Novel. – Reissued 1965, 'cheap edition', 255 p.

U.S. ed.: New York: Doubleday, 1954. 251 p.

*The collected stories*. London: Heinemann, 1955. viii, 416 p. Contents: The dilemma of Catherine Fuchsias – Boy with a trumpet – The nature of man – Canute – Fear – The benefit concert – The contraption – Revelation – The fashion plate – Alice's pint – Tomorrow – Resurrection – The foolish one – Arfon – Abraham's glory – Wrath – The dark world – The trip to London – The last struggle – Blodwen – The public house – The two friends – Gents only – Conflict in Morfa – Pleasures of the table – A man in haste – Mourning for Ianto – River, flow gently – The journey – The bard – Death in the family – Half-holiday – The farm – The zinnias – The wages of love – Glimpses of the moon – A human condition – Price of a wedding ring – Nightgown – Caleb's ark – Over at Rainbow Bottom – The pits are on the top – A dangerous remedy.

*No escape: a play in three acts from his novel* **Under the rose** / in collaboration with Archibald Batty. London: Evans Brothers, 1955. 72 p.: front.: pbk. Anthologized in *Ring up the curtain: four plays*. London: Heinemann, 1955. pp. 101-154.

*The perishable quality: a novel*. London: Heinemann, 1957. 238 p. – Reissued 1959, 'cheap edition', 244 p.

*The darling of her heart and other stories*. London: Heinemann, 1958. 233 p. Contents: All through the night – A spot of bother – Afternoon of a faun – The darling of her heart – A man up a tree – A visit to

Eggeswick Castle – The wedding at The Lion – Period piece – Tears, idle tears.

Hungarian trans.: *A mama kedvence*, tr. Klára Szöllösy. Budapest: Európa, 1959. 137 p.

*Girl waiting in the shade*. London: Heinemann, 1960. 207 p. Novel.

Norwegian trans.: *Piken i skyggen*, tr. Elizabeth Kostøl. Oslo: Green, 1969. 159 p.

*The chosen one and other stories*. London: Heinemann, 1967. 185 p. Contents: The chosen one – The little heiress – I will keep her company – The old Adam – Betty Leyshon's marathon – The shriving of Gwenny Treharne – Love kept waiting.

U.S. ed.: New York: Dodd, Mead, 1967.

*Print of a hare's foot: an autobiographical beginning*. London: Heinemann, 1969. 200 p. ISBN: 0-434-17801-2.

U.S. ed.: New York: Dodd, Mead, 1969.

*Nobody answered the bell*. London: Heinemann, 1971. 158 p. ISBN: 0-434-17802-0. Novel. – Extract: Rose and Martin. *Planet* 7 (1971) 58-72.

U.S. ed.: New York: Dodd, Mead, 1971. ISBN: 0-396-06373-X.

*Honeysuckle girl*. London: Heinemann, 1975. 165 p. ISBN: 0-434-17803-9. Novel.

*The best of Rhys Davies*. Newton Abbot: David & Charles, 1979. 191 p. ISBN: 0-7153-7756-6. Contents: The chosen one – The old Adam – Fear – I will keep her company – A vist to Eggeswick Castle – Nightgown – Gents only – A human condition – Boy with a trumpet – All through the night – Canute – The dilemma of Catherine Fuchsias.

## A (ii). Publications by Rhys Davies: Selected Contributions to Books and Periodicals

*The withered root*. Mr Rhys Davies and Welsh dialogue. *WM*, 30 Nov 1927, 9:C. Reply to *WM* review, 24 Nov 1927; ensuing correspondence (3, 8, 10 Dec) includes letters from T. Gwynn Jones.

The confessions of Rhys Davies. In *The Georgian confession book*, ed. Gilbert H. Fabes. London: Foyle, 1930. [2] p. Slender answers to questionnaire.

Foreword. In Liam O'Flaherty, *The wild swan and other stories*. London: Joiner & Steele, 1932. (The Furnival books; 10).

Writing about the Welsh. In John Gawsworth, *Ten contemporaries: notes towards their definitive bibliography*. London: Benn, 1932. pp. 41-43.

What is there to say? In *Full score*, ed. Fytton Armstrong. London: Rich & Cowan, 1933. pp. 216-220. Story.

The first patient. In *Path and pavement: twenty new tales of Britain*, ed. John Rowland. London: Eric Grant, 1937. pp. 65-74.

Deplorable story. *Wales* 3 (1937) 90-98.

Review of *New writing* (Spring 1939). *Life and Letters Today* 21,22 (1939) 126-128.

Review of Mulk Raj Anand, *The village*. *Life and Letters Today* 21,22 (1939) 142-143.

Review of Adrian Bell, *The shepherd's farm*. *Life and Letters Today* 22 (1939) 300-301.

Review of Elizabeth Inglis-Jones, *Pay thy pleasure*; Ted Allen, *This time a better earth*. *Life and Letters Today* 23 (1939) 247; 248.

A note on Mary Butts. *Wales* 6-7 (1939) 207. Review of Mary Butts, *Last stories*.

Phaedra. *Wales* 8-9 (1939) 219-224. Drama.

D.H. Lawrence in Bandol. *Horizon*, Oct 1940, 191-208.

Review of Dylan Thomas, *Portrait of the artist as a young dog*. *Life and Letters Today* 24 (1940) 336-338.

Review of Ruthven Todd, *The laughing mulatto: the story of Alexandre Dumas*. *Life and Letters Today* 25 (1940) 104-107.

From my notebook. *Wales* 2nd ser. 2 (1943) 10-12. Continued: 4,5 (1944) 64-70; 6,2 [22] (1946) 13-19.

Seine – Louvre. In *Modern Welsh poetry*, ed. Keidrych Rhys. London: Faber, 1944. pp. 33-34. Poetry.

The city. *Wales* 2nd ser. 5,8-9 (1945) 72-73. Poetry. – First published in *Transition* [Paris; The Hague] 3 (1927).

Review of Glyn Jones, *The water music and other stories*. *WR* 4 (1945) 68-69.

Time and the Welsh mountains. In *Countryside character*, ed. Richard Harman. London: Blandford Press, 1946. pp. 209-219.

A drop of dew. In *The mint: a miscellany of literature, art and criticism*, ed. Geoffrey Grigson. London: Routledge, 1946. pp. 102-113. On Dr William Price. – Reprinted *Wales* 2nd ser. 9,31 (1949) 61-71.

Harvest moon. In *Little reviews anthology, 1946*, ed. Denys Val Baker. London: Eyre & Spottiswoode, 1946. pp. 18-26.

Reply to *Wales* questionnaire 1946. *Wales* 2nd ser. 6,2 [22] (1946) 18-19.

Is this Rhondda picture true? *WM*, 11 Jul 1946, 3:F. In response to *WM* article, 4 Jul, 2: E-F.

Writing about the Welsh. *Literary Digest* 2,2 (1947) 18-19.

Tenth anniversary year message. *Wales* 2nd ser. 7,26 (1947) 262. Letter.

Davies, Rhys. In *Twentieth century authors: a biographical dictionary of modern literature. First supplement*, ed. Stanley J. Kunitz and Vineta Colby. New York: Wilson, 1955. pp. 263-264. Autobiographical note, with bibliography.

Our contributors, no. 1. Rhys Davies. *Wales* 3rd ser., Sep 1958, 7. Autobiographical note, with portrait.

Nina Hamnet [sic], bohemian. *Wales* 3rd ser., Sep 1959, 27-33.

The friendly stove. *House and Garden* [U.S.A.], Oct 1963, 216-217.

Introduction. In Anna Kavan, *Julie and the bazooka, and other stories*, ed. Rhys Davies. London: Peter Owen, 1970.

The bazooka girl: a note on Anna Kavan. *London Magazine*, Feb 1970, 13-16.

Anna Kavan. *Books and Bookmen*, Mar 1971, 7-10.

Charles Lahr. *Times*, 18 Aug 1971, 14:H. Obituary notice.

Prefatory note. In Anna Kavan, *Let me alone*. London: Peter Owen, 1974. pp. 5-6.

Introduction. In Anna Kavan, *My soul in China: a novella and stories*, ed. Rhys Davies. London: Peter Owen, 1975.

Incident in a bookshop (1938). In *Wales on the wireless: a broadcasting anthology*, ed. Patrick Hannan. Llandysul: Gomer in assoc. with BBC Cymru/Wales, 1988. pp. 1-2. Broadcast talk.

A bad home influence. *Planet* 89 (1991) 70-83. A previously unpublished story.

# B. Publications about Rhys Davies

ADAM, G.F. *Three contemporary Anglo-Welsh novelists: Jack Jones, Rhys Davies and Hilda Vaughan.* Bern: A. Franke, [1948]. Incl. Rhys Davies: regionalism as an expression of universal values, pp. 48-76.

[ANON]. Crude phases of Welsh life. Why author's work may seem cruel. *WM* 1 Feb 1927, 7:G. Incl. interview on Davies's background, writing and future plans.

—— Welsh novelist in France. *WM*, 2 Jan 1929, 6:C. Alludes to his stay on the Riviera, meeting with D.H. Lawrence and a recent visit to Wales.

BAKER, Denys Val. Writers of today, 9. Man from the valley. *John O'London's Weekly*, 24 Oct 1952, 961-962.

CALLARD, David. Rhys Davies and the Welsh expatriate novel. *Planet* 89 (1991) 84-87. Discusses in particular *Two loves I have*, published under the pseudonym Owen Pitman.

DAVIES, Aneirin Talfan. Ar ymyl y ddalen. *Barn*, Chw/Feb 1963, 100-101. Discusses Rhys Davies and Caradoc Evans. – [In the margin].

DAVIES, W. Pennar ['Davies Aberpennar']. Anti-nationalism among the Anglo-Welsh. *Welsh Nationalist*, Feb 1948, 3:A-D. Mainly on Rhys Davies, *The story of Wales*.

DICK, Kay. Obituary. *Times*, 24 Aug 1978, 17:F.

GAWSWORTH, John. *Ten contemporaries: notes towards their definitive bibliography.* London: Benn, 1932. Incl. The works of Rhys Davies, giving bibliographical descriptions of 14 items, pp. 42-52.

GOODWAY, David. Charles Lahr: anarchist, bookseller, publisher. *London Magazine*, Jun-Jul 1977, 46-55. On one of Davies's early publishers.

HUGHES, Glyn Tegai. The mythology of the mining valleys. In *Triskel two: essays on Welsh and Anglo-Welsh literature*, ed. Sam Adams and Gwilym Rees Hughes. Llandybïe: Christopher Davies, 1973. pp. 42-61.

JONES, Glyn. Dedicated professional. *Planet* 40 (1977) 53-54. Review article on David Rees, *Rhys Davies*.

JONES, Gwyn. Anglo-Welsh writers, 5. Rhys Davies. *WM*, 11 May 1949, 4:D-F.

MATHIAS, Roland. Rhys Davies. In *Contemporary novelists of the English language*, ed. James Vinson. 2nd ed. London: St. James Press; New York: St. Martin's Press, 1976. pp. 338-341.

MEGROZ, R.L. *Rhys Davies: a critical sketch.* London: Foyle, 1932. xiii, 50 p.

MITCHELL, J. Lawrence. Home and abroad: the dilemma of Rhys Davies. *Planet* 70 (1988) 78-90.

POL LE LAY, Jean. Rhys Davies as an Anglo-Welsh story-teller. Thesis. Faculté des Lettres et Sciences Humaines de Brest, 1968-69.

REES, David. Rhys Davies: professional author. *Wales* 3rd ser., Feb 1959, 70-73.

—— *Rhys Davies.* Cardiff: University of Wales Press [for] the Welsh Arts Council, 1975. 73 p.: front. port. (Writers of Wales). Incl. selected bibliography, pp. 65-70. – 'Limited to 1000 copies'.

ROBERTS, Glyn. Rhys Davies's polished prose. *WM*, 12 Sep 1933, 6:D-E.

# W.H. DAVIES (1871-1940)

A. Publications by W.H. Davies
  (i)   Individual books, selections
  (ii)  Collected editions
  (iii) Books and periodicals edited
  (iv) Selected contributions to books and periodicals

B. Publications about W.H. Davies

## A (i). Publications by W.H. Davies: Individual Books, Selections

*The soul's destroyer and other poems*. London: Of the Author: Farmhouse, Marshalsea Rd., S.E., [1905]. 108 p.: pbk.
—— Alston Rivers, [1907]. xlvi p.: pbk. (The contemporary poets). Contains 14 of 40 poems in first edition.
—— Cape, 1921. Reissue of 3rd Alston Rivers impression, 1910.

*New poems*. London: Elkin Mathews, 1907. 75 p. Reissued 1913, with title-page device and Cork St. (not Vigo St.) in imprint.
—— Cape, 1922. viii, 68 p. (The life and colour series; 15)

U.S. ed.: Boston: B. Humphries, [n.d.].

*The autobiography of a super-tramp* / with a preface by Bernard Shaw. London: Fifield, 1908. xiv, 295 p.
—— Fifeld, 1920. xiv, 304 p.: front. port. 'Fifth edition, with a note by the author and five poems, and a frontispiece from a photograph of 1908.'
—— Cape, 1923, with new foreword by author.
—— Cape, 1926. xvi, 304 p. (The travellers' library).
—— Cape, 1930. 318 p.: ill. (The life and letters series; 6). 'With four photographs of the author'.
—— Cape, 1942. (New English edition).
—— / edited with a preface by W.G. Bebbington. Allen & Unwin, 1951. 155 p. 'School edition'.
—— Cape, 1955. 253 p. Reissued 1976, pbk. ISBN: 0-224-60350-7.
—— Brown, Watson, 1960. 316 p. (Digit books).
—— Corgi, 1971. 254 p.: pbk. ISBN: 0-552-08861-7.
—— Oxford: Oxford University Press, 1980. 253 p.: pbk. ISBN: 0-19-281293-9. With author's note to 1920 edition and foreword to 1923 edition.

U.S. eds.: New York: A.A. Knopf, 1917. xx, 345 p. Reissued 1924, (Borzoi pocket books).

—— New York: J. Cape, H. Smith, 1929. 304 p. (The travellers' library).

German trans.: *Autobiographie eines Vagabunden*, tr. Ursula von Wiese. Zúrich: Manesse-Verlag, 1985. 384 p.

Irish trans.: *Féin scríbhinn fíor-shreaothaide*, tr. Colm ó Goara. Baile Atha Cliath [Dublin]: Oifig an tSoláthair, 1938. 328 p.

Italian trans.: *Autobiografia di un supervagabonda*. Milano: Rizzoli, 1948. 312 p.

*Nature poems and others*. London: Fifield, 1908. 62 p. Reissued 1916, pbk., cover with 'third edition'.
—— Cape, 1921. (The life and colour series; 6).

U.S. ed.: Boston: Humphries, [n.d.].

*Beggars*. London: Duckworth, 1909. vi, 300 p. Prose.

*Farewell to poesy and other pieces*. London: Fifield, 1910. 60 p. Cover reads 'and other poems'.
—— Cape, 1921. (The life and colour series; 4).

U.S. ed.: Boston: B. Humphries, [n.d.].

*A weak woman: a novel*. London: Duckworth, 1911. viii, 305 p.

*Songs of joy and others*. London: Fifield, 1911. 94 p.
—— Cape, 1921. (The life and colour series; 7).

U.S. ed.: Boston: B. Humphries, 1911.

*The true traveller*. London: Duckworth, 1912. viii, 291 p. Prose.

*Foliage: various poems*. London: Elkin Mathews, 1913. 64 p.
—— Cape, 1922. viii, 63 p. (The life and colour series; 16). 'New and revised edition'.

U.S. ed.: Boston: B. Humphries, [n.d.].

*Nature*. London: Batsford, 1914. 54 p. (Fellowship books). Mostly prose.

*The bird of paradise and other poems*. London: Methuen, 1914. 86 p.
—— Cape, 1926.

*Child lovers and other poems*. London: Fifield, 1916. 29 p.: pbk.
—— Cape, 1921. 28 p.

*A poet's pilgrimage*. London: Melrose, 1918. 378 p. Prose.
—— Cape, 1927. 255 p. (The travellers' library).
—— Cape, 1940. (The Saint Giles library; 13).

U.S. ed.: New York: J. Cape & H. Smith, 1929.

*Raptures: a book of poems*. London: Beaumont Press, 1918. 38 p. '22 copies
... printed on Japanese vellum signed by the author and numbered 1 to 22
and 250 copies on hand-made paper numbered 23 to 272.'

*Forty new poems*. London: Fifield, 1918. 53 p. Incl: 30 poems of *Raptures*
and 12 others.
—— Cape, 1924.

*The song of life and other poems* / with a frontispiece from a portrait by
Laura Knight. London: Fifield, 1920. 61 p.

*The captive lion and other poems*. New Haven: Yale University Press, 1921.
vii, 99 p. Contents: *Forty new poems* – *The song of life*.

*The hour of magic and other poems* / decorated by William Nicholson.
London: Cape, 1922. 34 p.: ill. Also signed edition; 'of this large paper
edition ... have been printed 110 copies'.

U.S. ed.: New York: Harper & Bros, 1922.

*True travellers: a tramp's opera in three acts* / with decorations by William
Nicholson. London: Cape, 1923. 52 p.: ill. Also signed edition, '100 copies
only for sale'.

U.S. ed.: New York: Harcourt, Brace, 1923.

*Selected poems* / decorated with woodcuts by Stephen Bone. London: Cape,
1923. 76 p.: ill. Incl. 26 woodcuts.

U.S. ed.: New York: Harcourt, Brace, 1925.

*Secrets*. London: Cape, 1924. 48p.: ill. Also signed edition, '100 copies'.

U.S. ed.: New York: Harcourt, Brace, 1924.

*A poet's alphabet*. London: Cape, 1925. 63 p.: ill. Decorations by Dora M.
Batty. – Also signed edition; 'of this edition ... 125 copies have been printed
for sale'.
—— Cape, 1927. (The travellers' library).

—— Cape, 1934. Cheap edition.

*Later days*. London: Cape, 1925. 223 p. Also signed edition, '125 copies for sale, signed and numbered by the author'.
—— Cape, 1927. (The travellers' library).
—— Oxford: Oxford University Press, 1985. 141 p.: pbk. ISBN: 0-19-281864-3.

U.S. eds.: New York: George H. Doran, 1926. 234 p.
—— New York: J. Cape & H. Smith, 1929. (The American travellers' library).

*The Augustan books of modern poetry: W.H. Davies*. London: Benn, [1925]. v, 32 p.: pamph. Selection of 30 poems.

*The adventures of Johnny Walker, tramp*. London: Cape, 1926. 256 p. Incl. material from *Beggars* and *The true traveller*. – Also signed edition; 'of this edition ... have been printed 125 copies for sale'.
—— Cape, 1927. (The travellers' library).
—— Cape, 1932. (Florin books).
—— Brown, Watson, 1963. 238 p.: pbk. (Digit books).
—— Howard Baker, 1970. ISBN: 0-09-308900-7.

*The song of love*. London: Cape, 1926. 61 p.: ill. Decorations by Dora M. Batty. – Also signed edition; 'of this edition 125 copies have been printed for sale'.

*A poet's calendar*. London: Cape, 1927. 61 p.: ill. Also signed edition; '125 copies for sale'. – Reissued 1934, 'cheap edition'.

U.S. ed.: New York: P. Smith, 1934.

*Dancing mad: a novel*. London: Cape, 1927. 224 p.

*Moss and feather*. London: Faber & Gwyer, 1928. 3p.: ill.: pamph. (The Ariel poems; 10). Illustrated by William Nicholson. – Also signed 'large-paper edition, printed on English hand-made paper ... limited to five hundred copies'.

*Forty-nine poems* / selected and illustrated by Jacynth Parsons. London: Medici Society, 1928. viii, 58 p.: ill. (some col.). Incl. preface by author. – Also signed edition; '110 copies have been printed, of which 100 are for sale.'

U.S. ed.: New York: J. Cape & H. Smith, 1929. viii, 56 p.: ill.

*Selected poems* / arranged by Edward Garnett with a foreword by the author. Newtown: Gregynog Press, 1928. vii, 91 p.: front. port. Portrait by Augustus John. – 'Edition is limited to three hundred and ten copies'. – Also specially bound edition of 25 copies.

*In winter*. The Poetry Bookshop, [1928]. 4 p.: ill. (Christmas card; 6).
—— London: Privately printed [for Terence Fytton Armstrong], 1931. [5] p.: ill.: pamph. 'Of this poem 290 numbered copies ... have been issued, all signed by the author, 250 copies for sale only. There is also an edition of 15 copies, lettered A – O, printed on an old style hand-made paper, 10 copies for sale only.'

*Ambition and other poems*. London: Cape, 1929. 32 p. Also signed edition. '210 copies only'.

*Poems, 1930-31*. London: Cape, 1932. 48 p.: ill. Also signed edition, 'limited to one hundred and fifty copies for sale'.

U.S. ed.: New York: J. Cape & H. Smith, 1932.

*My birds*. London: Cape, 1933. 128 p.: ill. Illustrations by Hilda M. Quick. – Poetry and prose.

*My garden* / with illustrations by Hilda M. Quick. London: Cape, 1933. 127 p.: ill. Poetry and prose.

*The lovers' song-book*. Newtown: Gregynog Press, 1933. v, 30 p. 'Edition is limited to two hundred and fifty copies'; 19 copies bound in light green levant morocco.
—— Newtown: Gwasg Greynog, 1993. ISBN: 0-948714-56-5. New ed. of 350 copies – With 100 sets of the 10 Gertrude Hermes engravings originally commissioned 1933.

*Love poems*. London: Cape, 1935. 60 p.: ill. Contents: *The lovers' song-book* – 20 additional poems.

U.S. ed.: New York: Oxford University Press, 1935.

*The birth of song: poems, 1935-36*. London: Cape, 1936. 32 p.: ill.

U.S. ed: New York: Oxford University Press, 1936.

*The loneliest mountain and other poems*. London: Cape, 1939. 32 p.

*My garden and my birds* / with illustrations by Hilda M. Quick. London: Cape, 1939. 128, 127 p.: ill. Reissue of the 1933 editions.

*Common joys and other poems*. London: Faber, 1941. 80 p.

*The essential W.H. Davies* / selected, with an introduction by Brian Waters.

London: Cape, 1951. 333 p. Contents: Introduction – Songs of Gwent – *The autobiography of a super-tramp* – London poems – The sport of fame [from *Beggars*] – Introduction to *Jewels of song* – Nature poems – *A poet's pilgrimage* – Love poems – *Later days* – Sweet stay-at-home – *My birds* – *My garden* – Poems of fancy.

*Young Emma* / with a foreword by C.V. Wedgwood. London: Cape, 1980. 158 p. ISBN: 0-224-01853-1. Incl. letter from George Bernard Shaw, pp. 157-158. – Autobiography.
—— Sevenoaks: Hodder & Stoughton, 1983. pbk. (Coronet books). ISBN: 0-340-32115-6.
—— Sevenoaks: Sceptre, 1987. 140 p.: pbk. ISBN: 0-340-40515-5.

U.S. ed.: New York: George Braziller, 1989.

Spanish trans.: *Joven Emma*, tr. Eduardo Goligorsky. Barcelona: Muchnik, 1983. 162 p.

*Selected poems* / chosen with an introduction by Jonathan Barker. Oxford: Oxford University Press, 1985. xlix, 206 p.: pbk. ISBN: 0-19-281432-X. Incl. Introduction, chronology of Davies's life and work, and selections from: *The soul's destroyer and other poems* – *New poems* – *Nature poems and others* – *Farewell to poesy and other pieces* – *Songs of joy and others* – *Foliage: various poems* – *The bird of paradise and other poems* – *Child lovers and other poems* – *A poet's pilgrimage* – *Forty new poems* – *The song of life and other poems* – *The hour of magic and other poems* – *The autobiography of a super-tramp* – *True travellers* – *Secrets* – *Later days* – *A poet's alphabet* – *The song of love* – *A poet's calendar* – *Ambition and other poems* – *Poems, 1930-31* – *My birds* – *My garden* – *Love poems* – *The birth of song: poems, 1935-36* – *The loneliest mountain and other poems*. – Reissued 1992, with corrections.

# A (ii). Publications by W.H. Davies: Collected Editions

*Collected poems by William H. Davies* / with a portrait in collotype from a pencil sketch by Will Rothenstein; and facsimile of author's script. London: Fifield, 1916. vii, 160 p.: front. port.
—— *Collected poems: first series by W.H. Davies*. London: Cape, 1923. Also special edition in parchment and lambskin.

U.S. ed.: *The Collected poems of William H. Davies* / with a portrait by William Rothenstein. New York: Knopf, 1916. 190 p.: front. port. With 12 additional poems.

*Collected poems: second series by W.H. Davies*. London: Cape, 1923. 157 p.: front. port. Incl. poems from: *New poems* – *Foliage* – *Forty new poems* – *The song of life* – *The hour of magic* – New poems. – 112 poems in all. –

Portrait by Augustus John. – Also signed edition, '106 copies …100 only for sale'.

U.S. ed.: New York: Harper, 1923.

*The collected poems of W.H. Davies, 1928.* London: Cape, 1928. xx, 399 p.: front. port. 431 poems. – Frontispiece of bust by Jacob Epstein.

U.S. ed.: New York: J. Cape & H. Smith, 1929.

*The poems of W.H. Davies.* London: Cape, 1934. 475 p. 533 poems.

U.S. ed.: New York: Oxford University Press, 1935.

*The poems of W.H. Davies, 1940.* London: Cape, 1940. 525 p.: front. port. 636 poems. – Portrait by Laura Knight.

*Collected poems of W.H. Davies.* London: Cape, 1942. xxviii, 525 p.: front. port. 636 poems. – 1940 frontispiece portrait acknowledged as 'by Harold Knight'. – 1943 impression with introduction by Osbert Sitwell.

U.S. ed.: *The poems of W.H. Davies* / introduction by Osbert Sitwell. New York: Transatlantic, 1946. xxviii, 525 p.

*The complete poems of W.H. Davies* / with an introduction by Osbert Sitwell; and a foreword by Daniel George. London: Cape, 1963. xxxiv, 616 p. 749 poems. – Reissued 1967, pbk.

U.S. ed.: Middletown, Conn.: Weslyan University Press, 1965. 630 p. ISBN: 0-8195-3055-7.


# A (iii). Publications by W.H. Davies: Books and Periodicals Edited

*Form: a monthly magazine of the arts,* 1-3, Oct 1921-Jan 1922. Edited by A.O. Spare and W.H. Davies. – With editorials by W.H. Davies.

*Shorter lyrics of the twentieth century, 1900-1922* / selected with a foreword by W.H. Davies. London: Poetry Bookshop, 1922. 192 p. – Also special edition, '200 copies on large paper'. – Reissued 1926, printed boards.

U.S. ed.: Folcroft, [n.d.].

*Jewels of song: an anthology of short poems* / compiled by W.H. Davies. London: Cape, 1930. xx, 250 p. Incl. Introduction, by W.H. Davies. – Reissued 1934, 'cheap edition'.
—— *An anthology of short poems* / compiled by W.H. Davies. London: Cape, 1938. xii, 250 p.

U.S. ed.: New York: P. Smith, 1934.


## A (iv). Publications by W.H. Davies: Selected Contributions to Books and Periodicals

This section draws attention to W.H. Davies's prose and to the influential *Georgian poetry* anthologies, where he was a substantial contributor. Sylvia Harlow, *W. H. Davies: a bibliography* (1993) is a definitive listing of publications by and about the author.

How it feels to be out of work. *English Review* 1 (1908) 168-171.

Short studies. The finder. *Nation*, 26 Feb 1910, 842-843. Story.

*Georgian poetry, 1911-1912*, ed. Edward Marsh. London: The Poetry Bookshop, 1912. Incl. 5 poems by W.H. Davies, pp. 55-63. – Davies appeared in all four subsequent *Georgian poetry* anthologies: *1913-1915* (with 9 poems), *1916-1917* (4 poems), *1918-1919* (8 poems), *1920-1922* (6 poems).

Short studies. A sea-captain. *Nation*, 3 Apr 1915, 17.

My memory of Edward Thomas. *Voices in Poetry and Prose* 4,4 (1920) 118-122.

Introduction. In Edmund X. Kapp, *Reflections: a second series of drawings*. London: Cape, 1922.

What I gained and lost by not staying at school. *Teachers World*, 13 Jun 1923, 543.

Review of Daniel Defoe, *Moll Flanders. New Statesman*, 23 Jun 1923, 330.

Poets and critics. *New Statesman*, 8 Sep 1923, 619.

Review of Walter de la Mare, *Songs of childhood* and *Come hither*, Wilfrid Scawen Blunt, *Poems. New Statesman*, 8 Dec 1923, 272.

Biographical note and introduction. In Daniel Defoe, *Moll Flanders.* London:

Simpkin, Marshall, Hamilton, Kent, 1924. (The Abbey classics). pp. [v]-xi.

Introduction. In Glen H. Mullin, *Adventures of a scholar tramp.* London: Cape, 1925.

Introduction [by 'W.J. Davies']. In Robert Burns, *Poetical works.* Glasgow: Collins, [1925?].

Introduction. In John Maplet, *A greene forest, or a naturall historie ...* London: Hesperides Press, 1930. Facsimile of 1567 edition. – 'Limited to 575 copies' .

*Jewels of song. New Statesman*, 22 Nov 1930, 204. Letter.

Rungs of the ladder. *Listener*, 18 May 1932, 724-725. On his early life.

Confessions of a down and out. *New Statesman*, 18 Mar 1933, 338, 340. Review of George Orwell, *Down and out in Paris and London.*

A Cotswold village. In *The English country: fifteen essays by various authors*, ed. H.J. Massingham. London: Wishart, 1934. pp. 97-109.

Rhys, Ernest. *Letters from limbo: with 63 reproductions of letters.* London: Dent, 1936. Incl. letters by W.H. Davies, pp. 216-218.

Epilogue. In W.J. Townsend Collins, *The romance of the echoing wood.* Newport: R.H. Johns, 1937, pp. 41-43.

Pharaoh the cat. *Gloucestershire Countryside*, Jan 1938, 303.

The poetry of life. *Gloucestershire Countryside*, Apr 1938, 329.

Alms and the supertramp: nineteen unpublished letters from W.H. Davies to Edward Thomas. *AWR* 70 (1982) 34-59. Edited by William Cooke.

## B: Publications about W.H. Davies

ADCOCK, Arthur St. John. The cripple poet. *Daily Mail*, 18 Aug 1905, 3:C-D.
—— *Gods of modern Grub Street: impressions of contemporary authors.* London: Sampson, Low, Marston, 1923. Incl. William Henry Davies, pp. 62-70 (with portrait by E.O. Hoppe).
[ANON]. *Shaded lights on men and books: essays selected from* Peace of mind *and* Serenity. London: Melrose, 1922. Incl. The apotheosis of W.H. Davies, pp. 88-94.
—— Journey's end of the tramp poet. *WM*, 27 Sep 1940, 4:D-F. Obituary.

—— Mr W.H. Davies: the 'tramp poet'. *Times*, 27 Sep 1940, 7:F. Obituary.

—— W.H. Davies. *TLS*, 5 Oct 1940, 508. Obituary.

ARMSTRONG, Martin D. W.H. Davies: the simple philosopher. *Listener*, 16 Jul 1942, 84-85.

BAYLEY, John. The undercover poet. *TLS*, 25 Jan 1985, 79-80. Review article on W.H. Davies, *Selected poems*.

BARKER, Jonathan. Songs of childhood, birds and flowers? *PW* 18,2 (1983) 46-56.

BAX, Clifford. *Some I knew well.* London: Phoenix House, 1951. Incl. W.H. Davies: the super-tramp, pp. 64-68.

BURKE, Thomas. *City of encounters: a London divertissement.* London: Constable, 1932. Discusses Davies's relationship with Frank Cazenove's literary agency, pp. 78-89.

CHURCH, Richard. W. H. Davies: the man and his work. *Fortnightly Review* 147 (1940) 80-86.

—— *Eight for immortality.* London: Dent, 1941. Incl. W.H. Davies: the man and his work, pp. 1-12.

—— Portrait of my friend W.H. Davies. *John O'London's Weekly*, 31 Dec 1943, 125.

—— *Son of London.* London: Herbert Jenkins, 1946. Reminiscences of W.H. Davies, pp. 201-204.

—— *The voyage home.* London: Heinemann, 1964. Incl. account of visit by W.H. Davies, pp. 44-47.

—— Remembering the tramp poet. *Country Life*, 24 Jun 1971, 1598-1599.

COLLINS, W.J. Townsend. *Monmouthshire writers: a literary history and anthology.* Newport: R.H.Johns, 1945. Incl. W.H. Davies, the tramp poet, pp. 94-99 (with photograph of Epstein bust).

CONRAN, Anthony. *The cost of strangeness: essays on the English poets of Wales.* Llandysul: Gomer Press, 1982. Incl. The tramp poems of W.H. Davies, pp. 21-51.

CULLUP, Michael. Recovering W.H. Davies. *PN Review* 47 (1985) 36-38. Review article on W.H. Davies, *Selected poems*.

DE LA MARE, Walter. *Private view.* London: Faber, 1953. Incl. W.H. Davies, pp. 134-137. – Reprinted from *TLS*, 8 Jun 1916.

DILLON, G.H. Mr Davies' poetry. *Poetry* [Chicago] 27,1 (1925) 44-48.

DUFF, Louis Blake. From a doss-house to Parnassus. *Colophon* 19 (1934).

EVANS, Caradoc. Tramp and poet. *WM*, 15 Jan 1916, 7:A-B.

—— *Fury never leaves us: a miscellany of Caradoc Evans*, ed. John Harris. Bridgend: Poetry Wales Press, 1985. Incl. W.H. Davies, pp. 126-130. – Reprinted from *WR* 3 (1944) 183-186.

FINNEY, Brian. *The inner I: British literary autobiography in the twentieth century.* London: Faber, 1985. Incl. W.H. Davies: *Autobiography of a super-tramp*, pp. 24-34.

FRANCIS, John. Sidelights on the supertramp. *WM* , 21 Jan 1961, [Weekend magazine] 1.

GARDINER, Wrey. *The poems of W.H. Davies, 1940. Poetry Quarterly* 2,2 (1940) 50-51.

GARNETT, David. *The golden echo.* London: Chatto & Windus, 1953. Incl. reminiscences of W.H. Davies, pp. 121-122, 238.

GIBBON, Monk. A great poet. In *Then and now: a selection ... from the first fifty numbers of* Now and Then, *1921-35.* London: Cape, 1935. pp. 55-58.

GRIFFITHS, Teifion. The Welsh influence on English verse. *Y Ddinas*, Aug 1956, 19.

GUTHRIE, James. *To the memory of Edward Thomas.* Flansham: Pear Tree Press, 1937. Summary of Edward Thomas's letters to W.H. Hudson (with references to W.H. Davies), pp. 21-31.

HAINES, John W. William Henry Davies: a poet of whom Gloucestershire should be proud. *Gloucester Journal*, 26 Jul 1941, 5:E-F.

HARDING, Joan N. Dau fardd Sir Fynwy. *Barn*, Chw/Feb 1973, 156-157. On W.H. Davies and Idris Davies.

HARLOW, Sylvia. *W.H. Davies: a bibliography.* Winchester: St. Paul's Bibliographies, 1993. xii, 259 p. (Winchester bibliographies of 20th century writers). 'It consists of his books, anthologies edited by him, those containing his work, his articles, broadcasts by and about him, and articles and books about the author.' – The definitive listing.

HASSALL, Christopher. *Edward Marsh, patron of the arts: a biography.* London: Longmans, 1959. Many references to W.H. Davies.

HOCKEY, Lawrence. Tramp poet of Gwent to be honoured by his country. *South Wales Argus*, 21 Sep 1938, 8:A-B; 22 Sep, 8:A-B. Articles celebrating erection of plaque at Church House Inn, Newport.

—— Irving and W.H. Davies. *TLS*, 5 Feb 1944, 67. Suggests distant family relationship between poet and actor. – Reply by Osbert Sitwell, 12 Feb 1944, 79.

—— The first book of W.H. Davies. *Poetry Review*, Jul-Aug 1945, 143-148.

—— Gwent's greatest poet: background to the genius of W.H. Davies. *South Wales Argus*, 11 Oct 1946, 3:C-D.

—— W.H. Davies and his family. *WR* 5 (1946) 191-195.

—— Edward Thomas and W.H. Davies. *WR* 7 (1948) 81-91.

—— W.H. Davies and Edward Thomas (1905-1907). *Poetry Review*, Oct-Nov 1949, 333-339.

—— Shaw could see 'a real poet' in W.H. Davies. *South Wales Argus*, 25 Nov 1950, 4:G-H; 27 Nov, 4:A-B.

—— Early days of W.H. Davies. *South Wales Argus*, 3 Feb 1951, 4:D-E.

—— The life and works of W.H. Davies. MA thesis. University of Wales (Cardiff), 1956. 287 p. Bibliography, pp. 276-287, citing unpublished material.

—— *W.H. Davies.* Cardiff: University of Wales Press [for] the Welsh Arts Council, 1971. 107 p.: front. port. (Writers of Wales). Incl. selected bibliography, pp. 101-103. – 'Limited to 750 copies'.

—— W.H. Davies: the man. *AWR* 20,46 (1972) 135-138.

—— *The soul's destroyer and other poems. AWR* 22,49 (1973) 58-68.

—— The poetry of W.H. Davies. *PW* 18,2 (1983) 80-88.

HOLLINGDRAKE, Sybil. *The super-tramp: a biography of W.H. Davies.* Newport: Hollydragon Books, 1980. 42 p. A reissue, with 3 new appendices, of *The super-tramp in Monmouthshire.* Aberdare: printed by George Selwyn, 1971.

—— W.H. Davies: the true traveller. *PW* 18,2 (1983) 25-45.

—— A bibliography of works by W.H. Davies. *PW* 18,2 (1983) 89-91. Arranged chronologically by month of publication.

JOHN, Augustus. *Augustus John: an autobiography.* London: Cape, 1975. Incl. reminiscences of W.H. Davies, pp. 169-170.

KERNAHAM, Coulson. *Five more famous living poets: introductory studies illustrated by quotation and comment.* London: Butterworth, 1928. Incl. W.H. Davies, pp. 17-48.

KNIGHT, Laura. *Oil paint and grease paint.* London: Ivor Nicholson & Watson, 1936. W.H. Davies's visits described, pp. 204, 233, 237.

—— W.H. Davies. *Cornhill Magazine*, Winter 1964-65, 282-292.

LARKIN, Philip. *Required writing: miscellaneous pieces, 1955-1982.* London: Faber, 1983. Incl. Freshly scrubbed potato [review of R. Stonesifer, *W.H. Davies*], pp. 164-167.

LLWYD, Alan. Trafod y meistri hyfedr: W.H. Davies ac R. Williams Parry. *Barddas* Rha/Dec 1977, 8; Ion/Jan, 1978, 6-7. [Discussing the skilful masters].

LOCK, D.R. The poetry of Mr W.H. Davies. *Holborn Review*, Oct 1927, 483-490.

LOOKER, Samuel J. Man and super-tramp: W.H. Davies, his life and work. *Bookman's Journal* 16 (1928) 363-370.

—— I remember W.H. Davies. *British Weekly*, 29 Mar 1951, 3.

LUCAS, Frank Lawrence. *Authors dead and living.* London: Chatto & Windus, 1926. Incl. discussion of W.H. Davies.

LYND, Robert. Letters to living authors, X. Mr W.H. Davies. *John O'London's Weekly*, 21 Dec 1929, 468.

MACLEISH, A. Four poets. *Yale Review* 14 (1925) 587-592.

MASSINGHAM, Harold John. *Letters to X.* London: Constable, 1919. Incl. discussion of W.H. Davies.

MAYNARD, Theodore. *Our best poets English and American.* London: Bretano's, 1924. Incl. W.H. Davies: a case of dual personality, pp. 107-115.

MENAI, Huw. Simplicity in poetry: a critical note on W.H. Davies. *Wales* 2nd ser. 2 (1943) 42-47.

MINHINNICK, Robert. On the Pill. *Planet* 62 (1987) 89-92. Incl. observations on W.H. Davies.

MOULT, Thomas. William H. Davies. *Bookman*, Nov 1921, 85-88. Incl. four portraits.

—— *W.H. Davies.* London: Thornton Butterworth, 1934. ix, 150 p. Incl. bibliography, pp. 147-150.

MURPHY, Gwendolen. Bibliographies of modern authors, no 3. W.H. Davies, part 1. *London Mercury*, Nov 1927, 76-80. Continued: Jan 1928, 301-304; Apr 1928, 684-688. – Incl. contributions to periodicals.

NORMAND, Lawrence. Authentic W.H. Davies. *PW* 21,2 (1985) 68-77.

—— Autobiography for a change: W.H. Davies's *Autobiography of a supertramp* and *Young Emma*. *NWR* 3,1 [10] (1990) 29-33.

OAK, Vera. W.H. Davies' visit to Neath. *Neath Antiquarian Society Transactions* (1977) 70-72.

OWEN, David. The supertramp in London. *Y Ddinas*, Dec 1950, 4,6.

PALMER, Herbert. W.H. Davies: the tramp poet. *John O'London's Weekly*, 11 Oct 1940, 34-36.

PARRY-WILLIAMS, T.H. W.H. Davies: the super-tramp. *Dragon*, Mar 1917, 89-96; Jun 1917, 150-157.

PEARSON, Fiona. W.H. Davies and contemporary artists. *PW* 18,2 (1983) 73-79.

PERKINS, David. *A history of modern poetry from the 1890s to the high modernist mode.* Cambridge, Mass.: Harvard University Press, 1976. Incl. discussion of W.H. Davies, pp. 220-222.

POUND, Ezra. William H. Davies, poet. *Poetry* [Chicago] 11,1 (1917) 99-102. Review of *Collected poems* (1916).

PRESS, John. W.H. Davies. In *Reference guide to English literature*, ed. D.L. Kirkpatrick. 2nd ed. 3 vols. Chicago; London: St James Press, 1991. Vol. 1, pp. 453-454.

QUENNELL, Peter. One-legged super-tramp. *Spectator*, 23 Feb 1985, 21-22. Review article on W.H. Davies, *Selected poems*.

RABINOWITZ, I.A. Words in themselves ordinary: a comment on five poems by W.H. Davies (1871-1940). *Unisa English Studies* 12,1 (1974) 22-26.

RHYS, Ernest. *Wales England wed: an autobiography.* London: Dent, 1940. Incl. impressions of W.H. Davies, pp. 170-171.

ROBERTS, Glyn. W.H. Davies: the poet who stands and stares. *WM*, 10 Oct 1933, 6:D-F.

ROGERS, Timothy. *Georgian poetry, 1911-1922: the critical heritage.* London: Routledge, 1977. Reprints contemporary response.

ROSS, Robert H. *The Georgian revolt: rise and fall of a poetic ideal, 1910-22.* London: Faber, 1967. Incl. discussion of W.H. Davies.

ROTHENSTEIN, Will. *Twenty-four portraits with critical appreciations by various hands. Second series.* London: Chatto & Windus, 1923. Incl. W.H. Davies.

SITWELL, Edith. *Aspects of modern poetry.* London: Duckworth, 1934. Incl. William H. Davies, pp. 90-98.

SITWELL, Osbert. Irving and W.H. Davies. *TLS*, 12 Feb 1944, 79. Reply to Lawrence Hockey.

—— *Noble essences or courteous revelations: being ... the fifth and last volume of Left hand, right hand!* London: Macmillan, 1950. Incl. W.H. Davies, pp. 207-244. – Reprinted from *Life and Letters Today* 34 (1942) 2-12, 81-91, 156-171.

STARK, J. W.H. Davies: a sketch. *WR* 1 (1939) 15-16.

STONESIFER, Richard James. W.H. Davies: a critical biography. PhD thesis. University of Pennsylvania, 1953.

—— W.H. Davies and his Disney world. *Approach* 44 (1962) 3-10.

—— *W.H. Davies: a critical biography.* London: Cape, 1963. 256 p.

STURGEON, Mary C. *Studies of contemporary poets.* London: Harrap, 1920. Incl.: William H. Davies, pp. 53-71 – Bibliography, pp. 433-440. – First published 1916.

SWANN, John H. The poetry of W.H. Davies. *Papers of the Manchester Literary Club* 52 (1926) 54-63.

SWINNERTON, Frank. *The Georgian literary scene, 1910-1935.* London: Hutchinson, 1969. Incl. brief references to W.H. Davies. – First published 1936.

THOMAS, Dylan. *The broadcasts*, ed. Ralph Maud. London: Dent, 1991. Brief comment on W.H. Davies, pp. 41-42.

THOMAS, Edward. A poet at last. *Daily Chronicle*, 21 Oct 1905, 3. Review of W.H. Davies, *The soul's destroyer and other poems*. – For list of Thomas's subsequent reviews of W.H. Davies see William Cooke, Alms and the supertramp: nineteen unpublished letters from W.H. Davies to Edward Thomas, *AWR* 70 (1982) 34-59.

THOMAS, Gwyn. *A Welsh eye.* London: Hutchinson, 1964. Discusses W.H. Davies, pp. 88-93.

THOMAS, Helen. The discovery of W.H. Davies. *Times*, 27 Mar 1963, 12:F-G.

—— *A memory of W.H. Davies.* Edinburgh: Tragara Press, 1973. [8]p. 'Edition limited to one hundred and fifty copies'. – Text dated 1963.

—— *Time and again: memoirs and letters*, ed. Myfanwy Thomas. Manchester: Carcanet, 1978. Incl. reminiscences of W.H. Davies, pp. 87-91.

THOMAS, R. George. Immortal moments: Edward Thomas and W.H. Davies. *PW* 18,2 (1983) 57-66.

—— *Edward Thomas: a portrait.* London: Oxford University Press, 1985. With interesting comment on W.H. Davies.

TWISTON-DAVIES, Suzanne. Famous people of Gwent: W.H. Davies, super-tramp. *Gwent Local History* 56 (1984) 43-45.

WATERS, Brian. *The Bristol Channel.* London: Dent, 1955. Incl. Newport and W.H. Davies, pp.12-22.

WILLIAMS, Charles. *Poetry at present.* Oxford: Clarendon Press, 1930. Incl. discussion of W.H. Davies, pp. 70-80.

WILLIAMS, E. Roland. The poetry of W.H. Davies. *Welsh Outlook*, Oct 1918, 304-307.

WILSON, George F. A bibliography of W.H. Davies. *Bookman's Journal* 5 (1922) 202; 6 (1922) 29, 59.

WRIGHT, H.G. *Studies in contemporary literature.* Bangor: Jarvis & Foster, 1918. Incl. W.H. Davies, pp. 31-67.

# CARADOC EVANS (1878-1945)

A. Publications by Caradoc Evans
  (i)  Books
  (ii) Selected contributions to books and periodicals

B. Publications about Caradoc Evans


## A (i). Publications by Caradoc Evans: Books

*My people: stories of the peasantry of west Wales*. London: Melrose, [1915].
276 p. Contents: A father in Sion – A heifer without blemish – The way of
the earth – The talent thou gavest – The glory that was Sion's – The devil
in Eden – The woman who sowed iniquity – A just man in Sodom – Be
this her memorial – The redeemer – As it is written – A bundle of life –
Greater than love – Lamentations – The blast of God. – Reissued 1919,
'cheap edition' ('sixth'), front. port. – Reissued 1924, printed boards.
—— Dobson, 1953. 155 p. Incl. Introduction, by Gwyn Jones, pp. 7-10.
—— / edited and introduced by John Harris. Bridgend: Seren Books, 1987.
153 p.: ill.: pbk. (Welsh writing in English). ISBN: 0-907476-81-3. Incl.:
Introduction: The banned, burned book of war, pp. 7- 47 – Bibliography.

U.S. eds.: *My people*. New York: Duffield, 1917. 276 p. Reissue of fifth
British edition, 1917.
—— New York: Boni & Liveright, 1918. Reissue of fifth British edition,
1917.


*Capel Sion*. London: Melrose, [1916]. 225 p. Contents: Redemption – The
word – The tree of knowledge – Three men from Horeb – The pillars of
Sion – The widow's mite – Calvary – Sons of their father – A mighty
man in Sion – A sacrifice unto Sion – The deliverer – Judges – A keeper
of the doors – The acts of Dan – The comforter.

U.S. ed.: New York: Boni & Liveright, 1918.


*My neighbours*. London: Melrose, 1919. 242 p. Contents: The two apostles
– According to the pattern – Earthbred – For better – Love and hate –
Treasure and trouble – Saint David and the prophets – Joseph's house –
Like brothers – A widow woman – Unanswered prayers – Lost treasure
– Profit and glory. – Published 1920.

U.S. eds.: *My neighbors*. New York: Harcourt, Brace & Howe, 1920. 248
p. Incl. preface, The Welsh people.
—— *My neighbors: stories of the Welsh people*. Freeport, N.Y.; Books for

Libraries Press, [1970]. 244 p. (*Short story index* reprint series). ISBN: 0-8369-3495-4.

*Taffy: a play of Welsh village life in three acts*. London: Melrose, [1924]. 86 p. Reissued 1925, pbk. – Play first performed 1923.

*Nothing to pay*. London: Faber, 1930. 311 p. Novel.
—— / with an afterword by John Harris. Manchester: Carcanet, 1989. 237 p. (Welsh writing in English). ISBN: 0-85635-771-5. Incl. Gazing at an inferno: an afterword, pp. 221-237.
—— Sphere, 1990. pbk. (A Cardinal book). ISBN: 0-7474-0717-7. Reissue of 1989 Carcanet edition.

U.S. ed.: New York: Norton, 1930. 286 p.

*Wasps*. London: Rich & Cowan, [1933]. 288 p. Novel. – Another edition [Hurst & Blackett, 1933, 304 p.] suppressed before publication.

*This way to heaven*. London: Rich & Cowan, 1934. 335 p. Novel.

*Pilgrims in a foreign land*. London: Andrew Dakers, 1942. 155 p. Contents: Your sin will find you out – Bliss is in the mist – Do not borrow your brother's head – Robbers do not look for treasure in coffins – A wife from off is well off – One repentant sinner is worth two pews in heaven – The hangman's rope is made of words – Do not praise your marriage day in the morning – Where faith is blind, God is bright – The capel always wins – Twins with one head, trouble; twins with two heads, peace – Changeable as a woman with child – Cobbler, stick to your bench – A widow with a full purse needs no husband – Pews for saints and fire for sinners, but no rest for the soulless – Who loses his money loses his brains – Bellyful of religion, bellyful of madness.

*Morgan Bible*. London: Andrew Dakers, 1943. 111 p. Novel.

*The earth gives all and takes all*. London: Andrew Dakers, 1946. xxxv, 65 p.: front. port. Contents: Without bitterness, by Marguerite Caradoc Evans, pp. v-vi – Caradoc, by George H. Green, pp. vii-xxxiv – The earth gives all and takes all – To keep a rainbow white – Oldest brother – Big servant – A Jew named Joshua – Pen Clook wanted a mint – Clogs for love. – Frontispiece portrait by Evan Walters.

*Mother's marvel*. London: Dakers, [1949]. 204 p. Novel.

*Fury never leaves us: a miscellany of Caradoc Evans* / edited by John Harris. Bridgend: Poetry Wales Press, 1985. 220 p.: ill.: hbk & pbk. ISBN: 0-907476-37-6 hbk, 0-907476-38-4 pbk. Contents: Caradoc Evans, 1878-1945: a biographical introduction, by John Harris, pp. 9-45 – First stories; A sovereign remedy, The pretender, The man who wouldn't die – 'An offender in Sion' [stories]; Judges, The day of judgement, An offender in Sion – Late stories; Your sin will find you out, To keep a rainbow white, Horse Hysbys and oldest brother – 'Self-portraits'; Self-portrait, Children and news, My preachers, A bundle of memories – Authors and authorship; The road with one fingerpost, Mary Webb, W.H. Davies, A talk on short-story writing, The Publicity Club address – Polemics; Letters to *Western Mail* and *Herald of Wales*, The Welsh miner, Do I insult the Welsh?, A tilt at the Eisteddfod – *Taffy: a play of Welsh village life* – Annotated bibliography.

*Selected stories* / edited by John Harris. Manchester: Carcanet, 1993. 192 p. ISBN: 0-85635-937-8. Contents: Our antagonist is our helper: an introduction, by John Harris, pp. 7-17 – A father in Sion – The way of the earth – Greater than love – Be this her memorial – The tree of knowledge – The pillars of Sion – The deliverer – Judges – The day of judgment – The acts of Dan – The word – The comforter – An offender in Sion – A widow woman – Joseph's house – Earthbred – According to the pattern – For better – Saint David and the prophets – Your sin will find you out – Changeable as a woman with child – A widow with a full purse – Horse Hysbys and oldest brother – The earth gives all and takes all – Bibliographical notes, pp. 191-192.

## A (ii): Publications by Caradoc Evans: Selected Contributions to Books and Periodicals

This section covers Caradoc Evans's uncollected stories and miscellaneous journalism, excepting his contributions to *Ideas*, the weekly that he edited between 1915 and 1917. The stories before 1915 were published under the pseudonym, D. Evans Emmott.

The star turn. *Freelance*, 19 Aug 1905, 4. Story.

King's evidence. *Chat*, 13 Oct 1906, 15. Story.

An inch from death. *Chat*, 27 Oct 1906, 53. Story. Under pseudonym, S. Wales.

The prodigal's return. *Chat*, 8 Dec 1906, 197. Story.

Royalty in retirement. *London Chat*, 25 May 1907, 779.

Wot's the good of washing? *London Chat*, 6 July 1907, 52. Story.

Hopkins on holiday: his expectations and realisations. *London Chat*, 3 Aug 1907, 147. Story.

Taffy at home: the humour and pathos of Welsh village life. *London Chat*, 21 Sept 1907, 327-328. Story. – Reprinted in Trevor Williams, *Caradoc Evans*.

At the feet of the virgin. *London Chat*, 9 Nov 1907, 495. Story.

The convict's Christmas. *London Chat*, 21 Dec 1907, 9. Story.

Her royal highness: a tale of slum life. *London Chat*, 28 Dec 1907, 9. Story.

Letter. *South Wales Echo*, 15 Apr 1915, 4:C-D. On his *English Review* stories.

A Welsh critic of Wales. *South Wales Daily News*, 21 Apr 1915, 7:F-G. Letter.

My answer. *Carmarthen Journal*, 23 Apr 1915, 5:D. Letter on his *English Review* stories.

The sorry illusions of Wales. *Cambria Daily Leader*, 24 Apr 1915, 5:C. Letter.

A Welsh critic on Wales. *South Wales Daily News*, 4 May 1915, 9:E. Letter.

A Welsh critic of Wales. *South Wales Daily News*, 14 May 1915, 9:D. Letter.

A libel on Wales. *WM*, 23 Nov 1915, 4:E. Letter.

Slanders on Wales. *South Wales Daily News*, 25 Nov 1915, 8:A. Letter.

The banned book. *WM*, 27 Nov 1915, 4:E-F. Letter.

*My people. WM*, 6 Dec 1915, 4:F. Letter.

Mr Caradoc Evans and his critics. *WM*, 22 Dec 1915, 7:A. Letter.

*My people. WM*, 6 Jan 1916, 8:B. Letter.

Tramp and poet. *WM*, 15 Jan 1916, 7:A-B. On W.H. Davies.

The banned book. *WM*, 22 Jan 1916, 6:G. Letter.

A Welshman's book received with a 'furore of indignation' in Wales. *Publishers' Circular*, 5 Feb 1916, 109. Letter.

Cardiff police and *My people. WM*, 15 Mar 1916, 7:B. Letter.

Review of Arthur Machen, *The great return. New Witness*, 23 Mar 1916, 640-641.

Mr Caradoc Evans: bitter attack on Welsh nonconformity. *WM*, 20 Dec 1916, 4:D. Letter.

Mr Caradoc Evans' standpoint. *WM*, 26 Dec 1916, 2:G. Letter.

Mr Caradoc Evans and the *Western Mail. WM*, 17 Jan 1917, 4:D. Reprinted from *Newspaper World*, Jan 1917.

Mr Caradoc Evans and his schoolmaster. *WM*, 23 Jan 1917, 3:D. Letter.

Chapel Prussianism. *New Witness*, 8 Feb 1917, 434. Review of Mary Webb, *The golden arrow*.

Caradoc Evans replies. *Everyman*, 2 Nov 1917, 93. Letter.

Welsh nonconformity. *WM*, 15 Nov 1917, 2:H. Letter.

Mr Caradoc Evans and his disciple. *WM*, 23 Mar 1918, 3:F. Letter on Edith Nepean.

Letter. *WM*, 1 May 1919, 6:C. Congratulates *Western Mail* on its Jubilee.

An honest Welshman. *New Witness*, 21 Nov 1919, 15. Review of Edith Nepean, *Welsh love.*

Letter. *WM*, 22 Mar 1920, 6:C. On review of *My neighbours.*

An appreciation. In Dennis H. Bradley, *Adam and Eve.* London: Laurie, 1923. pp. vii-ix.

The coffin. *Illustrated Review* 1,2 (1923) 85-87. Story. – Reprinted in *The Magic Valley travellers: Welsh stories of fantasy and horror*, ed. Peter Haining. London: Gollancz, 1974. pp. 151-156.

Letter. *Review of Reviews*, Jun-Jul 1924, 542. In response to Richard Hughes.

My people. *WM*, 28 July 1924, 7:G. Letter.

Mr Caradoc Evans replies to his most recent critics. *WM*, 12 Aug 1924, 7:E. Letter.

Advice to young authors. *Writer*, April 1925, 165-166.

The captive Welsh. *Sunday Express*, 16 Aug 1925, 5.

My dear old Welsh bible. *Sunday Express*, 13 Sep 1925, 7.

Downtrodden actors. *Sunday Express*, 20 Sep 1925, 7.

The Welsh as playgoers. *WM*, 19 Oct 1925, 7:F-G.

The Welsh people. *Faculty of Arts Journal* [University of London] 4 (1925) 56-57.

Caradoc at it once more. *WM*, 5 Nov 1926, 8:A-B. Partial text of address to the Tomorrow Club, London.

When Wales wins. *Sunday Express*, 1 May 1927.

A bundle of memories. In *The book of Fleet Street*, ed. Michael T. Pope. London: Cassell, 1930. pp. 92-98.

Caradoc Evans writes about his critics: Big Heads of the Swansea Art Gallery. *HW*, 7 Feb 1931, 4:A. Letter on the Evan Walters portrait of Caradoc Evans.

A nation of penny whistlers: no money, no Welsh Eisteddfod! *Evening News* [Glasgow], 10 Aug 1935, [Saturday supplement] 1:D-E. Reply by Geraint Goodwin, 24 Aug, [Saturday supplement] 1:A-C.

Talk Mr Caradoc Evans will not broadcast. *WM*, 3 Feb 1937, 10:A-C. Text of talk suppressed by Welsh Regional Station of the BBC.

Mary Webb. *Colophon* 3,1 (1938) 63-66.

Caradoc Evans' 'Pilgrims'. *WM*, 5 Feb 1943, 3:F. Letter.

Self-portrait. *Wales* 2nd ser. 3 (1944) 83-85.

Men and women, 1. Mary Webb. *WR* 3 (1944) 25-28.

Men and women, 2. W.H. Davies. *WR* 3 (1944) 183-186.

Who steals an egg will steal all. In *New voices: Atlantic anthology*, ed. Nicholas Moore and Dougals Newton. London: Fortune Press, 1945. pp. 136-139. Story.

The milky way. In *English story: sixth series*, ed. Woodrow Wyatt. London: Collins, 1945. pp. 51-60.

Men and women, 3. T.P. O'Connor. *WR* 4 (1945) 34-35.

Caradoc Evans' journal, 1939-44. *WR* 4 (1945) 104-111; 4 (1945) 201-208.

Williams, Trevor. Three early stories by Caradoc Evans. *AWR* 19,44 (1971) 129-137. Reprints: The star turn – On the morning – The convict's Christmas.

Williams, Trevor. Three unpublished stories by Caradoc Evans. *AWR* 20,45

(1971) 82-98. Incl.: Sweets for a sinner – [Untitled story] – Rock of ages: a love story.

Wisdom: an unpublished story. *Planet* 90 (1991) 38-43.


# B: Publications about Caradoc Evans

[ANON]. Caradoc Evans. *Times*, 13 Jan 1945, 6. Obituary.
—— Caradoc Evans. *WM*, 13 Jan 1945, 2,3. Obituary and editorial notice.
BAKER, Simon. Caradoc Evans's 'A father in Sion' and contemporary critical theory. *NWR* 3,3 [11] (1991) 46-50.
BARNIE, John. The impious artist. *Planet* 53 (1985) 64-69. Review article on *Fury never leaves us: a miscellany of Caradoc Evans*, ed. John Harris.
BELLRINGER, Alan W. *Mabon* [English] 1,3 (1970). 9-10. Review of Trevor Williams, *Caradoc Evans*.
BULLOCK, George. Caradoc Evans [1948]. In *Wales on the wireless: a broadcasting anthology*, ed. Patrick Hannan. Llandysul: Gomer; BBC Cymru/Wales, 1988. pp. 31-33.
CLARKE, Austin. *A penny in the clouds: more memories of Ireland and England.* London: Routledge, 1968. Incl. recollections of Caradoc Evans, pp. 184-186.
CONRAN, Anthony. *The cost of strangeness: essays on the English poets of Wales.* Llandysul: Gomer Press, 1982. Incl. A note on Caradoc Evans, pp. 155-161.
CUMBERLAND, Gerald [i.e. Charles F. Keynon]. *Written in friendship: a book of reminiscences.* London: Grant Richards, 1923. Incl. recollections of Caradoc Evans, pp. 39-40.
DAVIES, Aneirin Talfan. A question of language. *Welsh Anvil* 5 (1953) 19-31.
—— Ar ymyl y ddalen. *Barn*, Chw/Feb 1963, 100-101. Discusses Rhys Davies and Caradoc Evans. – [In the margin].
—— *Astudio byd.* Llandybïe: Llyfrau'r Dryw, 1967. Incl. discussion of D. Tecwyn Lloyd on Caradoc Evans, pp. 9-16.
DAVIES, D.T. Caradoc Evans: a defence and an appreciation. *WM*, 30 Aug 1924, 5:D-E.
DAVIES, Jacob. Family feuds. *Planet* 1 (1970) 71-74. Review of Trevor Williams, *Caradoc Evans*.
DAVIES, John and John Harris. Caradoc Evans and the forcers of conscience: a reading of 'A father in Sion'. *AWR* 81 (1985) 79-89.
EVANS, D.L. Caradoc Evans' boyhood days. *Wales* 2nd ser. 7,27 (1947) 381-382.
GRIFFITH, Jack. Soak yourself in the Russians: Caradoc Evans remembered. *Wales* 3rd ser., Apr 1959, 67-70.
GRUFFYDD, W.J. Is Caradoc Evans right? *T.P.'s and Cassell's Weekly*, 17 Oct 1925, 815.
HARRIS, John. Big Daddy meets the nogood boyos: Caradoc, Dewi Emrys and Dylan. *PW* 18,4 (1983) 43-47.

—— Caradoc Evans and the forcers of conscience: a reading of 'A father in Sion'. *AWR* 81 (1985) 79-89. Written jointly with John Davies.

—— A dissident among the dissenters. *BNW*, Spring 1985, 3-4.

—— Caradoc Evans as editor of *Ideas*. *Planet* 53 (1985) 52-63.

—— The early career of Caradoc Evans. PhD thesis. University of Wales (Aberystwyth), 1986. 369 p. Incl. bibliography, pp. 353-369.

—— Dai Lanlas: the schoolboy at Rhydlewis. *Ceredigion: Journal of the Ceredigion Antiquarian Society*, 10,4 (1987) 431-449.

—— Publishing *My people*: the book as expressive object. *NWR* 1,1 [1] (1988) 23-30.

—— 'Neighbours': Caradoc Evans, Lloyd George and the London Welsh. *Llafur: Journal of Welsh Labour History* 5,4 (1990) 90-98.

—— From his Presbyterian pinnacle: Caradoc Evans and Andrew Melrose. *Planet* 90 (1991) 31-37.

—— The devil in Eden: Caradoc Evans and his Wales. *NWR* 5,3 [19] (1993) 10-18. The 1992 Gwyn Jones lecture.

HART, Olive. *The drama in modern Wales: a brief history of Welsh playwriting from 1900 to the present day*. University of Pennsylvania, 1928. Incl. Caradoc Evans: a prophet in his own country, pp. 39-43. – Published PhD thesis.

JENKINS, David. Dai Caradog. *Taliesin* 20 (1970) 79-86.

—— Community and kin: Caradoc Evans at home. *AWR* 24,53 (1974) 43-57.

JENKINS, David Clay. Writing in twentieth century Wales: a defense of the Anglo-Welsh. PhD thesis. State University of Iowa, 1956. Incl. Caradoc Evans' distorting mirror, pp. 82-116.

JONES, Dedwydd. *Black book on the Welsh theatre*. London: Bozo, 1985. Incl. reprinted articles on Welsh drama, some relating to Caradoc Evans. – First pubished 1980; revised 1985.

JONES, Glyn. Three Anglo-Welsh prose writers. *Rann* 19 (1953) 1-5. On Caradoc Evans, Gwyn Thomas and Dylan Thomas.

—— *The dragon has two tongues: essays on Anglo-Welsh writers and writing*. London: Dent, 1968. Incl. Caradoc Evans, pp. 64-80.

—— Review of forgotten pioneer. *WM*, 21 Mar 1970, 6:C-E. Review of T.L. Williams, *Caradoc Evans*.

JONES, Gwyn. Author and reviewer. *WM*, 14 Jan 1943, 3:F. Letter on review of Caradoc Evans, *Pilgrims in a foreign land*.

—— Caradoc Evans. *WR* 4 (1945) 24-28.

—— The Welshman who became a legend. *Listener*, 17 Jan 1946, 79, 87.

—— *WR* 7 (1948) 146-147. Review of Oliver Sandys, *Unbroken thread*.

—— Caradoc Evans was envied, hated, but not ignored. *WM*, 23 Mar 1949, 4:F-H.

—— Language, style and the Anglo-Welsh. *Essays and Studies* 6 (1953) 102-114. On Dylan Thomas, Gwyn Thomas, Glyn Jones and Caradoc Evans.

—— *The first forty years: some notes on Anglo-Welsh literature*. Cardiff: University of Wales Press, 1957. (W.D. Thomas Memorial lecture). Comments on Caradoc Evans.

—— Caradoc was the daddy of us all. *WM*, 20 Aug 1960, 5:C-E.

—— Let *My people* go. *TLS*, 9 Jan 1969, 33-34.

—— *Background to Dylan Thomas and other explorations.* Oxford; New York: Oxford University Press, 1992. Incl. A mighty man in Sion: Caradoc Evans, 1878-1945, pp. 72-88.

JONES, Mary. The satire of Caradoc Evans. *AWR* 72 (1982) 58-65

—— A changing myth: the projection of the Welsh in the short stories of Caradoc Evans. *AWR* 81 (1985) 90-96.

JORDAN-SMITH, Paul. *For the love of books: the adventures of an impecunious collector.* New York: Oxford University Press. 1934. Incl. note on Caradoc Evans, pp. 259-265.

LLEWELYN, Lloyd. The best-hated man in Wales. *London Welshman*, Summer 1972, 10-11.

LLOYD, D. Tecwyn. Cynddaredd rhai gwenyn. *Barn*, Ion/Jan 1963, 78-79. Incl. discussion of Caradoc Evans. – [The madness of some bees].

MARRIOTT, Raymond. Caradoc Evans. *Wales* 2nd ser. 5,7 (1945) 61-64.

MORGAN, W. John. Evans, Thomas and Lewis. *Twentieth Century*, Oct 1956, 322-329. On Caradoc Evans, Dylan Thomas and Saunders Lewis. – Reprinted in *John Morgan's Wales: a personal anthology.* Swansea: Christopher Davies, 1993. pp. 167-174.

MURRAY, Nicholas. Mr Evans, Mr Rushdie and the white settlers. *NWR* 3,3 [11] (1991) 51-52.

NORRIS, Leslie. *Powys Review* 23 (1989) 71-72. Review of *My people* (1987).

PAGE, Alun. Dai Caradog a David Adams. *Barn*, Mai/May 1972, 184.

PHILLIPS, D.Z. *From fantasy to faith: the philosophy of religion and twentieth-century literature.* London: Macmillan, 1991. Incl. Distorting truth (Caradoc Evans), pp. 84-94.

POPE, T. Michael. Caradoc Evans. *Current Literature*, Aug 1930, 305-306, 314.

RAYMOND, David. Two replies to Caradoc Evans. *Wales* 2nd ser. 4 (1944) 92-93.

REES, J. Seymour. Caradoc Evans. *Yr Ymofynnydd* 52,12 (1952) 204-208.

REES, W.J. Inequalities: Caradoc Evans and D.J. Williams: a problem in literary sociology. *Planet* 81 (1990) 69-80.

ROBERTS, T. Glyn. The case of Caradoc Evans. *Saturday Review*, 1 Apr 1933, 311-312.

SANDYS, Nicholas. Dylan and the stormy petrel. *WM*, 7 Jan 1961, 5:A-E.

SANDYS, Oliver [i.e. Marguerite Caradoc Evans]. *Caradoc Evans.* London: Hurst & Blackett, [1946]. 167 p.: illus. Incl.: Caradoc's journal, pp. 125-142 – Caradoc Evans, by Arthur Machen, p. 146 – Caradoc, by Hannen Swaffer, pp. 147-149 – Caradoc, by Gwyn Jones, pp. 150-154 – Reminiscences, by Thomas Burke, George H. Green, Glyn Jones, Howell Evans, Frank Lewis, R.B. Marriott, pp. 155-164.

—— *Unbroken thread: an intimate journal of the daily life in the Welsh countryside of England's best-loved woman novelist.* London: Rider, [1948]. Incl. many references to Caradoc Evans.

SARNICOL [i.e. T.J. Thomas]. Caradoc Evans in a new light. *WM*, 20 Jul 1933, 11:F-G.

SMITH, A.J. and W.H. Mason. *Short story study: a critical anthology.* London: Arnold, 1961. Incl. Be this her memorial, pp. 64-71 [text and commentary].

STOKES, Sewell. *Personal glimpses.* London: Laurie, 1924. Incl. reminiscences of Evans, pp. 135-139.

THOMAS, Gwilym. Caradog Evans. *Y Cardi* 13 (1976) 15-17.

THOMAS, M. Wynn. *My people* and the revenge of the novel. *NWR* 1,1 [1] (1988) 17-22. Review article.

WEBB, Harri. *PW* 6,2 (1970) 60-63. Review of T.L. Williams, *Caradoc Evans.*

WEINGARTNER, Regina. The fight against sentimentalism: Caradoc Evans and George Douglas Brown. *Planet* 75 (1989) 86-92.

WILLIAMS, David Marcel. The presentation of character in the Anglo-Welsh novel: a study of techniques and influences. MA thesis. University of Wales (Swansea), 1959. Incl. Caradoc Evans, pp. 5-23.

WILLIAMS, T. Hefin. Mr Caradoc Evans a Chymru. *Efrydydd* 9 (1932) 344-346. [Mr Caradoc Evans and Wales].

WILLIAMS, Trevor. The life and works of Caradoc Evans. PhD thesis. University of Wales (Cardiff), 1970. 486 p.

—— *Caradoc Evans.* Cardiff: University of Wales Press [for] the Welsh Arts Council, 1970. 107 p.: front. port. (Writers of Wales). Incl. bibliography, pp. 101-103. – 'Limited to 750 copies'.

—— The birth of a reputation: early Welsh reaction to the work of Caradoc Evans. *AWR* 19,44 (1971) 147-171.

—— Caradoc Evans's sayings: an approach to the style of his later work. *AWR* 24,54 (1974) 58-66.

WRIGHT, Edward. Caradoc Evans. *Bookman*, Oct 1917, 6-7.

# GERAINT GOODWIN (1903-1941)

A. Publications by Geraint Goodwin
  (i)   Books
  (ii)  Selected contributions to books and periodicals

B. Publications about Geraint Goodwin

## A (i). Publications by Geraint Goodwin: Books

*A first sheaf.* London: London School of Printing, [1923]. 22 p: pamph.
Poetry.

*Conversations with George Moore.* London: Benn, 1929. 180 p.
—— Cape, 1937. (New library series). – With preface by Geraint Goodwin,
and 'A letter [to Goodwin] as postscript', by Bernard Shaw, pp. 17-19.
—— Cape, 1940. (The Saint Giles library; 36).

U.S. eds.: New York: A.A. Knopf, 1930. 175 p.
—— Philadelphia, Pa.: Folcroft, 1973. (Folcroft library editions). Reprint
of 1940 Cape edition.
—— New York: Haskell House, 1974. Reprint of 1940 Cape edition.
—— Philadelphia, Pa.: Norwood, 1975. Reprint of 1929 Benn edition.

*Call back yesterday.* London: Cape, 1935. 218 p.

*The heyday in the blood: a novel.* London: Cape, 1936. 287 p.
—— Harmondsworth: Penguin, 1954. pbk.
—— Bath: Chivers, 1970. (Portway reprints).

Welsh trans.: *Bwrlwm yn y gwaed*, tr. Mair Closs Roberts. Caernarfon:
Argraffty'r M.C., 1975.

*The white farm and other stories.* London: Cape, 1937. 288 p. Contents:
The white farm – Saturday night – The trial of Shoni Bach – Janet
Ifans' donkey – The auction – Into the dark – The picnic – The old
folk in the dead houses – The flying hours are gone – The young bull –
Come Michaelmas – The auld earth – The old man leaves home – The
coroner's officer – Late spring.
—— Bath: Chivers, 1968. (Portway reprints).

*Watch for the morning: a novel.* London: Cape, 1938. 372 p.
—— Bath: Chivers, 1969. (Portway reprints).

Welsh trans.: *Hyfryd fore*, tr. Mair Closs Roberts. Caernarfon: Gwasg Pantycelyn, 1980. pbk.

*Come Michaelmas: a novel*. London: Cape, 1939. 282 p.
—— Bath: Chivers, 1969. (Portway reprints).

*The collected short stories of Geraint Goodwin* / edited by Sam Adams and Roland Mathias. Tenby: H.G. Walters, 1976. 246 p.: front. port.: hbk & pbk. ISBN: 0-901906-24-7 hbk, 0-901906-13-1 pbk. Contents: Introduction, by Sam Adams, pp. 9-20 – The auld earth – The flying hours are gone – The old man leaves home – The coroner's officer – The young bull – The old folk in the dead houses – Late spring – Come Michaelmas – The auction – The picnic – The trial of Shoni Bach – The white farm – Saturday night – Into the dark – Janet Ifans' donkey – Fair day – Ap Towyn – The lost land – A handful of feathers – Huw Ifans – A sitting of eggs – The penny reading – The shearing.

# A (ii). Publications by Geraint Goodwin: Selected Contributions to Books and Periodicals

The 'Tess' of real life: what famous actress owes Wales: Miss Ffrangcon-Davies' girlhood days. *WM*, 31 Oct 1925, 9:B.

A Chelsea cameo: the record of a chance encounter. *Welsh Outlook*, Jun 1926, 159.

A Welsh singer as pioneer: evolution of a new entertainment: the first piano-song comedian. *WM*, 25 Mar 1927, 8:F. On John Parry.

Mystic poet and dramatist: how a Welshman came to fame: Richard Hughes' one act play in London. *WM*, 30 Jun 1927, 8:E.

An Edward Thomas revival. *Welsh Outlook*, Nov 1927, 297-298. Occasioned by the Gregynog Press edition of *The poems of Edward Thomas*.

Charles Wood: a tribute (by one who knew him). *Montgomeryshire Express*, 22 May 1928, 2:A. Obituary.

A new Welsh dramatist. *Welsh Outlook*, Nov 1928, 344-345. On Emlyn Williams.

George Moore: a portrait. *Welsh Outlook*, Jan 1929, 16-18.

Mary Webb: a memoir. *Everyman*, May 1929, 14-15.

Rhine soldiers come home without a cheer. *Daily Mail*, 16 Sep 1929, 14:B.

Thoughts on the Welsh novel. *Welsh Outlook*, Mar 1930, 72-74.

An artist of vision: the works of Rhys Griffiths. *Welsh Outlook*, Mar 1932, 78-80.

Are Celtic festivals worthwhile? *Evening News* [Glasgow], 4 Aug 1935, [Saturday supplement] 1:A-C. In reply to Caradoc Evans, 10 Aug 1935, [Saturday supplement] 1:D-E.

Welsh life as seen by writers: reply to Listener-in's criticism. *WM*, 5 Nov 1936, 11:B. Letter on article, 31 Oct 1936, 11:C-E.

Welsh life in novels today: writer deplores critic's taste. *WM*, 14 Nov 1936, 11:A.

Letter to a young writer. *Modern Reading 11-12* (1944) 8-9.

The Geraint Goodwin-Edward Garnett letters. *AWR* 22,49 (1973) 10-23; 22,50 (1973) 119-148. Introduced by Rhoda Goodwin.

## B: Publications about Geraint Goodwin

ADAMS, Sam. *Geraint Goodwin.* Cardiff: University of Wales Press [for] the Welsh Arts Council, 1975. 113 p.: front. port. (Writers of Wales). Incl. bibliography, pp. 107-109. – 'Limited to 1000 copies'.
—— Geraint Goodwin: a Montgomeryshire writer and his characters. *Planet* 29 (1975) 30-34.
[ANON]. Geraint Goodwin. *WM*, 20 Oct 1941, 3:D. Obituary.
—— Noted novelist's death: Mr Geraint Goodwin, Montgomery. *Montgomeryshire Express*, 25 Oct 1941, 6:D-E. Obituary.
REES, David M. Geraint Goodwin: a neglected Welsh writer. *AWR* 16,38 (1967) 126-129.

# RICHARD HUGHES (1900-1976)

A. Publications by Richard Hughes
  (i)   Books
  (ii)  Selected contributions to books and periodicals
  (iii)  Richard Hughes: translations

B. Publications about Richard Hughes


## A (i). Publications by Richard Hughes: Books

*Gipsy-night and other poems*. Waltham St. Lawrence: Golden Cockerel Press, 1922. 69 p.: front. port. Portrait by Pamela Bianco. – 'Edition of 750 copies'.

U.S. ed.: Chicago: W. Ransom, 1922. 65 p.: front. 'Of this first American edition of *Gipsy-night and other poems*, with a special proof of the lithograph portrait by Pamela Bianco, sixty-three copies, each signed by both author and artist, have been issued, of which thirty are for sale in America and twenty-four in England.'

*The sisters' tragedy*. Oxford: Blackwell, 1922. 32 p.: pamph.
—— *The sisters' tragedy: a play*. London: Chatto & Windus, [1924]. 35 p.: pbk.
—— *The sisters' tragedy: a play*. Carmarthen: Druid Press, 1948. 35 p.: pbk.

U.S. ed.: *The sisters' tragedy: a play in one act*. Boston: H. Baker, [1956]. 23 p.

*Lines written upon first observing an elephant devoured by a roc*. Waltham St. Lawrence: Golden Cockerel Press, [1922]. 7 p.: pamph.

*Meditative ode on vision*. [London]: Privately printed at the Curwen Press, 1923. 6 p.: pamph. 'Edition limited to 75 copies of which 25 are for sale.'

*The sisters' tragedy and three other plays*. London: Heinemann, 1924. vii, 159 p. Contents: The sisters' tragedy – The man born to be hanged – A comedy of good and evil – A comedy of danger.
—— *Plays: The sisters' tragedy, A comedy of good and evil, The man born to be hanged, Danger*. Chatto & Windus, 1928. vii, 191 p. (Phoenix library).
—— Chatto & Windus, 1966.

U.S. eds.: *A rabbit and a leg: collected plays*. New York: A.A. Knopf, 1924. vii, 159 p.

—— New York: Harper & Row, 1966. vii, 191 p.

*Ecstatic ode on vision*. [London]: Privately printed at the Curwen Press, 1925. 6 p.: pamph. 'Of this poem 75 copies have been printed for presentation.'

*Confessio iuvenis: collected poems*. London: Chatto & Windus, 1926. 95 p. Also signed limited edition, 80 copies.
—— Chatto & Windus, 1934 (Phoenix library).

U.S. ed.: University Microfilms, 1976.

*A moment of time*. London: Chatto & Windus, 1926. vii, 243 p. Contents: Lochinvárovic: a romantic story – The stranger – Locomotive – Llwyd – Poor man's inn – A moment of time – She caught hold of the toe – The vanishing man – Monoculism – Jungle – The cart – The swans – The ghost – Cornelius Katie – The sea – Leaves – Martha – The chest – The devil-stick – A night at a cottage – The Victorian room – And James – The diary of a steerage passenger.
—— Chatto & Windus, 1930. (Phoenix library).
—— Chatto & Windus, 1931. (Centaur library).
—— Chatto & Windus, 1941. (Pelham library).

U.S. ed.: University Microfilms, 1976. From first British edition.

*Danger: a play*. London: Chatto & Windus, [1928]. [175-191 p. From a copy recorded in *National Union Catalogue: Pre-1956 Imprints* with 'first published 1924; second edition 1928' and a label pasted on fly-leaf, 'Royalty notice: Walter H. Baker Company, Boston, Mass'. – *NUC* also records copies of *A comedy of good and evil*, 'Chatto & Windus, [2 ed. 1928]', and *The man born to be hanged*, 'Chatto & Windus, [1924?], cover title'. Pagination suggests that these also are bound-up sheets from *Plays*, 1928 (Phoenix library).

German ed.: *Danger: a play* / with questions and aids to comprehension, edited and annotated by Dieter Zeitz. Frankfurt a. M.: Verlag Moritz Diesterweg, 1975. 23 p.: pamph. (Diesterwegs Neusprachliche Bibliothek). ISBN: 3-425-04146-0.

*A high wind in Jamaica*. London: Chatto & Windus, 1929. 284 p. Also signed limited edition; 'one hundred and fifty copies are for sale: seven complimentary copies have been printed'. – First published in abridged form in *Life and Letters* 3 (1929) 83-242.
—— Chatto & Windus, 1931. (Phoenix library).
—— Chatto & Windus, 1931. (Centaur library).
—— Evergreen Books [Heinemann/Chatto & Windus], 1940. 254 p.: pbk. (Evergreen books; 5).
—— Chatto & Windus for British Publishers' Guild, 1943. 160 p.: pbk. (Guild books; S30). 'Services edition'.

—— Chatto & Windus, 1948. 144 p.: pbk.

—— Harmondsworth: Penguin, 1949. 192 p.: pbk. Reissued 1965, 192 p.: pbk. ISBN: 0-1400-0694-X. Subsequently reissued in 'Penguin modern classics' series.

—— Chatto & Windus, 1956. (New phoenix library).

—— Landsborough Publications, 1958. 192 p.: pbk. (Four square books; 60).

—— Chatto & Windus, 1964. 284 p. (Queen's classics).

—— Chatto & Windus, 1975. 388 p. ISBN: 0-7011-2153-X. 'Collected edition'. – Reissued 1993, ISBN: 0-7011-4903-5.

—— Bath: Lythway Press, 1976. 296 p. ISBN: 0-85046-679-2. Large print edition.

—— St. Albans: Triad/Panther, 1976. 173p.: pbk. ISBN: 0-586-04425-6.


U.S. eds.: *The innocent voyage*. New York: Harper & Bros., 1929. 399 p. Precedes U.K. edition.

—— New York: Grosset & Dunlap, 1929.

—— *A high wind in Jamaica (The innocent voyage)* / introduced by Isabel Patterson. New York: Random House, 1929. xiii, 339 p.: ill. (Modern library of the world's best books).

— *A high wind in Jamaica (The innocent voyage)*. New York: Harper & Bros., 1930. ix, 399 p.: ill. Incl. A note, by Burton Roscoe, pp. v-vii.

—— *A high wind in Jamaica (The innocent voyage)*. New York: Editions for the Armed Services, [1941?]. 255 p.

—— *The innocent voyage* / illustrated with lithographs in color by Lynd Ward; and with an introduction by Louis Untermeyer. New York: Heritage Press, 1944. vii, 221 p.: ill. Also bound in full morocco for Limited Editions Club, 1944.

— *The innocent voyage (A high wind in Jamaica)*. New York: Penguin, 1947. 186 p.: pbk. Precedes British Penguin edition.

—— *A high wind in Jamaica*. New York: Harper & Row, 1958. viii, 212 p. Incl. Introduction, by Burton Roscoe, pp. vii-viii.

—— *High wind in Jamaica*. New York: F. Watts, 1958. viii, 212 p. Large type edition.

—— *The innocent voyage (A high wind in Jamaica)* / with an introduction by Max Bogart. New York: Harper, 1959. 399 p. (Harper's modern classics).

—— *A high wind in Jamaica, or The innocent voyage* / with a foreword by Vernon Watkins. [New York]: New American Library, 1961. 192 p.: hbk & pbk. (Signet classic). Reissued 1965, pbk. (Signet P2468).

—— *A high wind in Jamaica* / with a new introduction by the author. New York: Time Inc., 1963. 241 p. (Time reading program special edition).

—— *A high wind in Jamaica*. New York: Harper & Row, 1972. pbk. ISBN: 0-06-083099-9.

—— *A high wind in Jamaica, or The innocent voyage*. Mattituck, N.Y.: Amereon, [n.d.]. IBSN: 0-88411-128-8.

—— *A high wind in Jamaica, or The innocent voyage*. New York: Harper/Collins, 1989. 224 p. ISBN: 0-06-091627-3.

— [dramatized version]. *Innocent voyage: based upon the novel* A high wind in Jamaica, *by Richard Hughes*. Chicago: Dramatic Publ. Co., 1946. 114 p.

German ed.: Leipzig: Tauchnitz, 1931.

*Burial* and *The dark child*. London: Privately printed [Curwen Press], 1930. 14 p.: pamph. Incl. poem and story. – 'Limited to sixty copies'.

*Richard Hughes: an omnibus*. New York: Harper & Bros., 1931. xxxvii, 426 p.: front. port. Contents: Autobiographical introduction – Travel piece – Lochinvárovic – The horse-trough – The sisters' tragedy – Meditative ode on vision – Ecstatic ode on vision – Burial of the spirit of a young poet – Unicorn mad – The cart – The swans – The sermon – The stranger – Gipsy-night – Poor man's inn – Tramp – Lines written upon first observing an elephant devoured by a roc – Time – Moon-struck – Storm – Enigma – The chest – Leaves – The ghost – Cornelius Katie – Danger – Lover's reply to good advice – Laughing at Netta – Lovers find something out – The singing furies – A moment of time – Gratitude – The limber horses – Weald – Winter – Landscape with horse – The bird's nester – Martha – The image – The jumping-bean – Gaza – Isaac Ball – Felo da se – Glaucopis – Old cat care – The bird – Steerage passenger – The ruin – Llwyd – A comedy of good and evil – When shall I see gold?

*The spider's palace and other stories* / with illustrations by George Charlton. London: Chatto & Windus, 1931. vii, 164 p.: ill. Contents: Living in W'ales – The dark child – As they were driving – The gardener and the white elephants – The man with a green face – Telephone travel – The glass-ball country – Nothing – The hasty cook – The three sheep – The spider's palace – The ants – The invitation – The three innkeepers – Inhaling – The china spaniel – The magic glass – The Christmas tree – The old queen – The school. – Also limited edition; '110 copies for sale of this special edition have been printed. 100 are for sale.' – Reissued 1933, 'cheap edition'.
—— Chatto & Windus, 1961. 166 p. Published Mar 1962.
—— Harmondsworth: Penguin, 1972. 158 p.: ill.: pbk. (Puffin books). ISBN: 0-1403-0519-X

U.S. eds.: New York: Harper & Bros., 1932. vii, 163 p.
—— New York: Random House, [1960]. 167 p.: ill. (Looking glass library).

*In hazard: a sea story*. London: Chatto & Windus, 1938. 273 p.
—— World Books, 1941. 273 p. 'This edition published 1941 by the Reprint Society Ltd by arrangement with Chatto & Windus.'
—— Chatto & Windus for British Publishers' Guild, 1944. 144 p.: pbk. (Guild books; S75). 'Services edition'.
—— Chatto & Windus, 1948. 144 p.: pbk.
—— Harmondsworth: Penguin, 1950. 173 p.: pbk.

—— Chatto & Windus, 1952. 273 p. (New phoenix library; 19).
—— Chatto & Windus, 1953. 154 p. (Queen's classics). 'Edited and slightly abridged by the author'.
—— Bath: Lythway Press, 1974. 263 p. ISBN: 0-85046-582-6. Large print edition. – Reissued 1977, pbk. ISBN: 0-85046-735-7.
—— Chatto & Windus, 1975. 272 p. ISBN: 0-7011-2154-8. 'Collected edition'. – Reissued 1992, ISBN: 0-7011-4993-0.
—— St. Albans: Triad/Panther, 1977. 155 p.: pbk. ISBN: 0-586-04486-8.

U.S. eds.: New York: Harper & Bros., 1938. 279 p.
—— New York: Harper & Row, [1962]. 279 p.: pbk. (Harper colophon books; CN 4).
—— Gloucester, Mass.: P. Smith, 1963. Harper & Row edition rebound.
—— / with a new introduction by the author. New York: Time Inc., [1963]. 241 p. (Time reading program special edition). Reissued 1966, pbk.
—— New York: Signet Books, 1971. 144 p.: pbk. (New American library).
—— / with an introduction by the author. Alexandria, Va.: Time-Life Books, 1982. xxiii, 229 p. (Time reading program special edition). ISBN: 0-8094-3729-5 de luxe, 0-8094-3730-9 pbk. Issued with John Cheever, *The Wapshot chronicle*.

German ed.: Leipzig: Tauchnitz, [1939].

***Don't blame me! and other stories*** / with illustrations by Fritz Eichenberg. London: Chatto & Windus, 1940. 145 p.: ill.

U.S. ed.: New York: Harper & Bros., [1940]. 159 p.: ill.

***The administration of war production.*** London: HMSO; Longmans, 1955. xii, 544 p. Written jointly with J.D. Scott.

***The human predicament. Volume one. The fox in the attic.*** London: Chatto & Windus, 1961. 353 p.
—— *The fox in the attic.* Bungay: Reprint Society, [1962]. 286 p.
—— Harmondsworth: Penguin, 1964. 332 p.: pbk. Reissued 1974, ISBN: 0-1400-2069-1.
—— *The fox in the attic.* Chatto & Windus, 1975. 352 p. ISBN: 0-7011-2155-6. 'Collected edition'. – Reissued 1993, ISBN: 0-7011-0772-3.
—— St. Albans: Triad/Panther, 1979. 349 p.: pbk. ISBN: 0-586-04883-9.

U.S. eds.: New York: Harper, [1962]. 352 p.
—— New York: Signet Books, 1963. 286 p.: pbk. (New American library).

***Liturgical language today.*** [Penarth]: Church in Wales Publications, [1962]. 11 p.: pamph.

***Gertrude's child*** / pictures by Rick Schreiter. Quist, 1967 [42] p.: ill. Published by Quist Publishing Ltd, distributed by W.H. Allen. – 'First British edition 1967', title-page verso.

U.S. ed.: / pictures by Nicole Claveloux. New York: Harlin Quist, 1974. [32] p.: ill. ISBN: 0-8252-0119-5, 0-8252-0120-9 library binding.

*Gertrude and the mermaid* / pictures by Nicole Claveloux. New York: Harlin Quist, 1968. Ill.

*The human predicament. Volume two. The wooden shepherdess.* London: Chatto & Windus, 1973. ix, 389 p. ISBN: 0-7011-1946-2.
—— Harmondsworth: Penguin, 1975. 397 p.: pbk. ISBN: 0-1400-3777-2.
—— *The wooden shepherdess.* St. Albans: Triad/Panther, 1980. 398 p.: pbk. ISBN: 0-586-05001-9.

U.S. ed.: *The wooden shepherdess.* New York: Harper & Row, 1973. ISBN: 0-06-011986-1.

*The wonder-dog: the collected children's stories of Richard Hughes* / illustrations by Anthony Maitland. London: Chatto & Windus, 1977. 180 p.: ill. ISBN: 0-7011-5091-2. Contents: Foreword, by Richard Hughes, pp. 9-11 – Living in W'ales – The dark child – The gardener and the white elephants – The man with a green face – Telephone travel – The glass-ball country – Nothing – The hasty cook – The spider's palace – The ants – The invitation – The three innkeepers – Inhaling – The china spaniel – The magic glass – The Christmas tree – The old queen – The school – The wonder-dog – The palace on the rock – The cat and the mouse – The motherly pig – Evacuation – A sea story – The jungle school – The elephant's picnic – Early closing – Don't blame me! – The doll and the mermaid – Gertrude's child.
—— Harmondsworth: Puffin, 1980. pbk. ISBN: 0-1403-1069-X.

U.S. ed.: New York: Greenwillow Books, 1977.

*In the lap of Atlas: stories of Morocco.* London: Chatto & Windus, 1979. 124 p. ISBN: 0-7011-2430-X . Contents: Introduction, by Richard Poole, pp. 7-17 – In the lap of Atlas – The fool and the fifteen thieves – Two pots of gold – The will – The effects of hashish – The country parson – The red lantern – The canary – The story of Judah ben Hassan – . . . And Sidi Heyar had a long beard but little wits – The cow – The vizier's razor – The eyes of Ben' Adi – A woman to talk to.

*Fiction as truth: selected literary writings by Richard Hughes* / edited and introduced by Richard Poole. Bridgend: Poetry Wales Press, 1983. 174 p.: front. port. ISBN: 0-907476-18-X. Contents: Introduction, by Richard Poole, pp. 7-13 – Autobiographical; A preface to his poetry, Illogic and the child, The birth of radio drama, Introduction to *A high wind in Jamaica* – Fear and *In hazard* – Introduction to *In hazard* – On *The human predicament* – On fiction; Under the nose and under the skin, The writer's duty, The novel behind your eyes: (i) literature and the plastic arts, (ii) Why do we read novels?, Fiction as truth – Four talks; The relation of nationalism to literature, The poet and the scientist, The voice and the pen, *Liturgical language today* – Books and authors; W.E. Henley, John Skelton, *Mrs. Dalloway, Seven pillars of wisdom*, The Lawrence letters, Robert Louis Stephenson: a centenary tribute, Mr. Forster's quandary, Virginia Woolf, Joyce Cary, George Borrow: victorian rebel, Dylan Thomas: the real tragedy, Laughter from the doldrums, On Welsh literature, Faulkner and Bennett – Bibliography.

## A (ii). Publications by Richard Hughes: Selected Contributions to Books and Periodicals

For bibliographies of Richard Hughes see *Fiction as truth: selected literary writings by Richard Hughes*, ed. Richard Poole (1983), Richard Poole, *Richard Hughes: novelist* (1987) and, especially, Paul Morgan, *The art of Richard Hughes: a study of the novels* (1993), pp. 149-175. This present section draws attention to a selection of Hughes's articles, prefaces and reviews, mostly on literary or Welsh topics.

Literature and the schools. *Nation and Athenaeum*, 25 Aug 1923, 633. Review article on Sir Arthur Quiller-Couch, *On the art of writing*.

Mr Davies writes an opera. *Weekly Westminster*, 8 Dec 1923, 192. Review of W.H. Davies, *True Travellers*.

Review of D.H. Lawrence, Birds, beasts and flowers. *Nation and Athenaeum*, 5 Jan 1924, 519-520.

A study of Chehov. *Weekly Westminster*, 5 Jan 1924, 320. Review of William Gerhardi, *Anton Chehov: a critical study*.

Goya interpreted. *Weekly Westminster*, 8 Dec 1924, 501. Review of Blamire Young, *The proverbs of Goya*.

Wales and the Welsh: drama among the mountains. *Review of Reviews*, May-Jun 1924, 641-646.

Aspects of the cinema. *Outlook*, 2 Jan 1926, 8.

Introduction. In Frank Penn Smith, *Hang!* London: Chatto & Windus, 1928. pp. v-x.

Introduction. In William Faulkner, *Soldiers' pay*. London: Chatto & Windus, 1930. pp. ix-xi.

Nightingales and daggers in Morocco. *Radio Times*, 17 Oct 1930, 161, 180.

Strange Christmasses. *Harper's Bazaar*, Dec 1930, 75, 96.

The relation of nationalism to literature. *Trans. Hon. Soc. Cymm.* (1930-31) 107-128.

Introduction. In William Faulkner, *The sound and the fury.* London: Chatto & Windus, 1931. pp. vii-ix.

Physics, astronomy and mathematics, or beyond common-sense. In *An outline for boys and girls and their parents*, ed. Naomi Mitchison. London: Gollancz, 1932. pp. 303-357.

Foreword. In Frank Penn Smith, *The unexpected.* London: Cape, 1933. pp. 11-12.

Cave drawings: a new theory. *New Statesman*, 1 Apr 1933, 414-415.

Northern Africa. *Listener*, 19 Apr 1933, 629.

Safe among lions. *Spectator*, 29 Jun 1934, 992-993.

The theatre in Wales. *Bookman*, Nov 1934, 97-98.

Everyship on the Welsh seas. In H.A. Piehler, *Wales for everyman.* London: Dent, 1935. pp. 13-16. Signed 'Dylan'.

Preface. In *Catalogue of Contemporary Welsh art exhibition, September 12 – October 3, 1935.* Swansea: Deffett Francis Art Gallery, 1935.

Numen inest. *Spectator*, 2 Aug 1935, 193. Review of T.E. Lawrence, *The seven pillars of wisdom.*

Open the door! *Time and Tide*, 4 Apr 1936, 473.

Notes on the way. *Time and Tide*, 19 Sep 1936, 1273-1275; 26 Sep, 1306-1308.

Review of Glyn Jones, *The blue bed. Observer*, 7 Feb 1937, 7:E.

Notes on the way. *Time and Tide*, 16 Oct 1937, 1361-1364. Continued: 23 Oct, 1393-1395; 30 Oct, 1428-1429.

The gentle pirate. *Listener*, 16 Jun 1938, 1268-1270.

Birth of a hurricane. *Listener*, 15 Sep 1938, 544-545.

Notes on the way. *Time and Tide*, 26 Nov 1938, 1638-1639. Continued: 3 Dec, 1686-1688; 10 Dec, 1777-1780.

Introduction. In Fred Rebell, *Escape to the sea.* London: John Murray, 1939. pp. ix-xxii.

Review of Daisy Bates, *The passing of the aborigines*. *Sunday Times*, 15 Jan 1939.

Jamaica today. *Geographical Magazine*, Dec 1939, 105-114.

Review of Hilaire Belloc, On sailing the sea. *New Statesman*, 10 Feb 1940, 182, 184.

Letter to editor. *WM*, 30 May 1940, 6:B. On defence of Welsh villages.

Notes on the way. *Time and Tide*, 29 Jun 1940, 684; 6 Jul, 708.

Comedy to tragedy. *TLS*, 5 Jan 1946, 5:A. Review of Gwyn Jones, *The buttercup field*.

Will radio develop a literature of its own? *World Review*, Nov 1946, 33-36.

Review of A.L. Rowse, *West country stories*. *TLS*, 8 Dec 1946, 585.

The second revolution: literature and radio. *Virginia Quarterly Review* 23 (1947) 33-44.

Review of G.M. Gilbert, *Nuremburg Diary*. *Sunday Times*, 1 Aug 1948.

Polish impressions. *Spectator*, 17 Sep 1948, 358-359.

Star Tiger down. *Spectator*, 8 Oct 1948, 457-458. On accident to a Tudor IV aircraft.

Politicians are specialists. *Our Time*, Oct 1948, 338.

Introduction. In John Voss, *The venturesome voyages of Captain Voss*. London: Hart-Davis, 1949. pp. v-x.

Dry land. *Time and Tide*, 26 Nov 1949, 1185-1186. Against the flooding of Welsh valleys.

Make parenthood possible. *World Review*, Dec 1949, 48-52.

Review of Thor Heyerdahl, *The Kon-Tiki expedition*. *Observer*, 2 Apr 1950, 364, 366-367.

Prologue [and] Epilogue. In Amabel and Clough Williams-Ellis, *Headlong down the years: a tale of today*. Liverpool: Liverpool University Press, 1951. pp. 7, 113-118. – Epilogue reprinted from *Time and Tide*.

Wales through the looking-glass. *Listener*, 24 May 1951, 838-839.

The coronation in Wales. *Time and Tide*, 6 Jun 1953, 742-743.

Review of Desmond McCarthy, *Humanities. Spectator*, 2 Oct 1953, 364, 366-367.

Albert Schweitzer. *Picture Post*, 12 Dec 1953, 16-17.

The Strachey family. *Spectator*, 5 Feb 1954, 156-157. Review of Charles R. Sanders, *The Strachey family*.

Success and failure. *Sunday Times*, 25 Apr 1954, 4:F. Review of Anthony Alpers, *Katherine Mansfield*.

Bloomsbury. *Spectator*, 11 Jun 1954, 716, 719. Review of J.K. Johnstone, *The Bloomsbury group*.

The lord of the rings. *Spectator*, 1 Oct 1954, 408-409. Review of J.R.R. Tolkien, *The fellowship of the ring*.

The meaning of semantics. *Sunday Times*, 15 May 1955, 5:D-E. Review of Stuart Chase, *The power of words*.

Old words with new meanings. *Sunday Times*, 26 Jun 1955, 5:C. Review of Harry Hodgkinson, *Double talk: the language of communism*.

Elinor Glyn: a study in love and money. *Sunday Times*, 24 Jul 1955, 5:C-D. Review of Anthony Glyn, *Elinor Glyn*.

The mind of genius. *Sunday Times*, 7 Aug 1955, 5:F-G. Review of Lionel Trilling, *The opposing self: nine essays in criticism*.

Review of David Garnett, *The flowers of the forest. Spectator*, 14 Oct 1955, 504.

Joe's imagination runs riot. *WM*, 26 Sep 1961, 6:B-E. Penultimate part of Sextet, a composite serial with six authors.

Last words from Augustus. *Sunday Telegraph*, 5 Nov 1961, 20. On Augustus John.

I live in Merioneth. *Homes and Gardens*, Mar 1962, 92-95.

I live where I like. *Vogue*, 15 Aug 1962, 72-73.

Introduction. In William Faulkner, *Mosquitoes: a novel*. London: Chatto & Windus, 1964.

Seven mirrors for parishes. In *Six lay voices: Joyce Evans, T.I. Jeffreys-Jones, R.*

*Gerallt Jones, Rhiannon Lewis, Richard Hughes, Owen Stable.* Penarth: Church in Wales Publications, 1964. pp. 29-35.

Poet with frying pan. *Sunday Telegraph*, 25 Jul 1965, 14: A-C. Reminiscences of the young Robert Graves.

A note on the artist. In *Edward Wolfe ARA: a retrospective catalogue of paintings and drawings.* London: Arts Council, 1967. pp. 7-8.

Shop talk by Richard Hughes. *Christian Science Monitor*, 2 Mar 1967, 5. Interview.

Foreword. In *Deudraeth Rural District Council ... : the official guide.* Penrhyndeudraeth: Deudraeth R.D.C., [1968]. p. [1].

Richard Hughes. *New Yorker*, 28 Jun 1969, 30-31. Interview.

A new church building? *Impact* 1,3 (1969) 61-63.

Not things, but persons. *Times*, 21 Mar 1970, [Saturday review] 1. 'On fiction's unique ability to convey, from within, the identity of other men.'

Of use and beauty. *Books* 1 (1970) 21-24.

You should have been here yesterday. *Observer*, 17 Jan 1971, 30. On a vanished Wales.

Without letters. *Times*, 10 Feb 1971, 13:D. On the absence of postal services.

A line and a half a day. *Guardian*, 6 Apr 1973, 10:A-C. Written jointly with Yvonne Thomas.

Thinker in action. *Sunday Times*, 6 May 1973, 39:A-B. Review of Hugh Thomas, *John Strachey*.

Foreword. In *The magic valley travellers: Welsh stories of fantasy and horror*, ed. Peter Haining. London: Gollancz, 1974. pp. 13-15.

Interview. In *The writer's place: interviews on the literary situation in contemporary Britain*, ed. Peter Firchow. Minneapolis: University of Minnesota Press, 1974. pp. 183-208.

A conversation with Richard Hughes. *Listener*, 23 Oct 1975, 546-547. With Alasdair Clayre.

Eheu fugaces. *Virginia Quarterly Review* 51 (1975) 258-263.

Six poems. *PW* 16,3 (1981) 52-59. The moonlit journey – On time – When shall I see gold? – Travel-piece – Burial of the spirit of a young poet – The limber horses. – Reprinted from *Confessio iuvenis* and the *New Statesman*.

Self -awareness (1950) – Terrible (1951). In *Wales on the wireless: a broadcasting anthology*, ed. Patrick Hannan. Llandysul: Gomer in assoc. with BBC Cymru/Wales, 1988. pp. 135; 159-160.

# A (iii). Richard Hughes: Translations

### Bulgarian

*Uragan na Jamajka*, tr. Jordan Kosturkov. Varna: G. Bakalov, 1982. 199 p. [*A high wind in Jamaica*].

*Lisica na tavana*, tr. Cvetan Petrov. Plovdiv: Hristo G. Danov, 1986. 296 p. [*The fox in the attic*].

### Czech

*Pohádky od Richarda Hughesa*, tr. Zdenka Schubertová. Praha: Nakladatelstvi Kruh, 1936. Illustrated by George Kobbe. [*The spider's palace and other stories*].

### Danish

*Storm over Jamaica*, tr. Jørgen Budtz-Jørgensen. København: Westermann, 1943. 232 p. [*A high wind in Jamaica*].
—— Achehoug, 1954. 186 p.
—— Gyldendal, 1966. 192 p.

*Barometeret falder*, tr. Jørgen Budtz-Jørgensen. København: Bestermann, 1944. 210 p. [*In hazard*].
—— København: Gyldendal, 1962. 192 p.

*Raeven på loftet*, tr. Jørgen Arup Hansen. København: Gyldendal, 1962. 319 p. [*The fox in the attic*].

*Gertrud og havfruen*, tr. Martin Berg. København: Berg, 1972. 32 p.: ill. [*Gertrude and the mermaid*].

*Gertruds barn*, tr. Martin Berg. København: Berg, 1975. 32 p.: ill. [*Gertrude's child*].

### Dutch

*Kinderen en piraten*, tr. Robert Peereboom. Amsterdam: Kosmos, [193?]. 278 p.: front. port. [*A high wind in Jamaica*].

—— Antwerp; Utrecht: Het Spectrum, 1955. 224 p.

*De vos op zolder (Het menselijk dilemma; 1)*, tr. Jos Pankuijsen. Utrecht: Fontein, 1962. 329 p. [*The fox in the attic*].
—— Merksem: Westland, 1962. 331 p.

*Orkaan: geautoriseerde vertaling*, tr. Johan van der Wonde. Den Haag: Zuid-Hollandsches Uitgevers Midj, n.d. 250 p.: ill. [*In hazard*].

## Finnish

*Rajumyrsky Jamaikassa*, tr. Tauno Tainio. Helsinki: Tammi, 1956. 226 p. [*A high wind in Jamaica*].

*Sattuman kourissa*, tr. Kaj Kauhanen. Helsinki: Tammi, 1959. 206 p. [*In hazard*].

*Kettu ullakolla*, tr. Auli Tarkka. Helsinki: Tammi, 1965. 348 p. [*The fox in the attic*].

## French

*Un cyclone à la Jamaïque: roman*, tr. Jean Talva. Paris: Plon, 1931. 282 p. (Feux croisés). Also issued 1931, 251 p. (Collection pourpre). [*A high wind in Jamaica*].
—— Paris: Nicholson & Watson, 1948. 251 p.
—— Bruxelles: Nicholson & Watson, 1949. 249 p.
—— Paris: Plon, 1952. 253 p. Reissued 1958. (Livres de poche). – Reissued 1962, 247 p.
—— Paris: Presses pocket, 1983. 251 p.

*Péril en mer*, tr. Jean Talva. Paris: Stock, 1939. 282 p. Preface by Gérard Boutelleau. [*In hazard*].
—— [Paris]: Le club français du livre, 1948. 285 p.

*Le renard dans le grenier: roman*, tr. M. Lebas. Paris: Stock, 1962. 416 p. [*The fox in the attic*]. – Also special edition for Le cercle du nouveau livre, 1962. 422 p.

*Gertrude et la sirène*, tr. François Ruy-Duval. Boissy St Leger: Éditions Quist-Vidal, 1971. [31] p.: ill. Illustrations by Nicole Claveloux, [*Gertrude and the mermaid*].

*La bergère des bois: roman*, tr. Colette-Marie Huet. Paris: Stock, 1975. 472 p. ISBN: 2-234-00098-X. Preface by Jean-Luis Curtis. [*The wooden shepherdess*].

*Un mouton pas comme les autres: nouvelles*, tr. Jean Queval. Paris: F. Nathan, 1983. 91 p.: ill. [*The spider's palace and other stories*].

## German

*Ein Sturmwind von Jamaika: Roman*, tr. E. MacCalman. Berlin: Erich Reiss Verlag, 1931. 268 p. [*A high wind in Jamaica*].

*Das Walfischheim: Märchen*, tr. Käthe Rosenberg. Berlin: S. Fischer Verlag, 1933. 155 p.: ill. Illustrated by George Kobbe. [*The spider's palace and other stories*].
—— Frankfurt a. M.: Suhrkamp, 1953. Reprint of 1933 edition.

*Von Dienstag bis Dienstag: eine Seegeschichte*, tr. Richard Möring and Alfred Newman. Berlin: S. Fischer Verlag, 1938. 260 p. [*In hazard*].
—— [Berlin]: Suhrkamp, 1948. 263 p.
—— *Hurrikan im Karibischen Meer*, tr. Richard Möring and Alfred Newman. Berlin; Frankfurt a. M.: Suhrkamp, 1956. 218 p. Reissued 1959, 1962.
—— *Hurrikan im Karibischen Meer*: eine Seegeschichte. Frankfurt a. M.: Suhrkamp, 1977. 176 p. (Suhrkamp Taschenbuch; 394). ISBN: 3-518-06894-6.

*Ein Sturmwind auf Jamaika: Roman*, tr. Annemarie Seidel. Berlin; Frankfurt a. M.: Suhrkamp, 1950. 296 p. [*A high wind in Jamaica*].
—— Zurich: Büchergilde Gutenberg, 1953. 254 p.
—— *Sturm über Jamaika*. Reinbek: Rowohlt, 1965. 154 p.
—— *Ein Sturmwind auf Jamaika*. Frankfurt a. M.: Suhrkamp, 1973. 296 p. Reissued 1984. (Suhrkamp Taschenbuch; 980). ISBN: 3-518-37480-X .

*Der Fuchs unterem Dach*, tr. Maria Wolff. Frankfurt a. M.: Insel-Verlag, 1963. 369 p. [*The fox in the attic*].

*Gertrude und das Meermädchen,* tr. Dörthe Marggraf and Uwe Friesel. Köln: Middelhauve, 1971. 32 p.: ill. [*Gertrude and the mermaid*].

*Gefahr*. Baden: Grasl, 1981. 81 p. [*Danger: a play*].

*Gertrudes Kind*, tr. Angelika Feilhauer; mit vielen Zeichnungen von Anne Wilsdorf. Zürich: Diogenes, 1985. 33 p.: ill. [*Gertrude's child*].

## Greek

[*A high wind in Jamaica*]. Athens: Angyra Publishing House, 1975. 175 p.

## Hebrew

*Ruah azza be-Jamaica*, tr. G Aryok. Tel-Aviv: Am oved, 1970. 190 p.

[*The fox in the attic*], tr. Hayim Glickstein. Tel-Aviv: Zamora-Bitan-Modan, 1980. 302 p.

[*The wooden shepherdess*]. Tel-Aviv: Zamora, Bitan, 1987.

*Armon ha-akavish*, tr. Nima Carasso & Isaac Izuz. Tel-Aviv: Zmora-Bitan, 1984. 135 p. [*The spider's palace*].

## Hungarian

*Szélvihar Jamaikában*, tr. Aladár Schöpflin. Budapest: Franklin, 1933. 217 p. (Külfoldi regényirók). [*A high wind in Jamaica*].

*Szélvihar Jamaikában: regény*, tr. Péter Balabán. Budapest: Európa, 1958. 212 p. [*A high wind in Jamaica*].
——— *Szélvihar Jamaikában. Örvényben*, tr. Péter Balabán and Iván Boldizsár. Budapest: Európa, 1969. 321 p. [*A high wind in Jamaica. In hazard*].
——— *Szélvihar Jamaikában*, tr. Péter Balabán. Budapest: Szépirodalmi Kiadó, 1974. 223 p.

*Örvényben*, tr. Iván Boldizsár. Budapest: Európa, 1957. 189 p. [*In hazard*].

*Róka a padláson*, tr. László Kéry. Budapest: Európa, 1964. 343 p. [*The fox in the attic*].

*A fából való pásztorlányka: regény*, tr. Istvan Bart. Budapest: Európa, 1978. 489 p. [*The wooden shepherdess*].

## Italian

*Un ciclone nella Giamaica: romanzo*, tr. Lila Jahn. Milano: Treves, 1933. 290 p.: front. port. (Scrittori stranieri moderni). [*A high wind in Jamaica*].
——— *Un ciclone sulla Giamaica*. Milano: Bompiani, 1955. 270 p.
——— Milano: Longanesi, 1967. 276 p.
——— Milano: Garzanti, 1967. 196 p.

*Nel pericolo*, tr. Ada Prospero. Torino: Frassinelli, 1939. xvi, 237 p. [*In hazard*].
——— Milano: Bompiani, 1949. 223 p. Reissued 1963, 244 p.
——— tr. Ada Marchesini Gobetti. Milano: Garzanti, 1967. 199 p.

*Il palazzo del rago e altre fiabe*, tr. Ermanno Medori & Bonaventura Tecchi. Milano: Bompiani, 1952. 154 p.: ill. [*The spider's palace and other stories*]. – Reissued 1964, 162 p.

*Quel momento*, tr. Maria Livia Serini. Milano: Bompiani, 1957. 234 p. [*A moment of time*].

*La volpe nella soffitta*, tr. Ester Negro. Milano: Rizzoli, 1963. 420 p. [*The fox in the attic*]. Reissued 1966. – Reissued 1980.

*La vicenda umana. 2. La pastorella di legno*, tr. Franca Cancogni. Milano: Rizzoli, 1976. 368 p. [*The wooden shepherdess*].

*Cane prodigio.* Milano: Bompiani, 1982. [*The wonder-dog: collected children's stories*].

## Japanese

Jamaika no reppû, tr. Takeshi Onodera. Tokyo: Chikuma Shobô, 1970. 254 p. [*A high wind in Jamaica*]. – Reissued 1978.
—— Tokyo: Shôbunsha, 1977. 254 p.

*Hirrota mahô no renzu*, tr. Shigeru Shiraki. Tokyo: Bunken Shuppan, 1974. 79 p. [*The spider's palace and other stories*].
—— *Kumo no kyûden*, tr. Yoshiko Yagita and Masako Suzuki. Tokyo: Hayakawa Shobô, 1979. 228 p.

*Aarashi*, tr. Katsuhiko Kitayama. Tokyo: Shôbun-Sha, 1975. 232 p. [*In hazard*].

*Janguru gakkô*, tr. Sumiko Yagawa. Tokyo: Iwanami Shoten, 1979. 94 p. [*Don't blame me! and other stories*].

## Lithuanian

*Uraganas Jamaikoje*, tr. Laima Grigaliuniene. Vil'njus: Vaga, 1980. 191 p. [*A high wind in Jamaica*].

## Norwegian

*Barometret faller*, tr. E. Boysen. Oslo: Gyldendal, 1939. 208 p. [*In hazard*].

*Storm over Jamaica*, tr. Gunnar Reiss-Andersen. Oslo: Gyldendal, 1951. 217 p. [*A high wind in Jamaica*]. – Reissued 1959.

*Reven på loftet*, tr. Carl Fredrik Engelstad. Oslo: Gyldendal, 1962. 309 p. [*The fox in the attic*].

*Spill I mørke*, tr. Finn Havrevold. Oslo, 1973. 26 p. [*Danger: a play*].

## Polish

*Orkan na Jamaice*, tr. J.P. Zajaczkowski. Warszawa: Rój, 1934. 265 p. [*A high wind in Jamaica*].

*Huragan (Opowiesc morska)*, tr. Tadeusz Borysiewicz. Warszawa: Pánstw. Instytut Wydawn, 1967. 228 p. [*In hazard*].

*Orkan na Jamajce*, tr. Ariadna Demkowska. Warszawa: Czytelnic, 1968. 291 p.
—— Warszawa: Ksiazka i Wiedza, 1979. 279 p.

## Portuguese

*Nas garras da tempestade*, tr. Marina Guaspari. Rio de Janiero: Vecchi, 1954. 187 p. [*In hazard*].

*Ciclone na Jamaica: romance*, tr. João Cabral do Nascimento. Lisboa: Estúdios Cor, 1957. 233 p. [*A high wind in Jamaica*].

## Russian

*Dervjannaja pastuška*, tr. T. Kudrjavceva. Moskva: Progress, 1979. 333 p. [*The wooden shepherdess*].

*Lisica na čerdake*, tr. T. Ozerskaja. Moskva: Progress, 1979. 308 p. [*The fox in the attic*].

*Lisica na čerdake. Dervjannaja pastuška*, tr. T. Ozerskaja and T. Kudrjavceva. Kisinev: Lumina, 1981. 543 p. [*The fox in the attic. The wooden shepherdess*].

## Slovak

*Vichor na Jamajke*, tr. Verona Chorvátová. Bratislava: Slovenský spisovatel', 1982. 182 p. [*A high wind in Jamaica*].

## Spanish

*Hurracan en Jamaica*, tr. Rafael Vazquez-Zamora. Barcelona: Ediciones Destino, [1944]. 266 p. [*A high wind in Jamaica*].

*Peligro en el mar*. Madrid: Ediciones Lauro, 1945. 228 p. [*In hazard*]

*El zorro en la bohardilla*, tr. Matilde de Horne. Buenos Aires: Sudamericana, 1963. 380 p. [*The fox in the attic*].
—*El zorro en el desván*, tr. Ana Marie de la Fuente. Barcelona: Plaza y Jans, 1964. 430 p.

*El perro prodigio*, tr. Emilianio Ramos. Madrid: Alfaguara, 1982. 187 p. [*The wonder-dog: collected children's stories*]. – Reissued 1983, 1986.

*En el regazo del Atlas: cuentos de Marruecos*, tr. Javier Lacruz. Madrid: Alfaguara, 1984. 178 p.: ill. [*In the lap of Atlas*]. – Reissued 1985, 1986.

## Swedish

*Storm på Jamaica*, tr. Aida Törnell. Stockholm: Norstedt, 1930. 253 p. [*A high wind in Jamaica*].
—— *Storm över Jamaica*. Stockholm: Norstedt, 1965. 224 p.

*Cyklonen: en berättelse från sjön*, tr. Nils Fredricson. Malmö: Allhem, 1952. 246 p. [*In hazard*].

*Räven pa vinden*, tr. Torsten Blomkvist. Stockholm: Norstedt, 1962. 322 p.
[*The fox in the attic*].
—Stockholm: PAN-Norstedt, 1974. 305 p.

*Herrdinnan i skogen*, tr. Thomas Warburton. Stockholm: Norstedt, 1974. 318
p. [*The wooden shepherdess*].


## B. Publications about Richard Hughes

Note that Paul Morgan, *The art of Richard Hughes* (1993) lists contemporary
reviews of Hughes's major publications.

[ANON]. Drama by wireless waves: encouraging first results. *Evening Standard*,
   16 Jan 1924, 5.
—— Richard Hughes: author of *The innocent voyage*. *Wilson Bulletin*, Nov
   1929, 660.
—— Notes on Richard Hughes's A high wind in Jamaica. London: Methuen,
   1971. 43 p. (Study-aid series).
ACTON, Harold. The short story and Mr Richard Hughes. *Cherwell*, 20 Feb
   1926, 138. Review article on *A moment of time*.
AHRENDS, Gunther. Richard Hughes, *The wooden shepherdess*. In *Englische
   Literatur der Gegenwart, 1971-1975*, ed. Rainer Lengler. Düsseldorf: Bagel,
   1977. pp. 227-241.
ALLEN, Walter. *Tradition and dream: the English and American novel from the
   twenties to our time*. London: Phoenix House, 1964. Incl. discussion of
   Richard Hughes, pp. 58-62, 87.
—— Richard Hughes. In *Novelists and prose writers*, ed. James Vinson.
   London: Macmillan, 1979. (Great writers of the English language). pp.
   675-678.
—— Richard Hughes. In *Reference guide to English literature*, ed. D.L. Kirk-
   patrick. 2nd ed. 3 vols. Chicago; London: St James Press, 1991. Vol. 2,
   pp. 753-755.
BAKEWELL, Michael. A life sentence: memories of Richard Hughes. *Listener*,
   10 May 1979, 658-659.
BEBB, Howard S. *The novels of William Golding*. Columbus: Ohio State Uni-
   versity Press, 1970. Incl. comparison with *A high wind in Jamaica*.
BENNETT, Arnold. *The Evening Standard years: books and persons, 1926-1930*,
   ed. Andrew Mylett. London: Chatto & Windus, 1974. Incl. comment on
   *A high wind in Jamaica*, p. 309.
BOSANO, J. Richard Hughes. *Études Anglaises* 16,3 (1963) 262-269.
BRADSHAW, Jon. Tolstoy in Wales. *Daily Telegraph Magazine*, 6 Aug 1971,
   27-28.
BROWN, Daniel R. *A high wind in Jamaica*: comedy of the absurd. *Ball
   State University Forum* 9,1 (1968) 6-12.
CLARKE, Gillian and John Davies. Editorial. *AWR* 26,57 (1977) 3-7. Incl.
   obituary and reminiscences of Richard Hughes.
DE JONG, John M. Richard Hughes and the Cartesian world. *Critique* 19,2
   (1977) 13-22.

DRAKAKIS, John. Introduction. In *British radio drama*, ed. J. Drakakis. Cambridge: Cambridge University Press, 1981. pp. 1-36. Incl. comment on Richard Hughes.

DUMBLETON, Susanne M. Animals and humans in *A high wind in Jamaica. AWR* 68 (1981) 51-61.

— *The fox in the attic* and *The wooden shepherdess*: a definition of the human predicament. *AWR* 73 (1983) 38-48.

ERDMENGER, Manfred. *Das Hörspiel: ein vernachlässigtes Kapitel der englischen Literaturgschichte. Die neueren Sprachen* 22 (1973) 405-409. Traces radio play from Richard Hughes's 'Danger'. – [The radio play: a neglected chapter in English literary criticism].

FLETCHER, Ian Kyrle. Richard Hughes: a Welsh playwright of distinction. *South Wales Daily News*, 31 Aug 1927, 6:E.

GORDAN, John D. Richard Hughes, *Bulletin of the New York Public Library* 71 (1967) 303.

GOODWIN, Geraint. Mystic poet and dramatist: how a Welshman came to fame: Richard Hughes' one act play in London. *WM*, 30 Jun 1927, 8:E. On 'The man born to be hanged'.

HART, Olive. *The drama in modern Wales: a brief history of Welsh playwriting from 1900 to the present day.* University of Pennsylvania, 1928. Incl. Richard Hughes, pp. 44-51. – Published PhD thesis.

HENIGHAN, T.J. Nature and convention in *A high wind in Jamaica. Critique* 9,1 (1966) 5-18.

HUGHES, Penelope. *Richard Hughes: author, father.* Gloucester: Alan Sutton, 1984. 194 p.: ill.

HUMFREY, Belinda. Richard Hughes. In *British novelists, 1930-1959. Part 1: A-L*, ed. Bernard Oldsey. Detroit: Gale, 1983. (Dictionary of literary biography; 15). pp. 186-194.

HUMPHREY, Richard. Der historische Roman und das Feindbild: Zu Richard Hughes' unvollendeter Faschismus-Trilogie *The Human Predicament* (1961-73). *Anglistik und Englischunterricht* 29-30 (1986) 157-172. [The historical novel and the picture of the enemy: on Richard Hughes's unfinished trilogy on fascism, *The human predicament*].

JONES, Dedwydd. *Black book on the Welsh theatre.* London: Bozo, 1985. Incl. discussion of Richard Hughes. – Revision of work first pubished in 1980.

JONES, Jack. Nofelau'r Cymry Seisnig. *Tir Newydd*, Mai/May 1937, 5-9. [Anglo-Welsh novels].

JONES, Jonah. The *Gallipoli diary.* Bridgend: Seren Books, 1989. Incl. Richard Hughes, pp. 75-87.

KERMODE, Frank. Out of class, out of touch. *Daily Telegraph*, 8 May 1976, 13. Obituary.

KRUSE, Hildegard. *Bauformen und Erzählverfahren in den Romanen von Richard Hughes.* Frankfurt a. M.: Lang, 1983. 393 p. (Studien zur englischen und americanischen Literatur; 2). Incl. bibliography listing English and German criticism, pp. 388-393. – Photo-reprint of doctoral thesis (University of Bochum). – [Structures and narrative process in the novels of Richard Hughes].

LEIBOLD, Roland. Unterrichtsreihen Englisch: Ballantyne's *The coral island*, Golding's *Lord of the flies*, Hughes's *A high wind in Jamaica*: eine literaturvergleichende Studie als Unterrichtsprojekt für den Leistungskurs Englisch. *Anglistik und Englischunterricht* 29-30 (1986) 277-307. [English teaching series: ... a comparative literary study as a teaching project for the English course].

MILLER, Richard Hugh. History and children in Richard Hughes's *The wooden shepherdess*. *Antigonish Review* 22 (1975) 31-35.

MILLIGAN, Ian. Richard Hughes's *A high wind in Jamaica* and Aaron Smith's *Atrocities of the pirates*. *Notes and Queries*, Aug 1979, 336-337.

—— *Richard Hughes*, A high wind in Jamaica: *notes*. London: Longman, 1980. 73 p. (York notes; 17). Incl. bibliography, pp. 71-72.

—— Richard Hughes and Michael Scott: a further source for *A high wind in Jamaica*. *Notes and Queries*, Jun 1986, 192-193.

MORGAN, Louise. Richard Hughes: artist and adventurer. *Everyman*, 9 Apr 1931, 327-329. With an interview.

MORGAN, Paul Bennett. Richard Hughes and 'Living in W'ales'. *AWR* 84 (1986) 91-103.

—— Richard Hughes: an author's library. *National Library of Wales Journal* 25 (1988) 341-346.

—— Biographica et bibliographica: Ex libris Richard Hughes: three bookplates. *National Library of Wales Journal* 25 (1988) 347-349.

—— *A moment of time*: the short stories of Richard Hughes. *NWR* 1,2 [2] (1988) 57-63.

—— The art of Richard Hughes: unity of theme and technique in the writings of Richard Arthur Warren Hughes. PhD thesis. University of Wales (Lampeter), 1989. 2 vols. 571 p. Incl. bibliography, pp. 538-571.

—— Richard Hughes's *A high wind in Jamaica*: a misattributed edition. *Notes and Queries*, March 1990, 67.

—— *The art of Richard Hughes: a study of the novels*. Cardiff: University of Wales Press, 1993. 177 p. Incl.: Appendix. *The human predicament*: the unpublished fragment, pp. 143-146 – Bibliography, pp. 149-175. – The appendix summarizes the first twelve chapters of *The human predicament* volume 3, drafted by Hughes 1973-1976.

OTTO, Erwin. The living are dead, the dead are alive: two very short ghost stories. *Anglistik und Englischunterricht* 18 (1982) 101-113. Discusses Ronald Duncan's 'When we dead awaken' and Richard Hughes's 'The ghost'.

PARKER, Geoffrey. Richard Hughes's *The spider's palace and other stories*. *Children's Literature in Education* [New York] 20 (1976) 32-40.

PERCY, Walker. Hughes's solipsism *malgré lui*. *Sewanee Review* 72 (1964) 489-495. On *The fox in the attic*.

POOLE, Richard. Irony in *A high wind in Jamaica*. *AWR* 23,51 (1974) 41-57.

—— Morality and selfhood in the novels of Richard Hughes. *AWR* 25,55 (1975) 10-29.

—— Fiction as truth: Richard Hughes's *The human predicament*. *AWR* 26,57 (1976) 57-92.

—— In hazard: the theory and practice of Richard Hughes's art. *Planet* 45-46 (1978) 68-77.

—— An afterword to Richard Hughes, 'A preface to his poetry' (1921). *PW* 16,3 (1981) 70-71.

—— Under the nose and under the skin. *BNW*, Spring 1983, 5-6.

—— *Richard Hughes: novelist.* Bridgend: Poetry Wales Press, 1987. 253 p. Incl. bibliography, pp. 241-245.

PRICE, Doris Seys. Novelist at home. *Country Quest*, Oct 1967, 45,

ROBERTS, Glyn. Richard Hughes, novelist and playwright. *WM*, 29 Aug 1933, 6:D-F.

SAVAGE, D.S. Richard Hughes, solipsist. *AWR* 68 (1981) 36-50. Discusses *The fox in the attic* and *The wooden shepherdess.* – Reprinted *Sewanee Review* 94 (1986) 602-613.

SCHONE, Annemarie. Richard Hughes: ein Meister der tragischen Ironie. *Germanisch-Romanische Monatsschrift* 40 (1959) 75-86.

SCHUCHARD, Margret. Richard Hughes. In *Englische Dichter der Moderne: ihr Leben und Werk*, ed. Rudolf Sühnel and Dieter Reisner. Berlin: Schmidt, 1971. pp. 385-92.

SIEVEKING, Lance. *The eye of the beholder.* London: Hulton Press, 1957. Incl. biographical section on Richard Hughes, pp. 163-187.

SULLIVAN, Walter. Old age, death, and other modern landscapes: good and indifferent fables for our time. *Sewanee Review* 82 (1974) 138-47. Discusses Richard Hughes, pp. 142-144.

SWINDEN, Patrick. *Unofficial selves: character in the novel from Dickens to the present day.* London: Macmillan, 1973. Incl. discussion of Richard Hughes, pp. 181-202.

—— *The English novel of history and society, 1940-1980: Richard Hughes, Henry Green, Anthony Powell, Angus Wilson, Kingsley Amis, V.S. Naipaul.* London: Macmillan, 1984. (Macmillan Studies in Twentieth Century Literature). Incl. Richard Hughes, pp. 24-56.

THOMAS, Peter. Measuring the wind: the early writings of Richard Hughes. *AWR* 20,45 (1971) 36-56.

—— *Richard Hughes.* Cardiff: University of Wales Press [for] the Welsh Arts Council, 1973. 103 p.: front port.. (Writers of Wales). Incl. bibliography, pp. 97-100. 'Limited to 1000 copies'.

—— In the Abbey shadow: the fortunes of the Portmadoc players. *AWR* 21,47 (1972) 89-95. Incl. account of first performance of Richard Hughes's 'The man born to be hanged'.

TRANTER, H.L. Set books. xviii. *A high wind in Jamaica. Use of English* 14,1 (1962) 36-41.

WOODWARD, Daniel H. The Delphic voice: Richard Hughes's *A high wind in Jamaica. Papers on Language and Literature* 3,1 (1967) 57-74.

# EMYR HUMPHREYS (b. 1919)

A. Publications by Emyr Humphreys
  (i)   Books
  (ii)  Selected contributions to books and periodicals
  (iii) Emyr Humphreys: television drama

B. Publications about Emyr Humphreys

## A (i). Publications by Emyr Humphreys: Books

*The little kingdom*. London: Eyre & Spottiswoode, 1946. 221 p. Novel.

Welsh trans.: *Darn o dir*, tr. W.J. Jones. Penygroes: Dwyfor, 1986. 162 p.: pbk. [A piece of land].

*The voice of a stranger*. London: Eyre & Spottiswoode, 1949. 304 p. Novel.

*A change of heart: a comedy*. London: Eyre & Spottiswoode, 1951. 239 p. Novel.

*Hear and forgive*. London: Gollancz, 1952. 238 p. Novel.
—— Macdonald, 1971. ISBN: 0-356-03798-3.

U.S. ed.: New York: Putnam, 1953. 249 p.

French trans.: *Écoute et pardonne*, tr. Jacques and Jean Tournier. Paris: Plon, 1955. 277 p.

*A man's estate*. London: Eyre & Spottiswoode, 1955. 255 p. Novel.
—— A man's estate: a novel. Readers Union, 1957.
—— Dent, 1988. pbk. (Everyman fiction). ISBN: 0-460-02496-5.

U.S. ed.: New York: McGraw-Hill, 1956. 279 p.

Swedish trans.: *En man arvedel*, tr. Torsten Blomkvist. Stockholm: Bonnier, 1957. 280 p.

Welsh trans.: *Etifedd y glyn*, tr. W.J. Jones. Llandysul, Gomer, 1981. 317 p. ISBN: 0-85088-935-9.

*The Italian wife*. London: Eyre & Spottiswoode, 1957. 255 p. Novel.

U.S. ed.: New York: McGraw-Hill, 1958. 228 p.

*A toy epic*. London: Eyre & Spottiswoode, 1958. 158 p. Novel. – Extract: A death in the street. *Wales* 3rd ser., Nov 1958, 21-25.
—— Arrow, 1961. 160 p.: pbk.
—— Severn House, 1981. 160 p. ISBN: 0-7278-0712-9.
—— / edited and introduced by M. Wynn Thomas. Bridgend: Seren, 1989. 200 p.: pbk. (Welsh writing in English). ISBN: 1-85411-009-8. Incl.: Introduction, pp. 7-14 – Afterword, by M. Wynn Thomas, pp. 122-150 – Bibliography and notes – Appendix. Michael Edwards, the nationalist at College.

Author's Welsh version: *Y tri llais: nofel*. Llandybïe: Llyfrau'r Dryw, 1958. 117 p. [The three voices].
—— [Penygroes]: Cyhoeddiadau Mei, 1985. pbk. ISBN: 0-905775-46-5.

*The gift*. London: Eyre & Spottiswoode, 1963. 317 p. Novel.

*Outside the house of Baal*. London: Eyre & Spottiswoode, 1965. 444 p. Novel.
—— Dent, 1988. 454 p.: pbk. (Everyman fiction). ISBN: 0-460-02495-7. Incl. additional chapter, first published *Mabon* [English] 1,1 (1969) 30-40.

*Natives*. London: Secker & Warburg, 1968. 255 p. ISBN: 0-436-20980-2. Contents: A mystical experience – The rigours of inspection – The hero – The suspect – With all my heart – An artistic mission – A list of good people – Mel's secret love – Dinas – A cheerful note. – Stories.

*Ancestor worship: a cycle of eighteen poems*. Denbigh: Gee, 1970. 40 p.: ill. Illustrations by Eric Malthouse.

*Dinas*. Llandybïe: Llyfrau'r Dryw, 1970. 95 p. Drama. Written jointly with W.S. Jones. – [The City].

*National winner*. London: Macdonald, 1971. 405 p. ISBN: 0-356-03597-2. Novel.

*Flesh and blood*. London: Hodder & Stoughton, 1974. 348 p. ISBN: 0-340-18547-3. Novel. – Reissued 1978, ISBN: 0-340-23082-7.
—— Hodder & Stoughton, 1986. 378 p.: pbk. ISBN: 0-7221-4785-6. With 'Emyr Humphries' on title-page.

*Diwylliant Cymru a'r cyfryngau torfol*. [Aberystwyth]: Cymdeithas yr Iaith Gymraeg, 1977. 28 p.: pamph. [Welsh culture and the mass media].

*The best of friends*. London: Hodder & Stoughton, 1978. 412 p. ISBN: 0-340-22964-0. Novel. – Extract: Two episodes, *Planet* 39 (1977) 24-34.

—— Sphere, 1987. 409 p.: pbk. ISBN: 0-7221-4202-1.

*Bwrdd datblygu teledu Cymraeg*. [Aberystwyth]: Cymdeithas yr Iaith Gymraeg, 1979. 12 p.: pamph. [Development board for Welsh television].

*The kingdom of Brân*. [Beckenham]: Keith Holmes, 1979. [33] p.: ill. 'Adapted from *The Mabinogi* by Emyr Humphreys. Text, illustrations and printing by Keith Holmes. 15 copies, i-xv vellum bound, 100 copies, 1-100 paper bound'. – Signed by author and printer.

*Landscapes: a sequence of songs* / illustrated by Keith Holmes. Beckenham: Chimaera Press, 1979. 22p.: ill. 150 copies for sale.

*Penguin modern poets 27: John Ormond, Emyr Humphreys, John Tripp*. Harmondsworth: Penguin, 1979. 171 p.: pbk. ISBN: 0-14042-192-0. Incl.: The *Ancestor worship* cycle, and other poems by Emyr Humphreys, pp. 67-123.

*Theatr Saunders Lewis*. Bangor: Cymdeithas Theatr Cymru, 1979. 30 p.: pamph. (Astudiaethau Theatr Cymru; 1).

*The anchor tree*. London: Hodder & Stoughton, 1980. 224 p. ISBN: 0-340-25408-4. Novel.

*Pwyll a Riannon* [sic]. [Beckenham]: Keith Holmes, 1980. [23]p.: ill. 'Adapted from the *Mabinogi* by Emyr Humphreys. Text, illustrations and printing by Keith Holmes. 15 copies ... vellum bound. 100 copies ... paper bound.' – Signed by author and printer.

*Miscellany two: Emyr Humphreys*. Bridgend: Poetry Wales Press, 1981. 146 p.: hbk & pbk. ISBN: 0-907476-05-8 hbk, 0-907476-06-6 pbk. Contents: Stories; Boys in a boat, A corner of a field, Down in the heel, The arrest – Poems; Interim verdict, A tree waiting, Partial recall, Two generations, Brân – Essays; Poetry, prison and propaganda, Arnold in wonderland, The loss of incantation, Television and us.

*The Taliesin tradition: a quest for the Welsh identity*. London: Black Raven Press, 1983. ix, 245 p.: ill. ISBN: 0-85159-002-0.
—— Bridgend: Seren Books, 1989. pbk. ISBN: 1-85411-020-9. This reissue with an afterword by the author, pp. 231-236, replacing bibliography.

*Jones: a novel*. London: Dent, 1984. 138 p. ISBN: 0-460-04660-8.

*Salt of the earth*. London: Dent, 1985. 182 p. ISBN: 0-460-04661-6. Novel.
—— Sphere, 1987. 214 p.: pbk. ISBN: 0-7221-4204-8.

*An absolute hero*. London: Dent, 1986. 194 p. ISBN: 0-460-04705-1. Novel. – Extract: *An absolute hero*: two chapters ... *Planet* 52 (1985) 81-96.

—— Sphere, 1988. 218 p.: pbk. ISBN: 0-7221-4192-0.

*Y gwir di-goll: fickle fact and sober fiction*. Bangor: Cymdeithas Celfyddydau Gogledd Cymru, 1986. [12] p.: pamph. (Ben Bowen Thomas memorial lecture). Bilingual text.

*Open secrets*. London: Dent, 1988. 224 p. ISBN: 0-460-04759-0. Novel.
—— Sphere, 1989. 320 p. ISBN: 0-747-40356-2.

*The triple net: a portrait of the writer Kate Roberts, 1891-1985*. London: Channel 4 Television, 1988. 56 p.: ill.: pamph. ISBN: 1-85144-007-0. Accompanies four television programmes, transmitted 1988.

*The crucible of myth*. Swansea: University College of Swansea, 1990. 20 p.: pamph. (W.D. Thomas memorial lecture). ISBN: 0-86076-070-7.

*Bonds of attachment*. London: Macdonald, 1991. 357 p. ISBN: 0-456-19134-6. Novel. – Extract: Fragile threads. *Planet* 77 (1989) 24-32.
—— Bath: Chivers, 1991. 468 p. ISBN: 0-7451-7518-X. Large print edition.

*Outside time* [cover title]. London: Channel 4 Television, 1991. 52 p.: ill.: pamph. Incl.: *The crucible of myth*, pp. 9-15 – *Pwyll a Riannon* [sic], pp. 17-29 – *The kingdom of Brân*, pp. 17-47. – *The crucible of myth* is the W.D. Thomas lecture, 1990. – The adapted translations are photo-litho reprints of privately printed editions, with calligraphy and illustrations by Keith Holmes, published in 1979 and 1980 respectively. – Booklet designed to accompany series of television programmes on The four branches of the Mabinogi, transmitted 1991.

## A (ii). Publications by Emyr Humphreys: Selected Contributions to Books and Periodicals

The Bangor Summer School. *Welsh Nationalist*, Sep 1939, 5.

A young man considers his prospects. *Wales* 6-7 (1939) 202-203. Poetry.

The curate. *Wales* 10 (1939) 270. Poetry.

To John Gwilym Jones (Acting) *Wales* 2nd ser. 3 (1944) 9-10. Poetry.

Piecepomb for Vjayday. *Wales* 2nd ser. 6,2 [22] (1946) 6. Poetry.

Reply to *Wales* questionnaire 1946. Wales 2nd ser. 6,3 [23] (1946) 27.

A season in Florence: 1945. *Wales* 2nd ser. 6,24 (1946) 120-124. Extracts from a journal.

Review of Jack Jones, *Off to Philadelphia in the morning*. *New English Review*, Oct 1947, 373-374.

On duty. *New English Review*, Dec 1947, 551-555. Story.

Michael Edwards: the nationalist at college. *Wales* 2nd ser. 7,26 (1947) 265-280. Story. -Continued as Michael Edwards at college. *Wales* 2nd ser. 7,27 (1947) 343-363. – Reprinted as appendix to *A toy epic* (1989).

Letter. *Wales* 2nd ser. 7,26 (1947) 264. On tenth anniversary of *Wales*.

At the frontier: Palestine. *Wales* 2nd ser. 8,30 (1948) 644-645. Poetry.

An imaginary encounter written for broadcasting: Saunders Lewis and Llewelyn ap Gruffydd. *Wales* 2nd ser. 9,31 (1949) 29-35.

Comment in the novel. *Time and Tide*, 5 May 1951, 410-411.

The protestant novelist. *Spectator*, 21 Nov 1952, 681-682.

*The anathemata* of David Jones. *Time and Tide*, 29 Nov 1952, 1400. Review.

The girl in the ice. *New Statesman*, 7 Feb 1953, 145-146. Short story.

The poet's communication. *Time and Tide*, 28 March 1953, 418. Review of Herbert Read, *The true voice of feeling*.

Review of *Dock Leaves*, vol. 3, no. 9. *Time and Tide*, 28 Mar 1953, 426.

A protestant view of the modern novel. *Listener*, 2 Apr 1953, 557-559.

Humble song – The rabbit ensemble. *Rann* 19 (1953) 9, 14. Poetry.

[Eisteddfod adjudication]. In *Eisteddfod Genedlaethol Frenhinol Cymru: Cyfansoddiadau a Beirniadaethau*, Ystradgynlais 1954. pp. 158-159.

The Eisteddfod at Pwllheli. *Time and Tide*, 30 Jul 1955, 993-994.

Hen wlad ei dadau. *Empire News*, 29 Jan 1956, 6:B-C.

My great aunt. *DL* 7,19 (1956) 8-9. Poetry.

Notes from an Aalborg sketchbook. In *Aalborg shows the way*. Aalborg Municipality, [1958?]. pp. 3-4, 15. Article in publicity brochure.

Introduction. In *Eric Malthouse: an exhibition of paintings, drawings and prints from 1947-1958, held at the National Museum of Wales, Turner House Gallery, 4 Apr to 3 May 1959*. Cardiff: National Museum of Wales, [1959]. [20] p.: ill. Two-page introduction.

Mrs. Armitage. In *Welsh short stories*, ed. George Ewart Evans. London: Faber, 1959. pp. 246-259.

[Eisteddfod adjudication]. In *Eisteddfod Genedlaethol Frenhinol Cymru: Cyfansoddiadau a Beirniadaethau*, Caernarfon 1959. pp. 195-197.

The death of Gwilym de Breos from the *Siwan* of Saunders Lewis. *AWR* 10,25 (1959) 22-27. Translated by Emyr Humphreys.

[Eisteddfod adjudication]. In *Eisteddfod Genedlaethol Frenhinol Cymru: Cyfansoddiadau a Beirniadaethau*, Caerdydd 1960. p. 220.

How the prince found a wife: Pwyll a Rhiannon. *Mabon* [English] 1,2 (1960) 33-38. Adapted from the *Mabinogion*.

*Siwan*. In *Plays of the year. Vol. 21. 1959-60*, ed. J.C. Trewin. London: Elek, 1961. pp. 113-186. Emyr Humphreys' translation of the Saunders Lewis play; reprinted in *Presenting Saunders Lewis*, ed. R. Alun Jones and Gwyn Thomas. Cardiff: University of Wales Press, 1983. pp. 251-300.

[Eisteddfod adjudication]. In *Eisteddfod Genedlaethol Frenhinol Cymru: Cyfansoddiadau a Beirniadaethau*, Dyffryn Maelor 1961. pp. 173-174.

Monologue for a horizontal patriot. *WM*, 11 Feb 1961, i. Poetry.

[Eisteddfod adjudication]. In *Eisteddfod Genedlaethol Frenhinol Cymru: Cyfansoddiadau a Beirniadaethau*, Llanelli 1962. pp. 211-213.

A true mirror of European thought. *WM*, 10 Nov 1962, 5:A-C. On European drama, particularly Brecht.

A view of Wales. *Anglia* [USSR] 3 (1962) 76-89. Russian translation of article on Wales.

Ysgrifennu cyfoes yng Nghymru, I. Y nofel. *Lleufer* 18,1 (1962) 4-8. [Contemporary writing in Wales, I. The novel].

Ysgrifennu cyfoes yng Nghymru, II. Y ddrama. *Lleufer* 18,2 (1962) 61-68. [Contemporary writing in Wales, II. The drama].

[Eisteddfod adjudication]. In *Eisteddfod Genedlaethol Frenhinol Cymru: Cyfansoddiadau a Beirniadaethau*, Maldwyn 1965. pp. 185-186.

Notes from an Aalborg sketchbook. In *Aalborg shows the way*. Aalborg Municipality, [1965?]. pp. 2-4, 14-15. Article in publicity brochure.

Meet Emyr Humphreys, novelist. *Welsh Nation*, May 1966, 2:E-F. Interview.

[Eisteddfod adjudication]. In *Eisteddfod Genedlaethol Frenhinol Cymru: Cyfansoddiadau a Beirniadaethau*, Y Bala 1967. pp. 186-188.

National Theatre: author resigns. *WM*, 4 Dec 1967, 2:F-H. Letter on resignation from National Theatre for Wales committee.

Fanatic. *PW* 4,1 (1968) 15. Poetry.

[Eisteddfod adjudication]. In *Eisteddfod Genedlaethol Frenhinol Cymru: Cyfansoddiadau a Beirniadaethau*, Y Fflint 1969. pp. 97-100.

*Traed mewn cyffion*. In *Cyfrol deyrnged Kate Roberts*, ed. Bobi Jones. Dinbych: Gwasg Gee, 1969. pp. 51-60. On the Kate Roberts novel.

Y celfyddydau yng Nghymru. In *Y chwedegau*. Cardiff: Avalon, 1970. pp. 75-88. Text of television lecture. – [The arts in Wales].

Personal column. *WM*, 16 Feb 1970, 6:C-F. On the meaning of 'Anglo-Welsh'.

Personal column. *WM*, 9 Mar 1970, 6:C-F. On BBC mentality.

The Welsh condition. *Spectator*, 28 Mar 1970, 411-412. Reprinted as Plaid Cymru pamphlet (Denbigh: Gee and Son, n.d.).

Personal column. *WM*, 30 Mar 1970, 6:C-F. On actors.

Personal column. *WM*, 20 Apr 1970, 6:C-D. On north- and south-Walian temperament.

In love with an island. *Spectator*, 22 Aug 1970, 181. Essay on Anglesey.

[Eisteddfod adjudications]. In *Eisteddfod Genedlaethol Frenhinol Cymru: Cyfansoddiadau a Beirniadaethau*, Bangor 1971. pp. 172-173, 174-175. With John Gwilym Jones.

Cymod cadarn: drama-ddogfen am hynt delfryd. *Llwyfan* 9 (1973) 13-40. Birthday tribute to Saunders Lewis. – [Steadfast reconciliation: drama documentary on the progress of an ideal].

[Eisteddfod adjudication]. In *Eisteddfod Genedlaethol Frenhinol Cymru: Cyfansoddiadau a Beirniadaethau*, Bro Myrddin 1974. pp. 224-225.

Nodyn ar natur sgwrs. In *John Gwilym Jones: cyfrol deyrnged*, ed. Gwyn Thomas. Llandybïe: Christopher Davies, 1974. pp. 49-55. [Notes on the nature of conversation].

Diwylliant Cymru a'r cyfryngau torfol. *Taliesin* 29 (1974) 9-30. [Welsh culture and the mass media].

[Eisteddfod adjudications]. In *Eisteddfod Genedlaethol Frenhinol Cymru: Cyfansoddiadau a Beirniadaethau*, Bro Dwyfor 1975. pp. 88-90, 144-146.

Y sianel Gymraeg. *Tafod y Ddraig*, Chw/Feb 1975, 14-17. [The Welsh TV channel].

Ffigys oddiar ysgall. *Barn*, Mai/May 1977, 150-151. [Figs from thistles].

Review of Kate Roberts, *Feet in chains*, tr. Idwal Walters and John Idris Jones. *Barn*, Rha/Dec 1977, 414-415.

Sweet research. *PW* 12,3 (1977) 40-41. Poetry.

A household in the south – Considering time. *Cyphers* 8 (1978) 46-47. Poetry.

Poetry, prison and propaganda. *Planet* 43 (1978) 17-23.

Arnold in wonderland. *PR* 3 (1978) 49-50. On Matthew Arnold and the Celtic peoples. – Welsh version: Arnold yng ngwlad hud. *Taliesin* 37 (1978) 10-23.

Poppies – Horses. *PW* 14,2 (1978) 89-90. Poetry.

Our American dream: Y baradwys bell. *PW* 14,3 (1978) 49. On the author's TV series.

Colli gorchan. *Y Traethodydd* 133 (1978) 126-134. [The loss of incantation].

Datganoli yn y meddwl. *Y Faner*, 5 Ion/Jan 1979, 5-6. [Devolution in the mind].

Yn trafod 'Pobl y cwm'. *Y Faner*, 2 Chw/Feb 1979, 5. [Discussing 'Pobl y cwm'].

Letter to editor. *WM*, 27 Feb 1979, 10:D. Welsh writers commend devolution.

Y genedl fawr. *Y Faner*, 2 Maw/Mar 1979, 5. [The great nation].

Uchelgais anrhydedd. *Y Faner*, 30 Maw/Mar 1979, 7. [The ambition of honour].

Taid T.S. Eliot. *Y Faner*, 27 Ebr/Apr 1979, 7. [T.S. Eliot's grandfather].

Uwchlaw'r cymylau. *Y Faner*, 25 Mai/May 1979, 6. [Above the clouds].

Carl Marcs newydd. *Y Faner*, 22 Meh/Jun 1979, 5. [A new Karl Marx].

Epistol poen. *Y Faner*, 20 Gor/Jul 1979, 8. On R. Williams-Parry. – [Epistle of pain].

Jones, y rheol aur. *Y Faner*, 17 Aws/Aug 1979, 8. On Samuel Milton Jones. – [Golden rule Jones].

Bys gwallgo. *Y Faner*, 14 Med/Sep 1979, 8. [The crazy finger].

Nid cyfalafiaeth chwaith. *Y Faner*, 12 Hyd/Oct 1979, 8. [Nor yet capitalism].

Ysbryd chwyldro. *Y Faner*, 9 Tach/Nov 1979, 10. [The spirit of revolution].

Gwraig yr hanesydd. *Y Faner*, 7 Rha/Dec 1979, 8. Story. – [The historian's wife].

Yr ewyllys yw'r unig beth sy'n brin. *Y Cymro*, 18 Rha/Dec 1979, 6:B-F. [The will's the only thing missing].

Seiliau protestannaidd y nofel fodern. *Y Traethodydd* 134 (1979) 4-12. [Protestant foundations of the modern novel].

Hanner call. *Y Faner*, 11 Ion/Jan 1980, 7. [Not all there].

Lawen chwedl. *Y Faner*, 8 Chw/Feb 1980, 7. [A happy tale].

Mater o addysg. *Y Faner*, 7 Maw/Mar 1980, 6. [A matter of education].

Anweledig gôr. *Y Faner*, 4 Ebr/Apr 1980, 6,7. [The invisible choir].

Egni aflonydd Balzac. *Y Faner*, 9 Mai/May 1980, 10. [Balzac's restless energy].

Yr anifail, y peiriant a'r bod dynol. *Y Faner*, 30 Mai/May 1980, 8,21. [The animal, the machine and the human being].

Hel achau: cyfrif y tystion. *Y Faner*, 27 Meh/Jun 1980, 8. [Family trees: counting the witnesses].

Dic Penderyn. *Y Faner*, 1 Aws/Aug 1980, 11.

Emyr Humphreys interviewed by Ioan Williams. *BNW*, Autumn 1980, 3-4.

The night of the fire. *Planet* 49-50 (1980) 74-94. On the Penyberth Bombing School fire, 1936.

Taliesin and Frank Lloyd Wright. *Welsh Books and Writers* [Welsh Books Council], Autumn 1980, 3-5.

Chasing shadows. *Arcade*, 6 Feb 1981, 21. On television and 'Anglo-worship'.

Y gelyn oddi mewn. *Y Ddraig Goch*, Chw/Feb-Maw/Mar 1981, 7. [The enemy within].

The chosen people. *Arcade*, 6 Mar 1981, 19. Discusses the Welsh condition.

Of poor Bertolt Brecht. *Arcade*, 26 Jun 1981, 20-21. Review of Bertolt Brecht, *Poems, 1913-1956*, ed. John Willett and Ralph Manheim.

Faith and a nation's fate. *Arcade*, 4 Sep 1981, 14-15. Review article on R. Tudor Jones, *Ffydd ac argyfwng cenedl: hanes crefydd yng Nghymru, 1890-1914*.

*Etifedd y glyn*. *Llais Llyfrau*, Hydref/Autumn 1981, 8-9. On his novel.

A perpetual curate. *PR* 8 (1981) 22-27. Essay on Evan Evans ('Ieuan Fardd'), eighteenth-century poet and scholar.

Sgwrs brawd a chwaer. *Taliesin* 43 (1981) 100-106. [Conversation between brother and sister].

Twee or not twee. *Arcade*, 5 Feb 1982, 9. Letter on use of 'Gwent'.

Llongyfarchion i Saunders Lewis ar ei ben-blwydd. *Barn*, Hyd/Oct 1982, 304. [Congratulations to Saunders Lewis on his birthday].

Newid gosgedd. *Taliesin* 44 (1982) 89-100. [Shape shifting].

Kate Roberts. In *Kate Roberts: ei meddwl a'i gwaith*, ed. Rhydwen Williams. Swansea: Christopher Davies, 1983. pp. 18-19. [Kate Roberts: her thought and work].

Outline of a necessary figure. In *Presenting Saunders Lewis*. Cardiff: University of Wales Press, 1983. pp. 6-13.

The Welsh identity, 1. Mythological fuel for the next generation. *WM*, 15 Jun 1983, 8:D-E. Interview with Terry Campbell.

The Welsh identity, 2. Encroaching power of American English. *WM*, 16 Jun 1983, 8:F. Interview with Terry Campbell.

Jones. *BNW*, Summer 1984, 5. Interviewed by Rheinallt Llwyd on publication of the novel.

Mr Emyr Humphreys: Dydd Mercher, 7 Awst. In *Eisteddfod Genedlaethol Cymru: llawlyfr ac adroddiad*, 1985. pp. 185-186. Presidential address to Rhyl Eisteddfod. – *WM*, 8 August 1985, 9:F-H, reports this, giving extracts in English.

Cyfieithu S.L.. *Y Faner*, 28 Meh/Jun 1985, 14-15. Review of *The plays of Saunders Lewis.* 2 vols (translations into English of six plays).

The road to Rhyl. *Planet* 52 (1985) 81-82. Prefatory comment on extract from *An absolute hero*.

Arcadia oes y cerrig. *Taliesin* 51 (1985) 65-73. [The stone age Arcadia].

Cysgod y pulpud. In *Y gair a'r genedl: cyfrol deyrnged R. Tudor Jones*, ed. E. Stanley John. Abertawe: Tŷ John Penry, 1986. pp. 216-225. [The shadow of the pulpit].

The size of soap. In *Lingue meno diffuse e mezzi d'informazione nella comunita' Europea: problemi della radio-televisione: documenti, relazioni, comunicazioni del Convegno Europeo*. Organizzato da ISPROM, Sardinia 2-5 Oct 1986. pp. 279-283. Conference paper on Welsh-language television.

Dau le: Ffilisota a Castro. *Y Faner*, 13 Maw/Mar 1986, 12-13. [Two places: Filisota and Castro]

The third difficulty. *Planet* 61 (1987) 16-25. Considers traditional art and the novel in relation to contemporary culture and media.

Consurio'r cosmos Cymraeg. *Barn*, Hydref/Autumn 1988, 10-16. Emyr Humphreys interviewed by Gerwyn Williams. – [Conjuring the Welsh cosmos].

Ebychiad. *Barn*, Hydref/Autumn 1988, 16. Poetry. – [Exclamation].

A writer and television. *BNW*, Autumn 1988, 4-5.

Interview: Emyr Humphreys. *NWR* 1,2 [2] (1988) 5-11. Interviewed by Penny Smith.

Under the yoke. *NWR* 1,3 [3] (1988) 9-13. On Kate Roberts.

The dissident condition: Emyr Humphreys interviewed by Murray Watts. *Planet* 71 (1988) 23-29. Edited version of a radio interview.

Native genius. *Sbec*, 4-10 Jun 1988, 4. On Kate Roberts.

Carchar gweir. *Taliesin* 63 (1988) 16-18. Poetry.

Cardiau post. *Taliesin* 65 (1988) 30-31. Poetry.

Ar y Guincho. *Barn*, Hyd/Oct 1989, 41. Poetry.

Postcards (Songs of exile). *PW* 25,2 (1989) 6-9. Poetry.

Poughkeepsie. *Taliesin* 67 (1989) 33-34. Poetry.

Cymodi â ffawd – Norchia. *Taliesin* 68 (1989) 26-27, 28-29. Poetry.

A lost leader? On the Britishness of Huw Weldon. *Planet* 83 (1990) 3-11.

Cara signora. *Taliesin* 71 (1990) 15-17. Poetry.

Aralleiro Montale – Montale, fwy neu lai. *Barn*, Maw/Mar 1990, 43. Poetry.

Tro yn yr allwedd. *Y Faner*, 21 Med/Sep 1990, 9. Text of address at opening of Saunders Lewis memorial, Clynnog Fawr. – [A turn of the key].

Cân serchus. In *Cymru yn fy mhen: casgliad o gerddi*, ed. Dafydd Morgan Lewis. Talybont: Y Lolfa, 1991. pp. 22-23. Poetry. – Text misprints 'heb' for 'hen' (l.4) and omits 'Hon', the first line of the poem.

Gwleidydda. *Golwg*, 7 Chw/Feb 1991, 21. Poetry.

I'r afael ag enaid Cymru: 20 mlynedd o nofelau Emyr Humphreys. *Golwg*, 14 Chw/Feb 1991, 19-22. Interviewed by Dylan Iorwerth. – [Grappling with the soul of Wales].

Y drwydded. *Golwg*, 27 Meh/Jun 1991, 18. Poetry.

Darllen. *Y Gwyliedydd* 51 (Ion/Jan 1992).

Show business. *Planet* 91 (1992) 17-18, Poetry.

Inscribing stones. *PW* 28, 2 (1992) 23-28. Bilingual poetry, English and Welsh.

S.L. i R.S. (Cyfarchiad dychmygol). *PW* 29,1 (1993) 10. Poem in sections numbered i-iv (the last in Welsh).

## A. (iii). Emyr Humphreys: Television Drama (1973-1992)

*The peak.* HTV, 19 Oct 1973, 10.30-11.00pm. Play by Humphreys based on short story of John Gwilym Jones.

*Our American dream.* HTV, 1976. Six-part series on history of the Welsh in America, written and co-produced by Humphreys. – Part 1 transmitted 25 Nov 1976, 10.35-11.20pm.

*Y gosb.* S4C, 6 Jan 1983, 9.30-10.40pm. Drama. 'A story about a Minister and a young boy – both have an experience which changes their life', *Sbec*. – [The penalty].

Ŵyn i'r lladdfa. S4C, 1 Mar 1984, 9.30-10.45pm. Drama. 'A political thriller set in North Wales. An American company wants to buy a disused quarry. Why? How will it affect the community?', *Sbec.* – [Lambs to the slaughter].

*Etifedd y glyn*: drama gyfres mewn chwe phennod gan Emyr Humphreys. BBC Wales, 6 Mar 1984, 12.15-12.45pm. Continued. – [Heir to the valley].

*Hualau.* S4C, 8 Mar 1984, 9.30-10.20pm. Drama. 'Why is Sioned so reluctant to leave the city smog of Birmingham to return home to the beautiful countryside of Anglesey?', *Sbec.* – [Fetters].

*Byw yn rhydd.* S4C, 18 Dec 1984, 9.05-10.55pm. Drama. 'A Welshman living in London faces early retirement. He reviews his life', *Sbec.* – [Living free].

*Angel o'r nef.* S4C, 17 Dec 1985, 9.00-10.25pm. Drama. 'It's Christmas time. A child goes missing', *Sbec.* – [Angel from heaven].

*Teulu Helga.* S4C, 2 Mar 1986, 9.00-10.45pm. Drama. 'Helga's ex-pupils are her "family". When a star pupil returns from London the pleasant façade begins to crumble and the past seems not as rosy as it did', *Sbec.* – [Helga's family].

*Twll o le.* S4C, 21 Apr 1987, 9.30-11.00pm. Drama. 'A play depicting the oppression of unemployment in a deprived area, showing the emotional influences upon its people', *Sbec.* – [Hole of a place].

*Cwlwm cariad.* S4C, 5 May 1987, 9.05-10.05pm. Drama. 'When Janet dies, her husband and daughter face their options for the future', *Sbec.* – [The knot of love].

*The triple net; a portrait of Kate Roberts.* Channel 4, 1988. Four films by Emyr Humphreys, transmitted 8.00-8.30 pm, 25 May, 1 8 15 June 1988. – Also shown S4C, 7.00-7.35pm, 28 May, 4 11 18 June.

*Tudalen '88.* S4C, 25 Jul 1988, 7.30-8.00pm. Includes interview with Emyr Humphreys.

*Yr alwad.* S4C, 24 Dec 1988, 8.55-10.25pm. Drama. 'A young teacher receives threatening phone calls. Whose victim is she?', *Sbec.* – [The call].

*Yr alltud.* S4C, 31 Dec 1989, 9.00-11.00pm. Drama. 'It is May 1945, and a widowed German countess has found refuge in Gwynedd', *Sbec.* – [The exile].

*Y dyn perig.* S4C, 1 Jan 1991, 8.15-9.50pm. Drama, in collaboration with W.S. Jones. 'Things are getting worse between Buddug and her father', *Sbec.* – [A dangerous man].

*Outside time.* Channel 4. Four programmes on the Four branches of the Mabinogi. Transmitted at weekly intervals, the first on 13 Aug 1991, 8.30-9.00pm.

*Dwr a thân.* S4C, 3 May 1992, 9.10-10.15pm. Drama set on Breton campsite. [Water and fire].

*Note also:*
The airy tomb. A film of R.S. Thomas's poem, directed by Emyr Humphreys, 1962. Read by Kenneth Griffiths. – Privately made, in conjunction with Richard, Lord Dynevor, and shot on location at Berthgoed, Pontrhydfendigaid.

## B. Publications about Emyr Humphreys

BARTELS, Irma. Wales in the works of Emyr Humphreys: a study of some of his novels and stories. Thesis. Johannes Gutenberg-Universitat, Mainz, 1982. 114 p. With a letter from Emyr Humphreys on the *Land of the living/Bonds of attachment* series.

BASINI, Mario. Top author lays famous Welsh family to rest. *WM*, 18 Feb 1991. On publication of *Bonds of attachment.* – Incl. brief interview with author.

DAVIES, E. Tegla. Nofel Gymraeg gan Emyr Humphreys. *Baner ac Amserau Cymru*, 25 Rha/Dec 1958, 5. Review article on *Y tri llais.*

DAVIES, Geraint E. The themes of childhood and education in the works of Dylan Thomas and Emyr Humphreys. MEd dissertation. University of Wales (Cardiff), 1981. Incl. The themes of childhood and education in the works of Emyr Humphreys, pp. 66-101.

GRUFFYDD, R. Geraint. Emyr Humphreys. *Taliesin* 71 (1990) 91-92. Presentation speech on occasion of award to Emyr Humphreys of a University of Wales honarary degree.

HOOKER, Jeremy. Land of the living. *Planet* 8 (1971) 68-72. Review article on *Hear and forgive* and *National winner.*

—— A seeing belief: a study of Emyr Humphreys' *Outside the house of Baal. Planet* 39 (1977) 35-43. Reprinted in *The poetry of place: essays and reviews, 1970-1981.* Manchester: Carcanet, 1982. pp. 93-105.

JONES, Bobi. Taliesin's identity kit. *BNW*, Autumn 1983, 3-4. Review article on *The Taliesin tradition.*

JONES, John Gwilym. Dawn Emyr Humphreys. *Yr Arloeswr Newydd* 1 (1959) 17-18. [Emyr Humphreys' talent].

LEWIS, Saunders. Athens and Bethel. *WM*, 28 Oct 1955, 4:C-D. Review article on *A man's estate.*

—— Welsh writers today. In *Presenting Saunders Lewis*, ed. Alun R. Jones and Gwyn Thomas. Cardiff: University of Wales Press, 1973. pp. 164-170. Briefly discusses *A toy epic and Y tri llais.*

LLOYD, Vernon. Variations on a theme by Aeschylus: Desmond Cory and Emyr Humphreys. *AWR* 73 (1983) 49-63.

LLWYD, Elin. Friendship with top author spanned 50 years. *Bangor-Anglesey*

*Mail*, 24 Apr 1991, 17. Emyr Humphreys on his memories of Graham Greene.

LLYWELYN-WILLIAMS, Alun. *Y llenor a'i gymdeithas.* London: B.B.C., 1966. 29 p. (BBC in Wales annual lecture). Incl. discussion of Emyr Humphreys, pp. 22-24. – [The writer and his society].

MATHIAS, Roland. Channels of grace: a view of the earlier novels of Emyr Humphreys. *AWR* 70 (1982) 64-88. Reprinted in *A ride through the wood: essays on Anglo-Welsh literature.* Bridgend: Poetry Wales Press, 1985. pp. 206-233.

—— Emyr Humphreys. In *British novelists, 1930-1959. Part 1: A-L*, ed. Bernard Oldsey. Detroit: Gale, 1983. (Dictionary of literary biography; 15). pp. 195-206.

—— Emyr Humphreys. In *Contemporary novelists*, ed. Lesley Henderson. 5th ed. Chicago; London: St James Press, 1991. pp. 465-466. Incl. listing of radio and TV plays.

MORGAN, André. Three voices: Emyr Humphreys' *A toy epic* and some comparisons with *Y tri llais. Planet* 39 (1977) 44-49.

—— Protestantism and nationhood in the novels of Emyr Humphreys. MA thesis. University of Wales (Aberystwyth), 1981. 233 p. Incl. bibliography, pp. 224-233.

MORGAN, Derec Llwyd. Emyr Humphreys: llenor y llwyth. In *Ysgrifau beirniadol VII*, ed. J.E. Caerwyn Williams. Denbigh: Gee, [1971]. pp. 285-303. [Emyr Humphreys: writer of the tribe].

MORRIS, Jan. Identifying the identity. *Encounter*, May 1984. 66-67. Review article on *The Taliesin tradition.*

NEWBY, P. H. *The novel, 1945-1950.* London: Longmans, Green for the British Council, [n.d.]. Incl. discussion of Emyr Humphreys, p.37.

ROBERTS, Ioan. Portread: Emyr Humphreys. *Y Bangoriad* 3,1 (1973) 28-32. [Portrait: Emyr Humphreys].

THOMAS, Karen. Cloffi rhwng dau feddwl. *Barn*, Ebr/Apr 1983, 115-117. Discusses *Outside the house of Baal.* – [In two minds].

THOMAS, M. Wynn. *Salt of the earth. BNW*, Summer 1985, 7-8. Review article.

—— *Open secrets. BNW*, Summer 1988, 5-6. Review article, setting novel in context of the *Land of the living/Bonds of attachment* series.

—— Hanes dwy chwaer: olrhain hanes *Y tri llais*, 1. Barn, Ion/Jan 1989, 23-25; Chw/Feb 1989, 23-25. Traces novel's compositional history. – [The story of two sisters: an outline of *Y tri llais*].

—— Ynddo mae Cymru'n un. *Golwg*, 20 Ebr/Apr 1989, 23. [Wales is one in him].

—— *Emyr Humphreys.* Caernarfon: Gwasg Pantycelyn, 1989. 96 p. (Llên y llenor). Incl. bibliography, pp. 94-96. – Critical study in Welsh.

—— Timely tribute to top writer. *WM*, 12 May 1989, 14:B-E. On Radio Cymru documentary to mark author's seventieth birthday.

—— The poetry of Emyr Humphreys. *PW* 25,2 (1989) 10-12.

—— The relentlessness of Emyr Humphreys. *NWR* 4,1 [13] (1991) 37-40. Review article on *Bonds of attachment.*

—— Emyr Humphreys: mythic realist. In *English studies 3: proceedings of the third conference om the literature of region and nation. Part 1*, ed. J.J. Simon and

Alain Sinner. Luxembourg: Centre Universitaire de Luxembourg, 1991. pp. 264-281.

—— *Internal difference: twentieth-century writing in Wales.* Cardiff: University of Wales Press, 1992. Incl.: Flintshire and the regional weather forecast, pp. 68-81 – A corner of Wales, pp. 82-106. – First essay, on *A toy epic* and Emlyn Williams, *The corn is green*, appeared in *NWR* 3,1 [9] (1990) 10-15. – Second reprinted from 1989 Seren Books edition of *A toy epic*.

Williams, Ioan. *Emyr Humphreys.* Cardiff: University of Wales Press [for] the Welsh Arts Council, 1980. 97 p.: front. port. (Writers of Wales). Incl. bibliography, pp. 89-93. – 'Limited to 1000 copies'.

—— The land of the living. *Planet* 52 (1985) 97-105.

—— Emyr Humphreys, *Open secrets. NWR* 1,2 [2] (1988) 11-14. Review article.

—— Y clymau byw. *Golwg,* 21 Chw/Feb 1991, 23. Review of *Bonds of attachment.*

Williams, Gerwyn. Options and allegiances: Emyr Humphreys and Welsh literature. *Planet* 71 (1988) 30-36.

—— Cymodi 'r gorffennol. *Barn,* Gor/Jul, 41-43. Review article on *Bonds of attachment.*

# DAVID JONES (1895-1974)

A. Publications by David Jones
   (i)   Books
   (ii)  Selected contributions to books and periodicals

B. Publications about David Jones
   (i)   Critical studies
   (ii)  *David Jones Society Newsletter*
   (iii) David Jones: exhibition catalogues


## A (i). Publications by David Jones: Books

*In parenthesis: seinnyessit e gledyf ym penn mameu*. London: Faber, 1937.
xv, 226 p.: 3 leaves of plates. Incl. frontispiece, endpiece and map by
author.
—— 1961. Incl. A note of introduction, by T.S. Eliot, vii-viii. – 'Limited
to seventy numbered copies, signed by the author and T.S. Eliot. Fifty copies
only are for sale.'
—— 1963. pbk. ISBN: 0-571-05661-X [1975- ]. 'For the 1978 impression a
few corrections have been made to the text, following information given by
David Jones before his death to Professor William Blissett.'

U.S. eds.: New York: Chilmark Press, 1962. 224 p.: ill.
—— New York: Viking Press, [1963]. pbk. (Compass books; C139).


*The anathemata: fragments of an attempted writing*. London: Faber, 1952.
243 p.: 9 plates. Incl. 7 inscriptions, 1 drawing, 1 engraving. – Reissued
1972, pbk. ISBN: 0-571-10127-5.

U.S. eds.: New York: Chilmark Press, 1964. 243 p.: ill.
—— New York: Viking Press, [1965]. 224 p.: ill. pbk. (Compass books;
C179).


*Epoch and artist: selected writings by David Jones* / edited by Harman
Grisewood. London: Faber, 1959. 320 p.: front. Contents: Autobiographical
talk – The preface to *In parenthesis* – Wales and the Crown – Changes
in the Coronation service – Welshness in Wales – Welsh Wales – Welsh
poetry – George Borrow and Wales – Art and democracy – Religion and
the muses – The preface to *The anathemata* – Past and present – Art
and sacrament – The utile, a note to 'Art and sacrament' – The viae, the
Roman roads in Britain – The heritage of early Britain – The Arthurian
legend – The myth of Arthur – The eclipse of a hymn – Abstract art –

A note on Mr. Berenson's views – If and perhaps and but – Christopher Smart – Eric Gill as sculptor – Eric Gill: an appreciation – James Joyce's Dublin. – Reissued 1973, pbk. ISBN: 0-571-10152-6.

U.S. ed.: New York: Chilmark Press, 1959.

*The fatigue: c. A.V.C. DCCLXXXIV tantis labor non sit cassus.* Cambridge: Rampant Lions Press, 1965. xii, 20 p. Incl.: Introductory note, by David Jones – List of subscribers. – 'Privately printed [for] the friends and admirers of David Jones on the occasion of his seventieth birthday ... The edition is limited to 298 copies of which fifty, numbered I to L in Roman numerals, are for presentation to David Jones ... seven, lettered A to G, are for presentation to the National Libraries of Great Britain and Ireland and to the Library of Congress ... and 241 are reserved for subscribers to the Birthday fund ... [printed] by Will and Sebastian Carter at the Rampant Lions Press.'

*The tribune's visitation.* London: Fulcrum Press, 1969. [33] p.: ill. Title-page design by the author. – '150 copies have been numbered and signed by the author.'

French trans.: La visite du tribun, tr. Louis Bonnerot, Lucien Malarmey and Jean Mambrino. *Études*, Avr/Apr 1973, 589-603.

*An introduction to 'The rime of the ancient mariner'.* London: Clover Hill Editions, 1972. 40 p.: ill. (Clover Hill editions; 7). Incl. Editorial note, by Douglas Cleverdon. – A continuation of Jones's foreword to his illustrated edition of the poem. – '115 copies numbered I-CXV signed by the author and 215 copies numbered 1-215 ... designed and printed by Will and Sebastian Carter at the Rampant Lions Press'.

*The sleeping lord and other fragments.* London: Faber, 1974. 111 p.: ill. ISBN: 0-571-10350-2. Contents: A,a,a, domine Deus – The wall – The dream of Private Clitus – *The fatigue* – *The tribune's visitation* – The tutelar of the place – The hunt – The sleeping lord – from 'The book of Balaam's ass'. – Also signed edition 1974, ISBN: 0-571-10584-X, with frontispiece and title-page inscribed by author; 150 copies.

French trans.: Le rêve du simple soldat Clitus, tr. Louis Bonnerot. *Agenda* 5, 1-3 (1967) 128-134.

*The Kensington mass.* London: Agenda Editions, 1975. 19 p.: 14 p. of plates: pbk. ISBN: 0-902400-15-0. 'Printed version tentatively constructed from the various drafts of this ms. by René Hague'. – Plates A-O reproduce worksheets.

*Use and sign: an essay.* Ipswich: Golgonooza Press, 1975. 10 p.: pamph. 'This edition is limited to 350 numbered copies.' – First published in *Listener*, 24 May 1962, as transcript of radio broadcast. – Reissued 1976,

ISBN: 0-903880-11-3; 'the present reprint consists of a further 250 unnumbered copies'.

*David Jones: letters to Vernon Watkins* / edited with notes by Ruth Pryor; foreword by Gwen Watkins. Cardiff: University of Wales Press, 1976. 79 p.: front. ISBN: 0-7083-0616-0. Incl. Note on David Jones [from the National Eisteddfod Catalogue, 1964], by Vernon Watkins.

*The dying Gaul and other writings* / edited with an introduction by Harman Grisewood. London: Faber, 1978. 230 p.: ill. ISBN: 0-571-11067-3. Contents: Introduction, pp. 9-13 – In illo tempore – On the difficulties of one writer of Welsh affinity whose language is English – A London artist looks at contemporary Wales – Notes on the 1930s – The dying Gaul – An aspect of the art of England – Wales and visual form – The Roland epic and ourselves – The death of Harold – The Welsh dragon – Welsh culture – Art in relation to war – A Christmas message, 1960 – Use and sign – *An introduction to 'The rime of the ancient mariner'.*

*Letters to William Hayward* / edited by Colin Wilcockson. London: Agenda Editions, 1979. 79 p.: 2 p. of plates: pbk. ISBN: 0-902400-24-X.

*Introducing David Jones: a selection of his writings* / edited by John Matthias; with a preface by Stephen Spender. London: Faber, 1980. 237 p.: ill.: hbk & pbk. ISBN: 0-571-11526-8 hbk, 0-571-11525-X pbk. Incl.: Introduction, by John Matthias, pp. 13-30 – A, a, a, domine Deus – Selections from: *In parenthesis, The anathemata, The sleeping lord and other fragments* [i.e. *The tribune's visitation*, The tutelar of the place, The hunt, The sleeping lord]. – With 1 map and 2 inscriptions.
—— *Selected works of David Jones from* In parenthesis, The anathemata, The sleeping lord / edited by John Matthias. Cardiff: University of Wales Press; Orono: University of Maine/National Poetry Foundation, 1992. 237 p.: pbk. ISBN: 0-7083-1169-5. – A reissue of the 1980 Faber selection, omitting the Stephen Spender preface and with a new prefatory note by John Matthias.

*Dai greatcoat: a self-portrait of David Jones in his letters* / edited by René Hague. London: Faber, 1980. 273 p.: front. port. ISBN: 0-571-11540-3.

*David Jones: letters to a friend* / [edited by] Aneirin Talfan Davies. Swansea: Triskele, 1980. 120 p.: front. port.: 4 p. of plates. ISBN: 0-904652-02-5. Incl.: Introduction, by Aneirin Talfan Davies, pp. 7-29 – Appendix I. An introduction to David Jones' 'Dream of Private Clitus' – Appendix II. Broadcasts by and about David Jones produced by Aneirin Talfan Davies – Appendix III. Introductions by David Jones to radio readings of 'The wall' and 'The tutelar of the place'.

*The narrows* / with an introduction by Roland Mathias. Budleigh Salterton: Interim Press, 1981. [20] p.: pamph. ISBN: 0-0904675-18-1. Incl. Narrows and the western empire, by Eric Ratcliffe.

French trans.: Le chenal, tr. Christine Pagnoulle. *Le Journal des Poètes*, Aou/Aug 1977, 12-14.

**The Roman quarry and other sequences** / edited by Harman Grisewood and René Hague. London: Agenda Editions, 1981. xxviii, 283 p.: ill.: hbk & pbk. ISBN: 0-902400-26-6 hbk, 0-902400-27-4 pbk. Contents: The Roman quarry – The narrows – Under Arcturus – *The Kensington Mass* – Caillech – The Grail Mass – The old quarry, part 1 – The agent – The old quarry, part 2 – The book of Balaam's ass – Commentary, by René Hague, pp. 213-283.

U.S. ed.: New York: Sheep Meadow Press, 1982. ISBN: 0-935296-25- 5 hbk, 0-935296-24-7 pbk.

**The engravings of David Jones: a survey** / by Douglas Cleverdon. London: Clover Hill Editions, 1981. x, 58 p.: 96 p. of plates. (Clover Hill editions; 12). Contents: A survey of the engravings of David Jones, by Douglas Cleverdon, pp. 1-20 – A list of engravings, pp. 21-58 – Selected engravings, pp. [1-96]. – '6 copies on vellum, lettered A to F, each with a portfolio containing sets of the engravings [full-leather binding, slipcase quarter leather], 105 copies on J. Barcham Green handmade paper ... numbered I-CV each with a portfolio containing a set of the engravings [quarter leather binding, slipcase cloth], 260 copies on vélin d'Arches numbered 1-260 [cloth binding, in cloth slipcase], 75 portfolios numbered i-lxxv each containing a set of the engravings [in cloth box].' – Designed and printed by Will and Sebastian Carter at the Rampant Lions Press. – Also printed, 500 copies of a 4-page Prospectus, with plate.

**Inner necessities: the letters of David Jones to Desmond Chute** / edited and introduced by Thomas Dilworth. Toronto: Anson-Cartwright Editions, 1984. 101 p.: ill. ISBN: 0-919974-09-0. Incl.: Introduction, pp. 9-19 – Appendix. Desmond Chute's review of *The anathemata* [*Downside Review*, Summer 1953], pp. 93-101. – With 3 wood engravings, 2 by David Jones. – 'One thousand copies have been printed.'

# A (ii). Publications by David Jones: Selected Contributions to Books and Periodicals

This selection mostly covers David Jones's letters, essays and interviews. For a full guide to his visual art see Cleverdon [above] and Gray [section B (i)]; below are listed his three outstanding early achievements.

*The Book of Jonah: taken from the authorized version of King James 1* / with engravings on wood by David Jones. Waltham St. Lawrence: Golden Cockerel Press, 1926. 15p.: ill. 'The edition is limited to [175] copies.'
—— 'authorised'. London: Clover Hill Editions, 1979. 19 p.: ill. (Clover Hill editions; 11). ISBN: 0-9500388-4-X. '10 copies on vellum, lettered A to J, with a portfolio containing sets of engravings ... 100 copies on ...

hand-made paper numbered I to C, with an extra set of the engravings on japon. 300 copies on mould-made paper, numbered 1 to 300, 60 sets of the engravings, printed on japon, in folders numbered i to lx ... The thirteen engravings .... were first printed in 1926 at the Golden Cockerel Press.' – 'Printed by Will Carter ... at the Rampant Lions Press, Cambridge.'

*The Chester play of the deluge* / edited by J. Isaacs; with engravings on wood by David Jones. Waltham St. Lawrence: Golden Cockerel Press, 1927. iv, 16 p.: ill. 'This edition is limited to [275] copies.' – 'In the opinion of some the engravings ... are the greatest graphic achievement of the Press. They are, however, very poorly printed in the book' (*Chanticleer: a bibliography of the Golden Cockerel Press*).
—— with ten wood-engravings by David Jones. London: Clover Hill Editions, 1977. 32p.: ill. (Clover Hill editions; 9). Incl. publisher's note, by Douglas Cleverdon. – '7 copies on vellum, lettered A to G ... bound ... in full morocco, with a separate portfolio containing three sets of the wood-engravings on vellum ... 80 copies on Barcham Green hand-made paper ... numbered I to LXXX, bound in quarter-morocco, with a separate set of the wood-engravings on japon ... 250 copies on Barcham Green mould-made paper, numbered 1 to 250 ... printed by Will Carter at the Rampant Lions Press, Cambridge.'

*The rime of the ancient mariner* / with ten engravings on copper by David Jones. Bristol: Douglas Cleverdon, 1929. 37 p.: 8 leaves of plates. 'Of this edition ... there have been printed ten copies numbered I to X [signed] ... sixty copies numbered 1 to 60 [signed] ... four hundred copies numbered 61 to 460.'

US ed.: / with a foreword by David Jones. New York: Chilmark Press, 1964. 37p.: 8 leaves of plates: in slipcase. (Clover Hill editions of the Chilmark Press; 1). 'Of this edition ... there have been printed 115 copies, numbered I to CXV and signed by the artist with a portfolio containing an extra set of fifteen engravings ... 200 copies, numbered 1 to 200 ... printed ... under the supervision of Douglas Cleverdon ... by Will and Sebastian Carter at the Rampant Lions Press.'

Reply to *Wales* questionnaire 1946. *Wales* 2nd ser. 6,2 [22] (1946) 84-88.

History and pre-history. *DL* 6,16 (1955) 18-21.

The Great War and the Welsh. *London Welshman*, Dec 1964, 3-4. Interview.

David Jones at seventy. *London Welshman*, Nov 1965, 4. An interview with Bryn Griffiths.

[Interview]. In *The poet speaks: interviews with contemporary poets*, ed. Peter Orr. London: Routledge, 1966. pp. 97-104.

Ray Howard-Jones: an introduction. *AWR* 17,39 (1968) 53-54.

Saunders Lewis introduces two letters from David Jones. *Mabon* [English] 1,5 (1972) 15-25. Reprinted in *Agenda* 11,4-12,1 (1973-4) 17-29.

A letter from David Jones. *PW* 8,3 (1972) 5-9.

Introduction. In *Presenting Saunders Lewis*, ed. Alun R. Jones and Gwyn Thomas. Cardiff: University of Wales Press, 1973. pp. xvii-xix.

Yr iaith. *Planet* 21 (1974) 3-5. 'Written ... for the adoption meeting of Valerie Wynne-Williams, Plaid Cymru parliamentary candidate for the Barry constituency.'

An awful outsider: some letters from David Jones [to Vernon Watkins], introduced by Gwen Watkins. *AWR* 24,54 (1975) 15-36.

David Jones: three letters, edited by Roland Mathias. *AWR* 61 (1978) 53-65. Two to Wyn Griffith, one to Mr Diffey, secretary of 15th (London Welsh) Battalion, Royal Welsh Fusiliers' Association.

Extract from a letter to Father Desmond Chute. *Agenda* 17,3-4/18,1 (1979-80) 273-277.

David Jones: letters to H. S. Ede, selected and edited by John Matthias. *PN Review* 22 (1981) 10-16.

David Jones: letters to H. S. Ede. *Notre Dame English Journal* 14,2 (1982) 129-144.

A new David Jones letter. *Notre Dame English Journal* 14,2 (1982) 145-146.

David Jones on art and culture: a distillation from his essays and letters. *Agenda* 26,4 (1988) 72-80. Selection by Edmund Gray.

Staudt, Kathleen Henderson. David Jones: eight previously unpublished letters to Vernon Watkins. *AWR* 87 (1988) 76-90.

An unpublished appreciation of Gerard Manley Hopkins, ed. Kathleen H. Staudt. *Agenda* 31,3 (1993) 72-80. Drafted 1968.

Dilworth, Thomas. A try-out: David Jones's 'A French version'. *London Magazine*, 33,12 (1993) 73-79. A previously unpublished essay dating from 1916 and the earliest surviving extended writing by David Jones.

# B (i). Publications about David Jones: Critical Studies

The list that follows is highly selective. The major guide is Samuel Rees, *David Jones: an annotated bibliography and guide to research* (1977), updated by

Rees in *David Jones: man and poet*, ed. John Matthias (1989). Note that there have been two collections of critical essays on David Jones, edited by Roland Mathias (1976) and John Matthias (1989). Their contents are given below.

ACTON, Carol Gillian. Paradox in parenthesis: a comparative study of the war poetry of Wilfred Owen, Charles Sorley, Isaac Rosenberg, Ivor Gurney and David Jones. PhD thesis. Queen's University at Kingston (Canada), 1989.

AYKROYD, Freda. Echoes in the work of Alun Lewis and David Jones. *PW* 23,2-3 (1988) 71-89.

ALEXANDER, Michael. David Jones, hierophant. *Agenda* 5,1-3 (1967) 116-123.

—— The secret princes: a study of David Jones's *In parenthesis. Mabon* [English] 1,7 (1974) 25-33.

—— David Jones. *Agenda* 16,2 (1978) 26-32. Review article on David Jones, *The dying Gaul*, Rene Hague, *A commentary on* The anathemata.

—— David Jones, an introduction: the unknown modernist. *Scripsi* [University of Melbourne] 2 (1984) 257-298.

—— The poetry of David Jones. In *English and American literature: continuity and change:* proceedings of the Fourth International Conference in English Studies, Cracow, 1987, ed. Marta Gibińska and Zygmunt Mazler. Cracow: Uniwersytet Jagielloński, 1989. pp. 93-100.

ALLCHIN, A. M. *The world is a wedding.* London: Darton, Longman & Todd, 1978. Incl. A discovery of David Jones, pp. 157-167. – Reprinted from *Theology*, Jun 1973, 283-291.

AUSTIN, Diana L. A study of *In parenthesis*, by David Jones. DPhil thesis. University of Oxford, 1983.

—— O sisters two what may we do?: musical allusion and the female in David Jones's *In parenthesis. English Studies in Canada* 15,1 (1989) 66-79.

BARD, Glenn Taylor. An elucidation of 'The sleeping lord', by David Jones. MA thesis. University of Wales (Bangor), 1978.

BARNARD, John. The murder of Falstaff: David Jones and the disciplines of war. In *Evidence in literary scholarship: essays in memory of James Marshall Osborn*, ed. René Wellek and Alvaro Ribeiro. Oxford: Clarendon Press, 1979. pp. 13-27.

BARTLETT, Neil. David Jones: 'Cara Wallia derelicta'. In *The Celtic consciousness*, ed. Robert O'Driscoll. New York: Braziller, 1982. pp. 489-497.

BELL, David. *The artist in Wales.* London: Harrap, 1957. Incl. discussion of David Jones, pp. 176-178.

BERGAN, Brooke. Sacred site: the poetics of piety. *Religion and Literature* 22,1 (1990) 39-57.

BERGONZI, Bernard. *Heroes' twilight: a study of the literature of the Great War.* London: Macmillan, 1980. Incl. Remythologising: David Jones's *In parenthesis*, pp. 198-212. – First published 1965.

BLAMIRES, David. 'Kynge Arthur ys nat dede'. *Agenda* 5,1-3 (1967) 159-171.

—— The ordered world: *The anathemata* of David Jones. Agenda 5,1-3 (1967) 101-111.

—— 'Roma aurea Roma' in the writings of David Jones. *AWR* 22,50 (1973) 44-57.

—— David Jones: the sacramental vision. *Quaker Monthly*, Dec 1977, 237-240. Reprinted from *Reynard* 30 (1976) 17-20.

—— *David Jones: artist and writer*. Manchester: Manchester Uuniversity Press., 1978. xiv, 220 p.: ill. Incl. select bibliography, pp. 207-213. – First published 1971.

—— Portrait of the artist. *Radio Times*, 29 Aug 1981, 13-14. Accompanying the broadcast of *In parenthesis*.

—— *David Jones and the nativity: a Christmas essay*. Manchester: [Author], 1982. 16 p.: ill. Incl. Animals kneeling, an engraving by David Jones.

—— The use of the Bible in 'The Roman quarry' of David Jones. In *Backgrounds for the Bible*, ed. Michael Patrick O'Connor and David Noel Freedman. Winona Lake: Eisenbrauns, 1987.

—— David Jones. In *Reference guide to English literature*, ed. D.L. Kirkpatrick. 2nd ed. 3 vols. Chicago; London: St James Press, 1991. Vol. 2, pp. 791-792.

BLISSETT, William. David Jones: himself at the cavemouth. *UTQ* 36 (1967) 259-273.

—— *In parenthesis* among the war books. *UTQ* 42 (1973) 258-288.

—— *The long conversation: a memoir of David Jones*. Oxford: Oxford University Press, 1981. 159 p., 8 p. of plates.

—— To make a shape in words. *Renascence* 38 (1986) 67-81.

BONNEROT, Louis. David Jones: down the traversed history-paths. *Agenda* 5,1-3 (1967) 124-127.

—— David Jones: poète du sacré. *Études*, Avr/Apr 1973, 575-588.

—— David Jones and the notion of fragments. *Agenda* 11,4-12,1 (1973-74) 76-89.

BRESLIN, John Bernard. David Jones: the making of a sacramental poetic. PhD thesis. Yale University, 1983. 284 p.

—— David Jones: the shaping of a poet's mind. *Renascence* 38 (1986) 83-102.

CAMPBELL, Andrew Marchant. Geology in modern poetry. PhD thesis. University of Kentucky, 1985. 168 p. Examines David Jones, Paul Metcalf, Hugh MacDiarmid, Ronald Duncan and Christopher Dewdney.

CASTAY, Marie-Thérèse. À propos de *L'anathemata* de David Jones. *Caliban* 13 (1976) 113-123.

CHARLES, R.L. David Jones: some recently acquired works. *Amgueddfa: Journal of the National Museum of Wales* 22 (1976) 2-13. With reproductions.

CLARK, Kenneth. Some recent paintings of David Jones. *Agenda* 5,1-3 (1967) 97-100.

CLEVERDON, Douglas. David Jones and broadcasting. *PW* 8,3 (1972) 72-81.

COHEN, Joseph. Depth and control in David Jones' *In parenthesis*. *PW* 17,4 (1982) 46-52.

COLLINS, Michael J. The achievement of David Jones. *PW* 17,4 (1982) 35-36.

[COOK], Diane DeBell. Strategies of survival: David Jones, *In parenthesis* and

Robert Graves, *Goodbye to all that*. In *The first world war in fiction: a collection of critical essays*, ed. Holger Klein. London: Macmillan, 1976. pp. 160-173.

—— Poetry and religion in the major writings of David Jones. PhD thesis. University of East Anglia, 1981.

COOPER, John Xiros. The writing of the seen world: David Jones's *In parenthesis*. *UTQ* 48 (1979) 303-312.

CORCORAN, Neil. David Jones's *The anathemata*: a study of its background and significance. MLitt thesis. University of Oxford, 1980.

—— *The song of deeds: a study of* The anathemata *of David Jones*. Cardiff: University of Wales Press, 1982. xi, 120 p. Incl. bibliography, pp. 115-118.

DALY, Anne Carson. The amphibolic structure of *The anathemata*: David Jones's rhetoric of 'anamnesis'. PhD thesis. Johns Hopkins University, 1980. 347 p.

—— Transubstantiation and technology in the work of David Jones. *Notre Dame English Journal* 14 (1982) 217-230.

—— *The anathemata*: a brilliant modernist poem. *PW* 17,4 (1982) 53-58.

—— The amphibolic title of *The anathemata*: a key to the structure of the poem. *Renascence* 35 (1982) 49-63.

—— Hills as the sacramental landscape in *The anathemata*. *Renascence* 38 (1986) 131-139.

DAVIE, Donald. *Under Briggflatts: a history of poetry in Great Britain, 1960-1988*. Manchester: Carcanet, 1989. Incl. discussion of David Jones, pp. 158-163.

DAVIES, Aneirin Talfan. Gyda gwawr y bore. Llandybïe: Llyfrau'r Dryw, 1970. Incl. Awenydd y pethe, pp. 46-55. – Essay on Jones reprinted from *WM*, 22 Nov 1965, 8.

—— A note on David Jones. *PW* 2,1 (1966) 33-36. Reprinted in *Agenda* 5,1-3 (1967) 172-175.

—— Ar ymyl y ddalen. *Barn*, Sep 1973, 477-478. [In the margin].

DAVIES, Pennar. London-Welsh islander. *PW* 8,3 (1972) 10-13.

DE SOMOGYI, Stephen. David Jones and the historic deposits of Wales and the island of Britain. *PW* 15,1 (1979) 81-103.

DEANE, Patrick. Raising a valid sign: a defence of the form of David Jones's *Anathemata*. PhD thesis. University of Western Ontario, 1986.

—— The fate of narrative in David Jones's, *The anathemata*. *UTQ* 57 (1987-88) 306-320.

DELANEY, Paul. Great illustrators: David Jones. *Antiquarian Book Monthly Review* 7 (1980) 480-487. Replies by Douglas Cleverdon, Paul Delaney, *ABMR* 7 (1980) 571-572.

DILWORTH, Thomas. The parenthetical liturgy of David Jones. *UTQ* 42 (1973) 241-257.

—— The technique of allusion in the major poems of David Jones. PhD thesis. University of Toronto, 1977.

—— David Jones's use of a geology text for *The anathemata*. *English Language Notes* 15 (1977) 115-119. On the poet's use of William Whitehead Watts, *Geology for beginners*.

—— *The liturgical parenthesis of David Jones*. Ipswich: Golgonooza Press, 1979. 34 p.

—— The anagogical form of *The anathemata*. *Mosaic* 12,2 (1979) 183-195.

—— A book to remember by: David Jones's glosses on *A history of the Great War*. *Papers of the Bibliographical Society of America* 74,3 (1980) 221-234. On *A history of the 38th (Welsh) division*, ed. Lt-Col. J. E. Munby (1920).

—— David Jones's glosses on *The anathemata*. *Studies in Bibliography* 33 (1980) 239-253.

—— Wales and the imagination of David Jones. *AWR* 69 (1981) 41-52.

—— Introducing David Jones. *Georgia Review* 35 (1981) 437-441.

—— *In parenthesis* as chronicle. *PW* 17,4 (1982) 37-45.

—— Arthur's wake: the shape of meaning in David Jones's 'The sleeping lord'. *AWR* 76 (1984) 59-72.

—— David Jones and Gerard Manley Hopkins. In *Hopkins among the poets: studies in modern responses to Gerard Manley Hopkins*. Hamilton, Ontario: International Hopkins Association, 1985. pp. 53-57.

—— The arts of David Jones. *Religion and Literature* 17 (1985) 89-98. Review article, with particular reference to Elizabeth Ward, *David Jones: mythmaker*.

—— Sex and the goddess in the poetry of David Jones. *UTQ* 54 (1985) 251-264.

—— David Jones and fascism. *Journal of Modern Literature* 13 (1986) 149-162.

—— Form versus content in David Jones's *The tribune's visitation*. *Renascence* 38 (1986) 103-116.

—— David Jones's 'The hunt'. *AWR* 85 (1987) 93-102.

—— The city at the centre of *The anathemata*. *Neohelicon* [Hungary] 14 (1987) 345-352.

—— *The shape of meaning in the poetry of David Jones*. Toronto: University of Toronto Press, 1988. xii, 434 p.: ill.

DORENKAMP, Angela G. Time and sacrament in *The anathemata*. *Renascence* 23 (1971) 183-191.

—— In the order of signs: an introduction to the poetry of David Jones. PhD thesis. University of Connecticut, 1974. 242 p.

DUNTHORNE, Kirstine Brander. *Artists exhibited in Wales, 1945-74*. Cardiff: Welsh Arts Council, 1976. Incl. list of David Jones's appearances in exhibitions, pp 164-166.

EAVES, Christine. The significance of *Y Gododdin* to David Jones's *In parenthesis*. *Ariel* 15,3 (1984) 51-59.

EDE, H.S. The visual art of David Jones. *Agenda* 5,1-3 (1967) 153-158.

ELIOT, T.S. A note on *In parenthesis* and *The anathemata*. *DL* 6,16 (1955) 21-23.

EVANS, Geraint Gwilym. The correspondence of Saunders Lewis and David Jones. MA thesis. University of Wales (Swansea), 1987.

FLEISHMAN, Avrom. Giants in the earth: recent myths for British poets. *ELH* 51 (1984) 185-205. Considers David Jones, Jeremy Hooker and others.

FOWKES, Robert. Helaethrwydd locer Dafydd Jones. *Ninnau* [USA] 4,5 (1979). [The abundance of David Jones's locker].

FRIEDMAN, Barton. Tolkien and David Jones: the Great War and the War of the Ring. *Clio* 11,2 (1982) 115-136.

FUSSELL, Paul. *The Great War and modern memory*. London, New York: Oxford University Press, 1975. Incl. The honourable miscarriage of *In parenthesis*, pp. 144-154.

GALLAGHER, E.J. The mythopoetic impulse in the poetry of David Jones. PhD thesis. University of Manchester, 1980.

GEMMILL, Janet Powers. *In parenthesis*: a study of narrative technique. *Journal of Modern Literature* 1 (1971) 311-328.

GIARDELLI, Arthur. Three related works by David Jones. *PW* 8,3 (1972) 60-71. On 'Manawydan's glass door', 'Cara Wallia derelicta', 'Y cyfarchiad i Fair'. – Reprinted in *Agenda* 11,4-12,1 (1973-74) 90-98. – Revised, in *David Jones: man and poet*, cd. John Matthias (1989).

—— 'Tristan ac Esyllt'. *Agenda* 11,4-12,1 (1973-74) 50-53. Welsh version: *Barn*, Med/Sep 1973, 498-500.

—— Artists as friends: Ceridwen Lloyd Morgan interviews Arthur Giardelli. *Planet* 77 (1989) 51-59.

GRANT, Patrick. *Six modern authors and the problems of belief.* London: Macmillan, 1979. Incl. Belief in religion: David Jones, pp. 67-92.

GRAY, Edmund. The representational art of David Jones and Ben Nicholson: an analysis and a moral. *Agenda* 12,4-13,1 (1975-76) 126-134.

GRAY, Nicolete. David Jones. *Signature* n. ser. 8 (1949) 46-56.

—— David Jones and the art of lettering. *Agenda* 5,1-3 (1967) 146-152.

—— *The painted inscriptions of David Jones.* London: Gordon Fraser, 1981. 113 p.: ill. Contents: Introduction, pp. 8-26 – Catalogue of inscriptions, list of minor inscriptions, book plates, book jackets, record sleeves, pp. 27-102 – Extracts from letters, pp. 103-109 – Select bibliography.

—— *The paintings of David Jones.* London: Lund Humphries in association with the Tate Gallery, 1988. [120] p.: ill.

GRISEWOOD, Harman. A personal memoir. *Blackfriars*, Feb 1941, 90-94.

—— David Jones. *Blackfriars*, Apr 1951, 151-155.

—— David Jones (1965). In *Wales on the wireless: a broadcasting anthology*, ed. Patrick Hannan. Llandysul: Gomer in assoc. with BBC Cymru/Wales, 1988. pp. 29-31.

—— *David Jones: artist and writer.* London: BBC, 1966. 32 p.: ill. (Annual lecture of the BBC in Wales; 1965). Frontispiece woodcut by David Jones, Y briodferch.

—— Remembering David Jones. *Journal of Modern Literature* 14 (1988) 565-576.

HAGUE, René. David Jones: a reconnaissance. *Agenda* 5,1-3 (1967) 57-75.

—— *David Jones.* Cardiff: University of Wales Press [for] the Welsh Arts Council, 1975. 91p.: front. port. (Writers of Wales). Incl. select bibliography, pp. 85-87. – 'Edition ... limited to 1000 copies'.

—— The clarity of David Jones. *Agenda* 12,4-13,1 (1975-76) 109-125.

—— *A commentary on* The anathemata *of David Jones.* Wellingborough: Christopher Skelton, 1977. xii, 264 p.: ill. Incl. Bibliography, pp. 263-264. – Frontispiece portrait by Eric Gill.

—— Myth and mystery in the poetry of David Jones. *Agenda* 15,2-3 (1977) 37-79.

HALSALL, T. Then-ness and now-ness: a study of modern and historical elements in the major works of David Jones. MPhil thesis, University of Warwick, 1977.

HEATH-STUBBS, John. Strata. *Agenda* 11,4-12,1 (1973-74) 64-67. Review article on *The sleeping lord and other fragments*.

HILL, Greg. The feminine principle in the works of David Jones. MA thesis. University of Wales (Aberystwyth), 1985. 103 p. Incl. bibliography, pp. 89-103.

HILLS, Paul. The radiant art of David Jones. *Agenda* 10,4-11,1 (1972-73) 125-137.

—— A list of works in public collections by David Jones. *Agenda* 11,4-12,1 (1973-74) 99-101.

HINCHLIFFE, Michael. Welsh and foreign words in David Jones's 'The sleeping lord'. *Caliban* 18 (1981) 33-43.

—— David Jones et la guerre de 1914-1918: le héros entre parenthèses. In *Le mythe du héros: actes du colloque interdisciplinaire, Centre Axois de Recherches Anglaises, 12-14 Mars 1982*, ed. N.J. Rigaud. Aix-en-Provence: Publications Université de Provence, 1982. pp. 165-183.

—— David Jones, poète épique: oralité et intertextualité dans 'The book of Balaam's ass'. In *Pays de Galles, Écosse, Irlande: actes du Congrès de Brest, Mai 1987*. Brest: Centre de Recherches Bretonnes et Celtiques, 1987. 366 p. (Cahiers de Bretagne Occidentale; 7). pp. 43-62.

—— Poétique de la foi dans l'oeuvre de David Jones. *Caliban* 24 (1987) 125-140.

HIRST, Désirée. Particularity and power. *PW* 8,3 (1972) 42-55.

—— *The anathemata* repeated. *PW* 14,1 (1978) 137-140. On broadcast version of the poem, BBC Radio 3, 31 Jan 1978.

—— Epic of attrition: David Jones' *In parenthesis*. In *The world I breathe: talks and lectures delivered to the Dylan Thomas Society of Great Britain*, ed. Hugh S. Price. [Swansea]: Dylan Thomas Society of Great Britain, 1991. pp. 54-63.

HOLLOWAY, John. *The colours of clarity: essays on contemporary literature and education*. London: Routledge & Kegan Paul, 1964. Incl. A perpetual showing: the poetry of David Jones, pp.113-123. – Review article on *In parenthesis* and *The anathemata*, reprinted from *Hudson Review* 16,1 (1963) 122-130.

HOLLOWAY, Watson Lee. Alone in Pellam's land: a prolegomenon to David Jones' *The anathemata*. PhD thesis. Emory University, 1983. 193 p.

—— The pagan liturgy of David Jones. *Antigonish Review* 53 (1983) 47-53.

—— Apocalypse and moment in the poetry of David Jones. *Faith and Reason* 10 (1984) 191-199.

HOOKER, Jeremy. The poetry of David Jones. *PW* 6,3 (1970) 5-12.

—— History as imagination: some aspects of the poetry of David Jones. In *Triskel one: essays on Welsh and Anglo-Welsh literature*, ed. Sam Adams and Gwilym Rees Hughes. Llandybïe: Christopher Davies, 1971. pp. 27-42.

—— Ends and new beginnings. *PW* 8,3 (1972) 22-31.

—— On *The anathemata*. *AWR* 22,50 (1973) 31-43.

—— *David Jones: an exploratory study of the writings*. London: Enitharmon Press, 1975. 68 p.

—— *John Cowper Powys and David Jones: a comparative study*. London: Enitharmon Press, 1979. 54 p. (Enitharmon Press Powys Series; 1).

—— *The poetry of place: essays and reviews, 1970-1981*. Manchester: Carcanet, 1982. Incl. Ends and new beginnings, On *The anathemata*, Brut's Albion, pp. 32-65.

—— *The presence of the past: essays on modern British and American poetry*. Bridgend:

Poetry Wales Press, 1987. Incl. The presence of the past [on David Jones, Basil Bunting, Geoffrey Hill], pp. 9-32.

—— The naked shingles of the world: modern poetry and the crisis of religious language. *NWR* 2,3 [7] (1989-1990) 46-53. With comment on David Jones.

HUGHES, Colin. *David Jones: the man who was on the field:* In parenthesis *as straight reporting.* Manchester: David Jones Society, 1979. 32 p.: ill. Incl. maps. – Revised, in *David Jones: man and poet,* ed. John Matthias (1989).

IRONSIDE, Robin. *David Jones.* Harmondsworth: Penguin, 1949. 18 p., 32 p. of plates: pbk. (Penguin modern painters).

JACOBS, Nicholas. David Jones a'r traddodiad Cymraeg. *Taliesin* 25 (1972) 12-25. [David Jones and the Welsh tradition.]

—— David Jones and the politics of identity. *Agenda* 11,4-12,1 (1973-74) 68-75.

JAMES, M. Ingli. Relating to David Jones. *AWR* 80 (1985) 64-75. Incl. discussion of the watercolour, 'Trystan ac Esyllt'.

JEFFFREY, Ian. Review article on Nicolete Gray, *The paintings of David Jones. NWR* 2,1 [5] (1989) 50-51.

JENNINGS, Elizabeth. *Seven men of vision: an appreciation.* London: Vision Press, 1976. Incl. David Jones: a vision of war, pp. 151-172.

JOHNSTON, John H. *English poetry of the first world war: a study in the evolution of lyric and narrative form.* London: Oxford University Press; Princeton: Princeton University Press, 1964. Incl. David Jones: the heroic vision, pp. 284-340.

JONES, Alun R. David Jones. *Mabon* [Welsh] 1,8 (1974) 4-6.

JONES, Bedwyr Lewis. David Jones. *Taliesin* 25 (1972) 26-34.

JONES, Jack. Epic of the war to end wars. *WM,* 15 Oct 1959, 4:F-H. On *In parenthesis.*

JONES, Jonah. *The Gallipoli diary.* Bridgend: Seren Books, 1989. Incl. David Jones and the vernacular tradition, pp. 87-93.

JONES, Mary. Shape and sign in the writings of David Jones. MA thesis. University of Sheffield, 1969.

—— Heroism in unheroic warfare. *PW* 8,3 (1972) 14-21.

KEEBLE, Brian. Epoch, art and utility: some notes on David Jones and the traditional doctrine of art. *AWR* 24,54 (1975) 39-54.

KEITH, W.J. Encounter with otherness: readings of David Jones. *UTQ* 50 (1981) 330-335.

KERMODE, Frank. *Puzzles and epiphanies: essays and reviews, 1958-1961.* London: Routledge, 1962. Incl. On David Jones, pp. 29-34.

KRANZ, Gisbert. Walisisches Erbe: erster Blick auf David Jones. *Stimmen der Zeit,* June 1979, 394-402. [Welsh heritage: first glance at David Jones].

—— 'Die Tellus der Ara Pacis Augustae' und andere Bildwerke in den Dichtungen von David Jones. *Anglia* 100,1-2 (1982) 92-102. ['The tellus of the ara pacis Augustae' and other works of art in the poems of David Jones].

—— David Jones und die Inklings. *Inklings: Jahrbuch fur Literatur und Asthetik* 4 (1986) 139-146.

—— Llongyfarchiadau: zum deutschen Ausgabe von David Jones'

*Anathemata. Inklings: Jahrbuch fur Literatur und Asthetik* 6 (1988) 187-200. [Congratulations: on the German edition of David Jones' *Anathemata*].

LEHMANN, John. *English poets of the First World War*. London: Thames & Hudson, 1981. Incl. illustrations by and discussion of David Jones, pp. 101-104, 125-131.

LEVI, Peter. The poetry of David Jones. *Agenda* 5,1-3 (1967) 80-89.

—— History and reality in David Jones. *Agenda* 11,4-12,1 (1973-74) 56-59.

—— *In memory of David Jones: the text of a sermon delivered in Westminster Cathedral at the solemn requiem for the poet and painter, David Jones, on 13 December, 1974.* London: *The Tablet*, 1975. [10] p. Incl. 'A, a, a, domine Deus', p. [1]. – Reprinted from *The Tablet*, 4 Jan 1975, 6-7; also in *PW* 10,4 (1975) 5-9.

—— *The noise made by poems.* London: Anvil Press, 1977. (Poetica; 2). Incl. discussion of David Jones, pp. 32-34.

LEVY, Edward. David Jones: life-out-there and the limits of love. *AWR* 61 (1978) 66-88.

LEWIS, Saunders. A note. *Agenda* 5,1-3 (1967) 90-91. Reprints foreword to 1954 Arts Council (Welsh Committee) exhibition catalogue. – Translated from the Welsh.

—— *Agenda* 5,1-3 (1967) 112-115. Review of *Epoch and artist*.

—— David Jones's inscriptions. *PW* 8,3 (1972) 56-59. Reprinted from *DL* 6,16 (1955) 24-26 ['Two inscriptions'].

LI, Victor Paw Hoon. The inward continuities: aesthetics, crisis and *The anathemata* of David Jones. MA thesis. University of British Columbia, 1975.

LLOYD, David. The structural dynamics of David Jones's *The tribune's visitation*. *Ariel* 18,1 (1987) 3-15.

LOCHHEAD, Douglas. *Word index of* In parenthesis *by David Jones*. Sackville, New Brunswick: Harrier Editions, 1983. v, 342 p. Incl. corrigenda by William Blissett, pp. 341-342. – 'This edition is limited to 100 copies.'

MCARTHUR, Kathleen. A vision of desolation: an examination of the Passchendaele section from the abandoned 'Book of Balaam's ass'. *PW* 20,3 (1985) 67-77.

MCPHILEMY, K.E. Towards open form: a study of process poetics in relation to four long poems: *The anathemata*, by David Jones, 'In memoriam James Joyce', by Hugh MacDiarmid, 'Passages', by Robert Duncan, and 'Gunslinger', by Edward Dorn. PhD thesis. University of Edinburgh, 1980.

MACSWEEN, R.J. The letters of David Jones. *Antigonish Review* 49 (1982) 45-49.

MANGLAVITI, Leo M. J. *The anathemata* of David Jones: notes on theme and structure. *Twentieth Century Literature* 15 (1969) 105-113.

—— David Jones and *The anathemata*: life as art. *PW* 17,4 (1982) 59-63.

MATHIAS, Roland. *David Jones: eight essays on his work as writer and artist:* being the first transactions of Yr Academi Gymreig (English section), ed. Roland Mathias. Llandysul: Gomer Press, 1976. 144 p.: ill. Contents: David Jones the artist: a brief autobiography collated and edited by Peter Orr, pp. 9-12 – David Jones and his recorded readings, by Peter Orr, pp. 13-21 – The efficacious word, by William Blissett, pp. 22-49 – The present

past in *The anathemata* and Roman poems, by N. K. Sandars, pp. 50-72
– The medieval inspiration of David Jones, by David Blamires, pp. 73-87
– The artist David Jones, by Arthur Giardelli, pp. 88-100 – Fragility and
force: a theme in the later poems of David Jones, by Désirée Hirst,
pp. 101-122 – Brut's Albion, by Jeremy Hooker, pp. 123-138 – Bibliography, pp. 139-144.

—— David Jones. *Welsh Books and Writers* [Welsh Books Council], Autumn
1980, 8-10

—— *A ride through the wood: essays on Anglo-Welsh literature.* Bridgend: Poetry
Wales Press, 1985. Incl. David Jones: towards the holy diversities, pp. 13-
56. – Reprinted from *THSC* (1981) 137-178.

—— David Jones: an introduction. *Spirit* 48 (1982) 56-62.

MATTHEWS, Caitlin and John. David Jones: alchemist of images. *Temenos* 2
(1982) 243-251. Review of recent publications.

MATTHIAS, John. *David Jones: man and poet*, ed. John Matthias. National
Poetry Foundation, University of Maine, [1989]. 580 p.: ill. Contents:
Introduction, by John Matthias, pp. 17-32 – Chronology [of David
Jones' life] adapted from Paul Hills' Tate Gallery catalogue with addi-
tions by Thomas Dilworth and John Matthias, pp. 33-38 – A note
on *In parenthesis* and *The anathemata*, by T.S. Eliot, pp. 41-42 – On
*In parenthesis*, On *The anathemata*, by W.H. Auden, pp. 43-49 – David
Jones, by Stephen Spender, pp. 50-53 – An identity of purpose, by
Hugh MacDiarmid, pp. 55-58 – [from] David Jones and the actually
loved and known, by Kathleen Raine, pp. 59-64 – [from] 'David Jones'
and 'The dream of the rood' (a translation for David Jones), by Michael
Alexander, pp. 65-71 – In love with all things made, by Guy Davenport,
pp. 73-75 – Poems, by R.S. Thomas, John Tripp, John Montague, Anne
Beresford, pp. 77-85 – [from] *Dai Greatcoat*, by René Hague, pp. 87-105
– David Jones, Letters to H.S. Ede, selected by John Matthias, pp. 107-
121 – [from] *The long conversation*, by William Blissett, pp. 123-141 –
David Jones and fascism, by Thomas Dilworth, pp. 143-159 – David
Jones: the man who was on the field: *In parenthesis* as straight reporting,
by Colin Hughes, pp. 163-192 – The syntax of violence, by William
Blissett, pp. 193-207 – Spilled bitterness: *In parenthesis* in history, by Neil
Corcoran, pp. 209-225 – The ineluctable monologuality of the heroic, by
Vincent Sherry, pp. 227-241 – The present past in *The anathemata* and
Roman poems, by N.K. Sandars, pp. 243-261 – In the labyrinth: an
exploration of *The anathemata*, by Jeremy Hooker, pp. 263-284 – The
shape of time in *The anathemata*, by Thomas Dilworth, pp. 285-305 –
The text as 'valid matter': language and style in *The anathemata*, by
Patrick Deane, pp. 307-329 – The Tribune and the Tutelar: the tension
of opposites in *The sleeping lord*, by Teresa Godwin Phelps, pp. 331-350
– Notes towards performing 'The sleeping lord', by Tony Stoneburner,
pp. 351-365 – Poems for Britain, poems for sons, by John Peck, pp.
367-392 – *The Roman quarry* of David Jones: extraordinary perspectives,
by Vincent Sherry, pp. 391-401 – [from] David Jones, by Eric Gill, pp.
405-407 – Some recent paintings by David Jones, by Kenneth Clark,
pp. 409-424 – Four related works by David Jones, by Arthur Giardelli,
pp. 413-424 – The pierced hermaphrodite: David Jones' imagery of the

crucifixion, by Paul Hills, pp. 425-440 – The decline of the west and the optimism of the saints: David Jones' reading of Oswald Spengler, by Kathleen Henderson Staudt, pp. 443-463 – Homo faber, homo sapiens, by Thomas R. Whitaker, pp. 465-487 – David Jones bibliography, by Samuel Rees, pp. 491-544 – A list of drawings, paintings, carvings and inscriptions by David Jones in public collections, by Paul Hills, pp. 545-551. – The essays by Colin Hughes, Vincent Sherry, N.K. Sanders, Arthur Giardelli, Jeremy Hooker and Thomas Dilworth are revised for republication.

——  *Reading old friends: essays, reviews, and poems on poetics, 1975-1990.* New York: State University of New York Press, 1992. Incl.: Robert Duncan and David Jones: some affinities, pp. 107-125 – *Dai Greatcoat*, pp. 126-139 – The later poetry of David Jones, pp. 140-150.

MILES, Jonathan. Coherent eclecticism: intellectual disposition, content and form in the work of David Jones. DPhil thesis. University of Oxford, 1984.

——  David Jones and the right-wing. *NWR* 2,1 [5] (1989) 57-61.

——  *Backgrounds to David Jones: a study in sources and drafts.* Cardiff: University of Wales Press, 1990. 232 p.

——  *Eric Gill and David Jones at Capel-y-Ffin.* Bridgend: Seren Books, 1992. 172 p.

MORGAN, Paul Bennett. David Jones: an artist's library. *NLWJ* 26 (1990) 337-341. On the 1800 volumes now housed in the National Library of Wales.

MORGAN, Gerald. David Jones a'r Gymraeg. *Taliesin* 42 (1981) 47-53. [David Jones and the Welsh language].

MURRAY, Atholl C.C. Medievalism in the works of David Jones and Charles Williams. MLitt thesis. University of Glasgow, 1970-71.

——  In perspective: a study of David Jones's *In parenthesis. Critical Quarterly* 16 (1974) 254-263.

NEVE, Christopher. A garden enclosed: David Jones's watercolour. *Country Life*, 29 May 1981, 1388-1389. With four plates.

——  Journey of a soul: David Jones. *Country Life*, 13 Aug 1981, 570-571.

NYE, R. Letter from England: Jones and Sisson. *Hudson Review* 28 (1975) 468-476.

ORR, Peter. Mr Jones, your legs are crossed: a memoir. *Agenda* 15,2-3 (1977) 110-125.

PACEY, Philip. *David Jones and other wonder voyagers: essays.* Bridgend: Poetry Wales Press, 1982. 134 p. Incl.: An outrage on nature: the landscape of war in the work of Paul Nash and David Jones, pp. 27-38 – A rare one for the locality: the feminine principle in the poetry of David Jones, pp. 39-47 – Why David Jones is not a household name, pp. 49-61 – A man detailed: the creative life in the letters of David Jones, pp. 63-67 – Celtic wonder-voyagers: Hugh MacDiarmid and David Jones, pp. 71-84 – Navigants of the obscure passage: five English poets in quest of the Grail, pp. 111-126.

PAGNOULLE, Christine. *David Jones: a commentary on some poetic fragments.* Cardiff: University of Wales Press, 1987. 162 p.

——  David Jones's Wales. In *Pays de Galles, Écosse, Irlande: actes du Congrès de*

*Brest, Mai 1987.* Brest: Centre de Recherches Bretonnes et Celtiques, 1987. (Cahiers de Bretagne Occidentale; 7). pp. 63-75.

—— Dramatic irony in David Jones's poem, 'The tribune's visitation'. In *Multiple worlds, multiple words*, ed. Hena Maes-Jelinek and others. Liège: Univ. de Liège, 1987. pp. 229-237.

PECK, John. Our politics and 'The dream of Private Clitus'. *Ploughshares* 6,4 (1981) 208-227.

PETTS, John. David Jones: an introduction. *DL* 6,16 (1955) 10-17.

PHELPS, Teresa Godwin. Empress of the labyrinth: the feminine in David Jones's poetry. PhD thesis. University of Notre Dame, 1980. 186 p.

—— David Jones's 'The hunt' and 'The sleeping lord': the once and future Wales. *PW* 17,4 (1982) 64-71.

PIGGOTT, Stuart. David Jones and the past of man. *Agenda* 5,1-3 (1967) 76-79. Reprinted in *Agenda* 11,4-12,1 (1973-74) 60-63.

PHILLIPS, Robert Kenney. The literary art of David Jones. PhD thesis. University of Virginia, 1977. 271 p.

PRICE-OWEN, Anne. Fragments of an attempted painting: some visual imagery in David Jones's *The anathemata. NWR* 2,1 [5] (1989) 51-57.

—— [ as Ann Pryce Owen]. Priodferch David Jones. *Taliesin* 68 (1989) 69-73. On 'The bride' engraving.

RAINE, Kathleen. *David Jones: solitary perfectionist.* Ipswich: Golgonooza Press, 1974. 11 p. 'This edition is limited to 350 numbered copies, of which 1 to 100 are signed by the author.' – Enlarged edition 1975, 17p., 'includes a third section occasioned by the publication of David Jones' 'The sleeping lord'.

—— *David Jones and the actually loved and known.* Ipswich: Golgonooza Press, 1978. 25 p.

—— David Jones. In *The Celtic consciousness*, ed. Robert O'Driscoll. New York: Braziller, 1982. pp. 483-487.

REES, David. Profile, 1: David Jones. *Wales* 3rd ser., Jun 1959, 74-78.

—— Sgyrsiau gyda David Jones. *Barn*, Hyd/Oct 1975, 844-845. Translated from the English. [Conversations with David Jones.]

—— David Jones and the matter of Wales. In *The world I breathe: talks and lectures delivered to the Dylan Thomas Society of Great Britain*, ed. Hugh S. Price. [Swansea]: Dylan Thomas Society of Great Britain, 1991. pp. 36-53.

REES, Samuel. The achievement of David Jones, Anglo-Welsh poet. PhD thesis. University of Washington, 1969. 185 p.

—— The impressionist's rage for order: David Jones and *In parenthesis. AWR* 20,46 (1972) 112-123.

—— The poetry of David Jones. *Modern Poetry Studies* 3,4 (1972) 161-169.

—— *David Jones: an annotated bibliography and guide to research.* New York, London: Garland, 1977. x, 97 p. (Garland reference library of the humanities; 68). Comprehensive listing of publications by and about Jones. – Also covers exhibitions, broadcasts and recordings.

—— *David Jones.* Boston: Twayne, 1978. 154 p.: front. port. (Twayne's English authors series; 246). Incl. selected bibliography, pp. 147-150.

RICHARDS, A. R. Poetry as prophecy: a study of the written work of David Jones. DPhil thesis. University of Oxford, 1987.

RICHARDS, Frances. *Remembering David Jones.* 1980. [4] p. 'Printed for the Enitharmon Press in an edition of [105]'.

ROBB, M.P. The sacramental vision: belief and art in the poetry of David Jones, Charles Williams and W.H. Auden. PhD thesis. University of Manchester, 1989.

ROSENTHAL, M. L. and Sally M. Gall *The modern poetic sequence: the genius of modern poetry.* New York; Oxford: Oxford University Press, 1983. Incl. discussion of David Jones, especially pp. 296-309.

ROWAN, Eric. *Art in Wales: an illustrated history, 1850-1980.* Cardiff: Welsh Arts Council; University of Wales Press, 1985. Incl. discussion of David Jones and reproductions of his work, pp. 82-85, 94-102.

SANDARS, N. K. The inward continuities. *Agenda* 5,1-3 (1967) 92-96.

—— Some thoughts arising from David Jones's latest published writings. *Agenda* 11,4-12,1 (1973-74) 36-45.

SANESI, Roberto. Il genius loci di David Jones. *Annali dell' Instituto di Lingue e Letterature Germanische* [Universita di Parma, Facolta di Magistero] 6 (1980-81) 9-43.

SANGER, Peter. Warden of stores: on the letters and conversation of David Jones. *Antigonish Review* 68 (1987) 95-101.

—— A chase for the wine-juice skipper: David Jones and Thomas Dilworth. *Antigonish Review* 77-78 (1989) 229-252.

SAVOIA, Daniella. *In parenthesis:* 'Art and sacrament' nella poesia di guerra. *Quaderni di Lingue e Letterature,* 3-4 (1978-79) 87-112.

—— Gerusalemme, 'signum' di *The anathemata. Quaderni di Lingue e Letterature* 5 (1980) 5-17.

—— L' ultimo Jones: l'universalizzazione dei 'Fragments'. *Studi di Letteratura Inglese e Americana* (1980) 127-146.

—— *Il soldato scalzo: la poesia di David Jones,* 1895-1974. Milan: Unicopli, 1985. 208 p.: 16 p. of plates. (Biblioteca di anglistika; 3). Incl. bibliography, pp. 107-202.

SCHMIDT, Michael. *An introduction to 50 modern British poets.* London: Pan, 1979. (Pan literature guides). Incl. David Jones, pp. 156-165.

SCHWARTZ, Joseph. The poetry of David Jones. *Renascence* 38 (1986).

SCOTT, David. David Jones (1895-1974). *New Fire* 5,38 (1978) 276-282.

SHERRY, Vincent B. Jr. The habit of monologue: poetic voices and literary tradition in David Jones's *In parenthesis.* PhD thesis. University of Toronto, 1979.

—— A new boast for *In parenthesis*: the dramatic monologue of David Jones. *Notre Dame English Journal* 14 (1982) 113-128.

—— David Jones's *In parenthesis*: new measure. *Twentieth Century Literature* 28 (1982) 375-380.

—— David Jones. In *British poets,* 1914-1945, ed. Donald E. Stanford. Detroit: Gale, 1983. (Dictionary of Literary Biography; 20). pp. 182-191.

—— Unmistakable marks: symbols and voices in David Jones's *In parenthesis. Critical Quarterly* 25,4 (1983) 63-73.

—— Current critical models of the long poem and David Jones's *The anathemata. English Literary History* 52 (1985) 239-255. Also considers works by Basil Bunting and Geoffrey Hill.

SILKIN, Jon. *Out of battle: the poetry of the Great War.* London: Oxford University Press, 1972. Incl. discussion of David Jones, pp. 315-340.

SMITH, A.J. A perpetual showing: apocalypse in *In parenthesis. Du verbe au geste: mélanges en l'honneur de Pierre Danchin.* Nancy: PUs de Nancy, 1986. pp. 275-288.

SPEARES, Monroe K. Shapes and surfaces: David Jones, with a glance at Charles Tomlinson. *Contemporary Literature* 12 (1971) 402-419.

—— *In parenthesis. New Republic,* 6 Mar 1976, 29-31.

STALLWORTHY, John. Survivors' songs in Welsh poetry. *TLS,* 4 Sep 1981, 1015-1016. Discusses *In parenthesis.*

STANCLIFFE, Michael. David Jones and the liturgy. *Temenos* 3 (1982) 13-25.

STAUDT, Kathleen Henderson. Metaphor, sign and sacrament: the problem of transcendence in Shelley, Mallarmé and David Jones. PhD thesis. Yale University, 1980. Incl.: David Jones and the poetics of sacrament, pp. 171-328 – Bibliography, pp. 368-384.

—— At the turn of a civilisation: Spenglerian vision and revision in David Jones's 'The sleeping lord'. *Contemporary Poetry* 5,2 (1983) 51-70.

—— The text as material and as sign: poetry and incarnation in William Blake, Arthur Rimbaud, and David Jones. *Modern Language Studies* 14,3 (1984) 13-30.

—— Incarnation reconsidered: the poem as sacramental act in *The anathemata* of David Jones. *Contemporary Literature* 26,1 (1985) 1-25.

—— Recent criticism on David Jones. *Contemporary Literature* 27,3 (1986) 409-422.

—— The language of T.S. Eliot's *Four quartets* and David Jones's *The anathemata. Renascence* 38 (1986) 118-130.

STONEBURNER, Charles Joseph. The regimen of the ship-star: a handbook for *The anathemata* of David Jones. PhD thesis. University of Michigan, 1966. 258 p.

STONEBURNER, Tony. The work in progress. *Agenda* 5,1-3 (1967) 135-145.

—— *A list of letters by David Jones.* Granville, Ohio: Limekiln Press, 1977. [41] p. Lists 'about 700 items addressed to about 75 persons'.

—— Triad from Great Britain: introduction to three recent longer poems and a trying-out to discover if faith coinheres there. *Semiea* 13 (1978) 93-129. Discusses 'The sleeping lord', Geoffrey Hill's *Mercian hymns,* and John Heath-Stubbs' *Artorius.*

—— David Jones: poet of catch-as-catch-can. *Cross Currents* 38,2 (1988) 211-218.

STREVENS, Peter. David Jones and his 'bits of lettering'. *AWR* 22,50 (1973) 58-64.

SUMMERFIELD, Henry. *An introductory guide to* The anathemata *and 'The sleeping lord' sequence of David Jones.* Victoria, B.C.: Sono Nis Press, 1979. 192 p.: ill. Incl.: 8 maps, pp. 11-18 – Bibliography, pp. 188-192.

TERPSTRA, John. 'Bedad he revives! See how he raises!': an introduction to David Jones's 'The sleeping lord'. *UTQ* 52 (1982) 94-105.

THWAITE, Anthony. *Poetry today: a critical guide to British poetry, 1960-1984.* London: Longman, 1985. Incl. Robert Graves and David Jones, pp. 3-6.

TOMLINSON, Charles. *The sense of the past: three twentieth-century British poets.* Liverpool: Liverpool University Press, 1983. 19 p. Lecture on David Jones, Basil Bunting and Geoffrey Hill.

WARD, Elizabeth. *David Jones: mythmaker.* Manchester: Manchester University Press, 1983. 236 p. Incl. Bibliography, pp. 226-230.

WATKINS, Vernon. Prose. *PW* 12,4 (1977) 52-65. Excerpts from lecture notes, including comment on David Jones.

WILBORN, William Francis. Sign and form in the poetry of David Jones: a study in the poetics of the image. PhD thesis. Cornell University, 1976. 114 p.

WILCOCKSON, Colin. Notes on some letters of David Jones. *Agenda* 14,2 (1976) 67-87.

—— David Jones and 'the break'. *Agenda* 15,2-3 (1977) 126-131.

WILLIAMS, Griffith. David Jones, writer and artist. *Welsh Nation*, 14 Nov 1974, 7:C-D

WILMER, Clive. An art of recovery: some literary sources for Geoffrey Hill's 'Tenebrae'. *Southern Review* 17,1 (1981) 121-141. David Jones discussed, pp. 126-132.

# B (ii). *David Jones Society Newsletter*

The contents of this periodical, edited by David Blamires, are listed selectively below. Most issues include detailed bibliographies of recent publications. Reviews are by the editor unless otherwise stated.

*The David Jones Society Newsletter* 1 (1976) 4 p. Incl.: Notes on founding of David Jones Society – Report on Aberystwyth conference – News of forthcoming *The Chester Play of the Deluge,* Clover Hill edition – Notices of recent radio broadcasts – Advance notice of conference (30 Oct 1976), Connaissance des poètes du Pays de Galles et de la poésie Anglo-Welsh: hommage au poète David Jones – [David Jones's] Corrigenda to *In parenthesis,* by William Blissett.

*DJSN* 2 (1976) 5 p. Incl.: Notes on Gregynog Press and St. Dominic's Press exhibitions – Further notes on *The Chester Play of the Deluge,* Clover Hill edition – Review, by Samuel Rees, of 'Steel be my sister: the poetry and painting of David Jones', HTV, 29 Feb 1976 – Bibliography, by Tony Stoneburner, of 'writings that contain incidental biographical and critical references to David Jones'.

*DJSN* 3 (1976) 3 p. Incl.: Review of *David Jones: letters to Vernon Watkins,* ed. Ruth Pryor – [David Jones's] Corrigenda to *The anathemata,* by Aneirin Talfan Davies.

*DJSN* 4 (1976) 4 p. Incl.: News on membership and forthcoming books – Note on original David Jones drawings, etc in possession of the Welsh Arts Council, the National Museum of Wales and the National Library of Wales – Corrigenda to *The anathemata,* by René Hague, Colin Wilcockson and (on Viking edition) Henry Summerfield.

*DJSN* 5 (1976) 2 p. Incl.: Reports on Manchester and Stirling exhibitions and on Academi Gymreig Lampeter conference on Poets of the First

World War – Note on acquisition of three David Jones works by Scottish National Gallery of Modern Art – Corrigenda to: *In parenthesis* (anon) – 'The sleeping lord' (William Blissett, approved by Jones) - *The anathemata* (Thomas Dilworth).

*DJSN* 6 (1977) 4 p. Incl.: Report on membership – Note on *The Chester Play of the Deluge*, Clover Hill edition – Note on the earliest published examples of David Jones's paintings – Provisional schedule, by Peter Orr, of recordings by David Jones – Note on The homoerotic imagination, a lecture by Michael Lynch referring to *In parenthesis*.

*DJSN* 7 (1977) 4 p. Incl.: Letter from Jones scholars dissociating themselves from Michael Lynch [see *DJSN* 6] – Note on works by David Jones in the Beaverbrook Gallery, Canada – David Jones anthologised [bibliography].

*DJSN* 8 (1977) 6 p. Incl.: Note on Barbara Bertram's *Anathemata* embroidery – List of members.

*DJSN* 9 (1977) 2 p. Incl. Textual problems in *The anathemata*, by Neil Corcoran.

*DJSN* 10 (1977) 4 p. Incl.: Note comparing the Clover Hill and Golden Cockerel Press editions of *The Chester Play of the Deluge* – Information on list of letters by David Jones, by Tony Stoneburner – Review of René Hague, *A commentary on* The anathemata *of David Jones* – Textual problems in *The anathemata*, by Thomas Dilworth.

*DJSN* 11 (1978) 3 p. Incl.: Notes on conferences of David Jones Society and Royal Foundation of St. Katharine's – Note on radio broadcast of *The anathemata*, 31 Jan 1978 – '79 Jones and '89 Jones in *In parenthesis*, by Chris O'Neill.

*DJSN* 12 (1978) 4 p. Incl.: Note on, and programme of, David Jones Society Conference – Note on 'Chapel in the park', Ganymede facsimile – '79 Jones and '89 Jones in *In Parenthesis*: replies from Thomas Dilworth and René Hague [see *DJSN* 11] – Grass as a substitute for Holy Communion [note on medieval literature], by David Blamires.

*DJSN* 13 (1978) 4 p. Incl.: Review of David Jones, *The dying Gaul and other writings*, ed. Harman Grisewood – '79 Jones and '89 Jones in *In Parenthesis*, by Nicholas Jacobs – Grass as a substitute for Holy Communion [see *DJSN* 12] – Note on Kevin Cecil, David Jones: the word and the visual image [undergraduate thesis].

*DJSN* 14 (1978) 6 p. Incl.: Note on Hilary Pepler centenary celebrations – Report on David Jones Society conference, Pembroke College, Cambridge, and on visit to Kettle's Yard – Review, by Diana Austin, of Kathleen Raine, *David Jones and the actually loved and known* – Note on cassette recording of David Jones reading his poetry.

*DJSN* 15 (1978) 4 p. Incl.: Inquiry, by Paul Hills, on whereabouts of David Jones paintings – David Jones anthologised: additions to bibliography – David? or David Jones? [letter from Neil Corcoran, preferring the latter].

*DJSN* 16 (1979) 6 p. Incl.: Review of Jeremy Hooker, *John Cowper Powys and David Jones: a comparative study* – Review, by Richard Outram, of David Blamires, *David Jones: artist and writer*, 2nd ed. – Report on Hilary Pepler centenary conference – David? or David Jones?:

letters from Arthur Giardelli, Peter Orr and Greg Hill [see *DJSN* 15].

*DJSN* 17 (1979) 4 p. Incl.: Review, by John Banks, of Samuel Rees, *David Jones* – David? or David Jones?: letters from Jeremy Hooker and Jonathan Miles.

*DJSN* 18 (1979) 4 p. Incl.: Review, by Neil Corcoran, of David Jones: letters to *William Hayward*, ed. Colin Wilcockson.

*DJSN* 19 (1979) 4 p. Incl.: Review, by Douglas Kerr, of Colin Hughes, *David Jones: the man who was on the field* – Note, by Alan Freer, on David Jones exhibition [Anthony d'Offay Gallery] – Review of Henry Summerfield, *An introductory guide to* The anathemata – Publications in German on David Jones [bibliography].

*DJSN* 20 (1979) 4 p. Incl.: Review, by Michael Stancliffe, of Thomas Dilworth, *The liturgical parenthesis of David Jones* – Note on Australian broadcast on David Jones – Note on Eric Gill exhibition at Kettle's Yard, Cambridge.

*DJSN* 21 (1980) 6 p. Incl.: Review of *The Book of Jonah*, Clover Hill edition – Note on, and inventory of, David Jones items in 'Strange meeting: the arts of the first world war', exhibition at Aberystwyth Arts Centre – Note on David Jones items in 'The thirties' exhibition at Hayward Gallery – Note on ms. letters of David Jones in America – Corrigenda, by Glenn Bard, to 'The sleeping lord'.

*DJSN* 22 (1980) 6 p. Incl.: Review of Brocard Sewell, *A checklist of books ... printed by H.D.C. Pepler at Saint Dominic's Press* – Review, by Martin Robb, of *Introducing David Jones*, ed. John Matthias – Review of *David Jones: letters to a friend*, ed. Aneirin Talfan Davies – Note on David Jones items on exhibition and in catalogue at Kettle's Yard, Cambridge – Note on 'Strict delight', Eric Gill exhibition at Whitworth Art Gallery – Additions [and corrections], by William Blissett, to Samuel Rees, *David Jones: an annotated bibliography*.

*DJSN* 23 (1980) 4 p. Incl.: Note on David Jones exhibition at University of Kent – Review of *Dai Greatcoat*, ed. René Hague – Note on Critics' Forum discussion of *Dai Greatcoat*, BBC Radio 3, 24 May 1980 – Note on *The engravings of David Jones*, forthcoming Clover Hill edition.

*DJSN* 24 (1980) 2 p. Incl.: Note on new acquisition by Whitworth Gallery, Manchester – Note on *The engravings of David Jones*, Clover Hill edition.

*DJSN* 25 (1980) 5 p. Incl.: Review, by Jamie Muir, of 'David Jones: inscriptions' exhibition, Anthony d'Offay Gallery.

*DJSN* 26 (1981) 4 p. Incl.: Obituary of René and Joan Hague – Note on The poetry of David Jones, BBC Radio 3 programme, 14 Mar 1981 – 'The buried rowan' [note on possible pun in 'The sleeping lord'].

*DJSN* 27 (1981) 4 p. Incl.: Note on 'The sleeping lord', BBC Radio 3 arrangement by Peter Orr, 21 Jul 1981 – Review, by Philip Pacey, of David Jones exhibition at Tate Gallery – Review, by John Banks, of William Blissett, *The long conversation...* – Note on David Jones letters at Boston College.

*DJSN* 28 (1981) 6 p. Incl.: Review, by Jonathan Miles, of *The Roman quarry* – Notes on the text of *The Roman quarry* [proposed corrections] – Note on readings from David Jones at the Tate Gallery

- Note on *In parenthesis*, BBC Radio 3, 30 Aug 1981 – Review, by John Banks, of John Lehmann, *The English poets of the First World War*.

*DJSN* 29 (1981) 6 p. Incl.: Note on text in 'The Narrows', as presented in *AWR*, *Agenda*, *The Roman quarry* and Interim Press edition – Note on David Jones exhibition at Harrow School – Corporals stay: Amos Niven Wilder and David Jones, by Michael Patrick O'Connor.

*DJSN* 30 (1982) 6 p. Incl.: 'The Narrows ' [further textual variations; see *DJSN* 29] – Review, by John Blamires, of Nicolete Gray, *The painted inscriptions of David Jones* and notes on its textual errors – Notes on Maurice Percival, and on Tony Appleton [bookseller's] *Catalogue 34* – Note on Tate Gallery exhibition at National Museum of Wales and associated lectures.

*DJSN* 31 (1982) 5 p. Incl.: Review, by Michael Taylor, of Douglas Cleverdon, *The engravings of David Jones: a survey* – Note on Eric Gill exhibitions – A new David Jones letter [to Douglas and Mea Woodruff].

*DJSN* 32 (1982) 6 p. Incl.: List of members – Review of Kathleen Raine, *The inner journey of the poet*.

*DJSN* 33 (1982) 4 p. Incl.: Review, by Barrie Paskins, of Colin Hughes, *Mametz: Lloyd George's 'Welsh army' at the battle of the Somme* – Review, by Martin Robb, of Jeremy Hooker, *The poetry of place* – Note on Douglas Cleverdon, *The engravings of David Jones*.

*DJSN* 34 (1983) 5 p. Incl.: Review of Philip Pacey, *David Jones and other wonder voyagers*.

*DJSN* 35 (1983) 6 p. Incl.: Review, by Bill Ruddick, of Neil Corcoran, *The song of deeds* – David Jones and the commemoration of the death of Llewelyn [report of James Nicholas's Eisteddfod address] – Review of Charles Tomlinson, *The sense of the past: three twentieth century British poets* – List of lectures on David Jones at academic conferences.

*DJSN* 36 (1983) 2 p. Incl.: Report on special David Jones session at MLA conference – Review of Douglas Lochhead, *Word index of* In parenthesis.

*DJSN* 37 (1984) 8 p. Incl.: Review, by Christine Pagnoulle, of Elizabeth Ward, *David Jones, mythmaker* – Note on David Jones at the Chicago Art Fair.

*DJSN* 38 (1984) 10 p. Incl.: Note on recordings by David Jones – Tate Gallery archive collection of David Jones [list of 30 items] – The dating of 'Guenever', 'Aphrodite in Aulis' and 'The four queens', by Douglas Cleverdon – Notes on sale of David Jones mss. at Sotheby's, and on David Jones fine bindings.


# B (iii). David Jones: Exhibition Catalogues

Arrangement is chronological. Reviews listed are of exhibitions, not exhibition catalogues.

*David Jones: watercolours and drawings*. London: Goupil Gallery, 1929. [4] p.
*Watercolours by David Jones*. London: Redfern Gallery, 1940. [3] p.
*An exhibition of the works of David Jones*. London: CEMA, 1944. 7 p. Review: *Wales* 2nd ser. 4 (1944) 91-92.

Arts Council of Great Britain (Welsh Committee). *An exhibition of paintings, drawings and engravings by David Jones.* Cardiff: Pwyllgor Cymreig Cyngor Celfyddyd Prydain Fawr, 1954. 27 p., [17] p. of plates: pamph. Incl.: Foreword, by Saunders Lewis, p. 3 – Introduction, by John Petts, pp. 4-11.

*Word and image IV: David Jones, b.1895.* London: National Book League, 1972. 63 p.: ill. Incl.: 24 p. of plates – Bibliography, p. 62. – Compiled by Douglas Cleverdon. – Reviews: *Art International*, May 1973, 22-23; *AWR* 22,49 (1973) 296-298 (Bryn Griffiths); *Burlington Magazine*, Jan 1973, 52.

*David Jones: writings and drawings: addenda.* Cardiff: National Museum of Wales, 1972. 13 p. Addenda to National Book League catalogue.

*David Jones, 1 November 1895-28 October 1974.* [Cambridge]: Kettle's Yard Gallery, [1975]. [14] p., 4 p. of plates.

*David Jones, 1895-1974.* London: Anthony d'Offay, 1975. [15] p. Incl. introduction by Douglas Cleverdon. – Reviews: *Apollo*, Jun 1975, 478; *Studio International*, Sep-Oct 1975, 162-163 (Paul Hills).

*David Jones: watercolours and drawings.* Stirling: MacRobert Centre Gallery, 1976. [8] p.: ill. Incl. introduction by Paul Hills.

*David Jones.* Cardiff: Oriel, 1976. 4p.: ill. 'Paintings, drawings and inscriptions recently acquired by the National Library of Wales, the National Museum of Wales and the Welsh Arts Council'.

*David Jones: peintiadau, lluniau ac arysgrifiadau ... paintings, drawings and inscriptions recently acquired by the National Library of Wales, the National Museum of Wales and the Welsh Arts Council.* Cardiff: Welsh Arts Council, [1977]. 12p.: ill.: pamph. Incl. Introduction, by David Fraser Jenkins.

*David Jones, 1895-1974.* London: Anthony d'Offay, 1979. [19] p., 8 leaves of plates. Incl. introduction by Paul Hills, pp. [1-3]. – Reviews: *Apollo*, May 1979, 401; *Burlington Magazine*, May 1979, 335; *Connoisseur*, May 1979, 75 (N. Usherwood); *Observer*, 13 May 1979, 14 (William Feaver).

*David Jones: inscriptions.* London: Anthony d'Offay, 1980. [12] p., [8] p. of plates. Incl. introduction by Nicolete Gray, pp. 1-3. – Reviews: *Art International*, Jan-Feb 1981, 102; *Art International* [Switz.], Jan-Feb 1981, 70-113 (Gerard Dou, partially dealing with this exhibition); *Arts Review* [UK], 21 Nov 1980, 539 (B. Wright).

*David Jones: poet and artist:* Kent University Library, Oct 20-Nov 1, 1980. [Canterbury]: Kent University Library, 1980. 19 p., 7 p. of plates. Compiled by Stephen Holland, with appendix by Canon A.M. Allchin.

*David Jones.* London: Tate Gallery, 1981. 144p.: ill (some col.). Incl.: The art of David Jones, by Paul Hills, pp. 19-71 – Reproductions of paintings, drawings, engravings and inscriptions, pp. 72-140 – Bibliography, pp. 141-142. – Reviews: *Arts Review*, 31 Jul 1981, 337 (H. Einzig); *Arcade*, 4 Sep 1981, 23 (Mollie Baxter); *Arcade*, 13 Nov 1981, 22 (Jonah Jones); *AWR* 71 (1982) 75-79 (Arthur Giardelli); *London Magazine*, Nov 1981, 63-68 (Andrea Rose); *PW* 17,3 (1982) 105-109 (Greg Hill); *TLS*, 4 Sep 1981, 1007-1008 (Robert Hewinson).

*David Jones.* Harrow: Harrow School, [1981]. [8] p.: ill.

*David Jones engravings.* London: Blond Fine Art, 1982. 20 p.: ill. Review: *Arts Review*, 8 Oct 1982, 519 (G. Burn).

*Tate gallery archive display: David Jones, 1895-1974.* London: Tate Gallery, 1984. [2] p.

*David Jones: an exhibition of wood engravings and other prints, 1923-32.* Cardiff: Andrew Knight Gallery, [1986]. [2] p.

# GLYN JONES (b. 1905)

A. Publications by Glyn Jones
   (i)  Books, and books edited
   (ii) Selected contributions to books and periodicals

B. Publications about Glyn Jones

## A (i). Publications by Glyn Jones: Books, and Books Edited

*The blue bed and other stories*. London: Cape, 1937. 245 p. Contents: I was born in the Ystrad Valley – The kiss – Knowledge – Wil Thomas – Eben Isaac – Cadi Hughes – Eden Tree – The blue bed – Porth-y-Rhyd.

U.S. ed.: New York: Dutton, 1938.

*Poems*. London: Fortune Press, [1939]. 44 p. (The fortune poets; 4). Incl. Sketch of the author, pp. 39-44.

*The water music and other stories*. London: Routledge, 1944. v, 162 p. Contents: The apple-tree – The saviour – The wanderer – The four-loaded man – The little grave – Explosion – An afternoon at Ewa Shad's – Wat Pantathro – The last will – Price-Parry – Bowen, Morgan and Williams – The water music.

*The dream of Jake Hopkins*. London: Fortune Press, 1954. 44 p. Incl. Author's note, pp. 42-44. – 'The title poem was commissioned by the BBC and broadcast in the Welsh Home Service in 1953.'

*The saga of Llywarch the old* / a reconstruction by Glyn Jones; with the verse interludes translated by T.J. Morgan; and an introduction by Sir Ifor Williams. London: Golden Cockerel Press, 1955. 38 p.: ill.: in slipcase. Colour engravings by D. Braby. – 'This edition limited to 200 numbered copies'. – 'The poems have been translated from the early Welsh by Dr T.J. Morgan and the narrative has been devised by Glyn Jones to replace the original prose saga.'

*The valley the city the village: a novel*. London: Dent, 1956. 316 p.
—— Severn House, 1980. hbk & pbk. ISBN: 0-7278-0617-3 hbk, 906461-04-9 pbk. Incl. Introduction, by David Smith.

*Codiad lloer* [*Moonrise*] / geiriau gan Glyn Jones; y gerddoriaeth gan Alun Hoddinott. Cardiff: University Council of Music; University of Wales Press, 1960. 8 p.: pamph. A part-song with words by Glyn Jones and music by Alun Hoddinott. – Text in Welsh, paraphrased in English by 'G.W.'.

*The learning lark*. London: Dent, 1960. 224 p. Novel.

Welsh trans.: *Miri dysgu*, tr. Harri Pritchard Jones. Llandysul: Gwasg Gomer, 1984. 129 p.: pbk. ISBN: 0-86383-033-1.

*The island of apples*. London: Dent, 1965. 256 p. Novel.
—— / with an introduction by Belinda Humfrey. Cardiff: University of Wales Press, 1992. xxiv, 256 p.: hbk & pbk. (Welsh writing in English). ISBN: 0-7083-1177-6 hbk, 0-7083-1176-8 pbk. Incl.: The island of apples: an introductory discussion, by Belinda Humfrey, pp. vii-xxxi – Glossary of Welsh words and phrases and Anglo-Welsh dialect forms appearing in the text, supplied by Glyn Jones, pp. xxxiii-xxiv.

U.S. ed.: New York: Day, 1965.

*The dragon has two tongues: essays on Anglo-Welsh writers and writing*. London: Dent, 1968. ix, 221 p. ISBN: 0-460-03650-5. Contents: Letter to Keidrych – Autobiography – Background – Introduction to short stories and novels – Three prose writers; Caradoc Evans, Jack Jones, Gwyn Thomas – Introduction to poetry – Three poets; Huw Menai, Idris Davies, Dylan Thomas – Conclusion – Bibliographical note.

*Selected short stories*. London: Dent, 1971. vi, 185p. ISBN: 0-460-03968-7. Contents: Knowledge – Wil Thomas – Eben Isaac – Cadi Hughes – The saviour – The four-loaded man – An afternoon at Ewa Shad's – Wat Pantathro – The last will – Price-Parry – Bowen, Morgan and Williams – The water music – Jordan – The boy in the bucket – It's not by his beak you can judge a woodcock.

*The beach at Falesá: opera in three acts*. London: Oxford University Press, 1974. 240 p.: pbk. Music by Alun Hoddinott, and libretto by Glyn Jones from Robert Louis Stevenson short story. – Also signed edition, 1974, hbk, 100 copies.
—— Oxford University Press, 1974. vii, 40 p.: pamph. Libretto only.

*Selected poems of Glyn Jones*. Llandysul: Gomer Press, 1975. 94 p. ISBN: 0-85088-308-3. Reprints 'Park' (*Wales* 4, 1938) as 'Island', and 'The garden' (*AWR* 9,4, 1959) as 'Dawn trees'.

*Poems '76: an anthology of poems by Welsh writers selected from work which has appeared during the last two years* ... / edited by Glyn Jones. Llandysul: Gomer Press, 1976. 89 p.: pbk. ISBN: 8-5088-000-0. Incl. About the editing, by Glyn Jones.

*Welsh heirs*. Llandysul: Gomer Press, 1977. 158 p. ISBN: 0-85088-495-0. Contents: Four tales; Robert Jeffreys, Mrs Jeffreys, Myra Powell, Gari – The tower of loss – Rhysie at Auntie Kezia's – Lias Lewis – Rhamant drist – The golden pony. – 'All the stories in this collection are new in the sense that they have not appeared in any of my previous volumes.'

*Profiles: a visitor's guide to writing in twentieth century Wales*. Llandysul: Gomer Press, 1980. xxxi, 382 p. ISBN: 0-85088-713-5. Incl.: Arthur Machen, pp. 203-208 – W.H. Davies, pp. 209-211 – John Cowper Powys, pp. 212-218 – Caradoc Evans, pp. 219-225 – Jack Jones, pp. 226-232 – David Jones, pp. 233-240 – Richard Hughes, pp. 241-247 – Rhys Davies, pp. 248-253 – Geraint Goodwin, pp. 254-256 – Gwyn Williams, pp. 257- 259 – Idris Davies, pp. 260-265 – Glyn Jones, pp. 266-271 – Vernon Watkins, pp. 272-277 – Gwyn Jones, pp. 278-284 – Gwyn Thomas, pp. 285-291 – R.S. Thomas, pp. 292-296 – Dylan Thomas, pp. 297-302 – Alun Lewis, pp. 303-307 – Roland Mathias, pp. 308-312 – Emyr Humphreys, pp. 313-319 – Harri Webb, pp. 321-322 – Ron Berry, pp. 323-325 – T.H. Jones, pp. 326-328 – Leslie Norris, pp. 329-331 – Dannie Abse, pp. 332-335 – John Ormond, pp. 336-338 – Raymond Garlick, pp. 339-341 – John Tripp, pp. 342-344 – Alun Richards, pp. 345-347 – Anthony Conran, pp. 348-350 – Raymond Williams, pp. 370-371. – Written jointly with John Rowlands. – The above profiles, and further notes on English-language authors, by Glyn Jones.

*When the rose bush brings forth apples: old Welsh verses* / translated and introduced by Glyn Jones. [Newtown]: Gwasg Gregynog, 1980. [11] p.: pamph. Incl. fourteen *hen benillion* or *penillion telyn*. – 'A limited edition of 400 numbered copies'.

*Random entrances to Gwyn Thomas*. Cardiff: University College Cardiff Press, 1982. 25 p.: pamph. (Annual Gwyn Jones lecture). ISBN: 0-906449-45-6. Discusses *A few selected exits*, *The dark philosophers* and *The alone to the alone*.

*Setting out: a memoir of literary life in Wales*. Cardiff: Dept. of Extra-Mural Studies, University College, 1982. iv, 16 p.: pamph. (Park Place papers; 13). ISBN: 0-946045-17-8. On channels of publication for Anglo-Welsh authors in the 1920s and 30s.

*Honeydew on the wormwood: a further selection of old Welsh verses* / translated and introduced by Glyn Jones. [Newtown]: Gwasg Gregynog, 1984. [14] p.: front.: pamph. Wood-engraved frontispiece by Colin Paynton. – Parallel Welsh and English texts; 'the *Hen Benillion* (old verses) translated here were composed in sixteenth and seventeenth century Wales.' – 'A limited edition of 400 numbered copies'.

*The meaning of fuchsias* / wood engraving by Sarah van Niekerk. Newtown: Gwasg Gregynog, 1988. [2] p.: ill.: pamph. (Gregynog poets; 2). ISBN: 0-948714-18-2. Text of single poem. – 'This edition consists of 400 copies.'

*Glyn Jones: selected poems, fragments and fictions*. Bridgend: Poetry Wales Press, 1988. 160 p.: pbk. ISBN: 0-907476-85-6. 'The poems in parts one, two and three ... have been chosen from those that appeared in my previous volumes of poetry. Part four has been written since ... "Prologue and Three fragments" is part of a long unfinished poem called "Seven keys to

Shaderdom".' – Glyn Jones, *BWA* 14 (1988) 7, discusses excluded poems and corrects a serious misprint.


## A (ii). Publications by Glyn Jones: Selected Contributions to Books and Periodicals

Three poems. *Poetry: a Magazine of Verse* 39 (1932) 252-255. Poet and peasant – The statue and the lord – The return of the Argo. – Published under the pseudonym, M.G. Gower.

Cassation. *Poetry: a Magazine of Verse* 41 (1933) 312-313. Published under the pseudonym, M.G. Gower.

Thoughts on the Burne-Jones exhibition. *Welsh Outlook* 20,10 (1933) 281-282. Discuses characteristics of Celtic art. – Published under the pseudonym, M.G. Gower.

Men who helped in revolution of poetry. *WM*, 22 Nov 1934, 11:C. Review of Edith Sitwell, *Aspects of modern poetry*, Constance Holm, *The trumpet in the dust*, S.B.P. Mais, *More books I like*.

Some old themes in modern dress. *WM,* 29 Nov 1934, 11:E. Review of Maurice Baring, *Unreliable history*, Martin Hare, *If this be error*, Duncan Fife, *Children of the chace*, [Various authors], *A mixed bag*.

Verse that is too easy. *WM*, 20 Dec 1934, 11:E. Review of E. Howard Harris, *Song cycle at the Worm and other poems*.

Review of F.W. Bateson, *English poetry and the English language*, A. Allen Brockington, *Mysticism and poetry*. *Adelphi* 9 (1935) 383-384.

Review of Max Eastman, *Art and the life of action*. *Adlephi* 10 (1935) 127.

Review of George Barker, *Poems*, Marianne Moore, *Selected poems*. *Adelphi* 10 (1935) 250-252.

Review of Rainer Maria Rilke, *Requiem and other poems*. *Adelphi* 11 (1935) 64.

Review of Archibald MacLeish, *Poems*. *Adelphi* 11 (1935) 128.

Review of Rayner Heppenstall, *First poems*. *Adelphi* 11 (1936) 251-252.

Review of Hugh Sykes Davies, *Petron*, Norman Cameron, *The winter house,* Clifford Dyment, *First day*. *Adelphi* 11 (1936) 256.

Review of C. Day-Lewis, *Noah and the waters*, Julian Bell, *Work for the winter,* Paul Selver, *A baker's dozen of tin trumpets*, Herbert E. Palmer, *The vampire*. *Adelphi* 12 (1936) 187-188, 190-192.

Review of W.J. Turner, *Songs and incantations,* James Reeves, *Natural seed. Adelphi* 12 (1936) 256.

Review of Michael Roberts, *Poems. Adelphi* 12 (1936) 318-319.

Reviews of Dylan Thomas, *Twenty five poems*; Ruth Pitter, *A trophy of arms, Adelphi* 13 (1936) 185-186; 192.

Nodiadau ar surrealistiaeth. *Tir Newydd,* Tach/Nov 1937, 11-14. [Notes on surrealism].

Satiric eye. *Twentieth Century Verse* 6-7 (1937). One-page comment on Wyndham Lewis.

The ripening Davies. *Wales* 1 (1937) 30-31. Review of Rhys Davies, *A time to laugh.*

Review of H.W.J. Edwards, *The good patch. Life and Letters Today* 18,12 (1938) 154-155.

Review of C.H. Peacocke, *Poems,* Brian Coffey, *Third person,* Idris Davies, *Gwalia deserta,* Frederic Prokosch, *The carnival,* [Various authors], *Proems. Life and Letters Today* 19,13 (1938) 123-125.

Review of Richard Hughes, *In hazard. Life and Letters Today* 19,13 (1938) 127-128.

Reviews of Leslie Halward, *The money's all right*; Maurice Thorez, *Son of the people. Life and Letters Today* 19,15 (1938) 104-105; 116-117.

Review of Rhys Davies, *Jubilee blues. Life and Letters Today* 20,16 (1938) 117-118.

Reviews of James Hanley, *People are curious*; Hugh Kingsmill, *D.H. Lawrence. Life and Letters Today* 20,17 (1939) 100; 110-112.

Review of Patrick White, *Happy valley. Life and Letters Today* 21,19 (1939) 101.

Hopkins and Welsh prosody. *Life and Letters Today* 21,22 (1939) 51-54.

Review of John Revell Reinhard, *Mediaeval pageant. Life and Letters Today* 21,22 (1939) 128-129.

Review of Wyndham Lewis, *The Jews: are they human? WR* 1 (1939) 355.

Review of B.L. Coombes, *These poor hands. WR* 2 (1939) 111.

Review of Dylan Thomas, *The map of love. WR* 2 (1939) 179-180.

Review of Idris Davies, *The angry summer. Wales* 2nd ser. 1 (1943) 86-87.

Review of Michael Gareth Llewellyn, *Sand in the glass. Life and Letters Today* 40,77 (1944) 62-64.

Irish expatriates, hikers and the law. *Wales* 2nd ser. 5,7 (1945) 107. Review of *They go – the Irish,* ed. Leslie Daiken, John Wood, *Quietest under the sun,* Thomas Artemus Jones, *Without my wig.*

[Reminiscences]. In Oliver Sandys, *Caradoc Evans*. London: Hurst & Blackett, [1946]. pp. 155-164. Describes meeting with Evans.

Reply to *Wales* questionnaire 1946. Wales 2nd ser. 6,3 [23] (1946) 26-27.

Tenth anniversary year message. *Wales* 2nd ser. 7,26 (1947) 257.

Review of Averyl Edwards, *Frederick Louis, Prince of Wales, 1707-1751. Wales* 2nd ser. 7,26 (1947) 322-323.

Review of Roland Mathias, *Break in harvest,* R.S. Thomas, *The stones of the field. WR* 6 (1947) 145-146.

Review of Cledwyn Hughes, *The inn closes for Christmas*, Cledwyn Hughes, *The different drummer*, George Ewart Evans, *The voices of the children. WR* 6 (1947) 300-302.

Review of William Glynne-Jones, *He who had eaten of the eagle,* Denys Val Baker, *The return of Uncle Walter. Wales* 2nd ser. 8,29 (1948) 549-550.

Romanticism and poetry. In *A new romantic anthology*, ed. Stephan Schimanski and Henry Treece. London: Grey Walls Press, 1949. pp. 167-169. Discusses the ambiguous nature of the romantic poet in modern society, by way of introducing his choice of poems by ten Welsh poets.

Review of Raymond Garlick, *Poems from the mountain-house. DL* 1,2 (1950) 58-60.

Review of Gwyn Thomas, *The world cannot hear you. DL* 2,6 (1951) 37-39.

Three memoirs. *Adam* 238 (1953) 11-13. Phillip Lindsay, David Daiches and Glyn Jones contribute to a Dylan Thomas memorial number.

Review of Idris Davies, *Selected poems. DL* 4,11 (1953) 53-54.

Three Anglo-Welsh prose writers. *Rann* 19 (1953) 1-5. Emphasizes individuality of style in Caradoc Evans, Gwyn Thomas and Dylan Thomas. – This Welsh number of *Rann* also includes poems by Glyn Jones.

Dylan Thomas and Welsh. *DL* 5,13 (1954) 24-25.

Review of Raymond Garlick, *The Welsh-speaking sea. DL* 6,16 (1955) 36-38.

Where are Wales' young writers? *News Chronicle*, 18 Apr 1956, 9:F-H.

I was born in Rhymney: Idris Davies, the man and his work. *Poetry and Drama Magazine* 9,2 (1957) 6-10.

Teenaged angel in a black polo-necked sweater. *WM*, 21 Apr 1958, 4:B-G. Continued: A prodigy among the down-beats, 22 Apr, 4:B-G; A roaring boy dying of welcome, 23 Apr, 6:B-E; The fallen angel with a tumbledown tongue, 24 Apr, 6:B-G. – Series with general title, Dylan Thomas: the other man.

Idris Davies: the man and the poet. *London Welshman*, June 1959, 10-11.

The literary scene. *Wales* 3rd ser., Dec 1959, 15-17. In response to Alun Richards' charge (*Wales* 3rd ser., Oct 1959, 27-29) that Anglo-Welsh authors have neglected the real Wales.

Slim volumes for a slim public. *WM*, 23 Jul 1960, 5:B-E. On the audience for poetry.

Cardiff: the largest, richest, loveliest city in Wales. *London Welshman*, Aug 1960, 4-8.

The man who walks alone. *WM*, 24 Sep 1960, 5:A-D. On Huw Menai.

Review of Roland Mathias, *The flooded valley. AWR* 10,26 (1960) 71-73.

Paths to penmanship. *WM*, 18 Feb 1961, 10:A-E. Review article on V.E.C. Gordon and Ruth Mock, *Twentieth century handwriting*.

A gun round the door starts Nick's day. *WM*, 21 Sep 1961, 8:B-E. Third part of 'Sextet', a composite serial with six authors.

*Yr ogof* in translation. *WM*, 16 Dec 1961, 6:D-E. Review of T. Rowland Hughes, *The story of Joseph of Arimathea*, tr. Richard Ruck.

Poetry rooted in suffering. WM, 12 Oct 1963, 6:E-F. Review of T.H. Jones, *The beast at the door*, R.S. Thomas, *The bread of truth*.

'Sgrifennu yn Saesneg. *Y Faner,* 7 Mai/May 1964, 6. [Writing in English].

Y llenorion Eingl-Gymreig. *Taliesin* 9 (1964) 50-63. [The Anglo-Welsh writers].

Strong contrasts at Cardiff exhibition. *Times* [early ed.], 28 Jul 1967. Art exhibition review. – 'From a correspondent', as are all Glyn Jones's art reviews in *The Times*.

The flowering of Wales. *WM*, 19 Aug 1967, 8:A-B. Review of *The Penguin book of Welsh verse*, ed. Anthony Conran.

Welsh painter's vision. *Times* [early ed.], 10 Nov 1967. Exhibition review.

A patch of dove-grey: reflections on poetry and painting. *AWR* 16,37 (1967) 101-105.

Review of Dylan Thomas, *Selected letters*. PW 3,1 (1967) 53-54.

Grave playfulness of John Piper. *Times* [early ed.], 12 Apr 1968. Art exhibition review.

Painter in love with Wales. *Times* [early ed.], 17 Apr 1968. On Donald McIntyre exhibition.

Paintings of more than charm and distinction. *Times* [early ed.], 17 Jul 1968. Exhibition review of Wyndham Lewis, Sidney Nolan, Walter Sickert and others.

Natural painter of all things Welsh. *Times* [early ed.], 16 Oct 1968. On Kyffin Williams exhibition.

Paintings of all shades and colours. *Times* [early ed.], 17 Dec 1968. Art exhibition review.

Voices of Wales. *TLS*, 19 Dec 1968, 1433. Letter on *The dragon has two tongues*.

Crumbling valleys. *PW* 4,1 (1968) 49-50. Review of Robert Morgan, *The night's prison*.

Foreword to Taliesin Congress, 14-20 September, 1969. In *Literature in Celtic Countries*, ed. J.E. Caerwyn Williams. Cardiff: University of Wales Press, pp. 21-24.

Introduction. In *Recording Wales, 2. Chapels*. Cardiff: Welsh Arts Council, 1969. pp. 3-4. Exhibition catalogue.

Bathsheba. *Outposts* 82 (1969). Uncollected poem.

Review of John James, *Men went to Catraeth*. PW 5,2 (1969) 60-61.

Whose flight is toil. In *Vernon Watkins, 1906-1967*. London: Faber, 1970. pp. 23-26. Recollections of Vernon Watkins.

Y dyn arall. *Barn*, Ion/Jan 1970, 77. Review of J.P. Ward, *The other man*.

Review of forgotten pioneer. *WM*, 21 Mar 1970, 6:C-E. Review of T.L. Williams, *Caradoc Evans*.

Jack Jones: 1884-1970. *Barn*, Gor/Jul 1970, 233. Obituary.

Jack Jones: 1884-1970. *AWR* 19,43 (1970) 17-21. Obituary.

Notes on Anglo-Welsh writing. *Études Anglaises* 23,3 (1970) 332-334.

Review of Rolfe Humphries, *Nine thorny thickets*. *PW* 5,3 (1970) 62-65.

Review of Leslie Norris, *Ransoms*. *PW* 6,2 (1970) 56-58.

[Autobiography]. In *Y llwybrau gynt*, ed. Alun Oldfield-Davies. Llandysul: Gwasg Gomer, 1971. pp. 61-93. Text of broadcast talk.

Llên y ddwy iaith. *Barn*, Hyd/Oct 1971, 353. Review of *Triskel one: essays on Welsh and Anglo-Welsh literature*, ed. Sam Adams and Gwilym Rees Hughes.

Review of Kusha Petts, *Necklace for a poor sod*, Glyn Hughes, *Neighbours*. *AWR* 19,44 (1971) 250-252.

Pant y Bril. *Planet* 5-6 (1971) 69-75. Translation of story by D. J. Williams. – Revised as 'A successful year' in *The Penguin book of Welsh short stories*, ed. Alun Richards.

*Letter*. *PW* 7,3 (1971) 7-14. On poetic climate before Dylan Thomas and the mood during the depression and war.

Second flowering: poetry in Wales. In *British poetry since 1960: a critical survey*, ed. M. Schmidt and G. Lindop. Manchester: Carcanet 1972. pp. 122-131. Discusses Anglo-Welsh poets of the 1960s and their concern for national identity.

O Bontypridd. *Barn,* Gor/Jul 1972, 247. Review of John L. Hughes, *Tom Jones slept here.*

Review of *Artists in Wales*. Vol. 1, ed. Meic Stephens. *AWR* 21,47 (1972) 212-214.

Review of Trevor Fishlock, *Wales and the Welsh*. *AWR* 21,48 (1972) 273-275.

Early Dylan. *Planet* 10 (1972) 75-78. Review of Dylan Thomas, *Early prose writings*, ed. Walford Davies, 'The world of Dylan Thomas' (gramophone record).

The large canvas widens. *WM,* 5 Apr 1973, 12:C-E. Review article on Richard Hughes, *The wooden shepherdess.*

Beirdd y cymoedd hiraeth. *Barn*, Meh/Jun 1973, 366-367. Review of Meic Stephens, *Exiles all*, Sam Adams, *The boy inside.*

Escaping from Satanic mills. *WM*, 15 Dec 1973, 11:E-F. Review of Moira Dearnley, *That watery glass*, Robert Nisbet, *Dreams and dealings*.

Poetry at the Casson: 'Womb to tomb' and 'Timeslip'. *AWR* 22,49 (1973) 290-294. Account of Casson Theatre poetry readings, with comment on performance styles of John Ormond and Leslie Norris.

Review of Rhydwen Williams, *Adar y gwanwyn. Y Genhinen* 23,3 (1973) 145-146.

Henffych – Ddafydd. *PW* 8,4 (1973) 77-79. In sequence, 'A garland for Dafydd ap Gwilym', by various poets.

*18 poems* again. *PW* 9,2 (1973) 22-26. On re-reading Dylan Thomas.

Bois y bont. *Planet* 22 (1974) 83-84. Review of Alun Richards, *Dai country*.

I country. *Planet 23* (1974) 78-80. Review of Alun Richards, *Home to an empty house*.

Review of Dyfnallt Morgan, *D. Gwenallt Jones. Y Traethodydd* 129 (1974) 72-74.

Leslie Norris – R.S. Thomas. In *Contemporary poets*, ed. James Vinson. 2nd ed. London: St. James Press; New York: St. Martins Press, 1975. pp. 1122-1123, 1539-1541.

Hen benillion. *Aquarius* 8 (1976) 16-20. *Penillion* translations.

Review of Vernon Watkins, *I that was born in Wales*, David Jones, *Letters to Vernon Watkins. BNW*, Autumn 1976, 18-19.

Artistiaid Cymreig, 2. John Elwyn. *Y Genhinen* 26,2 (1976) 69-74. [Welsh artists].

Duw, it's hard: notes on the short story. *Planet* 35 (1976) 6-8. On his practices as short-story writer.

Kate Roberts yn Saesneg. *Barn*, Chw/Feb 1977, 70. Review of Kate Roberts, *The living sleep*, tr. Wyn Griffith.

Bringing up the prodigal. *Guardian Weekly*, 1 May 1977, 23. Review of Paul Ferris, *Dylan Thomas*, Daniel Jones, *My friend Dylan Thomas*.

Yr Eingl-Gymry heddiw. *Y Faner*, 6 Mai/May 1977, 12-13. [The Anglo-Welsh today].

Harri'r werin. *Barn*, Tach/Nov 1977, 381. Review of Harri Webb, *Rampage and revel*.

Review of Cecil Price, *Gwyn Jones*, Julian Croft, *T.H. Jones. AWR* 26,58 (1977) 161-165.

Artistiaid Cymreig, 3. John Petts. *Y Genhinen* 27,2 (1977) 75-79.

Dedicated professional. *Planet* 40 (1977) 53-54. Review of David Rees, *Rhys Davies*.

['The beach at Falesá']. *Texas Arts Journal* 1 (1977). Article on his opera libretto.

Review of Leslie Norris, *Sliding. Madog* 2,1 (1978) 86-89.

Foreword. In Gwyn Jones, *Times like these*. London: Gollancz, 1979. pp. 5-7.

Letter. *WM*, 27 Feb 1979, 10:D. Welsh writers commend devolution.

Review of Mike Jenkins, *Rat city. Madog* 2,2 (1979) 106.

[Letter to editor]. *PW* 15,2 (1979) 10-12. On Anglo-Welsh literary criticism.

X = ?. In *Places: an anthology of Britain*, ed. Ronald Blythe. Oxford: Oxford University Press, 1981. pp. 97-103. Evocation of Llanstephan.

Writing *Profiles. BNW*, Spring 1981, 6.

A tribute to Gwyn Thomas. *AWR* 68 (1981) 4-5.

An interview with Glyn Jones. *Poetry* [Shih Feng Association, Hong Kong] 109 (1981) i-v.

Some letters of Idris Davies. *PW* 16,4 (1981) 76-84. Extracts from letters to Glyn Jones, with linking commentary.

Review of Jan Morris, *Wales. BNW,* Autumn 1982, 13.

Gwyn Jones. In *British novelists, 1930-1959. Part 1, A-L,* ed. Bernard Oldsey. Detroit: Gale, 1983. (Dictionary of literary biography; 15). pp. 232-236.

Review of John Pikoulis, *Alun Lewis: a life. BNW*, Autumn 1984, 9.

Shorts abroad. *BWA* (1984) 4. On recently published Russian translations of Anglo-Welsh short stories.

Review of Dannie Abse, *A poet in the family. BNW,* Spring 1985, 15.

A letter from Glyn Jones. *PW* 21,3 (1986) 73-75. On Leslie Norris. –

Reprinted as 'Poet of Merthyr' in *An open world: essays on Leslie Norris*, ed. Eugene England and Peter Makuck. Columbia: Camden House, 1993. pp. 26-28.

A. G. Prys-Jones. *BWA* 11 (1987) 4.

Keidrych Rhys: 1915-1987. *PW* 22,4 (1987) 12-15.

Foreword. In *The collected poems of A.G. Prys-Jones*, ed. Don Dale-Jones. Llandysul: Gomer 1988. pp. 5-8.

The poetry of meaning (1966). In *Wales on the wireless: a broadcasting anthology*, ed. Patrick Hannan. Llandysul: Gomer in assoc. with BBC Cymru/Wales, 1988. pp. 165-166.

Some inside authorial information: Glyn Jones on his *Selected poems, fragments and fictions*. *BWA* 14 (1988) 7. Discusses excluded poems and corrects a serious misprint.

[Robert Minhinnick interviews Glyn Jones]. *NWR* 1,1 [1] (1988) 7-11.

Letter. *Oriel Bulletin* 3 (1988) 6. Short note on his recent publications.

Review of *Wales on the Wireless: a broadcast anthology*, ed. Patrick Hannan, *Erkundungen: 28 walisische Erzähler*. *BWA* 16 (1989) 13-14.

Review of Robert Nisbet, *Downmarket*. *BWA* 17 (1989) 16.

Illuminations. *PW* 24,3 (1989) 42-45. Autobiography.

Review of Emyr Humphreys, *A toy epic*. *BWA* 19 (1990) 12.

Conference mosaic. *BWA* 20 (1990) 8. Brief impressions of the Welsh Academy conference, Tenby 1990.

At the Dylan Thomas School. *BWA* 21 (1990) 13. Brief impressions of the second Dylan Thomas Summer School, Aberystwyth 1990.

John Ormond, 1923-1990. *PW* 26,2 (1990) 3-5.

Yr awen addfwyn. *Golwg*, 3 Hyd/Oct 1991, 20-21. Interviewed by Dylan Iorwerth. – [The gentle muse].

Review of Harri Pritchard Jones, *Corner people*. *BWA* 24 (1991) 14.

[Autobiographical extract]. *NWR* 4,1 [13] (1991) 3. On publication of his first two books.

A welcome act of bridge-building. *NWR* 4,2 [14] (1991) 7-10. Review of

James A. Davies, *Leslie Norris,* Elwyn Evans, *Alun Llewelyn-Williams,* John Emyr, *Bobi Jones.*

Review of *The works,* ed. Nigel Jenkins. *NWR* 4,3 [15] (1991-1992) 70-71.

Shader Twm visits his retrospective exhibition. *PW* 28,2 (1992) 18-19. From the sequence, Seven keys to Shaderdom.

Dylan Thomas: The Boat House, Laugharne, Dyfed. *In Writers and their houses: a guide to the writers' houses of England, Scotland, Wales and Ireland: essays by modern writers,* ed. Kate Marsh. London: H. Hamilton, 1993. pp. 423-433.

# B. Publications about Glyn Jones

BEVAN, D.Tudor. Glyn Jones: the background to his writing. MA thesis. University of Wales (Swansea), 1989.

—— Glyn Jones's Wales. *BWA* 25 (1992) 5-7.

CHATALIC, Roger. Glyn Jones, or the exaltation of the commonplace. Mémoire de Diplôme d'Études Supérieures, University of Rennes, 1958.

CHOURLIN, Nicole. The Welsh element in Glyn Jones' selected short stories. Mémoire de Mâitresse thesis, University of Rouen, 1973. 98 p. Contents: A birds' eye view of Wales, pp. 6-16 – Life in Wales, pp. 17-39 – Tradition of thought in Wales, pp. 40-57 – Language and style, pp. 58-79 – Conclusion, notes, bibliography, pp. 80-98.

HARRIS, John and Sylvia Harris. A bibliography of Glyn Jones. *PW* 19,3 (1984) 90-96. Continued: *PW* 19,4 (1984) 66-69.

JONES, G. O. Glyn Jones. *BWA* 8 (1985) 1-2. On the occasion of Glyn Jones's 80th birthday.

JONES, Gwyn. Language, style and the Anglo-Welsh. *Essays and Studies* 6 (1953) 102-114. On Dylan Thomas, Gwyn Thomas, Glyn Jones and Caradoc Evans.

JONES, Jack. Nofelau'r Cymry-Seisnig. *Tir Newydd,* Mai/May 1937, 5-9. [Anglo-Welsh novels].

MATHIAS, Roland. Glyn Jones. In *Contemporary poets,* ed. James Vinson. 2nd ed. London: St. James Press; New York: St Martin's Press, 1975. pp. 796-799.

MINHINNICK, Robert. An uncommmon path: some thoughts on the poetry of Glyn Jones. *PW* 19,3 (1984) 63-71.

NORRIS, Leslie. *Glyn Jones.* Cardiff: University of Wales Press [for] the Welsh Arts Council, 1973. 95 p.: front. port. (Writers of Wales). Incl. selected bibliography, pp. 89-92. – 'Limited to 1000 copies'.

—— Glyn Jones. In *British novelists, 1930 to 1959. Part 1: A-L,* ed. Bernard Oldsey. Detroit: Gale, 1982. (Dictionary of literary biography; 15). pp. 226-231.

—— Glyn Jones. In *Contemporary novelists,* ed. Lesley Henderson. 5th ed. Chicago; London: St James Press, 1991. pp. 501-503.

PARRY, Idris, Glyn Jones. In *The concise encyclopaedia of modern world literature*, ed. Geoffrey Grigson. London: Hutchinson, 1963. pp. 240-241.

PRYS-JONES, A. G. A tribute to Glyn Jones. *BWA* 8 (1985) 2-3. On his 80th birthday.

PURSGLOVE, Glyn. In *Contemporary poets*, ed. Tracy Chevalier. 5th ed. Chicago; London: St James Press, 1991. pp. 486-487. Incl. comment by Glyn Jones.

SIMPSON, Mercer. Assimilation and synthesis: Glyn Jones as Anglo-Welsh poet. *PW* 19,3 (1984) 72-89.

—— Review article on Glyn Jones, *Selected poems, fragments and fictions*. *NWR* 1,1 [1] (1988) 11-14.

SMITH, Dai. A whole life. *Arcade*, 19 Feb 1982, 17. Profile of Glyn Jones based on interview.

STEPHENS, Meic. Glyn Jones. *South Wales Magazine*, Autumn 1970, 33. Under the pseudonym, Iolo Llwyd.

—— Wales's grand old man of literature. *WM*, 16 Feb 1991, [Weekender] 3:A-D. Incl. interview.

THOMAS, Dylan. *The broadcasts,* ed. Ralph Maud. London: Dent, 1991. Brief comment on Glyn Jones, pp. 45-46.

Williams, John Stuart. The poetry of Glyn Jones. *AWR* 16,38 (1967) 23-31.

# GWYN JONES (b. 1907)

A. Publications by Gwyn Jones
  (i)   Books
  (ii)  Books edited or translated
  (iii) Selected contributions to books and periodicals

B. Publications about Gwyn Jones

## A (i). Publications by Gwyn Jones: Books

*Richard Savage*. London: Gollancz, 1935. 607 p. Novel.

U.S. ed.: New York: Viking Press, 1935. 599 p.

*Times like these*. London: Gollancz, 1936. 319 p.
—— / with a foreword by Glyn Jones. Gollancz, 1979. hbk & pbk. ISBN: 0-575-02719-3 hbk, 0-575-02720-7 pbk.

*The nine days' wonder*. London: Gollancz, 1937. 448 p.

*Garland of bays*. London: Gollancz, 1938. 670 p. Novel based on life of Robert Greene.

U.S. ed.: New York: Macmillan, 1938.

*The buttercup field and other stories*. Cardiff: Penmark Press, 1945. vi, 138 p. Contents: The pit – The buttercup field – A man after God's own heart – All we like sheep – Kittens – Shacki Thomas – Ora pro boscis – The dreamers – A night at Galon-Uchaf – Gwydion Mathrafal – The passionate people – Their bonds are loosed from above – Take us, the little foxes.

*The green island: a novel* / engravings by John Petts. London: Golden Cockerel Press, 1946. 84 p.: ill. Frontispiece and 9 engravings by John Petts. – 'This edition is limited to 500 numbered copies. Nos 1-100 have been specially bound.'

*A prospect of Wales* / a series of water-colours by Kenneth Rowntree and an essay by Gwyn Jones. Harmondsworth: Penguin Books, 1948. 31 p.: ill.: ppb. (King Penguin; 43). With 20 colour plates and 3 text figures.

*The still waters and other stories*. London: Peter Davies, 1948. vi, 188 p. Contents: The green island – The still waters – Bad blood – Shining morn – A white birthday – Four in a valley – The prisoners – Down in the forest something stirred – Guto Fewel – Goronwy's house of gold.

*The flowers beneath the scythe.* London: Dent, 1952. 254 p.: hbk & pbk.

*Shepherd's hey and other stories.* London: Staples Press, 1953. 243 p. Contents: Shepherd's hey – The brute creation – Old age – Copy – All on a summer's day – Two women – A death on Sistersland.

*The first forty years: some notes on Anglo-Welsh literature.* Cardiff: University of Wales Press, 1957. 28 p.: pamph. (W.D. Thomas memorial lecture).

*The walk home: a novel.* London: Dent, 1962. 205 p.

U.S. ed.: New York: Norton, 1963.

*The Norse Atlantic saga: being the Norse voyages of discovery and settlement to Iceland, Greenland, America.* London: Oxford University Press, 1964. xiv, 246 p.: ill.
—— /A new and enlarged edition; with contributions by Robert McGhee, Thomas H. McGovern and colleagues, and Birgitta Linderoth Wallace. London: Oxford University Press, 1986. xv, 337 p.: ill.: hbk & pbk. ISBN: 0-19-215886-4 hbk, 0-19-285160-8 pbk.

Italian trans.: *Antichi viaggi di scoperta in Islanda, Groenlandia e America,* tr. Giorgio Romano. Milano: Bompiani, 1966. 322 p.

Spanish trans.: *El primer descubrimiento de América,* tr. J.A. Zabalbeascoa. Barcelona: Occidente, 1965. 319 p.

*A history of the Vikings.* London: Oxford University Press, 1968. xvi, 504 p.: ill. Reissued 1973, pbk. ISBN: 0-19-285063-6.
—— Book Club Associates, 1973.
—— London: Oxford University Press, 1984. xviii, 504 p.: ill.: hbk & pbk. ISBN: 0-19-215882-1 hbk, 0-19-285139-X pbk. 'New and extensively revised edition'.

Italian trans.: *I Vichinghi,* tr. Celso Balducci. Roma: Newton Compton editori, 1977. 519 p.: pbk.

Japanese trans.: Tokyo: Kobunsha, 1987. ISBN: 4-7704-0663-0.

*The legendary history of Olaf Tryggvason.* Glasgow: Jackson, 1968. 38 p.: pamph. (W.P. Ker memorial lecture; 22). ISBN: 0-85304-000-1.

*Kings, beasts and heroes.* London: Oxford University Press, 1972. xxvi, 176 p.: ill. ISBN: 0-19-215181-9. On 'Beowulf', the Welsh 'Culhwch and Olwen', and the Norse 'King Hrolf's saga'.

*Selected short stories.* London: Oxford University Press, 1974. xi, 173 p.:

pbk. ISBN: 0-19-281162-2. Contents: Introduction – The buttercup field
– All on a summer's day – Guto Fewel – Shacki Thomas – Kittens –
Ora pro boscis – All we like sheep – A man after God's own heart – A
white birthday – Four in a valley – The brute creation – The still waters
– Their bonds are loosed from above – The green island.

*Being and belonging: some notes on language, literature and the Welsh.*
BBC Publications, 1977. 25 p.: pamph. (BBC Wales annual radio lecture).
ISBN: 0-563-17473-0.

*Y nofel a chymdeithas: The novel and society.* Bangor: North Wales
Arts Association, 1981. [28] p.: pamph. (Ben Bowen Thomas lecture).
ISBN: 0-901833-99-1. Delivered Bangor 19 Sep 1980. – Text in English
and Welsh.

*Babel and the dragon's tongue.* Southampton: University of Southampton,
1981. 21 p.: pamph. (Gwilym James memorial lecture; 8). ISBN: 0-85432-
217-5. On Anglo-Welsh literature.

*Background to Dylan Thomas and other explorations.* Oxford; New York:
Oxford University Press, 1992. viii, 210 p. ISBN: 0-19-811283-1. Contents:
Background to Dylan Thomas: Anglo-Welsh literature, 1934-1946: a personal
view, pp. 1-19 – The Golden Cockerel Mabinogion, 1944-1948, pp. 20-51 –
Three poetical prayer-makers of the island of Britain [Cynddelw, Kitchener
Davies, Saunders Lewis], pp. 52-71 – A mighty man in Sion: Caradoc
Evans, 1878-1945, pp. 72-88 – Welsh Dylan, 1914-1953: an obituary, pp.
89-97 – Son of the late Earl Rivers: Richard Savage, 1697-1743, pp. 98-
114 – On first planting a library, pp. 115-121 – The novel and society,
pp. 122-138 – Here be dragons: a view of the nature and function of heroic
poetry, pp. 139-161 – The legendary history of Olaf Tryggvason, pp. 162-
185 – The Viking world, pp. 186-203 – Address to my friends, 24 May
1987, pp. 204-207.

# A (ii). Publications by Gwyn Jones: Books Edited or Translated

In addition to contributing to the works listed below, Gwyn Jones was
founder-editor of *The Welsh Review*, published monthly Feb-Nov 1939 (1,1
– 2,4) and quarterly Mar 1944-Winter 1948 (3,1 – 7,4). His editorials
appear in all 30 issues, excepting 7,1 and 7,3.

*Narrative poems for schools* / compiled by Gwyn Jones and E.M. Silvanus.
London: Rivingtons, 1935. 3 v. (viii, 183 p.; 177 p.; 246 p.): pbk.

*Four Icelandic sagas* / translated with an introduction and notes by Gwyn
Jones. Princeton: Princeton University Press, 1935. 164 p. Contents:
Introduction – Hrafnkel Freysgodi's saga – Thorstein the White's saga

– The Weaponfirthers' saga – The saga of the men of Keelness – Notes – Bibliography.

*Poems of six centuries: an anthology of verse from early times to the present day* / compiled by Gwyn Jones. London: Rivingtons, 1936. xii, 304 p.: pbk.

*Prose of six centuries: an anthology of prose from early times to the present day* / compiled by Gwyn Jones. London: Rivingtons, 1937. xi, 307 p.: pbk.

*Welsh short stories* / selected by Gwyn Jones. Harmondsworth: Penguin, 1940. 169 p.: pbk.
—— 1941. 154 p.: pbk.

*The Vatnsdalers' saga* / translated with an introduction and notes by Gwyn Jones. Princeton University Press for American-Scandinavian Foundation, 1944. 158 p.
—— New York: Kraus Reprint, 1973. ISBN: 0-527-92850-X.

*Alun Lewis: Letters from India* / with a note by Mrs. Alun Lewis; and a preface by A.L. Rowse. Cardiff: Penmark Press, 1946. 97 p.: ill. Includes facsimiles. – 'Selection of letters was made by Gweno Lewis and Gwyn Jones ... The edition is limited to 500 numbered copies, of which nos. 1-100 have been specially bound.'

*The Golden Cockerel Mabinogion: a new translation from the White Book of Rhydderch and the Red Book of Hergest* / by Gwyn Jones and Thomas Jones; with illustrations by Dorothea Braby. London: Golden Cockerel Press, 1948. 266 p.: ill. Incl. 20 engravings in wood and scraper board. – 'The edition is limited to 550 numbered copies of which copies numbered 1-75 are specially bound.'
—— *The Mabinogion* / translated with an introduction by Gwyn Jones and Thomas Jones. Dent, 1949. xxxiv, 282 p. (Everyman's library; 97). Revised, with expanded introduction.
—— Dent, 1974. xliv, 283 p.: hbk & pbk. (Everyman's library). ISBN: 0-460-00097-7 hbk, 0-460-01097-2 pbk. Revised, with supplementary introduction by Gwyn Jones. – Reissued 1989, pbk. (Everyman classics). ISBN: 0-460-15097-9, with maps and index of proper names.
—— / illustrated by Jeff Thomas. Dent, 1976. xliv, 273 p.: ill. ISBN: 0-460-04228-9. Incl. 16 plates.
—— / illustrated by Alan Lee. Netherlands: Dragon's Dream, 1982. 224 p.: ill.: hbk & pbk. ISBN: 90-6332-8613 hbk, 90-6332-9113 pbk. Incl. 45 coloured illustrations.

Bulgarian trans.: 1986.

Dutch trans.: partly published.

*Salmacis and Hermaphroditus: a poem attributed to Francis Beaumont* /

edited by Gwyn Jones; with engravings in colour by John Buckland-Wright. London: Golden Cockerel Press, 1951. 41 p.: ill. 'The edition is limited to 380 copies ... Copies 1-80 are specially bound and contain one extra plate.'

*Sir Gawain and the green knight* / a prose translation with an introductory essay by Gwyn Jones; with six engravings in colour by Dorothea Braby. London: Golden Cockerel Press, 1952. 95 p.: ill. Introduction, pp. 1-34. – 'The edition is limited to 360 numbered copies ... Numbers 1-60 are specially bound.'

Browne, William. *Circe and Ulysses: the Inner Temple masque presented by the gentlemen there, January 13, 1614* / ... edited with an essay on William Browne and the English masque by Gwyn Jones; seven wood-engravings by Mark Severin. London: Golden Cockerel Press, 1954. 61 p.: ill. Incl. William Browne and the English masque, by Gwyn Jones, pp. 39-61. – 'The edition is limited to 300 copies ... Numbers 1-100 are specially bound and contain four extra engravings.'

*Welsh legends and folk-tales* / retold by Gwyn Jones; illustrated by Joan Kiddell-Monroe. Oxford: Oxford University Press, 1955. 230 p.: ill. (Oxford myths and legends).
—— Harmondsworth: Puffin Books, 1979. 262 p.: ill. ISBN: 0-14-031097-5.

U.S. ed.: New York: H.Z. Walck, 1965. (Myths and legends).

*Welsh short stories* / selected and with an introduction by Gwyn Jones. London: Oxford University Press, 1956. xv, 330 p. (The world's classics; 551). Introduction, pp. ix-xv.

*Scandinavian legends and folk-tales* / retold by Gwyn Jones; illustrated by Joan Kiddell-Monroe. London: Oxford University Press, 1956. 222 p.: ill. (Oxford myths and legends). Reissued 1979, pbk. ISBN: 0-19-274124-1.

U.S. ed.: New York: H.Z. Walck, 1966. (Myths and legends).

Arabic trans.: *Asatirmin albuldan al scandinaviet*, tr. Muhammad Khaled Bashtawi. Damas, Syria: Wizaratal thaqafa, 1984. 343 p.

Japanese trans.: *Oxford sekai no minwa to densetsu, 9: Hokuo-hen*, tr. Yamamuro Shizuka. Tokyo: Kodansha, 1964. 242 p. Reissued 1978.

*Songs and poems of John Dryden* / chosen and introduced by Gwyn Jones; drawings by Lavinia Blythe. London: Golden Cockerel Press, 1957. 64 p.: ill. 'Limited to 500 numbered copies. The text has been prepared by James Kinsley ... Special copies (nos. 1-100), with an extra set of the eight pictures and eight of the [eleven] drawings.'

*The Metamorphoses of Publius Ovidius Naso translated by the most eminent hands* / a selection from the 1717 edition, with drawings by J. Yunge Bateman. London: Golden Cockerel Press, 1958. 284 pp.: ill. 'Limited to 200 numbered copies, of which nos. 1-75 are specially bound and accompanied by an extra set of the 11 drawings, together with 3 additional pictures not printed in the book.'

*Egil's saga* / translated from the Old Icelandic, with an introduction and notes by Gwyn Jones. Syracuse: Syracuse University Press, for American-Scandinavian Foundation, 1960. ix, 257 p.
—— New York: Twayne, 1975.

*The poems and sonnets of William Shakespeare* / edited by Gwyn Jones. London: Golden Cockerel Press, 1960. 245 pp. Incl. Editorial note, pp. 239-245. – 'Limited to 470 numbered copies, of which nos. 1-100 are specially bound'.

*Eirik the Red and other Icelandic sagas* / selected and translated with an introduction by Gwyn Jones. London: Oxford University Press, 1961. xvi, 318 p. (The world's classics; 582). Contents: Introduction, pp. vii-xvi – Sagas of Icelanders; Hen-Thorir, The Vapnfjord men, Thorstein Staff-struck, Hrafnkel the Priest of Frey, Eirik the Red, Thidrandi whom the Goddesses Slew, Authun the Bear, Gunnlaug Wormtongue – Saga of times past; King Hrolf and his champions. – Reissued 1975, ISBN: 0-19-250582-3. – Reissued 1980, hbk & pbk. ISBN: 0-19-251006-1 hbk, 0-19-281528-8 pbk.

*Twenty-five Welsh short stories* / selected by Gwyn Jones and Islwyn Ffowc Elis; with an introduction by Gwyn Jones. London: Oxford University Press, 1971. xvi, 239 p.: pbk. ISBN: 0-19-281099-5. Introduction, pp. ix-xvi. – Reissued 1992, as *Classic Welsh short stories*. pbk. ISBN: 0-19-282940-8.

*The Oxford book of Welsh verse in English* / chosen by Gwyn Jones. Oxford: Oxford University Press, 1977. xxxvii, 313 p. ISBN: 0-19-211858-7. Incl. introduction, pp. xvii-xxi. – Reissued 1983, pbk. ISBN: 0-19-281397-8.

*Fountains of praise: University College Cardiff, 1883-1983* / edited by Gwyn Jones and Michael Quinn. Cardiff: University College Cardiff Press, 1983. xv, 207 p.: ill. ISBN: 0-906449-52-9. Incl. Editorial, pp. xi-xiv.

# A (iii). Publications by Gwyn Jones: Selected Contributions to Books and Periodicals

This section covers Gwyn Jones's literary writings, including his many reviews for the *Times Literary Supplement*. His Northern scholarship is more selectively listed.

Review of *The Twickenham edition of the poems of Alexander Pope. Vol. IV. Imitations of Horace,* etc., ed. John Butt. *Life and Letters Today* 23 (1939) 128-132.

Reviews of *The Kingis quair*, ed. W. Mackay Mackenzie, Ha Rollo, *The*

*Edda of Asgard*; Howard Rollin Patch, *On re-reading Chaucer. Life and Letters Today* 23 (1939) 241-244; 377-378.

An unpublished poem of Charles Kingsley. *WR* 2 (1939) 165.

Review of W.H. Davies, *The loneliest mountain.* WR 2 (1939) 232-234.

Review of Oliver Elton, *Essays and addresses. Life and Letters Today* 24 (1940) 89-90.

Reviews of B. Ifor Evans, *Tradition and romanticism; Tudor translations: an anthology chosen by Judge Clements. Life and Letters Today* 24 (1940) 326-328; 329-332.

Reviews of Basil Willey, *The eighteenth century background;* E.J. Sweeting, *Studies in early Tudor criticism; The poems of Thomas Pestell,* ed. Hannah Buchan. *Life and Letters Today* 26 (1940) 81-84; 284-285; 286-288.

Reviews of Edith Weir Perry, *Under four Tudors;* C.J. Sisson, *The judicious marriage of Mr Hooker and the birth of* The laws of ecclesiastical polity; Logan Pearsall Smith, *Milton and his modern critics. Life and Letters Today* 27 (1940) 66-68; 144-146; 253-254.

At Beguildy. In *English story: first series,* ed. Woodrow and Susan Wyatt. London: Collins, 1941. pp. 175-186. Story.

The fool. *Argosy,* Sep 1941, 61-69. Story.

Review of William A. Nitze. *Arthurian romance and modern poetry and music. Life and Letters Today* 28 (1941) 73-74.

Review of *The Twickenham edition of the poems of Alexander Pope. Vol. II. The rape of the lock, and other poems,* ed. Geoffrey Tillotson. *Life and Letters Today* 29 (1941) 81-83.

Review of *The works of George Herbert,* ed. F.E. Hutchinson. *Life and Letters Today* 30 (1941) 66-68.

Review of Anthony Steel, *Richard II. Life and Letters Today* 31 (1941) 219-221.

Review of Aldous Huxley, *Grey eminence. Life and Letters Today* 32 (1942) 72-76.

Review of John Cowper Powys, *Owen Glendower. Life and Letters Today* 33 (1942) 130-132.

Notes on the Welsh short story writers. *Life and Letters Today* 34 (1942) 172-180. Continued: *LLT* 36 (1943) 156-163.

Author and reviewer. *WM*, 14 Jan 1943, 3:F. Letter on review of Caradoc Evans, *Pilgrims in a foreign land.*

Review of Walter Dowding, *Wales – know thyself. Life and Letters Today* 36 (1943) 186-187.

Brave and splendid Alun Lewis. *WM*, 20 Mar 1944, 2:G. Obituary.

Reviews of Margiad Evans, *Autobiography; The Twickenham edition of the poems of Alexander Pope. Vol. VI. The dunciad,* ed. James Sutherland. *Life and Letters Today* 40 (1944) 122-124; 184-188.

Review of *Hazlitt in the workshop: the manuscript of* The fight, ed. Stewart C. Wilcox. *Life and Letters Today* 43 (1944) 114-118.

Review of H.J.C. Grierson and J.C. Smith, *A critical history of English poetry. Life and Letters Today* 43 (1944) 170-174.

Letter. *Wales* 2nd ser. 3 (1944) 104. On revival of *The Welsh Review.*

Review of *Collected poems of W.H. Davies,* Idris Davies, *The angry summer, WR* 3 (1944) 69-74.

Alun Lewis (1915-1944). *WR* 3 (1944) 118-121. Obituary. – Reprinted in Alun Lewis, *In the green tree.* London: Allen & Unwin, 1948. pp. 137-141.

Review of Jack Jones, *The man David. WR* 3 (1944) 148.

Review of C.M. Bowra, *From Virgil to Milton. Life and Letters* 46 (1945) 128-132.

Caradoc Evans. *WR* 4 (1945) 24-28. – Reprinted in Oliver Sandys, *Caradoc Evans.* London: Hurst & Blackett, [1946]. pp. 150-154.

Review of *The midnight court: a rhythmical bacchanalia from the Irish of Bryan Merryman,* tr. Frank O'Connor. *WR* 4 (1945) 292.

The Welshman who became a legend. *Listener,* 17 Jan 1946, 79, 87. On Caradoc Evans.

Wales, the oldest brother. *English-Speaking World* 28,1 (1946) 385-392.

Review of Edith Sitwell, *Fanfare for Elizabeth. Life and Letters* 51 (1946) 44-46.

Mabinogi and Edda. *Saga-Book of the Viking Society for Northern Research* 13 (1946) 23-47.

Welsh profile, 1. Professor W.J. Gruffydd. *WR* 5 (1946) 33-35. Unsigned.

Review of Jack Jones, *Me and mine. WR* 5 (1946) 296-298.

Branwen, daughter of Llŷr. *Life and Letters Today* 52 (1947) 161-170.

Review of Malcolm Elwin, *The life of Llewelyn Powys. Life and Letters* 52 (1947) 213-216.

Review of Laurence Binyon, *The madness of Merlin. Life and Letters* 54 (1947) 74-76.

Review of Gwyn Thomas, *Where did I put my pity? WR* 6 (1947) 148.

Culhwch and Olwen. *Life and Letters Today* 58 (1948) 200-212.

Review of John Cowper Powys, *Rabelais. Life and Letters Today* 58 (1948) 244-246.

Review of Oliver Sandys, *Unbroken thread. WR* 7 (1948) 146-147.

Introduction. In A prospect of *Wales: twenty -one water-colour drawings of Wales by Kenneth Rowntree.* Cardiff: Arts Council, 1949. 1 folded sheet (6 p.). Exhibition catalogue.

Caradoc Evans was envied, hated, but not ignored. *WM*, 23 Mar 1949, 4:F-H.

Anglo-Welsh writers, 2. Jack Jones, patriarch of the Anglo-Welsh. *WM*, 30 Mar 1949, 4:D-F.

Anglo-Welsh writers, 3. Dylan Thomas, poet of elemental things. *WM*, 13 Apr 1949, 4:D-F.

Anglo-Welsh writers, 4. Wales will never see the best of Alun Lewis. *WM*, 27 Apr 1949, 4:F-H. Reprinted *WM*, 4 Mar 1961.

Anglo-Welsh writers, 5. Rhys Davies: his last book is his best. *WM*, 11 May 1949, 4:D-F.

Emlyn Williams: comedy and melodrama at his finger-ends. *WM*, 49, 1 Jun 1949, 4:D-E.

Review of George Woodcock, *The paradox of Oscar Wilde. WM,* 6 Jul 1949, 4:D.

The paradox of G.K.C. *WM*, 10 Aug 1949, 4:C-E. Review of G.K. Chesterton, *Autobiography*.

Dickens: literary man of action. *WM*, 24 Aug 1949, 4:A-B. Review of Hesketh Pearson, *Dickens: his character, comedy and career.*

The restless spirit of W.E. Henley. *WM*, 21 Sep 1949, 4:C-E. Review of John Connell, *W.E. Henley*, Joseph Szigeli, *With strings attached.*

Autobiography for today. *WM*, 5 Oct 1949, 4:C-D. Review of G.B. Stern, *Benefits forgot,* Aleric Jacob, *Scenes from a bourgeois life.*

Lives and ideas. *WM*, 2 Nov 1949, 4:C-E. Review of E.M. Hanson, *The four Brontes*, Graham Hough, *The last romantics, Oscar Wilde*, ed. V. Holland.

Brief candles. *WM*, 14 Dec 1949, 4:C-E. Review of John Aubrey, *Brief lives,* ed. Oliver L. Dick, Reginald L. Hine, *Charles Lamb and his Hertfordshire,* Duff Cooper, *Sergeant Shakespeare.*

Charles Tennyson, *Alfred Tennyson. Life and Letters* 63 (1949) 166-167.

The new Anglo-Welsh. *Welsh Anvil* 1 (1949) 56-62. Review of R.S. Thomas, *Stones of the field,* Roland Mathias*, Break in harvest,* Gwyn Thomas, *Where did I put my pity?,* Cledwyn Hughes, *The inn closes for Christmas,* Cledwyn Hughes, *The different drummer,* George Ewart Evans, *The voices of children.*

Review of Norman Ault, *New light on Pope. Life and Letters* 64 (1950) 65-67.

Judgment under Taurus. *Life and Letters* 64 (1950) 214-222. Story.

Egill Skallagrimsson in England. *Proceedings of the British Academy* 37 (1952) 127-144. Also published separately by the British Academy 1952 (Sir Israel Gollancz memorial lecture series).

History and fiction in the sagas of the Icelanders. *Saga-Book of the Viking Society for Northern Research* 13 (1952-53) 285-306.

Introduction. In Caradoc Evans. *My people: stories of the peasantry of west Wales.* London: Dobson, 1953. pp. 7-10.

Icelandic literature. *TLS*, 24 Aug 1953, 520. Review of E.O.G. Turville-Petre, *Origins of Icelandic literature.*

The great story of the north. *TLS*, 27 Nov 1953, i-ii. Review of *Tales of the Norse gods and heroes*, retold by Barbara Léonie Picard.

Language, style and the Anglo-Welsh. *Essays and Studies* 6 (1953) 102-114. On Dylan Thomas, Gwyn Thomas, Glyn Jones and Caradoc Evans.

Introduction. In Robert Louis Stevenson. *The treasure of Franchard.* London: Rodale Press, 1954. pp. vii-xiv.

Review of Dylan Thomas, *Under Milk Wood. WM,* 17 Mar 1954, 6:B-C.

The greatest of sagas. *TLS*, 24 Dec 1954, 836. Review of *Brennu-Njáls saga.*

Welsh Dylan. *Adelphi* 30 (1954) 108-117. Reprinted in *Background to Dylan Thomas* (1992), pp. 89-97.

Norse tales retold, *TLS*, 3 Jun 1955, 303. Review of *The prose Edda of Snorri Sturluson,* ed. and tr. Jean I. Young, *Njáls* saga, tr. Carl F. Bayerschmidt and Lee M. Hollander.

The blue day journey. *TLS*, 2 Dec 1955, 728. Poetry.

Hunter's moon. *Adelphi* 31 (1955) 144-146. Poetry.

Njála, the greatest of sagas. *American-Scandinavian Review*, 43 (1955) 160-162.

The old man of Powys. *WM*, 4 Jan 1956, 6:G. Review of Glyn Jones, *The saga of Llywarch the Old.*

The prose romances of medieval Wales. In *Wales through the ages. Vol 1. From the earliest times to 1485*, ed. A.J. Roderick. Llandybie: Christopher Davies, 1959. pp. 138-144.

Caradoc was the daddy of us all. *WM*, 20 Aug 1960, 5:C-E.

Forum needed for Welsh writers. *WM*, 27 Aug 1960, 5:A-E.

Dylan Thomas in London. *WM*, 3 Sep 1960, 5:B-D. Review article on Rayner Heppenstall, *Four absentees.*

Pennies from heaven. *WM*, 8 Oct 1960, 5:A-E. On arts funding.

A pay-dirt record? *WM*, 25 Mar 1961, 6:B-D. On Arts in Wales conference.

Introduction. In *Wace and Layamon Arthurian Chronicles*, tr. Eugene Mason. London: Dent, 1962. (Everyman's library). pp. v-xii.

Light on the great Norse explorers. *Times*, 14 Jul 1962, 9:F-G.

When Norse swords became ploughshares. *Times*, 4 Aug 1962, 7: F-G.

First church of the new world. *Times*, 1 Sep 1962, 7:F-G.

Introduction. In Geoffrey of Monmouth, *History of the Kings of Britain*. London: Dent, 1963. (Everyman's library). pp. v-xix.

The forms and places of Norse worship. *TLS*, 27 Feb 1964, 167. Review of E.O.G. Turville-Petre, *Myth and religion of the north: the religion of ancient Scandinavia.*

The first Europeans in America. *Beaver: Magazine of the North*, Winter 1964, 4-17.

Life and death of the Greenland settlements. *Icelandic Canadian* 22,4 (1964) 13-19.

The Anglo-Welsh: as it was and may be. In *St. David's National Festival Souvenir 1965*. London: London Welsh Trust, 1965. pp. 7-8.

The angry old men. In *Scandinavian studies presented to H.G. Leech,* ed. Carl F. Bayerschmidt and Erik J. Friis. University of Washington for American-Scandinavian Foundation, 1965. pp. 54-62. On the Icelander Egill Skallagrimsson and the Welshman Llywarch Hen.

Oral versus written. *TLS*, 8 Apr 1965, 279. Review of Theodore M. Andersson, *The problem of Icelandic saga origins*.

Westward who? *TLS*, 25 Nov 1965, 1076. Review of R.A. Skelton, Thomas E. Marston and George D. Painter, *The Vinland map and the Tartar relation*.

T. H. Jones. *PW* 1,1 (1965) 16. Obituary.

The first discovery of America. *Geographical Magazine*, Jan 1966, 649-656.

Norse studies in a School of English. *Lögberg-Heimskringla*, 3 Feb 1966, 7-8.

The first Europeans in North America: the literary record. *English Studies Today* [Rome] (1966) 377-394.

The Greenlanders' saga – The story of Einar Sokkason. In Knud J. Krogh, *Viking Greenland, with a supplement of saga texts*. Copenhagen: National Museum, 1967. pp. 141-182. Translations by Gwyn Jones.

Beyond the Celtic fringe. *TLS*, 2 Mar 1967, 165. Review of Richard Deacon, *Madoc and the discovery of America*.

Fond of war, fond of words. *TLS*, 8 Feb 1968, 138. Review of Myles Dillon and Nora K. Chadwick, *The Celtic realms*.

Manuscripts and crosses. *TLS*, 25 Apr 1968, 420. Review of Françoise Henry, *Irish art during the Viking invasions, 800-1020 A.D.*

Borealic wonders and horrors. *TLS*, 1 Aug 1968, 831. Review of *Gautrek's saga and other medieval tales*, tr. Herman Pálsson and Paul Edwards.

Voices of Wales. *TLS*, 14 Nov 1968, 1267. Review of Glyn Jones, *The dragon has two tongues*.

Celtic cult figures. *TLS*, 19 Dec 1968, 1429. Review of Stuart Piggott, *The druids*.

Reputations, IV. Let *My people* go. *TLS*, 9 Jan 1969, 33-34. On Caradoc Evans.

The craft of Anglo-poetic Welshness. *TLS*, 24 Jan 1969, 827. Review of *The lilting house,* ed. John Stuart Williams and Meic Stephens.

The historian and the jarl. *History Today*, Apr 1969, 232-239.

Rock sermons. *TLS*, 8 May 1969, 494. Review of Peter Gelling and Hilda Ellis Davidson, *The chariot of the sun.*

Columbus and after. *TLS*, 12 Jun 1969, 632. Review of Helge Ingstad, *Westward to Vinland*, tr. Erik J. Friis.

The boy from Clydach Vale. *TLS*, 19 Jun 1969, 664. Review of Rhys Davies, *Print of a hare's foot.*

Columbus's journal. *TLS*, 10 Jul 1969, 750. Review of *The journal of Christopher Columbus*, tr. Cecil Jane.

Down the dykes. *TLS*, 24 Jul 1969, 835. Review of Dorothy Sylvester, *The rural landscape of the Welsh borderland.*

Glorifying the warriors. *TLS*, 4 Sep 1969, 970. Review of *The Gododdin: the oldest Scottish poem,* ed. Kenneth Hurlstone Jackson.

The Icelandic microcosm. *TLS*, 11 Sep 1969, 1001-1002. Review of Halldor Laxness, *World light*, tr. Magnus Magnússon.

Sword-strokes of poetic genius. *TLS*, 9 Oct 1969, 1154. Review of *The poetic Edda. Vol.1. Heroic poems,* ed. Ursula Dronke.

Irish bulls. *TLS*, 18 Dec 1969, 1446. Review of *The Táin,* tr. Thomas Kinsella.

Free Welsh versions. *TLS*, 18 Dec 1969, 1446. Review of *Bardic heritage: a selection of Welsh poetry in free English translation*, ed. Robert Gurney.

Introduction. In *The Norse discoverers of America: The Wineland sagas translated and discussed by G.M. Gathorne-Hardy.* Oxford: Clarendon Press, 1970. pp. xvi-xxv. Reprint of 1921 edition.

Gwilym James: a memoir. In D.G. James, *Henry Sidgwick: science and faith in Victorian England.* London: Oxford University Press, 1970. pp. ix-xvi.

On more legs than one. *TLS*, 15 Jan 1970, 60. Review of *The elder Edda,* tr. Paul B. Taylor and W. H. Auden.

Sailor under Magellan. *TLS*, 12 Feb 1970, 167. Review of Antonia Pigafetta, *Magellan's voyage*, tr. and ed. R.A. Skelton.

The Vikings at home and abroad. *TLS*, 11 Jun 1970, 632. Review of Peter Foote and David M. Wilson, *The Viking achievement*, David M. Wilson, *The Vikings and their origins*.

Brief encounters. *TLS*, 25 Jun 1970, 680. Review of Brenda Chamberlain, *Alun Lewis and the making of the Caseg broadsheets*.

Forever alien. *TLS*, 31 Jul 1970, 849. Review of Joseph P. Clancy, *The earliest Welsh poetry*.

The Vikings and more. *TLS*, 23 Oct 1970, 1218. Review of *The art of Scandinavia*, Vol. 1, by Peter Anker, and Vol. 2, by Aron Andersson.

Greenland before 1700. *TLS*, 4 Dec 1970, 1405-1406. Review of Finn Gad, *The history of Greenland. Vol. 1. Earliest times to 1700*.

Sons and lovers. *TLS*, 4 Dec 1970, 1428. Review of Brynmor Jones, *A bibliography of Anglo-Welsh literature, 1900-1965*.

Jack Jones, May 1970. *Planet 1* (1970) 32-37.

Review of Raymond Garlick, *An introduction to Anglo-Welsh literature. PW* 6,1 (1970) 55-57.

Western voyages and the Vinland map. In *Proceedings of the Vinland Map Conference*. Chicago: University of Chicago Press, 1971. pp. 119-129.

Review of Anne Ross, *Everyday life of the pagan Celts. TLS*, 5 Mar 1971, 278.

A noble account of a less than noble Savage. *TLS*, 7 May 1971, 517-518. Review of Samuel Johnson, *Life of Savage*, ed. Clarence Tracy.

A nation's language and a way of life. *TLS*, 18 Jun 1971, 691. Review of Ned Thomas, *The Welsh extremist: a culture in crisis*.

Dolmens and mounds, amber and battle-axes. *TLS*, 18 Jun 1971, 702. Review of P.V. Glob, *Danish prehistoric monuments*.

Writing around the fringe. *TLS*, 15 Oct 1971, 1280. Review of *Literature in Celtic countries*, ed. J.E. Caerwyn Williams.

Second coming of the Europeans. *TLS*, 10 Dec 1971, 1547. Review of W.P. Cumming, R.A. Skelton and D.B. Quinn, *The discovery of North America*.

Where did America's culture come from? *TLS*, 21 Jan 1972, 77. Review of

*Man across the sea,* ed. Carroll L. Riley and others, Geoffrey Ashe and others, *The quest for America.*

Literature and criticism. *TLS*, 25 Feb 1972, 230. Review of William Morris and Eiríkr Magnússon, *The story of Kormack, the son of Ogmund.*

Rights and permissions. *TLS*, 3 Mar 1972, 249. Letter on publishing malpractice.

When Wales was Welsh. *TLS*, 21 Apr 1972, 451. Review of *Glamorgan county history. Vol. 3. The middle ages,* ed. T.B. Pugh.

Sense of place, 2. Writing for Wales and the Welsh. *TLS*, 28 Jul 1972, 869-870.

Wales as was. *TLS*, 18 Aug 1972, 965. Review of Iorwerth C. Peate, *Tradition and folk life: a Welsh view.*

Saints, seaways and settlements. *TLS*, 29 Sep 1972, 1168. Review of E.G. Bowen, *Britain and the western seaways.*

A land over there. *TLS*, 8 Dec 1972, 1504. Review of Cyrus H. Gordon, *Before Columbus.*

For Snowdon's sake. *TLS*, 22 Dec 1972, 1562. Review of Amori Lovins, *Eryri: the mountains of longing.*

Tripping along. TLS, 26 Jan 1973, 84. Review of Caradog Prichard, *Full moon,* tr. Menna Gallie.

Viewpoint. *TLS*, 13 Apr 1973, 418. On translating the *Mabinogion.*

On the Welsh side. *TLS*, 25 May 1973, 590. Review of *Presenting Saunders Lewis,* ed. Alun R. Jones and Gwyn Thomas.

Eisteddfodder. *TLS*, 20 Jul 1973, 826. Review of Kenneth A. Wright, *Gentle are its songs.*

Lib service. *TLS*, 14 Sep 1973, 1048. Review of Jean Markale, *La femme celte.*

Recasting the runes. *TLS*, 14 Dec 1973, 1545. Review of R.I. Page, *An introduction to English runes.*

Celtic continuity. *TLS*, 21 Dec 1973, 1568. Review of Ian Finlay, *Celtic art.*

Man of Menai. *TLS*, 4 Jan 1974, 4. Review of Kyffin Williams, *Across the straits.*

A magician and his universe: the true nature of John Cowper Powys. *TLS,* 8 Feb 1974, 121-122. Review of Glen Cavaliero, *John Cowper Powys: novelist,* John A. Brebner, *The demon within: a study of John Cowper Powys's novels,* Jeremy Hooker, *John Cowper Powys,* John Cowper Powys, *Weymouth Sands,* John Cowper Powys, *Rodmoor.*

The hardy north. *TLS,* 5 Apr 1974, 368. Review of Olaus Magnus, *De gentibus septentrionalibus.*

In our hour of deepest need. *TLS,* 10 May 1974, 507. Review of David Jones, *The sleeping lord and other fragments.*

Undecomposed. *TLS,* 14 Jun 1974, 633. Review of P.V. Glob, *The mound people,* tr. Joan Bulman.

The interests of the Eskimos. *TLS,* 9 May 1975, 516. Review of Henrik Rink, *Tales and traditions of the Eskimos,* Henrik Rink, *Danish Greenland: its people and products.*

The Kensington stone – The Norseman in America – Vinland. In *Dictionary of American history.* New York: Scribner, 1976. Encyclopedia articles.

Letter. *PW* 13,4 (1978) 108. On Edward Thomas.

In the cause of Denmark. *TLS,* 25 Jan 1980, 83. Review of Saxo Grammaticus, *The history of the Danes. Vol.1. Text,* tr. Peter Fisher.

What the invaders left behind. *Telegraph Sunday Magazine,* 27 Jan 1980, 18-27.

The spread of Scandinavia. *TLS,* 8 Feb 1980, 135. Review of *The northern world: the history and heritage of northern Europe, AD 400-1100,* ed. David M. Wilson; David M. Wilson, *The Vikings and their origins; Norges kongesagaer,* ed. Finn Hodnebo and Hallvard Mageroy.

Excelsior! *New York Review of Books,* 17 Jul 1980, 35-37. Review of Roland Huntford, *Scott and Amundsen.*

The fury of the northmen. *New York Review of Books,* 9 Oct 1980, 23-25. Review of James Graham-Campbell and Dafydd Kidd, *The Vikings;* G.C. James, *The Viking world;* 'The Vikings', an exhibition at the British Museum and the Metropolitan Museum of Art, New York.

Witness to a miracle. *Scandinavian Review* 68,3 (1980) 20-27. On the Second lay of Helgi Hundingsbana.

Three poetical prayer-makers of the island of Britain. *Proceedings of the British Academy* 67 (1981) 249-267. On Cynddelw, Kitchener Davies and Saunders

Lewis. – Published separately by the British Academy 1981 (Warton lecture on English poetry). ISBN: 0-85672-356-8. – Reprinted in *Background to Dylan Thomas* (1992). pp. 52-71.

Odin and his underlings. *TLS*, 17 Apr 1981, 441. Review of Kevin Crossley-Holland, *The Norse myths*.

The Atlantic voyages. In *The Viking world*. Chicago: *Chicago Tribune*, 1982. pp. 8-9. Background report prepared by the *Chicago Tribune* Educational Services Department.

Historical evidence for Viking voyages to the new world. In *Vikings in the west: papers presented at a symposium sponsored by the Archaeological Institute of America ...*, ed. Eleanor Guralnick. Chicago: Archaeological Institute of America, 1982. pp. 1-12.

The Vikings and North America. In *The Vikings*, ed. R. T. Farrell. Chichester: Phillimore, 1982. pp. 219-230.

Anglo-Saxon York. *TLS*, 25 Jun 1982, 694. Review of 'The Vikings in England' exhibition, Yorkshire Museum.

Domesticated pirates. *TLS*, 27 Aug 1982, 926. Review of Else Roesdahl, *Viking age Denmark*, tr. Susan Margeson and Kirsten Williams.

The Marcher mentality. *TLS*, 29 Oct 1982, 1199. Review of Robert Bartlett, *Gerald of Wales, 1146-1223*.

The colour of then. In *Fountains of praise: University College Cardiff, 1883-1983*, ed Gwyn Jones and Michael Quinn. Cardiff: University College Cardiff Press, 1983. pp. xi-xiv.

The rememberer. *TLS*, 8 Apr 1983, 349. Review of Neil Corcoran, *The song of deeds: a study of* The anathemata *of David Jones*, Philip Pacey, *David Jones and other wonder voyagers*.

Address by Professor Gwyn Jones. In *The National Library of Wales 75th anniversary celebration*. Aberystwyth: National Library of Wales, 1984. pp. [7-11]. Text in English and Welsh.

The Vinland sagas in translation. In Helge Ingstad, *The Norse discovery of America*. Vol. 2. Oslo: Norwegian University Press, 1985. pp. 495-537. 'The Greenlanders' saga' and 'Eirik the Red's saga' in Gwyn Jones's translations.

Reflections: John Barnie interviews Gwyn Jones. *Planet 63* (1987) 23-28.

Anglo-Welsh literature, 1934-46: a personal view. *THSC* (1987) 177-192. Reprinted in *Background to Dylan Thomas* (1992). pp. 1-19.

Alun Lewis (1944) – Gwyn Thomas (1981) – The survival of Welsh (1977). In *Wales on the wireless: a broadcasting anthology,* ed. Patrick Hannan. Llandysul: Gomer in assoc. with BBC Cymru/Wales, 1988. pp. 27-28; 33-34; 140-143.

Eldjárn, Nordal og Jones. *Mannlíff,* Feb 1988, 92-98. Interview with Asgeir Fridgeirsson.

Siglingar vkinga til vesturheims stadfestar. *Morgunbladid,* 26 Jul 1988, 12:D-E. Interview.

The Golden Cockerel Mabinogion, 1944-1948. *THSC* (1989) 181-209. On the translation, and the physical production of this edition. – Reprinted in *Background to Dylan Thomas* (1992). pp. 20-51.

Gwyn Williams, 1904-1990. *Planet* 85 (1991) 118-120. Obituary notice.

Castle Cottage bequest. In *Annual report of the University of Wales, Aberystwyth, 1991-92,* pp. 24-25. On a gift of 117 illustrated volumes, mostly from twentieth-century private presses. – Bilingual text, English and Welsh.

R.S. Thomas at seventy. In M.J.J. van Buuren, *Waiting: the religious poetry of Ronald Stuart Thomas, Welsh poet and priest.* Nijmegen: Katholieke Universiteit van Nijmegen, 1993. pp. 172-181. – Text of a broadcast, BBC Radio 3, 7 Dec 1983, with contributions by Gwyn Jones.

# B: Publications about Gwyn Jones

ADAMS, Sam. Prof Gwyn. *Oriel Bulletin* 4 (1988) 15-16.

BARBARINI, F. L'opera di Gwyn Jones e alcune questioni di storia dei Vichinghi. *Economia e Storia* 1 (1978) 1-51.

COLLINS, W.J. Townsend. *Monmouthshire writers: a literary history and anthology.* Newport: R.H. Johns, 1945. Incl. Gwyn Jones, pp. 140-147.

DAVIES, James A. Kinds of relating: Gwyn Thomas (Jack Jones, Lewis Jones, Gwyn Jones) and the Welsh industrial novel. *AWR* 86 (1987) 72-86.

HUGHES, Glyn Tegai. The mythology of the mining valleys. In *Triskel two: essays on Welsh and Anglo-Welsh literature,* ed. Sam Adams and Gwilym Rees Hughes. Llandybïe: Christopher Davies, 1973. pp. 42-61.

JONES, Glyn. Gwyn Jones. In *British novelists, 1930-1959. Part 1: A-L,* ed. Bernard Oldsey. Detroit: Gale, 1983. (Dictionary of literary biography; 15). pp. 232-236.

MORGAN, Paul Bennett. The writings of Gwyn Jones: a checklist. *NWR* 1,3 [3] (1988) 39-41.

—— Casgliad Castell Gwyn: the Gwyn Jones gift to the National Library of Wales. *National Library of Wales Journal* 26,1 (1989) 102-106. On Gwyn Jones's collection of rare books, mostly eighteenth-century.

ORTEGA, Ramon-Lopez. *La crisis economica 1929 y la novelistica de tema obrero en Gran Bretana en los anos trienta.* Salamanca, 1974. Discusses Gwyn Jones, Lewis Jones and B.L. Coombes.

PRICE, Cecil. *Gwyn Jones*. Cardiff: University of Wales Press [for] Welsh Arts Council 1976. 72 p.: front. port. (Writers of Wales). Incl. bibliography, pp. 61-69. – 'This edition ... is limited to 1000 copies.'

SMITH, Dai. A novel history. In *Wales the imagined nation: studies in cultural and national identity,* ed. Tony Curtis. Bridgend: Poetry Wales Press, 1986. pp. 131-158.

THOMAS, Roy. Gwyn Jones. In *Contemporary novelists,* ed. Lesley Henderson. 5th ed. Chicago; London: St James Press, 1991. pp. 502-504.

WILLIAMS, Raymond. *The Welsh industrial novel.* Cardiff: University College Cardiff Press, 1979. (Inaugural Gwyn Jones lecture).

# JACK JONES (1884-1970)

A. Publications by Jack Jones
(i) Books
(ii) Selected contributions to books and periodicals

B. Publications about Jack Jones

## A (i). Publications by Jack Jones: Books

*Rhondda roundabout*. London: Faber, 1934. 351 p. Reissued 1936, 'cheap edition'.
—— H. Hamilton, 1949. 272 p.
—— Bath: Chivers, 1965. (Portway reprints).

*Black parade*. London: Faber, 1935. 407 p. Reissued 1937, 'cheap edition'.
—— H. Hamilton, 1948. 312 p.
—— Bath: Chivers, 1965. (Portway reprints).

*Unfinished journey* / with a preface by the Rt. Hon. David Lloyd George. London: H. Hamilton, 1937. 318 p. Autobiography. – Reissued 1938, 'cheap edition'.
—— Readers Union, 1938.
—— Bath: Chivers, 1966. 304 p. (Portway reprints).

U.S. ed.: New York: Oxford University Press, 1937. 303 p.

*Land of my fathers: a play*. London: French, 1937. 119 p.: pbk. (French's acting edition; 71). Review article on London production, *HW*, 4 Jun 1938, 2:A-E.

Welsh trans.: *Hen wlad fy nhadau*, tr. Kitchener Davies. London: French, 1938. 139 p.: pbk. (Welsh drama series; 128).

*Bidden to the feast*. London: H. Hamilton, 1938. 446 p. Reissued 1940, 'cheap edition'. – Reissued 1955, pbk.
—— Transworld Publishers, 1955. (Corgi books; G105).
—— Bath: Chivers, 1965. (Portway reprints).
—— Pan, 1979. 382 p.: pbk. ISBN: 0-330-25658-0.
—— Remploy, 1979. ISBN: 0-7066-0827-5.

U.S. ed.: New York: Putnam, 1938.

*Rhondda roundabout: a play in three acts*. London: H. Hamilton, 1939. 128 p.: hbk & pbk.

*The man David: an imaginative presentation based on fact of the life of David Lloyd George from 1880 to 1914.* London: H. Hamilton, 1944. v, 248 p.: front. port.
—— Bath: Chivers, 1966. 256 p. (Portway reprints).

*Me and mine: further chapters in the autobiography of Jack Jones.* London: H. Hamilton, 1946. 428 p.
—— Bath: Chivers, 1967. (Portway reprints).

*Off to Philadelphia in the morning.* London: H. Hamilton, 1947. 372 p.
—— Harmondsworth: Penguin, 1951. 414 p.: pbk.
—— Bath: Chivers, 1966. (Portway reprints).
—— Corgi, 1971. 348 p.: pbk. ISBN: 0-552-08655-X.
—— Pan, 1978. 352 p.: pbk. ISBN: 0-330-25501-0.

*Transatlantic episode: a comedy in a prologue and three acts.* London: French, 1947. 102 p.: pbk. (French's acting edition; 167).

*Some trust in chariots.* London: H. Hamilton, 1948. 421 p.
—— Bath: Chivers, 1966. (Portway reprints).

U.S. ed.: New York: W. Sloane Associates, [1948]. 381 p.

*Give me back my heart: final chapters in the autobiography of Jack Jones.* London: H. Hamilton, 1950. 272 p.
—— Bath: Chivers, 1967. 284 p. (Portway reprints).

*River out of Eden.* London: H. Hamilton, 1951. 671 p. Serialized in *HW*, Jun 9 1951-18 Mar 1952 (39 weekly parts).
—— Bath: Chivers, 1965. (Portway reprints).
—— Corgi, 1970. 2 v. (348 p.; 381 p.). ISBN: 0-552-08333-X, v. 1, 0-552-08334-8, v.2.
—— Pan, 1979. pbk. ISBN: 0-330-25659-9.

*Lily of the valley.* London: H. Hamilton, 1952. xi, 210 p.
—— Bath: Chivers, 1966. 220 p. (Portway reprints).

*Lucky Lear.* London: H. Hamilton, 1952. 224 p.
—— Bath: Chivers, 1965. (Portway reprints).

*Time and the business.* London: H. Hamilton, 1953. 224 p.
—— Bath: Chivers, 1967. (Portway reprints).

*Choral symphony: a novel.* London: H. Hamilton, 1955. 223 p. Serialized, as 'Bessie', in *Empire News*, 19 Jun-4 Sep 1955 (12 weekly parts).
—— Bath: Chivers, 1967. (Portway reprints).

*Come night, end day! or, The theatre that came to stay: a novel.* London: H. Hamilton, [1956]. 279 p.
—— Bath: Chivers, 1967. (Portway reprints).

*Note:* 'Jack Reynolds', the pseudonymous author of *A sort of beauty* and *A woman of Bangkok* is not, as the *British Library general catalogue of printed books to 1975* suggests, Jack Jones (1884-1970). See *Contemporary authors, vol. 109,* ed. Hal May. Detroit: Gale, 1983. p. 233.

## A (ii). Publications by Jack Jones: Selected Contributions to Books and Periodicals

This section covers Jack Jones's stories and miscellaneous journalism, mostly in Welsh newspapers.

The miners' travail: hope in Liberal scheme. *South Wales Daily News,* 17 Sep 1927, 8:C-E.

Mr Jack Jones and his critics: challenge to Garw ballot. *South Wales Daily News,* 24 Sep 1927, 8:C-E. Attacks A.J. Cook.

A challenge: Mr. Jack Jones replies to Mr. Gwilym Richards. *WM,* 19 Feb 1929, 4:E.

A novelist on the stump: a Merthyr by-election. *Time and Tide,* 14 Jul 1934, 902-904.

The prestige of the National. *HW,* 28 Jul 1934, 1:A-C. Story.

Llew's Rhondda choir goes to town. *HW,* 1 Aug 1934, 1:F-G, 12:G. Story.

A bottom-bass like an organ. *HW,* 4 Aug 1934, 10:E-G, 10:E. Story.

He who beats Bandy Bowen. *HW,* 18 Aug 1934, 1:A-B. Story.

Derby in the Rhondda Valley. *HW,* 25 Aug 1934, 1:E-G. Story.

Beulah choir on an outing to Bracelet. *HW,* 1 Sep 1934, 1:F-G, 12:E. Story.

The death and burial of Dai Bach Dwl. *HW,* 8 Sep 1934, 1:E-G. Story.

Penuel chapel takes up George Bernard Shaw. *HW,* 15 Sep 1934, 1:F-G, 12:B. Story.

Attempt to save the theatre in Wales. *WM,* 16 Feb 1935, 11:A. Letter.

For one night only. *HW,* 22 Jun 1935, 1:C-F. Story.

*Black parade*: author agrees that critic is entitled to his opinion. *WM,* 3 Oct 1935, 11:A.

Old timer: the passing of Ponty Pete, the boxer. *HW*, 26 Oct 1935, 6:B-E. Story.

Ianto and Dai join the Fried Bread Fusiliers. *HW*, 16 Nov 1935, 1:A-F, 10:A. Story.

Merry, merry Christmas time! The three musketeers enter the realm of fancy. *HW*, 21 Dec 1935, 1:A-E. Story.

The Pandy players bring home the bacon. *HW*, 15 Feb 1936, 8:A-G. Story.

Three generations in the Rhondda. *HW*, 21 Mar 1936, 4:A-G.

Will Cardiff redeem failure of Welsh drama. *WM*, 2 Sep 1936, 11:C-D.

Welsh writers and critics. *WM*, 26 Feb 1937, 11:C-E.

For such is the kingdom. *HW*, 13 Mar 1937, 6:B-E. Story.

Is there a novelist who will write the story of Swansea? *HW*, 24 April, 1:A-D.

Nofelau'r Cymry Seisnig. *Tir Newydd*, Mai/May 1937, 5-9. [Anglo-Welsh novels.]

Author tells story of his play's inspiration. *HW*, 5 Mar 1938, 1:A-D. On *Land of my fathers*.

Is Wales being reborn in London? *WM*, 1 Nov 1938, 6:C-E. On London-Welsh cultural activities.

New era for Welsh drama: Mr Jack Jones on the realism of *Land of my fathers*. *WM*, 19 Nov 1938, 5:C.

Drama festival's premier award for worst play of the week. *WM*, 23 Jan 1939, 6:C-D. On the Treorchy Drama Festival.

Old engine shed that became a theatre. *WM*, 10 Apr 1939, 6:C-D. On the Aberdare Little Theatre.

Jack Jones urged to go on writing for the stage, but finds he can't work in London. *WM*, 19 Jun 1939, 9:C. Interview.

Building Welsh theatre within framework of 'National' week. *WM*, 7 Aug 1939, [Eisteddfod supplement] 11:C-D.

Carry on with Welsh drama weeks. *WM*, 6 Oct 1939, 9:A-B.

Drama in the mining valleys. *WM*, 14 Oct 1939, 9:A-B. Letter rebutting Keidrych Rhys, 12 Oct 1939, 7:A-B.

Revival of Welsh drama competitive festivals. *WM*, 31 Oct 1939, 9:A-B. Letter.

Collier boy of the gay Nineties. *WR* 1 (1939) 79-85. Story.

Shoni in Shaftsbury Avenue. *WR* 2 (1939) 40-44. On reception of 'Rhondda roundabout'.

Stage and morale of services. *WM*, 18 May 1940, 6:C. Letter.

American notes. *WM*, 23 Dec 1941, 2:E-G. Continued: 29 Dec, 2:D-F; 30 Dec, 2:D-G; 31 Dec 1941, 2:D-F.

Russian trade union visitors to city. *WM*, 6 Jan 1942, 3:F. Letter.

American notes [new series], 1. *WM*, 22 Jan 1942, 4:D-G. Continued: 31 Jan, 2:E-G; 2 Feb, 4:C-E; 3 Feb 1942, 2:E-G.

Workers must save to make future safe. *WM*, 10 Sep 1942, 2:E-G.

Let us drop our native reserve. *WM*, 11 Sep 1942, 2:E-G. Welcoming American troops.

America at war, 1. U.S. railmen doing a grand job of work. *WM*, 31 May 1943, 3:E-G. Continued: 1 Jun 1943, 2:E-G; 2 Jun 1943, 2:E-G; 3 June 1943, 2:C-D.

An open letter to Welsh miners. *WM*, 10 Mar 1944, 2:E-G. Against strike action.

Crucial May Day in our history. *WM*, 1 May 1944, 2:E-G. Jones's travels at home and abroad to promote the war effort.

Yes America, this is Wales. *WM*, 19 May 1944, 2:E-G. On American servicemen's impression of Wales.

My Whitsuntide roundabout. *WM*, 30 May 1944, 2:E-F. On the need for continued vigour in the war effort.

Dowlais Top revisited. *WM*, 17 Jul 1944, 2:E-F. Memories of childhood.

The boys of the black parade. *WM*, 29 Jul 1944, 2:E-G; 31 Jul, 2:E-G. On the Bevin boys.

My night-train up north. *WM*, 19 Oct 1944, 2:E-F. Continued: 20 Oct,

4:D-E; 21 Oct, 4:C-D; 23 Oct, 4:C-D; 24 Oct, 4:C-D. – Impressions of North Wales.

What Welsh acting did for the author. *WM*, 27 Nov 1944, 2:E-G. On production of 'Rhondda roundabout'.

Three weeks with our lads over there. *WM*, 13 Dec 1944, 2:E-G. With army in Normandy.

A gallery of grand chaps. *WR* 3 (1944) 130-135. Story.

Queues for sweets. How the army has changed. *WM*, 15 Jan 1945, 2:E-G. Continued: *WM* 16 Jan, 2:E-G; 20 Jan, 2:E-G; 22 Jan, 2:E-G. – Impressions of army life.

The troops say: houses? Yes, but when? *WM*, 22 Mar 1945, 2:E-F.

In search of Wales on the Italian front. *WM*, 29 May 1945, 2:E-G. Continued: 30 May, 4:C-D; 31 May, 2:E-G; 1 Jun, 3:B-C.

Grandma laughed at this. *WM*, 23 Jul 1945, 2:G. Review of 'Ten nights in a bar room', performed by Cardiff Unity Theatre Group.

The amateur theatre in Wales. *WM*, 14 Apr 1947, 2:E-G.

At His Majesty's. *New World News* 4,12 (1948) 3-4. Theatrical reminiscences.

Mr Jack Jones's new book. *WM*, 9 Feb 1949, 3:H. Letter on *Some trust in chariots* (U.S. edition).

My greatest living Welshman. *Y Ddinas*, Nov 1950, 10. On Thomas Jones.

One man's capital. *WM*, 31 May 1951, 2:F. Argues Cardiff's case for becoming Welsh capital.

Annual miracle of Llangollen. *Liverpool Daily Post*, 7 Jul 1954, [International Eisteddfod Supplement] 2:A-B.

Ll.G.: the love story that is still untold. *Empire News*, 21 Nov 1954, 4:A-E. Review of Frank Owen, *Tempestuous journey: Lloyd George, his life and times*.

Challenge at the docks. *Empire News*, 5 Dec 1954, 6:A-D. On Cardiff docks.

A seasoned playgoer at six. *Radio Times*, 29 Jun 1956, 9. Recollections of theatre-going in Merthyr and Pontypridd.

The old language. *Time and Tide*, 11 Aug 1956, 952.

Review of Wil Jon Edwards, *From the valley I came*. *WM*, 17 Nov 1956, 4:B-D.

A sinner and his saint. *Y Ddinas*, Mar 1957, 12, 26. St. David's Day piece.

The black Welshman. *Empire News*, 23 Jun 1957, 6. Continued: 30 Jun; 7 14 21 28 Jul; 4 11 18 25 Aug; 1 8 15 22 29 Sep; 6 13 Oct. – Serialized story. – Jones was scriptwriter on *The proud valley* (1939), a film starring Paul Robeson.

Looking back without anger. *WM*, 23 Sep 1957, 4:B-H. Continued daily to 27 Sep 1957.

My literary life. *WM*, 25 Nov 1957, 4:B-F. Continued daily to 28 Nov 1957.

American industry listens when the Welsh lion roars. *WM*, 30 Jul 1958, 4:B-H. On John L. Lewis, American trade unionist.

Jack Jones' bookshelf. *WM*, 16 Apr 1959, 4:A-E. Continued: 23 30 Apr; 7 14 21 28 May; 4 11 18 Jun; 13 20 27 Aug; 3 10 17 Sep; 8 15 (on David Jones, *In parenthesis*) 22 29 Oct; 4 26 Nov; 3 10 17 23 31 Dec; 7 14 21 28 Jan 1960; 4 11 18 25 Feb; 3 10 24 31 Mar; 7 21 Apr. – Regular column on favourite authors, from Herodotus to Kerouac.

Mabon – miners' friend or traitor? *WM*, 18 Nov 1959, 6:B-H.

From my place in a long line. *WM*, 24 Nov 1959, 4:B-D. Reflections on his 75th birthday.

Jack Jones' hundred best books. *WM*, 30 Apr 1960, 5. Continued: 7 14 21 28 May; 4 11 18 25 Jun; 2 9 16 23 30 Jul; 6 13 20 27 Aug; 3 10 17 24 Sep; 1 8 15 Oct. – Weekly column, succeeding 'Jack Jones' bookshelf'.

A briefing for crime. *WM*, 20 Sep 1961, 6:B-E. Second part of 'Sextet', a composite serial with six authors.

Boy on the old men's corner. *Merthyr Express*, 7 Nov 1964, 20:C-F. Continued: 13 20 27 Nov; 4 11 Dec. – Serial about Merthyr Tydfil.

Authorship is no light matter. *Merthyr Express*, 20 Nov 1964, 12:B-F. Interview on his 80th birthday.

The Saran stories. *Merthyr Express*, 19 Nov 1965, 5:A-D. Continued: 10 17 31 Dec; 14 28 Jan 1966; 11 25 Feb; 11 25 Mar; 8 22 Apr; 6 20 May; 3 17 Jun; 1 15 29 Jul; 12 26 Aug; 9 23 Sep; 7 21 Oct; 11 25 Nov; 9 23 Dec; 6 20 Jan 1967; 3 17 Feb; 3 17 31 Mar; 14 28 Apr; 12 26 May; 9 23 Jun; 7 21 Jul; 4 18 Aug; 1 15 29 Sep; 13 27 Oct; 11 24 Nov; 22 Dec; 18 Jan 1968. – Series of stories with central character, Saran. – Keri Edwards writes, 'I think it likely that for these [Jones] used some of the "quarter of a million words" of "my magnum opus" *Saran*, which he probably wrote 1932/3. The mss was ... published, much reduced in length, in 1935 with the title *Black parade.*'

Quarry row. *South Wales Echo*, 2 Oct 1967, 6:B-F. Continued daily to 12 Oct. – Serial about 'life in a fictional South Wales street in 1890'.

Schooldays remembered. *WM*, 23 Jan 1968, 1:F-H.

Wear and tear. *Mabon* [English] 1,3 (1970) 4-7. On the difficulties of writing at eighty-five years of age.

Rats, birds and bare knuckles (1964) – Women in adversity (1941) – A negation of humanity (1964). In *Wales on the wireless: a broadcasting anthology*, ed. Patrick Hannan. Llandysul: Gomer in assoc. with BBC Cymru/Wales, 1988. pp. 85; 103; 111.

## Addenda: Jack Jones reported

Jack Jones and the young voters. *WM*, 4 Jan 1929, 9:B. Speech to Neath Young Liberals.

Waiting for milk and honey: Mr Jack Jones on the Socialist wilderness. *WM*, 1 Oct 1929, 10:A-E. Speech to Merthyr Liberal Association.

Mr Jack Jones replies to Mr Saunders Lewis. *WM*, 14 Dec 1938, 8:E. Rebuts dismissive attitude to Anglo-Welsh literature.

Unity of north and south Wales is a myth, says Jack Jones. *WM*, 27 Mar 1939, 9:F-G. London lecture.

Tribute to Anglo-Welsh writers. *WM*, 28 Jun 1951, 3:E.

## B: Publications about Jack Jones

[ANON]. Welsh profile, 7: Jack Jones. *WR* 6 (1947) 168-171.
—— In memory of Jack Jones, 1884-1970. *Mabon* [English] 1,3 (1970) 2-4.
ADAM, G.F. *Three contemporary Anglo-Welsh novelists: Jack Jones, Rhys Davies and Hilda Vaughan*. Bern: A. Franke [1948]. Incl. Jack Jones's documentary realism, pp. 31-48.
DAVIES, Anthony. A mirror of Welsh life: Jack Jones at home and abroad. *Y Ddinas*, Jan 1947, 6,12.
—— When Dr Joseph Parry came to London to win fame: Jack Jones's vivid new novel. *Y Ddinas*, Nov 1947, 2, 12. On *Off to Philadelphia in the morning*.

DAVIES, James A. Kinds of relating: Gwyn Thomas (Jack Jones, Lewis Jones, Gwyn Jones) and the Welsh industrial experience. *AWR* 86 (1987) 72-86.

EDWARDS, Keri. The life and works of three Anglo-Welsh writers of East Glamorgan: Joseph Keating, Jack Jones, Lewis Jones. MA thesis. University of Wales (Aberystwyth), 1962. Incl.: Jack Jones ... the naturalist, pp. 184-289.

—— *Jack Jones.* Cardiff: University of Wales Press [for] the Welsh Arts Council, 1974. 93 p.: front. port. (Writers of Wales). Incl. bibliography, pp. 85-89. – 'Limited to 1000 copies'.

EVANS, Brian. Jack Jones of the Rhondda. *Radio Times*, 20 Nov 1953, 8.

GRIFFITHS, William. A distinguished Welshman. *Y Ddinas*, Nov 1950, 10-11.

HUGHES, Glyn Tegai. The mythology of the mining valleys. In *Triskel two: essays on Welsh and Anglo-Welsh literature,* ed. Sam Adams and Glyn Tegai Hughes. Llandybïe: Christopher Davies, 1973. pp. 42-61.

JONES, Glyn. *The dragon has two tongues: essays on Anglo-Welsh writers and writing.* London: Dent, 1968. Incl. Jack Jones, pp. 81-106.

—— Jack Jones, 1884-1970. *AWR* 19,43 (1970) 17-21. Obituary.

—— Jack Jones, 1884-1970. *Barn*, Gor/Jul 1970, 233. Obituary.

JONES, Gwyn. Anglo-Welsh writers, 2. Jack Jones, patriarch of the Anglo-Welsh. *WM*, 30 Mar 1949, 4:D-F.

—— Jack Jones, May 1970. *Planet* 1 (1970) 32-37. Recalls friendship with Jack Jones.

JONES, J.T. Vivian. In defence of Merthyr after reading *Black Parade. WM*, 2 Oct 1935, 11:C-E. Letter.

SMITH, Dai. *Wales! Wales?* London: Allen & Unwin, 1984. Includes discussion of Idris Davies, Jack Jones, Lewis Jones and Gwyn Thomas, pp. 134-151.

WILLIAMS, Emlyn. Jack Jones. *WR* 1 (1939) 205-208.

WILLIAMS, Raymond. Working-class, proletarian, socialist: problems in some Welsh novels. In *The socialist novel in Britain: towards the recovery of a tradition,* ed. H. Gustav Klaus. Brighton: Harvester Press, 1982. pp. 110-121.

# LEWIS JONES (1897-1939)

A. Publications by Lewis Jones
  (i) Books
  (ii) Selected contributions to books and periodicals

B. Publications about Lewis Jones

## A (i). Publications by Lewis Jones: Books

*From exchange and parish to the P.A.C.: for decency instead of destitution.*
Tonypandy: Evans & Short [for] Central Marchers' Council, 1934. 16 p.:
pamph.

*South Wales slave act special: full explanation of the unemployed allowances.*
Tonypandy: Evans & Short, 1935. 8 p.: pamph.

*Cwmardy: the story of a Welsh mining valley.* London: Lawrence & Wishart,
1937. x, 310 p.
—— Lawrence & Wishart, 1978. pbk. ISBN: 85315-468-6. Incl. Introduction, by Dai Smith.

German trans.: *Im Tal der schlagenden Wetter*, tr. Hans Löffler. Berlin: Volk
und Welt, 1969. 315 p.

*We live: the story of a Welsh mining valley.* London: Lawrence & Wishart,
1939. ix, 334 p.: front. port. Incl. Foreword by D.M. Garman. – Reissued
1940, 'cheap edition'. – Reissued 1941, (Workers' library).
—— Lawrence & Wishart, 1978. pbk. ISBN: 85315-469-4. Incl. Introduction, by Dai Smith.

## A (ii). Publications by Lewis Jones: Selected Contributions to Books and Periodicals

Young Dai. *Daily Worker*, 1 Jul 1932, 6:D. Story.

The power of the pit. *Daily Worker*, 23 Aug 1932, 4:D. Story.

Foreword. In *Monmouthshire hunger march of August 1933*, written and compiled
by members of the Monmouthshire Marchers' Council. Abertillery, 1933.

Boots, shiny, big and heavy. *Daily Worker*, 28 Apr 1933, 6:A. Story.

The pit cage. *Daily Worker*, 21 Jun 1933, 6:A. Story.

The Rhondda in 1934. *Daily Worker*, 19 May 1934, 6:B.

Tonypandy. *Left Review*, Apr 1937, 157-159.

Tory coalminer. *Left Review*, Aug 1937. Review of G.A.W. Thomlinson, *Coalminer*.


# B. Publications about Lewis Jones

[ANON]. *Daily Worker*, 2 Feb 1939, 1,8. Obituary, with extracts from Harry Pollitt's funeral speech.

CUNNINGHAM, Valentine. *British writers of the thirties.* Oxford: Oxford University Press, 1988. Discusses Lewis Jones, pp. 308-316.

DAVIES, James A. Kinds of relating: Gwyn Thomas (Jack Jones, Lewis Jones, Gwyn Jones) and the Welsh industrial novel. *AWR* 86 (1987) 72-86.

EDWARDS, Keri. The life and works of three Anglo-Welsh writers of East Glamorgan: Joseph Keating, Jack Jones, Lewis Jones. MA thesis. University of Wales (Aberystwyth), 1962. Incl. Lewis Jones ... the Communist, pp. 290-326.

FRANCIS, Hywel and Dai Smith. *The Fed: a history of the South Wales miners in the twentieth century.* London: Lawrence & Wishart, 1980. Incl. discussion of Lewis Jones.

GARMAN, Douglas. *Daily Worker*, 19 Apr 1939, 7. Brief article on Lewis Jones.

—— A revolutionary writer. *WR* 1 (1939) 263-267.

GEORGE, Philip. Three Rhondda working class writers. *Llafur: Journal of Welsh Labour History* 3,2 (1981) 5-13. On Huw Menai, Lewis Jones and Gwyn Thomas.

HASSEL, Monica and A. Cim Meyer, A. Litteratur og politik i 30ernes England: på jagt efter realismen: en analyse af Lewis Jones' *Cwmardy* og *We live.* Roskilde: Roskilde University Center, 1981. 306 p. Incl. discussion of Lewis Jones, pp. 153-268. – Advanced student thesis. – [The literature and politics of England in the 30s: on the hunt for realism: an analysis of Lewis Jones's *Cwmardy* and *We live*].

HOLDERNESS, Graham. Miners and the novel: from bourgeois to proletarian. In *The British working class novel in the twentieth century,* ed. Jeremy Hawthorn. London: Arnold, 1984. pp. 19-35.

HUGHES, Glyn Tegai. The mythology of the mining valleys. In *Triskel two: essays on Welsh and Anglo-Welsh literature,* ed. Sam Adams and Gwilym Rees Hughes. Llandybïe: Christopher Davies, 1973. pp. 42-61.

JOHNSTON, Dafydd. Dwy lenyddiaeth Cymru yn y tridegau. In *Sglefrio ar eiriau,* ed. John Rowlands. Llandysul: Gwasg Gomer, 1992. Discusses Lewis Jones, pp. 58-62.

KERMODE, Frank. *History and value*: the Clarendon lectures and Northcliffe lectures, 1987. Oxford: Clarendon Press, 1988. Incl. discussion of Lewis Jones, pp. 85-107.

ORTEGA, Ramon Lopez. *La crisis economica de 1929 y la novelistica de tema obrero en Gran Bretana en los anos treinta.* Salamanca, 1974. 81 p. Discusses Gwyn Jones, B.L. Coombes and Lewis Jones.

—— *Movimiento obrero y novela Inglesa.* Salamanca: Universidad de Salamanca, 1976.

—— Industrial conflict and the viewpoint of the English novel in the 1930s. *Gulliver* 4 (1979) 54-66.

—— The language of the working-class novel of the 1930s. In *The socialist novel in Britain: towards the recovery of a tradition,* ed. H. Gustav Klaus. Brighton: Harvester Press, 1982. pp. 122-144.

PIKOULIS, John. Lewis Jones. In *British novelists, 1930-1959. Part 1: A-L.,* ed. Bernard Oldsey. Detroit: Gale, 1983. (Dictionary of literary biography; 15). pp. 237-241.

—— Lewis Jones. *AWR* 74 (1983) 62-71.

SMITH, David [1938 – ]. *Socialist propaganda in the twentieth-century British novel.* London: Macmillan, 1978. Discusses Lewis Jones, pp. 67-68.

SMITH, Dai. Leaders and led. In *Rhondda past and future,* ed. K.S Hopkins. Rhondda: Rhondda Borough Council, [1975?]. pp. 37-65. Historical background.

—— Myth and meaning in the literature of the South Wales coalfield: the 1930s. *AWR* 25,56 (1976) 21-41. Discusses Lewis Jones, Richard Llewellyn and other writers.

—— Tonypandy 1910: definitions of community. *Past and Present* 87 (1980) 158-184. Historical background.

—— *Lewis Jones.* Cardiff: University of Wales Press [for] the Welsh Arts Council, 1982. 91 p.: front. port. (Writers of Wales). Incl. bibliography, pp. 83-87. – 'Limited to 1000 copies'.

—— *Wales! Wales?* London: Allen & Unwin, 1984. Includes discussion of Idris Davies, Jack Jones, Lewis Jones and Gwyn Thomas, pp. 134-151.

SNEE, Carole. Working class literature or proletarian writing? In *Culture and crisis in Britain in the thirties,* ed. Jon Clark and others. London: Lawrence & Wishart, 1979. pp. 165-191. Discusses Lewis Jones, Walter Greenwood and Walter Brierly.

THOMAS, M. Wynn. Literature in English. In *Glamorgan County history. Volume VI. Glamorgan society, 1780-1980,* ed. Prys Morgan. Cardiff: Glamorgan History Trust and University of Wales Press, 1980. pp. 353-365.

WALLIS, Owen John. A critical appreciation of Lewis Jones's novels. MA thesis. University of Wales (Cardiff), 1988.

WILLIAMS, Raymond. *The Welsh industrial novel.* Cardiff: University College Cardiff Press, 1979. (Inaugural Gwyn Jones lecture).

—— Working-class, proletarian, socialist: problems in some Welsh novels. In *The socialist novel in Britain: towards the recovery of a tradition,* ed. H. Gustav Klaus. Brighton: Harvester Press, 1982. pp. 110-121.

# T. HARRI JONES (1921-1965)

A. Publications by T. Harri Jones
  (i) Books
  (ii) Selected contributions to books and periodicals
B. Publications about T. Harri Jones

## A (i). Publications by T. Harri Jones: Books

*The enemy in the heart: poems, 1946-1956*. London: Hart-Davis, 1957. 80 p.

*Songs of a mad prince and other poems*. London: Hart-Davis, 1960. 71 p. Incl. Jones's translations of poems by Roberto Sanesi.

*The beast at the door and other poems*. London: Hart-Davis, 1963. 79 p.

*Dylan Thomas*. Edinburgh; London: Oliver & Boyd, 1963. 118 p.: pbk. (Writers and critics).

U.S. eds.: New York: Grove, 1963. (Evergreen pilot books; EP 23).
—— Gloucester, Mass.: P. Smith, 1964. 1963 edition rebound.
—— New York: Barnes & Noble, 1966. (Writers and critics).

*Cotton Mather remembers the trial of Elizabeth How: Salem, Massachusetts, June 30 1692*. [Newcastle, Australia: University of Newcastle], 1964. 1 folded sheet [8 p.]: ill. (Nimrod pamphlets; 1).

*The colour of cockcrowing and other poems*. London: Hart-Davis, 1966. 84 p. Incl. Preface, by D.C. Muecke, pp. 9-13.

*The collected poems of T. Harri Jones* / edited with an introduction by Julian Croft and Don Dale-Jones. Llandysul: Gomer Press, 1977. xix, 267 p. Contents: Introduction – *The enemy in the heart* – *Songs of a mad prince* – *The beast at the door* – *The colour of cockcrowing* – Uncollected poems, 1959-1964. – Reissued 1987, pbk. ISBN: 0-85088-412-8.

[Unpublished thesis]. *The imagery of the metaphysical poets of the seventeenth century*. MA thesis. University of Wales (Aberystwyth), 1949. 201 p.

## A (ii). Publications by T. Harri Jones: Selected Contributions to Books and Periodicals

Note that Jones in the 1960s also reviewed for the Australian periodical *Quadrant*.

Poem for Wales. *Dragon* 68,3 (1946) 13. During 1947 T.H. Jones edited this, the literary magazine of University College of Wales, Aberystwyth.

Two poems. *Dragon* 69,1 (1946) 3.

Ennui: Mediterranean. *Wales* 2nd ser. 8,30 (1948) 640-641. Poetry.

Review of Austin Warren, *Rage for order. Life and Letters* 60 (1949) 180-182.

Review of Rosemary Freeman, *English emblem books. Life and Letters* 61 (1949) 172-173.

Reviews of Edwin Muir, *Essays on literature and society; New directions,* ed. James Laughlin, *New road 5,* ed. Wrey Gardiner, *A new romantic anthology,* ed. Stefan Schimanski and Henry Treece, *Since 1939* 2. *Life and Letters* 63 (1949) 162-164; 185-190.

Review of Cledwyn Hughes, *A wanderer in North Wales,* D. Parry-Jones, *Welsh country upbringing. Life and Letters* 64 (1950) 82-84.

Review of H.L.R. Edwards, *Skelton: the life and times of an early Tudor poet. Life and Letters* 65 (1950) 251-252.

Review of Hamish Henderson, *Elegies for the dead in Cyrenaica,* E.N. da C. Andrade, *Poems and songs. Poetry Quarterly* 12,1 (1950) 45-46.

The riding strangers. *Dublin Magazine,* 26,1 (1951) 21-24. Story.

My grandfather would have me be a poet. *Life and Letters* 64 (1950) 30-38. Story.

The Anglo-Welsh. *DL* 4,11 (1953) 46. Poem dedicated to Aneirin Talfan Davies.

Holy deceptions. *The Glass* [Lowestoft] 8 [1953-4?] [1-4]. Story.

A day at the seaside. *DL* 5,15 (1954) 7-12. Story.

Home. *Dublin Magazine* 30,2 (1954) 24-33. Story.

The essential vulgarity of Henry James. *In Proceedings of the Ninth Congress of the Australasian Universities' Languages and Literature Association, 19-26 Aug 1964,* ed. Marion Adams. Melbourne: University of Melbourne, 1964. pp. 49-50.

Small protest from a native son. *University of Wales Review,* Summer 1965, 16. Poem, with extract from accompanying letter to the editor.

Rhiannon. *AWR* 17,39 (1968) 97-98. Original version of the poem, reprinted with accompanying letter to Raymond Garlick.

Saturday night. *Planet* 69 (1988) 77-81. Story.

## B. Publications about T. Harri Jones

BURNHAM, Richard. *The Dublin Magazine's* Welsh poets. *AWR* 27,60 (1978) 49-63.

CONRAN, Anthony. *The cost of strangeness: essays on the English poets of Wales.* Llandysul: Gomer Press, 1982. Incl. discussion of T. Harri Jones, pp. 275-283.

CROFT, Julian. A word not lightly said. *Poetry Magazine* [Sydney] 2 (1965) 3-7.

—— *T.H. Jones.* Cardiff: University of Wales Press [for] the Welsh Arts Council, 1976. 123 p.: front. port. (Writers of Wales). Incl. selected bibliography, pp. 117-119. – 'Limited to 1000 copies'.

DAVIES, Aneirin Talfan. Ar ymyl y ddalen. *Barn*, Chw/Feb 1968. 89-90. [In the margin].

FARRELLY, Alan. The Welshman and the beast. *Newcastle Morning Herald* [Australia], 13 Mar 1965.

JONES, Gwyn. T.H. Jones. *PW* 1,1 (1965) 16. Obituary.

JONES, P. Bernard. The anonymous lecturer: the early years of T. Harri Jones. *Planet* 69 (1988) 82-87.

MATHIAS, Roland. Editorial. *AWR* 15,36 (1966) 3-6. On T. Harri Jones.

MORGAN, Robert. Death of a poet. *London Welshman*, Jul-Aug 1965, 3-4. Obituary.

—— Farewell to poetry. *PW* 24,4 (1989) 3-7. Incl. reminiscences of T. Harri Jones.

[NATIONAL Library of Wales]. *T. Harri Jones.* [Aberystwyth: National Library of Wales], 1988. [12] p. Catalogue of exhibition at Ceredigion Museum, Aberystwyth, 17 Jun-23 Jul 1988.

PARTRIDGE, Colin John. The verse of T.H. Jones. *PW* 1,2 (1965) 3-7.

RUTHERFORD, Anna. Harri Jones: a tribute. Planet 49-50 (1980) 128-134. Review article on T. Harri Jones, *The collected poems*, ed. Julian Croft and Don Dale-Jones, Julian Croft, *T.H. Jones.*

SMITH, Peter. The dissatisfaction of T. Harri Jones. *Planet* 69 (1988) 88-92.

*T. HARRI Jones, 1921-1965, ed.* Pat Power, P. Bernard Jones and Liz Felgate. Cardiff: Welsh Arts Council, 1987. 104 p.: chiefly ill. (Writers' world). Incl. bio-bibliography, p. 103.

TALBOT, Norman. *The seafolding of T. Harri Jones.* [Newcastle, Australia: University of Newcastle], 1965. 1 folded sheet [8 p.]. (Nimrod pamphlets; 2).

—— To write simply: the poetry of T.H. Jones. *Quadrant* [Australia] 9,5 (1965) 35-42.

# ALUN LEWIS (1915-1944)

A. Publications by Alun Lewis
  (i) Books
  (ii) Selected contributions to books and periodicals
B. Publications about Alun Lewis

## A (i). Publications by Alun Lewis: Books

*Two poems*. Llanllechid: Caseg Press; Llandysul, Gomerian Press, [1941]. single sheet. (Caseg broadsheet; 1). Contents: Raiders' dawn – Song of innocence. – With wood engraving, 'Debris searcher', by John Petts.

*Raiders' dawn and other poems*. London: Allen & Unwin, 1942. 93p.: front. port.: ppb. Portrait and cover illustration from a woodcut by John Petts.

U.S. ed.: New York: Macmillan, 1943.

*The last inspection*. London: Allen & Unwin, 1942. 221 p. Contents: The last inspection – Flick – Private Jones – Almost a gentleman – Farewell binge – It's a long way to go – [Trilogy]; Change for dinner, The last day, The moon – Lance-jack – The wanderers – Picnic – The lapse – Interruption – The housekeeper – Acting Captain – The children – Ballerina – Cold spell – Dusty hermitage – The prisoners – They came. – Published 1943.

U.S. ed.: New York: Macmillan, 1943.

*Ha! Ha! among the trumpets: poems in transit* / foreword by Robert Graves. London: Allen & Unwin, 1945. 75 p.: front. port. Also limited edition, 50 copies.

U.S. ed.: New York: Macmillan, 1945.

*Letters from India* / with a note by Mrs. Alun Lewis; and a preface by A.L. Rowse. Cardiff: Penmark Press, 1946. 97 p.: ill. Incl. facsimiles. – 'Selection of letters was made by Gweno Lewis and Gwyn Jones ... The edition is limited to 500 numbered copies, of which nos. 1-100 have been specially bound.'

*In the green tree* / with a preface by A.L. Rowse; a postscript by Gwyn Jones; and a sonnet by Vernon Watkins; drawings by John Petts. London: Allen & Unwin, 1948. 141 p.: ill. Contents: Sonnet on the death of Alun Lewis – Preface – Letters from India; The voyage, Prospect of India, India, Burma – Short stories; Night journey, The raid, The earth is a syllable, Ward 'O' 3(b), The orange grove, The reunion – Postscript. – Frontispiece portrait from a sketch by John Petts. – Published 1949.

U.S. ed.: New York: Macmillan, 1949.

*Alun Lewis: selected poetry and prose* / with a biographical introduction by Ian Hamilton. London: Allen & Unwin, 1966. 214 p. Contents: Introduction, pp. 9-60 – Poetry [with 8 uncollected poems] – Prose; The last inspection, Private Jones, Almost a gentleman, Picnic, Dusty hermitage – They came – Ward 'O' 3(b) – The orange grove.

*Selected poems of Alun Lewis* / selected by Jeremy Hooker and Gweno Lewis; foreword by Robert Graves; afterword by Jeremy Hooker. London: Allen & Unwin, 1981. 112 p.: pbk. ISBN: 0-04-821048-X. Foreword, pp. 5-6 – Afterword, pp. 101-111.

*Alun Lewis: a miscellany of his writings* / edited by John Pikoulis. Bridgend: Poetry Wales Press, 1982. 171 p.: front. port.: hbk & pbk. (Miscellany; 3). ISBN: 0-907476-07-4 hbk, 0-907476-08-2 pbk. Contents: Critical preface and linking commentary, by John Pikoulis – Selected poetry, letters, stories and other prose arranged as; Beginnings, Student days, Marking time, Joining the war, Letters to Robert Graves, India, Burma.

*Alun Lewis: letters to my wife* / edited by Gweno Lewis. Bridgend: Seren Books, 1989. 427 p. ISBN: 1-85411-004-7. Incl. Preface, by Gweno Lewis, pp. 7-23.

*Collected stories* / edited by Cary Archard. Bridgend: Seren Books, 1990. 367 p. ISBN: 1-85411-012-8. Contents: Introduction, by Cary Archard, pp. 7-14 – *The last inspection* – *In the green tree* [6 stories] – From *The Bovian*; The death of Monga, The tale of a dwarf, The end of the hunt – From *The Dragon*; If such be nature's holy plan, The whirligig of fate, Attitude, Squibs for the guy – From *The Serpent*; The monk's tale, Chestnuts, The wedding breakfast – From the *Manchester Guardian*; The Cardinali crisis, The poetry lesson – Miscellaneous; Rain, The testimonial – Unpublished stories; And at my departing, Duration, It was very warm and welcome, Impasse, Enid didn't know what to do, Alexander's feast.

[Unpublished thesis]. *The English activities of Cardinal Ottobuono, Legate of the Holy See.* MA thesis. University of Manchester, 1937. vii, 231, xxxviii p.

# A (ii). Publications by Alun Lewis: Selected Contributions to Books and Periodicals

For a full listing see Ulrich Schäfer, *Alun Lewis: a bibliography* (1986), an impressively detailed and fully indexed guide.

Our grandparents at school, 1. *Aberdare Leader*, 23 Jul 1938, 3:C-D. Continued: 30 Jul 1938, 7:F-G, 8:A; 6 Aug 1938, 5:D-E.

Roger Leyburn and the pacification of England, 1265-7. *English Historical Review* 54 (1939) 193-214.

Review of James Hanley, *Between the tides*. *WR* 2 (1939) 110.

Review of The Tower Press Booklets. 3rd ser., Austin Clarke, *Night and morning*, Padraic Fallon, *Lighting-up time*, Padraic Colum, *Flower pieces*, Seamus O'Sullivan, *Poems*, Edward Sheehy, *God send Sunday*, J.L. Donaghy, *Selected poems*. *WR* 2 (1939) 172-174.

Review of *The Dublin Magazine*, vol. 14, nos. 1-4, 1939. *WR* 2 (1939) 231-232.

Review of Edward Thomas, *The trumpet and other poems*. *Horizon*, Jan 1941, 78, 80.

The creation of a class. *Horizon*, Sep 1941, 168-172. Published anonymously.

Why not war writers? A manifesto. *Horizon*, Oct 1941, 236-239. Signed by Arthur Calder-Marshall, Cyril Connolly, Bonamy Dobrée, Tom Harrisson, Arthur Koestler, Alun Lewis, George Orwell and Stephen Spender.

Coastal defence: diary for a Monday. *Journal of the South Wales Borderers and the Monmouthshire Regiment*, 21 Apr 1942, 18-19.

A sensitive plant. *Tribune*, 19 Jun 1942, 14. Review of *The Fortune Anthology*.

Messines. *Journal of the South Wales Borderers and the Monmouthshire Regiment*, 23 Apr 1943, 23-25.

The motherland. *Modern Reading* 6 (1943) 16-18. Story.

Grenadier. In *Bugle blast: an anthology from the services*. 2nd ser., ed. Jack Aistrop and Reginald Moore. London: Allen & Unwin, 1944. pp. 161-180.

Alun Lewis: letters from India. *WR* 4 (1945) 83-93. Selection differs from that in Alun Lewis, *Letters from India* (1946).

One modern poet at war. *TLS*, 12 Jul 1947, 350. Letters to Keidrych Rhys and Lynette Roberts, 1941-1943.

A sheaf of letters from Alun Lewis, 1941-1943: first selection. *Wales* 2nd ser. 7,28 (1948) 410-431. Addressed to Keidrych Rhys and Lynette Roberts.

Manuel. In *First view*, ed. George Frederick Green. London: Faber, 1950. pp. 217-220. Story. – First printed in *Lilliput*, Sep 1943, 201-203.

Alun Lewis to Robert Graves: three letters. *AWR* 16,37 (1967) 9-13.

The young historian: some letters from Alun Lewis. AWR 17,40 (1969) 3-21. To Reginald Treharne, Professor of History at Aberystwyth.

Bannerjee, Jacqueline. The Timothy Lewis collection: Alun Lewis memorabilia. *AWR* 21,48 (1972) 48-56. Incl.: Letters, 1938-1939, to Professor Timothy Lewis [the poet's uncle] – Spotlight on France [from *Aberdare Leader*, 8 Oct 1938].

Lewis, Gweno. Alun Lewis joins the Royal Engineers. *PW* 10,3 (1975) 9-25. Mostly Alun Lewis's letters, May-Jul 1940.

Prelude and fugue. *AWR* 63 (1978) 64-65. First printed in *More poems from the forces*, ed. Keidrych Rhys (1943) and not subsequently collected.

English weekend. *AWR* 65 (1979) 43-49. 1939 journal entries.

Last leaves of a civilian's journal. *AWR* 67 (1980) 32-42. 1939 journal entries.

# B. Publications about Alun Lewis

ABSE, Dannie. [Editor's introduction to Alun Lewis]. In *Corgi modern poets in focus. No. 3*. London: Corgi, 1971. pp. 89-95.

ALLEN, Walter. *The short story in English*. Oxford: Clarendon Press, 1981. Incl. discussion of Alun Lewis, pp. 301-305.

[ANON]. Alun Lewis: a chronology. *PW* 10,3 (1975) 7-8.

AYKROYD, Freda. Some letters of Alun Lewis. *Modern Reading* 22 (1952) 15-25. An article with liberal quotation.

—— Echoes in the work of Alun Lewis and David Jones. *PW* 23,2-3 (1988) 71-89.

—— An exchange of love poems. *NWR* 4,1 [13] (1991) 11-18.

BANNERJEE, Amitya. The muse and the wars: an examination of English poetry written during the two world wars. PhD thesis. University of Leicester, 1969.

—— *Spirit above wars: a study of the English poetry of the two world wars*. London: Macmillan, 1976. Incl. Alun Lewis, pp. 136-171.

BANNERJEE, Jacqueline. Alun Lewis: a study. PhD thesis. University of London (King's College), 1971.

—— Alun Lewis: the early stories. *AWR* 20,46 (1972) 77-82.

—— A faith-keeping act: the letters of Alun Lewis. *AWR* 21,47 (1972) 100-104. Incl. list of published and unpublished letters.

—— Seeking and still seeking: Alun Lewis in India. *PW* 10,3 (1975) 99-117.

—— Living more lives than are: three of Alun Lewis's poems from India. *AWR* 27,60 (1978) 69-79.

BERGONZI, Bernard. *The myth of modernism and twentieth century literature*. Brighton: Harvester Press, 1986. Incl. Poets of the 1940s (Bernard Spencer, Alun Lewis, G.S. Fraser), pp. 129-142.

BULLOUGH, Geoffrey. *The trend in modern poetry*. Edinburgh: Oliver & Boyd, 1949. Incl. discussion of Alun Lewis, pp. 248-252.

BURNHAM, Richard. *The Dublin Magazine's* Welsh poets. *AWR* 27,60 (1978) 49-63.

CHALFONT, Alun, *Lord*. Death of a poet.. *NWR* 6,1 [21] (1993) 2. Reports the opinion of Lewis's immediate senior officer, that the poet took his own life.

CHAMBERLAIN, Brenda. Alun Lewis. *Dublin Magazine* 19,3 (1944) 45-47. [Obituary].

—— *Alun Lewis and the making of the Caseg broadsheets*, with a letter from Vernon Watkins and a checklist of the broadsheets. London: Enitharmon Press, 1970. 44p.: ill. Incl. letters from Alun Lewis. – Reproduces Caseg broadsheet 1 [*Two poems*, by Alun Lewis]. – 'This edition is limited to 300 copies numbered 1 – 300 and 35 copies specially bound, numbered i-xxxv.'

COX, C.B. Poets at war. *Spectator*, 18 Nov 1966, 684. Discusses Keith Douglas and Alun Lewis.

CURREY, R.N. *Poets of the 1939-1945 war*. London: Longmans for the British Council and the National Book League, 1960. Incl. Alun Lewis, pp. 19-26.

CURTIS, Tony. *How to study modern poetry*. London: Macmillan, 1990. Discusses 'All day it has rained', pp. 60-67.

DAVIES, D. Jacob. *Cyfoeth cwm*. Abercynon: Cwmni Cyhoeddiadau Modern Cymraeg, 1965. 118 p. Incl. Alun Lewis, 1915-1943, p. 99. – [Valley heritage].

DAVIES, D.L. Alun Lewis, 1915-1944. *Hanes: Newsletter of the Cynon Valley History Society* 3 (1985) 1-2. D.L. Davies also contributes to this special issue: The Lewis family origins, pp. 2-3 – My Orphean uncle [Edward Lewis, 1879-1941], p. 4 – Our dreaming side [review article on John Pikoulis, *Alun Lewis: a life*], pp. 5-6. – Review supplies detail on Lewis family background.

DAVIES, D.R. A poet with a love of humanity. *Aberdare Leader*, 4 Mar 1961, 3:A-D.

DAVIES, Iolo. *A certaine schoole*. Cowbridge: D. Brown 1967. A history of Cowbridge Grammar School, with references to Alun Lewis, pp. 290-293.

DAVIES, John Alun. The poetry of darkness: Alun Lewis's Indian experience. MA thesis. University of Wales (Aberystwyth), 1969. 68 p.

—— The poetry of darkness: Alun Lewis's Indian experience. *AWR* 19,43 (1970) 176-183.

DAVIES, Pennar ['Davies Aberpennar']. Alun Lewis. *Welsh Nationalist*, Aug 1948, 3:B-D. Part of a BBC broadcast.

Devine, Kathleen. Alun Lewis: a debt to Wilfred Owen. *PW* 10,3 (1975) 84-98.

—— Alun Lewis's 'Almost a gentleman'. *AWR* 67 (1980) 79-84.

—— Alun Lewis's 'A fragment'. *PW* 19,1 (1983) 37-43.

—— The way back: Alun Lewis and Remarque. *Anglia* 103,3-4 (1985) 320-335.

—— Alun Lewis: the Manchester stories. *NWR* 4,1 [13] (1991) 24-29.

DUNCAN, Ronald H. Towards a re-examination of Alun Lewis. *Chance* 4 (1953) 87-92.

EVANS, George Ewart. The foils are poisoned that the good may die. *Wales* 2nd ser. 4 (1944) 4-5. Obituary notice.

EVANS, Keith. Alun Lewis, the development of a writer: an analysis or re-examination and explanation of Alun Lewis's poetry, short stories and letters. MA thesis. University of Lancaster, 1971.

FALCK, Colin. Alun Lewis. In *The modern poet: essays from* The Review, ed. Ian Hamilton. London: Macdonald, 1968. pp. 141-150.

—— A small salient gained: Alun Lewis and twentieth century romanticism. *New Review* 3,25 (1976) 53-59.

FENN, Mair. Outward challenge and inward search. *PW* 10,3 (1975) 26-30.

GRAVES, Robert. War poetry in this war. *Listener*, 23 Oct 1941, 566.

GRIFFITHS, Teifion. The Welsh influence on English verse. *Y Ddinas*, Aug 1956, 19.

HAMILTON, Ian. Poetry. The forties, 1. *London Magazine*, Apr 1964, 81-89.

HANNAN, Patrick. Alun Lewis. *London Welshman*, Jan 1965, 10-12.

HEWINSON, Robert. *Under siege: literary life in London,* 1939-1945. London: Weidenfeld & Nicholson, 1977. Discusses Alun Lewis, pp. 126-130.

HILL, Greg. Alun Lewis: the war, darkness, and the search for poetic truth. *Critical Survey* 2 (1990) 216-222.

—— The darkness that is there. *Planet* 86 (1991) 78-82. Review article on Alun Lewis, *Collected stories.*

HOUSTON, Ralph. The broken arch: a study of the poetry of Alun Lewis. *Adelphi* 28 (1951) 403-413.

HUTTON, W.R. The poetry of Alun Lewis. In *Bristol Packet 2*. Bristol: Bristol Writers' and Artists' Association, 1945. pp. 73-78.

JARKA, Horst. Alun Lewis: his short stories and poems. PhD thesis. University of Vienna, 1954. 205 p.

JOHN, Alun. Alun Lewis. WM, 3 Mar 1954, 6:E-F.

—— The life and works of Alun Lewis. PhD thesis. University of Wales (Cardiff), 1973. 234 p. Incl. bibliography, pp. 331-354.

—— *Alun Lewis.* Cardiff: University of Wales Press [for] the Welsh Arts Council, 1970. 97p.: front. port. (Writers of Wales). Incl. selected bibliography, pp. 91-94. – 'This edition ... limited to 750 copies.'

—— In retrospect. *PW*, 10,3 (1975) 124-127.

JONES, Brynmor. *Bibliographies of Anglo-Welsh literature: Alun Lewis 1915-1944: bibliographical note, original works and contributions to periodicals.* [Cardiff]: Welsh Arts Council Literature Department, 1968. [6] p.

JONES, Gwyn. Alun Lewis (1915-1944) *WR* 3 (1944) 118-121. Obituary.

—— Brave and splendid· Alun Lewis. *WM*, 20 Mar 1944, 2:G. Obituary.

—— Anglo-Welsh writer, 4. Wales will never see the best of Alun Lewis. *WM*, 27 Apr 1949, 4:F-H. Reprinted *WM*, 4 Mar 1961, i:A-G.

—— Alun Lewis (1944). In *Wales on the wireless: a broadcasting anthology,* ed. Patrick Hannan. Llandysul: Gomer in assoc. with BBC Cymru/Wales, 1988. pp. 27-28.

LEHMANN, John. A reader's notebook, iv. In *Penguin new writing 20,* ed. John Lehmann. Harmondsworth: Penguin, 1944. pp. 151-160. Under pseudonym, Jack Marlowe.

—— *The open night.* London: Longmans, 1952. Incl. A human standpoint, pp. 109-116.

LEWIS, E. Glyn. Some aspects of Anglo-Welsh literature. *WR* 5 (1946) 176-186.

LEWIS, Gwladys E. *Alun Lewis my son.* Aberystwyth: Cambrian News, [1968]. 52 p.

—— Remembering. *PW* 10,3 (1975) 31-37.

MACLAREN-ROSS, Julian. *The funny bone.* London: Elek, 1956. Incl. Second Lieutenant Lewis: a memoir, pp. 175-184. – Essay reprinted from *Penguin new writing* 27, ed. John Lehmann (1946), pp. 72-81; also in Julian Maclaren-Ross, *Memoirs of the forties.* London: Alan Ross, 1956. pp. 225-234.

MATHIAS, Roland. The Caseg letters: a commentary. *PW* 10,3 (1975) 47-77. Notes shortcomings in Brenda Chamberlain's editing. – Reprinted in Roland Mathias, *A ride through the wood: essays on Anglo-Welsh literature* (1985), pp. 58-185.

—— The black spot in focus: a study of the poetry of Alun Lewis. *AWR* 67 (1980) 43-78. Reprinted in Roland Mathias, *A ride through the wood: essays on Anglo-Welsh literature* (1985), pp. 125-157.

MEAD, Matthew. Alun Lewis the poet. *Satis* 1 (1960) 15-24.

MEREDITH, Christopher. Dai greatcoat, Insectman and Alun Lewis. *PW* 22,4 (1987) 59-65.

MORGAN, Gerald. Alun Lewis, 1915-44. *Barn*, Rha/Dec 1965, 43.

MORRIS, T.G. *WM*, 12 Mar 1954, 8:F. Letter on his meeting Alun Lewis in India.

NAGARAJAN, S. An Indian allusion in Alun Lewis. *Notes and Queries*, Jun 1980, 240-241.

PARKER, Jack. Alun Lewis. He died only 28 and Wales has lost a brilliant son. *South Wales Echo,* 8 Dec 1960, 5:C-G. Continued: 9 Dec 1960, 12:C-F; 10 Dec 1960, 3:G-H.

PIKOULIS, John. Alun Lewis: the way back. *Critical Quarterly* 14,2 (1972) 145-166.

—— Alun Lewis and the imagination. *PW* 10,3 (1975) 38-45.

—— East and east and east: Alun Lewis and the vocation of poetry. *AWR* 63 (1978) 39-65.

—— Alun Lewis and Edward Thomas. *Critical Quarterly* 23,4 (1981) 25-44.

—— Lynette Roberts and Alun Lewis. *PW* 19,2 (1983) 9-29.

—— The unknown Alun Lewis. *BNW*, Winter 1983, 3-4.

—— *Alun Lewis: a life.* Bridgend: Seren Books, 1991. 290 p.: ill. Extensively revised and rewritten paperback edition of a work first published (Bridgend: Poetry Wales Press) in 1984.

—— John Berryman's 'Elegy, for Alun Lewis'. *American Literature* 56,1 (1984) 100-101.

—— Alun Lewis to his wife. *NWR* 4,1 [13] (1991) 18-23. Review article on *Alun Lewis: letters to my wife*, ed. Gweno Lewis. – With a postscript on editorial practice in relation to Lewis's letters. – Pikoulis, *NWR* 4,1 [13] (1991) 32, also comments on the editorial practice of *Alun Lewis: collected stories*, ed. Cary Archard.

POOLE, Richard. Impersonality and the soldier poet: Alun Lewis and Keith Douglas. In *The Welsh connection: essays...*, ed. William Tydeman. Llandysul: Gomer Press, 1986. pp. 130-158.

PRESS, John. Poets of World War II. In *British writers*, vol. 8, ed. Ian Scott-Kilvert. New York: Scribner's, 1984. Discusses Alun Lewis, pp. 444-448.

REED, Henry. Poetry in war-time, ii. The younger poets. *Listener*, 25 Jan 1945, 100-101.

RICHARDS, Alun. When old ground starts to shift. *WM*, 19 Jul 1983, 8:B-F. Comments on Alun Lewis.

RHYS, Keidrych. Alun Lewis. *Tribune*, 2 Jun 1944, 19. Obituary.

ROWSE, A.L. Poets of today. *Listener*, 13 Jul 1944, 45-46.

SCANNELL, Vernon. *Not without glory: poets of the second world war*. London: Woburn Press, 1976. Incl. Alun Lewis, pp. 52-73.

SCHÄFER, Ulrich. *Alun Lewis: a bibliography*. 2nd workshop ed. Frankfurt A.M.: Anglo-Welsh Literature Circle, 1986. 114 p. Incl.: Primary texts, and translations – Secondary sources – Alun Lewis's letters available to the public. – A definitive listing.

SCOTT, A. H. English poetry of the Second World War. MLitt thesis. University of Aberdeen, 1967.

SHAYER, David. The poetry of Alun Lewis. In *Triskel two: essays on Welsh and Anglo-Welsh literature*, ed. Sam Adams and Gwilym Rees Hughes. Llandybïe: Christopher Davies, 1973. pp. 128-165.

—— Alun Lewis: the poet as combatant. *PW* 10,3 (1975) 79-83.

SHIRES, Linda M. Keeping something alive: British poetry, 1939-1956. PhD thesis. Princeton University, 1981. Incl. discussion of Alun Lewis, Dylan Thomas and Vernon Watkins.

—— *British poetry of the second world war*. London: Macmillan, 1985. Incl. Alun Lewis, pp. 86-99.

SMITH, Dai. Confronting the minotaur: politics and poetry in twentieth-century Wales. *PW* 15,3 (1979) 4-23.

—— The case of Alun Lewis: a divided sensibility. *Llafur: Journal of Welsh Labour History* 3,2 (1981) 14-27.

SYMES, Gordon. Muse in India: an aspect of Alun Lewis. *English* 6,34 (1947) 191-195.

THOMAS, Dylan. *The broadcasts*, ed. Ralph Maud. London: Dent, 1991. Brief comment on Alun Lewis, pp. 46-48.

THOMAS, M. Wynn. *Internal difference: twentieth-century writing in Wales*. Cardiff: University of Wales Press, 1992. Incl. The two Aluns, pp. 49-67. – On Alun Llewelyn-Williams and Alun Lewis. – English version of Y ddau Alun. *Taliesin* 64 (1988) 23-35.

THOMAS, W.D. Soldier poet. *Listener*, 4 May 1944, 497.

TOLLEY, A.T. *The poetry of the forties*. Manchester: Manchester University Press, 1985. Discusses Alun Lewis, pp. 220-227.

—— Alun Lewis. In *British poets, 1914-1945*, ed. Donald E. Stanford. Detroit: Gale, 1983. (Dictionary of literary biography; 20). pp. 207-210.

VALLETTE, Jacques. Trois poètes Anglais morts à la guerre. *Mercure de France*, 1 Apr 1947, 641-653.

WEBB, Harri. Alun Lewis: the lost leader. *PW* 10,3 (1975) 118-123.

WILLIAMS, John Stuart. The poetry of Alun Lewis. *AWR* 14,33 (1964) 59-71.

—— The short stories of Alun Lewis. *AWR* 14,34 (1964) 16-25.

—— The poetry of Alun Lewis. *PW* 2,2 (1966) 3-8.

—— Alun Lewis: a select bibliography. *AWR* 16,37 (1967) 13-15. Incl. reviews in English periodicals.

—— Alun Lewis. In *Reference guide to English literature*, ed. D.L. Kirkpatrick. 2nd ed. 3 vols. Chicago; London: St James Press, 1991. Vol. 2, pp. 866-867.

# ROLAND MATHIAS (b. 1915)

A. Publications by Roland Mathias
   (i)   Books
   (ii)  Books and periodicals edited
   (iii) Selected contributions to books and periodicals

B. Publications about Roland Mathias

## A (i). Publications by Roland Mathias: Books

*Days enduring and other poems*. Ilfracombe: Stockwell, 1943. 64 p.

*Break in harvest and other poems*. London: Routledge, 1946. 57 p.

*The roses of Tretower* / dust-cover and illustrations by Eric Peyman. [Pembroke Dock]: Dock Leaves Press, 1952. 66 p.: ill. Poetry.

*The eleven men of Eppynt and other stories*. [Pembroke Dock]: Dock Leaves Press, 1956. 199 p. Contents: Take hold on hell – Incident in Majorca – One bell tolling – Cassie Thomas – Block-system – Digression into miracle – The Rhine tugs – The neutral shore – A night for the curing – The palace – The eleven men of Eppynt – Agger makes Christmas – Ffynnon Fawr – Match.

*The flooded valley*. London: Putnam, 1960. 32 p. Poetry.

*Whitsun riot: an account of a commotion amongst Catholics in Herefordshire and Monmouthshire in 1605*. London: Bowes & Bowes, 1963. 153 p.

*Absalom in the tree and other poems*. Llandysul: Gwasg Gomer, 1971. 50 p. ISBN: 0-85088-114-5.

*Vernon Watkins*. Cardiff: University of Wales Press [for] the Welsh Arts Council, 1974. 127 p.: front. port.: pbk. (Writers of Wales). Incl. bibliography, pp. 121-124. 'Limited to 1000 copies'.

*The hollowed-out elder stalk: John Cowper Powys as poet*. London: Enitharmon Press, 1979. 158p.: hbk & pbk. ISBN: 0-90111-87-2 hbk, 0-90111-88-0 pbk.

*Snipe's castle*. Llandysul: Gomer Press, 1979. 89 p. ISBN: 0-85088-741-0. Poetry.

*Burning brambles: selected poems, 1944-1979*. Llandysul: Gomer Press, 1983. 163 p. ISBN: 0-85088-728-3. Contains poems from: *Break in harvest* – *The roses of Tretower* – *The flooded valley* – *Absalom in the tree* – *Snipe's castle* – Tide-reach: a sequence of Pembrokeshire poems written for music.

*The lonely editor: a glance at Anglo-Welsh magazines*. Cardiff: University College of Cardiff Press, 1984. 18 p.: pamph. (Annual Gwyn Jones lecture). ISBN: 0-906449-63-4.

*A ride through the wood: essays on Anglo-Welsh literature*. Bridgend: Poetry Wales Press, 1985. 320 p. ISBN: 0-907476-50-3. Contents: David Jones: towards the holy diversities – Lord Cutglass, twenty years after [on Dylan Thomas] – Any minute or dark day now: the writing of *Under Milk Wood* – Grief and the circus horse: a study of the mythic and Christian themes in the early poetry of Vernon Watkins – The black spot in focus: a study of the poetry of Alun Lewis – The Caseg letters: a commentary – Philosophy and religion in the poetry of R.S. Thomas – Channels of grace: a view of the earlier novels of Emyr Humphreys – Address for the Henry Vaughan service 1977 – Under the threatening train of steam engines and schoolmasters: the predicament of some Anglo-Welsh poets in the nineteenth century – *The lonely editor: a glance at Anglo-Welsh magazines*.

*Anglo-Welsh literature: an illustrated history*. Bridgend: Poetry Wales Press, 1987. 142 p.: ill.: pbk. (The illustrated history of the literatures of Wales; 4). ISBN: 0-907476-64-3.

*Craswall* / wood engraving by Peter Reddick. Newtown: Gwasg Gregynog, [1989]. [4] p.: ill.: pamph. (Beirdd Gregynog; Greynog poets; 9). ISBN: 0-948714-29-8. Text of single poem. – 'This edition consists of 400 copies.'

## A (ii). Publications by Roland Mathias: Books and Periodicals Edited

*Here To-day,* [1-4], [1944-45]. 'A review published in Reading'. – Edited by Pierre Edmunds and Roland Mathias.

*The Anglo-Welsh Review*, 11,27 – 25,56, 1961-1976. From issue 22,50 (1973) Roland Mathias was joint editor with Gillian Clarke; his editorials and reviews are presented in Section A (iii).

*The shining pyramid and other stories by Welsh authors* / edited by Sam Adams and Roland Mathias. Llandysul: Gwasg Gomer, 1970. xvi, 163 p. ISBN: 0-85088-079-3.

*Spirit: a Magazine of Poetry*, 41,2 (1974/75). Special issue ('Sixteen Welsh poets'), edited by Roland Mathias. – Incl. editorial note, pp. 2-4.

*The collected short stories of Geraint Goodwin* / edited by Sam Adams and Roland Mathias. Tenby: H.G. Walters, 1976. 246 p.: front. port.: pbk.

*David Jones: eight essays on his work as writer and artist:* being the first transactions of Yr Academi Gymreig (English section) / edited by Roland Mathias. Llandysul: Gomer Press, 1976. 144 p.: ill. ISBN: 0-85088-372-5.

*Anglo-Welsh poetry, 1480-1980* / edited and introduced by Raymond Garlick and Roland Mathias. Bridgend: Poetry Wales Press, 1984. 377 p.: hbk & pbk. ISBN: 0-907476-21-X hbk, 0-907476-22-8 pbk.

## A (iii). Publications by Roland Mathias: Selected Contributions to Books and Periodicals

The mental invalid and the modern novel. *Here To-day* [1945] 30-36.

Subite. In *For those who are alive: an anthology of new verse,* ed. Howard Sergeant. London: Fortune Press, 1946.

Robert Frost: an appreciation. *Poetry Review*, Mar-Apr 1947, 102-106.

Alpweg. *The Penfro* [Pembroke Dock Grammar School Magazine], Jul 1949, 2-5. Travel story, under pseudonym 'William O'Tell'.

A note on some recent poems by Vernon Watkins. *DL* 1,3 (1950) 38-49.

Review of Goronwy Rees, *Where no wounds were.* DL 1,3 (1950) 51-54.

Reviews of *The historical basis of Welsh nationalism* (Plaid Cymru pamphlet); E.H. Stuart Jones, *The last invasion of Britain.* DL 2,5 (1951) 44-46; 47-50.

Man on those hills of myrrh and flowers: a glimpse of Henry Vaughan's Breconshire. *DL* 3,7 (1952) 20-31.

Review of John Cowper Powys, *Porius.* DL 3,7 (1952) 40-46.

Review of Oliver Onions, *A penny for the harp.* DL 3,8 (1952) 40-42.

Reviews of *Llewelyn Powys: a selection of his writings,* ed. Kenneth Hopkins, John Cowper Powys, *The inmates*; Henry Treece, *The dark island. DL* 3,9 (1952) 50-54; 56-59.

Reviews of A. Tindal Hart, *William Lloyd: bishop, politician, author and prophet;* Vaughan Wilkins, *A king reluctant. DL* 3,10 (1953) 46-48; 49-50.

Reviews of John Cowper Powys, *In spite of*; A.H. Dodd, *Studies in Stuart Wales. DL* 4,11 (1953) 61-62; 64-67.

Review of Carl B. Cone, *Torchbearer of freedom: the influence of Richard Price on 18th century thought*, A.H. Dodd, *The character of early Welsh emigration to the United States*. *DL* 4,12 (1953) 51-55.

Review of *An anthology of contemporary verse*, ed. Margaret J. O'Driscoll. *Welsh Secondary Schools Review*, Dec 1953, 32-33.

In a co-educational grammar school in Wales. In *The school as Christian community*, ed. W.O. Lester Smith. London: S.C.M. Press, 1954. pp. 47-63.

Ticinese. *The Penfro* [Pembroke Dock Grammar School Magazine], Jul 1954, 2-4.

A merry manshape, or Dylan Thomas at a distance. *DL* 5,13 (1954) 30-39.

Reviews of Llewelyn Powys, *Black laughter*, Malcolm Elwin, *The life of Llewelyn Powys*; 'Wil Ifan', *Here and there*; T.H. Parry-Williams, *John Rhys, 1840-1915*; Arthur Clark, *Raglan Castle and the Civil War in Monmouthshire*. *DL* 5,13 (1954) 45-46; 48; 50-51; 51.

Reviews of Vernon Watkins, *The death bell; The laws of Hywel Dda*, tr. Melville Richards; V.E. Nash-Williams, *The Roman frontier in Wales*, E.A. Lewis and J. Conway Davies, *Records of the court of augmentations relating to Wales and Monmouthshire*. *DL* 5,14 (1954) 34-35; 42-43; 43-44.

Review of James Hanley, *The Welsh sonata*. *DL* 5,15 (1954) 49-50.

Reviews of John Cowper Powys, *Atlantis;* J.F. Rees, *The story of Milford*, Grahame E. Farr, *Chepstow ships*; E.G. Bowen, *The settlements of the Welsh saints in Wales*. *DL* 6,16 (1955) 41-42; 50-52; 53-55.

Reviews of Gwyn Jones, *Welsh legends and folk-tales*; R.A. Pritchard, *Thomas Charles, 1755-1814*. *DL* 6,17 (1955) 42-44; 47-48.

Reviews of Kingsley Amis, *That uncertain feeling*; Wilfred Watson, *Friday's child: poems*, *DL* 6,18 (1955) 36-39; 40-42.

Gwlad-yr-Haf. *DL* 7,19 (1956) 20-29. Essay on John Cowper Powys, *A Glastonbury romance*.

Reviews of Samuel Williams, *John Penry, 1563-1593*; Ivor Waters, *Chepstow Parish records*. *DL* 7,19 (1956) 51; 53-55.

Reviews of Emyr Humphreys, *A man's estate*, W. John Morgan, *The small world*, Henry Treece, *The great captains*; J. M. Cleary, *The Catholic recusancy of the Barlow family of Slebech...* *DL* 7,20 (1956) 58-61; 61-62.

Mallorcan notebook. *DL* 8,21 (1957) 9-24.

Reviews of T.O. Phillips, *Robert Roberts (y sgolar mawr), 1834-1885*; David Williams, *The Rebecca riots. DL* 8,21 (1957) 66-69; 73-76.

Review of Thom Gunn, *The sense of movement*, Ted Hughes, *The hawk in the rain. DL* 8,22 (1958) 56-61.

Reviews of Emyr Humphreys, *The Italian wife*; Llewelyn Powys, *Somerset and Dorset essays;* Geoffrey F. Nuttall, *The Welsh saints. AWR* 9,23 (1959) 80-85; 89-95; 96-99.

Review of Rhys Davies, *The darling of her heart. AWR* 9,24 (1959) 47-49.

John Evans, 1858 -. *AWR* 9,24 (1959) 79-92. Biographical article on Prof. John Evans (1858 – 1963).

Dutch diary. *AWR* 10,25 (1959) 73-93.

Review of Anne Ridler, *A matter of life and death. AWR* 10,25 (1959) 111-117.

Edward Thomas. *AWR* 10,26 (1960) 23-37.

Reviews of Anthony Conran, *Formal poems*; Ted Hughes, *Lupercal*, Robert Huff, *Colonel Johnson's ride*; Emyr Humphreys, *A toy epic. AWR* 10,26 (1960) 73-75; 78-81; 85-87

Take me over the border. *London Welshman*, Jan 1961, 8-12. Essay on the border country.

Editorial. *AWR* 11,27 (1961) 5-13. Incl. discussion of Raymond Williams, *Border country.*

Reviews of Oliver Bernard, *Country matters*, T. Harri Jones, *Songs of a mad prince*; David Verey, *A Shell guide to Mid-Wales. AWR* 11,27 (1961) 51-53; 61-64.

Reviews of Thom Gunn, *My sad captains*; Caroline Glyn, *Dream saga and other poems. AWR* 12,29 (1962) 65-70; 71-72.

Reviews of Jack Bevan, *Brief candles*; Thom Gunn, *Fighting terms*, Rosamund Stanhope, *So looked I down to Camelot*; Richard Hughes, *The fox in the attic. AWR* 12,30 (1962) 60-61; 62-66; 75-78.

Editorial. *AWR* 13,31 (1963) 3-14. Incl. discussion of R.S. Thomas's images of nature and the Welsh.

Reviews of Gloria Evans Davies, *Words – for Blodwen*, John Stuart Williams, *Last fall*, John Williams Andrews, *First flight, The manoeuvring sun*, ed. Alan

Craig, *Collected poems 1962*, ed. William G. Smith; E.C. Freeman and Edward Gill, *Nelson and the Hamiltons in Wales and Monmouthshire. AWR* 13,31 (1963) 88-94; 103-105.

Editorial. *AWR* 13,32 (1963) 3-6. Obituary tribute to John Cowper Powys.

Reviews of Thomas Kinsella, *Downstream*, H.R. Bramley, Verse one; Arthur Calder-Marshall, *The enthusiast: an enquiry into the life ... of the Rev. Joseph Leycester Lyne, alias Father Ignatius. AWR* 13,32 (1963) 77-79; 90-91.

Review of H.W. Williams, *Wind whispers*, Jeffrey Du Cann Grenfell-Hill, *New thoughts*, Asoka Weerasinghe, *Lotus and other poems. AWR* 14,33 (1964) 113-115.

The only road open. *AWR* 14,34 (1964) 105-109. Story.

Reviews of Brenda Chamberlain, *The water-castle;* Harri Webb, *Our national anthem. AWR* 14,34 (1964) 121-122; 127-128.

Editorial. *AWR* 15,36 (1966) 3-6. Obituary tribute to T. Harri Jones.

The poetry of Dannie Abse, 1. The head still stuffed with feathers. *AWR* 15,36 (1966) 107-123.

Reviews of G. Wilson Knight, *The Saturnian quest: a study of the prose works of John Cowper Powys; Welsh History Review,* vol. 2 , no. 3 (1965). *AWR* 15,36 (1966) 148-150; 153-155.

Reviews of R.S. Thomas, *Pietà;* Derek Langridge, *John Cowper Powys: a record of achievement.* AWR 16,37 (1967) 158-160; 165-166.

The poetry of Dannie Abse, 2. The one voice that is mine. *AWR* 16,38 (1967) 84-98.

Reviews of Kenneth Osborne, *Yawning in the wind, Merthyr politics: the making of a working-class tradition,* ed. Glanmor Williams, Richard Deacon, *Madoc and the discovery of America;* Goronwy Rees, *The Rhine. AWR* 16,38 (1967) 158; 188-192; 193-194.

Editorial. *AWR* 17,39 (1968) 3-5. Obituary tribute to Vernon Watkins.

Reviews of Leslie Norris, *Finding gold*; Robert Morgan, *The night's prison and Rainbow valley;* Kate Roberts, *Tea in the heather,* tr. Wyn Griffith. *AWR* 17,39 (1968) 185-188; 188-190; 197-198.

Reviews of Dannie Abse, *A small desperation*; Richard Tudor Edwards, *William Morgan*; Richard Deacon, *John Dee*; Leonard Clark, *Grateful Caliban. AWR* 17,40 (1969) 193-195; 210-212; 212-214, 216-217.

Meetings with Vernon Watkins. In *Vernon Watkins, 1906-1967*, ed. Leslie
Norris. London: Faber, 1970. pp. 61-69.

Editorial. *AWR* 18,41 (1970) 3-10. On the development of *Dock Leaves* and
*The Anglo-Welsh Review*.

Reviews of *Wales*, nos. 1-11 [reprint]; Raymond Garlick, *A sense of Europe*,
Roy Burnett, *Rhondda and The collected works of Dai Cottomy*, Robert Morgan,
*Poems and extracts*, Ellen Tifft, *The kissed cold kite: poems and fables*; Anthony
Powell, *The military philosophers*; Myles Dillon and Nora Chadwick, *The Celtic
realms, The quest for Arthur's Britain*, ed. Geoffrey Ashe; David Picton Jones,
*After Livingstone. AWR* 18,41 (1970) 194-196; 203-208; 218-220; 225-229;
230-232, .

Reviews of John Ormond, *Requiem and celebration*, John Tripp, *The loss of
ancestry*, Alan Perry, *Characters*, J.P. Ward, *The other man*, R. Gerallt Jones,
*Jamaican landscape*, A.G. Prys-Jones, *High heritage; A choice of William Morris's
verse*, ed. Geoffrey Grigson; John James, *Men went to Cattraeth; Studies in folk
life: essays in honour of Iorwerth C. Peate*, ed. Geraint Jenkins; Wynford Vaughan
Thomas and Alun Llewellyn, *The Shell guide to Wales, AWR* 18,42 (1970) 224-
233; 237-239; 242-245; 260-261; 270-274.

Editorial. *AWR* 19,43 (1970) 3-11. Discusses Anglo-Welsh literature,
including T.L. Williams, *Caradoc Evans*.

Reviews of Brenda Chamberlain, *Poems with drawings*, Brenda Chamberlain,
*Alun Lewis and the making of the Caseg broadsheets;* Dannie Abse, *Selected poems*,
John Crowe Ransom, *Selected poems*; John Idris Jones, *Barry Island and other
poems*, Christopher Pilling, *Snakes and girls*; Nora K. Chadwick, *Early Brittany*, Henry Myhill, *Brittany; Industrial South Wales, 1750-1914*, ed. W.E.
Minchinton, Oliver Jones, *The early days of Sirhowy and Tredegar. AWR* 19,43
(1970) 234-238; 243-245; 249-253; 287-292; 296-298.

Editorial. *AWR* 22,49 (1970) 3-8.

Review of Vernon Watkins, *Uncollected poems. PW* 5,3 (1970) 43-48.

Roland Mathias. In *Artists in Wales*, ed. Meic Stephens. Llandysul: Gwasg
Gomer, 1971. Autobiographical essay, pp. 160-168.

Reviews of Clifford Dyment, *Collected poems; The survival of poetry*, ed. Martin
Dodsworth; V.S. Naipaul, *The loss of Eldorado*, Alexander Winston, *No pur-
chase, no pay;* R.C.B. Oliver, *The family history of Thomas Jones the artist of
Pencerrig, Radnorshire*, Robert Owen, *Report to the County of Lanark* [and] *A
new view of society*, ed. V.A.C. Gatrell. *AWR* 19,44 (1971) 252-254; 284-291;
296-300.

Reviews of *The correspondence of John Owen (1616-1683)*, ed. Peter Toon;

Thomas Jones, *Rhymney memories*, Arthur Gray-Jones, *A history of Ebbw Vale.* *AWR* 20,45 (1971) 254-257; 266-271.

Letter. *PW* 7,3 (1971) 19-24. On the twenty-first number of *Poetry Wales*.

The sacrificial prince: a study of *Owen Glendower*. In *Essays on John Cowper Powys*, ed. Belinda Humfrey. Cardiff: University of Wales Press, 1972. pp. 233-261.

Thin spring and tributary: Welshmen writing in English. In *Anatomy of Wales,* ed. R. Brinley Jones. Peterston Super Ely, Glamorgan: Gwerin Press, 1972. pp. 187-205.

Reviews of Rhys Davies, *Nobody answered the bell*, Emyr Humphreys, *National winner;* Jean-Jacques Hatt, *Celts and Gallo-Romans*, Charles Thomas, *Britain and Ireland in early Christian times...*, John Beddoe, *The races of Britain;* John Wesley in Wales, ed. A.H. Williams, R.C.B. Oliver, *The squires of Penybont Hall, Radnorshire; The world of Dylan Thomas* (Gramophone record). *AWR* 20,46 (1972) 210-214; 236-242; 242-246; 265.

Editorial. *AWR* 21,47 (1972) 3-8. On *Welsh poets*, ed. A.G. Prys-Jones.

Reviews of Cyril Hodges, Coming of age; Nora Chadwick, *The Celts*, D. Aneurin Thomas, *The Welsh Elizabethan Catholic martyrs; Radical adventurer: the diaries of Robert Morris, 1772-1774*, ed. J.E. Ross, *Little Hodge: his letters and diaries of the Crimean War, 1854-56*, ed. The Marquess of Anglesey. *AWR* 21,47 (1972) 197-198; 223-227; 229-235.

Reviews of R.S. Thomas, *H'm,* Jack Clemo, *The echoing tip*; Leslie Alcock, *Arthur's Britain,* Richard Barber, *The figure of Arthur*; Peter J. French, *John Dee: the world of an Elizabethan magus*; David Jenkins, *The agricultural community in south-west Wales at the turn of the century. AWR* 21,48 (1972) 201-205; 227-232; 233-236; 243-245.

Philosophy and religion in the poetry of R.S. Thomas. *PW* 7,4 (1972) 27-45.

The Welsh language and the English language. In *The Welsh language today*, ed. Meic Stephens. Llandysul: Gomer Press, 1973. pp. 32-63.

Reviews of *The song of Roland*, tr. D.D.R. Owen; *Clough: the critical heritage,* ed. Michael Thorpe; Bernard Knight, *Lion rampant*; Geoffrey L. Fairs, *A history of The Hay. AWR* 22,49 (1973) 202-206; 209-212; 255-256; 283-285.

Reviews of E. G. Bowen, *Britain and the western seaways*, Leslie Alcock, *By South Cadbury is that Camelot: excavations at Cadbury Castle, 1966-70*, Michael Prestwich, *War, politics and finance under Edward I*; A.G. Prys-Jones, *The story of Carmarthenshire, vol. 2, Pembrokeshire life 1572-1843: a selection of letters*, ed. B.E. and K.A. Howells. *AWR* 22,50 (1973) 239-245; 260-264.

A view of the estuary. *Planet* 17 (1973) 56-67. Story.

A niche for Dylan Thomas. *PW* 9,2 (1973) 51-74.

Editorial. *AWR* 23,51 (1974) 3-4. On Cyril Hodges.

Reviews of *Poems of Ivor Gurney, 1890-1937; Triskel two,* ed. Sam Adams and Gwilym Rees Hughes; *Correspondence and records of the S.P.G. relating to Wales, 1701-1750,* ed. Mary Clement, Ivor Walters, *Henry Marten and the Long Parliament*; Dafydd Tomos, *Michael Faraday in Wales*; Idris Parry, *Stream and rock.* *AWR* 23,51 (1974) 156-159; 181-184; 194-199; 201-204; 212-213.

Editorial. *AWR* 23,52 (1974) 3-7. On Anglo-Welsh attitudes.

Reviews of Alun Richards, *Home to an empty house;* Alwyn Rees and Brinley Rees, *Celtic heritage: ancient tradition in Ireland and Wales,* Francis John Byrne, *Irish kings and high-kings*; E.G. Bowen, *David Samwell (Dafydd Ddu Feddyg), 1751-1798*; Robert Evans and Brian John, *The Pembrokeshire landscape.* *AWR* 23,52 (1974) 204-206; 224-228; 233-235; 253-255.

Reviews of Andrew Young, *Complete poems,* ed. Leonard Clark; Emyr Humphreys, *Flesh and blood*; John Morris, *The age of Arthur, AWR* 24,53 (1974) 192-196; 203-206; 236-241.

Anglo-Welsh bards and metropolitan reviewers. *PW* 9,4 (1974) 4-8.

Reviews of Barry Cunliffe, *Iron age communities in Britain...,* D.W. Harding, *The iron age in lowland Britain*; B.G. Charles, *George Owen of Henllys: Welsh Elizabethan;* Links with the past: Swansea and Brecon historical essays, ed. Owain W. Jones and David Walker, Eifion Evans, *Howel Harris evangelist*; J.M. Lewis, *Welsh monumental brasses.* *AWR* 24,54 (1975) 219-225; 225-228; 228-234; 235-237.

Editorial. *AWR* 25,55 (1975) 3-8. On R.S. Thomas, *Laboratories of the spirit* (Gregynog Press edition) and Max Boyce.

Reviews of Garnet Owen, *Earth receding*; David G. Hey, *An English rural community: Myddle under the Tudors and Stuarts,* Humphrey Lloyd, *The Quaker Lloyds in the Industrial Revolution;* John Odell, *Exhumation of a murder: the life and trial of Major Armstrong*; Edmund John Mason, *Portrait of the Brecon Beacons*; John Sang Kinross, *Fishguard fiasco;* Roger Jones, *Gower: fact and fable. AWR* 25,55 (1975) 145-148; 204-211; 229-232; 247-249; 254-255; 255-256..

The Caseg letters: a commentary. *PW* 10,3 (1975) 47-77. Compares Brenda Chamberlain's edited versions of the letters (*Alun Lewis and the making of the Caseg broadsheets*) with the originals.

In search of the Silurist. *PW* 11,2 (1975) 6-35. On Henry Vaughan.

Rhys Davies. In *Contemporary novelists of the English language*, ed. James Vinson. 2nd ed. London: St. James Press; New York: St. Martin's Press, 1976. pp. 338-341.

Editorial. *AWR* 25,56 (1976) 3-11. On Anglo-Welsh literature in higher education. *AWR* 26,57 (1976) 280-286 has replies by Sheenagh Pugh and Belinda Humfrey, and Roland Mathias's further response.

Reviews of *France before the Romans*, ed. Stuart Piggott and others, Stuart Piggott, *The druids*; J.M. Scott, *Boadicea*; J.P.D. Dunbabin, *Rural discontent in nineteenth century Britain*, E. Tegla Davies, *The master of Penybryn*. *AWR* 25,56 (1976) 213-219; 219-222; 222-228.

Review of Elizabeth Jenkins, *The mystery of King Arthur*, Guy Ragland Phillips, *Brigantia: a mysteriography*, John Sharkey, *Celtic mysteries: the ancient religion*. *AWR* 26,57 (1976) 221-226.

Reviews of *Pesnici vojvodine: poets of Voivodina; Diary of a Welsh swagman, 1869-1894*, ed. Williams Evans; Michael Hunter, *John Aubrey and the realm of learning;* A.H.A. Hogg, *Hill-forts of Britain;* R.H. Kinvig, *The Isle of Man: a social, cultural and political history;* Manxman: the poems of T.E. Brown, read by Sir John Betjeman and William Bealby-Wright [gramophone record]. *AWR* 26,58 (1976) 140-141; 157-161; 172-176; 198-201; 201-203; 218-219.

Roland Mathias looks back over twenty six years of *The Anglo-Welsh Review*. *BNW*, Summer 1976, 16-17.

Address for the Henry Vaughan service. *Madog* 1,2 (1977) 42-52.

Introduction. In *Green horse: an anthology by young poets of Wales*, ed. Meic Stephens and Peter Finch. Swansea: Christopher Davies, 1978. pp. 15-22.

Siams. *AWR* 27,60 (1978) 41-48. Story.

Reviews of Samuel Rees, *David Jones: an annotated bibliography and guide to research;* D. Ben Rees, *Chapels in the valley; The justices of the peace in Wales and Monmouthshire, 1541 to 1689*, ed. J.R.S. Phillips, *Calendar of ancient petitions relating to Wales*, ed. William Rees. *AWR* 27,60 (1978) 135-136; 167-169; 170-173.

David Jones: three letters. *AWR* 61 (1978) 53-65. Edited by Roland Mathias.

Review of Jean Markale, *Women of the Celts*. *AWR* 61 (1978) 128-131.

Reviews of James Tucker, *The novels of Anthony Powell; The Roman west country: classical culture and Celtic society*, ed. Keith Branigan and P.J. Fowler, Lloyd Laing, *The archaeology of late Celtic Britain and Ireland, c.400-1200*. *AWR* 62 (1978) 121-123; 159-161.

Reviews of Gwyn Williams, *The land remembers: a view of Wales;* Gerhard Herm, *The Celts. AWR* 63 (1978) 177-178; 184-187.

Layers of learning. *Planet* 44 (1978) 57. Review of René Hague, *A commentary on* The anathemata *of David Jones.*

Review of G. Wilson Knight, *The Saturnian quest. Powys Review* 4 (1978) 82-84.

Letter. *PW* 13,4 (1978) 112-114. Roland Mathias considers Edward Thomas's influence on his own writing.

Literature in English. In *The Arts in Wales, 1950-75*, ed. Meic Stephens. Cardiff: Welsh Arts Council, 1979. pp. 207-238. Welsh version: Llenyddiaeth yn Saesneg. In *Y Celfyddydau yng Nghymru, 1950-75,* ed. Meic Stephens. Caerdydd: Cyngor Celfyddydau Cymru, 1979. pp. 217-250.

Letter. *WM,* 27 Feb 1979, 10:D. Roland Mathias and other writers on devolution.

Review of David Jones, *The dying Gaul and other writings*, ed. Harman Grisewood. *AWR* 64 (1979) 105-108.

Letter. *PW* 15,2 (1979) 25-27. On Anglo-Welsh literary criticism.

Pe medrwn yr iaith. *Y Faner*, 29 Chw/Feb 1980, 9. [If I could speak the language].

Reviews of *The collected poems of Edward Thomas*, ed. R. George Thomas; Christopher Hood, *The other side of the mountain. AWR* 66 (1980) 77-82; 112-114.

The black spot in focus: a study of the poetry of Alun Lewis. *AWR* 67 (1980) 43-78.

Reviews of Samuel Rees, David Jones; Vernon Watkins, *The breaking of the wave; Gerard Manley Hopkins: the major poems,* ed. Walford Davies; Sally Jones, *Allen Raine. AWR* 67 (1980) 110-113; 120-122; 123-127; 128-132.

Letter. *AWR* 67 (1980) 201-202. On Leonard Clark's birthday.

Review of Sheenagh Pugh, *What a place to grow flowers. BNW*, Summer 1980, 9.

Review of Belinda Humfrey, *John Dyer. BNW*, Autumn 1980, 9.

Review of Jeremy Hooker, *Englishman's road. BNW*, Winter 1980, 9-10.

Review of Seamus Heaney, *Field work. PW* 15,4 (1980) 52-56.

Review of *David Jones: letters to a friend*, ed. Aneirin Talfan Davies, *Introducing David Jones,* ed. John Matthias. *PW* 16,2 (1980) 122-127.

David Jones. *Welsh Books and Writers* [Welsh Books Council], Autumn 1980, 8-10.

Poets of Breconshire. *Brycheiniog* 19 (1980-81) 27-49.

Introduction. In David Jones, *The Narrows.* Budleigh Salterton: Interim Press, 1981.

Prospects for Wales. *The Author*, Spring 1981, 16-18.

The steward's letter. *AWR* 68 (1981) 20-23. Poetry.

Reviews of Gordon Hopkins, *Llanthony Abbey and Walter Savage Landor*; Molly Miller, *The saints of Gwynedd; Boroughs of mediaeval Wales*, ed. R.A. Griffiths. *AWR 68 (1981) 142-144, 146-148; 148-152.*

Reviews of Barry Cunliffe, *The Celtic world*; S.C. Stanford, *The archaeology of the Welsh marches. AWR* 69 (1981) 119-122; 122-125.

Review of Dannie Abse, *Miscellany one. BNW*, Summer 1981, 11.

Review of William Blissett, *The long conversation: a memoir of David Jones. British Book News*, Dec 1981, 751-752.

David Jones: towards the holy diversities. *THSC* (1981) 137-178.

Death of a naturalist. In *The art of Seamus Heaney*, ed. Tony Curtis. Bridgend: Poetry Wales Press, 1982. pp. 13-25.

Channels of grace: a view of the earlier novels of Emyr Humphreys. *AWR* 70 (1982) 64-88.

Review of *The selected poems of Alun Lewis*, ed. Jeremy Hooker and Gweno Lewis. *AWR* 71 (1982) 90-92.

A kind of expiation – Signal – They, without us. *AWR* 72 (1982) 23-25. Poetry.

Review of R.S. Thomas, *Between here and now. BNW*, Summer 1982, 9-10.

Lying down in the word-hoard: an introduction to the poetry of Seamus Heaney. *BNW*, Autumn 1982, 7-9.

Review of *Critical writings on R.S. Thomas*, ed. Sandra Anstey. *BNW*, Autumn 1982, 10-11.

Ferns at Rossnakill. *Honest Ulsterman* 72 (1982) 21. Poetry.

Innocent dying. *Poetry Review* 72,2 (1982) 52. Poetry.

Review of Thomas O. Calhoun, *Henry Vaughan: the achievement of* Silex Scintillans. *PW* 18,1 (1982) 138-142.

Saturday morning – Cynog. *Spirit* 48 (1982) 13-14. Poetry.

David Jones: an introduction. *Spirit* 48 (1982) 56-62.

Emyr Humphreys. In *British novelists, 1930-1959. Part: A-L.*, ed. Bernard Oldsey. Detroit: Gale, 1983. (Dictionary of literary biography; 15). pp. 195-206.

Review of Sheenagh Pugh, *Earth studies and other voyages*, Duncan Bush, *Aquarium,* Robert Minhinnick, *Life sentences. BNW*, Summer 1983, 9-10.

Critical and affectionate look at Dannie. *WM*, 12 Nov 1983, 9:E. Review of *The poetry of Dannie Abse*, ed. Joseph Cohen.

A field at Vallorcines – On South Lord's Land. *Fine Madness* 3 (1983) 28-29. Poetry.

On discovering Daumier's 'Don Quixote reading' in the National Museum of Wales. *Poetry Review* 73,2 (1983) 53. Poetry.

Roland Mathias: an interview. *PW* 18,4 (1983) 58-63. Interviewed by Cary Archard.

Foreword. In A.G. Prys-Jones, *More nonsense.* Cowbridge: D. Brown, 1984. pp. 5-7.

Review of *100 contemporary Christian poets*, ed. Gordon Bailey. *AWR* 76 (1984) 100-101.

Review of Mike Jenkins, *Empire of smoke*, Tony Curtis, *Letting go*, Joyce Herbert, *Approaching snow*, Graham Thomas, *The one place*, Christine Evans, *Looking inland. BNW*, Spring 1984, 7-8.

Review of Bryan Aspden, *News of the changes*, Steve Griffiths, *Civilised airs. BNW*, Autumn 1984, 11-12.

Review of Edward Thomas, *Wales. Powys Review* 14 (1984) 93-96.

An interview with Roland Mathias. In *Common ground: poets in a Welsh landscape*, ed. Susan Butler. Bridgend: Poetry Wales Press, 1985. pp. 21-40.

Review of Emyr Humphreys, *Jones. AWR* 78 (1985) 89-90.

Review of *The works of Thomas Vaughan*, ed. Alan Rudrum. *AWR* 80 (1985) 120-123.

Review of Emyr Humphreys, *Salt of the earth*, Edward Thomas, *The south country. AWR* 81 (1985) 128-130, 136-139.

Review of J.P. Ward, *The clearing*, Christopher Meredith, *This. BNW*, Spring 1985, 12-13.

Review of John Tripp, *Passing through*, Jon Dressel, *Out of Wales. BNW*, Summer 1985, 9-10.

Review of *Bulwark and bridge...*, ed. Huw Williams. *BNW*, Autumn 1985, 18.

A separated place: Roland Mathias surveys the current Anglo-Welsh poetry scene. *Poetry Society Newsletter*, Oct 1985, 5.

Sanderlings. *Poetry Australia* 102 (1985) 50. Poetry.

John Cowper Powys and 'Wales': a limited study. *Powys Review* 17 (1985) 5-26.

Powys: the monster hole in the middle of Wales. *WM*, 28 Feb 1986, 16:A-D.

Mansel Thomas (1909-1986). *Welsh Music* 8,2 (1986) 14-16. One of a number of tributes.

Beginning at home. In *The literature of Wales in secondary schools: project undertaken by the Welsh Academy on behalf of the Welsh Office.* Cardiff: Welsh Office; Welsh Academy, 1987. pp. 98-110. A survey of early Anglo-Welsh literature.

The first civil war – The second civil war and interregnum. In *Pembrokeshire county history. Vol. 3. Early modern Pembrokeshire,* ed. Brian Howells. Haverfordwest: Pembrokeshire Historical Society, 1987. pp. 159-196, 197-224.

John Cowper Powys: an impression. A BBC radio broadcast, Welsh Home Service, 27 June 1957. *Powys Review* 24 (1989) 51-58. With brief contribution from Roland Mathias.

Emyr Humphreys. In *Contemporary novelists*, ed. Lesley Henderson. 5th ed. Chicago; London: St James Press, 1991. pp. 465-466. Incl. listing of radio and TV plays.

Leslie Norris. In *Contemporary Poets,* ed. Tracy Chevalier. 5th ed. Chicago; London: St. James Press, 1991. pp. 703-704.

The clear sea. *NWR* 6,2 [22] (1993) 25. Poetry.

The lamentation of Marchell. *PW* 29,2 (1993) 7. Poetry

# B. Publications about Roland Mathias

[ANON]. Roland Mathias. In *Contemporary authors*, vols. 97-100, cd. Frances
C. Locher. Detroit: Gale, 1981. pp. 352-353. Incl. interview with Roland
Mathias.

COLLINS, Michael J. Roland Mathias. In *Poets of Great Britain and Ireland,
1945-1960*, ed. Vincent B. Sherry. Detroit: Gale, 1984. (Dictionary of literary biography; 27). pp. 241-246.

—— The elegiac tradition in contemporary Anglo-Welsh poetry. *AWR* 76
(1984) 46-57. Incl. discussion of Roland Mathias.

HOOKER, Jeremy. The poetry of Roland Mathias. *PW* 7,1 (1971) 6-13.

—— *The presence of the past: essays on modern British and American poetry.* Bridgend:
Poetry Wales Press, 1987. Incl. Roland Mathias: the strong remembered
words, pp. 141-150.

—— Profile: Roland Mathias. *NWR* 1,4 [4] (1989) 17-22.

LLOYD, Megan Sue. Texts against chaos: Anglo-Welsh identity in the poetry
of R.S. Thomas, Raymond Garlick and Roland Mathias. PhD thesis.
University of Kentucky, 1992. 417 p.

WILLIAMS, John Stuart. Roland Mathias. In *Contemporary poets of the English
language,* ed. James Vinson. 2nd ed. London: St. James Press; New York:
St. Martin's Press, 1975. pp. 996-998.

# LESLIE NORRIS (b. 1921)

A. Publications by Leslie Norris
   (i) Books, and books edited
   (ii) Selected contributions to books and periodicals

B. Publications about Leslie Norris


## A (i). Publications by Leslie Norris: Books, and Books Edited

*Tongue of beauty*. London: Favil Press, [1943]. 13 p. (Resurgam younger poets; 9).

*Poems*. London: Falcon Press, [1946]. 48 p. (Resurgam books).

*Finding gold*. London: Chatto & Windus: Hogarth Press, 1967. 59 p. (The phoenix living poets).

*The loud winter*. Cardiff: Triskel Press, 1967. [14] p.: pamph. (The Triskel poets; 3).

*Vernon Watkins, 1906-1967* / edited by Leslie Norris. London: Faber, 1970. 105 p.: ill. ISBN: 0-571-08904-6. Incl. A true death [poem], by Leslie Norris, pp. 97-98.

*Ransoms*. London: Chatto & Windus: Hogarth Press, 1970. 40 p. (The phoenix living poets). ISBN: 0-7011-1595-5.

*His last autumn*. Rushden: Sceptre Press, 1972. [1] p.: pamph. Poem, headed 'For Andrew Young, 1885-1971'. – 'Limited to 100 copies ... with nos. 1 to 30 being signed by the poet.'

*Glyn Jones*. Cardiff: University of Wales Press [for] the Welsh Arts Council, 1973. 95 p.: front. port.: pbk. (Writers of Wales). 'Limited to 1000 copies'.

*Mountains polecats pheasants, and other elegies*. London: Hogarth Press, 1974. 48 p.: pbk. (The phoenix living poets). ISBN: 0-7011-2020-7.

*At the publishers'*. Berkhamsted: Priapus Press, 1976. [4] p.: pamph. ISBN: 0-905448-01-4. Contents: At the publishers' – Ravenna Bridge. – '150 copies, 25 of which are signed by the author'. – Poetry.

*Islands off Maine* / monotypes by Charles E. Wadsworth. Cranberry Isles, Maine: Tidal Press, 1977. [27] p.: ill. 'Five hundred and fifty copies ... fifty numbered copies, signed by the author and artist, have been boxed by Gray Parrot.' – Poetry.

*Ravenna Bridge*. Knotting: Sceptre Press, 1977. [3] p.: pamph. 'This edition is limited to 150 numbered copies ... Nos. 1-50 are signed by the poet.'

*Sliding: short stories*. London: Dent, 1978. 148p. ISBN: 0-460-12038-7. Contents: Waxwings – Sliding – Cocksfoot, crested dog's tail, sweet vernal grass – The highland boy – The mallard – A big night – A house divided – Three shots for Charlie Betson – Snowdrops – Prey – A moonlight gallop – Away away in China – A roman spring – Percy Colclough and the religious girls. – Reissued 1981, pbk. ISBN 0-460-02225-3.

—— *Sliding: fourteen short stories and eight poems* / with photographs by Jessie Ann Matthew; edited by Geoffrey Halson. Longman, 1981. x, 165 p.: ill.: pbk. ISBN: 0-582-22066-1. Incl.: Introduction, by Leslie Norris, pp. vii-x – Poems; At Usk, Man and boy, Deerhound, Curlew, The strong man, A February morning, Barn owl, A small war.

U.S. ed.: New York: Scribner, 1976. 148 p. ISBN: 0-684-14775-0.

*Andrew Young: remembrance and homage* / compiled and introduced by Leslie Norris; monotypes and wood-engravings by Charles E. Wadsworth. Cranberry Isles, Maine: Tidal Press, 1978. 63 p.: ill. ISBN: 0-930954-09-2 trade, 0-930954-10-6 de luxe. Incl.: A remembrance, by Leslie Norris, pp. 1-18 – His last autumn [poem], by Leslie Norris, p. 45. – '1250 copies ... trade edition of 1200 ... 50 de luxe numbered copies'.

*Merlin and the snake's egg: poems* / illustrated by Ted Lewin. New York: Viking Press, 1978. 48 p.: ill. ISBN: 0-670-47191-7.

*Hyperion*. Knotting: Sceptre Press, 1979. [3] p.: pamph. 'Limited to 150 numbered copies. Nos. 1-50 are signed by the poet.'

*Walking the white fields: poems, 1967-1980*. Boston: Little, Brown, [1980]. 118 p. (An Atlantic Monthly press book). ISBN: 0-316-61189-1. Contains selections from: *Finding gold* – *Ransoms* – *Mountains polecats pheasants*. – With two new poems.

*The Mabinogion* / translated by Lady Charlotte Guest, edited and introduced by Leslie Norris; wood engravings by Joan Freeman. London: Folio Society, 1980. 268 p.: ill.: in slipcase.

*Water voices*. London: Chatto & Windus: Hogarth Press, 1980. 48 p.: pbk. (The phoenix living poets). ISBN: 0-7011-2518-7.

*A tree sequence*. Seattle: Sea Pen Press & Paper Mill, 1984. [27] p.: ill. Wood engravings by Gretchen Daiber.
—— Seattle: Spring Valley Press, 1984. [19] p.

*Selected poems.* Bridgend: Poetry Wales Press, 1986. 142 p.: front. port.: pbk. ISBN: 0-907476-60-0. Contains selections from: *The loud winter – Finding gold – Ransoms – Mountains polecats pheasants – Water voices – New poems.*

**The girl from Cardigan.** Bridgend: Seren Books, 1988. 202 p.: front. port.: hbk & pbk. ISBN: 0-907476-95-3 hbk, 0-907476-96-1 pbk. Contents: The girl from Cardigan – A flight of geese – Sing it again, Wordsworth – The kingfisher – My uncle's story – Blackberries – The wind, the cold wind – Some opposites of good – In the west country – A professional man – Shaving – All you who come to Portland Bill – Lurchers – A seeing eye – The holm oak – Reverse for Dennis – Gamblers – Johnny Trevecca and the devil – A piece of archangel – Keening.

U.S. ed.: *The girl from Cardigan: sixteen stories.* Layton, Utah: G.M. Smith, 1988. 176 p. (A Peregrine Smith book). ISBN: 0-87905-296-1. Reissued 1989, pbk. ISBN: 0-87905-337-2.

*Norris's ark.* Cranberry Isles, Maine: Tidal Press, 1988. 64 p.: hbk & pbk.: ill. ISBN: 0-930954-28-9 hbk, 0-930954-30-0 pbk. Illustrated by Charles E. Wadsworth. – Incl. cassette. – Poetry.

*Ransoms* / wood engraving by Anne Jope. Newtown: Gwasg Gregynog, 1988. [2] p.: ill.: pamph. (Gregynog poets; 3). ISBN: 0-948714-19-0. Text of single poem. – 'This edition consists of 400 copies.'

*Sequences.* Layton, Utah: G.M. Smith, 1988. 64 p. (A Peregrine Smith book). ISBN: 0-87905-303-8. Poetry.

*A sea in the desert.* Bridgend: Seren Books, 1989. 64 p.: pbk. ISBN: 1-85411-015-2. Contents: as *Sequences*, plus 'A sea in the desert' and 'Decoys'. – Poetry.

*Without contraries there is no progression: Dylan Thomas, Vernon Watkins and the romantic tradition.* Treforest: Polytechnic of Wales (Centre for the Study of Welsh Writing in English), 1992. 24 p.: pamph. (Inaugural Rhys Davies lecture). Delivered 29 Apr 1992.

[Unpublished thesis]. The poetry of Vernon Watkins. MPhil thesis. University of Southampton, 1971-72. 200 p.

# A (ii). Publications by Leslie Norris: Selected Contributions to Books and Periodicals

Poem for Betty. In *Today's new poets: an anthology of contemporary verse.* London: Resurgam Books, [1944].

The poet (for Derrick Webly). *WR* 4 (1945) 199. Poetry.

Review of Idris Davies, *Tonypandy and other poems. WR* 4 (1945) 301.

In Merthyr now. *Wales* 2nd ser 6,2 [22] (1946) 10. Poetry.

Review of Islwyn ap Nicholas, *Dic Penderyn. WR* 5 (1946) 152.

Three poems. *Stand* 5,4 (1961) 44-45. Incl. The village of Lillinton.

Three poems. *Stand* 6,1 (1962) 59-60. Incl.: The bowl of roses – Elegy for an old man found dead on a hill.

Andrew Young: a tribute. *Priapus* 4 (1965) [2 p., between 11 and 12].

Verlaine and Rimbaud. *AWR* 15,36 (1966) 64-65. Poetry.

The poetry of Vernon Watkins. *PW* 2,3 (1966) 3-10.

Review of John Stuart Williams, *Green rain. PW* 3,2 (1967) 52-54.

Owls. *Priapus* 11-12 (1967-68) 6. Poetry.

Three men. *AWR* 17,40 (1969) 120-121. Incl. Harry the Black. – Poetry.

Review of Vernon Watkins, *Fidelities. PW* 4,3 (1969) 55-58.

Review of John Ormond, *Requiem and celebration. PW* 5,2 (1969) 47-53.

Where the crakeberries grow: Robert Graves gives an account of himself to Leslie Norris. *Listener*, 28 May 1970, 715-716.

Plus fours. *Atlantic Monthly*, Aug 1970, 84. Story.

Review of William Cooke, *Edward Thomas. PW* 6,1 (1970) 47-52.

The poetry of Edward Thomas. In *Triskel one: essays on Welsh and Anglo-Welsh literature,* ed. Sam Adams and Gwilym Rees Hughes. Llandybïe: Christopher Davies, 1971. pp. 164-178.

Review of Alun John, *Alun Lewis. AWR* 20,45 (1971) 245-246.

A quiet study. *Planet* 8 (1971) 75-76. Review of Alun John, *Alun Lewis*.

Review of Ted Hughes, *Crow. PW* 7,1 (1971) 77-81.

Letter. *PW* 7,3 (1971) 15-19. On the twenty-first number of *Poetry Wales*.

Review of Glyn Jones, *Selected short stories. AWR* 20,46 (1972) 205-207.

Review of Alexander Cordell, *The fire people. AWR* 21,48 (1972) 219-220.

Letter. *PW* 7,4 (1972) 118-121. On R.S. Thomas.

Seeing eternity: Vernon Watkins and the poet's task. In *Triskel two: essays on Welsh and Anglo-Welsh literature,* ed. Sam Adams and Gwilym Rees Hughes. Llandybïe: Christopher Davies, 1973. pp. 88-110.

Review of George Ewart Evans and David Thomas, *The leaping hare. AWR* 22,45 (1973) 285-287.

A complex clarity. *London Magazine,* Jun-Jul 1974, 132-135. Review of Andrew Young, *Complete poems.*

Eagle and hummingbird. *Atlantic Monthly,* Aug 1974, 21. Reply by Norris to a letter regarding his poem.

Review of Roland Mathias, *Vernon Watkins. PW* 10,2 (1974) 28-31.

Vernon Watkins. In *Contemporary poets,* ed. James Vinson. 2nd ed. London: St. James Press, 1975. pp. 1806-1809.

Review of Glyn Jones, *Selected poems. PW* 11,4 (1976) 82-90.

Review of Dora Polk, *Vernon Watkins and the spring of vision. PW* 12,4 (1977) 130-135.

Reviews of Jan Marsh, *Edward Thomas: a poet for his country;* Glyn Jones, *Welsh heirs. AWR* 62 (1978) 118-120; 150-152.

Review of R.S. Thomas, *Frequencies. AWR* 63 (1978) 130-133.

Land without a name. *PW* 13,4 (1978) 89-101. On Edward Thomas.

Review of Jeremy Hooker, *Landscape of the daylight moon, Solent shore. AWR* 65 (1979) 111-115.

Review of Roland Mathias, *Snipe's castle. Powys Review* 6 (1979) 86-88.

Review of John Davies, *At the edge of town. AWR* 70 (1982) 89-93.

Foreword. In Dylan Thomas, *The collected stories.* London: Dent, 1983. pp. vii-xv.

Foreword. In Gwen Watkins, *Portrait of a friend.* Llandysul: Gomer Press, 1983.

Glyn Jones. In *British novelists, 1930-1959. Part 1: A-L,* ed. Bernard Oldsey. Detroit: Gale, 1983. (Dictionary of literary biography; 15). pp. 226-231.

The sense of the actual: a conversation with Leslie Norris. *Literature and Belief* 3 (1983) 41-53. Interviewed by Bruce W. Jorgensen.

A profound simplicity: the poetry of Andrew Young. *New Criterion* 4,2 (1985) 41-44.

Trouble at a tavern – A recantation. *Quarterly West* [University of Utah] (1985). Translations from Dafydd ap Gwilym.

Review of R. George Thomas, *Edward Thomas: a portrait. Powys Review* 19 (1986) 81-83.

Dylan Thomas (1914-1953). In *British writers. Supplement 1. Graham Greene to Tom Stoppard,* ed. under auspices of British Council by Ian Scott-Kilvert. New York: Scribner's, 1987. pp. 169-184.

Merthyr Tydfil (1983). In *Wales on the wireless: a broadcasting anthology,* ed. Patrick Hannan. Llandysul: Gomer in assoc. with BBC Cymru/Wales, 1988. pp. 51-52.

Review of Raymond Garlick, *Collected poems: 1946-1986. NWR* 1,1 [1] (1988) 54-55.

[Translations]. In Rainer Maria Rilke. *The sonnets to Orpheus,* tr. Leslie Norris and Alan Keele. Columbia, S.C.: Camden House, 1989. Incl. A note from Leslie Norris, pp. vii-viii.

Review of Caradoc Evans, *My people. Powys Review* 23 (1989) 71-72.

To explain the inexplicable. *PW* 25,2 (1989) 42-44. On his approach to writing.

The Brighton midgets. *Sewanee Review* 97 (1989) 163-172. Story.

Borders (i.m. John Ormond, died 4 May 1990). *NWR* 3,3 [11] (1991) 33. Poetry.

Glyn Jones. In *Contemporary novelists*, ed. Lesley Henderson. 5th ed. Chicago; London St James Press, 1991. pp. 501-503.

Owen Sullivan and the horse – In Cefn Cemetery. *NWR* 4,4 [16] (1992) 32. Two sections from a long poem in progress.

Three [sic] extracts from work in progress: A boy – A round table – Ithaca – A carol for my wife. *PW* 28,2 (1992) 11-13.

## B. Publications about Leslie Norris

Note that a collection of critical essays on Leslie Norris, edited by Eugene England and Peter Makuck is forthcoming (1993); contents are given below.

ADAMS, Sam. The poetry of Leslie Norris. *PW* 7,2 (1971) 14-27.

BAKER, Simon C. Keeping short boundaries holy: a study of the short stories of Leslie Norris. MA thesis. University of Wales (Swansea), 1987.

CLWYD Centre for Educational Technology. *Anglo-Welsh Poets: Leslie Norris.* Mold: Clwyd Centre for Educational Technology, 1978. Incl.: Two booklets, one of poems by Norris, another reprinting Sam Adams' *Poetry Wales* article (1971) – Eight facsimile manuscripts – Cassette of the poet reading twelve poems, plus interview – Twelve slides relating to Leslie Norris. – Teaching pack. – Reviewed *AWR* 67 (1980) 197-198.

CURTIS, Tony. *How to study modern poetry.* London: Macmillan, 1990. Discusses 'Water', pp. 123-129.

DAVIES, James A. *Leslie Norris.* Cardiff: University of Wales Press, 1991. 103 p. (Writers of Wales). ISBN: 0-7083-1117-2. Incl. Bibliography, pp. 97-103.

—— The life and work of Leslie Norris: an introduction. In *English studies 3: proceedings of the third conference on the literature of region and nation. Part 1,* ed. J.J. Simon and Alain Sinner. Luxembourg: Centre Universitaire de Luxembourg, 1991. pp. 96-109.

DAVIES, John. Approximate rivers move: the sound of water in the poetry of Leslie Norris. *PW* 28, 2 (1992) 13-18. Reprinted in *An open world: essays on Leslie Norris,* ed. Eugene England and Peter Makuck (1993).

EMERY, Thomas. Leslie Norris. In *Poets of Great Britain and Ireland, 1945-1960,* ed. Vincent B. Sherry. Detroit: Gale, 1984. (Dictionary of literary biography; 27). pp. 264-269.

ENGLAND, Eugene. *An open world: essays on Leslie Norris,* ed. Eugene England and Peter Makuck. Columbia: Camden House, 1993. 220 p. Contents: Two interviews with Leslie Norris; At the edge of things, by Meic Stephens [and] A sound like a clear gong, by Stan Sanvel Rubin and Bruce Bennett – Poems for Leslie Norris, by William Stafford and Ted Hughes – Poet of Merthyr, by Glyn Jones – White roads: Norris's landscape, by Judith Kitchen – On the poetry of Leslie Norris [1968], by Ted Walker – Stony Wales and the soft south, by Peter Davison – Rereading *Ransoms,* by Brendan Galvin – Approximate rivers move: the sound of water in Norris's poetry, by John Davies – Leslie Norris, formal poet, by Robert Richman – A resonant wind: breath to breath in Norris, by Wendy Barker – The paradox of winter, by Sue Ellen Thompson – Standing stones and stanzas: 'The twelve stones of Pentre Ifan', by Scott Abbott – Place and identity in 'Cave paintings', by Thomas Reiter – Unmade amends, by William Matthews – Crossing borders: the recent long poems, by Eugene England – Intimations of mortality: 'A flight of geese', by Bruce Bennett – Anecdote into story: 'Some opposites of good', by Vern Rutsala – The rigor of brevity, by George Core – Painful journeys, many happy returns, by Mark Jarman – Place as theme: Wales in 'Away away in China' and 'A Roman spring', by C.W. Sullivan III – 'Sing it again, Wordsworth': English romanticism, music, and the pleasure of the phrase, by Richard Simpson – Exiles and kingdoms, by Peter Makuck – Norris's birds, by Tony Curtis – Powers of observation: the stone, the hawk, the solitary I, by Fred Chappell – Out of bounds with Leslie Norris, by Barbara Drake – Norris's book of transformations, by Christopher Merrill.

JENKINS, Mike. The inner exile: the Merthyr poems of Leslie Norris. *PW* 21,3 (1986) 76-82.

JENKINS, Randal. The poetry of Leslie Norris: an interim assessment. *AWR* 20,46 (1972) 26-36.

JONES, Glyn. Poetry at the Casson: 'Womb to tomb' and 'Timeslip'. *AWR* 22,49 (1973) 290-294. On readings by John Ormond and Leslie Norris.

—— Leslie Norris. In *Contemporary poets*, ed. James Vinson. 2nd ed. London: St. James Press; New York: St. Martin's Press, 1975. pp. 1122-1123.

—— *PW* 21,3 (1986) 73-75. Letter. – Reprinted as 'Poet of Merthyr' in *An open world: essays on Leslie Norris*, ed. Eugene England and Peter Makuck (1993).

MATHIAS, Roland. Leslie Norris. In *Contemporary poets,* ed. Tracy Chevalier. 5th ed. Chicago; London: St. James Press, 1991. pp. 703-704. Incl. comment by Leslie Norris.

MINHINNICK, Robert. Leslie Norris: insistent elegist. *PW* 21,3 (1986) 83-86.

POGREBIN, Robin. He'll always be a Welshman. *New York Times Book Review*, 22 May 1988, 9.

ROBERTS, Neil. People and places. *Delta* 58 (1978) 17-19.

SIMPSON, Mercer. Leslie Norris: reluctant exile, discovered alien. *PW* 21,3 (1986) 87-94.

SMITH, Dai. Confronting the minotaur: politics and poetry in 20th century Wales. *PW* 15,3 (1979) 4-23. Comments on Leslie Norris.

WALKER, Ted. On the poetry of Leslie Norris. *Priapus* 11-12 (1967-68) 7-12. Reprinted in *An open world: essays on Leslie Norris,* ed. Eugene England and Peter Makuck (1993).

# JOHN ORMOND (1923-1990)

A. Publications by John Ormond
  (i)   Books, and books edited
  (ii)  Selected contributions to books and periodicals
  (iii) John Ormond: television films

B. Publications about John Ormond

## A (i). Publications by John Ormond: Books, and Books Edited

*Indications*. London: Grey Walls Press, 1943. 40 p.: pbk. As John Ormond Thomas. – With James Kirkup and John Bayliss. – Poetry.

*Requiem and celebration*. Swansea: Christopher Davies, 1969. 83 p.

*Definition of a waterfall*. London: Oxford University Press, 1973. 48 p.; pbk. ISBN: 0-19-211830-7.

*Penguin modern poets 27: John Ormond, Emyr Humphreys, John Tripp*. Harmondsworth: Penguin, 1979. 171 p.: pbk. ISBN: 0-104042-192-0. Incl. 28 poems by John Ormond, pp. 13-62.

*Graham Sutherland, O.M.: a memorial address: anerchiad coffa: discorso commemorativo: éloge funèbre*. Cardiff: National Museum of Wales, 1981. [36] p.: port.: pbk. ISBN: 0-7200-0244-3. Text of an address delivered at the Mass of Thanksgiving for the artist's life, Westminster Cathedral, 29 Apr 1980. – With Welsh, Italian and French translations.

*In place of an empty heaven: the poetry of Wallace Stevens*. Swansea: University College of Swansea, 1983. 23 p.: pbk. (W.D. Thomas memorial lecture). ISBN: 0-86076-037-5.

*Selected poems*. Bridgend: Poetry Wales Press, 1987. 142 p.: front. port.: pbk. ISBN: 0-907476-73-2.

*John Tripp: selected poems* / edited by John Ormond. Bridgend: Seren Books, 1989. 180 p.: pbk. ISBN: 0-907476-97-X. Incl. Introduction, by John Ormond, pp. 9-13.

*Cathedral builders and other poems*; with drawings by the author. Newtown: Gwasg Gregynog, 1991. x, 66 p.: ill. ISBN: 0-948714-37-9 leather, 0-948714-38-7 cloth. Contents: Introduction, by Rian Ormond Thomas, pp. vii-x –

35 poems. – With 11 drawings. – 'The edition consists of 250 copies ... Fifty copies are bound in quarter leather numbered I-L and 200 copies in quarter leather numbered 1-200.' – 'He [John Ormond] had very specific ideas on design and setting, which have been realised in this volume, as in his earlier works', p. viii.

## A (ii). Publications by John Ormond: Selected Contributions to Books and Periodicals

For some early pieces the author appears as John Ormond Thomas.

Welsh honorary degrees. *WM*, 22 May 1943, 3:F. Letter on recognition for literature.

Section from a work in progress. *Dawn* [University College, Swansea] 18 (1943) 23. As J.O. Thomas. – Prose.

Bright candle, my soul. Dawn [University College, Swansea] 18 (1943) 25. As J.O. Thomas. – Poetry.

An elegy for Alun Lewis. *Wales* 2nd ser. 4 (1944) 5-6.

Birthday poem. *WR* 3 (1944) 252-255.

Review of Vernon Watkins, *The lamp and the veil*, William Sydney Graham, *2nd poems. Poetry Quarterly* 7,4 (1945) 163-165.

Slate town. *PP*, 25 May 1946, 16-19. On Blaenau Ffestiniog.

The village under water. *Lilliput*, Jun 1946, 491-493. Story.

The Christmas mockers. *PP*, 28 Dec 1946, 20-23. On the Stephen Potter and Joyce Grenfell radio programme, 'How to cope with Christmas'.

From 'The influences'. *WR* 5 (1946) 167-171. Incl.: First sleep – Portrait of my grandfather – Portrait of my mother – Portrait of my father – The unseen blind – For the children, Bronwen and Neil. – Partly collected in *Requiem and celebration*.

War office land grab: Wales protests. *PP*, 25 Jan 1947, 7-9.

A bronze for the academy. *PP*, 3 May 1947, 21-24. On sculpture casting.

Dark harmony. *PP*, 4 Oct 1947, 26-27. On The Ink Spots.

Trev of the dog-tracks. *PP*, 18 Oct 1947, 19-21.

El Greco's 'The agony in the garden'. *WR* 6 (1947) 20. Written jointly with Harry Green.

Coal ambassador. *PP*, 17 Apr 1948, 19-21. On a miner's visit to Denmark.

Wakefield goes to sea. *PP*, 7 Aug 1948, 19-21. On Hornsea Seaside School.

Camera that photographs time. *PP*, 28 Aug 1948, 8-11. On the photo-finish technique.

Clay's great day. *PP*, 11 Sep 1948, 24-25. On J.C. Clay, the cricketer.

W.B. Yeats comes home to Sligo. *PP*, 9 Oct 1948, 10-13. On the poet's reburial.

Windsor Forest fall. *WR* 7 (1948) 93.

The street corner with a roof on. *PP*, 5 Mar 1949, 28-33. On Liverpool youth centre.

The old singer of Gower. *PP*, 19 Mar 1949, 30-33, 41. On Phil Tanner, the folk singer.

A coster's funeral. *PP*, 23 Apr 1949, 23-25.

Emlyn Williams directs Emlyn Williams. *PP*, 30 Apr 1949, 23-25. On filming 'The last days of Dolwyn'.

There's a man in that box. *PP*, 4 Jun 1949, 26-28. On adjudicating brass-bandsmen.

Revue singer with a difference. *PP*, 11 Jun 1949, 28-29. On Muriel Smith.

This is everyone's weekend college. *PP*, 30 Jul 1949, 22-25. On Ashridge, Hertfordshire.

Radio's top-line reporters. *PP*, 6 Aug 1949, 28-31.

The garden of Eden. *PP*, 27 Aug 1949, 14-16. On David Davies of Abergwili, topiarist and poet.

The vision and art of Dylan Thomas. *South Wales Evening Post*, 8 Nov 1952, 4:G-I. Review of Dylan Thomas, *Collected poems*.

Dylan Thomas writes a film script. *South Wales Evening Post*, 16 May 1953, 4:F. Review of Dylan Thomas, *The doctor and the devils*.

Dylan Thomas; an appeal. *PP*, 5 Dec 1953, 8. Letter, with personal reminiscences, asking for contributions to the Dylan Thomas Fund.

Borrowed Pasture: notes on a film. *Journal of Film and Television Arts*, Summer 1961, 6-8.

Introduction. In Dylan Thomas, *The doctor and the devils*. New York: Times Inc., 1964. (Times reading program).

Horizons hung in air: Kyffin Williams. *London Welshman*, Nov 1966, 7-9. Transcript of BBC Wales TV interview by John Ormond.

Review of Douglas Cleverdon, *The growth of* Under Milk Wood. *PW* 5,2 (1969) 61-64.

A music restored. *Planet* 7 (1971) 75-77. Review of Glyn Jones, *Selected short stories*.

R.S. Thomas, priest and poet: a transcript of John Ormond's film for BBC Television, broadcast on April 2nd, 1972; introduced by Sam Adams. *PW* 7,4 (1972) 47-57.

Ceri Richards: root and branch. *Planet* 10 (1972) 3-11.

Ceri Richards. In *Arddangosfa goffa Ceri Richards 1973: Ceri Richards memorial exhibition 1973*. Cardiff: National Museum of Wales, 1973. pp. 7-11.

John Ormond. In *Artists in Wales 2*, ed. Meic Stephens. Llandysul: Gomer Press, 1973. Autobiographical essay, pp. 155-164.

John Ormond writes. In *Corgi modern poets in focus 5*, ed. Dannie Abse. London: Corgi, 1973. pp. 133-135. Introduces 11 poems by John Ormond.

Nearly jilted. *Second Aeon* 16-17 (1973) 193. Poetry.

Political poetry. *WM*, 5 Aug 1974, 4:D-E. Review of Harri Webb, *A crown for Branwen*.

Gwyn Thomas. In *Contemporary novelists of the English language*, ed. James Vinson. 2nd ed. London: St. James Press; New York: St. Martin's Press, 1976. pp. 1360-1362.

In certain lights: extracts from a work in progress. *Planet* 36 (1977) 37-39. Incl. Bad light stops play [prose] – Patagonian portrait [poetry].

Y Gwyn Thomas arall. *Barn*, Ebr/Apr 1978, 146-147. Review of Ian Michael, *Gwyn Thomas*.

Gwyn Thomas: Welsh aristocrat. *WM*, 18 May 1982, 8:C-G. On 'Laughter before nightfall', Ormond's stage entertainment on Gwyn Thomas.

Introduction. In *Kyffin Williams R.A.: a catalogue for a retrospective exhibition /*

*Catalog ar gyfer arddangosfa adolygol* ... Cardiff: National Museum of Wales; Llandudno: Mostyn Art Gallery, 1987. pp. 10-27. Bilingual text.

Picturegoers (1980) – *Selected poems* (1987). In *Wales on the wireless: a broadcasting anthology,* ed. Patrick Hannan. Llandysul: Gomer in assoc. with BBC Cymru/Wales, 1988. pp. 58-60; 166-168.

Letter from Tuscany. *PW* 24,1 (1988) 20-24. Prose.

Wartime letters pledge poet's love. *WM*, 8 Jul 1989, 8:D-G. Review of Alun Lewis, *Letters to my wife*, ed. Gweno Lewis.

Poole, Richard. Conversations with John Ormond. *NWR* 2,1 [5] (1989) 38-46.

Saint Teresa's drum – Blue bath-gown. *NWR* 2,1 [5] (1989) 46. Poetry.

# A (iii). John Ormond: Television Films

Below is a brief selection of some seventy films made by John Ormond for television.

Borrowed pasture. BBC, 1960. Produced by John Ormond. – On two Polish ex-servicemen farming in Carmarthenshire.

A sort of welcome to spring. BBC Wales, 21 Mar 1960, 10.45-11.00 pm. Reading by Meredith Edwards of poems selected by John Ormond. – Produced by John Ormond.

Once there was a time. BBC Wales, 1 Mar 1961, 10.00-10.30 pm. Drama. 'Two old men sit engrossed in talk ... the scene is the Rhondda valley' – *Radio Times*.

Y Cymru bell: taith i Batagonia. BBC Wales, 7 Oct 1962. 1.10-1.40 pm. Introduced by Nan Davies, directed by John Ormond. – Continued 11 Oct, 18 Oct.

The desert and the dream. BBC Wales, 20 Dec 1962, 10.20-10.50 pm. Produced by John Ormond. – On modern Welsh Patagonians.

Return journey: the story of [Dylan Thomas's] return journey to Swansea. BBC Wales, 27 Oct 1964, 9.50-10.20 pm. A film of Thomas's prose piece produced by John Ormond.

Songs in a strange land: a film. BBC Wales, 17 Dec 1964, 10.15-11.15 pm. Television film. 'Near Cardiff's waterfront ... eastern religions ... are flourishing' – *Radio Times*.

The Mormons: a film report by John Ormond. BBC Wales, 18 Feb 1965, 9.25-10.10 pm.

Troubled waters: Harry Soan investigates a crisis on our rivers. BBC Wales, 20 Sep 1965, 10.55-11.20 pm. Produced by John Ormond.

My time again: Richard Burton. BBC Wales, 1965. Produced by John Ormond.

Just look again: 1-5. BBC Wales, 1966. Produced by John Ormond.

Under a bright heaven: a film portrait of Vernon Watkins. BBC Wales, 13 Jan 1966, 10.50-11.20 pm. Narrated and produced by John Ormond.

Horizons hung in air: an impression of Kyffin Williams, painter, and of his work. BBC Wales, 20 Apr 1966, 7.00-7.30pm. Narrated and produced by John Ormond.

Music in midsummer. BBC 2, 4 Jul 1968, 8.00-8.30 pm. Film on Llangollen International Eisteddfod, producer John Ormond.

A bronze mask: a film in elegy for Dylan Thomas. BBC Wales, 8 Jun 1969, 9.55-10.25 pm. Producer John Ormond.

The fragile universe: a portrait of Alun Lewis, poet and soldier. BBC Wales, 15 Jun 1969, 9.35-10.35 pm. Poems spoken by Henley Thomas, narration Arthur Phillips, produced by John Ormond.

The ancient kingdoms: a view of Wales. BBC Wales, 25 Jun 1969, 10.50-11.20 pm. Film to mark the Prince of Wales's investiture: music by Daniel Jones, narrated by Meredith Edwards, produced by John Ormond.

Piano with many strings: the art of Ceri Richards. BBC Wales, 29 Jun 1969, 9.35-10.05 pm. Narrated and produced by John Ormond.

Private view of art and artists in Wales: Leslie Norris. BBC Wales, 16 Feb 1970, 9.40-10.05 pm. Narrated and produced by John Ormond.

The land remembers. BBC Wales, 15 Feb 1972, 10.15-10.45pm. 'A series in which Gwyn Williams travels the length and breadth of Wales ... a personal account of Welsh archeology and history ... producer John Ormond' – *Radio Times*. – Part 1, History of Wales. – Continued: Slow centuries of Stone, 22 Feb – When the gods lived in the sea, 29 Feb – A fringe of Caesar's empire, 7 Mar – Divided kingdom, 14 Mar – Conquerors from Normandy, 21 Mar (11.00-11.30 pm).

R.S. Thomas: priest and poet. BBC 2, 2 Apr 1972, 9.30-10.00 pm. Produced by John Ormond.

The land remembers. BBC Wales, 4 Mar 1974, 10.15-10.45 pm. 'Colour, new series ... introduced by Gwyn Williams ... producer John Ormond' – *Radio Times*. – Part 1, The time of Owain Glyndŵr. – Continued: A Welshman comes to the throne, 11 Mar – Fires of the martyrs, 18 Mar – Wales the source country, 25 Mar – Wales and the Civil War, 1 Apr – The mould for future centuries, 8 Mar.

A day eleven years long. BBC Wales, 12 Sep 1975, 10.45-11.36 pm. Film on the painter Josef Herman, narrated and produced by John Ormond.

One man in his time: the world of W.J.G. Beynon, FRS. BBC Wales, 8 Dec 1975, 11.05-11.40 pm. Produced by John Ormond.

Y teithwyr. BBC Wales, 27 Feb 1976, 7.25-7.50 pm. Cynhyrchydd, John Ormond. On the artist John 'Warwick' Smith, set in 1797. First broadcast as 'The travellers', BBC 2.

Sutherland in Wales. BBC Wales, 2 Oct 1977, 11.05-11.35 pm. 'A film in which the artist ... tells how he first became hooked and obsessed by the landscape of Pembrokeshire' – *Radio Times*. – Produced by John Ormond.

## B. Publications about John Ormond

ABSE, Dannie. Introduction. In *Corgi modern poets in focus 5*, ed. D. Abse. London: Corgi, 1973. pp. 127-133. Introduces 11 poems by John Ormond.
—— John Ormond. *Independent*, 8 May 1990, 18:B-D. Obituary notice.
—— John Ormond as portraitist. *PW* 26,2 (1990) 5-7.
BERRY, Ron. What comes after? *PW* 27,3 (1991) 54-55.
BROWN, Tony. At the utmost edge: the poetry of John Ormond. *PW* 27,3 (1991) 31-36
COLLINS, Michael J. The Anglo-Welsh poet John Ormond. *World Literature Today* 51 (1977) 534-537.
—— The gift of John Ormond. *PW* 27,3 (1991) 4-8.
—— Craftsmanship as meaning: the poetry of John Ormond. *PW* 16,2 (1980) 25-33.
—— John Ormond. In *Poets of Great Britain and Ireland, 1945-1960*, ed. Vincent B. Sherry. Detroit: Gale, 1984. (Dictionary of Literary Biography; 27). pp. 269-275.
—— The elegiac tradition in contemporary Anglo-Welsh poetry. *AWR* 76 (1984) 46-57.
CURTIS, Tony. Grafting the sour to sweetness: Anglo-Welsh poetry in the last twenty-five years. In *Wales the imagined nation: studies in cultural and national identity*, ed. Tony Curtis. Bridgend: Poetry Wales Press, 1986. pp. 99-126. Incl. discussion of John Ormond.
FELTON, Mick. *PW* 27,3 (1991) 62-63. Review of *Cathedral builders and other poems* (Gwasg Gregynog).

GARLICK, Raymond. A Gregynog cathedral. *Planet* 89 (1991) 93-94. Review of *Cathedral builders and other poems* (Gwasg Gregynog).

GINGERICH, Martin E. *Contemporary poetry in America and England, 1950-1975: a guide to information sources*. Detroit: Gale, 1983. (American literature, English literature and world literatures English information guide series; vol. 41). Incl. annotated bibliography of John Ormond, pp. 288-289.

HOOKER, Jeremy. The accessible song: a study of John Ormond's recent poetry. *AWR* 23,51 (1974) 5-12. Reprinted in Hooker, *The presence of the past: essays on modern British and American poetry* (1987). pp. 107-113.

JENKINS, Randal. The poetry of John Ormond. *PW* 8,1 (1972) 17-28.

JONES, Glyn. Poetry at the Casson: 'Womb to tomb' and 'Timeslip'. *AWR* 22,49 (1973) 290-294. On poetry readings by John Ormond and Leslie Norris.

—— John Ormond, 1923-1990. *PW* 26,2 (1990) 3-5.

MINHINNICK, Robert. The echo of once being here: a reflection on the imagery of John Ormond. *PW* 27,3 (1991) 51-53.

NORRIS, Leslie. *PW* 5 (1969) 47-53. Review article on *Requiem and celebration*.

O'NEILL, Chris. Notes towards a bibliography of John Ormond's works. *PW* 16,2 (1980) 34-38. Covers films and the publication of individual poems.

ORMOND, Glenys. 'J.O.' and 'Rod'. *PW* 27,3 (1991) 24-45. By his wife Glenys, whose pet name was Rod.

POOLE, Richard. The voices of John Ormond. *PW* 16,2 (1980) 12-24.

—— John Ormond and Wallace Stevens: six variations on a double theme. *PW* 27,3 (1991) 16-26.

RICHARDS, Alun. John Ormond. *Independent*, 8 May 1990, 18:B-C. Obituary.

SIMPSON, Mercer. John Ormond (1923-1990). *BWA* 20 (1990) 16.

SMITH, Dai. A cannon off the cush. *Arcade*, 14 Nov 1980, 13-14. Profile.

—— John Ormond. *Times*, 14 May 1990, 14:B-E. Obituary.

STEPHENS, Meic. From *Picture Post* to poetry. *Guardian*, 9 Jun 1990, 21:C-E. Obituary.

SWALLOW, Norman. *Factual television*. London: Focal Press, 1966. 228 p. Incl. reference to *Borrowed pasture*, pp. 176-177, 184.

TRIPP, John. John Ormond. In *Contemporary poets of the English language*, ed. James Vinson. 2nd ed. London: St. James Press; New York: St. Martin's Press, 1976. pp. 1153-1155. Quotes Ormond's comments in *Corgi modern poets in focus 5*, ed. Dannie Abse (1971).

WALTERS, Gwyn. The early John Ormond: a tribute. *NWR* 3,1 [9] (1990) 27.

# ALUN RICHARDS (b. 1929)

A. Publications by Alun Richards
   (i)   Books, and books edited
   (ii)  Selected contributions to books and periodicals
   (iii) Alun Richards: television plays and adaptations

B. Publications about Alun Richards

## A (i). Publications by Alun Richards: Books, and Books Edited

*The elephant you gave me.* **London:** Michael Joseph, 1963. 192 p. Novel.

*The home patch.* London: Michael Joseph, 1966. 191 p. Novel.

*A woman of experience.* London: Dent, 1969. 157 p. ISBN: 0-460-04901-1. Novel.

*Dai country: short stories.* London: Michael Joseph, 1973. 254 p. ISBN: 0-7181-1133-8. Contents: Effie – Dream girl – Fly-half – Dai Canvas – The drop-out – The scandalous thoughts of Elmyra Mouth – Bowels Jones – Frilly lips and the son of the Manse – Going to the flames – Dailogue – Beck and call – One life.

*Home to an empty house.* Llandysul: Gomer Press, 1973. 240 p. ISBN: 0-85088-220-6. Novel.

*Plays for players.* Llandysul: Gomerian Press, 1975. 367 p. ISBN: 0-85088-290-7. Contents: The big breaker – The victualler's ball – The snowdropper – The horizontal life.

*The former Miss Merthyr Tydfil: stories.* London: Michael Joseph, 1976. 221 p. ISBN: 0-7181-1413-2. Contents: Hon. sec. R.F.C. – Off the record – On location – Jehoidah's gents – Sweethearts – Groceries – The former Miss Merthyr Tydfil.

*The Penguin book of Welsh short stories* / edited by Alun Richards. Harmondsworth: Penguin, 1976. 358 p.: pbk. ISBN: 0-1400-4061-7.

*Ennal's point.* London: Michael Joseph, 1977. 239 p. ISBN: 0-7181-1507-4. Novel.
—— Harmondsworth: Penguin, 1979. 256 p.: pbk. ISBN: 0-1400-4803-0.
—— / ed. David Pickling. Oxford: Oxford University Press, 1980. pbk. (Alpha books). ISBN: 0-1942-4280-3. School textbook.

German trans.: *Die letzte Fahrt der 'Gay Lady'*. Berlin: Verlag Volk und Welt, 1987. 269 p.: pbk. ISBN: 3-353-00210-3.

*The Penguin book of sea stories* / edited by Alun Richards. Harmondsworth: Penguin, 1977. 437 p.: pbk. ISBN: 0-14-004211-3. Incl. Introduction, by Alun Richards, pp. 7-8.

*Against the waves* / [compiled by] Alun Richards. London: Michael Joseph, 1978. 412 p. ISBN: 0-7181-1687-9. Incl.: Introduction, by Alun Richards, pp. 7-11 – The search, by Alun Richards, pp. 172-191. – Anthology of sea stories.
—— *The second Penguin book of sea stories* / edited by Alun Richards. Harmondsworth: Penguin, 1980. 413 p.: pbk. ISBN: 0-1400-4855-3.

*The former Miss Merthyr Tydfil and other stories.* Harmondsworth: Penguin, 1979. 348 p.: pbk. ISBN: 0-1400-4635-6. Contents: The former Miss Merthyr Tydfil – Hon. sec. R.F.C. – Off the record – On location – Jehoidah's gents – Sweethearts – Groceries – Effie – Dream girl – Fly-half – The drop-out – The scandalous thoughts of Elmyra Mouth – Bowels Jones – Frilly lips and the son of the Manse – Going to the flames – Dai-logue – Beck and call.

German trans.: *Schneewittchen und der Klempner: Geschichten aus Wales,* tr. Rainer Ronsch. Berlin: Verlag Volk und Welt, 1984. 226 p. Stories from: *Dai Country* – *The former Miss Merthyr Tydfil.*

*Barque Whisper.* London: Michael Joseph, 1979. 221 p. ISBN: 0-7181-1773-5. Novel.
—— Harmondsworth: Penguin, 1982. pbk. ISBN: 0-1400-5441-3.

U.S. ed.: New York: St. Martin's Press, 1979. ISBN: 0-312-06707-0.

*A touch of glory: 100 years of Welsh rugby.* London: Michael Joseph, 1980. 176 p.: ill. ISBN: 0-7181-1938-X .

*Carwyn: a personal memoir.* London: Michael Joseph, 1984. ix, 165 p.: ill. ISBN: 0-7181-2420-0. On Carwyn James, Welsh rugby coach.

*Days of absence: autobiography (1929-55).* London: Michael Joseph, 1986. 278 p.: ill. ISBN: 0-7181-2703 X.

*The new Penguin book of Welsh short stories* / edited by Alun Richards. London: Viking, 1993. xi, 400 p. ISBN: 0-670-84530-2.

# A (ii). Publications by Alun Richards: Selected Contributions to Books and Periodicals

Thy people: a fable. *Wales* 3rd ser., Oct 1958, 63-67.

Everybody says it's for the best. *Wales* 3rd ser., Nov 1958, 56-59.

Love and hate and Matabele Hopkins (Cubicle J). Wales 3rd ser., Jan 1959, 33-46. Reprinted in *Pick of today's stories 11,* ed. John Pudney (1960).

Journals: one. *Wales* 3rd ser., Apr 1959, 44-54.

The never-never land. *Wales*, 3rd ser., Oct 1959, 27-29. On the Wales of the Anglo-Welsh short story.

The literary scene: a footnote. *Wales* 3rd ser., Dec 1959, 17-18. In response to Glyn Jones, pp. 15-17.

Almareira blues. In *Pick of today's short stories 13,* ed. John Pudney. London: Putnam, 1962. pp. 24-52.

Place and the writer. *Listener*, 18 Jul 1963, 89-90. On Anglo-Welsh literature.

A theatre for Denise. *Listener*, 8 Dec 1966, 858-859.

Era's end for out of towner. *WM*, 1 Oct 1969, 7:A-B.

The boxing life. *Planet* 3 (1970) 72-75. Review of Ron Berry, *So long, Hector Bebb*.

Alun Richards. In *Artists in Wales*. Llandysul: Gwasg Gomer, 1971. Autobiographical essay, pp. 55-66.

Preview. *Radio Times*, 10-16 Apr 1976, 15. Continued: 8-14 May, 13; 5-11 Jun, 13; 4-10 Dec, 19.

Preview. *Radio Times*, 1-7 Jan 1977, 19. Continued: 29 Jan-4 Feb, 15; 26 Feb-4 Mar, 15; 26 Mar-1 Apr, 13; 23-29 Apr, 19; 21-27 May, 17; 18-24 Jun, 13; 16-22 Jul, 15; 13-19 Aug, 15; 24-30 Sep, 17; 22-28 Oct, 17; 19-25 Nov, 17; 17-23 Dec, 18.

Preview. *Radio Times*, 28 Jan-3 Feb 1978, 17. Continued: 25 Feb-3 Mar, 21; 25-31 Mar, 19; 22-28 Apr, 19; 20-26 May, 17; 17-23 Jun, 17; 15-21 Jul, 15; 12-18 Aug, 15; 2-8 Sep, 17; 7-13 Oct, 23; 25 Nov-1 Dec, 19.

Preview. *Radio Times*, 20-26 Jan 1979, 19. Continued: 17-23 Feb, 19; 17-23 Mar, 23; 14-20 Apr, 2; 12-18 May, 27; 9-15 Jun, 21; 7-13 Jul, 17; 4-10 Aug, 17; 1-7 Sep, 19; 6-12 Oct, 29; 3-9 Nov, 29; 1-7 Dec, 31.

Preview. *Radio Times*, 12-18 Jan 1980, 33. Continued: 9-15 Feb, 25; 10-16 May, 23; 28 Jun-4 Jul, 19: 2-8 Aug, 25.

Bred of heaven. *Radio Times*, 25-31 Oct 1980, 21, 23. On his television film, 'A touch of glory', celebrating centenary of the Welsh Rugby Union.

Ship talk. *Radio Times*, 15-21 Nov 1980, 31. On Stan Hugill, seaman.

Dog days for diarists. *WM*, 17 May 1983, 8:B-C. First in his *WM* series 'This and that: extracts from a writer's journal'.

Face to face with a consuming passion. *WM*, 15 Jun 1983, 8:B-E.

A lifeboat of honour. *WM*, 29 Jun 1983, 8:B-F.

When old ground starts to shift. *WM*, 19 Jul 1983, 8:B-F. Comments on Alun Lewis, and on Gwen Watkins, *Portrait of a friend*.

The more gentle they are, the greater the gap. *WM*, 27 Jul 1983, 8:B-F. On Carwyn James, rugby coach.

Introducing Patrick Ignatius. *WM*, 10 Aug 1983, 8:B-E. On his dog.

Style at the opera and virtue in the corner shop. *WM*, 24 Aug 1983, 8:B-E.

Castle view of history. *WM*, 14 Sep 1983, 8:B-E.

So, how do you get three veg to the table on time? *WM*, 27 Sep 1983, 8:B-F.

Ralph the books and Jackson the flying tailor. *WM*, 19 Oct 1983, 8:B-F.

The spice of Gwyn. *WM*, 2 Nov 1983, 8:B-F. On presentation of Gwyn Thomas's library to the South Wales Miners' Library, Swansea.

Naming no names. *WM*, 23 Nov 1983, 8:B-E.

Baiting the big loaner. *WM*, 19 Dec 1983, 8:B-E. On fishing.

The genie and the lamp. *WM*, 10 Oct 1984, 8:B-D. First of his series, 'At large in Tokyo'.

Anyone here from Neath, Ponty, Machynlleth even. *WM*, 24 Oct 1984, 10:B-E.

Sailing in Tokyo. WM, 6 Nov 1984, 8:B-F.

Stealing the show with a smart salute. *WM*, 13 Nov 1984, 8:B-E.

Sing along with me, shipmates. *WM*, 27 Nov 1984, 8:B-E.

Carwyn. *Yr Enfys* 24 (1984) 9.

Passengers. *Planet* 54 (1985) 6-12. Account of a voyage with a group of Japanese ex-servicemen.

Carwyn (1983) – Disappearing Wales (1963) In *Wales on the wireless: a broadcasting anthology,* ed. Patrick Hannan. Llandysul: Gomer in assoc. with BBC Cymru/Wales, 1988. pp. 24-27; 152-154.

The lingerie set. *The Works* [Welsh Union of Writers] 1 (1988) 130-150. Story.

The wizadry of Oz. *Quadrant*, Jan-Feb 1989, 95-97. Text of broadcast talk on Australia's bicentenary.

Help for Miners' Library. *WUW News*, Aug 1989, 7. Letter to newsletter of the Writers Union of Wales.

The ferryman's daughter. *NWR* 1,4 [4] (1989) 38-53. Story.

John Ormond. *Independent*, 8 May 1990, 18:B-C. Obituary.

Captain Colenso. *NWR* 5,2 [18] (1992) 35-39. Story.

## A (iii). Alun Richards: Television Plays and Adaptations

Below are brief details of a selection of Alun Richards's work for television.

Going like a fox. BBC TV 1959. Play, 75 mins.

O captain, my captain. BBC TV 1960. Play, 60 mins. Broadcast as radio play, 1961.

Hear the tiger, see the bay. ABC TV 1961. Play, 60 mins.

Nothing to pay. ABC TV 1961. Play, 60 mins.

The big breaker. BBC radio 1962. Play, 75 mins. Televised BBC TV 1964.

The hot potato boys. ABC TV 1962. Play, 60 mins.

The elephant you gave me. BBC TV 1963. Adaptation of his novel, 75 mins.

Ready for the glory. ABC TV 1963. Play, 60 mins.

The schoolmaster. BBC TV 1965. Adapted from Simenon, 60 mins.

Albinos in black. BBC radio 1968. Play, 75 mins. Televised BBC TV 1969.

Acting captain. BBC Wales TV 1969. Adapted from Alun Lewis, 30 mins.

Vessel of wrath. BBC TV 1969. Adapted from Somerset Maugham, 60 mins.

The princely gift. BBC TV 1970. Episode in the 'Shadow of tower' series.

Tales of unease. LW TV 1970. Play, 30 mins.

Under the carpet. Granada TV 1970. Play, 60 mins.

Harry Lifters. Granada TV 1972. Play, 60 mins.

Love and Mr Lewisham. BBC TV 1971. Four-part adaptation from H.G. Wells.

The Onedin line. BBC TV 1971. Two episodes of series; 1972, two episodes; 1973, two episodes; 1974-75, seven episodes.

Sutherland's law. BBC TV 1972. One episode of series.

Crown Court. Granada TV 1974. Three episodes of series; 1975, three episodes of series.

Warship. BBC TV 1974. One episode of series.

A touch of glory. BBC TV 1980. For centenary of the Welsh Rugby Union.

Ennal's Point. BBC TV 1981. Adaptation of his novel in six 60-minute episodes.

*Note*: Amongst Alun Richards's plays for BBC radio are Rowley Morgan (1959, 60 mins.), The goldfish bowl (1960, 60 mins.), The breadman (1961, 75 mins.), Eye of the needle (1961, 60 mins.) and Sailor's song [adapted from James Hanley] (1963, 75 mins.).

## B. Publications about Alun Richards

[ANON]. Alun Richards. In *Contemporary authors, new revision series. Vol. 17,* ed. Linda Metzger and Deborah Straub. Detroit: Gale, 1986. p. 384. Incl. bibliography of TV plays.

MCCARTHY, Shaun. Home from sea: tradition and innovation in the novels of Alun Richards. *AWR* 78 (1985) 59-71.

SMITH, Dai. A novel history. In *Wales the imagined nation: studies in cultural and national identity,* ed. Tony Curtis. Bridgend: Poetry Wales Press, 1986. pp. 131-158. Incl. discussion of Alun Richards.

# DYLAN THOMAS (1914-1953)

A. Publications by Dylan Thomas
  (i)  Books
  (ii) Selected contributions to periodicals
  (iii) Dylan Thomas: translations

B. Publications about Dylan Thomas
  (i)  Books and articles
  (ii) Theses

## A (i). Publications by Dylan Thomas: Books

*18 poems*. London: *Sunday Referee* and the Parton Bookshop 1934. 36 p. 'This book, the second volume of the *Sunday Referee* poets series, is unaccompanied by either portrait or preface, at the author's request', Victor S. Neuburg [p.5].
—— London: Fortune Press, [1942]. 32 p. With '12 Buckingham Palace Road' in imprint. – Later impressions have 'London, S.W. 1' [1946?] and '21 Belgrave Road' [1954?].

*Twenty-five poems*. London: Dent, 1936. vii, 47 p.

*The map of love: verse and prose*. London: Dent, 1939. viii, 116 p.: front port. Contents: Verse [16 poems] – Prose; The visitor, The enemies, The tree, The map of love, The mouse and the woman, The dress, The orchards.

*The world I breathe*. Norfolk, Conn.: New Directions, 1939. 184 p. (A New Directions book). Contents: Poems [40] – Stories; The dress, The visitor, The map of love, The enemies, The orchards, The mouse and the woman, The holy six, A prospect of the sea, The burning baby, Prologue to an adventure, The school for witches. – 'Seven hundred copies printed'.

*Portrait of the artist as a young dog*. London: Dent, 1940. 254 p. Contents: The peaches – A visit to grandpa's – Patricia, Edith, and Arnold – The fight – Extraordinary little cough – Just like little dogs – Where Tawe flows – Who do you wish was with us? – Old Garbo – One warm Saturday.
—— Dent, for the British Publishers Guild, 1948. 128 p.: pbk. (Guild books; 250). Reissued 1956.
—— Dent, 1965. 128 p.: pbk. (Aldine paperback). Reissued 1979.

(Everyman paperback). – Reissued, 1983. 128 p.: pbk. (Everyman fiction). ISBN: 0-468-02258-X. – Reissued 1989. ISBN: 0-460-01077-8. – Reissued 1991, pbk. (Everyman's classics). ISBN: 0-460-87053-X.

U.S. eds.: Norfok, Conn.: New Directions, 1940. 186 p. (A New Directions book). Reissued 1955. pbk. (A New Directions paperbook; 51).
—— *The collected prose of Dylan Thomas*. 3 vols. New York: New Directions, 1969. (New Directions paperbooks; NDP 183, 51, 90). Incl.: *Adventures in the skin trade – Portrait of the artist as a young dog – Quite early one morning*. – In slip-case.

*From* **'In memory of Ann Jones'**. Llanllechid: Caseg Press, [1942]. 1 leaf: ill. (Caseg broadsheet; 5). Text of poem, minus first 9 lines, with drawing by Brenda Chamberlain.

*New poems*. Norfolk, Conn.: New Directions, 1943. [31 p.]. (Poets of the year). Contents: There was a saviour – Into her lying down head – And death shall have no dominion – Among those killed in the dawn raid – To others than you – Love in the asylum – The marriage of a virgin – When I woke – The hunchback in the park – On a wedding anniversary – Unluckily for a death – Ballad of the long-legged bait – Because the pleasure bird whistles – Once below a time – Request to Leda – Deaths and entrances – O make me a mask and a wall.

*Deaths and entrances: poems*. London: Dent, 1946. 66 p.
—— / illustrated by John Piper; edited and with an introduction by Walford Davies. Newtown: Gwasg Gregynog, 1983. xiv, 59 p.: ill. Introduction, pp. vii-xiv – Frontispiece and 7 double-page lithographs by John Piper. – 'Published in an edition of 268 copies'.

*Selected writings* / introduction by John L. Sweeney. New York: New Directions, 1946. xxiii, 184 p.: front. port. (A New Directions book). Contents: Introduction, pp. ix-xxiii – Poems [47] – Stories; The orchards, A prospect of the sea, The burning baby, The mouse and the woman, The peaches, One warm Saturday.

*Twenty-six poems*. London: Dent, 1950. 78 p. 'The edition consists of ten copies on Japanese vellum, numbered I to X, and 140 copies on Fabriano hand-made paper numbered, 11 to 150, of which numbers 11 to 60 are for sale in Great Britain, all signed by author. December Mcmxxxxix.'

U.S. ed.: Norfolk, Conn.: J. Laughlin, 1949. 75 p. Edition of 150 signed copies.

*In country sleep and other poems*. New York: New Directions, 1952. 36 p.: front. port. (A New Directions book). Contents: Over Sir John's Hill – Poem on his birthday – Do not go gentle into that good night – Lament – In the white giant's thigh – In country sleep. – Title-page has mounted portrait of Thomas from photograph by Marion Morehouse. – 'The first edition consists of one hundred copies on stone-ridgepaper, each signed by the author, and five thousand copies on Kilmory paper.'

*Collected poems, 1934-1952.* London: Dent, 1952. xiv, 178 p.: front. port. Impressions after 1956 have note by Vernon Watkins on the unfinished 'Elegy', pp. 181-182. – Also signed edition 1952; 'limited to 65 copies of which 60 are for sale'.
—— Readers Union/Dent, 1954.
—— Dent, 1966. xvi, 172 p. (Everyman's library; 581). ISBN: 0-460-020870-0. Reissued 1971, (Aldine paperback). ISBN: 0-460-020870-0. – Reissued 1977, pbk. (Everyman's library; 1581). ISBN: 0-460-01581-8. – Reissued 1984, pbk. (Everyman's classics).

U.S. ed.: *The collected poems of Dylan Thomas.* New York: New Directions, 1953. 199 p.: front. port. (A New Directions book). Front. port. tipped-in photograph by Marion Morehouse. – Reissued 1971, (A New Directions paperbook; 316). ISBN: 0-8112-0205-4.

*The doctor and the devils* / from the story by Donald Taylor. London: Dent, 1953. 138 p. Incl. The story of the film, by Donald Taylor, pp. 135-138.
—— Dent, 1968. (Aldine paperback). ISBN: 460-02078-1. Reissued 1985, pbk. (Everyman's classics).
—— / adapted for the stage by Guy Williams. London: Macmillan, [1970]. 54 p. (Dramascripts).

U.S. eds.: New York: New Directions, 1953. (A New Directions book).
—— / With a new introduction by John Ormond. New York: Time Inc, 1964. 177 p. (Time reading program).

*Under Milk Wood: a play for voices* / preface and musical settings by Daniel Jones. London: Dent, 1954. ix, 101 p. Incl.: Preface, pp. v-viii – Notes on pronunciation – Cast list of first broadcast – Settings of songs.
—— Readers Union, 1957.
—— *Under Milk Wood: a play in two acts* / preface and musical settings by Daniel Jones. [Acting edition]. Dent, 1958. 96 p.: front.: pbk. Incl.: Lighting plot, pp. 69-79 – Property and furniture plot, pp. 80-82 – Lighting and setting sheet, pp. 83-85 – Notes on pronunciation, p. 86 – Musical settings, pp. 87-96.
—— / preface by Daniel Jones. Dent, 1962. viii, 86 p. (Aldine paperback; 1). Preface, pp. v-viii.
—— *Under Milk Wood* / screenplay by Andrew Sinclair. Lorrimer, 1972. 95 p.: ill.: pbk. ISBN: 0-900855-55-X. Incl. Milk Wood and magic, by Andrew Sinclair, pp. 3-8.
—— / edited with an introduction by Douglas Cleverdon; lithographs by Ceri Richards. Folio Society, 1972. 93 p.: ill. Incl:. Introduction, pp. 3-9 – Appendix of discarded passages, pp. 91-93. – 9 lithographs.
—— / prefaces (1954 and 1974) by Daniel Jones. Dent, 1975. 64 p. ISBN: 0-460-04270-X. Prefaces, pp. 5-10. – Also de luxe edition 1975, ISBN: 0-460-04279-3.

—— Dent, 1976. xiv, 82 p.: pbk. (Everyman's library). ISBN: 0-460-00006-3. Reissued 1977, (Everyman paperback). ISBN: 0-460-01006-9. – Reissued 1983, pbk. (Everyman's classics).

—— / prefaces (1954 and 1974) by Daniel Jones. Dent, 1985. xiv, 92 p.: pbk. (Everyman's library). ISBN: 0-460-11006-3. Reset edition of 1977 Everyman paperback, with cover illustration by Paul Cox. – Reissued 1991, hbk & pbk. (Everyman's library). ISBN 0-460-86059-3 hbk, 0-460-87055-6 pbk. With cover illustration by Brian Horton.

—— Phoenix, 1992. 89 p.: pbk. ISBN: 1-85799-010-2.

U.S. eds.: New York: New Directions, 1954. 107 p. (A New Directions book). With note on the New York performance. – Reissued 1957, pbk. (A New Directions paperbook; 73).

—— *Under Milk Wood: a play for voices: a reproduction of the illuminated manuscript.* Santa Ana, Calif.: International Letter Arts Network, 1989. 88 p.: ill. ISBN: 0-9623131-0-6. Incl. Introduction, by Heather Child. – With illustrations by Sheila Waters.

**Quite early one morning: broadcasts** / preface by Aneirin Talfan Davies. London: Dent, 1954. x, 181 p.: front. Contents: Preface, pp. vii-x – Part I; Reminiscences of childhood (2 versions), Quite early one morning, Memories of Christmas, Holiday memory, How to begin a story, The crumbs of one man's year, The Festival exhibition 1951, The International Eisteddfod, A visit to America, Laugharne, Return journey – Part II; Wilfred Owen, Walter de la Mare as prose writer, Sir Philip Sidney, A dearth of comic writers, The English festival of spoken poetry, On reading one's own poems, Welsh poets, Wales and the artist, Three poems ['Over Sir John's Hill', 'In country sleep', 'In the white giant's thigh'], On poetry – Notes, by Aneirin Talfan Davies. – Reissued 1967, pbk.

—— Dent, 1978. (Everyman paperback; 1007). Reissued 1987, pbk. ISBN: 0-4601-2543-5.

U.S. ed.: *Quite early one morning.* New York: New Directions, 1954. viii, 240 p. (A New Directions book). Contents: Reminiscences of childhood – Quite early one morning – A child's Christmas in Wales – Holiday memory – A story – The crumbs of one man's year – Laugharne – Return journey – Our country – Welsh poets – Wilfred Owen – Sir Philip Sidney – Artists of Wales – Walter de la Mare as prose writer – A dearth of comic writers – The English Festival of Spoken Poetry – On reading one's own poems – Three poems – Replies to an enquiry – On poetry – How to be a poet – How to begin a story – The Festival Exhibition, 1951 – The International Eisteddfod – A visit to America. – Includes 'stories and articles published in magazines and not broadcast ... also ... the more finished versions of the broadcast talks, as Thomas revised them for publication' (publisher's note). – Reissued 1960, (A New Directions paperbook; 90).

—— *The collected prose of Dylan Thomas.* 3 vols. New York: New Directions, 1969. (New Directions paperbooks; NDP 183, 51, 90). Incl.: *Adventures in the skin trade* – *Portrait of the artist as a young dog* – *Quite early one morning.* – In slip-case.

*Two epigrams of fealty* [and] *Galsworthy and Gawsworth.* [1954?]. Two 8-page leaflets. Three uncollected poems. – 'Both items being privately printed [by John Gawsworth] for members of the Court of the Realm of Redonda.' – Each of 'thirty memorial copies'.

*Conversation about Christmas.* 'Printed at Christmas 1954 for the friends of J. Laughlin and New Directions.' 8 p.: pamph. Text of essay from *Picture Post*, 27 Dec 1947, 26.

*A prospect of the sea and other stories and prose writings* / edited by Daniel Jones. London: Dent, 1955. vii, 136 p.: front. Contents: Part I; A prospect of the sea, The lemon, After the fair, The visitor, The enemies, The tree, The map of love, The mouse and the woman, The dress, The orchards, In the direction of the beginning – Part II; Conversation about Christmas, How to be a poet, The followers, A story.
—— Dent, 1968. (Aldine paperback). ISBN: 460-02058-7.
—— / edited by Daniel Jones. London: Dent, 1979. vii, 136 p. ISBN: 0-460110136.

*Adventures in the skin trade and other stories.* New York: New Directions, 1955. viii, 275 p. (A New Directions book). Contents: Adventures in the skin trade – After the fair – The enemies – The tree – The visitor – The lemon – The burning baby – The orchards – The mouse and the woman – The horse's ha – A prospect of the sea – The holy six – Prologue to an adventure – The map of love – In the direction of the beginning – An adventure from a work in progess – The school for witches – The dress – The vest – The true story – The followers. – Reissued 1964, (A New Directions paperbook; 183).
—— *The collected prose of Dylan Thomas.* 3 vols. New York: New Directions, 1969. (New Directions paperbooks; NDP 183, 51, 90). Incl.: *Adventures in the skin trade – Portrait of the artist as a young dog – Quite early one morning.* – In slip-case.
—— New York: New American Library, 1956. 191 p. (Signet books; S1281). Reissued 1961, (A Signet classic; CD38). Incl. Afterword by Vernon Watkins, pp. 184-190.

*Adventures in the skin trade.* London: Putnam, 1955. 115 p. Incl. Foreword, by Vernon Watkins, pp. 7-14.
—— Ace Books, 1961. 124 p. (Ace books; H423)
—— / foreword by Vernon Watkins. Dent, 1965. 115 p. (Aldine paperback). Foreword, pp. 9-16.
—— / an adaptation for the stage by Andrew Sinclair; introduction by James Roose-Evans. Dent, 1967. xiii, 89 p. Introduction, pp. v-xi.
—— / foreword by Vernon Watkins. Dent, 1977. 115 p. (Everyman's Library; 1921).
—— / foreword by Vernon Watkins. Putnam, 1982. ISBN: 0-370-30928-6. Forword, pp. 9-16.
—— Dent, 1985. pbk. (Everyman's Classics). ISBN: 0-460119214.

U.S. ed.: / an adaptation for the stage by Andrew Sinclair; introduction by James Roose-Evans. New York, New Directions, 1968.

*A child's Christmas in Wales.* Norfolk, Conn.: New Directions, [1955]. 32 p. – Lettering by Samuel H. Marsh.
—— New York: New Directions, 1959. [unpaged]: pbk: ill. Woodcuts by Ellen Raskin.
—— / illustrated by Fritz Eichenberg. New York: New Directions, 1969. 31 p.: ill.
—— / illustrated by Edward Ardizzone. Boston, Mass.: Godine, 1980. 45 p.: chiefly ill.: hbk & pbk. ISBN: 0-87923-339-7 hbk, 0-87923-529-2 pbk.
—— / illustrated by Trina Schart Hyman. New York: Holiday House, 1985. 47 p.: chiefly ill. ISBN: 0-8234-0565-6.

U.K. eds.: *A child's Christmas in Wales* / with woodcuts by Ellen Raskin. London: Dent, 1968. [32] p.: ill.: pamph. ISBN: 0-460-03864-8.
—— / illustrated by Edward Ardizzone. Dent, 1978. 45 p.: chiefly ill. ISBN: 0-460-0686-7-7. Reissued 1986, pbk. ISBN: 0-460-02772-7. – Reissued 1991, pbk. ISBN: 0-460-86058-5.
—— Orion, 1993. 48 p.: ill. ISBN: 1-85881-011-6. With Ardizzone illustrations.

*Letters to Vernon Watkins* / edited with an introduction by Vernon Watkins. London: Dent; Faber, 1957. 145 p.: front. port. Introduction, pp. 11-21.

U.S. eds.: New York: New Directions, 1957.
—— Westport, Conn.: Greenwood Press, 1982. ISBN: 0-313-23746-8.

*Miscellany one: poems, stories, broadcasts.* London: Dent, 1963. vi, 118 p. (Aldine paperback; 13). ISBN: 0-460-02013-7. Contents: I. Poems [16] – II. Stories; The map of love, The mouse and the woman, The visitor, The followers – III. Broadcasts; Reminiscences of childhood, Memories of Christmas, Return journey. – Reissued 1973, hbk. ISBN: 0-460-04173-8.

*The beach of Falesá* / based on a story by Robert Louis Stevenson. London: Cape, 1964. 124 p. Reissued 1966, 122p.: pbk. (A Panther book).

U.S. eds.: New York: Stein & Day, 1963. 126 p.: pbk. (A Scarborough book). ISBN: 0-8128-6205-8.
—— New York: Ballantine Books, 1965. 158 p.

*A film script of* **Twenty years a-growing** / from the story by Maurice O'Sullivan. London: Dent, 1964. 91 p.

*Me and my bike* / foreword by Sydney Box; illustrated by Leonora Box. London: Triton, 1965. 55 p.: ill. Inc.: Foreword, p. [5] – Letter from Dylan Thomas to Ralph Keene, p. [6]. – Also limited edition, 500 copies.
—— *Two tales: Me and my bike* [and] *Rebecca's daughters* / illustrations by Leonora Box. Sphere Books, 1968. 139p.: ill.: pbk.

U.S. ed.: New York: McGraw-Hill, 1965.

*Rebecca's daughters.* London: Triton, 1965. 144 p.
—— Grafton Books, 1992. 144 p.: pbk. ISBN: 0-586-21525-5.
—— *Two tales: Me and my bike* [and] *Rebecca's daughters* / illustrations by Leonora Box. Sphere Books, 1968. 139p.: ill.: pbk.

U.S. eds.: New York: Little, Brown, 1966.
—— / with illustrations by Fritz Eichenberg. New York: New Directions, 1982. ISBN: 0-8112-0852-4. (A New Directions book). Reissued 1983, pbk. ISBN: 0-8112-0884-2.

*The doctor and the devils, and other scripts.* New York: New Directions, 1966. 229 p. Contents: The doctor and the devils, from the story by Donald Taylor – Twenty years a-growing: a film script, from the story by Maurice O'Sullivan – A dream of winter [poem] – The London model for Dylan Thomas's Under Milk Wood, by Ralph Maud – The Londoner. – Reissued 1970, (New Directions paperbook; 297). ISBN: 0-8112-0206-2.

*Miscellany two: A visit to grandpa's and other stories and poems.* London: Dent, 1966. v, 117 p.: pbk. (Aldine paperback; 49). Contents: I. Poems; Altarwise by owl-light, After the funeral, Once it was the colour of saying, A refusal to mourn, Deaths and entrances, In my craft or sullen art, Ceremony after a fire raid, Ballad of the long-legged bait, Fern Hill, Over Sir John's Hill, Poem on his birthday – II. Stories; A visit to grandpa's, Extraordinary little cough, Where Tawe flows, Who do you wish was with us?, A prospect of the sea – III. Broadcasts; Quite early one morning, A visit to America.
—— Dent, 1973. pbk. ISBN: 0-460-04174-6. Reissued 1985, pbk. (Everyman's classics). ISBN: 0-7605-04174-6.

*Selected letters of Dylan Thomas* / [ed.] Constantine FitzGibbon. London: Dent, 1966. xii, 420 p. Incl. Introduction, by Constantine FitzGibbon, vii-ix.

U.S. ed.: New York: New Directions, 1967. (A New Directions book).

*Poet in the making: the notebooks of Dylan Thomas* / edited by Ralph Maud. London: Dent, 1968. 364 p. Contents: Introduction, by Ralph Maud, pp. 9-44 – 1930 notebook – 1930-32 notebook – February 1933 notebook – August 1933 notebook – Notes to introduction and poems, pp. 273-334 – Appendix: additional poems 1930-34, pp. 335-349.

U.S. ed.: *The notebooks of Dylan Thomas.* New York: New Directions, 1967.

*Twelve more letters.* London: Turret, 1969. 23 p.: front. port. ISBN: 0-85469-011-5. Incl. Appendix: a note by Eric Walter White, p. [21]. – Supplement to *Selected letters.* – '175 numbered copies of this book have been printed, together with a further 26 copies from A to Z.

*A child's Christmas in Wales and other stories* / edited by Hans Muller. Paderborn: Schoningh, [196?]. 81 p.: pbk. Incl.: A child's Christmas in

Wales – Reminiscences of childhood – Quite early one morning – Laugharne – How to begin a story – A story – Our country – The International Eisteddfod – A visit to America.

*Selected writings* / edited by J.P. Harries. London: Heinemann Educational, 1970. xii, 139 p. (The twentieth century series). ISBN: 0-370-30928-6. Contents: Introduction, pp. vii-xii – Part 1: Autobiographical stories – Part 2: Adventures in the skin trade – Commentary, pp. 131-138 – Record list, p. 139.

*The poems* / edited with an introduction and notes by Daniel Jones. London: Dent, 1971. xix, 291 p. ISBN: 0-460-03830-3. Introduction, pp. xiii-xix. – 'It contains all the verse of the *Collected poems, 1934-1952*, plus over one hundred other poems ... the contents have been arranged so that all the poems appear in chronological order of composition.'
—— Dent, 1974. 'Revised'. ISBN: 0-460-04181-9. Incl. Appendix III. A pub poem, pp. 281-282. – Reissued 1978, pbk. ISBN: 0-460-02202-4. – Reissued 1991, pbk. (Everyman's classics). ISBN: 0-460-87057-2.

U.S. ed.: New York: New Directions, 1971. ISBN: 0-8112-0398-0.

*Early prose writings* / edited with an introduction by Walford Davies. London: Dent, 1971. xvi, 204 p. ISBN: 0-460-03990-3. Contents: Introduction, pp. vii-xvi – Part I [creative work]; Brember, Jarley's, The true story, The vest, In the garden, Gasper Melchior Balthasar, The burning baby, The end of the river, The horse's ha, The school for witches, The holy six, Prologue to an adventure, An adventure from a work in progress, The death of the king's canary (experts), Betty London (excerpt) – Part II [critical writing]; Modern poetry, The films, The sincerest form of flattery, The poets of Swansea, Genius and madness akin in world of art, To Pamela Hansford Johnson, Spajma and Salnady, Answers to an enquiry, The cost of letters, Poetic manifesto, Idioms, Reviews.

U.S. ed.: New York: New Directions, 1972. ISBN: 0-8112-0395-6.

*The outing: a story* / with illustrations by Meg Stevens. London: Dent, 1971. [34] p.: ill.: pamph. ISBN: 0-460-07840-2. Reissued 1976, ISBN: 0-460-02182-6. – Reissued 1991, ISBN: 0-460-86056-9.
—— / illustrated by Paul Cox. Dent, 1985. [26] p.: chiefly ill. ISBN: 0-460-04704-3.

*Living and writing: Dylan Thomas* / edited by Christopher Copeman. London: Dent, 1972. ix, 186 p.: ill.: pbk. ISBN: 0-460-09510-2. Selection of poetry and prose, with linking commentary.

*Holiday memory: a story* / with illustrations by Meg Stevens. London: Dent, 1972. [31] p.: ill.: pamph. ISBN: 0-460-07888-7. Reissued 1991, ISBN: 0-460-86057-7.

*Seven poems.* Camberwell: Art School Press, 1974. [32] p. Contents: Poem in October – Light breaks where no sun shines – In my craft or sullen art – Fern Hill – And death shall have no dominion – On the marriage of a virgin – Do not go gentle into that good night. – 'Cut in linoleum by Keith Holmes and printed by offset lithography ... 75 copies reprinted at Camberwell School of Art and Crafts.'

*Selected poems* / edited with an introduction and notes by Walford Davies. London: Dent, 1974. vii, 136 p.: pbk. ISBN: 0-460-09618-4. Introduction, pp. 1-20.
——Dent, 1993. xxxvii, 130 p.: pbk. (Everyman). ISBN: 0-460-8729-2. Introduction, pp. xi-xxxvii. – An expanded selection with new introduction and updated notes.

*The death of the king's canary* [by Dylan Thomas and John Davenport] / with an introduction by Constantine FitzGibbon. London: Hutchinson, 1976. x, 145 p. ISBN: 0-09-127510-5.
—— Harmondsworth: Penguin, 1978. pbk. ISBN: 0-14-004577-5.

U.S. ed.: New York: Viking, 1977. ISBN: 0-670-26230-7.

*The followers: a story* / with illustrations by Meg Stevens. London: Dent, 1976. [32] p.: ill.: pamph. (Aldine paperback). ISBN: 0-460-02182-6.

*Selected works.* London: Book Club Associates, 1976. 197 p. Introduction, by Michael O'Mara – Part One; The map of love, The mouse and the woman, The visitor, The followers, Reminiscences of childhood (first version), Memories of Christmas, Return journey – Part Two; Selected poems – Part Three; *Under Milk Wood.*

*Miscellany three: poems and stories.* London: Dent, 1978. 119 p.: pbk. (Everyman's Library). ISBN: 0-460-01108-1. Contents: I. Poems [17] – II. Stories; The fight, The peaches, Old Garbo, After the fair, The enemies, Conversation about Christmas, How to be a poet.

*Collected stories* / illustrated by Paul Hogarth. Franklin Center, Pa.: Franklin Library, 1980. 360 p.: ill. (The collected stories of the world's greatest writers). Incl. Notes from the editors (22 p., inserted). – Limited edition.

*The green fuse: a collection of poems and wood engravings* / poems by Dylan Thomas, wood engravings by Takao Hiwasaki; edited by Hiroaki Manabe. Tokyo: Tairiku No Taiwa Sha, 1982. [26] sheets : ill.: in portfolio. ISBN: 0-84-126310. Contents: The force that through the green fuse – Especially when the October wind – In the beginning – This bread I break – Ears in the turrets hear – When all my five and country senses see – Twenty-four years – The hunchback in the park – In my craft or sullen art – Lie still, sleep becalmed. – Ten wood engravings.

*The collected stories.* London: Dent, 1983. xv, 362 p. Incl. Foreword, by Leslie Norris, pp. vii-xv. ISBN: 0-460-04603-9. Reissued 1984, pbk. (Everyman fiction). ISBN: 0-460-02285-7.
—— Phoenix, 1992. 384 p.: pbk. ISBN: 1-85799-030-7. Lacking foreword and bibliographical notes.

U.S. ed.: New York: New Directions, 1984. ISBN: 0-8112-0918-0 hbk, 0-8112-0998-9 pbk.

*Poem on his birthday: In the mustardseed sun* / prints by Nicholas Parry. [Market Drayton]: Tern Press, 1983. [24] p.: ill. Incl. 8 prints. – 'In the mustardseed sun' ... is here printed in an edition of 85 copies.'

*A visit to grandpa's and other stories* / drawings by Robin Jacques. London: Dent, 1984. 122 p.: ill. ISBN: 0-460-06154-2. Contents: A visit to grandpa's – Extraordinary little cough – Quite early one morning – Holiday memory – The peaches – Who do you wish was with us? – The fight – A child's Christmas in Wales. – 15 full-page illustrations.

*The collected letters of Dylan Thomas* / edited by Paul Ferris. London: Dent, 1985. xxiii, 982 p.: front. port. ISBN: 0-460-04635-7.
—— Paladin, 1987. pbk. ISBN: 0-586-08578-5. Lacks front. port.

U.S. ed.: New York: Macmillan, 1985. ISBN: 0-0261-7630-0.

*Collected poems, 1934-1953* / edited by Walford Davies and Ralph Maud. London: Dent, 1988. x, 268 p. ISBN: 0-460-04747-7. Incl. textual and other notes, pp. 159-264. – Reissued 1989, pbk. (Everyman classics). ISBN: 0-460-01747-0. – Reissued 1991, pbk. ISBN: 0-460-87054-8.

*The notebook poems, 1930-1934* / edited by Ralph Maud. London: Dent, 1989. xvi, 288 p.: ill. ISBN: 0-460-04792-5. Incl. Introduction, pp. vii-xvi. – 'Definitive for all the poetry written between the ages of fifteen and nineteen'. – Reissued 1990, pbk. (Everyman's library). ISBN: 0-460-04782-5.

*The broadcasts* / edited by Ralph Maud. London: Dent, 1991. xviii, 307 p.: front. port. ISBN: 0-460-86011-9. Contents: Introduction, by Ralph Maud, pp. ix-xviii – Reminiscences of childhood (1943) – Quite early one morning – Reminiscences of childhood (1945) – Memories of Christmas – Welsh poetry – On reading poetry aloud – Poets on poetry – Poems of wonder – The Londoner – Wifred Owen – Margate: past and present – How to begin a story – What has happened to English poetry? – Holiday memory – Walter de la Mare as a prose writer – The crumbs of one man's year – Sir Philip Sidney – The poet and his critic – Return journey – A dearth of comic writers – The English Festival of Spoken Poetry – Living in Wales – Edward Thomas – On reading one's own poems – Swansea and the arts – Three poems – Poetic licence – Persian oil – The Festival Exhibition – Edgar Lee Masters – Home town: Swansea – The International Eisteddfod – A visit to America – Laugharne – Thomas's BBC engagements calendar, pp. 283-305.

U.S. ed.: *On the air with Dylan Thomas: the broadcasts.* New York: New Directions, 1992. ISBN: 0-8112-1209-2.

*A Dylan Thomas treasury: poems, stories and broadcasts* / selected by Walford Davies. London: Dent, 1991. vi, 186 p.: pbk. (Everyman's library). ISBN: 0-460-87075-0. Contents: I. Poems [36] – II. Stories; The vest, After the fair, The visitor, The tree, The dress, The peaches, Extraordinary little cough, Just like little dogs, The followers, A story – III. Broadcasts; Memories of Christmas, Holiday memory, The Festival Exhibition 1951, A visit to America, Return journey.

*The loud hill of Wales: poetry of place* / selected and introduced by Walford Davies. London: Dent, 1991. xx, 172 p.: pbk. (Everyman's library). ISBN: 0-460-87076-9. Introduction, pp. ix-xx. – A selection of poems, with the following prose pieces: Reminiscences of childhood (first version), Laugharne, *Under Milk Wood* (excerpts), The orchards, The enemies, A prospect of the sea, A visit to grandpa's, Who do you wish was with us?, The crumbs of one man's year.

## A (ii). Publications by Dylan Thomas: Selected Contributions to Periodicals

J.A. Rolph, *Dylan Thomas: a bibliography* (1956) and Ralph Maud, *Dylan Thomas in print* (1972) provide full guidance. This section lists mostly the early journalism, some of which is reprinted in Dylan Thomas, *Early prose writings*, ed. Walford Davies (*EPW* below).

Nellie Wallace's mimicry. *South Wales Daily Post*, 15 July 1931, 7:A. An interview with the comedienne.

The poets of Swansea. Walter Savage Landor to James Chapman Woods. *HW*, 9 Jan 1932, 7:C-F. Comments on George Borrow, Thomas Bowdler, W.S. Landor, Ann Julia Hatton (Ann of Swansea) and S.P. Chapman. – Reprinted *EPW*.

Tragedy of Swansea's comic genius. The story of Llywelyn Prichard. *HW*, 23 Jan 1932, 6:C-E. On the poet, actor and author of *Twm Shon Cati*. – Reprinted *EPW*.

'Caesar's wife' at Swansea. *HW*, 23 Jan 1932, 12:B. Review, attributed to Thomas, of a performace of Somerset Maugham's play.

Minor poets of old Swansea. *HW*, 20 Feb 1932, 4:C-F. Accounts of James John Evans, C.D. Morgan, H.A.W. Rott, 'Carl Morgannwg' (J.C. Manning), 'E.E', and George Thomas Hood. – Reprinted *EPW*.

Minor poets of old Swansea. A study of Pierre Claire. *HW*, 19 Mar 1932, 4. On S.C. Gamwell, poet and editor of The Cambrian. – Reprinted *EPW*.

Verse of James Chapman Woods. A critical estimate. *HW*, 23 Apr 1932, 4: B-F. Compares his poetry to Arnold's. – With 'Youth calls to age', a poem by Thomas. – Reprinted *EPW*.

A modern poet of Gower. Anglo-Welsh bards. *HW*, 25 Jun 1932, 8: A-C. Discussion of E. Howard Harris: 'his romantic verses are not particularly distinguished, but they contribute more to the revival of Welsh poetry than any writings I know'. – Reprinted *South Wales Evening Post*, 11 Nov 1963. – Reprinted *EPW*.

A Baroness journeys into Gower. Lady Barham's six chapels. The story of Paraclete. End of a great ministry. *HW*, 5 Nov 1932, 6:B- E. Thomas's uncle had just retired as minister of Paraclete.

Genius and madness akin in world of art. *South Wales Evening Post*, 7 Jan 1933, 7:E-F. Reprinted *EPW*.

A plea for intellectual revolution. Clean thinking – clean living – a clean world. *Swansea and West Wales Guardian*, 3 Aug 1934, 11.

Review of three poets. *Adelphi*, Sep 1934, 418-420. Review of William Soutar, *The solitary way*, William Montgomerie, Squared circle, Sydney Salt, *Thirty pieces*. – Reprinted *EPW*.

Mr Pudney's second volume. *Bookman*, Nov 1934, 132. Review of John Pudney, *Open to the sky*. – Reprinted *EPW*.

Fey, Dollfuss, Vienna. *New verse*, 12 (1934) 19-20. Review of Stephen Spender, *Vienna*. – Reprinted *EPW*.

Individual and collective. *Bookman*, Christmas 1934, 12. Review of Ruth Pitter, *A mad lady's garland*, Wilfred Gibson, *Fuel*, John Lehmann, *The noise of history, The best poems of 1934*, ed. Thomas Moult. – Reprinted *EPW*.

Answers to an enquiry. *New Verse*, 11 (1934) 8-9. – Reprinted *EPW*.

Review of M.K. Gandhi, *Songs from prison*. *Adelphi*, Jan 1935, 255-256. Reprinted *EPW*.

Review of three poets. *Adelphi*, Feb 1935, 312-314. Review of Lyle Donaghy, *Into the light and other poems*, John Lehmann, *The noise of history*, Ruth Pitter, *A mad lady's garland*. – Reprinted *EPW*.

Dictator in freedom. *Adelphi*, Feb 1935, 317-318. Review of Alfred Hy. Haffenden, *Dictator in freedom*. – Reprinted *EPW*.

Death on all sides. A batch of the newest thrillers. *Morning Post*, 5 Apr 1935, 19:D. Review of John Dickson Carr, Death-watch, H.C. Bailey, *Mr Fortune objects*, Angus MacVicar, *The screaming gull*, Robin Forsythe, *The ginger cat mystery*, Herbert Corey, *Crime at Cobb's House*.

Five thrillers à la mode. *Morning Post*, 12 Apr 1935, 17:C. Review of Ellery

Queen, *The Spanish Cape murder*, Francis D. Grierson, *Murder in black*, Lord Gorell, *Red lilac*, George Goodchild and Bechhofer Roberts, *The dear old gentleman*, Nigel Burnaby, *The clue of the green-eyed girl*.

Too many pigs on the wing. *Morning Post,* 7 May 1935, 5. Review of Carleton Kendrake, *The clue of the forgotten murder,* Q. Patrick, *Darker grows the valley,* Means Davies, *Murder without weapon,* M. Doriel Hay, *Death on the Cherwell,* Cecil Freeman, *The ten black pearls.*

Post-morticians. *Morning Post,* 14 May 1935, 17. Review of C. St. John Sprigg, *Death of a queen,* Roger East, *Twenty-five sanitary inspectors,* Freeman Wills Croft, *Crime at Guildford,* G.D.H. and M. Cole, *Dr Tancred begins.*

By hooks and by crooks. *Morning Post,* 24 May 1935, 17. Review of John Creasy, *Death round the corner,* E.R. Punshon, *Death of a beauty queen,* Anthony Weymouth, *The doctors are doubtful,* Eimar O'Duffy, *Head of a girl.*

Review of *The poems of John Clare,* ed. J.W. Tibble. *Adelphi,* Jun 1935, 179-181. Reprinted *EPW.*

A few corpses and puzzles. *Morning Post,* 21 Jun 1935, 17. Review of Augustus Muir, *Raphael M.D,* Moray Dalton, *The Belgrave Manor crime,* Willoughby Sharp, *Murder in Bermuda,* Elaine Hamilton, *Tragedy in the dark.*

Blood without thunder. *Morning Post,* 28 Jun 1935, 16. Review of Cornelius Cafyn, *The death riders,* Phoebe Atwood Taylor, *The mystery of the Cape Cod Tavern,* Florence Leighton, *As strange a maze,* John Rhode, *Hendon's first case,* Rose and Dudley Lambert, *The mystery of the golden wings.*

A.E.W. Mason: King Thriller. *Morning Post,* 5 Jul 1935, 16:F. Review of *They wouldn't be chessmen.*

Two thrillers. *Morning Post,* 9 Jul 1935, 16:C. Review of R. Philmore, *Riot act,* Leonard R. Gribble, *Mystery at Tudor Arches.*

New thrillers. *Morning Post,* 24 Sep 1935, 14:E-F. Review of M.G. Eberhart, *The house on the roof,* Donald Macpherson, *Go home, unicorn,* Jean Lilly, *Death in B minor,* Robert Curtis, *The children of light.*

Review of R.D. Jameson, *A comparison of literatures. Adelphi,* Oct 1935, 58-59. Reprinted *EPW.*

Queer things in Mexico. *Morning Post,* 4 Oct 1935, 17:E. Review of Todd Downing, *The cat screams,* R.C. Woodthorpe, *The shadow on the Downs,* David Hume, *Call in the Yard,* John Bude, *The Lake District murder.*

Frequent, gory and grotesque. *Morning Post,* 11 Oct 1935, 15:B-C. Review of John Dickson Carr, *The hollow man,* John Rhode, *Mystery at Olympia,* J.Y Dane, *Murder in college,* Mary M. Atwater, *Murder in midsummer.*

Revolver, sandbag, hand-grenade. *Morning Post*, 15 Oct 1935, 16:B-C. Review of Douglas G. Browne, *The stolen boat-train*, Grierson Dickson, *Gun business*, Miles Burton, *The milk churn murder*, Kathleen Moore Knight, *Death blew out the match*.

A choice of new thrillers. *Morning Post*, 25 Oct 1935, 15:B. Review of Rex Stout, *The league of frightened men*, Francis D. Grierson, *Death on deposit*, Arthur Somers Roche, *The case against Mrs Ames*.

Two thrillers. *Morning Post*, 1 Nov 1935, 14:C. Review of Dorothea Brande, *Beauty vanishes*, John Newton Chance, Murder in oils.

Grand goose flesh parade. *Morning Post*, 5 Nov 1935, 1:C. Review of *A century of horror*, ed. Dennis Wheatley, *50 years of ghost stories*.

Three new thrillers. *Morning Post*, 15 Nov 1935, 6:E. Review of Cecil Freeman Gregg, *Danger at Cliff House*, Mignon G. Eberhart, *The cases of Susan Dare*, William Gore, *Death in the wheelbarrow*.

Lord Peter does another job. *Morning Post*, 22 Nov 1935, 14:C. Review of Dorothy L. Sayers, *Gaudy Night*, Carter Dickson, *The Red Widow murders*, Henry Wade, *Heir presumptive*, Carroll John Daly, *Death's juggler*.

He was framed with a false eye. *Morning Post*, 29 Nov 1935, 16:F-G. Review of Erle Stanley Gardner, *The case of the counterfeit eye*, Bruce Graeme, *Not proven*, S.S. Van Dine, *The garden murder case*, Gavin Holt, *The emerald spider*.

Murders for the new year. *Morning Post*, 7 Jan 1936, 15:A. Review of Agatha Christie, *The ABC murders*, Miles Burton, *Death in the tunnel*, Peter Drax, *Murder by chance*.

Dead bodies, live villains. *Morning Post*, 17 Jan 1936, 14:G. Review of Todd Downing, *Vultures in the sky*, Richard Hull, *Murder isn't easy*, Colin Davy, *Agents of the League*, Gordon Volk, *Cliffs of Sark*.

Books and people. Introducing a review column. *Swansea and West Wales Guardian*, 17 Jan 1936, 5.

Murder from inside. *Morning Post*, 31 Jan 1936, 14:G. Review of Baroness Von Hutten, *Cowardly custard*, Ngaio Marsh and H. Jellett, *The nursing home murder*, Moray Dalton, *The strange case of Harriet Hall*, David Hume, *Meet the dragon*.

Scot's travels. *Swansea and West Wales Guardian*, 31 Jan 1936, 7. Review of A.G. MacDonnell, *A visit to America*.

Patient detection. *Morning Post*, 7 Feb 1936, 20:A. Review of Freeman Wills Crofts, *The loss of Jane Vosper*, Phoebe Atwood Taylor, *Sandbar sinister*, Hugh Austin, *It couldn't be murder*.

The week's blood and fun. *Morning Post*, 11 Feb 1936, 16:G. Review of R. Philmore, *The good books*, Stuart Palmer, *The puzzle of the briar pipe*, F.J. Whaley, *Reduction of staff*, Sutherland Scott, *Murder without mourners*.

Death and fun. *Morning Post*, 27 Mar 1936, 16:E. Review of Milward Kennedy, *Sic transit gloria*, D.H. Landels, *His Lordship the Judge*, James Street, *Death in an armchair*, Cecil M. Wills, *Defeat of a Detective*.

Four thrillers. *Morning Post*, 28 Aug 1936, 4:F. Review of Erle Stanley Gardner, *The case of the sleepwalker's neice*, Selden Truss, *Rooksmiths*, Lee Thayer, *Murder in the mirror*, H.H. Stanners, *Murder at Markendon Court*.

Mysteries. *Morning Post*, 11 Sep 1936, 14:B. Review of Mary Fitt, *Murder mars the tour*, Charman Edwards, *Fear haunts the roses*, Guy Morton, *Mystery at Hardacres*, Ruth Burr Sanborn, *Murder on the Aphrodite*.

The Amherst poet. *Time and Tide*, 9 Oct 1937, 1328. Review of *The poems of Emily Dickinson*, ed. Martha Dickinson and Alfred Leete Hampson, Edna St. Vincent Millay, *Conversation at midnight*. – Reprinted *EPW*.

Review of Djuna Barnes, *Nightwood*. *Light and Dark* 1,2 (1937), 27,29. Reprinted *EPW*.

W.H. Auden. *New Verse* 26-27 (1937) 25. One of six statements on the poet.

Recent novels. *New English Weekly*, 17 Mar 1938, 454-455. Review of Samuel Beckett, *Murphy*, William Carlos Williams, *Life along the Passaic River*. – Reprinted *EPW*.

Recent novels. *New English Weekly*, 21 Apr 1938, 34-35. Review of Eric Ambler, *Epitaph for a spy*, Sheila Radice, *Not all sleep*. – Reprinted *EPW*.

Recent novels. *New English Weekly*, 19 May 1938, 115-116. Review of A.H. Atkins, *Sinister Smith*, C. Daly King, *Arrogant alibi*, John P. Marquand, *Haven's End*, Norah Hurston, *Their eyes were watching God*.

Recent novels. *New English Weekly*, 1 Sep 1938, 312. Review of Cecil Lewis, *The trumpet is mine*, Patrick Kavanagh, *The green fool*, Fred Urquhart, *Time will knit*.

Taverns in general. *New English Weekly*, 22 Sep 1938, 360. Review of George N. List, *Pub survey*.

Recent fiction. *New English Weekly*, 13 Oct 1938, 11-12. Review of Kay Boyle, *Monday night*, Mary Butts, *Last stories*, F.V. Morley, *War paint*, Walter Brierley, *Dalby Green*.

Recent fiction. *New English Weekly*, 17 Nov 1938, 92-93. Review of H.G.

Wells, *Apropos of Dolores*, Rose Wilder Lane, Free land, Jane Allen, *I lost my girlish laughter*, Signe Toksvig, *Port of refuge*. – Reprinted *EPW*.

Dos Passos and Kafka. *New English Weekly*, 2 Feb 1939, 256-257. Review of John Dos Passos, *USA*, Franz Kafka, *America*. – Reprinted *EPW*.

Recent fiction. *New English Weekly*, 18 May 1939, 79-80. Review of Flann O'Brien, *At Swim-Two-Birds*, Ruthven Todd, *Over the mountain*, Erskine Caldwell, *Journeyman*. – Reprinted *EPW*.

Novels and novelists. *New English Weekly*, 14 Dec 1939, 133-135. Review of Frederic Prokosch, *Night of the poor*, Dorothy Parker, *Here lies*, Georg Kaiser, *A villa in Sicily*. – Reprinted *EPW*.

A dream of winter. *Lilliput*, Jan 1942, [65-72]. Eight 3-line verse captions to photographs of winter scenes.

Our country. *Wales* 2nd ser. 2 (1943) 76-78. From a Ministry of Information filmscript. – Reprinted in *Quite early one morning* (US edition, 1954).

Chelsea word-pictures. *Lilliput*, Aug 1944, 37-46. Anonymous prose commentaries on photographs of Chelsea taken by Bill Brandt. – Reprinted in John Ackerman, *A Dylan Thomas companion* (1991), pp. 266-271.

The cost of letters. *Horizon*, Sep 1946, 173-175. Answers to a questionnaire. – Reprinted *EPW*.

Love poems. In *Love poems selected by Dylan Thomas*. Hammersmith: Lyric Theatre, [1946]. Introduction, printed in programme for poetry recital at Lyric Theatre, 3 Nov 1946. – Readers: Peggy Ashcroft, Valentine Dyall, Dylan Thomas.

An introduction to the drawings of Mervyn Levy. In *An exhibition of work by Mervyn Levy*. Swindon: Arts Centre, 1948. p. [2]. Catalogue, with brief comment by Thomas (dated March 1948).

Address given by Dylan Thomas to the Scottish P.E.N. Centre. *Voice of Scotland*, Dec 1948, 22-23. Delivered 4 Sep 1948.

War can't produce poetry. In *A little treasury of modern poetry*, ed. Oscar Williams. New York: Scribner, 1950. p. 820. One in an appendix of statements by poets, included in later editions of this anthology.

Flamboyants all the way. *Observer*, 16 Dec 1951, 7:F-G. Review of Roy Campbell, *Light on a dark horse*. – Reprinted *EPW*.

Blithe spirits. *Observer*, 6 Jul 1952, 7. Review of Amos Tutuola, *The palm-wine drinkard*. – Reprinted *EPW*.

Llareggub, a piece for radio perhaps. *Botteghe Oscure* 9 (1952) 134-153. With an explanatory 'From a letter', pp. 154-155.

Interview with Dylan Thomas. *Occident* [University of California], Spring 1952, 5-6.

Under Milk Wood. *Mademoiselle* [New York], Feb 1954, 110-122, 144-156. Abridged version, with photographs by Rollie McKenna. – 'Editor's note: The week before Dylan Thomas went to hospital he gave us his latest revisions in *Under Milk Wood* and a few cuts (mainly the character of Cherry Owen). . .'

Artists of Wales. *London Magazine*, Aug 1954, 62-63. – Reprinted in *Quite early one morning* (US edition, 1954).

A note on Dylan Thomas. *Origen* 12 (1954) 256-258. Cid Corman's note prefaces a transcription of the poet's opening remarks at a Brandeis University reading, 2 May 1950.

I am going to read aloud. *London Magazine*, Sep 1956, 13-17. Introduction to a reading at the Massachusetts Institute of Technology, Boston, 3 Jul 1952.

Marjorie Adix. In *Dylan Thomas: the legend and the poet*, ed. E.W. Tedlock. London: Heinemann, 1960. pp. 60-66. Includes her record of Thomas's discussion with students at the University of Utah, Apr 1952..

Preface to a reading. *Canto* [University of California at Los Angeles] 1,2 (1960) 11-12. Transcribed from a tape recording. – Also printed on the Caedmon record sleeve.

Poetic manifesto. *Texas Quarterly* 4,4 (1961) 45-53. Reproduces holograph replies (paged 1-9) to five questions asked him by a research student in 1951. – With introductory note by Richard Jones. – Reprinted *EPW*.

Poetry and film: a symposium. *Film Culture* 29 (1963) 55-63. Transcribed discussion (28 Oct 1953) between Maya Deren, Arthur Miller, Dylan Thomas and Parker Tyler.

# A (iii). Dylan Thomas: Translations

## Catalan

*Poemes*, tr. Maria Manent. Barcelona: Ediciones 62, 1974. 53 p.

## Czech

*Zvláště když rínový vítr*, tr. Jiřina Hauková. Praha: SNKLHU, 1958. 84 p. Selected poems, English and Czech.

*Portrét umělce jako štěněte,* tr. Petr Pujman. Praha: SNKLU, 1961. 204 p. [*Portrait of the Artist as a Young Dog*].

*Kapradinový vrch,* tr. Jiřina Hauková. (2 vol.). Praha: Mlad fronta, 1965.

## Danish

*Portraet af kunstneren som hvalp,* tr. Jørgen Andersen and Jørgen Nash. København: Gyldcndal, 1955. 163 p. [*Portrait of the Artist as a Young Dog*]. – Reissued 1971.

*Forår i Milkwood: et spil for stemmer,* tr. Jørgen Nash. København: Gyldendal, 1956. 67 p. [*Under Milk Wood*]. – Reissued 1971.

*Rejsen tilbage,* tr. Jørgen Andersen and others. Fredensborg: Arena, 1958. 127 p. Return journey, and other stories. [*Quite Early One Morning*].
—— København: Hasselbalch, [1964], 140 p.

*En pelshandlers eventyr,* tr. Erik Thygesen. København: Hasselbalch, 1965. 72 p. [*Adventures in the Skin Trade*].

## Dutch

*Aals een jonge hond,* tr. Hugo Claus. Rotterdam: Donker, [1958]. 166 p. (Donker pockets; 24). [*Portrait of the Artist as a Young Dog*].
—— Utrecht: Bruna, 1967.
—— Antwerp: A.W. Bruna, 1967. 190 p.
—— Amsterdam: Arbeiderspers, 1978. 204 p.

*Onder het Melkwoud,* tr. Hugo Claus. Amsterdam: Bezige Bij, 1958. 88 p. Reissued 1964, (Literaire pocket; 10). [*Under Milk Wood*].

*Gedichten,* tr. Henk Tikkemeijer. Amsterdam: De Beuk, 1959. 32 p.
—— Amsterdam: Broekman & De Meris, 1962. 33 p.

*Avonturen aan den lijve,* tr. Max Schuchart. Rotterdam: Donker, 1959. 109 p.
—— Tricht: Goossens, 1986. 88 p. [*Adventures in the skin trade*].

*Uitzicht op zee en andere verhalen,* tr. Max Schuchart. Rotterdam: Donker, 1961. 123 p. (Anker bocken; 3). [*A Prospect of the Sea*].

*Avonturen aan den lijve – Uitzicht op zee en andere verhalen.* Tr. Max Schuchart. Antwerp: A.W. Bruna, 1967. 191 p. [*Adventures in the skin trade – A Prospect of the Sea*].

*De terugreis,* tr. Bert Voeten. Utrecht: Stichting De Roos, 1967. 32 p.: ill. [*Quite early one morning*].

*In winterforhael,* tr. D.A. Tamminga. Leeuwarden: Fryske Akademy, 1974. 24 p.: ill. [*A winter's tale*].

*Rebecca's dochters*, tr. Joop van Helmond. Amsterdam: Arbeiderspers, 1975. [*Rebecca's daughters*].

*Nooit zal hel rijk der doden heersen over ons*. Antwerpen: Soethoudt, 1977. (Kijkgatpaperback; 54). 75 p. [*And death shall have no dominion*]. – Selections in English and Dutch.

## Esperanto

*Historio de Dylan Thomas: Le ekskurso,* tr. Arnold Pitt. Abergavennny: Jubilee of the British Esperanto Congress, 1987. 12 p. ISBN: 0-9512-3020-4. [*The Outing*].

## Estonian

*Surmad ja sisenemised*, tr. N. Neidre. Tallinn: Eěsti Raamat, 1972. 77 p. [*Deaths and Entrances*].

*Piimmetsa vilus: mang baaltele*, tr. Paul-Eerik Rummo. Tallina: Perioodika, 1970. 71 p. [*Under Milk Wood*].

## Finnish

*Taiteilijan omakuva penikkavuosilta*, tr. Veli Sandell. Turku: Tajo, 1963. 176 p. [*Portrait of the Artist as a Young Dog*].

## French

*Portrait de l'artiste en jeune chien,* tr. Francis Dufau-Labeyrie. Paris: Éditions de minuit, 1947. 255 p. [*Portrait of the Artist as a Young Dog*].
—— Paris: Union générale d'éditions, 1971. 191 p.
—— Paris: Éditions du Seuil, 1983. 213 p.

*Le bois de lait*, tr. Roger Giroud. *Les Lettres Nouvelles*, Jan 1953, 1-24. Continued: Fev, 235-249, Mar 380-394. [*Under Milk Wood*].

*Poèmes choisis,* tr. Jean Simon. Paris: Pierre Seghers, 1957. 77 p.: front. port. (Autour du monde; 42). Incl.: Light breaks where no sun shines – I see the boys of summer – Especially when the October wind – This bread I break – Why east wind chills – Ears in the turrets hear – I have longed to move away – And death shall have no dominion – How shall my animal – Twenty-four years – Poem in October – A winter's tale – In my craft or sullen art – Fern Hill. – English and French.

Hélène Bokanowski and Marc Alyn. *Dylan Thomas*. Paris: Editions Pierre Seghers, 1962. 222 p.: ill. (Poètes d'aujourd'hui; 92). Incl.: 27 poems tr. Hélène Bokanowski, Jean Simon, Jean Wahl and Armand Guibert.

*A child's Christmas in Wales – Un Noel d'enfant au Pays de Galles,* tr. Monique Nathan. Paris: Lettres Modernes, 1967. 47 p. (Passeport; 19). English and French.

*Oeuvres* / édition établie sous la direction de Monique Nathan et Denis Roche.

2 vols. Paris: Éditions du Seuil, 1970. 432 p., 398 p. Vol. 1: Images de Dylan Thomas, by Lawrence Durrell, pp. 9-13 – Dylan Thomas, by Karl Shapiro, pp. 17-27 – Le spectacle de l'écriture, by Denis Roche, pp. 31-39 – Portrait de l'artiste en jeune chien, tr. Francis Dufau-Labeyrie – Vingt ans de jeunesse, tr. Patrick Reumaux – Au bois lacté, tr. Jacques B. Brunius – Poèmes, tr. Patrick Reumaux. Vol 2: Une vue de la mer, tr. Denise Van Moppès – Très tôt un matin, tr. Hélène Bokanowski – Aventures dans le commerce des peaux, tr. Claude Portail – Trois nouvelles, tr. Claude Portail and Nicole Juy; Le bébé qui brûlait, The horse's ha, La vérité-vraie – Moi et mon vélo, tr. Solange Lecomte – La plage de Falesá, tr. Guy Durand.

*N'entre pas sans violence dans cette bonne nuit, et autres poèmes,* tr. Alain Suied, Paris: Gallimard, 1979. 63 p. [Poems].

*Il n'y a pas d'issue: poèmes,* tr. Alain Suied. Clermont: Actuels, 1984. 91 p.

*La joueuse de flute,* tr. Suzanne Mayoux. Paris: Press de Renaissance, 1984. 220 p.

*Poupées russes.* Paris: Presses de la Renaissance, 1985. 279 p.

## German

*Tode und Tore,* tr. Reinhard Paul Becker. Heidelberg: Drei Brucken Verlag, 1952. 91 p. English and German. [*Deaths and Entrances*].
—— Heidelberg: F.H. Kerle Verla, 1952.

*Unter dem Milchwald: ein Spiel für Stimmen,* tr. Erich Fried. Heidelberg: Drei Brücken Verlag, 1954. 87 p. [*Under Milk Wood*].
—— Stuttgart: Reclam, 1975. 107 p. Reissued 1981.
—— Frankfurt am Main: Fischer-Taschenbuch-Verlag, 1984. 91 p.

*Am frühen Morgen: Autobiographisches, Radio-Essays, Gedichte und Prosa,* tr. Erich Fried. Heidelberg: Drei Brücken Verlag, 1957. 158 p. [*Quite Early One Morning*].
—— *Gang früh eines Morgens,* tr. Erich Fried. Frankfurt am Main: Fischer-Taschenbuch-Verlag, 1984. 156 p.

*Ein Blick aufs Meer,* tr. Erich Fried and Enzio Von Cramon. Heidelburg: Drei Brücken Verlag, 1959. 128 p. [*A Prospect of the Sea*].
—— Tr. Erich Fried. Frankfurt am Main: Fischer-Taschenbuch-Verlag, 1984. 157 p.

*Der Doktor und die Teufel,* tr. Erich Fried. Frankfurt: Fischer, 1959. 114 p. [*The Doctor and the Devils*].

*Unter dem Milchwald: Dramatisches, Erzahlendes, Lyrisches,* tr. Erich Fried and Reinhard Paul Becker. Augsburg: Rowohlt, 1960. 147 p. [*Under Milk Wood,* with selections from *Quite early one morning* and *Deaths and entrances*].

—— München: Desch, 1964. 105 p.

*Eines Kindes Weihnacht in Wales,* tr. Erich Fried. Zurich: Verlag der Arche, 1964. 48 p.: ill. [*A Child's Christmas in Wales*].

*Ausgewählte Gedichte,* tr. Erich Fried. München: Hanser, 1967. 78 p. English and German. [Selections from *Collected poems, 1934-1952*].
—— München: Heyne, 1984. 82 p.

*Abenteuer in Sachen Haut,* tr. Alexander Schmitz. München: Hanser, [1971]. 99 p. [*Adventures in the Skin Trade*].

*Unter dem Milchwald. Ganz früh eines Morgens. Ein Blick aufs Meer,* tr. Erich Fried. München: Hanser, 1973. 341 p. [*Under Milk Wood, Quite early one morning, A prospect of the sea*]. – Reissued under various imprints, 1974, 1975, 1979.

*Gedichte,* tr. Erich Fried. Berlin: Verlag Neues Leben, 1974. 31 p.: ill.

*Lausbubenweihnacht in Wales,* tr. Karl Baiser. Leinfelden: K.F. Reinking, 1974. 12 p. [*A child's Christmas in Wales*].

*Die Krumen von eines Mannes Jahr: Eirinnerungen u. Geschichten,* tr. Erich Fried. Berlin: Verlag Volk & Welt, 1976. 190 p. [*The crumbs of one man's year: recollections and stories*].

*Die Nachganger,* tr. Erich Fried. Hamburg: Raamin-Presse, 1977. 26 p.: ill. (Druck der Raamin Presse; 8). Incl. 19 engravings by Roswitha Quadflieg. – 'Auflage 80 deutsche and 40 englische numerierte und signierte Exemplare'. – English copies: 'with ten illustrations and seventeen pictorial marginals by Roswitha Quadflieg'.

*Dylan Thomas: eine Auswahl seiner Gedichte englisch und deutsch,* tr. Ilse Burger and others. Mannheim: [privately printed], 1982. 40 p.: ill. Incl.: In my craft or sullen art – And death shall have no dominion – When you have ground such beauty down to dust – Especially when the October wind – Was there a time – Poem in October – I have longed to move away – No man believes – Author's prologue.

*Dies Brot, das ich breche: Gedichte,* tr. Reinhard Harbaum. Gottingen: Verlag Altauito, 1983. 28 p.: ill.

*Porträt des Künstlers als junger Dachs,* tr. Friedrich Polakovics. München: Hanser, 1978. 174 p. [*Portrait of the artist as a young dog*].
—— Leipzig: Insel-Verlag, 1983. 181 p.: ill.

*Rebecca's Tochter,* tr. Wulf Teichman. Frankfurt am Main: Eichborn, 1983. 168 p. [*Rebecca's daughters*].

*Und dem Tod soll kein Reich mehr bleiben: Gedichte,* tr. Karl Heinz Berger and

others. Berlin: Volk und Welt, 1984. 196 pp.: ill. Incl. Afterword, by Karl
Heinz Berger, pp. 178-192. – English texts and German translations of 44
poems, taken from Dylan Thomas, *The poems,* ed. Daniel Jones.

*Note also:*

Görtschacher, Wolfgang. Nur die Schattseite des Dichters? Erich Fried als
Übersetzer von Dylan Thomas. In *Österreichische Dichter als Übersetzer: Salzburger
komparatistische Analysen,* ed. Wolfgang Pöckl. Vienna: Österreichische Akad.
der Wiss., 1991. On Erich Fried as translator of Dylan Thomas.

Meyer-Clason, Curt. Die Anstrengung des bersetzens: Dargestellt am Beispiel
der Ubertragung eines Gedichts von Dylan Thomas. *Neue Rundschau* 101,4
(1990) 105-119. On the German-language translation of 'Do not go gentle
into that good night'.

### Greek

*Kato apo to Galatodassos,* tr. Katerina Angelake-Rouk. Athens: Ermeias, 1972.
144 p. [*Under Milk Wood*].

*Piemata,* tr. Tassos Porfyres and Stefanos Rozanes. Athens: Pandora, 1972.
48 p. [*Collected poems*].

### Hebrew

*Milk Wood,* tr. A. Aharoni.. Tel Aviv: Aleph, 1965. 111 p.

### Hungarian

*Az iró arcképe kölyökkutya korából,* tr. Tamás Ungvari. Budapest: Európa
Konyvkiado, 1959. 204 p.: ill. Incl. Dylan Thomas, by Tamás Ungvari,
pp. 187-201. – Illustrations by Ágnes Gergely. – [*Portrait of the Artist as a
Young Dog*].

*Összegyüjtött versei,* tr. István Eörsi, András Fodor and others. Budapest:
Európa Kiadó, 1966. 298 p.: ill.

*Versei,* tr. István Eörsi and others. Budapest: Európa, 1979. 183 p. [*Poems*].

*Rebeka leányai,* tr. Mária Borbás and Dezsó Tandori. Budapest: Móra Kiadó,
1980. 134 p. [Rebecca's daughters].

### Italian

*Poesie di Dylan Thomas con testo a fronte,* tr. Robert Sanesi. Parma: Guanda,
1954. 203 p. (Collana fenice; 23). Incl. Introduzione a Dylan Thomas, by
Roberto Sanesi. pp. 7-34.
—— Parma: Guanda, 1962. 212 p.: ill.
—— Milano: Guanda, 1976. xxxvii, 180 p.

*Ritratto di giovane artista,* tr. Lucia Rodocanachi. Torino: Einaudi, 1955. 200 p. [*Portrait of the artist as a young dog*].
—— Milano: Mondadori, 1962.

*Poesie giovanili,* tr. Roberto Sanesi. Milano: Edizioni del Triangolo, 1958. 42 p.: ill. Incl.: Out of a war of wits – This is remembered – Shiloh's seed – Before we mothernaked fall – The almanac of time. – English and Italian. – With illustrations by Gianna Dova.

Roberto Sanesi, *Dylan Thomas.* Milano: Lerici Editori 1960. 202 p.: ill. Incl. Appendix of translations: Author's prologue – This side of the truth – A winter's tale – In my craft or sullen art – Lie still sleep becalmed. – Also lists Italian, French, German, Swedish and Danish translations of Dylan Thomas.
—— Milano: Garzanti, 1977.

*Poeti Inglesi del 900: testi e traduzioni,* tr. Roberto Sanesi. Milano: Bompiani, 1960. Incl. 9 poems by Dylan Thomas, pp. 468-493. – Endpapers by Ceri Richards.

*Prose e racconti.* Torino: Einaudi, 1961. 591 p. Contents: I; Ritratto dell'autore da cucciolo, tr. Lucia Rodocanachi – II ultimi racconti; Avventure nel commercio della pelle, Gli inseguitori, Una storia, tr. Floriana Bossi – III; Sotto il bosco di latte, tr. Carlo Izzo – IV; Il dottore e i diavoli, tr. Floriana Bossi – V; Prima racconti, tr. Floriana Bossi & Angelo Fauno.

*Molto presto di mattina,* tr. Floriana Bossi. Torino: Einaudi, 1964. 179 p. [*Quite Early One Morning*]. – Reissued 1980.

*Poesie,* tr. Ariodante Marianni and others. Torino: Einaudi, 1965. 200 p. English and Italian. – Reissued 1970. – Reissued 1981, *Poesie inedite,* xii, 161 p.

*Ritratto dell'autore da cucciolo – Avventure nel commercio della pelle – Gli inseguitori – Una storia.* Tr. Luciana Rodocanachi & Floriana Bosi. Torino: Einaudi, 1966. xxii, 236 p. [*Portrait of the artist as a young dog, Adventures in the skin trade, The followers, the outing*].

*Ritratto del poeta attraverso le lettere,* tr. Bruno Oddera. Torino: Einaudi, 1970. 470 p. [*Selected letters*].

*Lunch at Mussolini's,* tr. Roberto Sanesi. Milano: Miarte edizioni, 1972. 41 p.: ill.

*Sotto il bosco di latte – Il dottore e i diavoli,* tr. Carlo Izzo and Floriana Bossi. Milano, 1972. 225 p. [*Under Milk Wood, The doctor and the devils*].

*Il dottore e i diavoli, e altri racconti per il cinema,* tr. Florina Bossi and Ettore

Capriolo. Torino: Einaudi, 1974. 266 p. [*Twenty years a-growing, The beach of Falesá. The doctor and the devils*].

*Favole di cinema,* tr. Ida Omboni. Milano: Milano libri, 1976. 143 p.: ill. [*Rebecca's daughters, Me and my bike*].

*18 poems,* tr. Gianni Rovera. Torino: Giappichelli, 1982. English and Italian.

### Japanese

*Tô no naka no mini,* tr. Hiroaki Manabe. Tokyo: Kôkubun-sha, 1956. 92 p.

*Shishû.* Tokyo: Yuriika, 1960. 113 p. (Kaigai-no-shijin Sôsho; 8). Incl.: *18 poems, Twenty-five poems, The map of love, Deaths and entrances.*

*Koinu no yôna geijutsuka no shôzô,* tr. Naomi Matsuura. Tokyo: Shôshinsha, 1964. 301 p. [*Portrait of the artist as a young dog*].

*Dylan Thomas zenshishû,* tr. Seitarô Tanaka and Ken'ichi Haya. Tokyo: Kôkubun-sha, 1967. 403 p. [*Collected poems, 1934-1952*].

*Milk no mori de ôku koeno no tameno geki,* tr. Naomi Matsuura and Nobukazu Aoki. Tokyo: Kôkubun-sha, 1967. 195 p. [*Under Milk Wood*].

*Shiron-shû shi to genjitsu,* tr. Naomi Matsuura. Tokyo: Kôkubun-sha, 1968. 196 p. Translation of prose pieces by Dylan Thomas, including some of the letters to Vernon Watkins.

*Kawa shôbai no bôken,* tr. Kitamura Tar. Tokyo: Shôbunsha, 1971. 258 p. [*Adventures in the skin trade*].

*Miruku uddo no motoni,* tr. Hidetoshi Ui. Tokyo: Ikegami shoten, 1975. 144 p. [*Under Milk Wood*].

*Shi,* tr. Seitarô Tanaka & Ken'ichi Haya. Tokyo: Kôkubun-sha, 1975. 488 p. [*The poems*].

*The green fuse: a collection of poems and wood engravings* / poems by Dylan Thomas ... , ed. & tr. Hiroaki Manabe. Tokyo: Tairiku No Taiwa Sha, 1982. [26] sheets: ill.: in portfolio. ISBN: 0-84-126310. Contents: The force that through the green fuse – Especially when the October wind – In the beginning – This bread I break – Ears in the turrets hear – When all my five and country sense see – Twenty-four years – The hunchback in the park – In my craft or sullen art – Lie still, sleep becalmed. – Engravings by Takao Hiwasaki. – 'This is a limited publication of 200 copies: English edition, 100 copies; Japanese edition, 100 copies.'

*Rebecca no musume tachi,* tr. Ken'ichi Haya. Tokyo: Shôbunsha, 1985, 241 p. [*Rebecca's daughters*].

## Norwegian

*Milk Wood: et spill for stemmer,* tr. Inger Hagerup. Oslo: Cappelen, 1956. 69 p. [*Under Milk Wood*].

*Diki og andre tekster,* tr. Harald Sverdrup. Oslo: Bokklubben, 1972. 94 p.: ill.

## Polish

*Szczeniecy portret artysty,* tr. Tadeusz Jan Dehnel. Warszawa: Państwowy Instytut Wydawniczy, 1966. 286 p. [*Portrait of the artist as a young dog,* with *Adventures in the Skin Trade*].

*Wiersze wybrane,* tr. Stanislaw Baranczak. Kraków: Wydaw. Liter., 1974. 218 p. [*Collected poems, 1934-1952*].

*Szkola czarownic,* tr. Teresa Truszkowska. Kraków: Wydaw. Liter., 1976. 121 p.: ill. [*Adventures in the Skin Trade*].

*Plaza Falesy,* tr. Teresa Truszkowska. Kraków: Wydaw. Liter., 1980. 116 p. [*The beach of Falesá*].

*Pod Mleczna Droga: sztuka na glosy,* tr. Tymona Terleckiego. Londyn [London]: Oficyna Poetów i Malarzy, 1981. 49 p.: front. port. Incl. critical essay. [*Under Milk Wood*].

## Portuguese

*Retrato do artista quando jovem cão,* tr. Alfredo Margarido. Lisboa: Livros do Brasil, [1961]. 222 p. [*Portrait of the artist as a young dog*].

Joaquin Manuel Magalhaes. *Dylan Thomas: consequencia da literatura e do real na sua poesia.* Lisboa: Assiro e Alvim, 1982. 299 p. (Cadernos peninsulares. Ensaio especial; 7). Incl.: The hand that signed the paper – After the funeral – Twenty-four years – Poem in October – In my craft or sullen art – Ceremony after a fire raid – Among those killed in the dawn raid ('When the morning was waking') – Lie still, sleep becalmed – Over Sir John's Hill – Poem on his birthday – Elegy ('Too proud to die'). – English and Portuguese.

## Romanian

*Viziune și rugay,* tr. C. Abăluță and St. Stoenescu. Bucuresti: Editura Univers, 1970. 125 p. [*Collected poems, 1934-1952*]. – English and Romanian.

*Fiicele Rebecai,* tr. Marcel Pop-Cornis. Timişoara: Facla, 1982. 192 p.: ill. [*Rebecca's daughters*].

## Russian

*Dylan Thomas: izbrannaya lirika,* tr. M. Koreneva. Moscow: Molodaya Gvardiya, 1980. 64 p. Translations of 22 poems. – Reviewed in *Arcade,* 6 Feb 1981, 20 ('Sixty-five thousand copies have been printed').

## Other Slavonic Languages

*Pripovetke,* tr. Branka Petrović. Beograd: Prosveta, 1961. 208 p.

*Poezija,* tr. Nikica Petrak. Zagreb: Mladost, 1964. 94 p. (Biblioteka Orion). English and Serbo-Croat.

*Pod Mlečnom Šumom: drama za glasove,* tr. Svetozar Brkić. Beograd: Nolit, 1964. 117 p. [*Under Milk Wood*].

*Praprotni grič,* tr. Jože Udović. Ljubljana: Cankarjeva Založba, 1965. 275 p. Poetry and prose (including *Under Milk Wood*).

*Tento chlieb ktory lámem,* tr. Ján Stacho. Bratislava: Slov. spis. 1968. 93 p.: ill. [*Collected poems, 1934-1952.*].

## Spanish

*Poemas,* tr. Esteban Pujals. Madrid: Rialp, 1955. 88 p.

*Con distinta piel,* tr. Juan Ángel Cotta. Buenos Aires: Muchnik. 1957. 109 p. [*Adventures in the skin trade*].
—— Buenos Aires: Compania General Fabril Editora, 1962. 120 p.
—— Barcelona: Bruguera, 1982. 151 p.

*Poemas escogidas,* tr. Jorge Ferrer-Vidal. Madrid: Agora, 1958. 70 p.

*Bajo el bosque de leche,* tr. Victoria Ocampo and Felix della Paolera. Buenos Aires, 1959. [*Under Milk Wood*].
—— *Under Milk Wood: En el joven bosque,* tr. Tomas Ramos Orea. Kingston, Ont.: Queen's University, 1971. 74 p. English and Spanish.

*El doctor y los demonios,* tr. Luisa Josefina Hernandez. Xalapa, Mexico: Universidad Veracruzana, [1960?]. 170 p. [*The Doctor and the Devils*].

*Retrato del artista cachorro,* tr. Juan Ángel Cotta. Buenos Aires: Compania General Fabril Editora, 1962. 208 p. [*Portrait of the artist as a young dog*].
—— Barcelona: Seix Barral, 1985. 183 p.

*La playa de Falesá,* tr. Patricio Canto. Buenos Aires: Ediciones Siglo Veinte, [1968]. 150 p. [*The Beach at Falesá*].

*Cartas,* tr. Piri Lugones. Buenos Aires: Ediciones de la Flor, 1971. 330 p. [*Selected letters*].

*Retrato del artista como perro jóven,* tr. Jorge Oliver. Barcelona: Fontamara, 1974. 208 p. [*Portrait of the artist as a young dog*]. – Reissued 1979.

*El doctor y los demonios,* tr. Virgilio Moya. Madrid: Felmar, 1975. 204 p.: ill. [*The Doctor and the Devils*].

*El visitante y otras historias,* tr. Ignacio Álvarez. Madrid: Nostromo, 1975. 160 p. [*A Prospect of the Sea*].
—— Madrid: Alfaquara, 1977. 166 p.
—— Barcelona: Bruguera, 1981. 187 p. Reissued 1983.

*Poemas,* tr. Gabriel Rodriguez and others. Caracas: Dirección General de Cultura de la Gobernación del Distrito Federal, 1976. 48 p.

*Poemas, 1934-1952,* tr. Esteban Pujals. Madrid: Alberto Corazón, 1976. 118 p.

*De pronto al amanecer,* tr. Isabel Salido. Madrid: Felmar, 1977. 257 p. [*Quite early one morning*].

*Las hijas de Rebecca.* Barcelona: Edic. del Cotal, 1978. 187 p. [*Rebecca's daughters*].

*Veinte anos creciendo,* tr. Antonio Resines. Madrid: Felmar, 1978. 162 p. [*Twenty years a-growing*]. – Reissued 1979.

*Bajo el bosque lácteo,* tr. Emilio Olcina Aya and Jesús Pérez. Barcelona: Fontamara, 1979. 117 p. [*Under Milk Wood*].

*La muerte del canario del rey,* tr. Patricia Cruzalegui Sotelo. Barcelona: Montesinos, 1981. 183 p. [*The death of the king's canary*].

**Swedish**

*Porträtt av konstnären som valp,* tr. Erik Lindegren and Thorsten Jonsson. Stockholm: Albert Bonnier, 1954. 201 p. (Panache serien). Incl. One warm Saturday, tr. Thorsten Jonsson. [*Portrait of the artist as a young dog*].
—— Stockholm: Bokforlaget Aldus/Bonniers, 1963. (En delfinbok; D90). Reissued 1983.
—— Stockholm: Legenda, 1985, 164 p.
—— Stockholm: Atlantis, 1986. 157 p.

*Äventyr i skinnbranschen,* tr. Harald Aström. Stockholm: Rabén & Sjögren, 1956. 109 p. (Partisanserien; 8). [*Adventures in the skin trade*].

*19 dikter,* tr. Jan Berg. Stockholm: Bonnier, 1957. 32 p. (Lilla lyrikserien; 31).
—— *Nitton dikter.* Lund: Ellerström, 1985, 63 p.

*Intill Mjölkhagen: ett spel for roster.* tr. Thomas Warburton. Stockholm: Bonnier, 1958. 75 p. (Panache serien). [*Under Milk Wood*].

*39 dikter,* tr. Jan Berg. Stockholm: Coekelberghs, 1977. 92 p.

*I riktning mot begynnelsen: prosaberättelser, 1931-1953,* tr. Kenneth Engström and

Birger Heden. Stockholm: Atlantis, 1981. 246 p. [*In the direction of the beginning: prose writings, 1931-1953*].

*Äventyr i skinnbranschen* – *Porträtt av konstnären som valp.* Stockholm: Atlantis, 1983. 232 p. In translations of Erik Lindegren and Thorsten Jonsson

**Welsh**

*Dan y Wenallt,* tr. T. James Jones. Llandysul: Gwasg Gomer, 1968. 114 p.: ill. With 10 full-page illustrations by Gaynor Owen. – See T.J. Jones. *Planet* 8 (1971) 29-32. [*Under Milk Wood*]. – Reissued 1992, with new illustrations.

*Nadolig plentyn yng Nghymru,* tr. Bryan Martin Davies. Llandysul: Gwasg Gomer, 1978. 45 p.: ill. With illustrations by Edward Ardizzone. [*A Child's Christmas in Wales*].

# B (i). Publications about Dylan Thomas: Books and Articles

The major guides to critical and biographical writing about the poet are the bibliographies of Ralph Maud and Georg Gaston listed below. *Critical essays on Dylan Thomas*, edited by Gaston (1989), contains a useful introductory survey of Dylan Thomas criticism. This present highly selective listing concentrates on more recent studies.

### Bibliographies

HUFF, William H. Bibliography. In Elder Olson, *The poetry of Dylan Thomas.* Chicago: University of Chicago Press, 1954. pp. 102-146.

ROLPH, John Alexander. *Dylan Thomas: a bibliography.* London: Dent, 1956. xix, 108 p.: ill. Incl.: Foreword: the young Dylan Thomas, by Edith Sitwell, pp. xiii-xv – Section A. Literary biographies of poems by Dylan Thomas, 1933-56, pp. 1-38 – Section B. Books and pamphlets, pp. 39-66 – Section C. Contributions to periodicals, pp. 67-88 – Section D. Contributions to books, pp. 89-93 – Section E. Translations of books, pp. 95-96 – Section F. Gramophone recordings, pp. 97-98. – Reviews: *Papers of Bibliographical Society of America* 51 (1957) 98-100 (Gerald D. McDonald); *TLS*, 27 Jul 1956, 451 (Vernon Watkins). – Supplementary notes: *Book Collector* 6 (1957) 71-73 (William B. Todd); *Book Collector* 6 (1957) 73-74 (James Campbell).

MAUD, Ralph. *Dylan Thomas in print: a bibliographical history.* London: Dent, 1972. xi, 268 p. Contents: Section I. Books, anthologies, theses – Section II. Welsh periodicals and newspapers – Section III. London, etc., periodicals and newspapers – Section IV. United States and Canadian newspapers – Section V. Foreign-language publications – Index – Appendix. 1969-71, by Walford Davies. Lists publications by and about Dylan Thomas. – U.S. edition: University of Pittsburg, 1970. – Note also Ralph Maud, Dylan Thomas in Welsh periodicals. *National Library of Wales Journal* 15 (1968) 265-289.

THEISEN, Sister Lois. Dylan Thomas: a bibliography of secondary criticism. *Bulletin of Bibliography* 26,1 (1969) 9-28, 32; 26,2 (1969) 59-60.

GASTON, Georg M.A. *Dylan Thomas: a reference guide.* Boston, Mass.: G.K. Hall, 1987. xi, 213 p. Fully annotated bibliography of writings about Dylan Thomas, 1934-1985, chronologically arranged.

## Critical and biographical studies

Note that there have been six collections of critical essays on Dylan Thomas, edited by J.M. Brinnin (1960), E.W. Tedlock (1960), C.B. Cox (1966), Walford Davies (1972), Georg Gaston (1989) and Alan Bold (1990). Their contents are given below. All except the Walford Davies and Alan Bold volumes reprint previously published studies.

ABELEIRA, Juan. Las fuerzas vivas de Dylan Thomas. *Cuadernos Hispanoamericanos: Revista Mensual de Cultura Hispanica,* Feb 1990, 45-54.

ACKERMAN, Diane. Among soft particles and charms. *Parnassus: Poetry in Review* 14,1 (1987) 86-92.

ACKERMAN, John. *Dylan Thomas: his life and work.* London: Oxford University Press, 1964. 203 p.: front. port. New edition: Macmillan, 1991, with, Introduction 1990, pp. ix-xxix.

—— Review article on *Dylan Thomas: the poems,* ed. Daniel Jones, Clark Emery, *The world of Dylan Thomas. AWR* 20,46 (1972) 175-181.

—— *Welsh Dylan: an exhibition to mark the twentieth anniversary of the poet's death.* Cardiff: Welsh Arts Council 1973. [58] p. Profusely illustrated catalogue, with linking commentary.

—— The role of nature in the poetry of Dylan Thomas. In *Triskel two: essays on Welsh and Anglo-Welsh literature,* ed. Sam Adams and Gwilym Rees Hughes. Llandybïe: Christopher Davies, 1973. pp. 9-25.

—— *Welsh Dylan: Dylan Thomas' life, writing, and his Wales.* Cardiff: John Jones, 1979. vii, 128 p.: ill. Another edition: Granada, 1980. 143 p.: ill. (A Paladin book).

—— Poets as friends. *PW* 20,4 (1985) 59-65. Review article on Gwen Watkins, *Portrait of a friend.*

—— A la recherche du temps Gallois: Dylan Thomas's development as a prose writer. *AWR* 83 (1986) 86-95.

—— Review article on James A. Davies, *Dylan Thomas's places. AWR* 88 (1988) 121-123.

—— *A Dylan Thomas companion: life, poetry and prose.* London: Macmillan, 1991. xvi, 309 p.: ill. (Macmillan literary companions). Incl. Appendix. Chelsea word-pictures (1944) [previously unattributed prose by Dylan Thomas], pp. 266-271.

—— The colour of saying. *NWR* 4,4 [16] (1992) 14-20. On the narrative voice in the stories and their appeal to children. In the same issue, pp. 10-11, Ackerman reviews *Dylan Thomas: the broadcasts,* ed. Ralph Maud.

ADAMS, Robert Martin. Taste and bad taste in metaphysical poetry: Richard Crashaw and Dylan Thomas. *Hudson Review* 8 (1955) 61-77.

AIVAZ, David. The poetry of Dylan Thomas. *Hudson Review* 3 (1950) 382-404.

AMIS, Kingsley. *What became of Jane Austen? and other questions*. London: Cape, 1970. Incl.: Thomas the rhymer [review of *A prospect of the sea*], pp. 54-57 – An evening with Dylan Thomas, pp. 57-62.

—— Another Dylan (1987). In *Wales on the wireless: a broadcasting anthology*, ed. Patrick Hannan. Llandysul: Gomer in assoc. with BBC Cymru/Wales, 1988. p. 164.

ANDERSON, C.W. and C.E. McMaster. Modeling emotional tone in stories using tension levels in categorical states. *Computers and the Humanities* 20 (1986) 3-9. Incl. discussion of 'Poem on his birthday'.

ARDIZZONE, Edward. *Edward Ardizzone: the original illustrations for the book*, A child's Christmas in Wales, *by Dylan Thomas*. Aberystwyth: Welsh National Centre for Children's Literature, 1982. 24 p.: ill. Incl.: Edward Ardizzone, by Marcus Crouch, pp. 6-11 – Dylan Thomas, by Walford Davies, pp. 13-18 – A child's Christmas in Wales, by Paul Ferris, pp. 21-22. – Exhibition catalogue, in English and Welsh.

ARLOTT, John. Dylan Thomas and radio. *Adelphi* 30 (1954) 121-124.

—— Arlott on Dylan (1983). In *Wales on the wireless: a broadcasting anthology*, ed. Patrick Hannan. Llandysul: Gomer in assoc. with BBC Cymru/Wales, 1988. pp. 161-162.

ASTLEY, Russell. Stations of the breath: end rhyme in the verse of Dylan Thomas. *PMLA* 84 (1969) 1595-1605.

BAKER, A.T. The roistering legend of Dylan Thomas. *Esquire*, Dec 1957, 201-209. Perceptive summary of the life and work.

BAWER, Bruce. Dylan Thomas: the poet in his letters. *New Criterion* 4,8 (1986) 8-18.

BAYLEY, John. *The romantic survival: a study in poetic evolution*. London: Constable, 1957. Incl. Dylan Thomas, pp. 186-227.

BENTLEY, Gregory. Dylan Thomas in Arcadia: the Pan motif in the *Collected poems*. *AWR* 64 (1979) 91-104.

BERRYMAN, John. The loud hills of Wales. *Kenyon Review* 2 (1940) 481-485. Review article on Dylan Thomas, *The world I breathe*.

—— After many a summer: memories of Dylan Thomas. *TLS*, 3 Sep 1993, 13-14. Hitherto unpublished memoir, written in 1959.

BETZNER, Ray. Dylan Thomas and Sherlock Holmes. *Baker Street Journal* 37,2 (1987) 97.

BLACKBURN, Thomas. *The price of an eye*. London: Longmans, 1961. Incl. discussion of Dylan Thomas, pp. 111-123.

BLUNDEN, Allan. Beside the seaside with George Heym and Dylan Thomas. *German Life and Letters* 29 (1975-76) 4-14. Discusses 'One warm Saturday'.

BOKANOWSKI, Hélène and Marc Alyn. *Dylan Thomas*. Paris: Editions Pierre Seghers, 1962. 222 p.: ill. Incl.: Dylan Thomas, by Hélène Bokanowski, pp. 9-49 – Dylan Thomas, by Marc Alyn, pp. 53-146 – 27 poems by Dylan Thomas, tr. Hélène Bokanowski, Jean Simon, Jean Wahl and Armand Guibert – List of other French translations, pp. 216-217.

BOLD, Alan. *Dylan Thomas: craft or sullen art*, ed. Alan Bold. London: Vision Press; New York: St. Martin's Press, 1990. 181 p. Contents: Introduction, by Alan Bold, pp. 7-13 – Dylan Thomas's concept of the poet, by Jacob

Korg, pp. 15-34 – The lips of time, by Stewart Crehan, pp. 35-64 – A freak user of words, by Gareth Thomas, pp. 65-88 – Hitting the right note: the potency of cheap music, by Keith Selby, pp. 89-113 – Dylan Thomas and the individual talent: a dialogue, by Michael Hulse, pp. 114-124 – Living 'under the shadow of the bowler': *Portrait of the artist as a young dog,* by Margaret Moan Rowe, pp. 125-136 – Voices still singing: a revaluation of *Under Milk Wood,* by Daphne B. Watson, pp. 137-155 – Young heaven's fold: the second childhood of Dylan Thomas, by Alan Bold, pp. 156-174.

BOYD, Stephen J. Secular mysticism: Dylan Thomas's 'Fern Hill'. *Forum for Modern Language Studies* 27,2 (1991) 177-188.

BOZMAN, E.F. Dylan Thomas. *Books: Journal of the National Book League,* Dec 1953, 114-115.

BREIT, Harvey. *The writer observed.* London: Alvin Redman, 1957. Incl. Dylan Thomas, pp. 231-233.

BRINNIN, John Malcolm. *Dylan Thomas in America: an intimate journal.* Boston: Little, Brown 1955. 303 p.: ill. Incl. 5 pages of photographs. – U.K. edition: Dent, 1956. 245 p.: 10 plates.

—— *A casebook on Dylan Thomas,* ed. John Malcolm Brinnin. New York: Crowell, 1960. xiii, 322 p. (Crowell literary casebooks). Contents: 10 poems, by Dylan Thomas – Dylan Thomas, a pioneer, by Francis Scarfe, pp. 21-33 – Dylan Thomas, by G.S. Fraser, pp. 34-58 – The religious poet, by W.S. Merwin, pp. 59-67 – Dylan Thomas: a review of the *Collected Poems,* by John Wain, pp. 68-71 – The nature of the poet, by Elder Olson, pp. 72-79 – Gerard Manley Hopkins and Dylan Thomas, by Henry Treece, pp. 80-90 – Critics, style and value, by Derek Stanford, pp. 91-98 – Review of *Collected Poems* and *Under Milk Wood,* by William Empson, pp. 110-114 – How much me now your acrobatics amaze, by Geoffrey Grigson, pp. 115-124 – Dylan Thomas, by Edith Sitwell, pp. 125-127 – The romantic heritage of Dylan Thomas, by Horace Gregory, pp. 131-138 – Dylan Thomas and the religion of the instinctive life, by Stuart Holroyd, pp. 139-152 – American Dylan Thomas, by Elizabeth Hardwick, pp. 153-159 – Dylan Thomas, by Karl Shapiro, pp. 167-178 – Talks with Dylan Thomas, by Harvey Breit, pp. 193-197 – A visit to Laugharne, by Bill Read, pp. 266-272 – Recollections of Dylan Thomas, by Geoffry Grigson, pp. 256-262 – Other observations and analyses by: William Arrowsmith, Kenneth Rexroth, Robert Graves, Martin Shuttleworth, John Malcolm Brinnin, Caitlin Thomas, Alastair Reid, Pamela Hansford Johnson, Winfield Townley Scott, Augustus John, Daniel Jones, Louis MacNeice, Marjorie Adix, Howard Moss – Bibliography.

BROOKE-ROSE, Christine. *A grammar of metaphor.* London: Secker & Warburg, 1958. Incl. analysis of nine poems by Dylan Thomas.

BROY, Evelyn J. The enigma of Dylan Thomas. *Dalhousie Review* 45 (1965) 499-507.

BRUCE, D.W. Marooned in a cemetary: Paul Valery and Dylan Thomas. *Journal of European Studies* 18 (1988) 1-8.

BULLOUGH, Geoffrey. *The trend of modern poetry.* Edinburgh: Oliver & Boyd, 1949. Incl. discussion of Dylan Thomas, pp. 217-221.

BURDETTE, Robert Kenley. *The saga of prayer: the poetry of Dylan Thomas.* The Hague: Mouton, 1972. 160 p. (Studies in English literature; 67).

BURNS, Richard. *Ceri Richards and Dylan Thomas: keys to transformation.* London: Enitharmon Press, 1981. 137 p.: ill. Incl. 46 drawings by Ceri Richards, mostly to poems by Thomas, pp. 109-124.

—— Roberto Sanesi: an Italian among Welshmen. *PW* 17,2 (1981) 42-51.

*CAHIERS RENAUD-BARRAULT* 105 (1983): a Dylan Thomas issue, with the Lawrence Durrell correspondence and articles by Daniele Laruelle, Agnes Pierron and Ethel Ross. – Also includes a Dylan Thomas chronology, bibliography and discography.

CAMPBELL, Roy. Memories of Dylan Thomas at the BBC. *Poetry* 87 (1955) 111-114.

CASTAY, Marie-Thérèse. Nature and some some Anglo-Welsh poets. *PW* 15,2 (1979) 100-110.

CHANDRON, K. Narayana. Echoes of *The waste land* in Dylan Thomas's 'And death shall have no dominion'. *Notes and Queries* 236 (1991) 346-347.

CHURCH, Richard. *Speaking aloud.* London: Heinemann, 1968. Incl. Dylan Thomas, pp. 210-212.

CLEVERDON, Douglas. *The growth of Milk Wood,* with the textual variants of *Under Milk Wood.* London: Dent, 1969. x, 124 p.: ill.

—— Dylan Thomas and broadcasting. *PW* 9 (1973) 85-92.

COHEN, Marcelo. Dylan Thomas: donde los muertos son constelacion. *Quimera: Revista de Literatura* 37 (1984) 10-15.

CONRAN, Anthony. The English poet in Wales, 2. Boys of summer in their ruin. *AWR* 10,26 (1960) 11-21.

—— *The cost of strangeness: essays on the English poets of Wales.* Llandysul: Gomer Press, 1982. Incl: The age of Dylan Thomas, pp. 169-180 – After the funeral: the praise poetry of Dylan Thomas, pp. 180-187.

COSTELLO, Tom. Dylan Thomas and the October wind. *AWR* 63 (1978) 100-110.

COX, C.B. Dylan Thomas's 'Fern Hill'. In *Modern poetry: studies in practical criticism,* ed. C.B. Cox and A.E. Dyson. London: Arnold, 1963. pp. 122-127.

—— *Dylan Thomas: a collection of critical essays,* ed. C.B. Cox. Englewood Cliffs, N.J.: Prentice-Hall, 1966. 186 p. (Twentieth century views). Contents: Introduction, by C.B. Cox, pp. 1-8 – Dylan Thomas: a review of the *Collected poems,* by John Wain, pp. 9-13 – The poetry of Dylan Thomas, by David Daiches, pp. 14-24 – The Welsh background, by John Ackerman, pp. 25-44 – The universe of the early poems, by Elder Olson, pp. 45-59 – 'There was a saviour', by Winifred Nowottny, pp. 60-73 – Last poems, by Ralph Maud, pp. 74-83 – *Collected poems* and *Under Milk Wood,* by William Empson, pp. 84-88 – Dylan Thomas's Play for voices, by Raymond Williams, pp. 89-98 – A place of love: *Under Milk Wood,* by David Holbrook, pp. 99-116 – Dylan Thomas's prose, by Annis Pratt, pp. 117-129 – Crashaw and Dylan Thomas: devotional athletes, by Robert M. Adams, pp. 130-139 – Dylan Thomas, by John Bayley, pp. 140-168 – Dylan Thomas, by Karl Shapiro, pp. 169-180.

—— Welsh bards in hard times: Dylan Thomas and R.S. Thomas. In *The new Pelican guide to English literature. Vol. 8. The present,* ed. Boris Ford. Harmondsworth: Penguin, 1983. pp. 209-223.

COX, J. Stevens. *Dylan Thomas: judgment in an action by Mrs Caitlin·Thomas to recover from the Times Book Co. Ltd. the manuscript of Under Milk Wood.* St Peter Port, Guernsey: Toucan Press, 1967. 8 p. '100 copies printed'.

—— *Under Milk Wood: an account of an action to recover the original manuscript.* St Peter Port, Guernsey: Toucan Press, 1969. 17 p.: front. port. Incl. introduction, by Douglas Cleverdon. – '250 copies for sale'.

COX, R.G. The cult of Dylan Thomas. *Scrutiny* 16 (1949) 247-250. Review article on Henry Treece, *Dylan Thomas: dog among the fairies.*

CRAWFORD, Joan. *Dylan Thomas: Under Milk Wood.* Harmondsworth: Penguin, 1987. 72 p. (Penguin passnotes). 'Suitable for GCSE students'.

CURRELI, Mario. Dylan Thomas all Elba. *Studi dell'Istituto Linguistico* 2 (1979) 187-193.

CURTIS, Tony. *How to study modern poetry.* London: Macmillan, 1990. Discusses 'A refusal to mourn', pp. 73-80.

DAICHES, David. *Two studies.* London: Shenval Press, 1958. Incl. The poetry of Dylan Thomas, pp. 5-16.

DAVID, Hugh. *The Fitzrovians: a portrait of Bohemian society, 1900-55.* London: Michael Joseph, 1988. Incl. Enter Dylan Thomas, pp. 137-156.

DAVIE, Donald. *Trying to explain.* Manchester: Carcanet, 1980. Incl. The life of Dylan Thomas, pp. 63-65.

DAVIES, Aneirin Talfan. Dylan Thomas. *DL* 4,12 (1953) 5-7. Obituary notice.

—— The golden echo. *DL* 5,13 (1954) 10-17. On Dylan Thomas's work for the Welsh Home Service.

—— *The colour of saying: an anthology of verse spoken by Dylan Thomas,* ed. Ralph N. Maud and Aneirin Talfan Davies. London: Dent, 1963. Incl. Introduction, by Ralph N. Maud and Aneirin Talfan Davies, pp. xiii-xxv. – U.S. ed.: *Dylan Thomas's choice.* New York: New Directions, 1964.

—— *Dylan: druid of the broken body.* Swansea: Christopher Davies, 1977. 124 p. With additional essay, The influence of Welsh prosody on modern English poetry, pp. 86-124. – First published Dent, 1964. xi, 75 p. – 'The influence of Welsh prosody on modern English poetry' first appeared in *Proceedings of the Third Congress of the International Comparative Literature Association.* The Hague: Mouton, 1962. pp. 90-122.

DAVIES, Geraint. A tale of two Thomases: reflections on two Anglo-Welsh poets. In *Nationalism in literature/Literarischer Nationalismus: literature, language and national identity,* ed. Horst W. Drescher and Hermann Volkel. Frankfurt: Peter Lang, 1989. pp. 289-297. On Dylan and R.S. Thomas.

DAVIES, James A. Dylan Thomas' 'One warm Saturday' and Tennyson's 'Maud'. *Studies in Short Fiction* 14 (1977) 284-286.

—— A picnic in the orchard: Dylan Thomas' Wales. In *Wales the imagined nation: studies in cultural and national identity,* ed. Tony Curtis. Bridgend: Poetry Wales Press, 1986. pp. 45-65.

—— Crying in my wordy wilderness. *AWR* 83 (1986) 96-105. Review article on *The collected letters of Dylan Thomas,* ed. Paul Ferris.

—— *Dylan Thomas's places: a biographical and literary guide.* Swansea: Christopher Davies, 1987. 210 p.: ill.

DAVIES, Laurence. Dylan Thomas: Welsh poet? *Keltica* 2 (1983) 72-74.

DAVIES, Pennar. Sober reflections on Dylan Thomas. *DL* 5,15 (1954) 13-17.

DAVIES, Richard A. Dylan Thomas's image of the 'young dog' in the *Portrait. AWR* 26,58 (1977) 68-72.

DAVIES, Walford. *Dylan Thomas: new critical essays,* ed. Walford Davies. London: Dent, 1972. xv, 282 p. Contents: Introduction, by Walford Davies, pp. vii-xv – Druid of her broken body, by John Wain, pp. 1-20 – Self and word: the earlier poems, by Raymond Stephens, pp. 21-55 – Chains and the poet, by John Bayley, pp. 56-72 – Randy Dandy in the cave of spleen: wit and fantasy in Thomas (with comments on Pope, Wallace Stevens, and others), by C.J. Rawson, pp. 73-106 – The concept of mind and the poetry of Dylan Thomas, by Martin Dodsworth, pp. 107-135 – The wanton starer, by Walford Davies, pp. 136-165 – The code of night: the schizoid diagnosis and Dylan Thomas, by David Holbrook, pp. 166-197 – The cancered aunt on her insanitary farm, by John Fuller, pp. 198-220 – 'The conversation of prayers': an Anglo-Welsh poem, by F.W. Bateson, pp. 221-227 – Adder's tongue on maiden hair: early stages in reading 'Fern Hill', by Alastair Fowler, pp. 228-261 – Sex in Arcadia: *Under Milk Wood*, by Lawrence Lerner, pp. 262-282.

—— *Dylan Thomas*. Milton Keynes: Open University Press, 1986. 134 p. (Open Guides to Literature).

—— *Dylan Thomas: the poet in his chains*. Swansea: University College of Swansea, 1986. 28 p.: ill. (W.D.Thomas memorial lecture).

—— Dylan Thomas, 1914-1953. In *Read more about it: encyclopedia of information sources on historical figures and events*. Ann Arbor, Michigan: Pierian Press, 1989. pp. 693-696.

—— *Dylan Thomas*. Cardiff: University of Wales Press, 1990. vi, 68 p. Revised version of a study first published in the Writers of Wales series, 1972.

—— Bright fields, loud hills and the glimpsed good place: R.S. Thomas and Dylan Thomas. In *The page's drift: R.S. Thomas at eighty,* ed. M. Wynn Thomas. Bridgend: Seren Books, 1993. pp. 171-210.

DAVIN, Dan. *Closing time*. London: Oxford University Press, 1975. Incl. A spinning man: Dylan Thomas (1914-1953), pp. 121-150.

DAVIS, Cynthia. The voices of *Under Milk Wood. Criticism* 17 (1975) 74-89.

DAVIS, W. Eugene. The making of *A child's Christmas in Wales. Arizona Quarterly* 29 (1973) 342-351.

DAVIS, William V. Influence without anxiety: Dylan Thomas and W.S. Merwin. *Notes on Contemporary Literature* 19,5 (1989) 6-7. Considers Thomas's 'I dreamed my genesis' and Merwin's 'For the anniversary of my death'.

DEANE, Sheila. *Bardic style in the poetry of Gerard Manley Hopkins, W.B. Yeats, and Dylan Thomas*. Ann Arbor, Michigan: UMI Research Press, 1989.

DEUTSCH, Babette. *Poetry in our time*. New York: Columbia University Press, 1952. Discusses Thomas, pp. 330-344.

DEVAS, Nicolette. *Two flamboyant fathers*. London: Collins, 1966. 287 p. An autobiography by Caitlin Thomas's sister, with reminiscences of Dylan Thomas.

DUGDALE, J.S. *Brodie's notes on Dylan Thomas's* Under Milk Wood. Basingstoke: Macmillan, 1992. 92p.

DYLAN Thomas Society. *Dylan Thomas remembered.* Swansea: Dylan Thomas Society (Wales Branch), 1978. 72 p.: ill. Incl.: The Swansea of Dylan Thomas, by Peter Stead, pp. 8-25 – Dylan Thomas and America, by Martin E. Gingerich, pp. 26-34 – Conversations and reflections, by Gwen Watkins and Gilbert Bennett, pp. 35-46 – A reconsideration of the poems of Dylan Thomas, by R. George Thomas, pp. 47-60 – Prelude for organ: 'A refusal to mourn' [holograph music score], by Daniel Jones, pp. 61-68.

—— *The world I breathe: talks and lectures delivered to the Dylan Thomas Society of Great Britain,* ed. Hugh S. Price. [Swansea]: Dylan Thomas Society of Great Britain, 1991. 74 p. Contents: Annual birthday dinner addresses; Daniel Jones, Gwen Watkins, Walford Davies, pp. 1-19 – A refusal to mourn: an approach to the poetry of Edward Thomas, by R. George Thomas, pp. 20-35 – David Jones and the matter of Wales, by David Rees, pp. 36-53 – Epic of attrition: David Jones' *In parenthesis,* by Désirée Hirst, pp. 54-63 – The poet and his actor friend: Dylan Thomas and Richard Burton, by Peter Stead pp. 64-74.

EDMUNDS, Paul. Two poems about death. *Crux: Journal on the Teaching of English* 17,2 (1983) 31-36. Discusses Tennyson's 'Crossing the bar' and Thomas's 'Do not go gentle into that good night'.

EMERY, Clark. *The world of Dylan Thomas.* Coral Gables: Miami University Press, 1962. 318 p. – U.K. edition: Dent, 1971. 319 p.

EMPSON, William. Some more Dylan Thomas. *Listener,* 28 Oct 1971, 588-590. Review of *Dylan Thomas: early prose writings,* ed. Walford Davies, *Dylan Thomas: the poems,* ed. Daniel Jones.

FARRINGDON, Jillian M. and Michael G. *A concordance and word-lists to the poems of Dylan Thomas.* Oxford: Oxford Microform; Swansea: Ariel House, 1980. 30 p.: 5 microfiches. Keyed to the 1978 printing of *Dylan Thomas: the poems,* ed. Daniel Jones.

FERRIS, Paul. *Dylan Thomas.* London: Hodder & Stoughton, 1977. 399 p.: ill. Revised and enlarged edition: Harmonsworth: Penguin, 1985. xviii, 446 p. (Penguin literary biographies).

—— *Caitlin: the life of Caitlin Thomas.* London: Hutchinson, 1993. 320 p.

FINK, Howard. *Under Milk Wood: notes.* Toronto: Coles, 1970. 67 p. (Coles notes; 1108).

FIRMAGE, George J. *A garland for Dylan Thomas,* gathered and with a preface by George J. Firmage. New York: Clarke and Way, 1963. xvi, 171 p.: ill. Incl.: 84 poems in celebration of Dylan Thomas – Notes on the art of poetry [i.e. Poetic manifest], by Dylan Thomas, pp. 147-152. – U.K. edition: Vision Press, 1966.

FITZGIBBON, Constantine. *The life of Dylan Thomas.* London: Dent, 1965. ix, 422 p.: ill. Incl.: Appendix 1. Broadcasts by Dylan Thomas, pp. 395-399 – Appendix 2. Film scripts by Dylan Thomas, pp. 400-402 – Appendix 3. Lectures and readings from America by Dylan Thomas, pp. 403-410. – Another edition: Sphere, 1968. 383 p.

FITZGIBBON, Theodora. *With love.* London: Pan, 1983. Incl. recollections of Dylan Thomas.

FOSBERG, Mary Dee Harris. Dylan Thomas's use of *Roget's Thesaurus* during composition of 'Poem on his birthday'. *Papers of the Bibliographical Society of America* 72 (1978) 505-517.

—— Dylan Thomas, the craftsman: computer analysis of the composition of a poem. *Association for Literary and Linguistic Computing Bulletin* 7 (1979) 295-300. Discusses 'Poem on his birthday'.

FRANKENBURG, Lloyd. *Pleasure dome: on reading modern poetry.* New York: Gordion Press, 1968. Incl. Dylan Thomas, pp. 316-323. – First published 1949.

FRASER, George S. *Dylan Thomas.* London: Longmans for the British Council, 1972. 41 p.: front. port. (Writers and their work). Revision of work first published 1957. – Reprinted in *A casebook on Dylan Thomas,* ed. John Malcolm Brinnin (1960), G.S. Fraser, *Essays on twentieth-century poets* (1977).

FREEMAN, Donald C. The strategy of fusion: Dylan Thomas's syntax. In *Style and structure in literature: essays in the stylistics,* ed. Roger Fowler. Ithaca, New York: Cornell University Press, 1975. pp. 19-39.

FRIEDMAN, Stanley. Whitman and Laugharne: Dylan Thomas's 'Poem in October'. *AWR* 18,41 (1969) 81-82.

FRYER, Jonathan. *Dylan: the nine lives of Dylan Thomas.* London: Kyle Cathie, 1993. xiii, 276 p.

GACECILAZE, Z.G. *Dilan Tomasis poezia.* Tbilisi: Tbilisis Universitetis Gamomcemloba, 1984. 160 p.: ill. Summaries in English and Russian.

GALLO, Bruno. *La metropoli dei pesci: la poesia di Dylan Thomas.* Bergamo: Minerva Italica, 1976. 279 p. Incl. poems in Italian translation.

—— *Linguaggio come pornotopia in Dylan Thomas.* Bergamo: Minerva Italica, 1979. 411 p. With some Italian translations.

GARLICK, Raymond. Editorial. *DL* 5,13 (1954) 1-5.

—— The shapes of thoughts. *PW* 9,2 (1973) 40-48. On 'Vision and prayer'.

GASTON, Georg. *Critical essays on Dylan Thomas,* ed. Georg Gaston. Boston, Mass.: G.K. Hall, 1989. 197 p. (Critical essays on British literature). Contents: Introduction, by Georg Gaston, pp. 1-11 – Reviews by John Berryman, Conrad Aiken, William Empsom, Howard Nemerov, William York Tindall, Henry W. Wells – The posthumous life of Dylan Thomas, by Alfred Kazin, pp. 35-42 – Dylan Thomas and the ark of art, by John Logan, pp. 42-49 – Notes on the imagery of Dylan Thomas, by Richard Morton, pp. 50-58 – Ambiguity as poetic shift, by A.J. Smith, pp. 59-65 – [Sound and form in Dylan Thomas], by Harvey Gross, pp. 65-70 – Dylan Thomas and the 'biblical rhythm', by W.T. Moynihan, pp. 70-96 – Dylan Thomas: the literal vision, by W.E. Yeomans, pp. 96-105 – Stations of the breath: end rhyme in the verse of Dylan Thomas, by Russell Astley, pp. 106-124 – The black-stockinged bait and Dylan Thomas, by Horace Gregory, pp. 125-132 – The personal and impersonal in some of Dylan Thomas's lyrics, by Barbara Hardy, pp. 133-139 – *Portrait of the artist as a young dog:* Dylan's *Dubliners,* by Kenneth Seib, pp. 139-147 – Dylan Thomas (1914-1953), by Anthony Thwaite, pp. 147-154 – [A reader's guide to Dylan Thomas], by Michael Schmidt, pp. 154-157 – Argument of the hewn voice: the early poetry of Dylan Thomas, by J.M. Kertzer, pp. 158-176 – Dylan Thomas and public suicide, by Donald Hall, pp. 176-193.

GINGERICH, Martin E. Dylan Thomas and the ark of the covenant. *AWR* 19,44 (1971) 183-185.

—— Dylan Thomas: curse-bless. *AWR* 22,49 (1973) 178-182.

—— The timeless narrators of Dylan Thomas's 'In country heaven'. *Modern Poetry Studies* 7 (1976) 109-121.

—— 'Especially when the October wind' and the Welsh autumn. *AWR* 64 (1979) 67-73.

GITTENS, Rob. *The last days of Dylan Thomas.* London: Macdonald 1986. 220 p. Another edition: Futura, 1987.

GOODLANDS, Giles. Dylan Thomas and film. *NWR* 3,1 [9] (1990) 17-22.

GÖRTSCHACHER, Wolfgang. Nur die Schattseite des Dichters? Erich Fried als Übersetzer von Dylan Thomas. In *Österreichische Dichter als Übersetzer: Salzburger komparatistische Analysen*, ed. Wolfgang Pöckl. Vienna: Österreichische Akad. der Wiss., 1991. On Erich Fried as translator of Dylan Thomas.

GRABE, Ina. Metaphor and interpretation: an analysis of interaction processes in poetic metaphor, with special reference to Dylan Thomas's 'A process in the weather of the heart'. Pretoria: University of South Africa, 1985. vii, 57 p. (Manualia; 34).

—— Kommunikasiemiddele in die posie. *Journal of Literary Studies/Tydskrif vir Literaturwetenskap* 1,2 (1985) 14-33. Discussess 'This bread I break'.

GRAVES, Robert. *The crowning privilege.* London: Cassell, 1955. Incl. 'These be your gods, O Israel', pp. 112-135.

GREENWAY, William. Dylan Thomas and the flesh's vision. *College Literature* 16 (1989) 274-280.

—— Dylan Thomas: back in America. *NWR* 3,1 [9] (1990) 23-26. On the Dylan Thomas Society's performances of 'Under Milk Wood' in America.

—— The Gospel according to Dylan Thomas. *Notes on Contemporary Literature* 20,1 (1990) 2-4. On 'A refusal to mourn'.

GREGORY, Horace. Romantic heritage in the writings of Dylan Thomas. *Poetry* 69 (1947) 326-336.

GRIGSON, Geoffrey. Recollections of Dylan Thomas. *London Magazine*, Sep 1957, 39-45.

—— *Blessings, kicks and curses: a critical collection.* London: Allison & Busby, 1982. Incl.: American and Welsh Dylanism: a last word from a non-Dylanist [reprint of 1964 review of John Ackerman, *Dylan Thomas: his life and work*, Aneirin Talfan Davies, *Dylan: druid of the broken body*], pp. 13-16 – Dylan Thomas: yet another last word [reprint of 1976 review of *The death of the king's canary*], pp. 17-19.

GRINDEA, Miron, ed. *Adam* 238 (1953) [Dylan Thomas memorial number]. ii, 80 p.: ill. Contents: For Dylan, by Miron Grindea, pp. ii-7 – The opera that might have been, by Igor Stravinsky, p. 8 – The monogamous bohemian, by Augustus John, pp. 9-10 – Three memoirs, by Phillip Lindsay, David Daiches and Glyn Jones, pp. 11-13 – Une larme pour Adonais, by Roy Campbell, Stephen Spender, John Lehmann, Emmanual Litvinoff, Elizabeth Lutyens, pp. 13-14 – Poem. A swansong at Laugharne, by George Barker, pp. 15-16 – Poem. In memoriam Dylan [French], by Pierre Emmanuel, p. 16 – The Dylan I knew, by Runia Sheila Macleod, pp. 17-23 – Seventeen further memoirs by: Pamela Hansford Johnson, Mario Luzi, Derek Patmore, John Davenport, E.F. Bozman, Hugo Manning, Clifford Dyment, William Griffiths, Robert Pocock, R.B. Marriott, Michael Ayrton, Leslie Rees, Ralph Wishart, Hugh MacDiarmid, Phillip Burton, Cecil Price, Griffith Williams, pp. 17-39 – Victoire de la poésie, by Georges-Albert Astre, pp. 40 42 – French translations of 'Out of the sighs' and 'After the funeral', pp. 42-43 – To take to give is all, by Linden Huddlestone, pp. 44-47 – Adventures in the skin trade, chapts. 1 & 2, by Dylan Thomas, pp. 48-65 – His work and background, by Suzanne Roussillat, pp. 66-72 – The religious poet, by W.S. Merwin, pp. 73-78 – Poem. The sea (Dylan Thomas), by Ronald Bottrall, p. 78 – Poem. Dylan Marlais Thomas: in memoriam, by Ken Etheridge, pp. 79-80. – With portraits of Thomas by Michael Ayrton and Alfred Janes.

GURALNICK, Elissa S. Radio drama: the stage of the mind. *Virginia Quarterly Review* 61 (1985) 79-94. Discusses 'Under Milk Wood'.

GRUBB, Frederick. *A vision of reality: a study of liberalism in twentieth-century verse.* London: Chatto & Windus, 1965. Incl. Worm's eye: Dylan Thomas, pp. 179-187.

HALL, Donald. *Remembering poets, reminiscences and opinions: Dylan Thomas, Robert Frost, T.S. Eliot, Ezra Pound.* New York: Harper & Row, 1978. Incl. Dylan Thomas and public suicide, pp. 3-37.

HAMBURGER, Michael. *A mug's game: intermittent memoirs, 1924-1954.* Manchester: Carcanet, 1974. Incl. comment on Dylan Thomas.

HARDESTY, Margaret A. *That momentary peace, the poem.* Washington, D.C.: University Press of America, 1982. xxi, 156 p. Considers Dylan Thomas as 'mediator of a sacremental vision of man and the universe'.

HARDING, Joan. Dylan Thomas and Edward Thomas. *Contemporary Review*, Sep 1957, 150-154.

HARDY, Barbara. *The advantage of lyric: essays on feeling in poetry.* University of London: Athlone Press, 1977. Incl. The personal and the impersonal in some of Dylan Thomas's lyrics, pp. 112-120. – First published in *PW* 9,2 (1973) 75-83.

—— *Dylan Thomas's poetic language: the stream that is flowing both ways.* Cardiff: University College, Cardiff 1987. 12 p. (Annual Gwyn Jones lecture).

—— Region and nation: R.S. Thomas and Dylan Thomas. In *The literature of region and nation,* ed. R.P. Draper. London: Macmillan, 1989. pp. 93-107.

HARRIS, John. Big Daddy meets the nogood boyos: Caradoc, Dewi Emrys and Dylan. *PW* 18,4 (1983) 43-47.

—— Not a 'Trysorfa fach': Keidrych Rhys and the launching of *Wales.* *NWR* 3,3 [11] 28-33. Discusses Dylan Thomas's involvement in the magazine.

HART, Dominick. The experience of Dylan Thomas's poetry. *AWR* 26,58 (1977) 73-78.

HAVARD, Robert G. The symbolic ambivalence of 'green' in García Lorca and Dylan Thomas. *Modern Language Review* 67 (1972) 810-819.

HAWKES, Terence. Dylan Thomas's Welsh. *College English* 21 (1960) 345-347.

—— Playboys of the western world. *Listener*, 16 Dec 1965, 991-993. On J.M. Synge and Dylan Thomas.

—— Some 'sources' of 'Under Milk Wood'. *Notes and Queries*, Jul 1975, 273-275.

HAYA, Kenichi. *Dylan Thomas*. Kenkyusha, 1983. 218 p.

HEPPENSTALL, Rayner. My bit of Dylan Thomas. [n. p.] 1957. [24] p. '80 copies for private circulation to the friends of T.E.H. [T.E. Hanley]'.

—— *Four absentees*. London: Barrie & Rockcliff, 1960. Reminiscences of Eric Gill, George Orwell, Dylan Thomas and J. Middleton Murry. – Also issued in a private edition.

HILTON, Ian. The poetic medicine man: Dylan Thomas and Germany. *AWR* 63 (1978) 93-99.

HINCHCLIFFE, Peter. Hopkins and some poets of the Thirties. In *Vital candle: Victorian and modern bearings in Gerard Manley Hopkins,* ed. John S. North and Michael D. Moore. Waterloo: University of Waterloo Press, 1984. pp. 99-112. Discusses Thomas and W.H. Auden.

HOGLER, Raymond L. Dylan Thomas: the development of an idiom. *AWR* 21,47 (1972) 113-123; 21,48 (1972) 102-114.

HOLBROOK, David. Two Welsh writers: T.F. Powys and Dylan Thomas. In *The new Pelican guide to English literature. Vol. 7. The modern age,* ed. Boris Ford. Harmondsworth: Penguin, 1961. pp. 415-428.

—— Llareggub revisited: Dylan Thomas and the state of modern poetry. London: Bowes & Bowes, 1962. 255 p. – U.S. edition: *Dylan Thomas and poetic dissociation.* Carbondale, Ill.: University of Southern Illinois Press, 1964. vi, 182 p.

—— *Dylan Thomas: the code of night.* University of London: Athlone Press, 1972. 271 p.

HOLLEY, Linda Tarte. Dylan Thomas' 'Fern Hill': the breaking of the circles. *Concerning Poetry* 15,2 (1982) 59-67.

HOLROYD, Stuart. *Emergence from chaos.* London: Gollancz, 1957. Incl. Dylan Thomas and the religion of the instinctive life, pp. 77-94.

HORAN, Robert. In defense of Dylan Thomas. *Kenyon Review* 7 (1945) 304-310.

HORNICK, Lita. *The intricate image: a study of Dylan Thomas.* New York: Gallery Editions, 1972. xi, 151 p.

HUGHES, Richard. *Fiction as truth: selected literary writings by Richard Hughes,* ed. Richard Poole. Bridgend: Poetry Wales Press, 1983. Incl. Dylan Thomas: the real tragedy [review of *Under Milk Wood*], pp. 157-159 – Laughter from the doldrums [review of *Adventures in the skin trade*], pp. 160-161.

JACKAMAN, Rob. Man and mandala: symbol as structure in a poem by Dylan Thomas. *Ariel: A Review of International English Literature* [Calgary] 7,4 (1976) 22-33. On 'I see the boys of summer'.

JENKINS, David Clay. Dylan Thomas and *Wales* magazine. *Trace* 30 (1959) 1-8.

—— Poetry and places: Dylan Thomas's Laugharne. *Eleusis of Chi Omega* 65,1 (1963) 48-58.

—— Dylan Thomas' *Under Milk Wood*: the American element. *Trace* 51 (1963) 325-335.

—— Shrine of the boily boy: the Dylan Thomas notebooks at Buffalo. *AWR* 19,43 (1970) 114-129.

JOHN, Brian. Dylan Thomas's 'Over Sir John's Hill'. *AWR* 23,51 (1974) 17-24.

JOHNSON, Pamela Hansford. *Important to me: personalia*. London: Macmillan, 1974. Incl. Dylan, pp. 140-149.

JONES, Daniel. Dylan Thomas obituary notice. *DL* 4,12 (1953) 4-5.

—— *My friend Dylan Thomas*. London: Dent, 1977. xi, 116 p.: ill.

—— Overmilk'd wood: the myth of Dylan Thomas. *Encounter*, May 1977, 23-28.

—— The Dylan I knew, 1. The saddest truth of all. *WM*, 29 Oct 1983, 9:A-D. Interview with Terry Campbell.

JONES, Glyn. Three Anglo-Welsh prose writers. *Rann* 19 (1953) 1-5. On Caradoc Evans, Gwyn Thomas and Dylan Thomas.

—— Dylan Thomas and Welsh. *DL* 5,13 (1954) 24-25.

—— Teenaged angel in a black polo-necked sweater. *WM*, 21 Apr 1958, 4:B-G. Continued: A prodigy among the down-beats, 22 Apr, 4:B-G; A roaring boy dying of welcome, 23 Apr, 6:B-E; The fallen angel with a tumbledown tongue, 24 Apr, 6:B-G. – Series title: Dylan Thomas, the other man.

—— *The dragon has two tongues: essays on Anglo-Welsh writers and writing*. London: Dent, 1968. Incl. Dylan Thomas, pp. 172-203.

——*18 poems again*. *PW* 9,2 (1973) 22-26.

—— Dylan Thomas: The Boat House, Laugharne, Dyfed. In *Writers and their houses: a guide to the writers' houses of England, Scotland, Wales and Ireland: essays by modern writers*, ed. Kate Marsh. London: H. Hamilton, 1993. pp. 423-433.

JONES, Gwyn. Dylan Thomas, poet of elemental things. *WM*, 13 Apr 1949, 4:D-F.

—— Language, style and the Anglo-Welsh. *Essays and Studies* 6 (1953) 102-114. On Dylan Thomas, Gwyn Thomas, Glyn Jones and Caradoc Evans.

—— Welsh Dylan. *Adelphi* 30 (1954) 108-117. Reprinted in Gwyn Jones, *Background to Dylan Thomas* (1992), pp. 89-97.

—— *The first forty years: some notes on Anglo-Welsh literature*. Cardiff: University of Wales Press, 1957. (W.D. Thomas memorial lecture). Incl. discussion of Dylan Thomas.

—— Dylan Thomas in London. *WM*, 3 Sep 1960, 5:B-D. Review article on Rayner Heppenstall, *Four absentees*.

JONES, John Idris. *Under Milk Wood*. *NWR* 4,4 [16] (1992) 4-9.

JONES, Richard. The Dylan Thomas country. *Texas Quarterly* 4,4 (1961) 34-42. On Laugharne.

JONES, Richard. Delinquent free spirit or astute operator. *NWR* 4,4 [16] (1992) 24-27. Review article on George Tremlett, *Dylan Thomas: in the mercy of his means*. – With new evidence on the 'Majoda', New Quay, incident of 1945.

JONES, T. James. A bilingual Llaregyb. *Planet* 8 (1971) 29-32. On translating *Under Milk Wood* into Welsh.

JONES, T. Harri. *Dylan Thomas*. Edinburgh; London: Oliver & Boyd, 1963. 118 p. (Writers and critics).

JOSHI, Neeta. Influence of the Welsh bardic tradition in the poetry of Dylan Thomas. *Panjab University Research Bulletin* (Arts) 21,2 (1990) 95-104.

KARRER, Wolgang. Die Metaphorik in den *Collected Poems* von Dylan Thomas: Eine syntaktische Untersuch. Bonn: Bouvier Verlag Herbert Grundmann, 1971. 175 p.

KAZIN, Alfred. *Contemporaries*. London: Secker and Warburg, 1963. Incl. The posthumous life of Dylan Thomas, pp. 192-202.

KELLEY, Richard. The lost vision of Dylan Thomas' 'One warm Saturday'. *Studies in Short Fiction* 6 (1969) 205-209.

KELLNER, Bruce. 'The force that through the green fuse drives the flower'. In *Reference guide to English literature,* ed. D.L. Kirkpatrick. 2nd ed. 3 vols. Chicago; London: St James Press, 1991. Vol. 3, pp. 1592-1593.

KEMENY, Tomaso. *La poesia di Dylan Thomas: enucleazione della dinamica compositiva.* [Rome]: Cooperativa Scrittori, 1976. 160 p. (Poesia e prosa; 5).

KERSHNER, R.B. *Dylan Thomas: the poet and the critics.* Chicago: American Library Association, 1976. xiii, 280 p. (The poet and his critics). Incl.: Appendix A: Basic sources for Thomas, pp. 235-242 – Appendix C: Index of explications, pp. 245-266.

KERTZER, J.M. Argument of the hewn voice: the early poetry of Dylan Thomas. *Contemporary Literature* 30 (1979) 293-315.

KIDDER, Rushworth Moulton. *Dylan Thomas: the country of the spirit.* Princeton, N.J.: Princeton University Press, 1973. xi, 234 p.

KLEINMAN, Hyman H. *The religious sonnets of Dylan Thomas: a study in imagery and meaning.* Berkeley: California University Press, 1963. xii, 153 p. (Perspectives in criticism; 13).

KNEIGER, Bernard. Dylan Thomas: the Christianity of the 'Altarwise by owl-light' sequence. *College English* 23 (1962) 623-628.

KORG, Jacob. *Dylan Thomas.* New York: Twayne, 1965. 205 p. (Twayne English authors; 20).

—— Hopkins and Dylan Thomas. In *Hopkins among the poets: studies in modern responses to Gerard Manley Hopkins,* ed. Richard F. Giles. Hamilton, Ontario: International Hopkins Association, 1985. pp. 91-94.

LAING, Jeffrey M. Obsessional themes/magical words: John Hawkes's homage to Dylan Thomas. *Notes on Contemporary Literature* 17,5 (1987) 4-6.

LANDA, Clara. With Welsh and reverend rook: the biblical element in Dylan Thomas. *Queen's Quarterly* 65 (1958) 436-447.

LANE, Gary. *A concordance to the poems of Dylan Thomas.* Metuchen, N.J.: Scarecrow Press, 1976. ix, 697 p. (Scarecrow concordances; 5). Keyed to the 1971 printing of *Dylan Thomas: the poems,* ed. Daniel Jones.

LARKIN, Philip. Master voices. *New Statesman,* 2 Feb 1962, 170-171. On poetry recordings, including Dylan Thomas's.

LE BON, Pierre. Approche thématique, symbolique et rythmique du poème, 'After the funeral' de Dylan Thomas. *Repérages* 12 (1989) 26-35.

LENGELER, Rainer. Dylan Thomas' 'Over Sir John's Hill': eine moderne Theodizee. In *Tradition und Innovation in der englischen und amerikanischen*

*Lyrik des 20. Jahrhunderts,* ed. Karl Josef Holtgen and others. Tubingen: Niemeyer, 1986.

LERNER, Laurence. *The uses of nostalgia: studies in pastoral poetry.* London: Chatto & Windus, 1972. Incl. Sex in Arcadia [on *Under Milk Wood*], pp. 81-104.

LEVY, Mervyn. The Dylan I knew, 2. Myths and legends. *WM,* 31 Oct 1983, 8:B-E. Interview with Terry Campbell.

LEWIS, E. Glyn. Dylan Thomas. *WR* 7 (1948) 270-281.

LEWIS, Min. *Laugharne and Dylan Thomas.* London: Dennis Dobson, 1967. 128 p.: ill. Incl. 29 full-page sketches by Stanley Lewis.

LEWIS, Peter Elfed. 'Under Milk Wood' as radio poem. *AWR* 64 (1979) 74-90. Reprinted in *Poetry dimension* 7, ed. Dannie Absie. London: Robson Books, 1980. pp. 16-34.

—— Return journey to Milk Wood. *PW* 9,2 (1973) 27-38.

—— The road to Llareggub. In *British radio drama,* ed. John Drakakis. Cambridge: Cambridge University Press, 1981. pp. 72-110.

—— *Under Milk Wood.* In *Reference guide to English literature,* ed. D.L. Kirkpatrick. 2nd ed. 3 vols. Chicago; London: St James Press, 1991. Vol. 3, pp. 1914-1915.

LEWIS, Saunders. Dylan Thomas. *DL* 5,13 (1954) 8-9. Text in Welsh and English.

LINDSAY, Jack. Dylan and Philip. *Overland,* Sep 1986, 54-58. On Thomas and Philip Lindsay.

LLOYD, Bernard. A friend who lives on in a Dylan Thomas story. *AWR* 20,45 (1971) 231-233. On Dylan Thomas and Trevor Hughes.

LOESCH, Katherine Taylor. Welsh poetic syntax and the poetry of Dylan Thomas. *THSC* (1979) 159-202.

—— Welsh poetic stanza form and Dylan Thomas's 'I dreamed my genesis'. *THSC* (1982) 29-52.

—— An early work on Irish folklore and Dylan Thomas's 'A grief ago'. In *Celtic language, Celtic culture: a festschrift for Eric P. Hamp,* ed. A.T.E. Matonis and Daniel F. Melia. Van Nuys, California: Ford & Bailie, 1990. pp. 308-321. Considers possible influence of W.G. Wood-Martin's *Traces of the elder faiths of Ireland* (1902) on 'Alterwise by owl-light' and 'A grief ago'.

LEWELL, Robert. Thomas, Bishop and Williams. *Sewanee Review* 55 (1947) 493-503. Reviews Dylan Thomas, *Selected writings.*

LYONS, Robin. To be enjoyed, not revered. *NWR* 4,4 [16] (1992) 22-23. On an animated version of *Under Milk Wood.*

McCORMICK, Jane. Sorry, old Christian. *AWR* 18,42 (1970) 78-82. Considers Vernon Watkins' influence on Dylan Thomas.

McKAY, Don. Dot, line and circle: a structural approach to Dylan Thomas's imagery. *AWR* 18,41 (1969) 69-80.

—— Aspects of energy in the poetry of Dylan Thomas and Sylvia Plath. *Critical Quarterly* 16 (1974) 53-67.

—— What shall we do with a drunken poet? Dylan Thomas's poetic language. *Queen's Quarterly* 93 (1986) 794-807.

—— Crafty Dylan and the Altarwise sonnets: 'I build a flying tower and I pull it down'. *UTQ* 55 (1986) 375-394.

McKENNA, Rollie. *Portrait of Dylan: a photographer's memoir.* London:

Dent, 1982. 111 p.: chiefly ill. Incl. Introduction, by John Malcolm Brinnin.

MACLAREN-ROSS, Julian. *Memoirs of the forties.* Harmondsworth: Penguin, 1984. Incl. The polestar neighbour, pp. 118-134. – First published 1956.

MAGALHAES, Joaquin Manuel. Dylan Thomas: consequencia da literatura e do real na sua poesia. Lisbon: Assiro e Alvin, 1981. 299 p. (Cadernos peninsulares: Ensaio especial; 7) Incl. Portuguese translations of eleven poems.

MARUCCI, Franco. *Il senso interrotto: autonomia e codificazione nella poesia di Dylan Thomas.* Ravenna: Longo, [1976]. 199 p. (Il portico; 59: Sezione letteratura straniera).

MATHIAS, Roland. A merry manshape, or Dylan Thomas at a distance. *DL* 5,13 (1954) 30-39.

—— A niche for Dylan Thomas. *PW* 9,2 (1973) 51-74.

—— *A ride through the wood: essays on Anglo-Welsh literature.* Bridgend: Poetry Wales Press, 1985. Incl: Lord Cutglass, twenty years after [on Dylan Thomas], pp. 57-78 – Any minute or dark day now: the writing of *Under Milk Wood*, pp. 79-87.

MAUD, Ralph N. Dylan Thomas's poetry. *Essays in Criticism* 4 (1954) 411-420.

—— Dylan Thomas astro-navigated. *Essays in Criticism* 5 (1955) 164-168. Review article on Elder Olson, *The poetry of Dylan Thomas.*

—— Dylan Thomas's first published poem. *Modern Language Notes* 74 (1959) 117-118.

—— Obsolete and dialect words as serious puns in Dylan Thomas. *English Studies* 41 (1960) 28-30.

—— Dylan Thomas' *Collected poems*: chronology of composition. *PMLA* 76 (1961) 292-297.

—— *The colour of saying: an anthology of verse spoken by Dylan Thomas,* ed. Ralph N. Maud and Aneirin Talfan Davies. London: Dent, 1963. Incl. Introduction, by Ralph N. Maud and Aneirin Talfan Davies, pp. xiii-xxv.

—— *Entrances to Dylan Thomas' poetry.* Pittsburg: University of Pittsburg Press, 1963. ix, 175 p. (Critical essays in modern literature). – U.K. edition: Lowestoft: Scorpion, 1963.

—— Paul Ferris, *Dylan Thomas. AWR* 62 (1978) 198-200. Letter.

—— Corrections to *Selected letters of Dylan Thomas. National Library of Wales Journal* 21 (1980) 435-440.

—— Dylan Thomas and Charles Olson. *Planet* 68 (1988) 68-72.

—— The new Dylan: editing the new *Collected poems. Planet* 71 (1988) 18-22.

MELCHIORI, Giorgio. *The tightrope walkers: studies of mannerism in modern English literature.* London: Routledge and Kegan Paul, 1956. Incl. Dylan Thomas: the poetry of vision, pp. 213-242.

MELLER, Horst. Zum literarischen Hintergrund von Dylan Thomas' *Under Milk Wood. Die Neueren Sprachen* 15 (1966) 49-58.

MEYER-CLASON, Curt. Die Anstrengung des Übersetzens: Dargestellt am Beispiel der Ubertragung eines Gedichts von Dylan Thomas. *Neue Rundschau*

101,4 (1990) 105-119. On the German-language translation of 'Do not go gentle into that good night'.

MIDDLETON, David Edward. Green countries: Dylan Thomas studies today. *Southern Review* 13 (1977) 845-852. Review article.

—— The ultimate kingdom: Dylan Thomas's 'Author's prologue' to *Collected poems. AWR* 63 (1978) 111-123.

—— Dylan Thomas. In *British poets, 1914-1945,* ed. Donald E. Stanford. Detroit: Gale Research, 1983. (Dictionary of literary biography; 20). pp. 365-394.

MILLER, James E. and others. *Start with the sun: studies in the Whitman tradition.* Nebraska: University of Nebraska Press, 1960. Incl. Whitman and Thomas: of monkeys, nudes, and the good gray poet, by Bernice Slote and James E. Miller, pp. 169-190.

MILLER, James E. Whitman and Thomas: the yawp and the gab. In *The presence of Walt Whitman: selected papers from the English Institute,* ed. R.W.B. Lewis. New York: Columbia University Press, 1962. pp. 137-163.

MILLER, Michael. Whitman's influence on Dylan Thomas's 'Poem in October', *Walt Whitman Review* 27,4 (1981) 155-158.

MILLS, Ralph. Dylan Thomas: the endless monologue. *Accent* 20 (1960) 114-139.

—— Dylan Thomas: poetry and process. In *Four ways of modern poetry,* ed. Nathan A. Scott. Richmond, Virginia: John Knox Press, 1965. pp. 51-69.

MONTGOMERY, Brother Benilde. The function of ambiguity in 'A refusal to mourn the death, by fire, of a child in London'. *AWR* 63 (1978) 125-129.

MOORE, Geoffrey. Dylan Thomas. *Kenyon Review* 17 (1955) 258-277.

MORGAN, George. Llareggub: espace utopique, ou, la représentation de la ville dans *Under Milk Wood. Cycnos* 1 (1984) 5-13.

—— Structuring utopia: spaces and places in *Under Milk Wood.* In *Pays de Galles, Ecosse, Irlande: actes du Congrès de Brest, Mai 1987.* Brest: Centre de Recherches Bretonnes et Celtiques, 1987. (Cahiers de Bretagne Occidentale; 7). pp. 77-101.

—— Au-delà du seuil noir: une relecture de 'After the funeral' de Dylan Thomas. *Cycnos* 3 (1986-87) 129-145.

—— Dylan Thomas and the ghost of Shakespeare. *Cycnos* 5 (1989) 113-121.

MORGAN, W. John. Evans, Thomas and Lewis. *Twentieth Century,* Oct 1956, 322-329. On Caradoc Evans, Dylan Thomas and Saunders Lewis.

MORTON, Richard. Notes on the imagery of Dylan Thomas. *English Studies* 43 (1962) 155-164.

MOYNIHAN, William Trumbull. Dylan Thomas and the biblical rhythm. *PMLA* 79 (1964) 631-647.

—— *The craft and art of Dylan Thomas.* London: Oxford University Press, 1966. xvi, 304 p.

MURDOCH, Brian. Überhaupt nichts los: some comments on Alfred Andersch and Dylan Thomas. *Neophilologus* 75,1 (1991) 11-20. Compares *Sansibar and Under Milk Wood.*

MURDY, Louise Baughan. *Sound and sense in Dylan Thomas's poetry.* The Hague: Mouton, 1966. 172 p. Incl. bibliography, pp. 151-172.

MURPHY, B.W. Creation and destruction: notes on Dylan Thomas. *British Journal of Medical Psychology* 41 (1969) 149-168.

NEMAN, Beth. A stylistic study of Dylan Thomas's 'Altarwise by owl-light'. *Language and Style* 18,3 (1985) 302-315.

NISBET, Robert. Young dog in Swansea: Dylan Thomas's artistic relationship to the people of his native town. *Planet* 45-46 (1978) 37-41.

—— Dream and innocence: on Dylan Thomas's prose. *Planet* 48 (1979) 37-43.

NOSAKA, Masashi. On dualism and consciousness in Dylan Thomas. *Language and Culture* 1 (1982) 1-22.

NOWOTTNY, Winifred. *The language poets use.* University of London: Athlone Press, 1962. Chapt. 8, Symbolism and obscurity, pp. 174-222. – Analyses 'There was a saviour'.

OLSON, Elder. *The poetry of Dylan Thomas.* Chicago: University of Chicago Press, 1954. vii, 164 p. Incl. Appendix C: Bibliography, by William H. Huff, pp. 102-146.

ORME, David. *Under Milk Wood.* Hodder & Stoughton, 1987. 48 p.: ill.. (Q series). Notes 'for use with mixed-ability groups in the middle years of the secondary school'.

ORMEROD, David. The central image in Dylan Thomas' 'Over Sir John's Hill'. *English Studies* 49 (1968) 449-450.

ORMOND, John. The vision and art of Dylan Thomas. *South Wales Evening Post,* 8 Nov 1952, 4:G-I. Review of Dylan Thomas, *Collected poems.*

PAANANEN, Victor N. Dylan Thomas. In *St. James guide to biography, ed.* Paul E. Schellinger. Chicago; London: St. James Press, 1991. pp. 766-768. Surveys 13 biographical studies.

PAGE, Christopher. Dylan and the scissormen. *AWR* 23,52 (1974) 76-81.

PATRIDGE, A.C. *The language of modern poetry.* London: Deutsch, 1976. Incl. discussion of Dylan Thomas, pp. 319-324.

PEACH, Linden. *The prose writings of Dylan Thomas.* Basingstoke: Macmillan, 1988. xii, 144 p. (Macmillan studies in twentieth-century literature).

PENG, Su Soon. 'The force that through the green fuse drives the flower': a stylistic observation. *Southeast Asian Review of English* 12-13 (1986) 107-122.

PERKINS, D.C. *The world of Dylan Thomas.* Swansea: Celtic Educational (Services) Ltd., 1975. 79 p.: ill.

PESCHMANN, Hermann. Dylan Thomas, 1912 [sic]-1953: a critical appreciation. *English* 10,57 (1954) 84-87.

PETERS, Robert L. The uneasy faith of Dylan Thomas: a study of the last poems. *Fresco* [University of Detroit] 9 (1958) 25-29.

PFISTER, Manfred. Die Villanelle in der englischen Modern: Joyce, Empson and Dylan Thomas. *Archiv fur das Studium der Neueren Sprachen und Literaturen* 219 (1982) 296-312.

PHILLIPS, Arthur. Dylan under Milkwood. *South Atlantic Quarterly* 78 (1979) 428-435. On Thomas at Laugharne.

PIKOULIS, John. On editing Dylan Thomas. *AWR* 21,48 (1972) 115-128. Occasioned by *Dylan Thomas: the poems,* ed. Daniel Jones (1971).

POOLE, Richard. Dylan Thomas, Ted Hughes and Byron: two instances of indebtedness. *AWR* 24,54 (1975) 119-124. Reply by Aneirin Talfan Davies: 25,55 (1975) 127-129.

POST, Robert M. Performing syllabic verse. *Literature in Perfomance: a Journal of Literary and Performing Art* 4,2 (1984) 10-19. Considers 'Fern Hill', and poems by W.H. Auden and Marianne Moore.

PRATT, Annis Vilas. *Dylan Thomas' early prose: a study in creative mythology.* Pittsburg: University of Pittsburg Press 1970. 229 p.

PRATT, Terrance M. Adventures in the poetry trade: Dylan Thomas and Arthur Rimbaud. *English Language Notes* 24,4 (1987) 65-73.

PRESS, John. *Rule and energy: trends in British poetry since the second world war.* London: Oxford University Press, 1963. Incl. discussion of Dylan Thomas, pp. 32-38.

—— *A map of modern English verse.* London: Oxford University Press, 1969. Incl. Dylan Thomas, pp. 218-229.

PRYS-JONES, A.G. Death shall have no dominion. *DL* 5,13 (1954) 26-29.

PUDNEY, John. Wales loses a great poet. *PP,* 28 Nov 1953, 25.

READ, Bill. *The days of Dylan Thomas.* London: Weidenfeld and Nicolson, 1964. 189 p.: ill. With photographs by Rollie McKenna and others.

RECKWITZ, Erhard. *The fused vision: Dylan Thomas' Poetik der Simultaneitat.* Essen: Die Blaue Eule, 1989. 154 p.

REDDINGTON, Alphonsus M. *Dylan Thomas: a journey from darkness to light.* New York: Paulist Press, 1968. vii, 100 p.

REES, Alan. Dylan Thomas and the BBC. *Listener,* 18 Oct 1973, 516-517, 520-521.

REES, Goronwy. Back to the Boat House. *TLS,* 29 Apr 1977, 505. Review article on Paul Ferris, *Dylan Thomas*, Daniel Jones, *My friend Dylan Thomas*.

REID, B.L. Four winds. *Sewanee Review* 87 (1979) 273-288. Reminiscences of Dylan Thomas, Robert Frost, T.S. Eliot and Ezra Pound.

RING, Lars. Dylan Thomas: walesaren i Mjolkhagen. *Kulturtidskiften Horizont: Organ for Svenska Osterbottens Litteraturforening* 33,4 (1986) 88-92. *On Under Milk Wood.*

ROBERTS, Lynette. Parts of an autobiography. *PW* 19,2 (1983) 30-50. Incl. accounts of Dylan Thomas's visits.

RODWAY, Allan. *The craft of criticism.* Cambridge: Cambridge University Press, 1982. Incl. 'Poem in October': Dylan Thomas, pp. 17-24.

ROSENTHAL, M.L. *The modern poets.* New York: Oxford University Press, 1960. Incl. Dylan Thomas and recent British verse, pp. 203-224.

ROSS, Ethel. *Dylan Thomas and the amateur theatre.* Swansea: Swansea Little Theatre, [n.d.]. [8] p.: ill.

—— The Dylan I knew, 3. The myth of the rake's progress. *WM,* 1 Nov 1983, 8:B-E. Interview with Terry Campbell.

SANDQUIST, Eric J. 'In country heaven': Dylan Thomas and Rilke. *Camparative Literature* 31 (1979) 63-78.

SANDYS, Nicholas. Dylan and the stormy petrel. *WM,* 7 Jan 1961, 5. On Thomas and Caradoc Evans.

SANESI, Roberto. *Nella coscia del gigante bianco.* Pollenza: La Nuova Foglio, [1976?]. 96 p. Incl. Italian translation of 'In the white giant's thigh'.

—— *Dylan Thomas.* Milano: Garzanti, 1977. 225 p. (I Garzanti argomenti). First published 1960.

SASTRI, P.S. *Dylan Thomas: poet of the romantic revival.* Gwalior: Kitab Ghar, 1980. 95 p.

SAUNDERS, Thomas. Religious elements in the poetry of Dylan Thomas. *Dalhousie Review* 45 (1965) 492-497.

SCARFE, Francis. The poetry of Dylan Thomas. *Horizon,* Nov 1940, 226-239.

SCHERTING, Jack. Echoes of *Look homeward angel* in Dylan Thomas's *A child's Christmas in Wales. Studies in Short Fiction* 9 (1972) 404-406.

SCHMIDT, Michael. *An introduction to 50 modern British poets.* London: Pan, 1979. (Pan literature guides). Incl. Dylan Thomas, pp. 278-284.

SCHOPF, Alfred. 'Especially when the October wind' von Dylan Thomas: ein poetologisches Gedicht? *Literaturwissenschaftliches Jahrbuch im Auftrage der Gorres-Gesellschaft* 28 (1987) 99-113.

SCHVEY, Henry I. Dylan Thomas and surrealism. *Dutch Quarterly Review of Anglo-American Letters* 52 (1975) 83-97.

SCHWARZ, Daniel R. And the wild wings were raised: sources and meaning in Dylan Thomas' 'A winter's tale'. *Twentieth Century Literature* 25 (1979) 85-98.

—— Dylan Thomas. In *Reference guide to English literature,* ed. D.L. Kirkpatrick. 2nd ed. 3 vols. Chicago; London: St James Press, 1991. Vol. 2, pp. 1317-1319.

SEIB, Kenneth. *Portrait of the artist as a young dog:* Dylan's *Dubliners. Modern Fiction Studies* 24 (1978) 239-246.

SERGEANT, Howard. The religious development of Dylan Thomas. *Review of English Literature* 3,1 (1962) 59-67.

SEYMOUR, Tryntje Van Ness. *Dylan Thomas' New York.* Maryland: Stemmer House, 1978. [149] p.: chiefly ill. Text and photographs by T. Van Ness Seymour, with selections from *Under Milk Wood.* – Also limited edition: Salisbury, Conn.: Lime Rock Press, 1977. 500 copies.

SHAPIRO, Karl. Dylan Thomas. *Poetry* 87 (1955) 100-110.

SHEPHERD, Rupert. *Caitlin & Dylan: an artist's view of the Macnamara and Thomas background drawings & paintings, 1932-1977.* Cardiff: National Museum of Wales, 1977. [10] p.: ill. Exhibition catalogue.

SHIRES, Linda M. *British poetry of the second world war.* London: Macmillan, 1985. Incl. Dylan Thomas: the early poetry; Thomas in the 1940s, pp. 40-48.

SIMPSON, Louis. *Studies of Dylan Thomas, Allen Ginsberg, Sylvia Plath and Robert Lowell.* London: Macmillan, 1979. Incl. The colour of saying, pp. 3-42. – U.S. edition: *A revolution in taste.* New York: 1978.

SINCLAIR, Andrew. *Dylan Thomas: poet of his people.* London: Michael Joseph, 1975. 240 p.: ill. – U.S. edition: *Dylan Thomas: no man more magical.* New York: Holt, Rinehart & Winston, 1975.

SINNOCK, Don. *The Dylan Thomas landscape,* photographs and text by Don Sinnock; captions from the writings of Dylan Thomas. Swansea: Celtic Educational (Services) Ltd., 1975. 96 p.: chiefly ill.

SLOCOMBE, Marie and Patrick Saul. Dylan Thomas discography. *Recorded Sound: Journal of the British Institute of Recorded Sound* 1 (1961) 80-95.

SLOTE, Bernice and James Miller. Whitman and Thomas: of monkeys, nudes, and the good gray poet, by Bernice Slote and James E. Miller. In *Start with the sun: studies in the Whitman tradition,* by James Miller and others. Nebraska: University of Nebraska Press, 1960. pp. 169-190.

SMITH, A.J. Ambiguity as poetic shift. *Critical Quarterly* 4 (1962) 68-74. Considers Dylan Thomas' 'Our eunuch dreams'.

SNELL-HORNBY, Mary. Zur sprachlichen Norm in der literarischen Übersetzung. *Bulletin de la Commission Interuniversitaire Suisse de Linguistique Appliquée* 49 (1989) 51-60. Considers *A child's Christmas in Wales, Animal Farm,* and *Der Wegwerfer* by Heinrich Boll.

SPENDER, Stephen. *Poetry since 1939.* London: Longmans, 1946. Incl. discussion of Dylan Thomas, pp. 44-47.

STANFORD, Derek. *Dylan Thomas: a literary study.* London: Neville Spearman, 1954. 194 p. – New edition: 1964, with, A literary post-mortem, pp. 189-205.

——— *In defence of ignorance.* New York: Random House, 1960. Incl. Dylan Thomas, pp. 171-186.

STEAD, Peter. Rebecca's seed falls on stony ground. *NWR* 4,4 [16] (1992) 12-13. Review of the Karl Francis film,'Rebecca's daughters', based on an original script by Dylan Thomas.

STEARNS, Marshall W. Unsex the skeleton: notes on the poetry of Dylan Thomas. *Sewanee Review* 52 (1944) 424-440.

STEPHENS, Raymond. Dylan Thomas and the biographers. *Planet* 48 (1979). 34-37.

SUIED, Alain. Le poète du siècle: Dylan Thomas (1914-1955). *Courrier du Centre Internationale d'Études Poétiques,* Nov-Dec 1990, 5-17.

SWANSEA Public Libraries Committee. *Two Swansea poets: Dylan Thomas and Vernon Watkins: 3rd-12th July, 1969.* Swansea: Swansea Public Libraries Committee, 1969. 15 p. Incl. bibliographies. – Exhibition catalogue compiled by Stanley Yonge.

SYMONS, Julian. Obscurity and Dylan Thomas. *Kenyon Review* 2 (1940) 61-71.

TAIG, Thomas. Swansea between the wars. *AWR* 17,39 (1968) 23-32.

TEDLOCK, E.W. *Dylan Thomas, the legend and the poet: a collection of biographical and critical essays,* ed. E.W. Tedlock. London: Heinemann, 1960. x, 283 p. Contents: Part 1. The man; Biographical essays, by Suzanne Roussillat, Daniel Jones, Cecil Price, Pamela Hansford Johnson, Augustus John, William Jay Smith, Ralph Wishart, Lawrence Durrell, Roy Campbell, John Lehmann, Mario Luzi, Theodore Roethke, Alastair Reid, Richard Eberhart, David Daiches, Marjorie Adix, Philip Burton, George Barker, John Davenport, G.S. Fraser, Louis MacNeice, pp. 3-87 – Part 2. The poet; Map of Llareggub, by Hugh Gordon Porteus, pp. 91-95 – Dylan Thomas: a pioneer, by Francis Scarfe, pp. 96-112 – Unsex the skeleton: notes on the poetry of Dylan Thomas, by Marshall W. Stearns, pp. 113-131 – In defence of Dylan Thomas, by Robert Horan, pp. 132-140 – The poetry of Dylan Thomas, by D.S. Savage, pp. 141-147 – Comment on Dylan Thomas, by Edith Sitwell, pp. 148-150 – A comment, by Henry Gibson, pp. 151-154 – How much me now your acrobatics amaze, by Geoffrey Grigson, pp. 155-167 – Dylan Thomas, by E. Glyn Jones, pp.

168-185 – The poetry of Dylan Thomas, by David Aivaz, pp. 186-210
– One ring-tailed roarer to another, by Theodore Roethke, pp. 211-213
– Dylan Thomas: yes and no [reviews by John Graddon and Geoffrey
Johnson], pp. 214-222 – Dylan Thomas: rhetorician in mid-career, by
Cid Corman, pp. 223-228 – The poetry of Dylan Thomas, by Elder
Olson, pp. 229-235 – The religous poet, by W.S. Merwin, pp. 236-247
– Dylan Thomas, by Geoffrey Moore, pp. 248-268 – Dylan Thomas,
by Karl Shapiro, pp. 269-283.

THOMAS, Aeronwy [as Aeronwy Thomas-Ellis]. *Christmas and other memories:
a daughter remembers Dylan.* London: Amwy Press, [198?]. 16 p.: ill. Incl.:
Going back to Laugharne, pp. 3-7 – Our poisonous tea party for an
amorous student, pp. 9-12 – Christmas: when Dad showed goodwill
toward children, pp. 12-16. – Reprinted from *WM*, 30 May 1981, 8; 6
Nov 1978, 10; 7 Nov 1978, 8. – Also in Aeronwy Thomas, *Poesie e ricordi:
poems and memories,* ed. Francesca Albarosa Acanfora. Turin: Pedrini, 1987.
English and Italian.

—— Memories: memento mori. *NWR* 4,4 [16] (1992) 28-29. On a recent
visit to the Boat House.

THOMAS, Caitlin. *Leftover life to kill.* London: Putnam, 1957. 240 p.

—— *Not quite posthumous letter to my daughter.* London: Putnam, 1963.
174 p.

—— *Caitlin: a warring absence.* London: Secker & Warburg, 1986. xvi, 212
p.: ill. Written jointly with George Tremlett. – Dust wrapper title: *Caitlin:
life with Dylan Thomas.* – U.S. edition: *Caitlin: life with Dylan Thomas.* New
York: Holt, 1987.

THOMAS, Gwyn. Dylan had unique gift of patriotic expression. *WM,* 29
Jan 1954, 3:F. Incl. extracts from talk on Dylan Thomas given to Barry
Rotarians.

—— *A Welsh eye.* London: Hutchinson, 1964. Discusses Thomas, pp. 94-
97.

THOMAS, M. Wynn. Unfamiliar affections: Dylan Thomas and the novelists.
*Swansea Review* 10 (1993) 45-93. On the role of the poet in Kingsley Amis,
*The old devils* and Marcel Williams, *Diawl y Wenallt.*

THOMAS, R. George. Bard on a raised hearth: Dylan Thomas and his craft.
*AWR* 12,30 (1962) 11-20.

—— Dylan Thomas: a poet of Wales? *English* 14 (1964) 140-145.

—— Dylan Thomas and some early readers. PW 9,2 (1973) 3-19.

THOMPSON, Kent. An approach to the early poems of Dylan Thomas. *AWR*
14,34 (1964-65) 81-89.

THURSLEY, Geoffrey. *The ironic harvest: English poetry in the twentieth century.*
London: Arnold, 1974. Incl. Dylan Thomas: Merlin as sponger, pp.
121-136.

THWAITE, Anthony. Dylan Thomas. In *Contemporary poets,* ed. James Vinson.
2nd ed. London: St James Press; New York, St Martin's Press, 1975. pp.
1802-1806.

—— *Twentieth-century English poetry: an introduction.* London: Heinemann,
1978. Incl. Dylan Thomas, pp. 72-80.

TINDALL, William York. *A reader's guide to Dylan Thomas.* London: Thames
& Hudson, 1962. 317 p. A poem-by-poem analysis.

—— The poetry of Dylan Thomas. In *On contemporary literature,* ed. Richard Kostelanetz. New York: Avon Books, 1964. pp. 607-615.

TINKLER, Valerie. Dylan Thomas as poet and story teller. *Dutch Quarterly Review* 11 (1981) 222-237.

TOLLEY, A.T. *The poetry of the thirties.* London: Gollancz, 1975. Incl. discussion of Dylan Thomas, pp. 252-277.

—— *The poetry of the forties.* Manchester: Manchester University Press, 1985. Incl. The lovely gift of the gab: Dylan Thomas, pp. 87-100.

TREMLETT, George. *Dylan Thomas: in the mercy of his means.* London: Constable, 1991. xxxviii, 206 p.: ill. A biography.

TREECE, Henry. *Dylan Thomas: dog among the fairies.* London: Lindsay Drummond, 1949. xiii, 159 p. New edition: Benn, 1956.

—— Chalk sketch for a genius. *DL* 5,13 (1954). 18-23.

TRICK, Bert. The young Dylan Thomas. *Texas Quarterly* 9,2 (1966) 36-49.

TRIPP, John. Llareggub revisited. *London Welshman,* Summer 1972, 11. On Welsh premiere of film of *Under Milk Wood.*

UNTERMEYER, Louis. *Lives of the poets.* New York: Simon & Schuster, 1959. With chapter on Dylan Thomas.

VERGHESE, C. Paul. Religion in Dylan Thomas's poetry. *Literary Criterion* 8 (1969) 35-41.

VOLSIK, Paul. Neo-Romanticism and the poetry of Dylan Thomas. *Études Anglaises* 42 (1989) 39-54.

WAIN, John. *Preliminary essays.* London: Macmillan, 1957. Incl. Dylan Thomas: a review of his *Collected poems,* pp. 180-185.

—— Dylan Thomas. In *English poetry,* ed. Alan Sinfield. London: Sussex, 1977. pp. 216-228.

WATKINS, Gwen. A newly discovered letter: Dylan Thomas to Vernon Watkins. *AWR* 21, 48 (1972) 29-34.

—— *Portrait of a friend.* Llandysul: Gomer Press, 1983. 226 p.: ill. – U.S. edition: *Dylan Thomas and Vernon Watkins: portrait of a friendship.* Seattle: University of Washington Press, 1983.

WATKINS, Vernon. Mr. Dylan Thomas: innovation and tradition. *Times,* 10 Nov 1953, 11:D. Obituary.

—— A poem by Dylan Thomas. *Times,* 2 Aug 1955, 9:G. On 'Do not go gentle into that good night'.

—— Dylan Thomas in America. *Encounter,* Jun 1956, 77-79. Prompted by John Malcolm Brinnin's *Dylan Thomas in America.*

—— Dylan Thomas. *Observer,* 1 Dec 1957, 6:G. Letter in reply to Stephen Spender's review of *Letters to Vernon Watkins,* 24 Nov 1957. – Further letters: 8 Dec (Spender), 15 Dec (Watkins).

—— Behind the fabulous curtain. *Poetry,* May 1961, 124-125. Review of *Dylan Thomas: the legend and the poet,* ed. E.W. Tedlock.

—— Swansea. *Texas Quarterly* 4,4 (1961) 59-64. In this issue Vernon Watkins also contributes (p. 54) an introduction to 'A painter's studio', a draft of a television programme partly by Dylan Thomas.

—— Dylan Marlais Thomas. In *The concise encyclopedia of English and American poets and poetry,* ed. Stephen Spender and Donald Hall. 2nd ed. London: Hutchinson, 1970. pp. 306-307.

WEINBERGER, C.J. Dylan Thomas's Paradise and Calvary. *AWR* 21,47 (1972) 148-149. Discusses 'In the beginning'.

WEST, Paul. Dylan Thomas: the position in calamity. *Southern Review* (1967) 922-943.

WILLIAMS, A.R. A dictionary for Dylan Thomas. *DL* 3,9 (1952) 30-36.

WILLIAMS, Forrest. Detour to Laugharne. *Colorado Quarterly* 3 (1954) 94-95.

WILLIAMS, Marcel. *Diawl y Wenallt.* Talybont: Y Lolfa, 1990. 157 p. Controversial novel (in Welsh) concerning Dylan Thomas. Review: *Planet* 84 (1990-91) 93-95 (Twm Morys).

WILLIAMS, Raymond. Dylan Thomas's play for voices. *Critical Quarterly* 1 (1959) 18-26.

WILLIAMS, Robert Coleman. *A concordance to the* Collected poems of Dylan Thomas. Lincoln, Nebraska: University of Nebraska Press, 1986. 582 p. Keyed to the 1954 printing of *Collected poems*.

WINTERS, Shelley. *Best of times, worst of times.* London: Muller, 1989. Describes Thomas in Hollywood, pp. 30-40.

WOODCOCK, George. Notes on the poetry, 2. Dylan Thomas and the Welsh scene. *Poetry and Poverty* 7 (1954) 20-25.

—— Dylan Thomas and the Welsh environment. *Arizona Quarterly* 10 (1954) 293-305.

YOUNG, Alan. Image as structure: Dylan Thomas and poetic meaning. *Critical Quarterly* 17 (1975) 333-345.

ZHOU, Jiang. Dylan Thomas. *Foreign Literatures* 11 (1986) 58-66.

# B (ii). Publications about Dylan Thomas: Theses

ACKERMAN, John [as J.A. Jones]. The works of Dylan Thomas in relation to his Welsh environment. MA thesis. University of London (Kings), 1959.

—— The role of nature in the poetry of Edward Thomas, Dylan Thomas, Vernon Watkins and R.S. Thomas. PhD thesis. University of London (Birkbeck), 1981.

ADACHI, Kenneth. Theme and technique in the poetry of Dylan Thomas. MA thesis. University of Toronto, 1958.

ASTLEY, Russell. The stations of the breath: a study of end-rhyme in the poetry of Dylan Thomas. MA thesis. Temple University, 1967.

BROWNING, Grayson D. The poetry of Dylan Thomas. MA thesis. University of Texas at Austin, 1955.

BURDETTE, Robert Kenley. Dylan Thomas and the Gnostic religion. PhD thesis. University of Michigan, 1964. 200 p.

BURKE, Thomas Edmund. A descriptive catalogue of the Dylan Thomas collection at the University of Texas at Austin. PhD thesis. University of Texas at Austin, 1972. 343 p.

CARROLL, Sherman Louis. The early poetry of Dylan Thomas. PhD thesis. Harvard University, 1974.

CHANDLER, Patricia Gail. Gerard Manley Hopkins and Dylan Thomas: a study in computational stylistics. PhD thesis. Louisiana State University, 1970. 151 p.

CHANELES, Sol. The metaphor of Dylan Thomas. MA thesis. New York University, 1949.

CLAIBORNE, Jay W. The rub of love: a study of humor in the writings of Dylan Thomas. MA thesis. University of Texas at Austin, 1965.

CUMMINGS, David E. The langauge of Dylan Thomas. MA thesis. Columbia University, 1954.

DANIELS, John H. The legend of the green chapel: a study in the background and attitude of Dylan Thomas. MA thesis. Syracuse University, 1955.

DAVIES, Geraint E. The themes of childhood and education in the works of Dylan Thomas and Emyr Humphreys. MEd dissertation. University of Wales (Cardiff), 1981. 119 p. Incl. The themes of childhood and education in the works of Dylan Thomas, pp. 31-65.

DAVIES, Walford D. A critical study of the prose works of Dylan Thomas, with a consideration of uncollected and unpublished poems. BLitt thesis. University of Oxford, 1966.

DEANE, Sheila McColm. Bardic style in the poetry of Gerard Manley Hopkins, William Butler Yeats, and Dylan Thomas. PhD thesis. University of Western Ontario, 1987.

DELAP, Anne M. The development of Dylan Thomas' use of private symbolism in poetry. MA thesis. Oklahoma State University, 1967.

DHALL, A.D. Dylan Thomas: a critical analysis and re-appraisal of the earlier poetry. MA thesis. University of Manchester, 1962.

DOLZANI, Michael. Unending lightning: Dylan Thomas and the theory of metaphor. PhD thesis. University of Toronto, 1987.

DOWNS, Richard Walter. Dylan Thomas' verse considered in the light of his poetic aims. MA thesis. University of Wales (Swansea), 1978.

FAULK, Carolyn Sue. The Apollonian and Dionysian modes in lyric poetry and their development in the poetry of W.B. Yeats and Dylan Thomas. PhD thesis. University of Illinois at Urbana (Champaign), 1963. 377 p.

FAUST, Richard L. A study of Dylan Thomas. MA thesis. Columbia University, 1956.

FERGUSON, Suzanne C. The bellowing ark: Dylan Thomas's 'Ballad of the long-legged bait'. MA thesis. Vanderbilt University, 1961.

FOSBERG, Mary Dee Harris. Computer collation of manuscript poetry: Dylan Thomas' 'Poem on his birthday'. PhD thesis. University of Texas at Austin, 1975. 196 p.

FRANCO, June W. The living skein: a stylistic study of Dylan Thomas. PhD thesis. North Texas State University, 1978. 158 p.

GHAREEB, M.A. Studies in the vocabulary of Dylan Thomas's poetry. PhD thesis. University of Sheffield, 1987.

GILBERTSON, Philip Nathan. Time and the timeless in the poetry of T.S. Eliot, Dylan Thomas, and Edwin Muir. PhD thesis. University of Kentucky, 1971. 215 p.

GINGERICH, Martin E. The intricate image: two poems of Dylan Thomas. MA thesis. University of Maine, 1961.

—— Time and persona in the poetry of Dylan Thomas. PhD thesis. Ohio University, 1967. 165 p.

GRAVES, Allen Wallace. Difficult contemporary short stories: William

Faulkner, Katherine Ann Porter, Dylan Thomas, Eudora Welty and Virginia Woolf. PhD thesis. University of Washington, 1954.

GREENWAY, William Henry. The poetic diction of Dylan Thomas. PhD thesis. Tulane University, 1984. 141 p.

GRIMES, Dorothy Gatlin. Phonemes, distinctive acoustic features, and phonesthemes in Dylan Thomas's *Collected poems*: a chronological study. PhD thesis. Auburn University, 1978. 382 p.

HAGGARD, Ann B. A morphological study of the process of compounding in the poetry of Dylan Thomas. MA thesis. Auburn University, 1969.

HALE, Terence John. Aspects of the lexis, syntax and semantics of Dylan Thomas's 'Fern Hill'. MA thesis. University of Wales (Bangor), 1984.

HALPEREN, Max. Moonless acre: the poetry of Dylan Thomas. MA thesis. Florida State University, 1952.

HARDESTY, Margaret Anne. An examination of the sacremental vision of Dylan Thomas: its sources, analogues, and its expression in his poetry. PhD thesis. State University of New York at Binghamton, 1974. 213 p.

HAUSMAN, Margaret Jane. Syntactic disordering in modern poetry: index, icon, symbol (Peirce). PhD thesis. Brown University, 1988. 146 p. Incl. discussion of Dylan Thomas.

HAVEMANN, C.P. Obscurity and mythic quest for shape: a discussion of Dylan Thomas' 'Altarwise by owl-light'. MA thesis. Rice University, 1968.

HELMSTETTER, Carol Ruth. The prose fiction of Dylan Thomas. PhD thesis. Northwestern University, 1968. 198 p.

HOGGINS, Carolyn. The nightmare world of Dylan Thomas. MA thesis. Texas Technological University, 1964.

HOGLER, Raymond Louis. Diction and metaphor in the poetry of Dylan Thomas. PhD thesis. University of Colorado at Boulder, 1972. 218 p.

HORNICK, Lita. The intricate image: a study of Dylan Thomas. PhD thesis. Columbia University, 1958. 258 p.

HUANG, C-H. Dylan Thomas's 'Fern Hill': a stylistic interpretation in the context of poetry and the teaching of English as a foreign language. MLitt thesis. University of Edinburgh, 1980.

JASIECKI, Dorothy. The preposition in the poetry of Dylan Thomas. MA thesis. Barry College, 1966.

JO, Sue-Jin. Dylan Thomas and the tradition of the romantic journey. MA thesis. Columbia University, 1966.

JONES, Benjamin W. A study of four poems by Dylan Thomas. MA thesis. Columbia University, 1956.

KANNEL, Gregory Joseph. Word, structure, and meaning in the poetry of Dylan Thomas. PhD thesis. Kent State University, 1969. 116 p.

KAPPUS, Dieter. Die dichterische Entwicklung von Dylan Thomas. Doctoral thesis. University of Freiburg, 1961.

KARRER, Wolgang. Die Metaphorik in den *Collected poems* von Dylan Thomas: eine syntaktische Untersuchung. PhD thesis. University of Bonn, 1971.

KIDDER, Rushworth Moulton. Religious imagery in the poetry of Dylan Thomas. PhD thesis. Columbia University, 1969. 265 p.

KLEINMAN, Hyman H. The religious sonnets of Dylan Thomas. MA thesis. Columbia University, 1950.

KOHAK, Frances MacPherson. Concepts of time in the poetry of Dylan Thomas. PhD thesis. Boston University Graduate School, 1969. 176 p.

LAFLEUR, Thomas Walter. An explication of the religious sonnets of Dylan Thomas. MA thesis. Texas A & I University, 1987. 171 p.

LAMONT, Colin C. A survey of criticism of Dylan Thomas's poetry from 1934 to 1954, and a bibliography from 1934 to 1966. PhD thesis. University of Edinburgh, 1976. 473 p. Bibliography, pp. 415-473.

LANDER, Clara. Wheel of fire: the dynamics of Dylan Thomas. MA thesis. University of Manitoba, 1956.

LAWNICZAK, Donald. The recurrent image: a study of Dylan Thomas. MA thesis. University of Toledo, 1961.

LIGHTNER, Barbara E. Some creative-destructive processes in Dylan Thomas' poetry. MA thesis. University of Idaho, 1966.

LOESCH, Katherine Taylor. Prosodic patterns in the poetry of Dylan Thomas. PhD thesis. Northwestern University, 1961. 363 p.

McBREIN, William Augustine. Likeness in the themes and prosody of Gerard Manley Hopkins and Dylan Thomas. PhD thesis. St. John's University, 1959.

McGANN, Mary Evelyn. Voices from the dark: a study of the radio achievement of Norman Corwin, Archibald MacLeish, Louis MacNeice, Dylan Thomas, and Samuel Beckett. PhD thesis. Indiana University, 1979. 316 p.

McKAY, Donald Fleming. Mythological elements in the work of Dylan Thomas. PhD thesis. University of Wales (Swansea), 1971.

McNEES, Eleanor Jane. Towards a poetics of real presence: eucharistic poetry of John Donne, Gerard Manley Hopkins, Dylan Thomas and Geoffrey Hill. PhD thesis. University of Colorado at Boulder, 1984. 275 p.

MAUD, Ralph N. Language and meaning in the poetry of Dylan Thomas. PhD thesis. Harvard University, 1958.

MIDDLETON, David Edward. Subject-object relations: the romantic version of an epistemological problem and its transformation in the poetry of Dylan Thomas. PhD thesis. Louisiana State University, 1979. 2 vols. 787 p.

MILLER, Joseph J. The grammar of Dylan Thomas in *Collected poems*. MA thesis. Columbia University, 1959.

MILLS, Ralph J. The development of the apocalyptic vision in five modern poets. PhD thesis. Northwestern University, 1963.

MOFFETT, Ethel A. Dylan Marlais Thomas: man and metaphor. MA thesis. George Washington University, 1954.

MONRO, Colin J. The existentialist void and the divine image: the poetry of Dylan Thomas. MA thesis. University of British Columbia, 1962.

MORGAN, Nicholas David. The significance of dualism and paradox in the work of Dylan Thomas. MA thesis. University of Wales (Swansea), 1986.

MOYNIHAN, William Trumbull. Dylan Thomas and the auditory correlative. MA thesis. University of Connecticut, 1957.

—— The poetry of Dylan Thomas: a study of its meaning and unity. PhD thesis. Brown University, 1962. 236 p.

MURDY, Louise Baughan. Sound and meaning in Dylan Thomas's poetry. PhD thesis. University of Florida, 1962. 226 p.

NICHOLS, Margaret Foster. Singing towards anguish: the later works of Dylan Thomas. PhD thesis. Cornell University, 1983. 246 p.

NOVICK, Donald. The poetry of Dylan Thomas and his shaping conscience. MA thesis. Columbia University, 1958.

OCHSHORN, Myron. The poetry of Dylan Thomas. MA thesis. University of New Mexico, 1953.

O'HARA, James D. The religious poetry of Dylan Thomas. MA thesis. Columbia University, 1957.

PALMER, Richard Allen. Dylan Thomas and the metaphysical mode: a study of shared sensibilities. PhD thesis. University of Illinois at Urbana (Champaign), 1976. 292 p.

PARKINSON, S.C.M. Obscurity in the *Collected poems* of Dylan Thomas. PhD thesis. Trinity College, Dublin, 1982.

PHILLIPS, Louis J. The screen plays of Dylan Thomas. MA thesis. Hunter College, 1968.

PIORKOWSKI, Stephen. Dylan Thomas: poet and dramatist. MA thesis. Hunter College, 1964.

PRATT, Annis Vilas. The early prose of Dylan Thomas. PhD thesis. Columbia University, 1965. 179 p.

PYLE, Paul Christian. The idealist artist: five early stories by Dylan Thomas. MA thesis. Acadia University, 1974.

REESE, Bette. Dylan Thomas: a discussion of macabre and humorous elements in his early prose. MA thesis. Utah State University at Logan, 1967.

REIFER, May. Supernatural stories of Dylan Thomas. MA thesis. Columbia University, 1956.

RONAN, John J. Dylan Thomas' use of the Bible. MA thesis. University of Illinois at Chicago Circle, 1969.

RUARK, Henry G. Death is all metaphors: a study of the death theme in the poetry of Dylan Thomas. MA thesis. University of Massachusetts, 1965.

SANDERS, Charles. Poetic characteristics and problems of Dylan Thomas. MA thesis. University of North Carolina, 1958.

SCHOFF, Gretchen Holstein. The major prose of Dylan Thomas. PhD thesis. University of Wisconsin (Madison), 1966. 338 p.

SEARFOSS, Kristin. Hopkinsian influences on the poetry of Dylan Thomas. MA thesis. McGill University, 1990. 110 p.

SENNISH, Robert Brady. The early prose of Dylan Thomas. MA thesis. Columbia University, 1956.

SHIRES, Linda Marguerite. Keeping something alive: British poetry, 1939-1956. PhD thesis. University of Princeton, 1981. 280 p. Incl. discussion of Dylan Thomas, Vernon Watkins and Alun Lewis.

SMOOT, George Albert. Metamorphosis and Dylan Thomas' 'Ballad of the long-legged bait': the poetics of harmonious conflict. MA thesis. Syracuse University, 1967.

—— The poetry of Dylan Thomas: processes in the weather of the heart. PhD thesis. Syracuse University, 1974. 208 p.

SPANGLER, Donald R. A collection of explications of the poetry of Dylan Thomas. MA thesis. University of Pittsburg, 1954.

SPEYSER, Patricia Earle. The 'Ballad of the long-legged bait' worksheets. MA thesis. University of Buffalo, 1959.

STAFFORD, Tony J. Dylan Thomas: the obscurant. MA thesis. University of Texas at El Paso, 1961.

STALKER, James Curtis. The stylistic and interpretative functions of relative clauses in Dylan Thomas's poetry: a transformational analysis. PhD thesis. University of Wisconsin (Madison), 1970. 201 p.

STARK, Bruce Roderick. An essay in the linguistic analysis of literature: Bloomfieldian linguistics and Dylan Thomas' 'After the funeral'. PhD thesis. Columbia University, 1970. 395 p.

STEVENS, Elizabeth G. The symbolic imagery of sea, liquid and water in the early poems of Dylan Thomas. MA thesis. Columbia University, 1956.

THOMPSON, K.E. Dylan Thomas in Swansea. PhD thesis. University of Wales (Swansea), 1966.

THOMPSON, Thomas Norman. Patterns of imagery in the poetry of Dylan Thomas. PhD thesis. University of Pennsylvania, 1969. 259 p.

TIMMONS, Grace E. A study of the Welsh influence on Dylan Thomas' poetry. MA thesis. West Texas State University, 1967.

TREW, Claudia Smith. Blake's concept of the contrary states of innocence and experience applied to Dylan Thomas. MA thesis. Florida Atlantic University, 1989. 97 p.

VOGEL, Joseph F. Religious thought in the poetry of Dylan Thomas. MA thesis. University of Miami, 1960.

WEICK, G.P. 'I, in my intricate image': the poetic self-portrait in the poetry of Dylan Thomas. PhD thesis. University of London (Queen Mary), 1957.

WILLIAMS, Alix. Dylan Thomas' 'Under Milk Wood': radio play, stage play, opera, film, German translation. Doctoral thesis. University of Innsbruck, 1975.

WILLIAMS, Harry S. Some characteristics of the visionary poet: William Blake and Dylan Thomas. MA thesis. University of Maryland at College Park, 1969.

WOLFE, Leslie Rosenberg. The poems and poetics of Dylan Thomas: the life of his art. PhD thesis. University of Florida, 1970. 204 p.

YOUNG, A. Aspects of the reaction to dadaism and surrealism in English literature, 1916-46, with particular reference to the writings of Dylan Thomas. PhD thesis. University of Manchester, 1974.

ZIMAN, Anna P. 18 poems: with Dylan Thomas's accent on death. MA thesis. Columbia University, 1955.

# GWYN THOMAS (1913-1981)

A. Publications by Gwyn Thomas
  (i)  Books
  (ii) Selected contributions to books and periodicals

B. Publications about Gwyn Thomas

## A (i). Publications by Gwyn Thomas: Books

*The dark philosophers.* Boston: Little, Brown, 1947. 178 p.
—— In *Triad one,* ed. Jack Aistrop. London: Dobson, 1946. pp. 81-193.
—— *The sky of our lives: three novellas.·* Hutchinson, 1972. pp. 93-205.
—— *The alone to the alone* with *The dark philosophers* / afterword by Michael
Parnell. Carmarthen: Golden Grove Editions, 1988. 278 p.: front port.:
pbk. ISBN: 1-870876-15-6. Incl.: *The dark philosophers*, pp. 157-269 –
Afterword, pp. 273-278.

German trans.: *Die Liebe des Reverend Emmanuel,* tr. L . Ṭankhauser, ill. Frans
Masereel. Zürich: Büchergilde Gutenberg, 1951. 140 p.: ill.: pbk.

Norwegian trans.: *Pastor Emmanuel og Hans Kjærlighet,* tr. Fredrik Wulfsberg.
Oslo: Tiden, 1948. 143 p.

Russian trans.: *Bezvestnye filosofy,* tr. M. Abkina. Moscow: Izd. Inostr. Lit.,
1958. 112 p.: pbk.

*Where did I put my pity?: folk tales from the modern Welsh.* London:
Progress Publishing, 1946. 193 p. Contents: Oscar – Simeon – The couch,
my friend, is cold – Dust in the lonely wind – A spoonful of grief to taste
– Myself my desert.

*The alone to the alone.* London: Nicholson & Watson, 1947. 164 p.
—— *The alone to the alone* with *The dark philosophers* / afterword by Michael
Parnell. Carmarthen: Golden Grove Editions, 1988. 278 p.: front port.: pbk.
ISBN: 1-870876-15-6. Incl.: *The alone to the alone, pp.* 13-154 – Afterword,
pp. 273-278.

U.S. ed.: *Venus and the voters.* Boston: Little, Brown, 1948. 254 p.

Italian trans.: *Venere e gli elettori: romanzo.* Milano: Feltrinelli, 1957.

*All things betray thee.* London: Michael Joseph, 1949. 318 p.
—— Lawrence & Wishart, 1986. pbk. ISBN: 0-85315-664-6. Incl. introduction by Raymond Williams, pp. iii-x.
U.S. eds.: *Leaves in the wind.* Boston: Little, Brown, 1949. 307 p.
—— / with a new introduction by Maxell Geismar. New York: Monthly

Review Press, 1968. 307 p.

German ed.: Leipzig: Paul List Verlag, 1956. 337 p.: pbk. (Panther Books).

Bulgarian trans.: *Vsicko ti izmenja: roman,* tr. Boris Mindov. Sofia: Narodna Kultura, 1961. 332 p.

Polish trans.: *Liscie na wietrze: powiesc,* tr. Tadeusz Dehnel. Warszawa: Panstw. Instytut Wydawn., 1955. 400 p.: pbk.

Rumanian trans.: *Totul ti-e potrivnic,* tr. Ticu Arhip. Bucuresti: Editura Pentru Literatura Universala, 1962. 341 p.: pbk.

Russian trans.: *Vse izmenjaet tebe,* tr. I.A. Gorkin. Moscow: Izd. Inostr. Lit., 1959. 342 p.

*The world cannot hear you: a comedy of ancient desires.* London: Gollancz, 1951. 288 p.
—— Bath: Chivers, 1968. (Portway reprints).

U.S. ed.: Boston: Little, Brown, 1952.

Hungarian trans.: *Ösi vágyak komédiája: regény,* tr. Tamás Kaposi. Budapest: Európa Könyvkiadó, 1959. 420 p. Incl. Gwyn Thomas, by Mihaly Sükösd, pp. 411-420.

*Now lead us home.* London: Gollancz, 1952. 256 p.
—— Bath: Chivers, 1968. (Portway reprints).

*A frost on my frolic.* London: Gollancz, 1953. 285 p.
—— Bath: Chivers, 1968. (Portway reprints).

*The stranger at my side: a novel.* London: Gollancz, 1954. 255 p.

*A point of order: a novel.* London: Gollancz, 1956. 224 p.

*Gazooka and other stories.* London: Gollancz, 1957. 200 p. Contents: By that same door – O brother man – As it was in the beginning – Not even then – Gazooka – Little Fury – Where my dark lover lies – The teacher – Tomorrow I shall miss you less – The leaf that hurts the hand – A team of shadows – Have you counted the tooth marks? – The pot of gold at Fear's End.

*The love man: a novel.* London: Gollancz, 1958. 221 p.

U.S. ed.: *A wolf at dusk: a novel.* New York: Macmillan, 1959.

Italian trans.: *L'uomo dell'amore: romanzo,* tr. Bruno Tasso. Milano: Feltrinelli, 1960. 283 p.: pbk.

*Ring delirium 123.* London: Gollancz, 1960. 192 p. Contents: The fixers – Mamba my darkling – The living lute – Cantor Agonistes – Darkness and a face turning – The unquiet fleece – New every morning – Brightest

and best – The speaking shade – Bacchus bach – That vanished Canaan
– Arrayed like one of these – Land! Land! – After you Mr. Zeigfeld –
Hugo my friend – Pass the can – On leaving a lover – What's behind
you, Silcox? – A pace or two apart – An excessive autumn – Will you
have honey on them? – He knows, he knows – Clout that dreamer –
Say, watchman – Wind of innocence – A clutch of iron thrushes.

*The keep.* London: Elek Books, 1962. 116 p. A play in two acts. – First
published in *Plays of the year*, vol. 24, ed. J.C. Trewin. London: Elek, 1961.
pp. 119-232.
—— French, 1962. 'Acting edition'.

German trans.: *Das Nest (The keep): Komödie,* tr. Karl Fruchtmann.
Reinbek bei Hamburg: Rowohlt Theater-Verlag, [n.d.]. 148 p.: pbk.
Incl. Autobiographical note, pp [1-4].
—— *Träume in der Mäusefalle: Komödie,* tr. Karl Fruchtmann. Reinbek bei
Hamburg: Rowohlt, 1963.

*A Welsh eye* / drawings by John Dd. Evans. London: Hutchinson, 1964.
176 p.: ill. Reissued 1984, pbk. ISBN: 0-09-154061-5.

U.S. ed.: Battleboro, Vt.: Stephen Greene Press, 1965.

*A hatful of humours* / edited by Brian Hammond; illustrated by Peter Rush.
London: Schoolmaster Publishing Co., [1965]. 164 p.: pbk.: ill. Selection of
articles from *The Teacher.*

*The loot.* London: Cassell, 1965. 21 p.: pbk. (Eight plays; 8). Incl. Note on
the author, pp. 20-[21]. – Also in *Eight plays: book 2,* ed. Malcolm Stuart
Fellows. London: Cassell, 1965. pp. [1-20].

*A few selected exits.* London: Hutchinson, 1968. 212 p. ISBN: 0-09-
088350-0.
—— Bridgend: Seren Books, 1985. ISBN: 0-907476-57-0.

U.S. ed.: *A few selected exits: an autobiography of sorts.* Boston: Little, Brown,
1968. 239 p.: ill. Text slightly expanded.

*The lust lobby: stories.* London: Hutchinson, 1971. 223 p. ISBN: 0-09-
105470-2. Contents: Who that up there? – Good night Julius – Loud
noises, soft voices, no voices – The cordial return – The two-stool blues
– The touch – The foot and the snare – A time for time – Blue print –
The pelt of the Celt that bit me – A horse called Meadow Prospect – The
joyful – Blue ribbons for a black epoch – The treatment – The short spell
– A zone of hush – Another scalp for Willie Silcox – The virgin bands –
The oompa – Show me – A purgative influence – Ewart knew my father
– The spoil-sports – An ample wash – Lo, hear the jumping gene – The
hoods – Off the beam – The everlasting Noah – The heart's ease.

*The sky of our lives: three novellas.* London: Hutchinson, 1972. 252 p.
ISBN: 0-09-112370-4. Contents: Oscar – *The dark philosophers* – Simeon.

—— *The sky of our lives.* Quartet Books, 1973. 215 p.: pbk. ISBN: 0-704-31045-7.

U.S. ed. Boston: Little Brown, 1972. ISBN: 0-09-112370-4.

*The subsidence factor.* Cardiff: University College of Cardiff Press, 1979. 16 p.: pamph. (Annual Gwyn Jones lecture). ISBN: 0-906449-03-0.

*Selected short stories.* Bridgend: Poetry Wales Press, 1984. 137p.: hbk & pbk. ISBN: 0-907476-30-9 hbk, 0-90-7476-29-5 pbk. Contents: And a spoonful of grief to taste – Arrayed like one of these – My fist upon the stone – Myself my desert – The couch, my friend, is cold – Where my dark lover lies – The pot of gold at Fear's End – The teacher – Oh brother man – That vanished Canaan – Land! Land! – Hugo, my friend – The joyful – Blue ribbons for a black epoch – Off the beam – The ample wish – A horse called Meadow Prospect.
    —— / foreword by Michael Parnell. Bridgend: Seren Books, 1988. 204 p.: hbk. & pbk. ISBN: 0-85411-000-4 hbk, 1-85411-001-2 pbk. Contents as 1984 edition, with: Foreword, pp. 7-15 – The hands of Chris – The leafless land – Violence and the big male voice – The leaf that hurts the hand – The cavers – Hastings.

*High on hope: extracts from the* **Western Mail articles** / edited by Jeffrey Robinson and Brian McCann. Cowbridge: Brown, 1985. 117 p. ISBN: 0-905928-40-7.

*Sorrow for thy sons.* London: Lawrence & Wishart, 1986. 275 p.: pbk. ISBN: 0-85315-665-4. Incl. Introduction, by Dai Smith, pp. 5-10. – Novel.

*The thinker and the thrush.* London: Lawrence & Wishart, 1988. 256 p.: pbk. ISBN: 0-85315-708-1. Incl. Introduction, by Michael Parnell, pp. 5-15. – Novel.

*Three plays* / edited by Michael Parnell. Bridgend: Seren Books, 1990. 236 p.: pbk. (Welsh writing in English). ISBN: 1-85411-017-9. Contents: Introduction, by Michael Parnell, pp. 7-21 – The keep – Jackie the jumper – Loud organs – Appendices: Introduction to 'The keep' [and] After the chip shop: introduction to 'Jackie the jumper', pp. 220-226 – Notes, pp. 227-236.

*Meadow Prospect revisited* / edited by Michael Parnell. Bridgend: Seren Books, 1992. 212 p.: pbk. ISBN: 1-85411-065-9. Contents: Introduction, by Michael Parnell, pp. 7-10 – The face of our jokes – The silences of passion – Down with the libido – The hard word – The walking compulsion – Growing up in Meadow Prospect; Brotherly love, Change here for strangeness, Stay as beat as you are, Explosion point, Lapsed policy, Reluctant trouper – Water boy – Sitting the monsoon out – The heist – The seeding twenties; A paling darkness; Scalping party, It figures, I am trying to tell you, So they came and took him away – The putters-out –

Nothing to declare – The stammering hammer – The Welsh dreamer –
A thought for the dragon – The appeal – We are not living, we're hiding
– Into the sunrise – A wish to know – The comeback – Ripe, I cry –
After you with the illusion – No dancing on the nerve-ends, please – The
little baron – Cover my flank – As on a darkling plain – Thy need –
Postcript [sources and bibliography], pp. 211-212. – 'The stories in this
collection were written and published at various times and in various places
between 1946 and 1979.'


## A (ii). Publications by Gwyn Thomas: Selected Contributions to Books and Periodicals

See also Michael Parnell's bibliography in his *Laughter from the dark* (1988),
listing Thomas's plays and features for radio and television, as well as his
theatre plays.

The dark philosophers, 1946. See section A(i).

The limp in my longing. In *Modern Reading* 15 (1947) 131-138. Story.

Then came we singing. *Coal*, Feb 1948, 24-25. First version of 'Gazooka',
with interview.

The miners call it 'our film'. *Coal*, Jul 1948, 20-21. Review of 'The blue
scar', a film by Jill Craigie.

Queue for song. *Coal*, Aug 1948, 20-21. On Govent Garden opera chorus
tour of South Wales.

Barry's literary phenomenon: Mr Gwyn Thomas makes his reply. *Barry
Herald*, 4 July 1952, 3:D-E. Response to T.H. Corfe and G. Ingli James,
27 Jun 1952, 2:B-D.

My heart sang on a hilltop. *Empire News*, 13 Mar 1953, 2:A-E.

[Article]. *Empire News*, 24 Mar 1953, 2.

Dylan had unique gift of patriotic expression. *WM*, 29 Jan 1954, 3:F. Extracts
from talk on Dylan Thomas given to Barry Rotarians.

Of all the saints. *Punch*, 13 Oct 1954, 460-462.

And some before the tavern shouted. *Punch*, 26 Oct 1955, 490-492. Reflections
on licensing laws.

Lie low, Jason. *Punch*, 17 Oct 1956, 452-454.

If you want, I'll act it for you. *Punch*, 10 Apr 1957, 460-462.

A Rhondda Bethel. *TES*, 24 May 1957, 736.

Saturnalia Cambriensa. *Punch*, 10 Jun 1958, 811-812.

Bread and Cymric circuses. *Punch*, 16 Jul 1958, 79-80. On the Commonwealth Games at Cardiff.

Education. *Punch*, 17 Dec 1958, 372-375. In series, New book of snobs.

The eleven plus. *Punch*, 18 Mar 1959, 372-375. In series, From cradle to university.

Oh you frabjous asses. *Punch*, 12 Aug 1959, 4-6. In series, Once again assembled here.

I think, therefore I am thinking. *AWR* 10,25 (1959) 19-21.

The unquiet fleece. *WM*, 30 Apr 1960, 6:B-F. Reprinted from *Punch*.

The speaking shade. *WM*, 7 May 1960, 8:C-F.

Comfort me with apples. *Punch*, 22 Jun 1960, 877-879. First of nine pieces in series, 'Gwyn Thomas's schooldays'. – Continues: Grace and gravy, 29 Jun, 912-914; Flannelled fools, 6 Jul, 16-18; Disintegration of the umpire, 13 Jul, 52-54; Vaulting ambition, 20 Jul, 90-92; Outward bound, 27 Jul, 126-128; Round the bend in the gym, 3 Aug, 164-166; A rugged winter, 10 Aug, 198-200; Whistling in the dark, 17 Aug, 234-236.

Comfort me with apples. *WM*, 9 Jul 1960, 6:D-G.

Catching the stage. *WM*, 30 Jul 1960, 6.

Chancellor, who are you hounding now? *Punch*, 7 Dec 1960, 800-802. In series, Shadowed cabinet.

A night called concern. *Punch*, 21 Dec 1960, 883-885.

Journey through Wales. *Holiday*, Sep 1960, 34-44, 132, 135.

A view of the valley. *New Statesman*, 24 Feb 1961, 300-301.

The neighbourly love of a phalanx of sages. *WM*, 19 Sep 1961, 6:B-E. First part of 'Sextet', a composite serial with six authors. – Thomas also contributed the final part, 'Curtains', 27 Sep, 6:B-E.

The banner, *Punch*, 27 Dec, 940-942. One of six stories under general title, 'The seeding twenties' (the others are reprinted in *Meadow Prospect revisited,* 1992).

A quiet place. In *The compleat imbiber 5,* ed. Cyril Ray. London: Vista Books, 1962. pp. 179-183. On Llanwonno and the Brynffynnon Arms.

The opening. *Spectator,* 2 Feb 1962, 134. On Sunday licensing laws.

To the hills. *Punch,* 7 Mar 1962, 385-387.

I dreamt that I dwelt. *Punch,* 16 May 1962, 756-758. On hotel life.

A season for wizards. *Punch,* 29 Aug 1962, 306-308. First of seven articles under general title, 'The man with the chalk'. – Continues: The cool eye, 5 Sep, 340-342; Exit, 12 Sep, 376-378; A view of the earth, 19 Sep, 409-410; Beau, 26 Sep, 452-454; Matins, 3 Oct, 488-490; The talent, 10 Oct, 524-526.

Exit. *Punch,* 12 Sep 1962, 376-378.

We are not living, we're hiding. *Punch,* 19 Dec 1962, 891-893. Recalls march on London from Welsh valleys.

Report from the outdoors. *Punch,* 9 Jan 1963, 61-62.

Jackie the jumper. *Plays and Players,* Feb 1963, 26-44. Reprinted in *Plays of the year,* vol. 26, ed. J.C. Trewin. London: Elek, 1963. pp. 209-297.

The fringe. *Punch,* 6 Feb 1963, 191-193. On Welsh and Irish temperaments.

The fragrant time. *Punch,* 10 Apr 1963, 525-526.

To the coast. *Punch,* 28 Aug 1963, 312-313.

The leaking ark. *Punch,* 11 Dec 1963, 853-854.

Making society smile. *Teacher,* 13 Dec 1963, 8.

Martin Luther: the new piety. *Holiday,* Jan 1964, 62, 95-96, 99, 135, 140, 145.

The atonal. *Teacher,* 21 Feb 1964, 18. On difficulties of teaching music.

The wilderness of wit. *Teacher,* 6 Mar 1964, 16.

Hitting the track. *Punch,* 8 Apr 1964, 533-535.

Tranquillity and warm beer: the Cotswold inns. *Holiday,* May 1964, 80-81, 157-158, 160-161, 167-168.

Fighting fit. *Punch,* 13 May 1964, 705-708.

One of the memorable. *Teacher*, 15 May 1964, 20. On his brother John.

Bowdler, what are you Bowdling now? *Punch*, 27 May 1964, 787-789.

A Welsh eye. *Spectator*, 14 Aug 1964, 207-208.

Come back next week. *Teacher*, 21 Aug 1964, 6.

Under the influence of literature. *Punch*, 7 Oct 1964, 532-534.

The traffic lights wink: a look around the frontal lobes. *Teacher*, 16 Oct 1964, 16.

Gimme, gimme. *Teacher*, 13 Nov 1964, 14. On rapaciousness of children.

Party of one: a joyful noise. *Holiday*, Dec 1964, 10, 14-18.

In the sun. *Teacher*, 19 Feb 1965, 18. Reflections on day at Barry Island.

Why I gave up walking. *Punch*, 10 Mar 1965, 356-357.

The Camelot syndrome. *Teacher*, 12 Mar 1965, 18.

Party of one: the passionate authors. *Holiday*, Apr 1965, 10, 16, 18, 20-24.

The geometry of grace. *Teacher*, 9 Apr 1965, 16. On houses and housing.

Time out of mind: a bit of Welsh topography. *Teacher*, 21 May 1965, 20. On Caerleon and Chepstow.

The slipping agenda. *Teacher*, 4 Jun 1965, 15. On local government.

In touch with the gravy: the elusive art of the businessman. *Teacher*, 18 Jun 1965, 14.

Some books for the beach. *Teacher*, 9 Jul 1965, i.

The insurgent psyche. *Teacher*, 16 Jul 1965, 10. Classroom contacts between teachers and pupils.

The westward fancy. *Punch*, 4 Aug 1965, 156-159.

The sol-fah set. *Teacher*, 24 Sep 1965, 16.

Private members' bill. *Punch*, 29 Sep 1965, 452-454.

A cry of collective poets. *Teacher*, 8 Oct 1965, 16. On international poetry conference at Cardiff.

Our four-legged masters. *Teacher*, 29 Oct 1965, 14.

Odysseus in a motor coach. *Teacher*, 19 Nov 1965, 16.

The alone and the alone. *Teacher*, 3 Dec 1965, 12.

A cloud of plans. *Teacher*, 17 Dec 1965, 8. Against planning and the power it gives to fools.

The longest evening. *WM*, 24 Dec 1965, 6:C-G. Story.

Among the blessed of the earth. *Teacher*, 30 Dec 1965, 6. On joys of teaching.

The Spanish flavour-buds. *Teacher*, 4 Feb 1966, 18. On Spanish literature.

The voices of the scattered kinsmen. *Teacher*, 18 Feb 1966, 22. Return to the Rhondda.

In search of Luther. *Teacher*, 4 Mar 1966, 16.

A touch of the boasts. *Punch*, 23 Mar 1966, 421-422. In series, Uninhibited confessions.

On to a sure thing. *Teacher*, 25 Mar 1966, 24. On gambling.

The ghost – hang on to it. *Teacher*, 20 May 1966, 18.

How I made my first ... *Punch*, 1 Jun 1966, 796-798.

A place, but not to rest. *Teacher*, 17 Jun 1966, 18. On lecturing to the unemployed.

Serrations of an old rake. *Teacher*, 5 Aug 1966, 15. The tediousness of libertinism.

A taste of yesterday. *Teacher*, 30 Sep 1966, 21. On *Sorrow for my sons* and Porth background.

Death moves in the valleys like a busy bagman. *Teacher*, 28 Oct 1966, 29. On Aberfan disaster.

Plaster saints in the valleys. *Twentieth Century* 174 (1966) 25-27.

There were hazards in my classroom. *Teacher*, 3 Feb 1967, 12.

Washington Irving slept here. *Punch*, 31 May 1967, 798-800.

Not all ruins are old. *Teacher*, 11 Aug 1967, 9. On Llanthony Abbey.

The antis. *Punch*, 23 Aug 1967, 280-282.

Our cloak of yesterdays. *Teacher*, 8 Sep 1967, 12.

Walking away from the impotent halls. *Punch*, 13 Sep 1967, 382-385. On his career as a teacher.

Growing helmsman. *Punch*, 10 Jan 1968, 59-61.

The call. *Punch*, 17 Apr 1968, 565-567. His relationship with Oxford.

First exit. *Punch*, 5 Jun 1968, 809-811. On going to Oxford for interview.

The flannel panel. *Teacher*, 28 Jun 1968, 11.

The improver. *Punch*, 9 Oct 1968, 503-506.

The pausing places. *Punch*, 23 Oct 1968, 587-588. Recalls some favourite pubs.

Some inns in Wales. In *Pub: a celebration*, ed. Angus McGill. London: Longmans, 1969. pp. 161-176.

Keeping up with the Joneses. *Guardian*, 28 Jun 1969, 7. 'On what it takes to be Welsh'.

Gwyn Thomas. In *Artists in Wales*, ed. Meic Stephens. Llandysul: Gwasg Gomer, 1971. pp. 67-80. Autobiographical essay.

The Romano-British. In *Treasures of the British Museum*, introduced by Sir John Wolfenden. London: Collins, 1971. pp. 96-109.

Tragi-comic dilemmas of human living. *WM*, 15 May 1971, 10:E-F. Review of Glyn Jones, *Selected short stories*.

Visionary vagabond who hung on a spider's web. *WM*, 24 Jul 1971, 8:A-C. Review of Sybil Hollingdrake, *The super-tramp in Monmouthshire*, L. Hockey, *W.H. Davies*.

My day. *Vogue*, Feb 1972, 17.

Journey from the Rhondda. *New Statesman*, 26 May 1972, 712. Review of Will Paynter, *My generation*.

Paint brush politics. *Daily Telegraph Magazine*, 3 Aug 1973, 5.

Foreword. In *Old Rhondda in photographs*, with commentaries by Cyril Batstone. Barry: Stewart Williams, 1974.

Valley pilgrims to the valley shrine. In *The Cardiff book. Vol. 2*, ed. Stewart Williams. Barry: Stewart Williams, 1974. pp. 11-19.

Traitors who make the dragon blanch. *WM*, 5 Aug 1974, 4:D-E. Review of Emyr Humphreys, *Flesh and blood*, Aldryd Haines, *The drift*.

Mr. Barrie and Mr. Shaw. *Listener*, 14 Aug 1975, 218-219. On broadcast of Thomas's play, 'The ghost of Adelphi Terrace'.

Variations on a Welsh theme for four male voices. *Listener*, 2 Oct 1975, 429-430. With Raymond Williams and others.

The last of the salmon sandwiches. *Guardian*, 10 Aug 1976, 6:A-E.

All gas and godliness. *Guardian*, 17 Aug 1976, 6:A-E.

Forbidden fruit. *Guardian*, 24 Aug 1976, 6:A-E.

Perfect pitch. *Guardian*, 31 Aug 1976, 13:A-E.

Mind the promised land doesn't become paradise lost. *WM*, 18 Nov 1976, 8:C-F. On contemporary Wales, marking first performance of 'The breakers'.

Foreword. In *Old Barry in photographs*, ed. Brian C. Luxton. Barry: Stewart Williams, 1977.

Foreword. In *Old Pontypridd and district in photographs*. Barry: Stewart Williams, 1977.

Sidelights. In *Contemporary authors. Vols. 65-68*, ed. Jane A. Bowden. Detroit: Gale, 1977. p. 586.

A dry run through old Wales. *WM*, 9 Sep 1978, 10:C-F. Review of Emyr Humphreys, *The best of friends*.

Letter. *WM*, 27 Feb 1979, 10:D. Argues, with other writers, for devolution,

Sound and fury in Wales. *Geo*, May 1980, 128-150.

Rich compost. *Arcade*, 31 Oct 1980, 10. Letter on first issue.

Wales. In *Travel in* Vogue. London: Macdonald, 1981. pp. 218-219.

Torchbearers of uneasiness. *Arcade*, 1 May 1981, 16-18.

The first waves. In *Fountains of praise: University College Cardiff, 1883-1983*, ed. Gwyn Jones and Michael Quinn. Cardiff: University College Cardiff Press, 1983. pp. 123-133.

Rhondda (1980) – Aberfan (1967) – Gazooka (1953) – Come off it, Mr

Chips (1960). In *Wales on the wireless: a broadcasting anthology,* ed. Patrick
Hannan. Llandysul: Gomer in assoc. with BBC Cymru/Wales, 1988. pp.
48-50; 63-64; 93-94; 184-185.

## B. Publications about Gwyn Thomas

[ANON]. Literary profile: Gwyn Thomas. *WM*, 7 May 1952, 3.
—— Mr Gwyn Thomas: novelist who captured Welsh experience. *Times*,
18 Apr 1981, 16:G-H. Obituary.
—— Gwyn Thomas, 1913-1981. In *Contemporary authors, new revision series.
Vol. 9,* ed. Ann Evory and Linda Metzger. Detroit: Gale, 1983. pp. 494-
495. Incl.: bibliography of stage, television and radio plays. – With
comment by Thomas on his work.
BURTON, P. Ever green was his valley. *Saturday Review*, 26 Apr 1969, 53.
DAVIES, James A. Kinds of relating: Gwyn Thomas (Jack Jones, Lewis Jones,
Gwyn Jones) and the Welsh industrial novel. *AWR* 86 (1987) 72-86.
FAST, Howard. *Literature and reality.* New York: International Publishers Co.
Inc., 1950. Discuss Gwyn Thomas, pp. 67-77.
FISHLOCK, Trevor. Gwyn Thomas: writer with a preacher's impulse. *Times*,
23 Nov 1974, 14:G-H.
GEORGE, Philip. Three Rhondda working class writers. *Llafur: Journal of
Welsh Labour History* 3,2 (1981) 5-13. On Huw Menai, Lewis Jones and
Gwyn Thomas.
GOLIGHTLY, Victor. Gwyn Thomas's American 'Oscar'. *NWR* 6,2 [22]
(1993) 26-31. On the background of his short story.
HUMFREY, Belinda. Gwyn Thomas. In *British novelists, 1930-1959. Part 2:
M-Z,* ed. Bernard Oldsey. Detroit: Gale, 1983. (Dictionary of literary
biography; 15). pp. 514-519.
JONES, Glyn. Three Anglo-Welsh prose writers. *Rann* 19 (1953) 1-5. On
Caradoc Evans, Gwyn Thomas and Dylan Thomas.
—— *The dragon has two tongues: essays on Anglo-Welsh writers and writing.*
London: Dent, 1968. Incl. Gwyn Thomas, pp. 107-123.
—— A tribute to Gwyn Thomas. *AWR* 68 (1981) 4-5.
—— *Random entrances to Gwyn Thomas.* Cardiff: University College Press,
1982. 25 p.: pamph. (Annual Gwyn Jones lecture). ISBN: 0-906449-45-6.
JONES, Gwyn. Language, style and the Anglo-Welsh. *Essays and Studies* 6
(1953) 102-114. On Dylan Thomas, Gwyn Thomas, Glyn Jones and
Caradoc Evans
—— Gwyn Thomas (1981). In *Wales on the wireless: a broadcasting anthology,*
*ed.* Patrick Hannan. Llandysul: Gomer in assoc. with BBC Cymru/Wales,
1988. pp. 33-34.
JONES, Graham. Play notices: 'Sap', by Gwyn Thomas. *AWR* 24,54 (1975)
276-282. Review article centred on Cardiff production.
—— Theatre review: 'The breakers', by Gwyn Thomas. *AWR* 26,58 (1977)
215-217. Review of the Cardiff production.
JONES, Roger Stephens. Absurdity in the novels of Gwyn Thomas. *AWR*
25,56 (1976) 43-52.
MICHAEL, Ian. *Gwyn Thomas.* Cardiff: University of Wales Press [for] the

Welsh Arts Council, 1977. 86 p.: front. port. (Writers of Wales). Incl. bibliography, pp. 73-81. – 'Limited to 1000 copies'.

ORMOND, John. Gwyn Thomas. In *Contemporary novelists of the English language,* ed. James Vinson. 2nd. ed. London: St. James Press; New York: St. Martin's Press, 1976. pp. 1360-1362.

PARNELL, Michael. Years of apprenticeship: the early life of Gwyn Thomas. *Planet* 59 (1986) 64-70.

—— Editing Gwyn Thomas. *BWA* 15 (1988) 4-5, 12.

—— *Laughter from the dark: a life of Gwyn Thomas.* London: John Murray, 1988. xiii, 241 p.: ill. ISBN: 0-7195-4426-2. Incl. Selected bibliography, pp. 225-232.

—— Mrs Lyn Thomas. *NWR* 3,1 [10] (1990) 57-58. Obituary notice of the wife of Gwyn Thomas. – Lists some of the author's unpublished writings.

RAYNOR, Henry. Gwyn Thomas. In *Contemporary dramatists,* ed. James Vinson. 2nd ed. London: St. James's Press; New York: St Martin's Press, 1977. pp. 758-761.

RICHARDS, Alun. The spice of Gwyn. *WM,* 2 Nov 1983, 8:B-F. On the presentation of Thomas's library to the South Wales Miners' Library, Swansea.

SMITH, Dai. Leaders and led. In *Rhondda past and future,* ed. K.S. Hoskins. Rhondda: Rhondda Borough Council, [1975?]. pp. 37-65. Background.

—— Explosive in the mind. *Arcade,* 9 Jan 1981, 19-20. Profile. Reply by Leo Simon, 16 Jan 1981, 10.

—— *Wales! Wales?* London: Allen & Unwin, 1984. Includes discussion of Idris Davies, Jack Jones, Lewis Jones and Gwyn Thomas, pp. 134-151.

—— Reading Gwyn Thomas. *BNW,* Autumn 1984, 3-4.

—— Breaking silence: Gwyn Thomas and the pre-history of Welsh working-class fiction. In *Artisans, peasants and proletarians, 1760-1860: essays presented to Gwyn A. Williams,* ed. Clive Emsley and James Walvin. London: Croom Helm, 1985. pp. 104-123.

—— The early Gwyn Thomas. *THSC,* 1985, 71-89.

—— *Gwyn Thomas, 1913-1981.* Cardiff: Welsh Arts Council, 1986. 83 p.: chiefly ill. (Writer's world). Incl. bibliography, p. 82.

—— A novel history. In *Wales the imagined nation: studies in cultural and national identity,* ed. Tony Curtis. Bridgend: Poetry Wales Press, 1986. pp. 131-158.

—— Satellite pictures and close-ups: the Welsh working-class novel. *Planet* 101 (1993) 88-92. On Gwyn Thomas, particularly the publishing of *Sorrow for thy sons.*

WILLIAMS, Raymond. *The Welsh industrial novel: the inaugural Gwyn Jones lecture.* Cardiff: University College Cardiff Press, 1979.

—— Working-class, proletarian, socialist: problems in some Welsh novels. In *The socialist novel in Britain: towards the recovery of a tradition,* ed. H. Gustav Klaus. Brighton: Harvester Press, 1982. pp. 110-121.

ZINOBER, Pearl. A study of Gwyn Thomas's humour. MA thesis. Iowa State University of Science and Technology, 1970.

# R.S. THOMAS (b. 1913)

A. Publications by R.S. Thomas
  (i)   Books
  (ii)  Books edited
  (iii) Selected contributions to books and periodicals

A. Publications about R.S. Thomas


## A (i). Publications by R.S. Thomas: Books

*The stones of the field.* Carmarthen: Druid Press, 1946. 48 p.

*An acre of land.* Newtown: Montgomeryshire Printing Co., 1952. 38 p.: pamph.

*The minister.* Newtown: Montgomeryshire Printing Co., 1953. 24 p.: pamph. First broadcast in the Welsh Home Service, 18 Sep 1952.

*Song at the year's turning: poems, 1942-1954* / with an introduction by John Betjeman. London: Hart-Davis, 1955. 115 p. Incl. poems from: *The stones of the field, An acre of land, The minister* – Later poems.

Japanese trans.: *R.S. Thomas: Shishu,* tr. Yaguchi Yorifumi. Sapporo: Soei Shuppan, 1974. 189 p.

*Poetry for supper.* London: Hart-Davis, 1958. 48 p.

*Judgment day.* London: Poetry Book Society, 1960. [4] p.: pamph. Facsimile holograph of 21-line poem. – Cover design by Ceri Richards. – 1000 copies.

*Tares.* London: Hart-Davies, 1961. 48 p.

*Penguin modern poets 1: Lawrence Durrell, Elizabeth Jennings, R.S. Thomas.* Harmondsworth: Penguin, 1962. 119 p.: pbk. Incl. poems from: *Song at the year's turning* – *Poetry for supper.*

*The bread of truth.* London: Hart-Davis, 1963. 48 p.

*Words and the poet: the W.D.Thomas memorial lecture delivered at the University College of Swansea on November 19, 1963.* University of Wales Press, 1964. 25 p.: pamph.

*Pietà*. London: Hart-Davis, 1966. 45 p.

*The mountains* / illustrated with ten drawings by John Piper; engraved on the wood by Reynolds Stone; with a descriptive note by John Piper. New York: Chilmark Press, 1968. 42 p.: ill.: in slipcase. Incl.: A descriptive note, by John Piper, pp. 5-11 – The mountains, by R.S. Thomas, pp. 13-42. – 'This edition consists of 350 copies as follows: 110 copies numbered I-CX, signed by the author, artist and engraver, and with an extra set of the ten engravings; and 240 copies numbered 1-240.'

*Pergamon poets 1* / by Roy Fuller and R.S. Thomas; selected by Evan Owen. Oxford: Pergamon Press, 1968. 65 p.: pbk. Incl. 34 poems by R.S. Thomas, pp. 41-65.

*Not that he brought flowers*. London: Hart-Davies, 1968. 45 p. ISBN: 0-246-98580-1.

*R.S. Thomas*. London: Longmans, 1969. 30 p.: pamph. (Longmans' poetry library). ISBN: 0-582-34198-1. Selection of 29 poems.

*H'm: poems*. London: Macmillan, 1972. vi, 37 p.: hbk & pbk. ISBN: 0-333-13630-6 hbk, 0-333-13807-4 pbk.

*Young and old*. London: Chatto & Windus, 1972. 32 p. (Chatto poets for the young). ISBN: 0-7010-0492-4 non-net, 0-7011-5004-1 net.

*Selected poems: 1946-1968*. London: Hart-Davis; MacGibbon, 1973. 134 p. ISBN: 0-246-10775-8. Incl. poems from: *Song at the year's turning* – *Poetry for supper* – *Tares* – *The bread of truth* – *Pietà* – *Not that he brought flowers*.
—— St. Albans: Granada, 1979. ISBN: 0-246-10775-8.
—— Newcastle upon Tyne: Bloodaxe Books, 1986. 125 p.: pbk. ISBN: 0-906427-96-7.

U.S. ed.: New York: St. Martin's, 1974.

*What is a Welshman?* Llandybïe: Christopher Davies, 1974. 12 [i.e. 24] p.: hbk. & pbk. ISBN: 0-7154-0067-3.

*Laboratories of the spirit*. London: Macmillan, 1975. vi, 65 p.: hbk & pbk. ISBN: 0-333-18510-2 hbk, 0-333-18511-0 pbk.
—— Newtown: Gwasg Gregynog, 1976. 72 p. 'Published by the University of Wales Press and printed by Michael Hutchins on the Albion Press at Gregynog ... This edition limited to 215 copies for sale.' – Edition subsequently reduced by 25 copies.

U.S. ed.: Boston: Godine, 1976. ISBN: 0-97923-170.

*The bright field.* [n.p.]: [1975]. [4] p.: ill. From *Laboratories of the spirit.*
– Parallel English text and German translation. – Edition of 50 copies.

*Abercuawg: y ddarlith lenyddol flynyddol Eisteddfod Genedlaethol Cymru Aberteifi a'r Cylch.* Llandysul: Gwasg Gomer, 1976. 18 p.: pamph. (Annual National Eisteddfod lecture).

*The way of it: poems* / drawings by Barry Hirst. Sunderland: Ceolfrith Press, 1977. 35p.: ill.: pbk. (Ceolfrith; 37). ISBN: 0-904461-20-3, 0-904461-22-X signed. 1925 ordinary copies, 75 numbered copies signed by poet and artist.

*Frequencies.* London: Macmillan, 1978. 52 p.: hbk & pbk. ISBN: 0-333-23650-5 hbk, 0-333-23712-9 pbk.

*Between here and now.* London: Macmillan, 1981. 110 p.: ill.: hbk & pbk. ISBN: 0-333-32186-3 hbk, 0-333-32629-6 pbk. Contents: Impressions [with 33 reproductions of Impressionist paintings in the Louvre] – Other poems.

*Das helle Feld: The bright field: Gedichte von R.S. Thomas* / englisch und deutsch gelesen von K.A. Perryman; Illustrationen von K.A. Perryman. [München: Babel], 1983. [20] p.: ill.: pamph. With music. – 'Printed on the occasion of the reading, recital and exhibition, "Das helle Feld", at the British Council in Munich, 21st Nov 1983.'

*Later poems: a selection by R.S. Thomas.* London: Macmillan, 1983. 224 p. ISBN: 0-333-34560-6. Incl. poems from: *H'm* – *Young and old* – *What is a Welshman?* – *Laboratories of the spirit* – *The way of it* – *Frequencies* – *Between here and now.* – With 43 new poems. – Cover title: *Later poems: 1972-1983.* – Reissued 1984, pbk. ISBN: 0-333-37055-4.

*Poets' meeting.* Stratford upon Avon: Celandine Press, 1983. [8] p.: ill.: pbk. With one line-block illustration by Geoffrey Whitney. – 125 copies printed, the first 85 signed by the poet.

*Selected prose* / edited by Sandra Anstey; with an introduction by Ned Thomas. Bridgend: Poetry Wales Press, 1983. 187 p.: front. port. ISBN: 0-907476-27-9. Contents: Introduction, pp. 7-16 – The depopulation of the Welsh hill country (1945) – Some contemporary Scottish writing (1946) – Two chapels (1948) [trans. of 'Dau gapel'] – Anglo-Welsh literature (1952) [trans. of 'Llenyddiaeth Eingl-Gymreig'] – The qualities of Christmas (1959) – Introduction to *The Penguin book of religious verse* (1963) – Words and the poet (1964) – A frame for poetry (1966) – The mountains (1968) – The making of a poem (1969) – Introduction to *A choice of Wordsworth's verse* (1971) – The paths gone by [trans. of 'Y llwybrau gynt 2'] – Where do we go from here? (1974) – *Abercuawg* (1976) – The creative writer's suicide

(1978) – Review of Dee Brown, *Bury my heart at Wounded Knee* (1978) – Bibliography, pp. 182-187. – Reissued 1986, pbk. ISBN: 0-907476-69-4.

*Ingrowing thoughts*. Bridgend: Poetry Wales Press, 1985. 49 p.: ill.: hbk & pbk. (Poetry Wales poets series; 3). ISBN: 0-907476-44-9 hbk, 0-907476-40-6 pbk. Incl. 21 reproductions of 20th-century paintings.

*Neb* / golygwyd gan Gwenno Hywyn. Caernarfon: Gwasg Gwynedd, 1985. 131 p.: pbk. (Cyfres y Cewri; 6). Autobiography. – [Nobody].

*Destinations* / with illustrations by Paul Nash. Halford: Celandine Press, 1985. 30 p.: ill. ISBN: 0-948795-01-8 cloth, 0-948795-00-x leather, 0-948795-04-2 quarter leather. Incl. 18 poems, 11 reprinted in *Experimenting with an amen*. – With 3 colour plates. – '300 copies designed ... and printed for the Celandine Press by Sebastian Carter at the Rampant Lions Press, Cambridge ... The first 75 copies signed by the author.' – Issued in cloth, leather and quarter leather bindings.

*Poems of R.S. Thomas*. Fayetteville: University of Arkansas Press, 1985. xiii, 196 p.: hbk & pbk. ISBN: 0-938626-46-9 hbk, 0-938626-47-7 pbk. Incl. poems from: *Song at the year's turning* – *Poetry for supper* – *Tares* – *The bread of truth* – *Pietà* – *Not that he brought flowers* – *H'm* - *Young and old* – *What is a Welshman?* – *Laboratories of the spirit* – *The way of it* – *Frequencies* – *Between here and now*. – With 43 new poems.

*Experimenting with an amen*. London: Macmillan, 1986. vi, 70 p. ISBN: 0-333-41982-0. Reissued 1988, pbk. ISBN: 0-333-46832-5.

*Welsh airs*. Bridgend: Poetry Wales Press, 1987. 55 p.: hbk & pbk. ISBN: 0-907476-72-4 hbk, 0-907476-75-9 pbk.

*Pe medrwn yr iaith ac ysgrifau eraill* / wedi ei olygu gan Tony Brown a Bedwyr L. Jones. Abertawe: Christopher Davies, 1988. 165 p.: pbk. ISBN: 0-7154-0688-4. Contents: Arian y swydd (1946) – Gobaith (1947) – Dau gapel (1948) – Llythyr: yr eglwys a Chymru (1949) – Maldwyn (1951) – Llenyddiaeth Eingl-Gymreig (1952) – Adaryddiaeth: beth amdani? (1967) – Y llwybrau gynt (1972) – Adolygiad ar *Bury my heart at Wounded Knee* (1974) – Abercuawg (1976) – O'n cwmpas (1977) – Hunanladdiad y llenor (1977) – Miwsig yn fy mywyd (1977) – Yr ynys dawel (1978) – Pe medrwn yr iaith (1980) – Gwrthod gwaith y diafol (1982) – Alltud (1983) – Nadolig niwcliar (1983) – Yr ateb i ddifodiant (1984) – Undod (1985) – Llyfryddiaeth o ryddiaith Gymraeg R.S. Thomas [Bibliography of Welsh publications by R.S. Thomas]. – [If I knew the language and other essays].

*The echoes return slow*. London: Macmillan, 1988. 121 p. ISBN: 0-333-

46806-6. Parallel sequences of prose and poetry. – Reissued 1989, pbk. ISBN: 0-333-48281-6.

*Three poems.* Child Okeford, Dorset: Words Press, 1988. 8 p.: ill.: pamph. (Mir poets; 15). ISBN: 1-871299-75-6, 1-871299-80-2 signed. Contents: The un-born – Caught – Requests. – 'Edition limited to 200 copies. Nos. 1-75 are signed by the author.'

*A blackbird singing* / wood engraving by Christopher Wormwell. Newton: Gwasg Gregynog, [1989]. [4] p.: ill.: pamph. (Beirdd Gregynog; Gregynog poets; 9). ISBN: 0-948714-27-1. Text of single poem. – 'This edition consists of 400 copies.'

*Counterpoint.* Newcastle upon Tyne: Bloodaxe Books, 1990. 64 p.: hbk & pbk. ISBN: 1-85224-116-0 hbk, 1-85224-117-9 pbk.

*Blwyddyn yn Llŷn.* Caernarfon: Gwasg Gwynedd, 1990. 98 p.: ill.: pbk. ISBN: 0-86074-060-9. A monthly diary. – [A year in Llŷn].

*Cymru or Wales?* Llandysul: Gomer, 1992. 32 p.: pbk. (Changing Wales; 1). ISBN: 0-86383-896-0.

*Mass for hard times.* Newcastle upon Tyne: Bloodaxe Books, 1992. 96 p.: hbk & pbk. ISBN: 1-85224-228-0 hbk, 1-85224-229-9 pbk.

*Frieze.* Schondorf am Ammersee: Babel, 1992. 38 p. 30 poems, mostly uncollected. 'The edition is limited to five hundred copies, of which four hundred are softbound ... and one hundred, numbered and signed by the author, are hardbound, the first twenty being bound in leather.'

*Collected poems: 1945-1990.* London: Dent, 1993. xii, 548 p. ISBN: 0-460-97266 (cased), 0-460-86113-1 (special). With indexes of titles and first lines. – Presents roughly three-quarters the contents of twenty-one published volumes (excluding *The echoes return slow* and *Counterpoint,* from which no poems are reprinted). – The selections from *The stones of the field* and *An acre of land* differ from those in *Song at the year's turning.* – Special edition: 250 signed copies in slip-case; with 'Sick visits' in facsimile holograph as frontispiece.

**Note** the following Italian translation:

*Un prete e la sua gente, e altre poesie,* tr. Augusta Canegallo and R.A. Henderson. Roma: Bulzoni, 1992. 154 p. Incl. Introduction, by R.A. Henderson, pp. 7-36. – Fifty poems in translation (with accompanying English texts), taken from eleven volumes up to and including *The echoes* return slow. – See Ruth Anne Henderson, Translating the silence. *NWR* 5,4 [20] (1993) 30-34.

## A (ii). Publications by R.S. Thomas: Books Edited

*The Batsford book of country verse* / edited by R.S. Thomas. London: Batsford, 1961. 128 p.: ill. Incl. Preface, by R.S. Thomas, pp. 7-8. 'This anthology is mainly for young people.'

*The Penguin book of religious verse* / introduced and edited by R.S. Thomas. Harmondsworth: Penguin, 1963. 192 p.: pbk. (The Penguin poets; D66). Introduction, pp. 7-11.

*Selected poems by Edward Thomas* / selected and introduced by R.S. Thomas. London: Faber, 1964. 63 p.: pbk. ISBN: 0-571-06067-6. Introduction, pp. 11-14.

*A choice of George Herbert's verse* / selected with an introduction by R.S. Thomas. London: Faber, 1967. 95 p.: hbk & pbk. Introduction, pp. 7-17.

*A choice of Wordsworth's verse* / selected with an introduction by R.S. Thomas. London: Faber, 1971. 136 p.: hbk & pbk. ISBN: 0-571-09258-6 hbk, 0-571-09259-4 pbk. Introduction, pp. 11-19.

## A (iii). Publications by R.S. Thomas: Selected Contributions to Books and Periodicals

This section covers prose writings by R.S. Thomas, including reviews and miscellaneous journalism. Sandra Anstey's doctoral thesis (1981) has a list of 'poems in manuscript, printed form or broadcast, that have not so far been collected', while her essay in *The page's drift*, ed. M. Wynn Thomas (1993) provides details of uncollected poems up to and including 1955. A bibliography of R.S. Thomas's writings in Welsh appears in *Pe medrwn yr iaith ac ysgrifau eraill*, ed. Tony Brown (1988).

Review of Rosalind Murray, *The good pagan's failure. Dublin Magazine* 16,3 (1941) 67-68.

Letter. *Wales* 2nd ser. 4 (1944) 106-107. On the resumption of *The Welsh Review*.

Adar y plwyfi. *Y Llan*, 28 Med/Sep 1945, 5. [Birds of the parishes].

Adar y gaeaf. *Y Llan*, 28 Rha/Dec 1945, 8. [Winter birds].

The depopulation of the Welsh hill country. *Wales* 2nd ser. 5,7 (1945) 75-80.

Wales in literature. *WM*, 12 Mar 1946, 3:F. Letter in reply to E.V. Dowds, 7 Mar 1946.

Save Europe now. *WM*, 24 Sep 1946, 3:F. Letter on the Save Europe Now fund.

Reply to *Wales* questionnaire 1946. *Wales* 2nd ser. 6,3 [23] (1946) 22-23.

Some contemporary Scottish writing. *Wales* 2nd ser. 6,3 [23] (1946) 98-103.

Arweinyddiaeth. *Y Llan*, 7 Maw/Mar 1947, 6. Letter.

Gobaith. *Y Llan,* 14 Maw/Mar 1947, 8.

Tenth anniversary year message. *Wales* 2nd ser. 7,26 (1947) 257. In Welsh.

Review of Roland Mathias, *Break in harvest and other poems. Wales* 2nd ser. 7,26 (1947) 323.

Anglo-Welsh literature. *Welsh Nationalist*, Dec 1948, 3:B-C.

*The guests*, by Dilys Cadwaladr. Wales 2nd ser. 8,29 (1948) 541-543. Translation by R.S. Thomas from the Welsh.

A Welsh view of the Scottish renaissance: substance of a talk given to the Dunedin Association. *Wales* 2nd ser. 8,30 (1948) 600-604.

Wales in world literature. *WM*, 26 Aug 1949, 4:H. Letter in reply to B.P. Rees, 19 Jul 1949.

Review of E. Morgan Humphreys, *The gorse glen. Y Fflam* 8 (1949) 55-56.

Y comisiwn. *Y Llan*, 3 Chw/Feb 1950, 8. Letter. [The commission].

Review of R.G. Lloyd Thomas, *Welsh Odyssey. Y Fflam* 10 (1951) 53-54.

Review of Roland Mathias, *The roses of Tretower. DL* 3,8 (1952) 34-35.

A Cymric survey. *New Statesman*, 24 Mar 1956, 286. Review of Thomas Parry, *A history of Welsh literature,* tr. H. Idris Bell.

The Welsh parlour. *Listener*, 16 Jan 1958, 119. On books about Wales.

The qualities of Christmas. *Wales* 3rd ser., Nov 1959, 17-20. Prose.

Review of *Dragons and daffodils: contemporary Anglo-Welsh verse,* ed. John Stuart Williams and Richard Milner. *Listener,* 8 Sep 1960, 393.

The making of poetry. *Listener,* 17 Aug 1961, 250. Text of broadcast in the BBC Home Service.

R.S. Thomas writes. *Poetry Book Society Bulletin,* Sep 1961, [1-2]. On his inability to discuss *Tares,* the PBS autumn choice. – With poem 'To a young poet'.

Review of *The Oxford book of Welsh verse,* ed. Thomas Parry. *Listener,* 26 Apr 1962, 740, 743.

*The bread of truth. Listener,* 14 Nov 1963, 797. Response to P.N. Furbank's review, 7 Nov 1963, 756.

Benedict Nightingale talks to the Rev R.S. Thomas. *Guardian,* 4 Mar 1964, 9:D.

Religion and the arts, IV. A frame for poetry. *TLS,* 3 Mar 1966, 169.

Preface. In *MacDiarmid: the Scottish National Library exhibition catalogue.* Edinburgh: National Library of Scotland, 1967. pp. 3-4.

Bachgen oeddwn i yng Nghaergybi – nid Cymro. *Y Cymro,* 20 Tach/Nov 1967, 12. Interviewed by Dyfed Evans. [I was a boy in Holyhead – not a Welshman].

Review of Daniel Hoffman, *Barbarous knowledge,* Donald D. Torchiana, *W.B. Yeats and Georgian Ireland,* Leonard Unger, *T.S. Eliot: moments and patterns,* William T. Moynihan, *The craft and art of Dylan Thomas. Critical Quarterly* 9,4 (1967) 380-383.

St. David's. In *By request from 'Ten to eight' on Radio 4.* London: BBC, 1968. pp. 26-27. Text of talk broadcast 1 March 1968.

R.S. Thomas writes. *Poetry Book Society Bulletin* 59 (1968) [1-2]. On his poetry and its appeal. – *Not that he brought flowers* was the PBS Christmas choice.

Poets on the Vietnam war. *Review: a Magazine of Poetry and Criticism* 18 (1968) 43-44. Answer to questionnaire.

The making of a poem. In *Llyfrgelloedd yng Nghymru: report of the proceedings of the thirty-fifth conference of library authorities in Wales and Monmouthshire ... Barry, 1968,* ed. Leslie M. Rees. Swansea: 1969. pp. 32-38.

Letter. *AWR* 18,41 (1969) 187. On the 'Morgan' of his poem, 'Llanrhaeadr ym Mochnant'.

Defenders of Welsh. *Times*, 28 May 1971, 17:E. Letter, with other Welsh writers, on the 'contemptuous injustice to the Welsh language'.

[Autobiography]. In *Y llwybrau gynt 2,* ed. Alun Oldfield-Davies. Llandysul: Gwasg Gomer, 1972. pp. 7-25.

Y *New Statesman* a Chymru. *Barn,* Maw/Mar 1972, 125.

[Interview with Timothy Wilson]. *Guardian*, 15 Sep 1972. 8: A-D. On the publication of *H'm*.

Ynys Enlli. *Barn*, Tach/Nov 1972, 16-17. [Bardsey].

Sgwrs efo R.S. Thomas. *Ffenics* [University College of North Wales, Bangor] 2,2 (1972) 8-12. Interviewed by William R. Lewis.

R.S. Thomas, priest and poet: a transcript of John Ormond's film for B.B.C. Television, broadcast on April 2nd, 1972; introduced by Sam Adams. *PW* 7,4 (1972) 47-57. Incl. interview.

Gwilym Rees Hughes yn holi R.S. Thomas. *Barn*, Gor/Jul 1973, 386-387. [Gwilym Rees Hughes interviewing R.S. Thomas].

Where do we go from here? *Listener*, 8 Aug 1974, 177-178. Discussion of immortality.

Cronfa cartref John Jenkins. *Y Faner*, 16 Ion/Jan 1976, 5:F-H. Letter to editor, with others.

Yr 'Union Jack'. *Y Faner*, 20 Mai/May 1977, 16. Letter.

Gwahaniaethu. *Y Faner*, 19 Aws/Aug 1977, 19. [Differences].

Prynu Enlli: datganiad y cadeirydd. *Llanw Llŷn,* Ebr/Apr 1978, 1.

'Dwyieithedd? Dim perygl!' *Y Faner,* 25 Aws/Aug 1978, 6. Letter. [Bilingual? No fear!].

Owens, Gwenda. Cyfarfod ag R.S. Thomas am y tro cyntaf. *Lleufer* 27,1 (1978) 24-26. [Meeting R.S. Thomas for the first time].

The creative writer's suicide. *Planet* 41 (1978) 30-33. Translation of 'Hunanladdiad y llenor'.

Letter. *WM*, 27 Feb 1979, 10:D. With other Welsh writers, in support of devolution.

Wil Ifans, Enlli. *Llanw Llŷn*, Mai/May 1979, 1.

Achub y Gymraeg. *Y Faner*, 20 Gor/Jul 1979, 5. Letter. [Saving the Welsh language].

Trychineb! *Y Faner*, 27 Gor/Jul 1979, 4. Letter. [Disaster!].

Nid yw Enlli yn eiddo'r genedl. *Y Faner*, 12 Hyd/Oct 1979, 5. Letter. [Bardsey does not belong to the nation].

A prince among poets: Christine Webb talks to R.S. Thomas. *WM*, 26 May 1980, 5:A-C.

Llythyr agored. *Y Faner*, 20 Meh/Jun 1980, 4. Open letter to William Whitelaw, signed by Thomas and others, on role of Welsh language.

Llanw Llŷn. *Y Faner*, 7 Tach/Nov 1980, 10. On nuclear threat.

Letter. *Llanw Llŷn*, Maw/Mar 1981, 13. On nuclear threat.

Atal y dreth incwm. *Y Faner*, 22 Mai/May 1981, 3. Letter. [Avoiding income tax].

Difaterwch llethol. *Y Faner*, 17 Gor/Jul 1981, 4. Letter. [Absolute indifference].

Lorna Keating, 1890-1981. *Llanw Llŷn*, Med/Sep 1981, 19.

Letter. *Llanw Llŷn,* Tach/Nov 1981, 3. On Welsh language in Llŷn.

Neges R.S. Thomas. *Y Faner*, 30 Ebr/Apr 1982, 1. On nuclear energy.

Anerchiadau llywyddion y dydd: y parchedig R.S. Thomas, Dydd mercher Awst 3 1983. In *Llawlyfr Eisteddfod Genedlaethol Cymru.* 1983. pp. 105-107.

Cau ceg er mwyn chwe chant? *Y Faner*, 15 Ebr/Apr 1983, 18. Letter. [Keeping quiet for the sake of six hundred?].

Araith R.S. Thomas. *Y Glorian*, 6 Aug 1983, 2. Special Eisteddfod issue containing his speech to the Llangefni Eisteddfod.

Owen, Rhys. *Pais* yn sgwrsio â R.S. Thomas. *Pais*, Med/Sep 1983, 8-9,20. [*Pais* talking to R.S. Thomas].

R.S. Thomas talks to J.B.Lethbridge. *AWR* 74 (1983) 36-56. Interview on his religious, political and poetic beliefs.

A thicket in Lleyn. In *Britain: a world by itself.* London: Aurum Press, 1984. pp. 92-101.

Yr ateb i ddifodiant. *Y Faner*, 3 Chw/Feb 1984, 10. Review.

Letter. *Llanw Llŷn*, Maw/Mar 1984, 15.

Dim llai brad ar y bobl. *Y Cymro*, 5 Meh/Jun 1984, 1:E-G, 6:C-E. Letter on Gwynedd Health Authority, signed by the poet and others.

Pa amddiffyn sifil? *Y Faner*, 7 Med/Sep 1984, 5.

Cyfeillion Llŷn. *Llanw Llŷn*, Gor/Jul 1985, 1.

Cyngrhair Gwynedd ddi-niwcliar. *Llanw Llŷn*, Gor/Jul 1985, 12. Letter.

Adar Pen Llŷn. *Cynefin*, Hyd/Oct 1985, 10. Letter.

Neb. *Llais Llyfrau*, Gaeaf/Winter 1985, 5-6.

R.S. Thomas, 1913 -. In *Contemporary authors: autobiography series. Vol. 4*, ed. Adele Sarkissian. Detroit: Gale, 1986. pp. 301-313. Autobiographical essay. – An English précis of *Neb*. – Reprinted in *Miraculous simplicity: essays on R.S. Thomas*, ed. William V. Davis (1993). pp. 1-20.

Letter. *Llanw Llŷn*, Maw/Mar 1986, 4. On nuclear winter.

Swyddfa 'Araf'. *Y Faner*, 2 Mai/May 1986, 2. Letter.

Achub yr Indiad. *Y Faner*, 20 Meh/Jun 1986, 17. Letter.

Letter. *Llanw Llŷn*, Meh/Jun 1986, 10. On Welsh language in commerce.

Y twyll mawr. *Y Cymro*, 2 Gor/Jul 1986, 6. Letter.

Pris bach i'w dalu. *Y Cymro*, 17 Med/Sep 1986. 6:A-C. Letter.

Dylanwadau. *Y Faner*, 7 Tach/Nov 1986, 12-13. [Influences].

Letter. *Llanw Llŷn*, Maw/Mar 1987, 23. On Welsh language in Llŷn.

Tynged yr iaith '87. *Sbec*, 24-30 Jun 1987, 17. [The fate of the language '87].

Dirywiad ers 1962. *Barn*, Tach/Nov 1987, 430-431.

Gwladgarwch nid cenedlaetholdeb. *Y Ddraig Goch* [Eisteddfod number] (1987) 4-5. [Patriotism not nationalism].

What fate for the language? *Planet* 61 (1987) 30-31. Contribution to a symposium on Saunders Lewis's 1962 radio lecture.

Letter. *Llanw Llŷn*, Hyd/Oct 1988, 15.

Unity. *Planet* 70 (1988) 29-42. Translation by Katie Jones of 'Undod', the J.R. Jones memorial lecture delivered at University College Swansea, 9 Dec 1985.

Arwahanrwydd cenedl ac ansawdd ei hiaith. *Taliesin* 65 (1988) 88-90. [The separateness of a nation and the quality of its language].

Language, exile, a writer and the future. *The Works* [Welsh Union of Writers] 1 (1988) 22-43. Transcript of talk and ensuing discussion at annual conference of the Welsh Union of Writers, Coleg Harlech, Sep 1987.

Y baich ar ein gwar. *Y Faner*, 30 Meh/Jun 1989, 12-14. TV lecture given on 'Y byd ar bedwar', 26 Jun 1989. [The burden on our back].

Annwyl gadeirydd Bwrdd yr Iaith. *Y Faner*, 2 Chw/Feb 1990, 4. Letter.

Y bardd yn erbyn y byd? Tyndra bywyd a gwaith R.S. Thomas. *Golwg*, 5 Ebr/Apr 1990, 22-25. Interviewed by Dylan Iorworth. – [The poet against the world? Tension in the life and work of R.S. Thomas].

Siarad fel bardd. *Y Cymro*, 26 Med/Sep 1990, 14:B-G. Interviewed by Annes Glyn. – [Talking like a poet].

Probings: an interview with R.S. Thomas. *Planet* 80 (1990) 28-52. Interviewed by Ned Thomas and John Barnie.

Reflections on a speech at Machynlleth. *Planet* 84 (1990) 3-6.

Cyfeillion Llŷn. *Y Faner*, 22 Chw/Feb 1991, 17. Letter.

R.S. Thomas at seventy. In M. J.J. van Buuren, *Waiting: the religious poetry of Ronald Stuart Thomas, Welsh poet and priest.* Nijmegen: Katholieke Universiteit van Nijmegen, 1993. pp. 172-181. – Text of a broadcast, BBC Radio 3, 7 Dec 1983, with contributions by the poet.

Tribute to a poet in the trenches. *WM*, 11 Mar 1993, 10:A-G. On Wilfred Owen.

Cyfraith a threfn ... cyfraith a thrais. *Barn*, Maw/Mar 1993, 6-7. On the circumstances under which violence may be justifiable.

Ett ramverk för poesin. *Härnstorm* [Uppsala] 45-46 (1993) 41-43. Article, translated and abridged by Magnus Ringgren. – With translations (by Lars Nyström and Bo Gustavsson) of 11 R.S. Thomas poems.

Birding. *Planet* 98 (1993) 9-15. On ornithological trips to Poland and Greece.

– This issue also contains (p.42) 'Although my flesh is straw', R.S. Thomas's translation of a poem by Ehedydd Iâl (William Jones).

## B. Publications about R.S. Thomas

There have been six collections of critical essays on R.S. Thomas, two edited by Sandra Anstey (1982; 1992), two by M. Wynn Thomas (1990; 1993) and one each by A.E. Dyson (1990) and William V. Davis (1993). Their contents are given below. Anstey and Dyson reprint published criticism, as does Davis (1993) for the most part. The M. Wynn Thomas collections consist of essays published for the first time. The bibliography in Anstey (1992) extensively lists reviews of R.S. Thomas.

ABBS, Peter. The revival of the mythopoeic imagination: a study of R.S. Thomas and Ted Hughes. *PW* 10,4 (1975) 10-27. – Reprinted, with slight changes, in *Root and blossom: essays on the philosophy, practice and politics of English teaching.* London: Heinemann Educational, 1976. pp. 106-119.

ACKERMAN, John. Man and nature in the poetry of R.S. Thomas. *PW* 7,4 (1972) 15-26.

—— [as J.A. Jones]. The role of nature in the poetry of Edward Thomas, Dylan Thomas, Vernon Watkins and R.S. Thomas. PhD thesis. University of London (Birkbeck), 1981.

—— R.S. Thomas: poet for our time. *AWR* 85 (1987) 103-111. Review article on *Experimenting with an amen.*

ADAMS, Sam. A note on four poems. *PW* 7,4 (1972) 75-81. Discusses 'Service', 'In church', 'Kneeling' and 'They'.

ADKINS, Joan. R.S. Thomas and 'A little point'. *Little Review* 13-14 (1980) 15-19.

ALLCHIN, A.M. Generously as bread: a study of the poetry of R.S. Thomas. *New Blackfriars*, Jun 1970, 274-280.

—— The poetry of R.S. Thomas: an introduction. *Theology*, Nov 1970, 488-495.

—— Emerging: a look at some of R.S. Thomas' more recent poems. *Theology*, Sep 1978, 352-361.

—— Out of the silence. *Planet* 85 (1991) 98-100. Review of *Counterpoint.*

—— An inexplicable note of hope. *NWR* 5,4 [20] (1993) 10-14.

ANSTEY, Sandra. A study of R.S. Thomas's literary achievement, with a full bibliography. PhD thesis. University of Wales (Swansea), 1981. 349 p. Incl. Bibliography, with alphabetical and chronological lists of poems, and list of 'poems in manuscript, printed form or broadcast, that have not so far been collected', pp. 253-349.

—— *Critical writings on R.S. Thomas,* ed. Sandra Anstey. Bridgend: Poetry Wales Press, 1982. 162 p. Contents: Introduction, by Sandra Anstey, pp. 9-16 – The poetry of R.S. Thomas, by Cecil Price, pp. 21-25 – A true poet, by Kingsley Amis, pp. 29-30 – Hewer of verses, by Benedict Nightingale, pp. 33-35 – Humanus sum: a second look at R.S. Thomas, by R. G. Thomas, pp. 39-48 – The Iago Prytherch poems of R.S. Thomas, by H.J. Savill, pp. 51-64 – R.S. Thomas, by Timothy Wilson, pp. 67-71 –

R.S. Thomas: occasional prose, by Randal Jenkins, pp. 75-89 – Review of *What is a Welshman?*, by Lyndon Pugh, pp. 93-97 – The revival of the mythopoeic imagination: a study of R.S. Thomas and Ted Hughes, by Peter Abbs, pp. 101-115 – Emerging: a look at some of R.S. Thomas' more recent poems, by A.M. Allchin, pp. 119-129 – Signs from the periphery, by John Mole, pp. 133-136 – The topography of R.S. Thomas, by Brian Morris, pp. 139-152 – Select bibliography, pp. 155-162.

—— New edition. Bridgend: Seren Books, 1992. 235 p. Contents: Introduction, by Sandra Anstey, pp. 7-12 – The poetry of R.S. Thomas, by Cecil Price, pp. 13-18 – Humanus sum: a second look at R.S. Thomas, by R. G. Thomas, pp. 19-29 – The Iago Prytherch poems of R.S. Thomas, by H.J. Savill, pp. 30-45 – R.S. Thomas: occasional prose, by Randal Jenkins, pp. 46-61 – Philosophy and religion in the poetry of R.S. Thomas, by Roland Mathias, pp. 62-82 – The revival of the mythopoeic imagination: a study of R.S. Thomas and Ted Hughes, by Peter Abbs, pp. 83-99 – Emerging: a look at some of R.S. Thomas' more recent poems, by A.M. Allchin, pp. 100-111 – The topography of R.S. Thomas, by Brian Morris, pp. 112-127 – Attempts to evade: R.S. Thomas's 'Impressions', by James A. Davies, pp. 128-144 – Across the grain, by John Barnie, pp. 145-153 – R.S. Thomas and his readers, by Tony Bianchi, pp. 154-181- On the screen of eternity: some aspects of R.S. Thomas's prose, by Tony Brown, pp. 182-201 – Exploring the God-space: the later poetry of R.S. Thomas, by K.E. Smith, pp. 202-211 – Out of the silence, by A.M. Allchin, pp. 212-216 – Collections of R.S. Thomas's poetry, p. 217 – Bibliography of critical materials on R.S. Thomas's writings, pp. 218-235.

ASPDEN, Brian. Prams. *PW* 29,1 (1993) 24-25. 'Some thoughts on R.S. Thomas'.

BABEL 1 (1983). R.S. Thomas section, pp. 3-61, with poems and prose by the author (original and translated), articles by Heinz Willkomm and Marie-Thérèse Castay, and biographical and bibliographical notes.

BARNIE, John. *The king of ashes*. Llandysul: Gomer Press, 1989. Incl.: Beauty and bread [on *Pe medrwn yr iaith ac ysgrifau eraill*], pp. 3-13 – Never forget your Welsh [on *Welsh airs*], pp. 14-19 – Across the grain [on *Neb*], pp. 20-27. – Reprinted from *Planet* 71 (1988) 54-63; *Planet* 68 (1988) 95-98; *Planet* 56 (1986) 101-106.

—— The candle in the window. *Planet* 86 (1991) 68-77. Review article on R.S. Thomas, *Blwyddyn yn Llŷn*.

BEDIENT, Calvin. On R.S. Thomas. *Critical Quarterly* 14 (1972) 253-268.

—— *Eight contemporary poets*. London: Oxford University Press, 1974. Incl. R.S. Thomas, pp. 51-68.

BIANCHI, Tony. R.S. Images for a divided identity. *Welsh Books and Writers* [Welsh Books Council], Autumn 1980, 15-18. On R.S. Thomas and the Welsh-language poet Gwyn Thomas.

—— R.S. Thomas and his readers. In *Wales: the imagined nation: studies in cultural and national identity*, ed. Tony Curtis. Bridgend: Poetry Wales Press, 1986. pp. 71-95.

BLACKBURN, Thomas. *The price of an eye*. London: Longmans, 1961. Incl. discussion of Thomas, pp. 158-159.

BROWN, Tony. Language, poetry and silence: some themes in the poetry of R.S. Thomas. In *The Welsh connection: essays ...*, ed. William Tydeman. Llandysul: Gomer Press, 1986. pp. 159-185.

—— On the screen of eternity: some aspects of R.S. Thomas's prose. *PR* 21 (1987-88) 5-15.

—— The romantic nationalism of R.S. Thomas. In *The literature of place*, ed. Norman Page and Peter Preston. London: Macmillan, 1993. pp. 156-169.

BUUREN, M.J.J. van. *Waiting: the religious poetry of Ronald Stuart Thomas, Welsh poet and priest*. Nijmegen: Katholieke Universiteit van Nijmegen, 1993. 183 p. Incl. as appendix the text of a broadcast, R.S. Thomas at seventy, BBC Radio 3, 7 Dec 1983 (with contributions by Kevin Crossley Holland, Andrew Waterman, Robin Young, Gwyn Jones, D.Z. Phillips, and the poet himself). – Doctoral thesis.

BURNHAM, Richard. *The Dublin Magazine's* Welsh poets. *AWR* 27,60 (1978) 49-63.

CARPANINI, Rudolf G. Romanticism in the poetry of R.S. Thomas. *Annali dell' Instituto di Lingue e Letterature Germaniche* [Universita di Parma] 6 (1980-81) 113-148.

—— *Deictic subversion and intertextuality in R.S. Thomas's* 'Here': *a stylistic approach to poetic discourse*. Parma: Edizioni Universitarie Casanova, 1984. 13 p.

CASTAY, Marie-Thérèse. From *The stones of the field* to *Pietà* by R.S. Thomas: a poetry of hunger. Maîtresse des Lettres thesis. University of Toulouse, 1967. 110 p. Contents: R.S. Thomas, a portrait – R.S. Thomas and the Welsh predicament – R.S. Thomas and the country world – Towards a philosophy of nature – The expression of a personal hunger – The relevance of R.S. Thomas's message – Bibliography.

—— Un poète gallois contemporain: R.S. Thomas. *Caliban* 5 (1968) 147-156.

—— Les images dans la poésie de R.S. Thomas. *Caliban* 7 (1970) 115-120.

—— English enriched by Celtic poets. *Spoken English* 10,3 (1977) 101-108.

—— R.S. Thomas. *Apex* 3 (1978) 8-27.

—— Nature and some Anglo-Welsh poets. *PW* 15,2 (1979) 100-110.

—— Développement de la poésie anglo-galloise (1930-1980). *Caliban* 18 (1981) 21-32.

—— Trajectoires dans la vie et l'oeuvre de R.S. Thomas. In *Pays de Galles, Écosse, Irlande: actes du Congrès de Brest, Mai 1986*. Brest: Centre de Recherches Bretonnes et Celtiques, 1987. (Cahiers de Bretagne Occidentale; 7). pp. 33-41.

CHAN Man Fong, Gisela. Themen und Bilder in der Dichtung von Ronald Stuart Thomas. MA thesis. University of Kiel, 1969. 50 p. Contents: Die Zeitgenössische Englische Lyrik – Wales, ein Existenzhintergrund – Der Dichter, Die Süche nach Identität – Zusammenfassung – Benutzte Literatur. – Review: *PW* 7,4 (1972) 112-115 (Glyn Tegai Hughes). – [Themes and images in the poetry of R.S. Thomas].

COLLINS, Michael J. The elegiac tradition in contemporary Anglo-Welsh poetry. *AWR* 76 (1984) 46-58.

CONRAN, Anthony. The English poet in Wales, 2. Boys of summer in their ruin. *AWR* 10,26 (1960) 11-21. Considers Dylan Thomas, R.S. Thomas and Vernon Watkins.

—— Anglo-Welsh poetry today. Part 2. *PW* 5,1 (1969) 9-12.

—— R.S. Thomas and the Anglo-Welsh crisis. *PW* 7,4 (1972) 67-74.

—— R.S. Thomas as a mystical poet. *PW* 14,4 (1979) 11-25.

—— *The cost of strangeness: essays on the English poets of Wales.* Llandysul: Gomer Press, 1982. Incl. Aspects of R.S. Thomas, pp. 220-262.

—— What a passionate poet this man is! *NWR* 5,4 [20] (1993) 15-19. Review article on *Collected poems: 1945-1990.*

COX, C.B. Welsh bards in hard times: Dylan Thomas and R.S. Thomas. In *The new Pelican guide to English literature. Vol. 8. The present,* ed. Boris Ford. Harmondsworth: Penguin, 1983. pp. 209-223.

—— [and A.E. Dyson]. *Modern poetry: studies in practical criticism.* London: Arnold, 1963. Incl. 'A blackbird singing', by R.S. Thomas, pp. 133-166.

—— [and A.E. Dyson]. *The practical criticism of poetry: a textbook.* London: Arnold, 1965. Incl. Exercise 2. A seminar on R.S. Thomas's 'Here', with questions, pp. 35-45.

CURTIS, Tony. *How to study modern poetry.* London: Macmillan, 1990. Discusses 'A peasant', pp. 82-90.

DAFIS, Dewi T. R.S. Thomas: rhai agweddau. *Ffenics* [University College of North Wales, Bangor] 2,1 (1971) 28-32. [R.S. Thomas: some aspects].

DAVIE, Donald. R.S. Thomas's poetry of the Church in Wales. *Religion and Literature* 19,2 (1987) 35-48.

—— *Under Briggflatts: a history of poetry in Great Britain, 1960-1988.* Manchester: Carcanet, 1989. Incl. R.S. Thomas, pp. 147-150.

DAVIES, Geraint. A tale of two Thomases: reflections on two Anglo-Welsh poets. In *Nationalism in literature/Literarischer Nationalismus: literature, language and national identity,* ed. Horst W. Drescher and Hermann Volkel. Frankfurt: Peter Lang, 1989. pp. 289-297. On Dylan and R.S. Thomas.

DAVIES, James A. Participating readers: three poems by R.S. Thomas. *PW* 18,4 (1983) 72-84. Discusses 'The airy tomb', 'The country clergy' and 'Poste Restante'.

—— Attempts to evade: R.S. Thomas's 'Impressions'. *AWR* 79 (1985) 70-83.

DAVIES, Jason Walford. Adleisiau'n dechrau dihuno. *Taliesin* 83 (1993) 59-71. On R.S. Thomas's references to Welsh literature.

DAVIES, Walford. R.S. Thomas: the poem's harsher conditions. *NWR* 3,3 [11] (1991) 15-25. See also D.Z. Phillips, Poetry and philosophy: a reply, *NWR* 3,4 [12] 64-68, and Walford Davies, Poetry and philosophy: a rejoinder, *NWR* 3,4 [12] 68-71.

DAVIS, William V. An abstraction blooded: Wallace Stevens and R.S. Thomas on blackbirds and men. *Wallace Stevens Journal* 8,2 (1984) 79-82.

—— R.S. Thomas: poet-priest of the apocalyptic mode. *South Central Review* 4,4 (1987) 92-106.

—— *Miraculous simplicity: essays on R.S. Thomas,* ed. William V. Davis. Fayetteville: University of Arkansas Press, 1993. xiv, 248 p. Contents: Autobiographical essay, by R.S. Thomas, pp. 1-20 – Probings: an interview with R.S. Thomas, by Ned Thomas and John Barnie, pp. 21-46 – The topography of R.S. Thomas, by Brian Morris, pp. 47-60 – Keeping his pen clean: R.S. Thomas and Wales, by M. Wynn Thomas, pp. 61-79 – Humanus sum: a second look at R.S. Thomas, by R. George Thomas, pp. 80-88 – Via negativa: absence and presence in the recent poetry of R.S. Thomas, by J.D. Vicary, pp. 89-101 – R.S. Thomas: the landscape of near-despair, by Robert Nisbet, pp. 102-109 – R.S. Thomas: poet-priest of the apocalyptic mode, by William V. Davis, pp. 110-126 – R.S. Thomas's poetry of the Church in Wales, by Donald Davie, pp. 127- 140 – Negativity and language in the religious poetry of R.S. Thomas, by Vimala Herman, pp. 140-161 – The gap in the hedge: R.S. Thomas's emblem poetry, by Belinda Humfrey, pp. 162-169 – R.S. Thomas and the vanishing God of form and number, by Julian Gitzen, pp. 170-181 – On the screen of eternity: some aspects of R.S. Thomas's prose, by Tony Brown, pp. 182-199 – The unmanageable bone: language in R.S. Thomas's poetry, by Patrick Deane, pp. 200-224 – Pessimism and its counters: *Between here and now* and after, by James A. Davies, pp. 225-243 – Bibliography, pp. 244-248. – All are reprinted essays, except for those by M. Wynn Thomas and James A. Davies; the Tony Brown essay is revised.

DEANE, Patrick. The unmanageable bone: language in R.S. Thomas's poetry. *Renascence* 42,4 (1990) 213-236.

DYSON, A.E. The poetry of R.S. Thomas. *Critical Quarterly* 20,2 (1978) 5-31.

—— *Yeats, Eliot and R.S. Thomas: riding the echo.* London: Macmillan, 1981. Incl. discussion of Thomas, pp. 285-326.

—— *Three contemporary poets: Thom Gunn, Ted Hughes and R.S. Thomas: a case-*book ed. A.E. Dyson. London: Macmillan, 1990. Incl. Thomas on himself and poetry, pp. 199-203 – Natural magic and moral profundity (1974), by Calvin Bedient, pp. 204-215 – On the recent poetry of R.S. Thomas (1978), by John Mole, pp. 215-222 – Untenanted cross (1978), by Kevin Nichols, pp. 222-228 – Poet of vision (1979), by Anthony Conran, pp. 229-232 – Mr Thomas's present concerns (1979), by Brian Morris, pp. 232-242 – The adult geometry of the mind (1980), by I.R.F. Gordon, pp. 242-247 – R.S. Thomas and 'a little point' (1980), by Joan F. Adkins, pp. 248-258 – Riding the echo (1981), by A.E. Dyson, pp. 259-282.

EDWARDS, Emrys. Dwylath i'm hysbrydoli: portread o R.S. Thomas. *Barddas,* Hyd/Oct 1976, 3. [A six-footer to inspire me: portrait of R.S. Thomas].

GARLICK, Raymond. Editorial. *DL* 6,18 (1955) 1-9. On R.S. Thomas.

—— Editorial. *AWR* 9,24 (1958) 3-8. Incl. discussion of Thomas's Iago Prytherch poems.

GINGERICH, Martin E. *Contemporary poetry in America and England, 1950-1975: a guide to information sources.* Detroit: Gale Research, 1983. (American literature, English literature and world literatures: English information guide series; vol. 41). Incl. annotated bibliography of R.S. Thomas, pp. 384-388.

GITZEN, Julian. British nature poetry now. *Midwest Quarterly* 15 (1974) 323-327. Incl. discussion of Thomas.

—— R.S. Thomas and the vanishing God of form and number. *Contemporary Poetry* 5,2 (1983) 1-16.

GORDON, I.R.F. The adult geometry of the mind: the recent poetry of R.S. Thomas. *Little Review* 13-14 (1980) 12-14.

GOUGH, Penelope E.A. The theology of R.S. Thomas. PHD thesis. University of Nottingham, 1991. 2 vols. 484 p.

GRAVIL, Richard. Wordsworth's second selves? *Wordsworth Circle* 14 (1983) 191-201.

GREEN, Harry. Poet-parson with the Welsh moors as his parish. *WM*, 1 Oct 1958, 6:B-H.

GRUFFYDD, Peter. The poetry of R.S. Thomas. *PW* 2,1 (1966) 13-17.

HAINSWORTH, J.D. Extremes in poetry: R.S. Thomas and Ted Hughes. *English* 14 (1963) 226-230.

HARDY, Barbara. Region and nation: R.S. Thomas and Dylan Thomas. In *The literature of region and nation,* ed. R.P. Draper. London: Macmillan, 1989. pp. 93-107.

—— Imagining R.S. Thomas's amen. *PW* 29,1 (1993) 21-22

HASSAN, Hasan Marhama. Jewels of blood: an Arab perspective on R.S. Thomas. PhD thesis. University of Wales (Aberystwyth), 1985. xii, 393 p. Contents: The Welsh heritage, a brief study – The concept of the past in Anglo-Welsh poetry – R.S. Thomas's role in preserving the past – Badr Shakir Al-Sayyub and the voyage to the past – Wales under English domination – The land of lost hope: R.S. Thomas's image of Wales – The envoy of a wound: Mahmoud Darwish's poetry on Palestine – The growth of Welsh nationalism – R.S. Thomas and Welsh nationalism – Ahmad Abdl Muti Hijazi and the party of revolution – Conclusion – Transcript of a personal interview with R.S. Thomas, pp. 328-365 – Bibliography, pp. 366-393.

HENDERSON, Ruth Anne. Translating the silence. *NWR* 5,4 [20] (1993) 30-34. On difficulties of translating R.S. Thomas into Italian.

HERMAN, Vimala. The priest as poet: a study of George Herbert, Gerard Manley Hopkins and R.S. Thomas. PhD thesis. University of Exeter, 1976.

—— Negativity and language in the religious poetry of R.S. Thomas. *ELH* 45,4 (1978) 710-731.

HIGNETT, D. J. *A selection of poetry by R. S. Thomas: GCE set book notes for O level students.* Formby: Hignett Schools Services, 1977. 12 p.

HOOKER, Jeremy. Review article on *H'm. PW* 7,4 (1972) 89-93.

—— *The presence of the past: essays on modern British and American poetry.* Bridgend: Poetry Wales Press, 1987. Incl. R.S. Thomas: Prytherch and after, pp. 128-140.

HUMFREY, Belinda. The gap in the hedge: R.S. Thomas's emblem poetry. *AWR* 26,58 (1977) 49-57.

HURST, J.S. Poetry is religion: the evolution of R.S. Thomas. *Expository Times,* Apr 1986, 195-200.

JASPER, David. Two or three gathered in his name: reflections on the English pastoral tradition in religious poetry. *Christianity and Literature* 38,1 (1988) 19-32.

JENKINS, Randal. R.S. Thomas: occasional prose. *PW* 7,4 (1972) 93-108.

JONES, Bobi. R.S. Thomas a'r genedl. *Barddas* 198 (1993) 20-23. First of an extended series of articles considering R.S. Thomas in the context of nation, the Movement, the Anglo-Welsh, and 'gwacter llawn' [full emptiness].

JONES, Glenys. Yn Abercuawg yt ganant gogeu. *Y Faner*, 10 Med/Sep 1976, 2:A-D. [In Abercuawg cuckoos sing].

JONES, Glyn. R.S. Thomas. In *Contemporary poets,* ed. James Vinson. 2nd. ed. London: St. James Press; New York: St. Martin's Press, 1975. pp. 1539-1541.

KEITH, W.J. *The poetry of nature: rural perspectives in poetry from Wordsworth to the present.* Toronto: Toronto University Press, 1980. Incl. R.S. Thomas, pp. 186-195.

—— R.S. Thomas. In *Poets of Great Britain and Ireland, 1945-1960,* ed. Vincent B. Sherry. Detroit: Gale, 1984. (Dictionary of Literary Biography; 27). pp. 346-356.

KNAPP, James Franklin. R.S. Thomas and the plain style in British poetry. PhD thesis. University of Connecticut, 1966.

—— The poetry of R.S. Thomas. *Twentieth Century Literature* 17,1 (1971) 1-9.

KORBI, Jill Kristin. R.S. Thomas and God: issues of language and communication with special reference to Thomas's later poems. MA thesis. University of Wales (Bangor), 1984.

LETHBRIDGE, J.B. Reciprocating touch: man in the poetry of R.S. Thomas. M. Phil thesis. University of Dundee, 1982.

—— R.S. Thomas. In *Reference guide to English literature,* ed. D.L. Kirkpatrick. 2nd ed. 3 vols. Chicago; London: St James Press, 1991. Vol. 2, pp. 1321-1322.

LEWIS, H.D. The later poetry of R.S. Thomas. *PW* 14,4 (1979) 26-30.

LLOYD, Megan Sue. Texts against chaos: Anglo-Welsh identity in the poetry of R.S. Thomas, Raymond Garlick and Roland Mathias. PhD thesis. University of Kentucky, 1992. 417 p.

MAGARASEVIC, Mirko. Pjesnistvo R.S. Tomasa. *Savremenik* 56,11 (1982) 495-499. Serbo-Croat. – [The poetry of R.S. Thomas].

MATHIAS, Roland. Editorial. *AWR* 13,31 (1963) 3-14.

—— *A ride through the wood: essays on Anglo-Welsh literature.* Bridgend: Poetry Wales Press, 1985. Incl. Philosophy and religion in the poetry of R.S. Thomas, pp. 186-205. – Reprinted from *PW* 7,4 (1972) 27-45.

MATTHEWS, Laurella. The poetry of R.S. Thomas. *Province* 11,4 (1960) 132-140.

MEIR, Colin. The poetry of R.S. Thomas. In *British poetry since 1970: a critical survey,* ed. Peter Jones and Michael Schmidt. Manchester: Carcanet, 1980. pp. 1-13.

MERCHANT, W. Moelwyn. The art of R.S. Thomas. *Province* 9,4 (1958) 116-125, 142.

—— R.S. Thomas. *Critical Quarterly* 2 (1960) 341-351.

—— *R.S. Thomas.* Cardiff: University of Wales Press, 1989. 77 p. ISBN: 0-7083-1034-6. Selected bibliography, pp. 74-76. – Reissue of volume first published in the Writers of Wales series, 1979.

—— The sense of place in the poetry of Henry Vaughan and R.S. Thomas. *THSC,* 1983, 69-80.

MINHINNICK, Robert. Living with R.S. Thomas. *PW* 29,1 (1993) 11-14.

MOLE, John. On the recent poetry of R.S. Thomas. *New Poetry* 43 (1978) 6-11.

—— Signals from the periphery. *TLS*, 2 Jun 1978, 608. Review article on *Frequencies*.

MORRIS, Brian. Mr Thomas's present concerns. *PW* 14,4 (1979) 31-42.

—— The topography of R.S. Thomas. *Little Review* 13-14 (1980) 5-11.

MORRIS, John S. The hail of love: self-recognition in R.S. Thomas. *Little Review* 13-14 (1980) 30-36.

NEWMAN, Elizabeth. Voices and perspectives in the poetry of R.S. Thomas. In *Linguistics and the study of literature*, ed. Theo D'haen. Amsterdam: Rodopi, 1986. pp. 56-71.

NICHOLS, Kevin. Untenanted cross: the poetry of R.S. Thomas. *Clergy Review*, Mar 1978, 82-85.

NISBET, Robert. R.S. Thomas: the landscape of near-despair. *Planet 35* (1976) 26-30.

NORRIS, Leslie. Letter. *PW* 7,4 (1972) 118-121. On R.S. Thomas.

NYE, Robert. A proper language for the telling of truth. *WM* (Literary Review), 17 Jul 1964, 7:A-D.

OPPEL, Horst. R.S. Thomas: 'The meeting'. In *Die moderne englische Lyrik: Interpretationen,* ed. Horst Oppel. Berlin: E. Schmidt, 1967. pp. 309-316.

ORMOND, John. R.S. Thomas, priest and poet: a transcript of John Ormond's film for BBC Television, broadcast on April 2nd, 1972; introduced by Sam Adams. *PW* 7,4 (1972) 47-57.

OXLEY, William. The taste of faith: a commentary on the poetry of R.S. Thomas. In *On poets and poetry, 4th series,* ed. James Hogg. Salzburg: Institut fur Anglistik und Amerikanistik, 1982. (Salzburg studies in English literature, poetic drama & poetic theory; 27). pp. 64-82.

PEZZINI, Domenico. La poesie della passione nelle tradizione letteraria inglese: dal *Sogno della croce* a R.S. Thomas. *Revista di storia e letteratura religiosa* [Florence] 26,3 (1990) 460-507.

PHILLIPS, D.Z. *Through a darkening glass: philosophy, literature and cultural change.* Oxford: Blackwell, 1982. Incl. Seeking the poem in the pain: order and contingency in the poetry of R.S. Thomas, pp. 165-190.

—— *R.S. Thomas, poet of the hidden God: meaning and mediation in the poetry of R.S. Thomas.* Basingstoke: Macmillan, 1986. xviii, 186 p. Incl. bibliography, pp. 180-184.

—— *From fantasy to faith: the philosophy of religion and twentieth century literature.* London: Macmillan, 1991. Incl. Revealing the hidden (R.S. Thomas), pp. 201-211.

—— On his knees with his eyes open. *NWR* 5,4 [20] (1993) 20-23. Review article on *Mass for hard times*.

PIKOULIS, John. R.S. Thomas's existential agony. *PW* 29,1 (1993) 26-32.

PIPE, Chris. Honest doubts. *Third-Way* 3,3 (1979) 27-28.

PITTMAN, Philip McM. The real language of men: Wordsworth and R.S. Thomas. *Little Review* 13-14 (1980) 20-25.

POOLE, Richard. R.S. Thomas at 80. *PW* 29,1 (1993) 2-6. Surveys recent publications by and about the poet.

PRESS, John. *Rule and energy: trends in British poetry since the second world war.*

London: Oxford University Press, 1963. Incl. discussion of R.S. Thomas, pp. 139-149.

PRICE, Cecil. The poetry of R.S. Thomas. *Welsh Anvil* 4 (1952) 82-86.

PUGH, Lyndon. A critical analysis of the poetry of R.S. Thomas in relation to Wales and the Anglo-Welsh tradition. MA thesis. University of Wales (Aberystwyth), 1975. 205 p. Contents: The Anglo-Welsh; a definition, pp. 1-36 – *Song at the year's turning; Stones of the field; An acre of land;* later poems, 1952-1958, pp. 37-113 – Poems, 1958-1966, pp. 114-169 – Poems, 1969-1974; *Not that he brought flowers; H'm,* pp. 170-199 – Bibliography, pp. 200-205.

REES, Ioan Bowen. Review article on *The mountains. PW* 7,4 (1972) 109-112.

ROBINSON, Marion. And now we have the movement, mostly still: a study of a group of contemporary British poets. PhD thesis. University of Exeter, 1964. Incl. The mind's scansion: R.S. Thomas, pp. 74-171.

ROGERS, Byron. The enigma of Aberdaron. *Telegraph Sunday Magazine,* 7 Nov 1975, 25-29.

ROKKAN, Elizabeth. Wales and the Welsh. In *Papers from the First Nordic Conference for English studies, Oslo, 17-19 Sep 1980,* ed. Stig Johansson and Bjorn Tysdahl. Oslo: Institute of English Studies, University of Oslo, 1981. pp. 170-182.

ROPER, Edward Benson. A study of the cycle of nature in the early poetry of R.S. Thomas. PhD thesis. University of Alabama, 1989. 195 p.

ROWLANDS, John. John Rowlands yn rhoi ei argraffiadau am ddarlith R.S. Thomas, *Abercuawg. BNW,* Winter 1976, 19. [John Rowlands giving his impressions on R.S. Thomas's lecture, *Abercuawg*].

RUNCIE, C.A. The poetry of R.S. Thomas. *Poetry Australia* 8,43 (1972) 56-58.

SAVILL, H.J. The Iago Prytherch poems of R.S. Thomas. *AWR* 20,45 (1971) 143-154.

SCHMIDT, Michael. *An introduction to 50 modern British poets.* London: Pan, 1979. (Pan literature guides). Incl. R.S. Thomas, pp. 260-265.

SHIVPURI, Jagdish. Two contemporary poets in English: Jon Silkin and R.S. Thomas. *Siddha* 10 (1975) 1-25.

SISSON, C.H. R.S. Thomas: a vivid stubbornness. *PW* 29,1 (1993) 9.

SMITH, Dorothy Anita. R.S. Thomas: the poet as querulous. PhD thesis. St. John's University, N.Y., 1970.

SMITH, Ken Edward. Exploring the God-space: the later poetry of R.S. Thomas. *Planet* 73 (1989) 54-61.

SMITH, Stan. R.S. Thomas. In *Contemporary poets,* ed. Tracy Chevalier. 5th ed. Chicago; London: St. James Press, 1991. pp. 988-989.

STACY, Tom. Andrew Young, R.S. Thomas and the parson poets. *Essays by Divers Hands* 42 (1982) 91-108.

SUTTON, Max Keith. Truth and the pastor's vision in George Crabbe, William Barnes and R.S. Thomas. In *Survivals of pastoral,* ed. Richard F. Hardin. Lawrence: University of Kansas, 1979. pp. 33-59.

TATHAM, M.A. The long dialectic of rain and sunlight. *New Blackfriars,* Jun 1977, 273-285.

THOMAS, Dafydd Elis. The image of Wales in R.S. Thomas's poetry. *PW* 7,4 (1972) 59-66.

THOMAS, Ethel M. A Welsh poet and the English reader: a short study of aspects of the work of R.S. Thomas. MA thesis. University of Wales (Cardiff), 1967. 101 p.

THOMAS, Gwilym. Rheithoriaid a beirdd ym Manafon. *Barddas,* Gor/Jul 1988, 36-38. On William Wynn, Evan Evans, Walter Davies, William Morgan and R.S. Thomas. – [Rectors and poets in Manafon].

THOMAS, M. Wynn. *R.S. Thomas: y cawr awenydd,* ed. M. Wynn Thomas. Llandysul: Gwasg Gomer, 1990. xxiv, 116 p.: ill. ISBN: 0-86383-543-0. Contents: Rhagymadrodd, by M. Wynn Thomas, pp. xiii-xxiv – Barddoniaeth R.S. Thomas, by Gwyn Thomas, pp. 1-22 – Agweddau ar farddoniaeth y chwedegau, by M. Wynn Thomas, pp. 23-41 – Y cwestiwn ynglŷn â thechnoleg, by Ned Thomas, pp. 42-50 – Painter, with your impressed brush: yr elfen arlunio ym marddoniaeth R.S. Thomas, a'i gerddi darlun, by Gareth Alban Davies, pp. 51-76 – Y Duw cudd, a conversation between M. Wynn Thomas, Gwyn Erfyl and Dewi Z. Phillips, pp. 77-95 – Yr ymchwiliwr crefyddol, by Pennar Davies, pp. 96-114. – Reviews: *Planet* 83 (1990) 18-23 (A.M. Allchin); *Poetry Wales* 26,2 (1990) 64-67 (Tony Brown). – See also Walford Davies. *NWR* 3,3 [11] (1991) 15-25.

—— *Internal difference: twentieth-century writing in Wales.* Cardiff: University of Wales Press, 1992. Incl.: R.S. Thomas: the poetry of the Sixties, pp. 107-129 – Songs of ignorance and praise: R.S. Thomas's poems about the four people in his life, pp. 130-155. – Shorter version of first essay published in Welsh in *R.S. Thomas: y cawr awenydd,* ed. M. Wynn Thomas (1990).

—— *The page's drift: R.S. Thomas at eighty,* ed. M. Wynn Thomas. Bridgend: Seren Books, 1993. Contents: The one [poem], by R.S. Thomas, p. [7] – Introduction, by M. Wynn Thomas, pp. 9-21 – Some uncollected poems and variant readings from the early work of R.S. Thomas, by Sandra Anstey, pp. 22-35 – The uses of Prytherch, by Anne Stevenson, pp. 36-56 – R.S. Thomas and painting, by Helen Vendler, pp. 57-81 – Adult geometry: dangerous thoughts in R.S. Thomas, by Rowan Williams, pp. 82-98 – The verbal hunger: the use and significance of 'gaps' in the poetry of R.S. Thomas, by William W. Davis, pp. 99-118 – The self and the other: the autobiographical element in R.S. Thomas's poetry, by Marie-Thérèse Castay, pp. 119-147 – Over seventy thousand fathoms: the sea and self-definition in the poetry of R.S. Thomas, by Tony Brown, pp. 148-170 – Bright fields, loud hills and the glimpsed good place: R.S. Thomas and Dylan Thomas, by Walford Davies, pp. 171-210 – R.S. Thomas and Wales, by Ned Thomas, pp. 211-220 – The poet [poem], by Gillian Clarke, p. 221 – Select bibliography, pp. 222-225.

—— Bardd enbydrwydd bywyd. *Barn,* Mai/May 1993, 40-41. Extended review of *Collected poems.*

—— Reviewing R.S. *Books in Wales,* Summer 1993, 5-7. On his reputation, mainly in England.

THOMAS, Ned. R.S. Thomas. *Welsh Books and Writers* [Welsh Books Council], Autumn 1982, 3-4.

—— Achos R.S. Thomas. *Taliesin* 63 (1988) 87-91. [R.S. Thomas in the dock].

—— R.S. Thomas: the question about technology. *Planet* 92 (1992) 54-60.

—— Welsh bards and English reviewers: the reception of R.S. Thomas's *Collected poems. Planet* 100 (1993) 22-24.

THOMAS, R. George. The poetry of R.S. Thomas. *Review of English Literature* 3,4 (1962) 85-95.

—— [and Leonard Clark]. *Andrew Young and R.S. Thomas.* London: Longmans for the British Council and National Book League, 1964. (Writers and their work). Incl. R.S. Thomas, by R. George Thomas, pp. 27-41.

—— Humanus sum: a second look at R.S. Thomas. *AWR* 18,42 (1970) 55-62. Reprinted in Anstey (above) and in *Triskel one: essays on Welsh and Anglo-Welsh literature,* ed. Sam Adams and Gwilym Rees Hughes. Llandybïe: Christopher Davies, 1971. pp. 186-197.

—— Review article on *H'm. PW* 7,4 (1972) 82-88.

TOLLEY, A.T. *The poetry of the forties.* Manchester: Manchester University Press, 1985. Incl. discussion of Thomas, pp. 153-157.

TOWNSEND, M.J. God after the silence: an introduction to the poetry of R.S. Thomas. *Encounter* [Christian Theological Seminary], Winter 1978, 45-57.

TRIGGS, Jeffery Alan. The halo upon the bones: R.S. Thomas's journey to the interior. *The Library Review: An International Journal of Contemporary Writing* [Madison, NJ] 32,2 (1989) 140-152.

—— A kinship of the fields: farming in the poetry of R.S. Thomas and Wendell Berry. *North Dakota Quarterly* 57,2 (1989) 92-102.

TRIPP, John. The lean world of R.S. Thomas. *London Welshman,* Feb 1966, 8-11.

VICARY, J.D. Via negativa: absence and presence in the recent poetry of R.S. Thomas. *Critical Quarterly* 27,3 (1985) 41-51.

VOLK, Sabine. *Grenzpfähle der Wirklichkeit: approaches to the poetry of R.S. Thomas.* Frankfurt am Main; London: Peter Lang, 1985. 277 p. (Neue Studien zur Anglistik und Amerikanistik; 31). Incl. bibliography. – [Outposts of reality].

WALROND, David Alan John. The religious poetry of Edwin Muir and R.S. Thomas. MA thesis. University of Exeter, 1981. Incl.: R.S. Thomas, pp. 154-287.

WARD, J.P. *The poetry of R.S. Thomas.* Bridgend: Poetry Wales Press, 1987. 151 p. Incl. bibliography, pp. 143-145.

—— R.S. Thomas's poems of Wales. *PW* 23,2-3 (1988) 20-25.

WATERMAN, Andrew. Closing the shutters: *Frequencies* and the poetry of R.S. Thomas. *PW* 14,4 (1979) 90-103. Review article.

WEBB, Harri. Letter. *PW* 7,4 (1972) 121-123. On R.S. Thomas.

WHALEN, Terry. *Philip Larkin and English poetry.* London: Macmillan, 1986. Discusses R.S. Thomas, pp. 130-137.

WITMER, Robert. On R.S. Thomas. *Poetry Nippon,* Dec 1973, 25-28.

WOOD, Carol Lloyd. Welsh characteristics in the poetry of R.S. Thomas. *McNeese Review* 25 (1978-79) 17-28.

WOODEN, Warren W. A question of influence: George Herbert and R.S.

Thomas. *Little Review* 13-14 (1980) 26-29.
ZAGANO, Phyllis. R.S. Thomas and Gerard Manley Hopkins: priest-poets. PhD thesis. State University of New York at Stony Brook, 1979.

# VERNON WATKINS (1906-1967)

A. Publications by Vernon Watkins
   (i) Books, and books edited
   (ii) Selected contributions to books and periodicals

B. Publications about Vernon Watkins

## A (i). Publications by Vernon Watkins: Books, and Books Edited

*Ballad of the Mari Lwyd and other poems*. London: Faber, 1941. 92 p. 'For the second edition [1947] Watkins rewrote the poem 'The eastern window' and lengthened the prose note to the 'Mari Lwyd'' (Jane McCormick, *West Coast Review* 4,1 [1969]).

*The lamp and the veil: poems*. London: Faber, 1945. 61 p.

*The lady with the unicorn*. London: Faber, 1948. 104 p.

*Selected poems*. Norfolk, Conn.: New Directions, 1948. 92 p. Selected from: *The ballad of the Mari Lwyd – The lamp and the veil*.

*The death bell: poems and ballads*. London: Faber, 1954. 112 p.

U.S. ed.: Norfolk, Conn.: J. Laughlin, 1954.

*Heinrich Heine: The North Sea* / translated by Vernon Watkins. London: Faber, 1955. viii, 95p. Incl. Note on *The North Sea*, by Vernon Watkins, pp. vii-viii.

U.S. ed.: New York: New Directions, 1951.

*Dylan Thomas: Letters to Vernon Watkins* / edited with an introduction by Vernon Watkins. London: Dent; Faber, 1957. 145 p.: front. port. Introduction, pp. 11-21.

U.S. eds.: New York: New Directions, 1957.
—— Westport, Conn.: Greenwood Press, 1982. ISBN: 0-313-23746-8.

*Landmarks and voyages: poetry supplement* / edited by Vernon Watkins. London: Poetry Book Society, Christmas 1957. 12 p.: pamph.

*Cypress and acacia*. London: Faber, 1959. 102 p.

U.S. ed.: New York: New Directions, 1960.

*Affinities:* poems. London: Faber, 1962. 99 p.

U.S. ed.: Norfolk, Conn.: New Directions, 1963.

*Selected poems, 1930-1960.* London: Faber, 1967. 80 p.: pbk.

U.S. ed.: *Selected poems.* New York: New Directions, 1967. (New Directions paperbooks; 221)

*Fidelities.* London: Faber, 1968. 103 p. ISBN: 0-571-08519-9.

U.S. ed.: New York: New Directions, 1969.

*Pergamon poets IV* / by Kathleen Raine and Vernon Watkins; selected by Evan Owen. Oxford: Pergamon Press, 1968. 87 p.: pbk. (Pergamon English library). ISBN: 0-08013077-1. Incl. selections from Vernon Watkins, pp. 43-85.

*Vernon Watkins: uncollected poems* / with an introduction by Kathleen Raine. London: Enitharmon Press, 1969. iii, 32p. 'The edition consists of 300 numbered copies ... the endpapers are from a design by Brenda Chamberlain.'

*Vernon Watkins and Jon Silkin.* London: Longmans, 1969. 30 p.: pamph. (Longmans' poetry library). ISBN: 0-582-34207-4. Incl. selections from Vernon Watkins, pp. 1-17.

*I that was born in Wales: a new selection from the poems of Vernon Watkins* / chosen and introduced by Gwen Watkins and Ruth Pryor. Cardiff: University of Wales Press, 1976. 73 p. ISBN: 0-7083-0615-2.

*The influences.* Hayes: Bran's Head Books, 1976. [40] p. Incl. Introduction, by Gwen Watkins, pp. [v-viii]. ISBN: 0-905220-08-0. 'This is a limited edition of 350 copies of which 330 are for sale.' – Published January 1977.

*Selected verse translations: with an essay on the translation of poetry* / introduction by Michael Hamburger; textual editor Dr. Ruth Pryor. London: Enitharmon Press, 1977. 79 p.: hbk & pbk. ISBN: 0-90111-75-9 hbk, 0-90111-76-7 pbk.

*Elegy for the latest dead* / with an introductory note by Gwen Watkins. [Edinburgh: Tragara Press, 1977]. [11] p.: pamph. 'This edition is limited to [120] copies ... [25] ... numbered 1 to 25 ... have been signed by Gwen Watkins.' – Previously published in *Botteghe Oscure* 13 (1954) 103-105 and *A garland for Dylan Thomas,* ed. George Firmage (1963).

*Unity of the stream: a new selection of poems.* Llandysul: Gomer Press;

Cardiff: Academi Gymreig, 1978. 108 p.: pbk. (Academi Gymreig reprint). ISBN: 0-85088-810-7. Incl.: Foreword, by Gwen Watkins, p. [7] – Poems from: *Ballad of the Mari Lwyd* – *The lady with the unicorn* – *The death bell* – *Cypress and acacia* – *Affinities* – *Fidelities* – *Uncollected poems*.

U.S. ed.: *Unity of the stream: selected poems*. Redding Ridge, CT.: Black Swan Books, [1983]. 123 p. ISBN: 0-933806-05-1.

**The ballad of the outer dark and other poems** / with an introduction by Kathleen Raine; textual editor Dr. Ruth Pryor. London: Enitharmon Press, 1979. 79 p.: hbk & pbk. ISBN: 0-905289-15-3 hbk, 0-905289-20-X pbk. Introduction, pp. 9-13. – Cover design by Ceri Richards.

**The breaking of the wave.** Ipswich: Golgonooza Press, 1979. 40 p.: pamph. Incl. Introduction, by Gwen Watkins and Ruth Pryor, pp. 5-6.

**Yeats and Owen: two essays.** Frome: Hunting Raven, [1981]. 30 p.: pbk. ISBN: 0-905220-11-0.

**The collected poems of Vernon Watkins** / [edited by Ruth Pryor]. Ipswich: Golgonooza Press, 1986. xvii, 495 p. ISBN: 0-903880-33-4. Incl. Foreword, by Ruth Pryor, p. [v]. – Also limited edition, ISBN: 0-903880-36-9. The limited edition includes two previously unpublished poems in holograph, with printed texts opposite, and a drawing by Ceri Richards accompanying 'Ode to Nijinski'. – 200 copies, signed by Gwen Watkins.

Note: **Vernon Watkins in Italian Translation**

*Vernon Watkins* / traduzione e scelta a cura di Roberto Sanesi. Milano: stampato per gli Amici di [Poiesis (Gk. alph.)], 1962. 28 p. (I libri del centro; 3).

*Poesie, con testo a fronte* / introduzione, versioni e note di Roberto Sanesi. Parma: Guanda, 1968. 128 p.: pbk. Incl. Introduzione: Vernon Watkins, o delle mutazioni naturali, by Roberto Sanesi, pp. 13-23 – Selected poems, English texts with Italian translations – Bibliography, citing Italian translations and critical studies.

*Elegiac sonnet con due litografie.* Milano: M'arte edizioni, 1970. [18] p.: ill. (Immagini e testi; 3). English and Italian. – Illustrated by Ceri Richards. – Edition of 149 numbered copies.

# A (ii). Publications by Vernon Watkins: Selected Contributions to Books and Periodicals

Review of David Jones, *In Parenthesis*. *Wales* 5 (1938) 184.

Reply to *Wales* questionnaire. *Wales* 2nd ser. [23] 6,3 (1946) 23-24.

The translation of poetry. *Gate* 1,3 (1947) 35-39.

Tenth anniversary year message. *Wales* 2nd ser. 7,26 (1947) 255.

Sailors on the moving land (to Dylan Thomas). *Life and Letters* 61,141 (1949) 140-145. Poetry.

All that matters. *Observer*, 26 Feb 1950, 5:A. Letter on the marketability of poetry.

[Afterword]. In Dylan Thomas, *Collected poems: 1934-1952*. London: Dent, 1952. pp. 181-182. Watkins's note, on the unfinished 'Elegy', appears in impressions from 1956 onwards.

Mr. Dylan Thomas: innovation and tradition. *Times*, 10 Nov 1953, 11:D. Obituary.

First choice. *Poetry Book Society Bulletin*, May 1954, 1.

Dylan Thomas and the spoken word. *TLS*, 19 Nov 1954, 731. Review of *Quite early one morning*. – See also Watkins's letter, 17 Dec 1954, 821, in reply to Aneirin Talfan Davies,

Foreword. In Dylan Thomas, *Adventures in the skin trade*. London: Putnam, 1955. pp. 7-14. – U.S. ed.: New York: New American Library, 1960 (Signet classics), with afterword by Vernon Watkins, pp. 184-190.

A poem by Dylan Thomas. *Times*, 2 Aug 1955, 9:G. On 'Do not go gentle into that good night'.

Prose writings by Dylan Thomas. *TLS*, 5 Aug 1955, 446. Review of *A prospect of the sea*.

Letter. *Poetry*, Oct 1955, [title-page verso]. In support of the magazine.

Dylan Thomas in America. *Encounter*, Jun 1956, 77-79. Prompted by John Malcolm Brinnin, *Dylan Thomas in America*.

The writings of Dylan Thomas. *TLS*, 27 Jul 1956, 451. Review of John Alexander Rolph, *Dylan Thomas: a bibliography*.

In memoriam Roy Campbell. *Poetry Book Society Bulletin*, May 1957, 2.

Dylan Thomas. *Observer,* 13 Oct 1957, 8. On the editorial re-paragraphing of a letter from Dylan Thomas, published in the *Observer*, 6 Oct 1957.

Dylan Thomas. Observer, 1 Dec 1957, 6:G. Letter on Stephen Spender's review of Dylan Thomas, *Letters to Vernon Watkins*, 24 Nov 1957.

Dylan Thomas. *Observer*, 15 Dec 1957, 6:F-G. In reply to Spender's letter, 8 Dec 1957.

In defence of sound. *Time and Tide*, 13 Dec 1958, 1526. Compares TV and radio.

[Aphorisms on poetry]. *Poets on Poetry*, Mar 1960, 153-154.

Vernon Watkins' 43rd year of poetry making. *Swansea Voice*, Apr 15 1960, 10. Interview with Ron Berry.

Foreword. In Richard Hughes, *A high wind in Jamaica, or, The innocent voyage.* [New York]: New American Library, 1961.

[Translations]. In Hugo von Hofmannsthal, *Poems and verse plays,* ed. Michael Hamburger. London: Routledge, 1961.

Behind the fabulous curtain. *Poetry* [Chicago], May 1961, 124-125. Review of *Dylan Thomas: the legend and the poet,* ed. E.W. Tedlock, with poem 'Exegesis'.

A painter's studio. *Texas Quarterly* 4,4 (1961) 54-57. Background to radio programme featuring Dylan Thomas, with introductory note by Vernon Watkins.

Swansea. *Texas Quarterly* 4,4 (1961) 59-64. Prose and poetry.

Commentary on 'Poet and goldsmith'. In *Poet's choice,* ed. Paul Engle and Joseph Langland. New York: Dial Press, 1962. pp. 90-91.

Context. *London Magazine,* Feb 1962, 43-44. Replies to questionnaire on poetry.

The need of the artist. *Listener,* 8 Nov 1962, 756-757. On Swansea's annual Festival of Arts.

W.B. Yeats: the religious poet. *University of Texas Studies in Literature and Language* 3 (1962) 475-488. Review article on W.B. Yeats, *The collected poems.* – First published as W.B. Yeats: le poète religieux. *Critique* [France], Nov 1953, 915-930.

Thomas, Dylan Marlais. In *The concise encyclopedia of English and American poets and poetry,* ed. Stephen Spender and Donald Hall. London: Hutchinson, 1963. 2nd ed. 1970, pp. 306-307.

The second pressure in poetry. *Unicorn* [Exeter], Spring 1963, 9-10.

Research and perception. *Poesia e Critica,* Dec 1963, 94-99. English and Italian.

La cathédrale engloutie. In *Catalogue of a selective retrospective exhibition of the work of Ceri Richards, March 7th to 31st, 1964.* Swansea: Glynn Vivian Art Gallery, 1964. p. [3].

Foreword. In Kenneth Grahame, *The golden age* and *Dream days.* New York: New American Library, 1964. (Signet classics).

The joy of creation. *Listener,* 30 Apr 1964, 720-721. On relationship between poetry, music and the visual arts.

Dylan Thomas. *Spectator,* 25 Sep 1964, 399. Letter in reply to John Tripp.

Exuberance. *Viewpoint* 1,7 (1964) 12-16. On Ceri Richards.

New year 1965. *Listener,* 7 Jan 1965, 22-23. Broadcast talk.

[Interview]. In *The poet speaks: interviews with contemporary poets,* ed. Peter Orr. London: Routledge, 1966. pp. 267-271. Interviewed 10 Oct 1960.

[Translations]. In Attila Jozsef, *Poems,* ed. Thomas Kabdebo. London: Danubia Book Co., 1966.

[Comment]. In *Authors take sides on the Vietnam war,* ed. Cecil Woolf and John Bagguley. London: Peter Owen, 1967. p. 103.

[Translations]. In *Tribute to Gyula Illyes: poems.* Washington: Occidental, 1968.

The mare – A dry prophet. *AWR* 17,39 (1968) 18-20. Incl. Ceri Richards's drawing for the former poem and a facsimile holograph of letter from Watkins to Neville Masterman.

Letter. In Brenda Chamberlain, *Alun Lewis and the making of the Caseg broadsheets.* London: Enitharmon Press, 1970. p. 44.

Four unpublished poems by Vernon Watkins. *AWR* 22,50 (1973) 65-68. Water under the bell – Abroad thoughts from home – The redpoll – Arrival in East Shelby.

Eight translations from Hölderlin. *AWR* 24,54 (1975) 55-59.

Note on David Jones. In *David Jones: letters to Vernon Watkins,* ed. Ruth Pryor. Cardiff: University of Wales Press, 1976. Taken from the National Eisteddfod catalogue, 1964.

Six new poems. *PW* 12,4 (1977) 36-43. I have no name – Delicate fire – Note towards a poem – [three untitled poems].

Prose. *PW* 12,4 (1977) 52-60. Excerpts from lecture notes used at University College Swansea, 1966 [on Style, Order and luck, Protest and gift, Pity and war, Theory and act] – Two sets of aphorisms – Address to the Poetry Society of Great Britain, 7 May 1966.

Correspondence with Ceri Richards. *PW* 12,4 (1977) 60-63. Five letters (1959-1960), three from Watkins, two from Richards,

Vernon Watkins and W.B. Yeats. *PW* 12,4 (1977) 64-65. Extract from Watkins's lectures at University College Swansea, 1966, with Gwen Watkins's letter to J.P. Ward, 1976.

Visit to Yeats in Dublin, Spring 1938. *PW* 12,4 (1977) 66-77. Transcript of notes made immediately after the visit. – With facsimile holograph and Watkins's photograph of Yeats.

War and poetry: the reactions of Owen and Yeats. *Labrys* [London] 1 (1978) [8 p.].

La Belle, Jenijoy. Vernon Watkins: some observations on poetry. *AWR* 65 (1979) 100-106. Aphoristic statements from Watkins's University of Washington class, 1964.

Dedication for a critical magazine. *PW* 15,2 (1979) 40-41. Poetry.

[Translations]. In *Johann Wolfgang von Goethe: selected poems,* ed. Christopher Middleton. Boston: Suhrkamp/Insel, 1983.

First pledges – Spring song – Autumn – Articulations, May 1985 – Holderlin's grave – The bond – Verses for my children – Moments – Beginning of an autobiographical poem. *Temenos* 8 (1987) 126-132. Poetry.

Selected letters to Michael Hamburger. *Temenos* 8 (1987) 133-145.

Selected quotations from letters to Francis Dufeau-Labeyrie. *Temenos* 8 (1987) 146-155.

Swansea (1961). In *Wales on the wireless: a broadcasting anthology,* ed. Patrick Hannan. Llandysul: Gomer in assoc. with BBC Cymru/Wales, 1988. pp. 57-58.

# B. Publications about Vernon Watkins

[ANON]. The poet who was at Lloyd's. *Swansea Evening Post,* 10 Oct 1967, 6:F-G. The paper published additional tributes to Watkins, 9 Oct 1967, 1:A; 11 Mar 1968, 2:E-G.

ACKERMAN, John [as J.A. Jones]. The role of nature in the poetry of Edward Thomas, Dylan Thomas, Vernon Watkins and R.S. Thomas. PhD thesis. University of London (Birkbeck), 1981.

—— The light which love has kindled: Vernon Watkins' *Collected poems.* *AWR* 88 (1988) 78-82. Review article.

—— Poets as friends. *PW* 20,4 (1985) 59-65. Review article on Gwen Watkins, *Portrait of a friend.*

BLACKBURN, Thomas. *The price of an eye.* London: Longmans, 1961. Incl. discussion of Watkins, pp. 129-131.

BLAMIRES, David. Vernon Watkins. In *Reference guide to English literature,* ed. D.L. Kirkpatrick. 2nd ed. 3 vols. Chicago; London: St James Press, 1991. Vol. 2, pp. 1372-1373.

BULLOUGH, Geoffrey. *The trend in modern poetry.* Edinburgh: Oliver & Boyd, 1949. Incl. discussion of Watkins, pp. 232-233.

BURNS, Richard. Roberto Sanesi: an Italian among Welshmen. *PW* 17,2 (1981) 42-51.

CASTAY, Marie-Thérèse. Nature and some Anglo-Welsh poets. *PW* 15,2 (1979) 100-110.

COLLINS, Michael J. Vernon Watkins. In *British poets, 1914-1945,* ed. Donald E. Stanford. Detroit: Gale, 1983. (Dictionary of literary biography; 20). pp. 394-402.

CONRAN, Anthony. The English poet in Wales, 2. Boys of summer in their ruin. *AWR* 10,26 (1960) 11-21.

DAVIES, Aneirin Talfan. Ar ymyl y ddalen. *Barn*, Ion/Jan 1963, 68. Discusses Vernon Watkins and Dylan Thomas. – [In the margin].

DAVIES, Eryl. *AWR* 17,39 (1968) 7-10. Tribute to Vernon Watkins.

DUFAU-LABEYRIE, Francis. Notes in memory of the Dublin visit. *PW* 12,4 (1977) 78-83. The author accompanied Vernon Watkins in 1938.

EASTAUGH, Kenneth. The bard of Pennard Cliffs. *Daily Mirror*, 27 Aug 1967, 12-13.

ELLIS, John. Vernon Watkins: poet in a shadow. *Dragon* 96 (1968) 25-30.

GROSS, Harvey. *Sound and form in modern poetry: a study of prosody from Thomas Hardy to Robert Lowell.* Ann Arbor: University of Michigan Press, 1964. Incl. analysis of poems by Watkins.

HAMBURGER, Michael. Die Aufnahme Hölderlins in England. *Hölderlin-Jahrbuch* 14 (1965-66) 20-34. Incl. comment on Watkins.

—— *A mug's game: intermittent memoirs, 1924-1954.* Manchester: Carcanet, 1974. Incl. references to Watkins, pp. 256-264.

HEATH-STUBBS, John. Pity and the fixed stars: an approach to Vernon Watkins. *Poetry Quarterly* 12,1 (1950) 18-23.

HILTON, Ian. Vernon Watkins and Hölderlin. *PW* 12,4 (1977) 101-117.

HIRST, Désirée. Vernon Watkins and the influence of W.B. Yeats. *PW* 12,4 (1977) 84-100.

JONES, Brynmor. *Bibliographies of Anglo-Welsh literature: Vernon Watkins 1906-1967: biographical note, original works and contributions to periodicals, critical articles.* [Cardiff]: Welsh Arts Council Literature Department, 1968. [6] p.: pamph.

JONES, Elizabeth M. *AWR* 17,39 (1968) 10-12. Tribute to Vernon Watkins.

KEEBLE, Brian. Vernon Watkins and the wisdom of poetry. *PW* 11,1 (1975) 10-23.

LARKIN, Philip. Mr Vernon Watkins. *Times*, 10 Oct 1967. 10:F-G. Obituary.

—— *The north ship*. London: Faber, 1973. With introductory comment on Vernon Watkins, pp. 7-10. – Reprinted in Philip Larkin, *Required writing: miscellaneous pieces, 1955-1982*. (1983). pp. 27-30.

—— *Required writing: miscellaneous pieces, 1955-1982*. London: Faber, 1983. Incl. Vernon Watkins: an encounter and a re-encounter, pp. 40-44. – Reprinted from *Mabon* [English] 1,1 (1969) 6-10. – Welsh version: *Mabon* [Welsh] 1,1 (1969) 24-28. – Also reprinted in *Vernon Watkins, 1906-1967*, ed. Leslie Norris (1970), pp. 28-33.

LEGONNA, John. Vernon Watkins, Swansea. *London Welshman*, Jul-Aug 1964, 18. Review of a poetry reading.

McCASLIN, Susan. The baptism of the bardic spirit: an examination of Vernon Watkins' Taliesin poems – The sense of the metaphysical in the poetry of Vernon Watkins. In *On poets and poetry, 4th series,* ed. James Hogg. Salzburg: Institut fur Anglistik und Amerikanistik, 1982. (Salzburg studies in English literature, poetic drama & poetic theory; 27). pp. 3-37; 38-51.

—— Vernon Watkins, metaphysical poet. PhD thesis. University of British Columbia, 1984.

McCORMICK, Jane. The identity of the Mari Lwyd. *PW* 4,2 (1968) 3-6. On origin of Mari Lwyd ceremony.

—— The prose of Vernon Watkins. MA thesis. Simon Fraser University, British Columbia, 1969.

—— Vernon Watkins: a bibliography. *West Coast Review,* 4,1 (1969) 42-48. Contents: Books and selected uncollected poems – Selected books and anthologies including Watkins' poems and translations – Uncollected reviews, essays, letters, other prose and recordings by the poet – Selected criticism on Watkins, and prizes awarded him. – Annotated.

—— Sorry old Christian. *AWR* 18,42 (1970) 78-82. Considers Vernon Watkins's influence on Dylan Thomas.

—— I sing a placeless and a timeless heaven: a study of several themes in the poetry of Vernon Watkins. PhD thesis. Lehigh University, 1975.

MASTERMAN, Neville. *AWR* 17,39 (1968) 12-16. Tribute to Vernon Watkins.

MATHIAS, Roland. A note on some recent poems by Vernon Watkins. *DL* 1,3 (1950) 38-49.

—— Editorial. *AWR* 17,39 (1968) 3-5.

—— Grief and the circus horse: a study of mythic and Christian themes in the early poetry of Vernon Watkins. In *Triskel one: essays on Welsh and Anglo-Welsh literature,* ed. Sam Adams and Gwilym Rees Hughes. Llandybïe: Christopher Davies, 1971. pp. 96-138. Reprinted in Roland Mathias, *A ride through the wood: essays on Anglo-Welsh literature.* Bridgend: Poetry Wales Press, 1985. pp. 88-124.

—— *Vernon Watkins*. Cardiff: University of Wales Press [for] the Welsh Arts Council, 1974. 127 p.: front. port. (Writers of Wales). Incl. bibliography, pp. 121-124 – 'Edition ... limited to 1000 copies'.

MOORE, Geoffrey. *Poetry today.* London: Longmans for the British Council and the National Book League, 1958. (Writers and their work). Incl. discussion of Watkins, pp. 34-35.

MORGAN, George. Le mythe de Taliesin dans l'oeuvre de Vernon Watkins. *Annales de la Faculté des Lettres et Sciences Humaines de Nice* (1978) 209-219. Reprinted in *Hommage à Emile Gasquet* (1927-1977), ed. Pierre Marambaud. Paris: Belles Lettres, 1979.

MURPHY, B.W. Creation and destruction: notes on Dylan Thomas. *British Journal of Medical Psychology* 41 (1969) 149-168. Considers his relationship with Watkins.

NORRIS, Leslie. The poetry of Vernon Watkins. *PW* 2,3 (1966) 3-10.

—— *Vernon Watkins, 1906-1967,* ed. Leslie Norris. London: Faber, 1970. 105 p.: ill. Contents: Vernon Watkins 1906-1967, by Gwen Watkins, pp. 15-18 – In memory of Vernon Watkins [poem], by Nelson Bentley, pp. 19-22 – Whose flight is toil, by Glyn Jones, pp. 23-26 – For Vernon Watkins 1906-1967 [poem], by John Heath-Stubbs, p. 27 – Vernon Watkins: an encounter and a re-encounter, by Philip Larkin, pp. 28-33 – The bank clerk [poem], by R.S. Thomas, p. 34 – The poetry of Vernon Watkins, by Kathleen Raine, pp. 35-43 – Who so well [poem], by Marianne Moore, p. 44 – For Vernon Watkins, by David Wright [poem], p. 45 – Vernon Watkins: a memoir, by Michael Hamburger, pp. 46-56 – At the grave of Vernon Watkins [poem], by George Barker, p. 57 – Paragraphs from a letter, by James Laughlin, pp. 59-60 – Meetings with Vernon Watkins, by Roland Mathias, pp. 61-69 – Elegia a Vernon Watkins, by Roberto Sanesi, pp. 70-73 – Vernon Watkins as translator, by Ian Hamilton, pp. 74-89 – October [poem], by Michael Hamburger, pp. 90-92 – Vernon Watkins 1906-1967, by Hugo Williams, pp. 93-94 – Remembering Vernon, by Ceri Richards, pp. 95-96 – A true death [poem], by Leslie Norris, pp. 97-98 – In Gower, by Ted Walker, pp. 99-105.

—— The poetry of Vernon Watkins. MPhil thesis. University of Southampton, 1971-72. 200 p. Contents: *Ballad of the Mari Lwyd and other poems,* pp. 1-16 – A note on the ballad of the Mari Lwyd, pp. 17-26 – *The lamp and the veil,* pp. 27-42 – Emergent themes in *The lady with the unicorn,* pp. 43-76 – Consolidation and the theme of time in *The death bell,* pp. 77-96 – Taliesin and the poet's task: the poems in *Cypress and acacia,* pp. 97-135 – Ploughing old ground: the poems in *Affinities,* pp. 136-169 – Old and new manners in *Fidelities* and *Uncollected poems,* pp. 170-190 – Conclusion, pp. 191-200 – Unpaginated appendices on Blake and Watkins, and Watkins on poetry – Bibliography citing books, selected translations, contributions to anthologies, uncollected prose and recordings by the poet, selected criticism on him, and prizes gained.

—— Seeing eternity: Vernon Watkins and the poet's task. In *Triskel two: essays on Welsh and Anglo-Welsh literature,* ed. Sam Adams and Gwilym Rees Hughes. Llandybïe: Christopher Davies, 1973. pp. 88-110.

—— *Without contraries there is no progression: Dylan Thomas, Vernon Watkins and the romantic tradition.* Treforest: Polytechnic of Wales (Centre for the Study of Welsh Writing in English), 1992. (Inaugural Rhys Davies lecture). Discusses Watkins, pp. 15-20.

OLDROYD, R.E. *An index of the worksheets of the poems of Vernon Watkins presented to the National Manuscripts Collection of Contemporary Poets.* Hull: University of Hull, 1966. 25, xv p.

POLK, Dora. Vernon Watkins: an ambience for reading the 'Ballad of the Mari Lwyd' and other poems. PhD thesis. University of California (Irvine), 1970. 322 p.

—— Gateways to the vision of Vernon Watkins. *AWR* 20,45 (1971) 131-140.

—— *Vernon Watkins and the spring of vision.* Swansea: Christopher Davies, 1977. 161 p. Incl. bibliography, pp. 158-161.

PRESS, John. *Rule and energy: trends in British poetry since the second world war.* London: Oxford University Press, 1963. Incl. discussion of Watkins, pp. 62-69.

PRICE, Cecil. *PW* 3,3 (1967) 1. Speech at the ceremony awarding the poet the degree of DLitt.

PRYOR, Ruth. Wisdom is hid in crumbs: Vernon Watkins and Dante. *AWR* 23,52 (1974) 94-101.

—— The pivotal point in poetry: Vernon Watkins and the Taliesin legend. *AWR* 26,59 (1977) 51-60.

—— The Palethorpe papers, or, a bibliographer's nightmare. *PW* 12,4 (1977) 44-51. On the complexities of arranging the poet's posthumous papers.

RAINE, Kathleen. *Defending ancient springs.* London: Oxford University Press, 1967. Incl. Vernon Watkins and the bardic tradition, pp. 17-34. – First published as Vernon Watkins: poet of tradition. *AWR* 14,33 (1964) 20-38. – Also in *Texas Quarterly* 7,2 (1964) 173-189.

—— Intuition's lightning: the poetry of Vernon Watkins. *Poetry Review*, Jun 1968, 47-54.

RICHARDS, Ceri *AWR* 17,39 (1968) 16-17. Tribute to Vernon Watkins.

ROSS, Alan. *Poetry 1945-50.* London: Longmans, 1951. Incl. discussion of Watkins, pp. 46-47.

SANESI, Roberto. *Poeti inglesi del 900: testi, traduzione a cura di Roberto Sanesi.* Milano: Bompiani, 1960. Incl. discussion of Watkins, pp. 82-84.

—— Vernon Watkins: poesie. *Poesia e Critica*, Apr 1963, 91-117. Incl. translations by Sanesi.

—— Vernon Watkins. *Temenos 8* (1987) 102-125.

SHIRES, Linda Marguerite. Keeping something alive: British poetry, 1939-1956. PhD thesis. University of Princeton, 1981. Incl. discussion of Dylan Thomas, Vernon Watkins and Alun Lewis.

SINGER, Burns. Sins and symbols. *Encounter*, Oct 1954, 79-82. Review of *The death bell*.

SOMERTON, Elizabeth M. Vernon Watkins and Kierkegaard: the poetry of eternity. MA thesis. Memorial University of Newfoundland, 1988. 158 p.

SPENDER, Stephen. *Poetry since 1939.* London: Longmans & Green, 1946. Incl. discussion of Vernon Watkins, pp. 40-41.

STANFORD, Derek. *Movements in English poetry.* London: Centaur, 1959. Incl. brief discussion of Dylan Thomas and Vernon Watkins.

SWANSEA Public Libraries Committee. *Two Swansea poets: Dylan Thomas and*

*Vernon Watkins: 3rd-12th July, 1969.* Swansea: Swansea Public Libraries Committee, 1969. 15 p. Incl. bibliographies. – Exhibition catalogue compiled by Stanley Yonge.

TAIG, Thomas. Swansea between the wars. *AWR* 17,39 (1968) 23-32.

TOLLEY, A.T. *The poetry of the thirties.* London: Gollancz, 1975. Incl. discussion of Vernon Watkins, and the magazine *Wales*, pp. 288-295.

—— *The poetry of the forties.* Manchester: Manchester University Press, 1985. Incl. Vernon Watkins, pp. 129-136.

VLLETTE, Jacques. La poésie de Vernon Watkins. *Mercure de France*, Oct 1948, 249-256.

WAIDSON, H.M. Vernon Watkins and German literature. *AWR* 21,47 (1972) 124-137. Incl. list of Watkins' translations published in journals.

—— Review of *Poetry Wales*, Vernon Watkins special number. *AWR* 27,60 (1978) 141-142.

WATKINS, Dorothy. *Vernon Phillips Watkins, 1906-1967: the early years.* Falmouth: Arwenack Press, [n.d.]. 48 p. 'Recollected by his younger sister with all the bias of total affection.'

WATKINS, Gwen. *Vernon Watkins: poet of the elegiac muse.* Swansea: University College, [1974]. 20 p. (W.D.Thomas memorial lecture). Delivered November 13, 1973.

—— An awful outsider: some letters from David Jones. *AWR* 24,54 (1975) 15-36.

—— *Portrait of a friend.* Llandysul: Gomer Press, 1983. 226 p.: ill. Incl. foreword, by Leslie Norris, p. [xi]. – U.S. ed.: *Dylan Thomas and Vernon Watkins: portrait of a friendship.* Seattle: University of Washington Press, 1983.

WILLIAMS, Hugo. Vernon Watkins. *Poetry Book Society Bulletin,* Dec 1967, 2. Obituary.

WRIGHT, David. Essay on Vernon Watkins. *Nimbus* 3,1 (1952) 12-17.

—— Introduction [to Vernon Watkins special number]. *PW* 12,4 (1977) 7-10.

# HARRI WEBB (b. 1920)

A. Publications by Harri Webb
  (i)  Books
  (ii) 'Periodicals edited
  (iii) Selected contributions to books and periodicals

B. Publications about Harri Webb


## A (i). Publications by Harri Webb: Books

*Dic Penderyn and the Merthyr rising of 1831.* Swansea: Gwasg Penderyn, 1956. 16 p.: pamph.

*Triad: thirty three poems* / by Peter Griffith, Meic Stephens, Harri Webb; with an introduction by Anthony Conran. Merthyr Tydfil: Triskel Press, 1963. 58 p.: pamph. Incl. 11 poems by Harri Webb, pp. 45-57. – 'These poems are printed in a limited edition of five hundred copies, numbered 1 to 500.'

*Our national anthem: some observations on 'Hen wlad fy nhadau'.* Merthyr Tydfil: Triskel Press, 1964. 24 p.: pamph.

*The green desert: collected poems, 1950-1969.* Llandysul: Gwasg Gomer, 1969. 74 p.

*Libraries and the arts: an address delivered to the Conference of Library Authorities in Wales at Brecon on Tuesday June 8th, 1971.* [Mountain Ash: The Author], 1971. 9 p.

*A crown for Branwen.* Llandysul: Gwasg Gomer, 1974. 76 p. ISBN: 0-85088-250-8. Poetry.

*Rampage and revel.* Llandysul: Gomer Press, 1977. 63 p.: pbk. ISBN: 0-85088-443-8. Poetry.

*Words written on the occasion of the official opening of St David's Hall, Cardiff,* in the gracious presence of her Majesty Queen Elizabeth, The Queen Mother. Cardiff: [1983]. 4 p.: pamph.

*Poems and points.* Llandysul: Gomer Press, 1983. 43 p.: pbk. ISBN: 0-85088-526-4.

*Tales from Wales* / retold by Harri Webb; illustrated by Lesley Bruce. London: Dragon Books, 1984. 95 p.: ill. ISBN: 0-246-12088-6.

*A crown for Branwen* / wood engraving by Yvonne Skargon. Newtown: Gwasg Gregynog, [1989]. [4] p.: ill.: pamph. (Beirdd Gregynog; Gregynog poets; 5). ISBN: 0-948714-25-5. Text of single poem. – 'This edition consists of 400 copies.'

## A (ii). Publications by Harri Webb: Periodicals Edited

*The Welsh Republican: Y Gweriniaethwr,* 1-7, 1950-51 – 1956-57. Harri Webb was successively managing editor, general editor and editor of *The Welsh Republican.* His signed contributions are listed in section A (iii). Also listed are his anonymous contributions to the column, 'Glorious figures from the past, or what they don't allow to be taught in Welsh schools'. This regular feature, running from Dec 1952 to the last issue of the periodical, he shared with Ivor Wilks.

*Welsh Nation.* Harri Webb edited this, the official newspaper of Plaid Cymru, between 1961 and 1964. His signed contributions are listed in section A (iii). He also contributed the satirical Land of Pong column about events in 'Cwmgrafft' (sometimes under the pseudonym, John Spang).

## A (iii). Publications by Harri Webb: Selected Contributions to Books and Periodicals

A theatre for Wales. *Wales* 2nd ser. 8,29 (1948) 552-553, Letter advocating a national theatre.

The clustered stars are lonelier. *WM,* 12 Mar 1949, 2:G. Poetry.

The Anglo-Welsh writers. *WM,* 28 Mar 1949, 3:G. Letter.

The cruellest month. *WM,* 11 Apr 1949, 2:G. Poetry.

Desert victory. *Life and Letters* 64 (1950) 137. Poetry.

Welsh White Paper. *Welsh Republican* 1,3 (Dec 1950-Jan 1951) 3.

We believe in the Welsh people: the basis of our action. *Welsh Republican* 1,4 (Feb-Mar 1951) 4.

Who's living in the past? A cracked record. *Welsh Republican* 1,5 (Apr-May 1951) 4. Review of Huw T. Edwards, *They went to Llandrindod.*

Compromise be damned! Wales wants independence. *Welsh Republican* 2,2 (Oct-Nov 1951) 4.

Wales will not be tricked: concessions mean nothing. *Welsh Republican* 2,5 (Apr-May 1952) 4.

Aneurin versus Bevan. *Welsh Republican* 2,6 (Jun-Jul 1952) 2. Review of Aneurin Bevan, *In place of fear.*

The English monarchy: symbol of Welsh subjection. *Welsh Republican* 3,1 (Aug-Sep 1952) 3.

The Merthyr rising, 1831. *Welsh Republican* 3,3 (Dec 1952-Jan 1953) 4.

Unconquered! The saga of Welsh resistance. *Welsh Republican* 3,4 (Feb-Mar 1953) 4.

The tithe war. *Welsh Republican* 3,5 (Apr-May 1953) 4.

The North Wales quarrymen. *Welsh Republican* 4,1 (Aug-Sep 1953) 4.

Tonypandy. *Welsh Republican* 4,3 (Dec 1953-Jan 1954) 4.

The heroes. *Welsh Republican* 4,5 (Apr-May 1954) 4.

Dic Penderyn. *Welsh Republican* 5,1 (Aug-Sep 1954) 4.

Lewis the Huntsman. *Welsh Republican* 5,3 (Dec 1954-Jan 1955) 4.

Welsh wizards who went wrong: T.E. Lawrence and Lloyd George. *Welsh Republican* 5,4 (Feb-Mar 1955) 3. Review of Frank Owen, *Tempestuous journey: Lloyd George, his life and times,* Richard Aldington, *T.E. Lawrence.*

Dai'r Cantwr [David Davies]. *Welsh Republican* 5,5 (Apr-May 1955) 4.

Llythyr VI. *Baner ac Amserau Cymru,* 18 Mai/May 1955, 2. Translation of poem by W.S. Graham. – [Letter VI].

Atgof am Ambrose Bebb. *Welsh Republican* 5,6 (Jun-Jul 1955) 4.

Labour's next step. *Welsh Republican* 5,6 (Jun-Jul 1955) 2. Continued: Aug-Sep 1955, 2; Oct-Nov 1955, 2; Dec-Jan 1956, 2; Jun-Jul 1956, 3. – A collection of these articles in pamphlet form, advertised as forthcoming by Gwasg Penderyn, Swansea, was seemingly not published.

Ieuan Gwynedd. *Welsh Republican* 6,1 (Aug-Sep 1955) 4.

Bedd Dai'r Cantwr. *Baner ac Amserau Cymr,* 28 Med/Sep 1955, 2. Poetry. – [Grave of Dai Cantwr].

The disclaimers. *Welsh Republican* 6,2 (Oct-Nov 1955) 3. Poetry. Written under pseudonym 'Gŵyrfab'.

Sut daeth Merthyr Tudful yn fwrdeisdref. *Baner ac Amserau Cymru,* 23 Tach/Nov 1955, 3. [How Merthyr became a borough].

'The nightfishing': an appreciation of the poem by W.S. Graham read by the author on BBC Third Programme, 6 November 1955. *Promenade* [Cheltenham] 72 (Nov 1955) 15-17.

Dr William Price. *Welsh Republican* 6,3 (Dec 1955-Jan 1956) 4.

Lewis Humphreys, bugler of liberty. *Welsh Republican* 6,5 (Apr-May 1956) 4.

The man in the cloth cap. *Welsh Republican* 7,1 (Aug-Sep 1956) 4. On Keir Hardie.

Dic Penderyn. *Welsh Nation*, 17 Nov 1956, 7:B. Letter on Webb's membership of the Labour Party.

A lesson from Switzerland. *Welsh Nation*, 24 Nov 1956, 4:B-E; 3:E.

Aaron Williams. *Welsh Republican* 7,3 (Dec 1956-Jan 1957) 4.

Emrys ap Iwan. *Welsh Republican* 7,5 (Apr-May 1957) 4.

'Heresi': llwyr ymwrthod. *Baner ac Amserau Cymru,* 17 Hyd/Oct 1957, 4. Letter, with poem. – [Heresy: total abstinence].

Trawsfynydd. *Times*, 12 Feb 1958, 9:F-G. On nuclear power station plans.

Song, by Federico García Lorca. *Wales* 3rd ser., Oct 1958, 61. Translation by Harri Webb.

Yet another Aberystwyth anthology: a treasury of school verse? *Wales* 3rd ser., Nov 1959, 62-67. Review of *Presenting Welsh poetry: an anthology,* ed. Gwyn Williams.

Letter from Wales: Merthyr Tydfil – the neon-lit sheep-track. *London Welshman*, Dec 1959, 10.

A year's garnering. *London Welshman*, Dec 1960, 4-5. Review of the year's books.

Llyfrau'r flwyddyn. *London Welshman*, Jan 1961, 19-21. Review of the year's Welsh books.

Ateb i Mr David Thomas. *Baner ac Amserau Cymru,* 14 Med/Sep 1961, 8. Letter.

Intellectuals and trade unionists? *WM,* 19 Sep 1961, 6:F-H. Letter.

Cofia, Gymru, dy ddyddiau fu. *Baner ac Amserau Cymru,* 26 Hyd/Oct 1961, 2. Poetry. – [Remember, Wales, your past].

We stand for the integrity of Wales. *Welsh Nation,* Nov 1961, 1, 8.

A ward for Wales. *Welsh Nation,* Mar 1962, 5:D-E.

Dewch adre o Lundain. *Baner ac Amserau Cymru,* 19 Ebr/Apr 1962, 3. Letter.

Days of battle. *Welsh Nation,* May 1962, 5:A-B. On aims of Plaid Cymru. Also poem 'Excelsior' on Saunders Lewis (1:C under Gŵyrfab).

Augustus John: artist and patriot. *Welsh Nation,* Aug 1962, 4:A-E, 7:A.

Cerydd o'r Beibl. *Baner ac Amserau Cymru,* 22 Tach/Nov 1962, 7. Letter.

Rhyfela hyd marw – The Cross Foxes. In *Caneuon rhyddid Cymru: Songs of Welsh freedom,* ed. Meic Stephens. Merthyr Tydfil: Triskel Press, 1963. pp. iv, vii. A collection of patriotic songs, mostly to Irish rebel tunes, by Meic Stephens, Harri Webb and others.

The only way. *Welsh Nation,* Feb 1964, 2:D-F.

Editorial. *Welsh Nation,* Feb 1964, 5:A-B.

Has Goronwy Rees a future? *Welsh Nation,* Apr 1964, 3. In reply to Goronwy Rees, Has Wales a future?, *Encounter,* Mar 1964.

Swansea proclaims its Welshness. *Welsh Nation,* Sep 1964, 8:B-E.

The gathering storm: Plaid Cymru in the light of the election. *Welsh Nation,* Oct 1964, 2:A-D.

Un babell lyfrau. *Llais Llyfrau,* Gaeaf/Winter, 1964, 8-9.

Calling the tune. *Welsh Nation,* Feb-Mar 1965, 8:A-C.

Bristol Channel challengers. *WM,* 19 March 1965, 6:C-G. On commercial rivalry between Cardiff and Bristol.

The faces of Wales. *Welsh Nation,* Apr 1965, 4:A-D.

Whose funeral? *Welsh Nation,* Apr 1965, 8:E-F. Poetry.

New Anglo-Welsh poets. *WM,* 10 Jul 1965, 10:E-G.

Profligate rebel or national hero. *WM,* 4 Sep 1965, 10:C-G. On Owain Glyndwr.

Poetic evening. *WM,* 14 Sep 1965, 9:A-B.

He learnt Welsh: his first book. *Welsh Nation,* Sep 1965, 2. Review of Gerald Morgan, *Yr afal aur.*

An open letter to Mr Goronwy Roberts. *Welsh Nation,* Sep 1965, 5.

Summer scene: pleasure at the National Eisteddfod. *Welsh Nation,* Sep 1965, 8:B-C.

Ten per cent poetry. *WM,* 2 Oct 1965, 9:A-D. On a poetry conference at the Cardiff Commonwealth Arts Festival.

Owain Glyndŵr: one of the greatest episodes in our history. *Welsh Nation,* Oct 1965, 3:A-F. Continued: Nov, 6:A-F; Dec, 6:A-F. – Summer school lecture.

Babylon has the edge on Zion. *WM,* 6 Nov 1965, 9:A-G.

From Maxen Wledig to Lloyd George – and after. *WM,* 4 Dec 1965, 7:C-G.

Review of *Young Commonwealth poets,* ed. P.L. Brent. *PW* 1,2 (1965) 28-29.

Our modern myths. *WM,* 5 Feb 1966, 9:A-C.

Poetry of the Scots. *WM,* 2 Apr 1966, 8:D-F. Review of *Modern Scottish poetry,* ed. Maurice Lindsay.

Creidiol, poet and temperate local patriot. *WM,* 9 Apr 1966, 7:A-C.

Over the sea to Wales. *WM,* 7 May 1966, 7:D-G.

Owen Glyn Dŵr: a hero for our time. *Welsh Nation,* Jul 1966, 3:D-F. Review of Glanmor Williams, *Owen Glendower.*

A ballad for the fourteenth of July. *Welsh Nation,* Sep 1966. 3:E-F. Begins, 'When Gwynfor got in for Carmarthen'.

Two cheers for Tudor. *London Welshman,* Sep 1966, 9. On Carmarthenshire by-election.

Letter. *PW* 2,3 (1966) 35-38. In response to Raymond Garlick's views on Anglo-Welsh literature, *PW* 2,2 (1966) 41-43.

Mapped. *London Welshman,* Mar 1967, 14. Review of L.G. Bullock, *A historical map of Wales.*

Landslide conference, says Harri Webb. *Welsh Nation,* Sep 1967, 5:D-F; 6:D-F. Report of Plaid Cymru Conference, Dolgellau.

Review of *The Oxford book of Scottish verse,* ed. John MacQueen. *PW* 3,1 (1967) 49-52.

From 'Imram: voyage'. *PW* 3,3 (1967) 29-31. Translation from Breton of Maodez Glanndour. – Poetry.

Compromise or appeasement. *Welsh Nation,* Jan 1968, 4:A-D.

Brittany on the boil. *Welsh Nation,* Jun 1968, 4:C-F.

One man's Wales. *Welsh Nation,* Jun 1968, 8:E-F. Continued: Jul 1968, 4:E-F; Aug 1968, 8:E-F.

Why not? (A conversation in Bargoed). *Welsh Nation,* Aug 1968, 3:A-F. Poetry

Lack of organisation resulted in Celtic subjugation. *Welsh Nation,* Sep 1968, 4:C-F.

Internal debates in the next decades. *Welsh Nation,* Dec 1968, 3:A-F. Review of Owen Dudley Edwards and others, *Celtic nationalism.*

Return visit. *PW* 4,1 (1968) 45. Poetry.

Radio and television in the 1970s. *Welsh Dominion* 2 (1968) 53-64.

One man's Wales. *Welsh Nation,* Jan 1969, 8:D. Continued: Mar, Apr, Aug, 8:E.

Posturing in the last agony. *Welsh Nation,* Jul 1969, 7:E-F. Poetry.

Ffabiaid. *Barn,* Aws/Aug 1969, 270. Letter. – [Fabians].

The moggie I see in my dreams. *Welsh Nation,* Oct 1969, 7.

Review of *This world of Wales,* ed. Gerald Morgan. *PW* 4,3 (1969) 50-53.

The tree – The starry bay. *PW* 5,1 (1969) 41-42. Translation from the Provencal of Frederic Mistral and the Sardinian of Antioco Casula. – Poetry.

Review of A.G. Prys-Jones, *High heritage. PW* 5,1 (1969) 76-69.

Harri Webb says. In *Plaid Cymru: build the new Wales.* Cardiff: Plaid Cymru, [1970]. broadsheet. Election address. – Harri Webb was Plaid Cymru candidate for Pontypool, 1970.

*Libraries and the arts,* ed. David E. Gerard. London: Bingley, 1970. Reports

Webb's contributions to the discussion at this symposium held at the College of Librarianship Wales, 1-6 Sep 1969.

Happy new year to Carlo, Caio, Wales. *Welsh Nation,* Jan 1970, 3:C-F.

Something has gone right somewhere. *Welsh Nation,* Apr 1970, 2:C-F.

Struldbugs must go! and soon. *Welsh Nation,* May 1970, 7:A-B. Political comment.

One man's Wales. *Welsh Nation* (Election special), June 1970, 2.

History passes Labour by as unions reject their weird allies. *Welsh Nation,* Sep 1970, 7:A-E.

Why did Hooson lurch to the right. *Welsh Nation,* Nov 1970, 7:A-B.

Gas sahibs for the colony. *Welsh Nation,* Dec 1970, 4:C-E.

Review of T.L. Williams, *Caradoc Evans. PW* 6,2 (1970) 60-63.

Review of *The Penguin book of Scottish verse,* ed. Tom Scott, *The Penguin book of Irish verse,* ed. Brendan Kenelly, *British poetry since 1945,* ed. Edward Lucie-Smith. *PW* 6,3 (1970) 66-69.

There was an amazing gap on that history shelf. *Welsh Nation,* Sep 1971, 6:A-F. Review of Gwynfor Evans, *Aros mae.*

The Burgos trials, by Jean-Paul Sartre. *Planet* 9 (1971) 3-21. Translated by Harri Webb.

Letter to the editor. *PW* 7,3 (1971) 39-41. On the twenty-first number of *Poetry Wales.*

Four castles: a scena for St. David's day. *Welsh Nation,* 2 Mar 1972, 3:A-D. Three poems: 1. Caernarvon: a Roman soldier – 2. Caerffili: a Gwent tribesman – 3. Harlech: a Gwynedd chieftain. – Poem 4. Cardiff: a young man, appears in *Welsh Nation,* 9 Mar 1972, 8:C-D.

To the memory of a friend. *Welsh Nation,* 23 Mar 1972, 5:C-D. Poetry.

Heil Stan! *Welsh Nation,* 16-22 Jun 1972, 7:A. Signed 'A contributor'.

The red, white and green. *Welsh Nation,* 23-29 Jun 1972, 2:E-F. Poetry.

It's time for us to learn the basics. *Welsh Nation,* 22 Dec 1972, 5:D-E.

From Aber without love. *Planet* 11 (1972) 94-96. Review of Goronwy Rees, *A chapter of accidents.*

Letter to the editor. *PW* 7,4 (1972) 121-123. On R.S. Thomas.

Webb on Thomas. *Welsh Nation,* 11 Jan 1973, 6:E. Review of Gwyn Thomas, *The sky of our lives.*

Le Pays de Galles. *L'Europe en Formation,* Avr/Apr 1973, 23-27.

Why Plaid must let Gwynfor go. *Welsh Nation,* 31 Jan 1974, 5:B-F.

Welsh channel. *Welsh Nation,* 7 Feb 1974, 6:B. Letter to editor.

A tour of inspection leaves the Doctor unmoved. *WM,* 31 Aug 1974, 8:A-F. On Samuel Johnson in Wales.

Galicia. *Planet* 24-25 (1974) 47-53.

Cymdeithas yr iaith Gymraeg: the manifesto. *Planet* 26-27 (1974) 77-136. Translation of the Welsh Language Society manifesto, originally drafted by Cynog Davies.

Review of *Welsh poems: sixth century to 1600,* ed. Gwyn Williams. *PW* 9,4 (1974) 92-94.

Down with the mandarins. *PW* 10,1 (1974) 100-102. Reply to Roland Mathias's letter, Anglo-Welsh bards and metropolitan reviewers, *PW* 9,4 (1974) 4-8.

Life in Cwmgrafft. *Welsh Nation,* 1974 (Election special), 3.

Some thoughts on Mr Hearne. *Welsh Nation,* 9-15 May 1975, 6.

The Jews of the diaspora, or the vocation of a minority, by Richard Marienstras. *European Judaism,* Summer 1975, 6-22. Translated by Harri Webb.

Alun Lewis: the lost leader. *PW* 10,3 (1975) 118-123.

Review of Euros Bowen, *Poems.* PW 10,3 (1975) 135-138.

Nid serch pethe ifanc. *Taliesin* 30 (1975) 118-121. Review of *Storiau 74,* ed. Gwilym Rees Hughes and Islwyn Jones. – [Not the love of young things].

Hynafgwyr yw ein beirdd gorau? *Taliesin* 31 (1975) 135-137. Review of *Cerddi '74,* ed. T. Gwynn Jones. – [Old men our best poets?].

Rhagolwg. *Radio Times,* 20 Dec 1975-2 Jan 1976, 18. [Preview].

Morfydd's celebration. In *The Penguin book of Welsh short stories,* ed. Alun

Richards. Harmondsworth: Penguin, 1976. pp. 241-247. Webb's translation of a story by Harri Pritchard Jones.

Is Wales really there? *Radio Times,* 28 Feb 1976, 12-13. On his television film, *How green was my father.*

Preview. *Radio Times,* 11-17 Sep 1976, 15. Continued: 16-22 Oct 1976, 15; 20-26 Nov 1976, 15.

The political drought. *Welsh Nation,* Oct 1976, 5:A-D.

Thoughts on an anniversary. *Welsh Nation,* Nov 1976, 7:A-D.

Cheers for the Coal Exchange. *Welsh Nation,* Dec 1976, 7:A-D.

Review of *Poems '76,* ed. by Glyn Jones, *Dragon's hoard,* ed. Sam Adams, Dylan Thomas and John Davenport, *The death of the king's canary. BNW,* Winter 1976, 13-14.

Webb's progress. *Planet* 30 (1976) 23-28. Autobiographical.

Homecoming. *Planet* 35 (1976) 9-22. Verse drama.

The historical context of Welsh translation. *PW* 11,3 (1976) 49-59.

Review of John Heath-Stubbs, *Artorius. PW* 11,3 (1976) 132-136.

Harri Webb. In *Artists in Wales 3,* ed. Meic Stephens. Llandysul: Gomer Press, 1977. Autobiographical essay, pp. 87-96.

*Preview. Radio Times,* 22-28 Jan 1977, 15. Continued: 19-25 Feb, 15; 19-25 Mar 1977, 17; 14-20 May, 17; 11-17 Jun, 15; 9-15 Jul 1977, 13; 6-12 Aug 1977, 13; 10-16 Sep, 21; 15-21 Oct, 17; 5-11 Nov, 21; 12-18 Nov, 19; 10-16 Dec, 17.

Andy: the Swansea Jack-in-the-box. *Welsh Nation,* Feb 1977, 5:A-C.

As Wales waits. *Welsh Nation,* Mar 1977, 8-9.

The lesson: the future of Wales is in our hands. *Welsh Nation,* Apr 1977, 7:A-D.

Remember the stars of the chamber of horrors. *Welsh Nation,* May 1977, 14:A-D.

Review of Gwyn Williams, *The land remembers. Resurgence,* May-June 1977, 29-30.

Canmlwyddiant trychineb. *Y Faner,* 10 Meh/Jun 1977, 14. On the Tynewydd mining disaster, Apr 1877. – [Centenary of a catastrophe].

Portread o hanes. *Y Faner,* 12 Aws/Aug 1977, 20. Review of Alexander Cordell, *This sweet and bitter earth.* – [Portrait of history].

By the light of the Czar's jewels. *Welsh Nation,* Aug 1977, 10:B-D

Bevan a great man and yet. *Welsh Nation,* Oct 1977, 3:A-D.

Llyfrau dwy ganrif yn ôl. *Y Faner,* 11 Tach/Nov 1977, 17. [Books two centuries ago].

Stori antur. *Y Faner,* 2 Rha/Dec 1977, 20. Review of Lynn Hughes, *Hawkmoor adventures of Twm Sion Catti.* – [Adventure story].

For Princess Nest. *AWR* 26,58 (1977) 47. Poetry.

Review of Philip Pacey, *Hugh MacDiarmid and David Jones: Celtic wonder-voyagers. PW* 13,3 (1977) 99-100.

Review of A.O.H. Jarman and Gwilym Rees Hughes, *A guide to Welsh literature. Vol. 1. PW* 12,3 (1977) 115-119.

Preview. *Radio Times,* 18-24 Feb 1978, 19. Continued: 18-24 Mar, 19; 15-21 Apr, 19; 13-19 May, 19; 10-16 Jun, 17; 21-27 Jun, 15; 8-24 Jul, 17; 9-15 Sep, 15; 30 Sep-6 Oct, 21; 28 Oct-3 Nov, 25; 4-10 Nov, 25; 2-8 Dec, 27.

A journey through one man's mind. *WM,* 6 Jul 1978, 7. Review of David Cole, *Mount of Angels and other poems.*

The boffin who assembled an historical jigsaw. *WM,* 26 Aug 1978, 8:A-C. On Thomas Pennant.

Englyn. *AWR* 62 (1978) 29-30. Translation from the Welsh of J.T. Jones. – Poetry.

The master draper. *AWR* 62 (1978) 30-31. Poetry.

Pure propaganda. *Planet* 45-46 (1978) 122. Review of *The socialist poems of Hugh MacDiarmid,* ed. T.S. Law and Thurso Berwick.

Preview. *Radio Times,* 13-19 Jan 1979, 21. Continued: 10-16 Mar, 21; 7-13 Apr, 27; 5-11 May, 27; 2-8 Jun, 21; 30 Jun-6 Jul, 21; 28 Jul-3 Aug, 17; 25-31 Aug, 19; 22-28 Sep, 29; 20-26 Oct, 27; 17-23 Nov, 29; 15-21 Dec, 27.

The day that the trattoria was drained dry of vino. *WM* [St. David's Day Special supplement], 1 Mar 1979, 2-3, 5.

1979: pethau sy'n llenwi'r cof. *Y Faner,* 21-28 Rha/Dec 1979, 6. [Things that fill the memory].

A visit to the waterworks. *Planet 48* (1979) 56-58.

Preview. *Radio Times,* 26 Mar-1 Feb 1980, 25. Continued: 23-29 Feb, 21; 29 Mar-4 Apr, 25; 26 Apr-2 May, 21; 19-25 Jul, 17; 23-29 Aug, 17.

Coalfield art. *Radio Times,* 13-19 Nov 1980, 25. On Jack Crabtree.

Then and now. *Arcade,* 14 Nov 1980, 14. Comparisons with the 1930s.

A chronicle of decline. *Radio Times,* 22-28 Nov 1980, 32-33. On Blaenavon.

Bwrw amheuon annheilwng. *Y Faner,* 13 Chw/Feb 1981, 21. Letter. – [Casting unworthy doubts].

Review of *A people and a proletariat,* ed. David Smith. *Welsh Republic* [1], Jan-Feb 1982, 10.

Bannau Macchu Picchu. *Barn,* Maw/Mar 1982, 61-64. Translation into Welsh of 'The heights of Macchu Picchu', by Pablo Neruda.

The way we were. *Radio Times,* 26 Jun 1982, 63.

Eisteddfodau Abertawe. *Barn,* Aws/Aug 1982, 199-200. [Swansea eisteddfods].

Llongyfarchion i Saunders Lewis ar ei ben-blwydd. *Barn,* Hyd/Oct 1982, 303. [Congratulations to Saunders Lewis on his birthday].

Down memory lane. *Radio Times,* 23-29 Oct 1982, 75.

Llew Llywel – dawn a anghofiwyd. *Y Faner,* 10 Rha/Dec 1982, 10.

Review of Kenneth O. Morgan, *Rebirth of a nation: Wales, 1880-1980. Welsh Republic* 6 (1982) 10.

Local Boyce makes good. *Radio Times,* 23-29 Apr 1983, 13.

The friendly festival. *Radio Times,* 16-22 Jul 1983, 17. On the International Eisteddfod, Llangollen.

Lampeter's eisteddfod. *Radio Times,* 4-10 Aug 1984, 14.

English? That's the dying language. *WM,* 2 Apr 1985, 8:B-E. Interviewed by Mario Basini.

*Note also:* Anglomaniac anthem. Talybont: Y Lolfa, [n.d.]. Poster poem.

## B. Publications about Harri Webb

BIANCHI, Tony. Propaganda'r prydydd. *Y Faner,* 27 Ion/Jan 1978, 9-11, 13. [A poet's propaganda].

CAMPBELL, T. Poetry of the valleys. *South Wales Echo,* 24 Apr 1974, 11. Includes interview with Harri Webb.

CLWYD Centre for Educational Technology. *The poems of Harri Webb.* Mold: Clwyd Centre for Educational Technology, 1979. Incl.: Booklet of 10 poems – Reprint of 'Webb's progress' (*Planet* 30, 1976) – Facsimile letter – 12 colour slides – Biographical and introductory notes. – Teaching pack.

CURTIS, Tony. Grafting the sour to sweetness: Anglo-Welsh poetry in the last twenty-five years. In *Wales the imagined nation: studies in cultural and national identity,* ed. Tony Curtis. Bridgend: Poetry Wales Press, 1986. pp. 99-126. Incl. discussion of Harri Webb.

HUMFREY, Belinda. Harri Webb in the wrong language. *AWR* 21,48 (1972) 9-17.

JENKINS, Nigel. The poetry of Harri Webb. *Planet* 83 (1990) 18-23.

JONES, Glyn. Harri'r werin. *Barn,* Tach/Nov 1977, 381. Review of *Rampage and revel.*

JONES, Harri Pritchard. Not a daffodil for miles. *Radio Times,* 3 Apr 1975, 18-19. On the appeal of Webb's poetry.

JONES, Sally Roberts. A matter of choices: the poetry of Harri Webb. *PW* 26,2 (1990) 27-30.

MORRIS, Brian. *Harri Webb.* Cardiff: University of Wales Press, 1993. 113 p.: pbk. (Writers of Wales). ISBN: 0-7083-1225-X.

O'NEILL, C.B. Harri Webb and nationalist poetry. *AWR* 65 (1979) 90-99. Incl. bibliography covering records and broadcasts.

ORMOND, John. Political poetry. *WM,* 5 Aug 1974, 4: D-E. Review of *A crown for Branwen.*

ROBERTS, Ioan. Bardd sy'n sgrifennu at y bobl am y bobl. *Y Cymro,* 7 Gor/Jul 1971, 20. [A poet who writes for the people about the people].

SIMPSON, Mercer. Harri Webb, poetic canvasser or rebel joker? *PW* 23,2-3 (1988) 37-40.

STEPHENS, Meic. Poet with dragon fire in his verse. *WM,* 7 Sep 1990, 11:A-C. On the occasion of Harri Webb's 70th birthday.

— The Garth Newydd years: halcyon days in Merthyr. *Planet* 83 (1990) 18-23. Recollections of Harri Webb.

TRIPP, John. Harri Webb. In *Contemporary poets,* ed. James Vinson. 2nd. ed. London: St. James Press; New York: St. Martin's Press, 1975. pp. 1640-1641.

WILKS, Ivor. Harri's web: Harri Webb and Welsh republicanism. *Planet* 83 (1990) 13-17.

WILLIAMS, Griffith. £5,000 to spend on books. *WM,* 15 Jul 1964, 6: E-G. On Harri Webb's appointment as librarian at Mountain Ash.

# RAYMOND WILLIAMS (1921-1988)

A. Publications by Raymond Williams
   (i)   Books
   (ii)  Books and periodicals edited
   (iii) Selected contributions to books and periodicals
   (iv)  Raymond Williams: translations

B. Publications about Raymond Williams


## A (i). Publications by Raymond Williams: Books

*Reading and criticism.* London: Muller, 1950. x, 142 p. (Man and society).

*Drama from Ibsen to Eliot.* London: Chatto & Windus, 1952. 283 p. Revised as *Drama from Ibsen to Brecht,* 1968 (see below).
—— Harmondsworth: Penguin, 1964. 315 p.: pbk. (Peregrine books).

U.S. ed.: New York: Oxford University Press, 1953.

*Preface to film.* London: Film Drama, 1954. 129 p. Written jointly with Michael Orrom.

U.S. ed.: Ann Arbor: University Microfilms, 1979.

*Drama in performance.* London: Muller, 1954. 128 p.: ill. (Man and society).
—— Watts, 1968. x, 198 p.: ill. (New thinker's library). ISBN: 0296-34704-3. Revised, with new discussion of Ingmar Bergman's film 'Wild strawberries', pp. 159-171.
—— Harmondsworth: Penguin, 1972. ix, 194 p.: ill. (Pelican books). ISBN: 0-1402-1459-3. Revised and extended, with discussion of 'Wild strawberries', pp. 157-169.
—— / with a new introduction and bibliography by Graham Holderness. Milton Keynes: Open University, 1991. 184 p.: ill.: pbk. ISBN: 0-335-0958-1. Bibliography, pp. 175-182.

U.S. eds.: Chester Springs: Dufour, 1961. 128 p.: ill.
—— New York: Basic Books, 1968. x, 198 p.: ill. (Culture and discovery).

*Culture and society, 1780-1950.* London: Chatto & Windus, 1958. xx, 363 p.
—— Harmondsworth: Penguin, 1961. 348 p.: pbk. (Pelican books).

Reissued 1963, with postscript by the author, pp. 324-325. – Reissued 1971, ISBN: 0-1402-0520-9.
—— *Culture and society: Coleridge to Orwell* / new foreword by the author. Hogarth, 1987. xx, 363 p.: pbk. ISBN: 0-7012-0792-2.

U.S. eds.: New York: Columbia University Press, 1958. 363 p.
—— New York: Doubleday, 1960. xviii, 382 p. (Anchor books).
—— New York: Harper, 1966. xviii, 363 p.: pbk. (Harper torchbooks; The academy library).
—— *The sociology of culture.* New York: Schocken Books, 1982. 248 p.: pbk. ISBN: 0-8052-0696-5.
—— New York: Columbia University Press, 1983. xx, 362 p.: hbk & pbk. ISBN: 0-231-02287-5, 0-231-05701-6 pbk.

**Border country: a novel.** London: Chatto & Windus, 1960. 351 p. Reissued 1978, ISBN: 0-0711-23761.
—— Readers Union, 1962.
—— *Border country.* Harmondsworth: Penguin, 1964. 334 p.: pbk.
—— *Border country.* Hogarth, 1988. 351 p.: pbk. ISBN: 0-7012-0807-4.

U.S. ed.: New York: Horizon, 1962. 350 p.

**The long revolution.** London: Chatto & Windus, 1961. xiv, 370 p. Contents: The creative mind – The analysis of culture – Individuals and societies – Images of society – Education and British society – The growth of the reading public – The growth of the popular press – The growth of 'Standard English' – The social history of English writers – The social history of dramatic forms – Realism and the contemporary novel – Britain in the 1960s.
—— Harmondsworth: Penguin, 1965. 399 p.: pbk. (Pelican books). Reissued 1984, ISBN: 0-1402-0762-7.

U.S. eds.: New York: Columbia University Press, 1961. 369 p.
—— New York: Harper, 1966. 375 p.: pbk. (Harper torchbooks; The academy library).
—— Westport, Conn.: Greenwood Press, 1975. xiv, 369 p. ISBN: 0-8371-8244-1. Reissued 1984.

**Communications and community.** Birmingham: Printed by F.H. Wakelin, 1961. 16 p. The William F. Harvey memorial lecture, given at Bedford College, London University, 8 Apr 1961.

**Britain in the sixties: communications.** Harmondsworth: Penguin, 1962. 134 p.: pbk. (Penguin special).
—— *Communications.* Chatto & Windus, 1966. 196 p. Revised edition.
—— *Communications.* Harmondsworth: Penguin, 1968. 185 p.: pbk. (Pelican books). 'Third edition' revised, with Retrospect and prospect, 1975, pp. 180-189. – Reissued 1976, 192p.: pbk. ISBN: 0-1402-0831-3.

U.S. eds.: Baltimore: Penguin, 1962. 134 p.: pbk. (Penguin special).
—— New York: *Communications.* Barnes & Noble, 1967. 196 p. Revised.

*The existing alternatives in communications.* London: Fabian Society, 1962. 15p.: pamph. (Fabian tracts; 337).

*Second generation: a novel.* London: Chatto & Windus, 1964. 347 p. Reissued 1978, ISBN: 0-7011-1218-2.
—— Hogarth, 1988. pbk. ISBN: 0-7012-0808-2.

U.S. ed.: New York: Horizon Press, 1965.

*Modern tragedy.* London: Chatto & Windus, 1966. 288 p. Incl. 'Koba', a drama by Raymond Williams, pp. 207-282.
—— Verso, 1979. 226 p.: pbk. ISBN: 0-86091-711-8. Incl. Afterword, 1979, pp. 207-219. – Omits 'Koba'.

U.S. ed.: Stanford, California: Stanford University Press, 1966. 208 p.

*Drama from Ibsen to Brecht.* London: Chatto & Windus, 1968. 352 p. A revision of *Drama from Ibsen to Eliot,* 1952.
—— Harmondsworth: Penguin, 1973. 408 p.: pbk. (Pelican books). ISBN: 0-14-021492-5. Revised edition. – 2nd revised edition, 1976. ISBN: 0-14-021492-5.
—— Hogarth, 1987. x, 352 p.: pbk. ISBN: 0-7012-0793-0.

U.S. ed.: New York: Oxford University Press 1969. 352 p.

*The English novel from Dickens to Lawrence.* London: Chatto & Windus, 1970. 196 p. ISBN: 0-7011-1542-4.
—— St. Albans: Paladin, 1974. 159 p.: pbk. ISBN: 0-586-08185-2.
—— Hogarth, 1984. 196 p.: pbk. ISBN: 0-7012-0558-X.

U.S. ed.: New York: Oxford University Press, 1970. ISBN: 0-19-519078-5.

*Orwell.* London: Fontana, 1971. 95 p.: pbk. (Modern masters). ISBN: 0-00-0632437-1.
—— Flamingo, 1984. 128 p.: pbk. ISBN: 0-00-654078-3. Incl. Afterword, *Nineteen eighty four* in 1984, pp. 95-126.

U.S. eds.: *George Orwell.* New York: Viking Press, 1971. 102 p. (Modern masters). ISBN: 0-670-33702-1.
—— New York: Columbia University Press, 1981.

*The country and the city.* London: Chatto & Windus, 1973. 335 p. ISBN: 0-7011-1371-5.

—— St. Albans: Paladin, 1975. 399 p.: pbk. ISBN: 0-586-08183-6.
—— Hogarth, 1985. 335 p.: pbk. ISBN: 0-7012-1005-2.

U.S. ed.: New York: Oxford University Press, 1973.


*Television: technology and cultural form.* London: Fontana, 1974. 160
p.: pbk. (Technosphere). ISBN: 0-00-633571-3.
—— / edited by Ederyn Williams. Routledge, 1990. 176 p. pbk. ISBN:
0-415-03047-1. Incl. Notes to the second edition, by Ederyn Williams,
pp. 153-156.

U.S. ed.: New York: Schocken Books, 1975. 160 p.: hbk & pbk. ISBN:
0-8052-0501-2 hbk, 0-8052-3597-3 pbk. Reissued 1987.


*Drama in a dramatised society:* an inaugural lecture delivered at the University of
Cambridge on 29 October 1974. Cambridge: Cambridge University Press,
1975. 21 p.: pamph. ISBN: 0-521-20932-3.


*Keywords: a vocabulary of culture and society.* London: Croom Helm,
1976. 286 p. ISBN: 0-85664-289-4.
—— Fontana, 1976. pbk. (Fontana communications series). ISBN: 0-00-
633479-2.
—— Flamingo, 1983. 341 p.: pbk. ISBN: 0-00-654021-X. Revised and
expanded.

U.S. eds.: New York: Oxford University Press, 1976. ISBN: 0-19-519854-
9 hbk, 0-19-519855-7 pbk.
—— New York: Oxford University Press, 1985. 349 p.: pbk. ISBN: 0-19-
520469-7. Revised and expanded.


*Marxism and literature.* Oxford: Oxford University Press, 1977. 218 p.:
hbk & pbk. (Marxist introductions). ISBN: 0-19-876056-6 hbk, 0-19-
876061-2 pbk.


*The volunteers.* London: Eyre Methuen, 1978. 208 p. ISBN: 0-413-45530-
0. Novel. Extract: *Madog* [Polytechnic of Wales] 1,2 (1977) 21-24. With
typescript emendations.
—— Hogarth, 1985. pbk. ISBN: 0-7012-1016-8.


*The fight for Manod.* London: Chatto & Windus, 1979. 207 p. ISBN: 0-
7011-2412-1. Novel.
—— Hogarth, 1988. pbk. ISBN: 0-7012-0809-0.


*The Welsh industrial novel: the inaugural Gwyn Jones lecture.* Cardiff: University College Cardiff Press, 1979. 20 p.: pamph. ISBN: 0-906449-02-2.
Delivered 21 Apr 1978.

*Politics and letters: interviews with* **New Left Review.** London: NLB [New Left Books], 1979. 444 p. ISBN: 0-86091-000-8. Contents: Biography – Culture; *Culture and Society, The long revolution, Keywords* – Drama; *Drama from Ibsen to Eliot,* Brecht and beyond – Literature; *Reading and criticism, The English novel from Dickens to Lawrence* – The Welsh trilogy, *The volunteers, The country and the city, Marxism and literature* – Politics; Britain 1956-78, *Orwell,* The Russian revolution, Two roads to change.
—— Verso, 1981. pbk. ISBN: 0-86091-735-5.

U.S. ed.: New York: Schocken, 1979.

*Problems in materialism and culture: selected essays.* London: Verso, 1980. viii, 277 p.: hbk & pbk. ISBN: 0-86091-028-8 hbk, 0-86091-729-0 pbk. Contents: A hundred years of *Culture and anarchy* – Literature and sociology – Base and superstructure in Marxist cultural theory – Means of communication as means of production – Ideas of nature – Social Darwinism – Problems of materialism – Social environment and theatrical environment: the case of English naturalism – The Bloomsbury fraction – Advertising: the magic system – Utopia and science fiction – *The Welsh industrial novel* – Notes on Marxism in Britain since 1945 – Beyond actually existing socialism.

U.S. ed.: New York: Schocken, 1981.

*Culture.* London: Fontana, 1981. 248 p.: pbk. (Fontana new sociology). ISBN: 0-00-635627-3.

U.S. ed.: *The sociology of culture.* New York: Schocken, 1982.

*Socialism and ecology.* London: Socialist Environment and Resources Association, [1982]. 20 p.: pamph.

*The Arts Council: politics and policies: the 1981 W.E. Williams memorial lecture given at the National Theatre on 3 November 1981* / by C.B. Cox and Raymond Williams. London: Arts Council of Great Britain, [1983?]. 16 p.: pbk. ISBN: 0-7287-0317-3. Incl. Lecture, by Raymond Williams, pp. 9-16.

*Cobbett.* Oxford: Oxford University Press, 1983. 89 p.: hbk & pbk. (Past masters). ISBN: 0-19-287576-0 hbk, 0-19-287575-2 pbk.

*Towards 2000.* London: Chatto & Windus; Hogarth, 1983. 273 p. ISBN: 0-7011-2685-X. Contents: Towards 2000 – Britain in the sixties – 'Industrial' and 'post industrial' society – Democracy old and new – Culture and technology – Class, politics and socialism – The culture of nations – East-west, north-south – War: the last enemy – Resources for a journey of hope
—— Harmondsworth: Penguin, 1985. pbk. ISBN: 0-1402-2534-X.

U.S. ed.: *The year 2000.* New York: Pantheon Books, 1983. xiii, 273 p. ISBN: 0-394-53552-9. Incl. preface to American edition.

*Writing in society.* London: Verso, 1983. 271 p.: hbk & pbk. ISBN: 0-86091-072-5 hbk, 0-86091-772-X pbk. Contents: *Drama in a dramatized society* – Form and meaning: Hippolytus and Phedre – On dramatic dialogue and monologue (particularly in Shakespeare) – Notes on English prose, 1780-1950 – David Hume: reasoning and experience – The fiction of reform – Forms of English fiction in 1848 – The reader in *Hard Times* – Cambridge English, past and present – Crisis in English studies – Beyond Cambridge English – Region and class in the novel – The ragged-arsed philanthropists – On first looking into *New Lines* – The tenses of imagination [discussing Williams's Welsh trilogy].

*Loyalties.* London: Chatto & Windus, 1985. 378 p. ISBN: 0-7011-2843-7. Novel. – Reissued 1989, pbk. ISBN: 0-7012-0897-X.

*Country and city in the modern novel.* Swansea: University College of Swansea, 1987. 16 p.: pbk. (W.D. Thomas memorial lecture). ISBN: 0-860760456.

*Resources of hope: culture, democracy, socialism* / edited by Robin Gale; with an introduction by Robin Blackburn. London: Verso, 1989. xxiii, 334 p.: hbk & pbk. ISBN: 0-86091-229-9 hbk, 0-86091-943-9 pbk. Contents: Introduction, pp. ix-xxiii – Defining a democratic culture; Culture is ordinary, Communications and community, The idea of a common culture – State, administration and the arts; The Arts Council – Solidarity and commitment; Why do I demonstrate?, You're a Marxist, aren't you?, The writer: commitment and alignment, Art: freedom as duty – Resources of class and community; Welsh culture, The social significance of 1926, The importance of community, Mining the meaning: key words in the miners' strike – Beyond Labourism; The British left, Ideas and the Labour movement, An alternative politics, Problems of the coming period, Socialists and coalitionists – The challenge of the new social movements; The politics of nuclear disarmament, Socialism and ecology, Between country and city, Decentralism and the politics of place – Redefining socialist democracy; The forward march of Labour halted?, Democracy and parliament, Walking backwards into the future, Hesitations before socialism, Towards many socialisms, The practice of possibility – Select bibliography.

*Raymond Williams on television: selected writings* / edited by Alan O'Connor. London: Routledge, 1989. xvii, 223 p.: pbk. ISBN:0-415-02627-X. Contents: Preface, by Raymond Williams, pp. ix-xii – Introduction, by Alan O'Connor, pp. xiii-xvii. – Part I. Television: cultural form and politics; *Drama in a dramatised society*, Distance, What happened at Munich, Impressions of U.S. television – Part II. *Listener* columns: television forms and conventions – Part III. An interview with Raymond Williams, Television and teaching – Bibliography, pp. 216-218. – Drawn largely from Williams's regular *Listener* column, 1968-1972.

*What I came to say* [edited by Francis Mulhern]. London: Hutchinson

Radius, 1989. 280 p.: hbk & pbk. ISBN: 0-09-175789-4 hbk. Contents: Preface, by Francis Mulhern – My Cambridge – Seeing a man running – Fiction and the writing public – Desire – Distance – Writing, speech and the 'classical' – Community – Wales and England – The city and the world – A kind of Gresham's law – Middlemen – Gravity's Python – Isn't the news terrible? – The press and popular culture: an historical perspective – Film history – The future of 'English literature' – Adult education and social change – The red and the green – Communications, technologies and social institutions – Marx on culture – A defence of realism – On Solzhenitsyn: 1. Literature and revolution; 2. Russia betrayed: a note on August 1914 – Commitment – Brecht – Lukács: a man without frustration. – Reissued 1990, pbk. ISBN: 0-09-174441-5.

***The politics of modernism: against the new conformists*** / edited and introduced by Tony Pinkney. London: Verso, 1989. xi, 208 p.: hbk & pbk. ISNB: 0-86091-241-8 hbk, 0-86091-955-2 pbk. Contents: Editor's introduction: modernism and cultural theory, pp. 1-29 – When was modernism? – Metropolitan perceptions and the emergence of modernism – The politics of the avant-garde – Language and the avant-garde – Theatre as a political forum – Afterword to *Modern tragedy* – Cinema and socialism – Culture and technology – Politics and policies: the case of the Arts Council – The future of cultural studies – The uses of cultural theory – Appendix: Media, margins and modernity: Raymond Williams and Edward Said [discussion].

***People of the Black Mountains. I. The beginning*** ... London: Chatto & Windus, 1989. 361 p. ISBN: 0-7011-2845-3. Novel.
—— Paladin, 1990. pbk. ISBN: 0-586-09058-4.

***People of the Black Mountains. II. The eggs of the eagle.*** London: Chatto & Windus, 1990. 330 p. ISBN: 0-7011-3564-6. Incl. Postscript, by Joy Williams, pp. 318-323. Novel.
—— Paladin, 1992. pbk. ISBN: 0-586-09059-2.

***Border country: Raymond Williams in adult education*** / edited by John McIlroy and Sallie Westwood. Leicester: National Institute of Adult Continuing Education, 1993. iv, 343 p.: pbk. ISBN: 1-872941-28-1. Contents: The unknown Raymond Williams, by John McIlroy, pp. 3-25 – Section 2: Cultural policies; For continuity in change, Culture and crisis, The reading public and the critical reader, Soviet literary controversy in retrospect, The state and popular culture: a note, The idea of culture, The new party line?, A kind of Gresham's Law, Culture is ordinary, Our debt to Dr Leavis, Fiction and the writing public, Working class attitudes, The press and popular education, London letter: the New British Left – Section 3: Teaching and learning; Some notes on aim and method in university tutorial classes, A note of Mr Hoggart's appendices, Some experiments in literature teaching, The way we read now, Critics and criticism, Literature in relation to history: 1850-75, Books for teaching 'culture and envirnment', The teaching of public expression, Film as a tutorial subject, Review of *Drama from Ibsen to Eliot,* by J.R. Williams [with Raymond Williams's reply], Text and context

– Section 4: Adult education; Figures and shadows, Standards, Class and classes, Going on learning, An open letter to WEA tutors, The common good, The roots of education, Sensible people, Workers' college, Voices of socialism: R.H. Tawney, Different sides of the wall, Open teaching, Adult education, Adult education and social change. – Retrospect and prospect; Border country: Raymond Williams in adult education, by John McIlroy, pp. 269-323 – Excavating the future: towards 2000, by Sallie Westwood, pp. 324-336. – A collection of Williams's writings, mostly from the period 1947-1961, arranged in three sections, each with its detailed introduction.

# A (ii). Publications by Raymond Williams: Books and Periodicals Edited

*Cambridge University Journal,* Apr-Jun 1940. For Williams's contributions see bibliography by Alan O'Connor, in his *Raymond Williams: writing, culture, politics* (1989).

*Outlook: a selection of Cambridge writing.* Cambridge: 1941. 64 p. Edited with Fred Parker and others.

*Twenty-one,* Apr-Oct 1945. The weekly newspaper of the 21st Anti-Tank Regiment, Royal Artillery, printed at Pinneberg, Germany. – Edited under pseudonym, Michael Pope.

*Politics and letters: a quarterly survey of intellectual background,* Summer 1947-Summer 1948. Edited by Raymond Williams, with Clifford Collins and Wolf Mankowitz. – Incorporates *The critic: a quarterly review of criticism,* 1,1 – 1,2. (1947), a companion periodical edited by Williams, Collins and Mankowitz. – Williams's contributions are listed in Alan O'Connor's bibliography (in his *Raymond Williams: writing, culture, politics,* 1989).

*1967 New Left May Day manifesto.* London: May Day Manifesto Committee, 1967. 46 p.: pamph. Edited with Stuart Hall and E. P. Thompson.

*May Day manifesto 1968* / edited by Raymond Williams. Harmondsworth: Penguin, 1968. 190 p.: pbk. (Penguin specials).

*The Pelican book of English prose. Volume 2. From 1780 to the present day* / edited by Raymond Williams. Harmondsworth: Penguin, 1969. 506 p. ISBN: 0-1402-1069-5. Incl. Preface and introduction, by Raymond Williams, pp. 19-55.

*D.H. Lawrence on education* / edited by Joy and Raymond Williams. Harmondsworth: Penguin Education, 1973. 242 p.: pbk. ISBN: 0-14-081202-4.

*George Orwell: a collection of critical essays* / edited by Raymond Williams.

Englewood Cliffs, N.J.: Prentice-Hall, 1974. viii, 182 p.: hbk & pbk. (Twentieth century views). ISBN: 0-13-647719-4 hbk, 0-13-647701-1 pbk. Incl. Observation and imagination in Orwell, by Raymond Williams, pp. 52-61.

*English drama: forms and development: essays in honour of Muriel Clara Bradbrook* / edited by Marie Axton and Raymond Williams. Cambridge: Cambridge University Press, 1977. x, 263 p. ISBN: 0-521-21588-9. Incl.: Introduction, by Raymond Williams, pp. vii-x – Social environment and theatrical environment: the case of English naturalism, by Raymond Williams, pp. 203-223.

*Contact: human communication and its history* / edited by Raymond Williams. London: Thames & Hudson, 1981. 272 p: ill. ISBN: 0500-01239-3. Incl. Communications techniques and social institutions, by Raymond Williams, pp. 8-19.

*John Clare: selected poetry and prose* / edited by Merryn and Raymond Williams. London: Methuen, 1986. viii, 252 p.: pbk. (Methuen English texts). ISBN: 0-416-41120-7. Incl. Introduction, by Raymond Williams, pp. 1-22.

# A (iii). Publications by Raymond Williams: Selected Contributions to Books and Periodicals

The most comprehensive bibliography of Raymond Williams is undoubtedly Alan O'Connor's, published in his *Raymond Williams: writing, culture, politics* (1989), pp. 128-175, and in *Raymond Williams: critical perspectives,* ed. Terry Eagleton (1989), pp. 184-227. This present bibliography makes no attempt to list Williams's book reviews in the *Guardian* (over 200) and *New Society,* articles in *Tribune* and the *Nation;* and letters to *The Times.* Nor in general does it note the first appearance of essays subsequently collected in book form. Here too O'Connor provides full details.

Sugar. In *Outlook: a selection of Cambridge writings,* ed. Raymond Williams and others. Cambridge, 1941. pp. 7-14.

Sack labourer. In *English story: third series,* ed. Woodrow Wyatt. London: Collins, 1942. pp. 71-79.

This time. *New Writing and Daylight* 2 (1942-43) 158-164. Story.

A dialogue on actors. *Critic* 1,1 (1947) 17-24.

Saints, revolutionaries, carpetbaggers, etc. *Critic* 1,1 (1947) 52-54. Review of E.W. Martin, *The new spirit, Writers of today,* ed. Denys Val Baker.

Ibsenites and Ibsenite-antis. *Critic* 1,2 (1947) 65-68. Review of Brian

W. Downs, *Ibsen: the intellectual background,* M.C. Bradbrook, *Ibsen the Norwegian.*

The delicacy of P.H. Newby. *Critic* 2,2 (1947) 79-81. Review of P.H. Newby, *Agents and witnesses.*

Lower fourth at St. Harry's. *Politics and Letters* 1,2-3 (1947) 105-106. On Hollywood McCarthyism.

Radio drama. *Politics and Letters* 1,2-3 (1947) 106-109.

Dali, corruption and his critics. *Politics and Letters* 1,2-3 (1947) 112-113. Review of Salvador Dali, *Hidden faces.*

And traitors sneer. *Politics and Letters* 1,4 (1948) 66-68.

Review of Llewellyn White, *The American radio. Politics and Letters* 1,4 (1948) 86-87.

A fine room to be ill in. In *English story: eighth series,* ed. Woodrow Wyatt. London: Collins, 1949. pp. 63-78.

Ibsen's non-theatrical plays. *Listener,* 22 Dec 1949, 1098-1099. Text of Third Programme broadcast.

The idea of culture. *Essays in Criticism* 1 (1953) 239-266.

Editorial commentary. *Essays in Criticism* 4 (1954) 341-344. On literary periodicals.

Second thoughts: T.S. Eliot on culture. *Essays in Criticism* 6 (1956) 302-318.

The new party line? *Essays in Criticism* 7 (1957) 68-76. Review of Colin Wilson, *The outsider.*

Fiction and the writing public. *Essays in Criticism* 7 (1957) 422-428. Review of Richard Hoggart, *The uses of literacy.*

The uses of literacy: working class culture. *Universities and Left Review* 1,2 (1957) 29-32.

Culture and society. *TLS,* 3 Oct 1958, 561. Letter.

The present position in dramatic criticism. *Essays in Criticism* 8 (1958) 290-298. Review of Ronald Peacock, *The art of drama.*

Priestley against Topside. *New Statesman,* 10 Jan 1959, 47-48. Review of J.B. Priestley, *Topside, or the future of England.*

Tribune's majority. *New Statesman*, 24 Jan 1959, 124. Review of *Tribune 21*, ed. Elizabeth Thomas.

The bearing of literature. *New Statesman*, 21 Mar 1959, 410. Review of William Walsh, *The uses of the imagination*, Vincent Buckley, *Poetry and morality*.

Science and culture. *New Statesman*, 25 Apr 1959, 584. Review of Cyril Bibby, *T.H. Huxley: scientist, humanist and educator*.

The critic as biographer. *New Statesman*, 9 May 1959, 662-663. Review of J. Middleton Murray, *Katherine Mansfield and other literary studies*.

Going on learning. *New Statesman*, 30 May 1959, 750-751.

Definitions of culture. *New Statesman*, 25 Jul 1959, 114. Review of F.R. Cowell, *Culture in private and public life*.

Literature and morality. *New Statesman*, 31 Oct 1959, 588-590. Review of Dorothea Krook, *Three traditions of moral thought*, William Robbins, *The ethical idealism of Matthew Arnold*.

Verse and drama. *New Statesman*, 26 Dec 1959, 916. Review of Dennis Donoghue, *The third voice*.

Dylan Thomas's play for voices. *Critical Quarterly* 1 (1959) 18-26.

The realism of Arthur Miller. *Critical Quarterly* 1 (1959) 140-149.

Our debt to Dr. Leavis. *Critical Quarterly* 1 (1959) 245-247.

Critical forum. *Essays in Criticism* 9 (1959) 432-437. On *Culture and society*.

A practical critic. *New Statesman*, 5 Mar 1960, 338-339. Review of Laurence Lerner, *The truest poetry*.

Ibsen restored. *New Statesman*, 2 Jul 1960, 23-24. On 'Brand', 'The lady from the sea', 'John Gabriel Borkman', 'When we dead awake'.

Oxford Ibsen. *New Statesman*, 24 Sep 1960, 447-448. Review of *Ibsen. Vol. 7*, tr. J.W. McFarlane, and 'An enemy of the people', 'The wild duck', 'Rosmersholm', tr. J.W. McFarlane.

Lawrence and Tolstoy. *Critical Quarterly* 2 (1960) 33-39.

Working class attitudes. *New Left Review* 1 (1960) 26-30. Revised transcript of conversation with Richard Hoggart.

[Witness for the defence]. In *The trial of Lady Chatterley: Regina v. Penguin Books Limited: the transcript of the trial,* ed. C.H. Rolph. Harmondsworth: Penguin, 1961. pp. 133-135.

Three-quarters of a nation. *New Statesman,* 3 Mar 1961, 351. Review of David Holbrook, *English for maturity.*

Hope deferred. *New Statesman,* 19 May 1961, 802. Review of production of 'Waiting for Godot'.

Work and leisure. *New Statesman,* 25 May 1961, 926-927.

Definitions of culture. *New Statesman,* 2 Jun 1961, 882. On Richard Wollheim, *Socialism and culture.*

Shame the world. *New Statesman,* 9 Jun 1961, 932-933. Review of production of Brecht, 'The visions of Simone Marchard'.

The figure in the rug. *New Statesman,* 7 Jul 1961, 20-21. Review of Richard Cordell, *Somerset Maugham.*

The future of Marxism. *Twentieth Century,* July 1961, 128-142.

The law and literary merit. *Encounter,* Sep 1961, 66-69.

Virtuous circle. *Listener,* 30 Nov 1961, 933-934. Review of Margaret Cole, The *story of Fabian socialism.*

My performances. *New Statesman,* 8 Dec 1961, 892-893. On Thomas Bewick, *Memoir.*

The achievement of Brecht. *Critical Quarterly* 3 (1961) 153-162.

Thoughts on a masked stranger. *Kenyon Review* 23 (1961) 698-702. Review of Hannah Arendt, *Between past and future.*

Freedom and ownership in the arts. *Overland* [Melbourne] 3,20 (1961) 23-27.

The deadlock. *Encounter,* Jan 1962, 14-15.

Sensible people. *New Statesman,* 5 Jan 1962, 21-22. Review of J.F.C. Harrison, *Learning and living, 1790-1960.*

Into the wilderness. *New Statesman,* 2 Mar 1962, 305-306. Review of J.M.S. Tompkins, *The popular novel in England, 1770-1800.*

From Scott to Tolstoy. *Listener,* 8 Mar 1962, 436-437. Review of Georg Lukács, *The historical novel.*

Review of David Holbrook, *Llareggub revisited. Listener,* 12 Apr 1962, 651-652.

To the north. *Listener,* 17 May 1962, 868, 870. Review of F.L. Lucas, *Ibsen and Strindberg.*

Strong feelings? *Listener,* 4 Oct 1962, 529-530. Review of Brian Magee, *The new radicalism.*

Review of *The classic theatre,* vols. 1-4, ed. E.R. Bentley. *Massachusetts Review* 4,1 (1962) 219-222.

A dialogue on tragedy. *New Left Review* 13-14 (1962) 22-35.

Fiction and delusion: a note on *Auto da fé,* by Elias Canetti. *New Left Review* 15 (1962) 103-106.

Influence of Strindberg on American and British drama. *World Theatre* 9,1 (1962). Written jointly with John Gassner.

Review of Georg Lukács, *The meaning of contemporary realism. Listener,* 28 Feb 1963, 385.

Going into Europe. *Encounter,* Mar 1963, 68.

Liberal breakdown. *Listener,* 30 May 1963, 926, 929. Review of C.B. Cox, *The free spirit.*

What kind of education? *Listener,* 18 Jul 1963, 91. Review of Marjorie Cruickshank, *Church and state in English education,* Robert Peers, *Fact and possibility in English education,* Kenneth Richmond, *Culture and general education.*

Radical history. *Listener,* 5 Dec 1963, 938, 941. Review of E.P. Thompson, *The making of the English working class.*

Tolstoy, Lawrence and tragedy. *Kenyon Review* 25,4 (1963) 633-650.

From hero to victim: notes on the development of liberal tragedy. *New Left Review* 20 (1963) 54-68.

Books 12: Raymond Williams. *Twentieth Century,* Summer 1963, 137. E.E. Hirschmann's *On human unity* as a neglected book.

David Hume: reasoning and experience. In *The English mind: studies in the English moralists presented to Basil Willey,* ed. Hugh Sykes Davies and George Watson. Cambridge: Cambridge University Press, 1964. pp. 123-145.

Social criticism in Dickens: some problems of method and approach. *Critical*

*Quarterly* 6 (1964) 214-227. Correspondence with J.C. Maxwell follows, *CQ* 6 (1964) 373.

Thomas Hardy. *Critical Quarterly* 6 (1964) 341-351.

Labour's cultural policy. *Views* 5 (1964) 40-44.

Tragic inquiry. *Spectator,* 8 Jan 1965, 46. Review of Leo Aylen, *Greek tragedy and the modern world.*

The achievement of Balzac. *New Society,* 4 Nov 1965, 28-29. Review of Andre Maurois, *Prometheus.*

Prelude to alienation. *Stand* 7,4 (1965) 36-44. On William Blake.

A critic in business. *New Society,* 6 Jan 1966, 23-24. Review of *The collected works of Walter Bagehot,* ed. Norman St. John Stevas.

New left Catholics. *New Blackfriars* 48 (1966) 74-77.

General profile – Criticism. In *Your Sunday paper,* ed. Richard Hoggart. London: University of London Press, 1967. pp. 13-29, 150-163.

Recent English drama. In *The Pelican guide to English literature. Vol. 7. The modern age,* ed. Boris Ford. 3rd ed. Harmondsworth: Penguin, 1967. pp. 531-545.

Literature and rural society. *Listener,* 16 Nov 1967, 630-632. Text of Third Programme talk.

Literature and the city. *Listener,* 23 Nov 1967, 653-656. Text of Third Programme talk.

The meanings of work. In *Work: twenty personal accounts,* ed. Ronald Fraser. Harmondsworth: Penguin, in assoc. with *New Left Review,* 1968. pp. 280-298.

Paradoxically, if the book works it to some extent annihilates itself. In *McLuhan: hot and cold,* ed. Gerald E. Stearn. Harmondsworth: Penguin, 1968. pp. 216-219.

How television should be run. *Listener,* 11 Jul 1968, 33-35.

Die Ablehnung der Tragödie: über Bertolt Brechts Dramen. *Forum* [Wien] 15 (1968) 99-104.

Public inquiry. *Stand* 9,1 (1968) 15-53. Text of television drama, broadcast BBC1, 15 Mar 1967.

Introduction. In D.H. Lawrence, *Three plays: A collier's Friday night, The daughter-in-law, The widowing of Mrs. Holroyd.* Harmondsworth: Penguin, 1969. pp. 7-14.

A social commentary. In *The press: a case for commitment,* ed. Eric Moonman. London: Fabian Society, 1969. (Fabian tract; 391). pp. 1-4.

National convention of the left: why CND must be there. *Sanity,* Mar 1969, 6.

Dramatic changes. *Listener,* 24 Apr 1969, 582-583. Review of F.P. Wilson, *The English drama, 1485-1585,* Glynne Wickham, *Shakespeare's dramatic heritage.*

Crisis in communications: a new mood of submission. *Listener,* 31 Jul 1969, 138,140. Considers appropriation of public media by advertisers and other private interests.

The knowable community in George Eliot's novels. *Novel* 2 (1969) 255-268.

Introduction. In Charles Dickens, *Dombey and son,* ed. Peter Fairclough. Harmondsworth: Penguin, 1970. pp. 11-34.

Radical and/or respectable. In *The press we deserve,* ed. Richard Boston. London: Routledge, 1970. pp. 14-26.

Dickens and social ideas. In *Dickens 1970: centenary essays,* ed. Michael Slater. London: Chapman & Hall, 1970. pp. 77-98.

On reading Marcuse. In *The Cambridge mind,* ed. Eric Homberg and others. London: Cape, 1970. pp. 162-166. Reprinted review of Herbert Marcuse, *Negations.*

The intellectual in politics. *Spokesman,* 3 May 1970, 508-509.

Shadowing Orwell. *Listener,* 13 Aug 1970, 218. Review of *The best of Hugh Kingsmill,* ed. Michael Holroyd.

The popularity of the press. *Listener,* 15 Oct 1970, 508-509.

An experimental tendency. *Listener,* 3 Dec 1970, 785-786. Review of *The new left,* ed. Maurice Cranston.

Ideas of nature. *TLS,* 4 Dec 1970, 1419-1421. Text of lecture given at the Institute of Contemporary Arts.

An introduction to reading in culture and society. In *Literature and environment: essays in reading and social studies,* ed. Fred Inglis. London: Chatto & Windus, 1971. pp. 125-140.

In praise of films. *Listener,* 20 May 1971, 633-635.

Going into Europe-again? *Encounter,* Jun 1971, 13.

Radical intellectuals. *Listener,* 24 Jun 1971, 821. Review of T.C. Worsley, *Fellow travellers.*

Raymond Williams thinks well of the Open University. *Listener,* 14 Oct 1971, 507-508.

Literature and sociology: in memory of Lucien Goldmann. *New Left Review* 67 (1971) 3-18.

A letter from the country. *Stand* 12,2 (1971) 17-34. Text of television drama, first broadcast in alternative version, BBC 2, Apr 1966.

Introduction. In Lucien Goldmann, *Racine,* tr. Alastair Hamilton. Cambridge: Rivers Press, 1972. pp. vii – xxii.

Raymond Williams writes that free speech is being curtailed, and in ways that are not generally understood. *Listener,* 13 Jan 1972, 60-61. On television coverage of Ulster.

Letter to editor. *TLS,* 10 Mar 1972, 276. In response to article on Cambridge, *TLS,* 25 Feb 1972.

Lucien Goldmann and Marxism's alternative tradition. *Listener,* 23 Mar 1972, 375-376.

News values. *Listener,* 29 Jun 1972, 876-877.

Social Darwinism. In *The limits of human nature: essays based on a course of lectures given at the Institute of Contemporary Arts, London,* ed. John Benthall. London: Allen Lane, 1973. pp. 115-130. Reprinted from *Listener,* 23 Nov 1972, 696-700.

Images of Solzhenitsyn. *Listener,* 29 Sep 1973, 750-751. Review of Zhores Medvedev, *Ten years after Ivan Denisovich,* Alexander Solzhenitsyn, *Candle in the wind.*

Pastoral versions. *New Statesman,* 27 Sep 1974, 428-429. Review of J.P.D. Dunbabin, *Rural discontent in 19th-century Britain, Land and industry: the landed estate and the industrial revolution,* ed. J.T. Ward and R.C. Wilson.

The English language and the English tripos. *TLS,* 15 Nov 1974, 1293-1294. Text of Cambridge lecture.

Communication as cultural science. *Journal of Communication* [Philadelphia] 24,3 (1974) 17-25.

Welsh culture. In *Culture and politics: Plaid Cymru's challenge to Wales*. Cardiff: Plaid Cymru, 1975. pp. 6-10.

The referendum choice. *New Statesman*, 30 May 1975, 719.

Variations on a Welsh theme for four male voices. *Listener*, 2 Oct 1975, 429-430. Incl. Raymond Williams on 'the Welsh fixation with the past'.

How can we sell the protestant ethic at a psychedelic bazaar? *New York Times Book Review*, 1 Feb 1976, 3. Review of Daniel Bell, *The cultural contradictions of capitalism*.

Legal? Honest? Decent? Truthful? An argument on advertising. *Listener*, 16 Oct 1976, 331-332. Transcript of broadcast, including contribution by Raymond Williams. – Winston Fletcher replies, 30 Oct, 417.

The bomb and democracy – you can't have it both ways. *Sanity*, Oct-Nov 1976, 10. Reprinted from *Sanity*, Apr 1965.

Contemporary drama and social change in Britain. *Revue des Langues Vivantes* 42 (1976) 624-631.

Developments in the sociology of culture. *Sociology* 10 (1976) 497-506.

Literature in society. In *Contemporary approaches to English studies,* ed. Hilda Schiff. London: Heinemann Educational, 1977. pp. 24-37.

Foreword. In *The critical twilight: explorations in the ideology of Anglo-American literary theory from Eliot to McLuhan,* ed. John Fekete. London: Routledge, 1977. pp. xi-xiv.

Wessex and the Border. In *The English novel: developments in criticism since Henry James,* ed. Stephen Hazell. London: Macmillan, 1977. pp. 190-205.

Talking with the folks back home. *New York Times Book Review*, 27 Feb 1977, 3. Review of Melvyn Bragg, *Speak for England: an oral history of England, 1900-1975.*

The fiction of reform. *TLS,* 25 Mar 1977, 330-331. Review article on Gary Kelly, *The English Jacobin novel.*

Television and the mandarins. *New Society,* 31 Mar 1977, 651-652.

The paths and pitfalls of ideology as an ideology. *Times Higher Education Supplement,* 10 Jun 1977, 13.

The social significance of 1926. *Llafur: Journal of Welsh Labour History* 2,2 (1977) 5-8.

Notes on British Marxism since the war. *New Left Review* 100 (1977) 81-94.

Interview with Raymond Williams: Marxism, poetry, Wales. *PW* 13,3 (1977) 16-34. On 'poetry and the differences between cultural traditions in various parts of Britain'.

The press we don't deserve. In *The British press: a manifesto,* ed. James Curran. London: Macmillan, 1978. pp. 15-28.

A book at bedtime. *New Society,* 4 May 1978, 264-265. Review of J.A. Sutherland, *Fiction and the fiction industry.*

The god that failed all over again. *New Society,* 23 Nov 1978, 469-470. Review of Leszek Kolakowski, *Main currents of Marxism.*

[Interview]. *Anglistica* [Naples] 21 (1978). Interviewed by Paola Splendore.

Commitment. *Stand* 20,3 (1978) 8-11.

Utopia and science fiction. In *Science fiction: a critical guide,* ed. P. Parrinder. London: Longman, 1979. pp. 52-66.

Art: freedom as duty. In *Art, duties and freedoms: a symposium.* Aberystwyth: University College of Wales (Dept. of Extra-Mural Studies); Cardiff: Welsh Arts Council, 1979. pp. 1-11.

Introduction. In *The arts in Wales, 1950-75,* ed. Meic Stephens. Cardiff: Welsh Arts Council, 1979. pp. 1-4.

Letter to editor. *WM,* 27 Feb 1979, 10:D. Williams and other Welsh writers argue for devolution.

A man confronting a very particular kind of mystery. *Times Higher Education Supplement,* 5 May 1979. 10. On F.R. Leavis.

Hardy and social class. In *Thomas Hardy,* ed. Norman Page. London: Bell & Hyman, 1980. pp. 29-40. (The writer and his background). Written jointly with Merryn Williams.

What is anti-capitalism. *New Society,* 24 Jan 1980, 189-190. Review of Michael Lowy, *Georg Lukács: from romanticism to bolshevism.*

From communism to Marxism. *New York Times Book Review,* 13 Apr 1980, 11. Review of Robert L. Heilbroner, *Marxism: for and against.*

The popularity of the melodrama. *New Society,* 24 Apr 1980, 170-171. Review of *Performance and politics in popular drama,* ed. David Bradby and others.

The role of the literary magazine. *TLS,* 6 Jun 1980, 637. Answer to a questionnaire.

Realism again. *New Society,* 20 Nov 1980, 381-382. Review of Georg Lukács, *Essays on realism.*

Remaking Welsh history. *Arcade,* 12 Dec 1980, 18-19. Review article on Hywel Francis and David Smith, *The Fed: a history of the South Wales miners in the twentieth century; A people and a proletariat: essays in the history of Wales.* ed. David Smith.

Yasar Kemal's novels. *Edebiyat* 5,1-2 (1980) 83-85.

Foreword. In *The language of television: uses and abuses,* ed. Albert Hunt. London: Eyre Methuen, 1981. pp. vii-x.

Black mountains. In *Places: an anthology of Britain,* ed. Roland Blythe. Oxford: Oxford University Press, 1981. pp. 215-222.

Editor's introduction. In Janet Coleman, *English literature in history, 1350-1400: medieval readers and writers.* London: Hutchinson, 1981. (English literature in history). pp. 9-12. Raymond Williams acted as series editor.

Foreword. In *A good night out: popular theatre: audience, class and form.* ed. John McGrath. London: Methuen, 1981. pp. vii-xi.

Freedom and a lack of confidence. *Arcade,* 17 Apr 1981, 16-17. On Anglo-Welsh novels, by way of introducing Welsh Academy and University College Cardiff novel competition.

Talking to ourselves. *Cambridge Review,* 27 Apr 1981, 160-164.

Review of Bernard Crick, *George Orwell: a life. Marxism Today,* Jun 1981, 28-29.

Society of Socialists. *Arcade,* 24 Jul 1981, 17. Proposes its formation.

Marxism, structuralism and literary analysis. *New Left Review* 129 (1981) 51-66.

Ideas and the Labour movement. *New Socialist* 2 (1981) 28-33.

'Exiles'. In *James Joyce: new perspectives,* ed. Colin MacCabe. Brighton: Harvester, 1982. pp. 105-110.

Working-class, proletarian, socialist: problems in some Welsh novels. In *The socialist novel in Britain: towards the recovery of a tradition,* ed. H. Gustav Klaus. Brighton: Harvester Press, 1982. pp. 110-121.

The man who shifted the tide. *New Society,* 29 Apr 1982, 188-189. Review of George Spater, *William Cobbett: the poor man's friend.*

Beyond specialisation. *TLS,* 10 Dec 1982, 1362. Contribution to a symposium on the study of English.

Monologue in Macbeth. In *Teaching the text,* ed. Susanne Kappeler and Norman Bryson. London: Routledge, 1983. pp. 180-202.

The estranging influence of post-modernism. *New Society,* 16 Jun 1983, 439-440. Review of Peter Fuller, *The naked artist: aesthetics after modernism.*

The Prof's approach to 2000 AD. *WM,* 10 Nov 1983, 9:A-D. Interviewed by Terry Campbell.

The Robert Tressel memorial lecture, 1982. *History Workshop* 16 (1983) 74-82. Extract from an address on Tressel.

Problems of the coming period. *New Left Review* 140 (1983) 7-18.

State culture and beyond. In *Culture and the state,* ed. Lisa Appignanesi. London: Institute of Contemporary Arts, 1984. pp. 3-5.

*Nineteen eighty-four. Morning Star,* 3 Jan 1984.

*Nineteen eighty-four* in 1984. *Marxism Today,* Jan 1984, 12-16.

How socialists and ecologists can get together. *Guardian,* 11 Jun 1984, 10:A-G.

Nationalisms and popular socialism: Phil Cooke talks to Raymond Williams. *Radical Wales* 2 (1984) 7-8.

Afterword. In *Political Shakespeare: new essays in cultural materialism,* ed. Jonathan Dollimore and Alan Sinfield. Manchester: Manchester University Press, 1985. pp. 231-239.

Wales and England. In *The national question again: Welsh political identity in the 1980s,* ed. John Osmond. Llandysul: Gomer Press, 1985. pp. 18-31.

The metropolis and the emergence of modernism. In *Unreal city: urban experience in modern European literature and art,* ed. Edward Timms and David Kelley. New York: St. Martin's Press, 1985. pp. 13-24.

Community. *London Review of Books,* 24 Jan 1985, 14-15. Review of Emyr Humphreys, *The Taliesin tradition: a quest for the Welsh identity,* Emyr Humphreys, *Jones: a novel,* Dai Smith, *Wales! Wales?,* Jan Morris, *The matter of Wales: epic views of a small country.*

Ruskin among others. *London Review of Books,* 20 Jun 1985, 18. Review of Tim Hilton, *John Ruskin: the early years.*

Torches for superman. *London Review of Books,* 21 Nov 1985, 17-18. Review of August Strindberg, *By the sea,* Olaf Lagercrantz, *August Strindberg,* Michael Meyer, *Strindberg: a biography.*

Introduction. In Gwyn Thomas, *All things betray thee.* London: Lawrence & Wishart, 1986.

Foreword. In *Languages of nature: critical essays on science and literature,* ed. L.J. Jordanova. London: Free Association Books, 1986. pp. 10-14. First published in America, 1981.

Pierre Bourdieu and the sociology of culture: an introduction. In *Media, culture and society,* ed. Richard Collins and others. London: Sage, 1986. pp. 116-130. Written jointly with Nicholas Garnham.- Reprinted from *Media, Culture and Society (1980).*

An interview with Raymond Williams. In *Studies in entertainment: critical approaches to mass culture,* ed. Tania Modleski. Bloomington: Indiana University Press, 1986. pp. 3-17. Interviewed by Stephen Heath and Gillian Skirrow.

Review of *The Oxford companion to the literature of Wales,* ed. Meic Stephens. *Guardian,* 27 Feb 1986, 23.

The uses of cultural theory. *New Left Review* 152 (1986) 19-31.

Language and the avant-garde. In *The linguistics of writing: arguments between language and literature,* ed. Nigel Fabb and others. Manchester: Manchester University Press, 1987. pp. 33-47.

Past masters. *London Review of Books,* 25 Jun 1987, 13-14. Review of Marjorie Reeves and Warwick Gould, *Joachim of Fiore and the myth of the eternal evangel in the 19th century,* Hilary Fraser, *Beauty and belief: aesthetics and religion in Victorian literature, The correspondence of John Ruskin and Charles Eliot Norton,* ed. John Bradley and Ian Ousby.

The practice of possibility. *New Statesman,* 7 Aug 1987, 19-21. Terry Eagleton interviews Raymond Williams. – Reprinted in *Raymond Williams: critical perspectives,* ed. Terry Eagleton (1989).

People of the Black Mountains: John Barnie interviews Raymond Williams. *Planet 65* (1987) 3-13.

Introduction: the politics of the avant-garde – Theatre as a political form. In *Visions and blueprints: avant-garde culture and radical politics in early twentieth-century Europe,* ed. Edward Timms and Peter Collier. Manchester: Manchester University Press, 1988. pp. 1-15; 307-320.

Fact and fiction. *In International encyclopedia of communications,* ed. Eric Barnouw and others. Vol. 2. London: Oxford University Press, 1988. pp. 148-151.

Art: freedom and duty. *Planet* 68 (1988) 7-14. Edited version of a tape-recorded lecture.

Interview: Raymond Williams and Pierre Vicary. *Southern Review* [Adelaide] 22 (1989) 163-174. Text of a broadcast on Radio Helicon, 28 Mar 1983.

Interview with Raymond Williams: the politics of literacy. *Pretexts: Studies in Writing and Culture* [Cape Town] 3,1-2 (1991) 136-143. Interview of 1988, conducted by John Higgins.

# A (iv). Raymond Williams: Translations

## Catalan

*Cultura i societat,* tr. Jem Cabanes. Barcelona: Laia, 1974. 495 p. [*Culture and society*].

## Danish

*Massemedierne,* tr. Hans Hertel. København: Fremad, 1963. 197 p. [*Britain in the sixties: communications*].

*Orwell,* tr. Allan Hilton Andersen. København: Tiderne Skifter, 1984. 113 p.

## French

*George Orwell,* tr. Michel Morvan. Paris: Seghers, 1972. 159 p.

## German

*Gesellschaftstheorie als Begriffsgeschichte: Studien z. histor. Semantik von Kultür,* tr. Heinz Blumensath. München: Rogner & Bernhard, 1972. 427 p. [Culture and society].

*Innovationen: über den Prozesscharakter von Literatur und Kultur* / herausgegeben und übersetzt von H. Gustav Klaus. Frankfurt am Main: Syndikat Autoren- & Verlagsges., 1977. 229 p. A collection of book extracts and previously published articles, translated into German. – Reissued: Frankfurt am Main: Suhrkamp, 1983.

## Hungarian

*A kommunikáció,* tr. János Zentai. Budapest: Magyar Rádió es Televizió, 1968. 69 p. [*Britain in the sixties: communications*].

*A televizió-technika és a kulturális forma,* tr. Julia Veres. Budapest: Tömegkommunikációs Kutatóközpont Szakkönyvtára, 1976. 185 p. [*Television: technology and cultural form*].

## Italian

*Cultura e rivoluzione industriale Inghilterra, 1780-1950,* tr. Maria T. Grendi. Torino: Einaudi, 1968. 408 p. [*Culture and society*].

*La lunga rivoluzione,* tr. Paola Splendore. Rome, 1979. [*The long revolution*].

*Marxismo e letteratura,* tr. Mario Stetrema. Bari: Laterza, 1979. 287 p. [*Marxism and literature*].

*Televisione: tecnologia e forma culturale,* tr. Celestino E. Spada. Bari: De Donate, 1981. 229 p. [*Television: technology and cultural form*].

*Materialismo e cultura.* Naples, 1983. [*Problems in materialism and culture*].

*Sociologia della cultura.* Bologno, 1983. [*Culture*].

## Japanese

*Bunka to shakai,* tr. Shigenobu Wakamutsu and Mitsuaki Hasegawa. Kyôtô: Minerva shobo, 1968. 288 p. [*Culture and society*].

*Communication,* tr. Hiromoto Tachihara. Tokyo: Gôdô Shuppan, 1969. 215 p. [*Britain in the sixties: communications*].

*Henkyô,* tr. Takeshi Onodera. Tokyo: Kodansha, 1972. 373 p. [*Border country*].

*Kiwâdo jiten,* tr. Kôichi Okazaki. Tokyo: Shôbunsha, 1980. 417 p. [*Keywords: a vocabulary of culture and society*].

*Nagai kakumei,* tr. Wakamatsu Shigenobu. Kyoto: Mineruva Shobo, 1983. 307 p. [*The long revolution*].

*Bunka towa,* tr. Tamio Koike. Tokyo: Shôbunsha, 1985. 300 p. [*Culture*].

*Inaka to tokai,* tr. Kazuhei Yamamoto. Tokyo: Shôbunsha, 1985. 425 p. [The country and the city].

## Korean

*I-nyeom-gwa munhag,* tr. Lee Il Hwan. Seoul: Munhag-gwa jiseongsa, 1982. 264 p. [*Marxism and literature*].

*Munhwasahoehag,* tr. Jun Gyu Seol and Seung Cheol Song. Seoul: Ggachi, 1984. 254. [*Culture*].

*Orwell-gwa 1984 nyeon,* tr. Byeong Ig Kim. Seoul: Munhag-gwa jiseongsa, 1984. 249 p. [*Orwell*].

*Hyeondae bi-geugron,* tr. Sun Heui Im. Seoul: Hagmunsa, 1985. 267 p. [*Modern tragedy*].

### Portuguese

*Marxismo y literatura,* tr. Waltensir Dutra. Rio de Janeiro: Zahar, 1979. 215 p. [*Marxism and literature*].

### Russian

*Vtroroe pokolenie,* tr. I. Arhangel'skaja and I. Bernstejn. Moskva: Progress, 1975. 400 p.: ill. [*Second generation*].

### Spanish

*Los medios de comunicación social,* tr. Manuel Carbonell. Barcelona: Peninsula, 1971. 203 p. [*Britain in the sixties: communications*]. – Reissued 1978.

*El teatro de Ibsen a Brecht,* tr. José M. Alvarez. Barcelona: Peninsula, 1975. 411 p. [*Drama from Ibsen to Brecht*].

*Marxismo y literatura,* tr. Pablo di Masso. Barcelona: Peninsula, 1980. 250 p. [*Marxism and literature.*].

*Cultura: sociologia de la communicación y del arte,* tr. Graziella Baravalle. Barcelona: Paidos, 1982. 231 p. [*Culture*].

Hacia el año 2000, tr. Paloma Villegas. Barcelona: Critica, 1984. 312 p. [*Towards 2000*].

### Swedish

*Marx och kulturen: en diskussion kring marxistisk kultur-och litteraturteori,* tr. Anette Rydstrom. Stockholm: Bonnier, 1980. 174 p. [*Marxism and literature*].

# B. Publications about Raymond Williams

Note that there have been two collections of critical essays on Raymond Williams, edited by Terry Eagleton (1989), and Denis L. Dworkin and Leslie G. Roman (1993). Their contents are given below.

ABDUL-FATAH, Abdullah Moutasim. The literary and cultural criticism of Raymond Williams. *Neohelicon* [Budapest] 14,2 (1987) 33-40.
ADLER, Louise. Historiography in Britain: rethinking history: time, myth, writing. *Yale French Studies* 59 (1980) 243-253.

ALLOR, Martin F. Cinema, culture and the social formation: ideology and critical practice. PhD thesis. University of Illinois at Urbana (Champaign), 1984. 168 p. 'The first principles of the culturalist approach are discussed in relationship to the work of Raymond Williams.'

BARNETT, Anthony. Raymond Williams and Marxism: a rejoinder to Terry Eagleton. *New Left Review* 99 (1976) 47-64.

BENETT, James R. The novel, truth and the community. *D.H. Lawrence Review* 4,1 (1971) 74-89.

BENNETT, Tony. Formalism and Marxism. London: Methuen, 1979. Incl. discussion of Raymond Williams, pp. 13-15.

—— Holding spaces. *Southern Review* [Adelaide] 22 (1989) 85-88.

BHATTACHARYA, Minhir. Developing a science of literature: Marxism and Raymond Williams. *Journal of the School of Languages, New Delhi* 7,1-2 (1980) 20-23.

BILAN, R.P. Raymond Williams: from Leavis to Marx. *Queens Quarterly* [Ontario] 87 (1980) 211-223.

BINDING, Wyn. Some observations on the novels of Raymond Williams. *AWR* 16,37 (1967) 74-81.

BLACKBURN, Robin. Raymond Williams and the politics of a new left. *New Left Review* 168 (1988) 12-22.

BODINGER de Uriarte, Cristina. Opposition to hegemony in the music of Devo: a simple matter of remembering. *Journal of Popular Culture* 18,4 (1985) 57-71. Applies Williams' theories to rock music lyrics.

BORKLUND, Elmer. *Contemporary literary critics.* 2nd ed. London: Macmillan, 1982. Incl. Raymond Williams, pp. 563-567.

BRANTLINGER, Patrick. Raymond Williams: from culture to community. *Postscript* 3 (1986) 19-25.

—— Raymond Williams: culture is ordinary. *Ariel: A Review of International English Literature* [Calgary] 22,2 (1991) 75-81. Review article on *Raymond Williams: critical perspectives,* ed. Terry Eagleton, Jan Gorak, *The alien mind of Raymond Williams,* Alan O'Connor, *Raymond Williams: writing, culture, politics.*

BRYANT, B.A.D. The new left in Britain, 1956-1968: the dialectic of rationality and participation. PhD thesis. London School of Economics, 1981. Chapt. 9, Raymond Williams and new leftism.

BULL, John. Raymond Williams: his country. *Delta* 52 (1974) 26-34.

BURTON, Robert S. Raymond Williams. In *Reference guide to English literature,* ed. D.L. Kirkpatrick. 2nd ed. 3 vols. Chicago; London: St James Press, 1991. Vol. 2, pp. 1404-1406.

—— Revitalising an old tradition: the 'organic' writings of Raymond Williams and John Fowles. *Studies in Medievalism* [Holland] 4 (1992) 270-275.

BUTTS, Dennis. Holding the connections: Raymond Williams's fiction. *New Universities Quarterly* 34 (1980) 235-240.

COLLITS, Terry. Raymond Williams in history. *Southern Review* [Adelaide] 22 (1989) 89-96.

CRANNY-FRANCIS, Anne. 'Nineteen eighty-four in 1984' in 1989: Raymond Williams and George Orwell. *Southern Review* [Adelaide] 22 (1989) 152-162.

CREADON, Mary Ann. Wittgenstein's door to historical criticism (language, politics, literary theory, representation, philosophy). PhD thesis. Northwestern University, 1986. 'I conclude with a chapter analyzing the work of Raymond Williams.'

DAS GUPTA, Kalyan. Principles of literary evaluation in English Marxist criticism: Christopher Caldwell, Raymond Williams and Terry Eagleton. PhD thesis. University of British Columbia, 1985.

DAVE, Jagdish V. 'Koba': a tragedy of revolution. *Indian Journal of English Studies* 14 (1973) 113-127.

DAVEY, K. The development of the work of Raymond Williams, 1939-1961. MA thesis. University of Kent, 1985.

DOCKER, John. Williams' challenge to screen studies. *Southern Review* [Adelaide] 22 (1989) 129-136.

DUCKWORTH, Alistair M. Raymond Williams and literary history. *Papers on Language and Literature* 11 (1975) 420-441. Review article on *The country and the city.*

DURING, Simon. After death: Raymond Williams in the modern era. *Critical Inquiry* 15 (1989) 681-703.

DWORKIN, Dennis L. *Views beyond the border country: Raymond Williams and cultural politics,* ed. Dennis L. Dworkin and Leslie G. Roman. New York & London: Routledge, 1993. xii, 346 p. Contents: Series editor's introduction, by Michael W. Apple, pp. vii-xii – Introduction: the cultural politics of location, by Dennis L. Dworkin and Leslie G. Roman, pp. 1-7 – Autobiography and the 'structure of feeling' in *Border country,* by Laura Di Michele, pp. 21-37 – Cultural studies and the crisis in British radical thought, by Dennis L. Dworkin, pp. 38-54 – Placing the occasion: Raymond Williams and performing culture, by Loren Kruger, pp. 55-71 – Realisms and modernisms: Raymond Williams and popular fiction, by Jon Thompson, pp. 72-88 – Rebuilding hegemony: education, equality and the New Right, by Michael W. Apple, pp. 91-114 – Raymond Williams, affective ideology, and counter-hegemonic practices, by Wendy Kohli, pp. 115-132 – Williams on democracy and the governance of education, by Fazal Rizvi, pp. 133-157 – 'On the ground' with anti-racist pedagogy and Raymond Williams's unfinished project to articulate a socially transformative critical realism, by Leslie G. Roman, pp. 158-214 – Raymond Williams and British colonialism: the limits of metropolitan cultural theory, by Gauri Viswanathan, pp. 217-230 – Country and city in a postcolonial landscape: double discourse and the geo-politics of truth in Latin America, by Julie Skurski and Fernando Coronil, pp. 231-255 – Raymond Williams and the inhuman limits of culture, by Forest Pyle, pp. 260-274 – Cultural theory and the politics of location, by R. Radhakrishnan, pp. 275-294 – Notes, pp. 295-353.

EAGLETON, Terry. Criticism and politics: the work of Raymond Williams. *New Left Review* 95 (1976) 3-23.

—— Raymond Williams e il populismo. *Calibano* 1 (1977) 159-184. With Franco Moretti.

—— *Criticism and ideology: a study in Marxist literary theory.* London: Verso, 1978. Incl. discussion of Raymond Williams, pp. 21-43. – Previously published 1976.

—— *The function of criticism: from* The Spectator *to post-structuralism.* London: Verso, 1984. Incl. discussion of Raymond Williams, pp. 108-115.

——. Professor Raymond Williams. *Independent,* 28 Jan 1988, 25:C-F. Obituary.

—— *Raymond Williams: critical perspectives,* ed. Terry Eagleton. Cambridge: Polity Press, 1989. ix, 235 p.: ill. Contents: Introduction, by Terry Eagleton, pp. 1-11 – Raymond Williams and the 'Two faces of modernism', by Tony Pinkney, pp. 12-33 – Relating to Wales, by Dai Smith, pp. 34-53 – Politics and letters, by Stuart Hall, pp. 54-66 – *Towards 2000*, or news from you-know-where, by Francis Mulhern, pp. 67-94 – Raymond Williams and the Italian left, by Fernando Ferrara, pp. 95-107 – Raymond Williams: a photographic sketch, compiled by Robin Gable [12 p, folllowing p. 107] – Homage to Orwell: the dream of a common culture, and other minefields, by Lisa Jardine and Julia Swindells, pp. 108-129 – In whose voice? The drama of Raymond Williams, by Bernard Sharratt, pp. 130-149 – Jane Austen and empire, by Edward W. Said, pp. 150-164 – Base and superstructure in Raymond Williams, by Terry Eagleton, pp. 165-175 – The politics of hope: an interview, by Raymond Williams and Terry Eagleton, pp. 176-183 – A Raymond Williams bibliography, by Alan O'Connor, pp. 184-227 – Index, by Mary Madden, pp. 228-235.

EFRON, Arthur. Why radicals should not be Marxists. *Sphinx* 3,4 (1981) 1-18.

FAIRBANKS, N. David. The class character of working-class fiction in post-war England. *Literature and Ideology* 11 (1972) 25-36. Incl. discussion of Raymond Williams.

FREE, William J. Robert Bolt and the Marxist view of history. *Mosaic* 14,1 (1981) 51-59.

GIDDENS, Anthony. *Profiles and critiques in social theory.* London: Macmillan, 1982. Incl. Literature and society, pp. 133-143.

GOLDSTEIN, Leonard. Aspects of Raymond Williams' *Second generation.* In *Essays in honour of William Gallacher,* ed. P.M. Kemp-Ashraf and Jack Mitchell. Berlin: Humboldt Universitat, 1966. pp. 221-233.

GORAK, Jan. *The alien mind of Raymond Williams.* Columbia (Missouri): University of Missouri Press, 1988. 132 p.

GREEN, Michael. Raymond Williams and cultural studies. *Cultural Studies* [University of Birmingham] 6 (1974) 31-48.

GREENFIELD, Cathy and Peter Williams. Raymond Williams: the political and analytical legacies. *Southern Review* [Adelaide] 22 (1989) 137-142.

HALEY, Eileen. Crossing the sexual frontier: Raymond Williams' concept of culture. *Refractory Girl* 1 (1972-73) 22-28.

HALL, Stuart. Only connect: the life of Raymond Williams. *New Statesman,* 5 Feb 1988, 20-21. Obituary.

HARVEY, J.R. Criticism, ideology, Raymond Williams and Terry Eagleton. *Cambridge Quarterly* 8 (1978) 56-65. Review article on *Marxism and literature* and *Keywords.*

HEATH, Stephen. Raymond Williams: a tribute. *NWR* 1,2 [2] (1988) 19-22. Text of an address given at the memorial service for Raymond Williams held in the chapel of Jesus College, Cambridge, on 21 May 1988.

—— and Colin MacCabe. Raymond Williams, 1921-1988. *Critical Quarterly* 30,1 (1988) 3-5.

HESS, James Cameron. Literary production and consumption. PhD thesis. University of Pennsylvania, 1981. 238 p. Discusses Raymond Williams, amongst others.

HEWISON, Robert. *In anger: culture in the cold war, 1945-60.* London: Weidenfeld & Nicolson, 1981. Incl. discussion of Williams, pp. 169-180.

HIGGINS, John. Raymond Williams and the problem of ideology. *Boundary 2: A Journal of Postmodern Literature and Culture* 11,1-2 (1982-83) 145-154.

—— Critical resources: Raymond Williams, 1921-1988. *Pretexts:Studies in Writing and Culture* [Cape Town] 1,1 (1989) 79-91.

—— A missed encounter: Raymond Williams and psychoanalysis. *Journal of Literary Studies* [Pretoria] 6, 1-2 (1990) 62-76.

HOOKER, Jeremy. *The poetry of place: essays and reviews, 1970-1981.* Manchester: Carcanet, 1982. Incl. Raymond Williams: a dream of a country, pp. 106-115. – Reprinted from *Planet* 49-50 (1980) 53-61.

HOWKINS, Alun. The discovery of rural England. In *Englishness: politics and culture, 1880-1920,* ed. Robert Colls and Philip Dodd. London: Croom Helm, 1986. pp. 62-88. Incl. comment on Williams.

INGLIS, Fred. *Radical earnestness: English social theory, 1880-1980.* Oxford: Martin Robertson, 1982. Incl. Culture and politics: Richard Hoggart, the *New Left Review,* and Raymond Williams, pp. 158-184.

IVASHEVA, Valentina. Literary encounters. *Anglo-Soviet Journal* 35,1-2 (1974) 26-31. Incl. impressions of Raymond Williams. – Translated from *Literaturnaya Gazeta.*

JARDINE, Lisa. Girl talk (for boys on the left), or marginalising feminist critical praxis. *Oxford Literary Review* 8,1-2 (1986) 208-217.

JOHNSON, Lesley. *The cultural critics: from Matthew Arnold to Raymond Williams.* London: Routledge, 1979. Incl. Raymond Williams, pp. 150-173.

JOHNSON, R.W. *Heroes and villains: selected essays.* London: Harvester Wheatsheaf, 1990. Incl. Raymond Williams and E.P. Thompson, pp. 136-146.

JONES, Bobi. Y Marcsydd beirniadol, 2. Raymond Williams. *Barddas,* Tach/Nov 1988, 13-15. In the series The critical Marxist.

KANWAR, A. S. The fictional theories of Arnold Kettle and Raymond Williams, with special reference to selected nineteenth-century novels. DPhil thesis. Sussex University, 1986. 395 p.

KAYE, Lawrence H. A voice from the Border: the fiction of Raymond Williams (Wales). PhD thesis. Brandeis University, 1987. 230 p.

KERMODE, Frank. Professor Raymond Williams. *Independent,* 28 Jan 1988, 25:C-F. Obituary.

KETTLE, Arnold. Culture and revolution: a consideration of the ideas of Raymond Williams and others. *Marxism Today* 5 (1961) 301-307.

KLAUS, H. Gustav. Raymond Williams. In *Contemporary novelists,* ed. D.L. Kirkpatrick. 4th ed. London: St James Press, 1986. pp. 881-884. With comment by Raymond Williams.

KNIGHT, Stephen. Personal substance: the novels of Raymond Williams. *NWR* 1,2 [2] (1988) 28-32.

—— The materialisation of a history: Raymond Williams' novels. *Southern Review* [Adelaide] 22 (1989) 143-148.

KROEBER, Karl. Fictional theory and social history: the need for a synthetic criticism. *Victorian Studies* 19 (1975) 99-106. Review article including discussion of *The country and the city.*

KRUGER, Loren. Exile and modernity. *Pretexts: Studies in Writing and Culture* [Cape Town] 3,1-2 (1992) 144-151. On *The politics of modernism,* ed. Tony Pinkney.

LANGE, Gerhard W. Materialistische Kulturtheorie im Vergleich: Raymond Williams, Terry Eagleton und die deutsche Tradition. Munster: Lit Verlag, 1984. [Materialist theories of culture, a comparison: Raymond Williams, Terry Eagleton and the German tradition].

LAWSON, Sylvia. Raymond Williams. *Southern Review* [Adelaide] 22 (1989) 81-84.

LEVY, Bronwen. Speaking a committed position: work in progress. *Southern Review* [Adelaide] 22 (1989) 104-111.

LOCKWOOD, Bernard. Four contemporary British working-class novelists: a thematic and critical approach to the fiction of Raymond Williams, John Braine, David Storey and Alan Sillitoe. PhD thesis. University of Wisconsin, 1984. 311 p.

LOVELL, Terry. Knowable pasts, imaginable futures. *History Workshop: A Journal of Socialist and Feminist Historians* 27 (1989) 136-140.

MACINTYRE, Stuart. Raymond Williams and history. *Southern Review* [Adelaide] 22 (1989) 149-151.

MCLAREN, John. Divisions and connection: Raymond Williams and the literature of displacement. *Southern Review* [Adelaide] 22 (1989) 97-103.

MATHIAS, Roland. [Editorial]. *AWR* 11,27 (1961) 5-13. Incl. discussion of *Border country.*

MAZUREK, Raymond A. Totalisation and contemporary realism: John Berger's recent fiction. *Critique: Studies in Modern Fiction* 25 (1984) 136-146. Discusses Berger in light of *The country and the city.*

MERRILL, Michael. Raymond Williams and the theory of English Marxism. *Radical History Review* 19 (1978-79) 9-31.

MILLER, Jane. *Seductions: studies in reading and culture.* London: Virago, 1990. Chapt. 2, The one great silent area, pp. 38-39, discusses women and women's politics in the work of Raymond Williams.

MILNER, Andrew. Williams and the new left. *Southern Review* [Adelaide] 22 (1989) 119-127.

—— *Cultural materialism.* Melbourne: Melbourne University Press, 1993. 140 p. With extended discussion of Williams's theories.

MOHAPATRA, Himansu Sekhar. Raymond Williams and the limits of realist discourse. PhD thesis. University of East Anglia, 1989. 353 p.

O'CONNOR, Alan. The knowable community: writing and politics in Raymond Williams. PhD thesis. York University (Canada), 1987.

—— *Raymond Williams: writing, culture, politics.* London: Blackwell, 1989. xi, 180 p.: hbk & pbk. Incl. A Raymond Williams bibliography, pp. 128-175.

OSMOND, John. Welsh mind behind a revolution. *WM,* 19 Jun 1990,

11:E-G. John Osmond scripted the Channel 4 profile of Raymond Williams, 'A journey of hope', filmed by Karl Francis.

PAGE, Malcolm. Raymond Williams. In *Contemporary novelists,* ed. James Vinson. 3rd ed. London: Macmillan, 1982. pp. 696-697. With comment by Raymond Williams.

PARRINDER, Patrick. The accents of Raymond Williams. *Critical Quarterly* 26,1-2 (1984) 47-57.

—— Raymond Williams, 1921-88. *Science Fiction Studies* 15 (1988) 250.

—— *The failure of theory: essays on criticism and contemporary fiction.* Brighton: Harvester, 1987. Incl. *Culture and society* in the 1980s, pp. 58-71 – Utopia and negativity in Raymond Williams, pp. 72-84.

PECHEY, Graham. *Scrutiny,* English Marxism, and the work of Raymond Williams. *Literature and History* 11,1 (1985) 65-76.

PINKNEY, Tony. *Raymond Williams.* Bridgend: Seren Books, 1991. x, 144 p. ill. (Border lines). 'The first critical study of the novels'.

RAO Ramdas. Cultural historicism: a study of major postwar British critics, 1950-1975. PhD thesis. Pennsylvania State University, 1987. 'Chapter 3 analyzes the cultural criticism of Richard Hoggart and Raymond Williams.'

ROBERTS, G.N. A way of remembering: Raymond Williams's last novel. *Planet* 78 (1989-90) 38-44. On *People of the Black Mountains.*

ROWLANDS, Graham. Raymond Williams' recent developments. *Westerly,* Jun 1972, 55-57.

RUTHVEN, K.K. Unlocking ideologies: 'keyword' as a trope. *Southern Review* [Adelaide] 22 (1989) 112-118.

RYAN, Kiernan. Socialist fiction and the education of desire: Mervyn Jones, Raymond Williams and John Berger. In *The socialist novel in Britain: towards the recovery of a tradition,* ed. H. Gustav Klaus. Brighton: Harvester Press, 1982. pp. 166-185.

SAID, Edward. *The world, the text and the critic.* London: Faber, 1984. Incl. discussion of Raymond Williams, esp. pp. 237-242.

—— Last dispatches from the border country: Raymond Williams, 1921-1988. *The Nation,* 5 Mar 1988, 312-314. Obituary notice.

SAMUEL, Raphael. Philosophy teaching by example: past and present in Raymond Williams. *History Workshop: A Journal of Socialist and Feminist Historians* 27 (1989) 141-153.

SCRUTON, Roger. *Thinkers of the new left.* London: Longman, 1985. Incl. Raymond Williams, pp. 54-65.

SEEHASE, Georg. Abbild des Klassenkampfes. *Zeitschrift fur Anglistik und Americanistik* [Berlin] 17 (1969) 392-405. [Image of class war].

SHARRATT, Bernard. Questioning critics: Hardy and Williams. *New Blackfriars* 50 (1978) 65-76.

—— *Reading relations: structures of literary production: a dialectical text/book.* Brighton: Harvester, 1982. Incl. discussion of *Marxism and literature,* pp. 35-40.

—— Communications and image studies: notes after Raymond Williams. *Comparative Criticism: A Yearbook* [Cambridge] 11 (1989) 29-50.

SHASHIDHAR, R. From literary criticism to Marxism: an analysis of the holistic writings of Raymond Williams. PhD thesis. University of Manchester. 1989.

SIEGMUND-SCHULTZE, Dorothea. Raymond Williams' concept of culture. *Zeitschrift fur Anglistik und Amerikanistik* [Berlin] 22,2 (1974) 131-145.

SKOVMAND, Michael. Culture, anger, community: Williams, Hoggart and the strange conjuncture of the late fifties. *Dolphin* 4 (1980) 59-80.

SKYDSGAARD, Niels Jorgen. Cultural creativity in the industrial society: an important theme in Raymond Williams' thought. In *Papers from the first Nordic conference for English studies, Oslo, 17-19 Sep., 1980,* ed. Stig Johansson and Bjorn Tysdahl. Oslo: Institute of English Studies, University of Oslo, 1981. pp. 211-224.

SMITH, Dai. The Welsh identity of Raymond Williams. *Planet* 76 (1989) 88-98.

—— The history of Raymond Williams. *NWR* 3,4 [12] (1991) 34-55. Discusses *People of the Black Mountains.*

SONG, Seung-Cheol. Politics and letters: the formation of Raymond Williams. PhD thesis. University of South Carolina, 1991. 308 p.

SPARKS, Colin. Raymond Williams, culture and Marxism. *International Socialism* 9 (1980) 131-144.

STEIN, Walter. *Criticism as dialogue.* Cambridge: Cambridge University Press, 1969. Incl. Humanism and tragic redemption, pp. 183-246.

SWANN, C.S.B. The keys of the republic. *Delta* 56 (1977) 20-24. On *Keywords.*

TATTON, Derek. The tension between political commitment and academic neutrality in the W.E.A. PhD thesis. Open University (UK), 1987. 439 p. Incl. discussion of Raymond Williams.

THOMAS, M. Wynn. Raymond Williams's medium. *BNW,* Autumn 1988, 5-6. On Williams as television critic.

THOMAS, Ned. Review article on Raymond Williams, *The fight for Manod. AWR* 67 (1980) 176-180.

—— From Raymond Williams to post-modernism? An oblique retrospect on *The Welsh extremist. Planet* 81 (1990) 18-23.

THOMPSON, E.P. *The long revolution. New Left Review* 9 (1961) 24-33; 10 (1961) 34-39. Review article.

—— Last dispatches from the border country: Raymond Williams, 1921-1988. *The Nation,* 5 Mar 1988, 310-312. Obituary notice.

THOMPSON, John O. Tragic flow: Raymond Williams on drama. *Screen Education* 35 (1980) 45-58.

TRACHTENBERG, Alan. Man and tradition: land and landscape. *Yale Review* 63 (1973-74) 610-621. Review article on *The country and the city.*

TREDELL, Nicolas. Uncancelled challenge: the work of Raymond Williams. Nottingham: Paupers Press, 1990. 96 p.

WARD, J.P. *Raymond Williams.* Cardiff: University of Wales Press [for] the Welsh Arts Council, 1981. 83 p.: front. port. (Writers of Wales). Incl. bibliography, pp. 77-79. – 'Limited to 1000 copies'.

—— Raymond Williams as inhabitant: the Border trilogy. *NWR* 1,2 [2] (1988) 23-27.

WATKINS, Evan. *The critical act: criticism and community.* New Haven;

London: Yale University Press, 1978. Incl. Raymond Williams and Marxist criticism, pp. 141-157.

—— Conflict and consensus in the history of recent criticism. *New Literary History* 12 (1981) 345-365.

WATSON, Garry. Criticism and the English idiom, I. A debate on the left. *New Universities Quarterly* 31 (1977) 316-340. Continued: Criticism and the English idiom, II. The significance of Raymond Williams, *NUQ* 31 (1977) 467-495.

WATSON, George. Raymond Williams (1921-88): the return of the sage. *Encounter* 74,1 (1990) 53-58.

WILLIAMS, Merryn. Raymond Williams, 1921-88. *Planet* 68 (1988) 3-6.

ZINMAN, Rosalind. Raymond Williams: toward a sociology of culture. PhD thesis. Concordia University (Canada), 1984. 268 p.